BUSINESS TRAVELLER'S HANDBOOK
A Guide To
AFRICA

Other areas covered by books in the BUSINESS TRAVELLER'S HANDBOOK series:

The Middle East
Europe
Latin America
Asia, Australia and the Pacific
The United States and Canada

BUSINESS TRAVELLER'S HANDBOOK

A Guide To AFRICA

Regional Editor: Toby Milner

Facts On File, Inc.
460 Park Avenue South
New York, N.Y. 10016

BUSINESS TRAVELLER'S HANDBOOK
A Guide To
AFRICA

Copyright © 1981 by Paddington Press Ltd.

All rights reserved. No part of this book may be reproduced or utilized in any form or by any means, electronic or mechanical, including photocopying, recording or by any information storage and retrieval systems, without permission in writing from the Publisher.

Library of Congress Cataloging in Publication Data
Main entry under title:

The Business traveller's handbook, Africa.

   Includes index.
   1. Africa—Description and travel—1977—Guide-books. I. Milner, Toby.
DT2.B87   1981   916'.04328   80-27391
ISBN 0-87196-341-8
ISBN 0-87196-347-7 (pbk.)

Printed in the United States of America
10 9 8 7 6 5 4 3 2 1

Acknowledgements

For their help and co-operation in the compilation of this handbook, the publishers and writers wish to acknowledge: Aeroflot; Air Afrique; Air Algérie; Air France; Air India; Air Malawi; Air Tanzania; Air Zaïre; Algerian Embassy, London; American Express; Arab League Office, London; Avis; Barclays Bank International Ltd; Botswana High Commission, London; British Airways; British Caledonian; British Overseas Trade Board, Export Services and Promotions Division; Cameroon Embassy, London; Commonwealth Institute, London; Thomas Cook Group Ltd; Diners Club; Egypt Air; Egyptian Embassy, London; Ethiopian Airlines; Europcar; Gabonese Embassy, London; Gambia High Commission, London; Ghana Airways; Ghana High Commission, London; Hertz; Kenya Airways; Kenya High Commission, London; Kenya Tourist Office, London; KLM; Lesotho High Commission, London; Liberian Embassy, London; Libyan Arab Airlines; Lloyds Bank International Ltd; Lufthansa; Malawi High Commission, London; Mauritius High Commission, London; Midland Bank International Ltd; Moroccan Embassy, London; National Westminster Bank; Nigeria Airways; Nigeria High Commission, London; Royal Commonwealth Society; SABENA; Senegal Embassy, London; Seychelles High Commission, London; Sierra Leone High Commission, London; TAP; Tunis Air; Tunisian Embassy, London; United Nations Information Centre, London; United States Embassy, London; UTA; Zaïre Embassy, London; Zambia Airways; Zambian High Commission, London.

Special thanks are due to Diana Hubbard and A. S. Atkinson for their invaluable help in checking the statistical information; and also to Suzanne Rich, Brigid Hampton, Margaret Solomon and Ian Sinclair, for their aid and support in preparing the final manuscript.

CONTENTS

Acknowledgements 5
Introduction 9
Health Information 12
African Social Customs and Attitudes 18
International and Regional Organisations . 21
Key to Symbols 28

Algeria 29
Angola 39
Benin 45
Botswana 55
Burundi 64
Cameroon 72
Central African Republic 82
Chad 89
Congo 98
Djibouti 107
Egypt 115
Equatorial Guinea 126
Ethiopia 131
Gabon 142
Gambia 151
Ghana 159
Guinea 169
Guinea-Bissau 178
Ivory Coast 186
Kenya 196
Lesotho 210
Liberia 219
Libya 228

CONTENTS

Madagascar 238
Malawi 248
Mali 258
Mauritania 267
Mauritius 274
Morocco 285
Mozambique 298
Namibia 307
Niger 315
Nigeria 322
Rwanda 336
Senegal 344
Seychelles 354
Sierra Leone 363
Somalia 372
South Africa 380
Sudan 401
Swaziland 411
Tanzania 420
Togo 431
Tunisia 442
Uganda 452
Upper Volta 459
Zaïre 467
Zambia 477
Zimbabwe 489

Appendices 499
Index 508

Africa

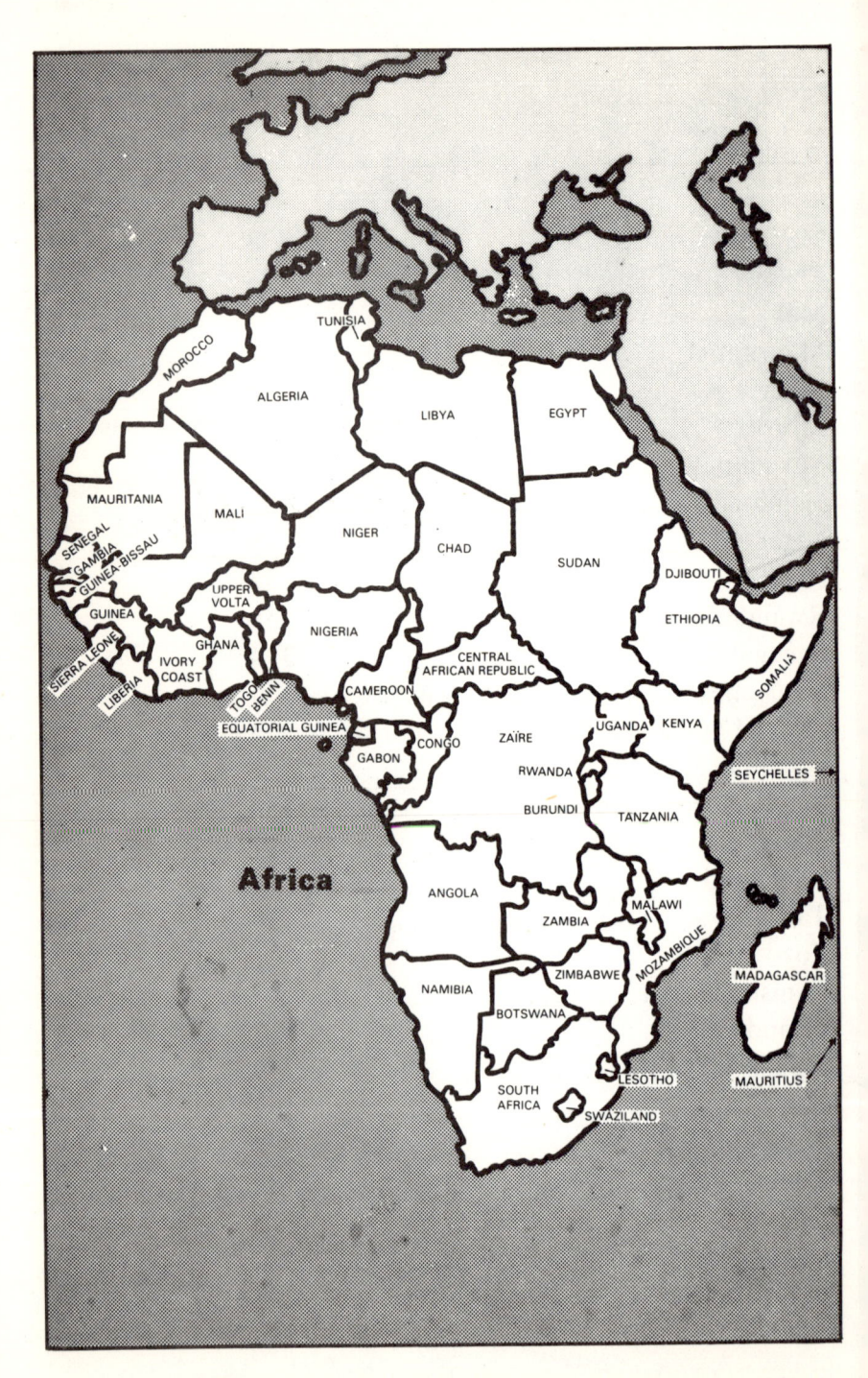

INTRODUCTION

The Business Traveller's Handbook: Africa is one of a series of travel guides designed especially for today's business traveller. Each handbook in the series covers one of the world's regions, country by country, giving detailed economic and business information as well as practical travel advice. The needs of the business traveller, so different from those of the tourist, have been thoroughly researched and considered. The result is a handbook which is not merely a convenient travel guide but, more importantly, an invaluable reference book that can be used by any business person at home or abroad.

Today more business travellers are visiting Africa than ever before, as improved transportation and communication systems have made more of the continent easily accessible. Steady expansion of agricultural, industrial and mineral production, much of which is now essential to the industrialised world, has generated growing interest among the business community the world over. Yet to many people Africa remains a continent of unknown dimensions, with a way of life in sharp contrast to that of the Western world. Business customs and practices, traditions and habits are different in the various regions of the continent, making the need for information about the countries even greater. The material contained in this handbook will help to dispel the apprehensions of the first-time visitor and provide valuable up-to-date facts and figures about an area of the world that has undergone dramatic change in the past 20 years.

By way of introduction, the handbook begins with several preliminary chapters designed to provide an overview of various medical, social and economic/political aspects of the continent that the business traveller should be aware of when planning a trip. First is a section on 'Health Information', which looks at the special problems and health risks that visitors may encounter in a tropical climate. Ranging from vaccination and immunisation schedules to discussions of malaria, bilharzia, gastro-intestinal upsets and even jet-lag, the section offers invaluable advice on how to remain in good health and get the most out of a business trip. Next is a brief survey of 'African Social Customs and Attitudes', which is essential reading for anyone visiting the continent, particularly for the first time. Featured in this section is a general explanation of the Islamic faith and its effect on the Muslim's way of life, together with practical information about Muslim etiquette and practices. And finally there is a section entitled 'International and Regional Organisations', which gives valuable background on the nature and purpose of the various organisations – such as the OAU, ACP, ECOWAS, etc. – found under the 'International Affiliations' listing in 'The Economy' section of each country.

The main portion of the handbook contains extensive chapters on 49 African countries, including the islands of Mauritius and the Seychelles. Each country is treated in a similar manner to facilitate the reader's quest for

INTRODUCTION

information, with reference material, important statistics and useful addresses clearly distinguished from the informative descriptions of the economy, geography, business climate and touristic descriptions of the major cities and towns. Each chapter begins with general information about the country under consideration – basic facts about the size and population, religion, language and government, as well as a description of the country's geography, climate and agriculture. Also included in this preliminary section is a detailed map showing the country's main physical features, cities, towns, major roads, railways and international airports. This is immediately followed by a section on the economy, which combines basic data with concise details of foreign trade, major industries, development programmes, inflation, balance of payments and much more.

Next is a section entitled 'How to Get There', which covers the various means of travel to the country available from Europe, North America and other parts of the world, together with information about visas and other entry requirements, health regulations, customs formalities and regulations governing the import of commercial samples and duty-free allowances.

The 'Practical Information for the Visitor' section presents an abundance of information, including addresses of major domestic and foreign commercial banks, details of the electricity supply and system of weights and measurements, currency, the media, medical care, telephone and telex services, public holidays, internal transport, car hire, tipping and social customs. Following this is a list of 'Useful Addresses', including foreign embassies and consulates, cultural organisations, local tourist information centres and major international travel agents.

The 'Business Information' section outlines general business conditions and gives an indication of the trade opportunities for foreign suppliers and manufacturers. The sections on 'Business Services' and 'Useful Business Addresses' lists names and addresses of companies and organisations dealing with advertising, forwarding and clearing agents, shipping, insurance and translation facilities as well as chambers of commerce, major Government ministries, and trade and professional associations.

Although business visitors have little time for sightseeing and recreational activities, a visit to some of the more beautiful and unusual attractions within a country can be both profitable and relaxing. Thus in the final section of each chapter a brief résumé of the principal historical sights and attractions of the major cities and towns in each country is given, as are suggestions for short trips and excursions. Also included is a selection of the better hotels in each city, giving details of their location in relation to the city centre and airport, and the facilities and services offered by each; particular attention has been paid to the services which are of use to the business visitor, such as secretarial and translation services, public telex facilities, availability of audio-visual equipment and the capacity of conference and banquet rooms. Restaurants and nightclubs are also listed, together with sports and social clubs, cultural attractions, local sporting events and a selection of local shops and markets, which will make the task of gift-buying much easier.

INTRODUCTION

It must be stressed that some of the information in this guide is subject to constant change. On the simplest level, it is widely accepted that the regulations governing visa and health requirements are frequently altered and revised. More importantly, there is the volatile nature of the political climate in certain areas of Africa to be considered. Political instability in a number of countries has led to changes of government and new policy orientations even as this guide was being compiled, and in some of the more extreme instances economic and tourist information has been virtually nonexistent. Where coverage seems sparse, it is hope that the reader will understand the problems involved in gathering relevant data. At the time of writing, several nations – notably the former Portuguese colonies of Angola, Mozambique and Guinea-Bissau and countries like Uganda and Zimbabwe – were engaged in the work of reconstruction after years of internal turmoil and war, and other areas – including Chad, Namibia, the Western Sahara and the Ogaden Desert region – were being disrupted by fitful guerrilla warfare. Whilst every effort has been made to ensure that the information given is both accurate and up to date, the writers and publishers are unable to assume any responsibility in this connection. If in any doubt, travellers are advised to contact the nearest diplomatic mission or tourist office of the country they intend to visit.

It is hoped that no aspect of a business visit has been overlooked in the compilation of this handbook, and that the presentation and arrangement of the various sections within each chapter make this a readable guide as well as a book to be used for quick and easy reference.

HEALTH INFORMATION

Any traveller visiting a tropical region will be exposed to health risks which are rarely found in the more temperate areas of Europe and North America. These risks may take the form of epidemic diseases, many of which have now been eradicated or brought under control through a wide-scale vaccination programme and against which a number of vaccinations are readily available. Or, more commonly, these risks are the minor complaints caused by a drastic change of climate, general insanitary conditions, a change of diet or the lack of immunity against local diseases and infections.

Whilst good health can never be totally guaranteed in a different climate and environment, there are many steps which you can take personally to ensure that your visit abroad is free from illness and health problems. Precautions such as vaccinations are amongst the more obvious ones, and indeed entry regulations into many tropical countries require that the visitor be in possession of certain International Certificates of Vaccination. General caution about food and drink, the water supply and the type of clothing suitable for a hot climate is not so obvious, and it is these small points which the traveller often forgets about and suffers from in the long run.

The advice and recommendations listed here apply in general to most tropical regions. Where a more uncommon disease is endemic in a particular country, travellers should seek additional advice from their doctor or should contact the nearest diplomatic mission of that country or the World Health Organisation (WHO). Travellers suffering from a chronic illness or with a personal medical history of illness may need to take extra precautions and, once again, the advice of a doctor should be sought. The information given here is aimed at the traveller who already enjoys good health and who should, if the advice given here is heeded, remain that way.

Vaccination Schedule

The schedules listed below are intended for international travel. Schedule I is designed for those travellers who have sufficient time to complete the course – it provides the maximum immunity, but can be modified according to individual requirements and circumstances. Schedule II gives a lesser degree of immunity, but provides adequate protection for those who have to arrange a long-distance trip at short notice.

International Certificates of Vaccination are issued for smallpox, yellow fever and cholera only.

Schedule I
Week 1 Yellow fever vaccination: Available at special centres only. A certificate will only become valid 10 days after the inoculation. The period of immunity is 10 years.

4 Smallpox vaccination (primary or re-vaccination): Certificates

HEALTH INFORMATION

become valid 8 days after a primary vaccination or from the day of a re-vaccination for a period of 3 years.
- **5** Reading of smallpox vaccination.
- **7** TAB or T (typhoid) (1) and tetanus toxoid (1).
- **10** Polio (oral) vaccination (1).
- **13** TAB or T (typhoid) (2) and tetanus toxoid (2).
- **16** Polio (oral) vaccination (2).
- **22** Polio (oral) vaccination (3).
- **39** TAB or T (typhoid) (3) and tetanus toxoid (3).

Schedule II
- **Day 1** Yellow fever, cholera (1) and polio (oral) (1).
- **5** Smallpox, TAB or T (typhoid) (1) and tetanus toxoid (1).
- **11** Cholera (2).
- **13** Reading of smallpox vaccination.
- **28** Polio (oral) (2), TAB or T (typhoid) (2) and tetanus toxoid (2).

Malaria

Although malaria has been eradicated from many parts of the world and brought under control in others, it is still the main cause of illness and death among people living in the tropics and is the principal health hazard to visitors from malaria-free countries who have not acquired immunity from the disease. The risk of malaria varies according to altitude and temperature and does not usually occur when the mean annual temperature is less than 15.6°C/60°F.

In all there are 4 types of malaria that affect humans, and common to all of them is the fact that they are transmitted only by the female anopheline mosquito. When the mosquito bites, the malaria parasites are inserted into the bloodstream from where they spread to other parts of the body.

Preventative Measures

The anopheline mosquito usually bites only after dark and therefore you should keep well covered at night – long sleeves and long trousers or skirts should be worn. The use of an effective insect repellent such as Flypel or Skeet-o-Stick or any other preparation containing DET (diethyl toluamide) on the exposed areas of the body, combined with protective clothing as suggested above, will considerably reduce the risk of malaria. Mosquito nets should always be used at night in unscreened bedrooms; an insecticidal spray is also useful in the bedroom.

However, the most successful and effective means of prevention is the anti-malarial tablet or prophylactic. Most of these are taken on a daily basis throughout the stay in the malarial area, for 1 week prior to the visit and for at least 28 days after departure from the risk area. Some tablets need only be taken once or twice a week, but it is generally easier to remember to take a daily tablet, and the consequences of forgetting 1 daily tablet are less serious than if the weekly tablet is forgotten. The drugs mentioned below are manufactured under a variety of names, some of which are listed in brackets.

Proguanil (Paludrine or Chlorguanide) is among the most effective tablets and is taken daily as described above. Weekly tablets include Pyrimethamine (Daraprim), Chloroquine (Aralen, Avlocor, Nivaquine, Resochin) and Amodiaquine (Camoquin, Floroquine). In their recommended doses, Proguanil, Pyrimethamine and Chloroquine are considered safe during pregnancy. Note that prophylactics which contain sulphonamides should be avoided during pregnancy.

The main symptoms of malaria are fever, enlargement of the spleen and progressive anaemia caused by the destruction of the red blood cells. If, despite taking anti-malarial tablets, you develop any of these symptoms you should consult a doctor immediately. The incubation period of the disease is 10–14 days and it is essential that prophylactics are taken for at least 28 days after leaving a malaria area. If you should fall ill a few weeks after returning home, you should visit your doctor immediately and explain where you have been.

Bilharzia

Bilharzia, more commonly known as schistosomiasis, is one of the most widespread and debilitating diseases in tropical Africa. It is caused by blood flukes (schistosomes) of which 3 species commonly infect man. 2 species (*Schistosoma haematobium* and *S. mansoni*) are commonly found in Africa, while *S. japonicum* is most prevalent in Asia.

The life cycle of the 3 species is similar. Eggs are deposited in the veins of the abdomen by adult male and female worms. These eggs work their way through to the bladder (*S. haematobium*) or the bowels (*S. mansoni* and *S. japonicum*) and are subsequently discharged in the faeces or urine. Upon reaching water, larvae hatch from the eggs and must then enter the bodies of certain aquatic snails – of the genus Bulinus in the case of *S. haematobium* and Biomphalaria in the case of *S. mansoni*. Failure to find a suitable snail within about 48 hours results in death for the larvae. Once inside a snail, they grow for 4 weeks before the young flukes (cercariae) pass back into the water where they await a human host. Again, they must find a host within 1 or 2 days to survive. Back in the human body, they develop, mate and move to the veins where the eggs are laid.

The relative importance of the groups of schistosomiasis varies from area to area in Africa and other species occur in other mammals. The aquatic snails favour shallow water near lake shores or in streams, tending to be more abundant in lightly polluted water near human habitation and, in general, they are more likely to be present in stagnant (rather than moving) waters and in water containing vegetation. Swimming pools may well be infected, especially if water is drawn from a stream. The ability of the Bulinus snail to aestivate in dry mud means that even the draining of infested water may not be effective; indeed, this ability of the snail is essential for its survival over much of East Africa.

The symptoms of the disease may start with an otherwise inexplicable fever, followed by a discharge of blood in the faeces or urine. When fully developed, schistosomiasis is painful and crippling as adult flukes can remain in the veins for several years laying eggs and causing repeated and cumulative damage. Any possible risk of contraction should be avoided and effective treatment should be sought as soon as possible once the disease is diagnosed. The most frequently used remedy is antimony, in the form of Astiban. The effectiveness of the cure, however, is dependent upon the general physical condition of the victim. Swimmers in tropical Africa may also experience a mild itch from related species of schistosoma which usually breed in other mammals; these species can enter the human skin and cause local irritation without developing further.

The best prevention lies in avoiding infected water by boiling all drinking and washing water or leaving water covered for a minimum of 4 days before use. Long-term hopes for a reduction in the general level of the disease lie in training people to refrain from urinating or defecating near water. Large-scale application of molluscicide to infected water is also effective. Where contact with water likely to be infected is unavoidable, an insecticide should be applied to the skin. Immediate and thorough drying also reduces the risk of infection.

Infectious Hepatitis

This is endemic in many parts of Africa and Asia as well as throughout South America, and is often caught by travellers to these areas. The best means of prevention is to eat only well-prepared food, avoid drinking water which you suspect may be contaminated and pay careful attention to personal hygiene. An injection of human immuno-globulin (gammaglobulin) will give added protection lasting for between 4 and 6 months. No preventative vaccine for infectious hepatitis is yet available.

Intestinal Upsets

Few travellers escape stomach upsets of one kind or another when visiting hot, tropical areas, and although the result is usually nothing more serious than an attack of diarrhoea lasting a few days, this can be very unpleasant and may prevent the business traveller from carrying out a planned schedule of meetings and visits.

Intestinal upsets are largely the result of unhygienic food preparation and other generally insanitary conditions. The chances of suffering from this complaint can be reduced if the following precautions are taken:

- Avoid eating uncooked vegetables, unpeeled fruit and salads.
- Keep away from restaurants which are fly-infested or have an otherwise grubby appearance. Do not buy food from street vendors.
- Take particular care with shellfish. It is best to see them alive and make sure the cooked product is the same that you have chosen.

HEALTH INFORMATION

● Tap water is safe to drink in most large cities and towns but if in any doubt, drink only filtered or boiled water. Bottled water is usually available in places where the water supply is considered unsafe. Alternatively water-sterilising tablets can be used. Milk should also be boiled unless you are sure that it has been properly pasteurised. (Further information about the water supply in individual countries is given in the 'Medical Care' section of each chapter.)

The most effective drugs against diarrhoea are Diphenoxylate with Atropine (e.g., Lomotil), Kaolin and Morphine, Paregoric and Codeine Phosphate. Travellers affected by vomiting in addition to diarrhoea should take Metoclopramide (Maxolon, Primperan, Berk) in tablet or injection form. Streptotriad tablets have proven relatively effective as an anti-diarrhoea measure.

If you suffer a more serious outbreak of diarrhoea, accompanied by severe abdominal pain, fever and passing of blood, it is likely that you are suffering from dysentery and medical advice should be sought immediately.

Heat

Acclimatisation to high temperatures usually takes at least 2 weeks and most visitors, unused to working in extreme heat conditions, feel tired and apathetic. This is even more noticeable where the relative humidity is high. Drink plenty of liquids and take extra salt with your food – alternatively, additional salt can be taken in tablet or solution form, but this is less effective.

It is most important to encourage perspiration by wearing clothes that will absorb sweat and therefore encourage you to sweat more. Cotton is the ideal fabric for hot climates; man-made fibres should be avoided wherever possible as they do not absorb sweat, leaving the skin permanently moist and susceptible to 'prickly heat'.

Although you may be tempted in excessive heat to take a quick dip in a fresh-water lake or river, avoid doing this as the water is more than likely contaminated and there is a high risk of schistosomiasis or bilharzia (*see above*).

Altitude

Visitors to high altitude areas (in general those over 3,000m/9,480ft) may be susceptible to *soroche*, or mountain sickness. This can be avoided if you rest for a few hours on arrival and avoid the consumption of alcohol and greasy food. Heavy smokers should try to cut down on cigarettes while in high altitude areas.

A gentle process of acclimatisation is essential, so avoid rushing about and over-exertion of any kind – a good lesson in how to move around can be learnt from the local people. You may feel breathless and suffer from heart pounding together with insomnia, but these are general conditions mainly caused by the lack of oxygen and should not give cause for alarm.

The symptoms of *soroche* are headache, dizziness, nausea, flatulence and vomiting – pain-killers (avoid aspirin-based ones) can be taken for headaches and anti-emetics for vomiting.

Air Travel

Despite the comfort and ease of modern air travel, even the most experienced traveller can fall victim to a number of disorders ranging from sickness and general discomfort to the common complaint of jet-lag. There are no hard and fast rules for avoiding these problems, but the following hints and suggestions may go a long way to overcoming them and ensuring trouble-free air travel.

Air sickness is usually caused by a bumpy flight combined with excitement, worry or any form of mental strain which the traveller may be experiencing. Turbulence can affect the inner ear and thus the balance mechanism of the individual, resulting in sickness. Try to avoid all greasy and fatty foods served on the aircraft, and drink and smoke in moderation. Keep your head as still as possible.

Dehydration may occur on long flights due to the rather dry atmosphere within the aircraft cabin. Drink plenty of fluids, but avoid alcohol as this will increase dehydration rather than reduce it.

Pressurisation discomfort may occur as the gases in the body, and particularly in the intestines, expand due to the changing pressure conditions in the aircraft cabin. Avoid overeating and fizzy drinks as these will cause the body gases to expand further. It is advisable to wear loose clothing and loose-fitting shoes or the socks provided on long-distance flights by some airlines (this will also help those who suffer from swollen feet and ankles).

The change of pressure during take-off and landing can cause a popping sensation in the ears or ear-ache and sometimes partial deafness. Repeated yawning or swallowing will overcome this. Sinus trouble is often aggravated when flying, and the use of nose drops helps to alleviate this. Smokers are particularly affected by cabin pressure and the decrease in oxygen often causes headaches and dizziness. The obvious remedy is to reduce smoking and, if possible, omit it altogether during a flight.

Jet-lag will affect any traveller on a journey involving a change of time zone, whether from east to west or vice versa. The body is programmed to a 24-hour clock and cannot immediately adjust to changes where, for example, bedtime occurs several hours later or earlier than usual. Sleeping and eating habits are usually affected, and travellers may suffer from constipation. Your general alertness and reactions will be much slower, in general for a period of 2–3 days. The effects of jet-lag appear to be greater on west–east flights than on westbound flights, as it is far more difficult to adjust to a daily routine several hours *ahead* of your habitual one.

General medical advice on the question of jet-lag is to allow a 24-hour rest period after a 5-hour time change; similarly, 48 hours are recommended for a 10-hour time change. On arrival, try to get to bed as close as possible to your normal bedtime. Do not arrange to attend any important meetings or business functions immediately after your arrival and avoid having to make important decisions until you feel fully acclimatised to the time change.

AFRICAN SOCIAL CUSTOMS AND ATTITUDES

More than any other factor, it is the geographical diversity of Africa that has necessitated the adoption of a wide variety of modes of livelihood. The shifting patterns of population as people migrated from region to region over the centuries, sometimes quickly but more often gradually, created cultural barriers of language and custom giving rise to the different tribal identities which many African politicians are striving to discourage in favour of a new and unfamiliar nationalism.

Yet, for all the readily perceivable variations in social customs, from the standpoint of the business traveller practices are not likely to be particularly strange. The colonial experience common to nearly all African countries (the exceptions being Ethiopia and Liberia), although varying in length and consequences, has in many places continued to provide the model for the conduct for business and government affairs even after independence, especially in dealings with the representatives of foreign companies.

The spread of Islam southwards into West Africa particularly, but also to Central and East Africa, following traditional trade routes, has added the code of behaviour derived from Islamic law to the African customs of which the business visitor should be aware.

Trade in many African countries is largely in the hands of various ethnic groups – for example, the Lebanese in West Africa, Indians in East and South Africa, and Greeks in Central Africa. Where British and French colonial interests have been strong, somewhat 'old-fashioned' social attitudes might still prevail, various countries in southern Africa being particularly conservative in matters of dress and behaviour.

Business visitors to those African states which have undergone protracted liberation struggles or a socialist revolution should be aware of the feeling of national and international solidarity expressed by people and Government. Care should be taken not to offend with outspoken support or with criticism of the system of government in the states.

The principal languages in use in commercial circles in African countries are the various languages of the colonial powers, that is English, French, Portuguese, Spanish, German and Italian. Also widely spoken are Swahili in East Africa, Afrikaans in South Africa, Arabic in North Africa and Hausa in West Africa, while Creole languages are common in West African countries. The African continent is extremely complex linguistically with over 2,000 named languages.

MUSLIM SOCIAL CUSTOMS

It is useful for any business visitor to Africa to have some knowledge of Muslim social customs and mores as many of the countries dealt with in this handbook are Muslim states or have a large Muslim population. Many of the customs and practices encountered by travellers to these countries seem strange and often contrary to their own beliefs, and visitors often find themselves in an embarrassing situation where they have offended their hosts quite innocently and unwittingly. Such a situation can easily be avoided if the visitor has some previous knowledge of the Muslim traditions and practices which play such an important role in all aspects of life.

The information given here is intended to clear up many of the misunderstandings and questions which occur time and time again in the mind of the non-Muslim. We have dealt with the most common beliefs and practices which, in general, apply to all Muslim countries, but it is important to remember that every country also has its own particular customs and mores which may differ from those stated here.

Muslims, or Muhammadans, belong to the Islamic faith and observe, to varying degrees, the following basic tenets of Islam: profession of the faith, prayer (5 times a day), alms giving, fasting, and pilgrimage or *Hajj*. Faith and the ritual accompanying such faith are extremely important to the Muslim believer. Islamic teaching provides the basis for many of the prevailing customs and practices, and the non-Muslim may find these easier to understand when seen in the light of their traditional significance.

The month of *Ramadan* is perhaps the best known of all the Muslim religious festivals – this is the major event of the Muslim calendar and is a time of fasting for all Muslims. Strict Muslims must refrain from eating, drinking and smoking during daylight hours, and non-Muslims are also expected to respect this tradition and refrain from such practices, at least while in public places. (In some countries meals are served during the daytime to non-Muslims in their hotel rooms.) It is important not to infringe the laws of *Ramadan* as this would cause considerable offence to many Muslims and may be punishable in some of the stricter Muslim countries.

Business visitors will find that the month of *Ramadan* is best avoided in predominantly Muslim countries as business comes to a virtual standstill in many cities, particularly during the 3–4 day festival of *Eid el Fitr* at the end of the month, and it is difficult to accomplish much work during this period.

The Muslim stance on alcohol is extremely important to be aware of. Indeed the mention of the word is virtually taboo in some places. Generally speaking, Muslims consider that alcohol damages personal health and efficiency and diminishes the emotional control of the individual – for this reason alcohol is prohibited under Islamic law. Alcohol is not readily available in many Muslim countries, although it can be purchased and consumed by foreigners in hotels and restaurants in the more liberal countries. Visitors should acquaint themselves with the alcohol laws of a particular country

MUSLIM SOCIAL CUSTOMS

before commencing their visit, and it is best to avoid the temptation of smuggling alcohol past the customs authorities on arrival. Infringement of the laws relating to alcohol is a punishable offence in many Muslim states, and quite frankly it is not worth risking a fine or imprisonment or jeopardising valuable business relationships. More detailed information can be found within the individual chapters in the handbook.

The Arabs are noted for their generous hospitality, but non-Muslims are often intimidated by the rituals of receiving and entertaining guests within the Muslim world. There is no reason to feel ill at ease with these practices if the following basic points of general etiquette are observed.

Handshaking is mandatory on arrival and departure, and an Arab may often keep hold of your hand while engaging you in conversation. The most common greeting used in the Middle East is '*Salaam alaykum*', meaning 'Peace be with you' – to which the reply is '*Wa alaykum as-salaam*', meaning 'And on you be peace'. The correct form of address when speaking to a male is '*Sayyid*' and to a female '*Sayida*' or '*Sitt*'. In Egypt and the eastern Arab states, an alternative form of address is '*Abu*' (father of) or '*Umm*' (mother of) followed by the name of the eldest son. In some areas it has become common practice to use the name of the eldest daughter if she is the firstborn.

When calling upon a Muslim, never make the sole of your foot plainly visible as this is considered rude. When offered anything, always receive it in the right hand; similarly, always give with the right hand. If coffee is offered, it should be accepted, and the cup should be taken and given back with the right hand. It is preferable to drink at least 2 cups – if no further coffee is required, simply shake the cup when returning it to your host or hostess and this will signify your refusal. When returning hospitality to an Arab, remember that the consumption of alcohol and pig meat is forbidden by Muslim law and neither of these should be offered.

Female business visitors may encounter more difficulty than their male counterparts. Women are viewed in a special way in the Arab world and the Western visitor will notice a definite discrimination against women, although this is less severe in countries such as Egypt and the West African nations.

Women should dress soberly and avoid clothes which might be considered in any way revealing. In the more conservative countries, women may find themselves excluded from certain business and social functions and, although this often seems unreasonable, there is nothing one can do other than accept this practice. In general, Arab men do not talk about their womenfolk and would not expect, for example, to be asked about the health of their wife.

The various social customs and practices outlined here are not intended as a definitive summary of the Muslim code of behaviour. We have tried to highlight the more important points of etiquette and law which are most likely to affect the non-Muslim visitor. Observance of these few rules should ensure an enjoyable and trouble-free visit and, more importantly, should enable the development of lasting and profitable relationships with Muslim business contacts who, for their part, will take note of and appreciate the respect shown for their way of life.

INTERNATIONAL AND REGIONAL ORGANISATIONS

The following organisations represent the interests of African countries and are amongst the 'International Affiliations' referred to in each chapter under 'The Economy'.

United Nations (UN)
There are several UN agencies of particular importance to African states.

Economic Commission for Africa (ECA)
The ECA was created in 1948 to assist the economic development of member nations of which there are now 49, with Namibia, France and the United Kingdom accorded associate membership. An annual Conference of Ministers determines general policy, initiates action and reviews progress. Programmes under way include 5 Trans-African Highways, the Pan-African Telecommunications Network (PANAFTEL) and teaching at various centres for applied research into agriculture, energy and mineral resources, technology and social development. The ECA is based in Addis Ababa, Ethiopia.

Food and Agriculture Organisation (FAO)
The FAO was established in 1945 to coordinate efforts to reduce world food shortages and to improve nutritional levels. The organisation promotes educational and training schemes and has sought to bring government, business and scientific representatives together in pursuit of its aims. Aid is donated by various countries and international institutions. The FAO is based in Rome, Italy.

International Bank for Reconstruction and Development (IBRD)
Also known as the World Bank, the IBRD makes loans to governments and companies in member nations where private capital is unavailable or too expensive, in order to promote economic development. Affiliated institutions include the International Development Association (IDA) and the International Finance Corporation (IFC). The IBRD is based in Washington, D.C.

United Nations Development Programme (UNDP)
Established in 1965, the UNDP assists in the development of the natural and human resources of member nations through technical co-operation projects. A number of international development organisations, including other UN agencies and several regional development banks, are involved in UNDP schemes. Policies are decided by a Governing Council composed of representatives from 48 member nations. The UNDP is based in New York City.

The UN promotes educational and health programmes in many African countries through the United Nations Educational, Scientific and Cultural

Organisation (UNESCO) and the World Health Organisation (WHO). In addition, there are 3 General Assembly Committees especially concerned with Africa: the Committee of Trustees of the United Nations Trust Fund for South Africa, the Special Committee against Apartheid and the United Nations Council for Namibia.

Organisation for African Unity (OAU)

The OAU charter was signed in May 1963 and the organisation now counts all African states as members, except Namibia and South Africa. Zimbabwe is expected to become the 50th member of the OAU. The objectives of the OAU are to promote unity and mutual support amongst the independent African states in accordance with the principles of the Charter of the United Nations and to encourage coordinated attempts to improve living standards throughout the continent. An annual Assembly of Heads of State and a twice-yearly Council of Ministers debate, decide and coordinate policies, whilst a number of departments of the General Secretariat administer the different areas of concern to the OAU (Economic and Social, Educational and Cultural, Legal, Press and Information, etc.). In addition, there are several specialised committees and commissions. The OAU is based in Addis Ababa, Ethiopia.

The African, Caribbean and Pacific group of countries (ACP)

The ACP states are those countries which have come together to negotiate trade and aid agreements with the European Economic Community (EEC) at the Lomé Conventions of 1975 (Lomé I) and 1979 (Lomé II). The purpose of Lomé I and II was to establish a comprehensive formula for the coordination of trade arrangements and financial assistance between the industrialised EEC nations and the 'underdeveloped' ACP states. The agreements signed at Lomé I have proved to be of mutual benefit to the 2 blocs of countries involved as a successful and practical, albeit imperfect, framework within which trade and aid can be conducted.

There are now a total of 57 ACP states claiming associate membership of the EEC. Administration is kept to a minimum, with representatives from each ACP and EEC country forming the Council of Ministers and the Committee of Ambassadors. The Consultative Assembly is composed of equal numbers of representatives from the EEC and ACP blocs. A numbers of committees and sub-committees direct operations relating to specific commodities and aspects of trade concerning member states.

The introduction of the STABEX scheme was one of the most important provisions of Lomé I. The central feature and advantage of STABEX to the ACP countries is that export volume and earnings have been largely fixed in advance (for the first time in the case of many independent ACP nations) facilitating more accurate economic planning in the countries often dependent on one or two commodities for their economic well-being in fluctuating world markets. Of equal importance are the trade arrangements whereby most ACP exports are permitted tariff-free entry to EEC markets. The few products disallowed are those which might compete with or disrupt production under the Common Agricultural Policy (CAP). Some 20% of EEC aid to developing nations is channelled through bodies associated with the Lomé Conventions, the most important of which are the European Development Fund (EDF) and the European Investment Bank (EIB). EDF project contracts are open to tenders from all companies in ACP or EEC countries. Other bodies associated with the Lomé Conventions include the Centre for Industrial Development in Brussels and a soon to be opened Technical Centre for Agricultural Co-operation.

African Development Bank (ADB)
The ADB commenced operations in 1966, having been created with ECA help in 1964; all OAU member states are now also members of the ADB. Administration is in the hands of an elected President, Board of Directors and a Board of Governors, each of whom is nominated by a member country. ADB Loans have gone to projects in all regions of Africa, mostly to agriculture and related industries. 4 associated institutions, the African Development Fund, the Nigeria Trust Fund, the African Reinsurance Corporation (AFRICARE) and the Société Internationale Financière pour les Investissements et le Développement en Afrique (SIFIDA), have been established by the ABD, and the Bank co-operates extensively with other development finance establishments including the World Bank and BADEA.

Arab League (AL)
The League of Arab States was formed in 1945 to strengthen economic and cultural links between Arab countries. 8 African states are now members. Regular summit and ministerial conferences have been held, and a growing number of specialised agencies and committees now operate under the aegis of the League. League members are involved in attempts to establish common duties and taxes on trade and in the coordination of industrial development. However, the League is basically a consultative body and specific measures must be agreed to separately by the states concerned. The Arab Monetary Fund (AMF), established by Arab League nations, plays an important role in Arab financial affairs by redistributing contributions received from the oil-rich states in the form of loans to countries experiencing financial difficulties.

Arab Bank for Economic Development in Africa (BADEA)
BADEA was established by the Arab League in 1973 to further economic development in Africa by contributing financial and technical assistance. The Bank commenced operations in 1975 under a Board of Governors and a Board of Directors dispensing aid contributed by Arab League members (except Djibouti, Somalia, and North and South Yemen) to OAU countries. BADEA loans and grants have helped to finance numerous projects in Africa with most money being channelled to West Africa. Aid is distributed according to the priorities determined by recipient countries. The Special Arab Assistance Fund for Africa (SAAFA) merged with BADEA in 1976. BADEA is based in Khartoum, Sudan.

The Commonwealth
The Commonwealth, formerly the British Commonwealth formed in 1931, is now a free association of former British colonies and territories holding regular conferences of prime ministers and finance ministers to discuss matters of mutual interest. A number of associated organisations in the cultural, educational and sporting fields link member nations, but economic co-operation is limited. The Commonwealth is based in London.

Organisation of Petroleum Exporting Countries (OPEC)
OPEC was formed in 1960 with the object of unifying the petroleum policies of members to give the exporting states greater strength in price negotiations with the oil companies. Although the unity envisaged in the original agreement has not been achieved, OPEC has become a very powerful organisation controlling the vast majority of oil traded in the world. There are now 4 African member states (Algeria, Gabon, Libya, Nigeria). The Council of Representatives draws up policy and is OPEC's highest decision-making body. A Board of Governors, composed of 1 governor from each member state, is responsible for the annual budget and for carrying out decisions made by the conference. The Secretariat under a Secretary-General supervises the running of OPEC affairs with several specialised departments and committees to deal with different areas of interest. OPEC is based in Vienna.

Organisation of Arab Petroleum Exporting Countries (OAPEC)
OAPEC was established in 1968 for mutual economic co-operation relating to petroleum production amongst members. Originally members states had to be predominantly reliant upon oil revenue, but since 1970 membership has been extended to smaller producers. The resources of member countries have been utilised on a number of joint projects and various funds and companies have been set up under the aegis of OAPEC. OAPEC has always closely coordinated its policies with those of OPEC. A twice-yearly Council of Ministers made up of the oil ministers of the member states formulates general policy and decides upon the rules governing members. The Executive Committee makes recommendations and is responsible for the implementation of Council resolutions. The General Secretariat, divided into a number of departments, is the executive body. OAPEC is based in Kuwait.

Communaute Economique de l'Afrique de l'Ouest (CEAO)
The Community was established in 1974 and, like the West African Customs Union (UDEAO) which it replaced, it is composed of former French West African colonies. At present, there are 6 member countries, with Benin and Togo accorded observer status. The main aims of CEAO are to coordinate the trade and customs regulations of member states and to formulate development programmes for transport and communications, industry, energy, tourism, research and external trade for the mutual benefit of member nations. All non-manufactured and most manufactured goods produced in the CEAO states do not attract customs duties or taxes when exported to other member states; instead a Regional Co-operation Tax is paid. In addition to

encouraging trade within the Community, the CEAO also contributes financial assistance to projects in member countries. The highest authority of the CEAO is the Conference of Heads of State held at least once a year. The Council of Ministers meets twice yearly for detailed consultations. The General Secretariat is the executive body. The CEAO is based in Ouagadougou, Upper Volta.

Economic Community of West African States (ECOWAS)

ECOWAS was created by the Treaty of Lagos in 1975 to promote trade and further economic links between the 16 member states. The reduction of customs duties, taxes on trade and restrictions on the movement of people and capital within the Community is envisaged with the formation of a Customs Union over the next 15 years. A summit meeting of the heads of state is the supreme authority with a Council of Ministers to discuss and decide upon policy details and administrative matters. An Executive Secretariat organises operations with 4 commissions working on particular areas of interest. The Fund for Co-operation, Compensation and Development, to which Nigeria is the major contributor, provides compensation for member countries adversely affected by the application of the provisions of the treaty and other financial assistance to reduce disparities in development. At present, research is under way to determine the economic and social development needs of ECOWAS members. ECOWAS is based in Lagos, Nigeria.

Franc Zone

The Franc Zone consist of countries with currencies linked and fully convertible with the French franc at a fixed rate of exchange and with at least 65% of their reserves held in French francs. Agreements between the 14 countries and France form the basis of the Zone. All members have their own central bank of issue, the Central Bank of West African States (BCEAO), the Central African Bank (BEAC) and the West African Monetary Union (UMAO) being the major institutions associated with the Franc Zone in Africa. The CFA franc is used in all African Franc Zone countries except Mali, where the Mali franc is used. CFA stands for Communauté Financière Africaine in the West African states and for Coopération Financière en Afrique Centrale in Central African member states. France also provides financial and technical assistance to Franc Zone countries administered by 3 Paris-based institutions: Fonds d'Aide et Coopération (FAC), Caisse Centrale de Coopération Economique (CCCE) and Bureau de Liaison des Agents de Coopération Technique (BLACT).

Organisation Commune Africaine et Mauricienne (OCAM)

OCAM was founded in 1965 and exists to assist the economic and social development of its members, having decided to largely abandon its role in political affairs. Since its inception, objectives have been changed from an all African Common Market to a confederacy of African economic communities within which mutual assistance in economic and social affairs may be more effective and which can provide a united front for negotiations with the industrialised nations and other organisations. Biannual Conferences of heads of state and an annual Council of Ministers are the highest authorities of OCAM with the Council administering the Secretariat General in the execution of policy decisions. Numerous agencies, departments and other specialised institutions are associated with OCAM. OCAM is based in Bangui, Central African Republic.

Economic Community of the Great Lakes (CEPGL)
The CEPGL was founded in 1976 to promote the development of the resources of the Ruzizi Valley and Lakes Kivu and Tanganyika to the benefit of the 3 member countries, Burundi, Rwanda and Zaïre. The formation of a common market is anticipated. The CEPGL is based in Kisenyi, Rwanda.

Gambia River Development Organisation (GRDO)
The GRDO was formed in 1973 by Senegal and Gambia. Planned projects include the construction of 3 dams on the Gambia River.

Kagera River Basin Organisation (KRBO)
The KRBO was formed in 1977 between Burundi, Rwanda and Tanzania to exploit the natural resources of the area and to improve agricultural productivity, transport facilities and to encourage tourism and trade.

Lake Chad Basin Commission (LCBC)
Created in 1964, the Commission consists of 4 member countries – Cameroon, Chad, Niger and Nigeria – and exists to coordinate the development of the Chad Basin, particularly water resources for agricultural use. Livestock, fisheries, transport and communications are to be improved with UN, French and US aid. All activities are administered by the Executive Secretary and 2 representatives from each member state who make up the Commission which is based in N'Djamena, Chad.

Mano River Union (MRU)
The Mano River Declaration of 1973 laid the basis for what may become a full customs and economic union between Liberia and Sierra Leone. A common external tariff was established in 1977 and further joint economic development is planned. Policy decisions are made by the Joint Ministerial Committee. The Mano River Union is based in Freetown, Sierra Leone.

Niger River Commission (NRC)
The Commission was set up in 1963 to research, administer and develop the River Niger. Projects include navigability studies, flood control surveys and a 5-year programme for the development and the regulation of the river. A Council of Ministers decides policy to be carried out by the Executive Secretariat. The Commission is based in Niamey, Niger.

Organisation pour la Mise en Valeur du Fleuve Sénégal (OMVS)
OMVS was created in 1973 to succeed the Organisation des Etats Riverains

du Sénégal (OERS) with the principal objective of developing the resources of the Senegal River Basin. The 3 members of OMVS are Senegal, Mali and Mauritania, whose heads of state meet to make policy decisions, leaving the Council of Ministers to negotiate general policy and review progress. Plans originally centred on controlling the River Senegal have now been broadened to include a number of projects related to the river, amongst which are a hydro-electric dam, irrigation projects and a programme of river port and harbour improvements to which a number of American, European and Arab countries and development agencies are to contribute financial and technical assistance. OMVS is based in Dakar, Senegal.

South African Customs Union (SACU)

SACU was created by the Customs Union Agreement which came into operation in 1970. The 4 member countries, Botswana, Lesotho, South Africa and Swaziland, benefit from shares in the common fund made up of customs, excise and sales duties levied within the Customs Union area. Shares in the common pool are determined by the level of imports, exports and production of each member state. Most goods produced in SACU member countries may be exported to other member countries without attracting any taxes; however, there are provisions to protect certain sectors of the developing economies of Botswana, Lesotho and Swaziland. Within the Rand Monetary Area (RMA), formed by monetary agreement between South Africa, Lesotho and Swaziland, the South African rand is acceptable as legal tender, although both Swaziland and Lesotho have now introduced their own currencies.

L'Union Douanière et Economique de l'Afrique Centrale (UDEAC)

The UDEAC was created by the Brazzaville Treaty in 1964 to replace the Union Douanière Equatoriale and has been in effect since 1966. There are 4 member states – Cameroon, Central African Republic, Congo and Gabon – with Chad retaining observer status. The supreme authority with UDEAC is the Council of Heads of State which meets regularly. The Executive Council, composed of Finance Ministers and other government representatives concerned with economic development, meets at least twice yearly to discuss policy. A General Secretariat executes policy decisions through its 2 divisions – Customs, and Fiscal and Economic Development. The objectives of the UDEAC are to extend economic integration beyond the existing limits of co-operation, and a number of vital industrial projects are planned within the UDEAC area. At present the Customs Union ensures duty-free trade between member states with a common principal import tariff, a common code for investment policy, a similar tax system and the right of people to move freely between the 4 countries. The UDEAC is based in Bangui, Central African Republic.

KEY TO SYMBOLS

Hotels
- ✱ Air conditioning in rooms
- ▥ Central heating in rooms
- ▤ Credit cards
- ☎ Direct-dial telephones in rooms
- FC Foreign currency exchanged
- ⚐ Laundry and valet service
- 📻 Radio in rooms
- ▽ Room service available
- S Secretarial services
- ☐ Television in rooms
- ♂ Translation services
- TC Travellers' cheques exchanged
- ㉔ 24-hour room service available

Maps
- ——— National boundaries
- ═══ Major roads
- ┈┈┈ Major railways
- ✈ International airport
- ⚓ Port
- ⚓ River port
- ▨ Disputed territory
- - - - - Cease-fire line

ALGERIA
Democratic and Popular Republic of Algeria

Geography	29
The Economy	31
How to Get There	32
Entry Regulations	32
Practical Information for the Visitor	33
Useful Addresses (General)	35
Business Information	35
Business Services	36
Useful Addresses (Business)	36
Algiers	36
Oran	38

Size: 2,381,741 sq.km/919,594 sq.miles.

Population: 18.91 million (1978).

Distribution: 30% in urban areas.

Density: 7 persons per sq.km/20 per sq.mile.

Population Growth Rate: 3.2% p.a. (1970–7).

Ethnic Composition: The population is largely of Arabo-Berber stock and includes some 70,000 Europeans, mainly French and Spanish.

Capital: Algiers Pop. 2 million (1978).

Major Cities: Oran Pop. 700,000; Constantine Pop. 600,000; Annaba Pop. 500,000.

Language: Arabic is the official language, but French is widely used in Government and business circles.

Religion: Islam is the official religion, and the majority are Muslims. The European population is mainly Roman Catholic, with Protestant and Jewish minorities.

Government: Algeria gained independence from France in 1962. The country is governed by a National Revolutionary Council, presided over by the President, who also heads the Cabinet of Ministers. Legislative power is held by the Assemblée Nationale Populaire. The Front de Libération Nationale (FLN) is the only recognised political party.

GEOGRAPHY

The landscape is dominated by desert and mountains, but a wide, fertile belt (80km/50 miles across) runs alongside the coast. The highest point is Mount Tahat in the Sahara, which rises to a height of 3,000m/9,850ft.

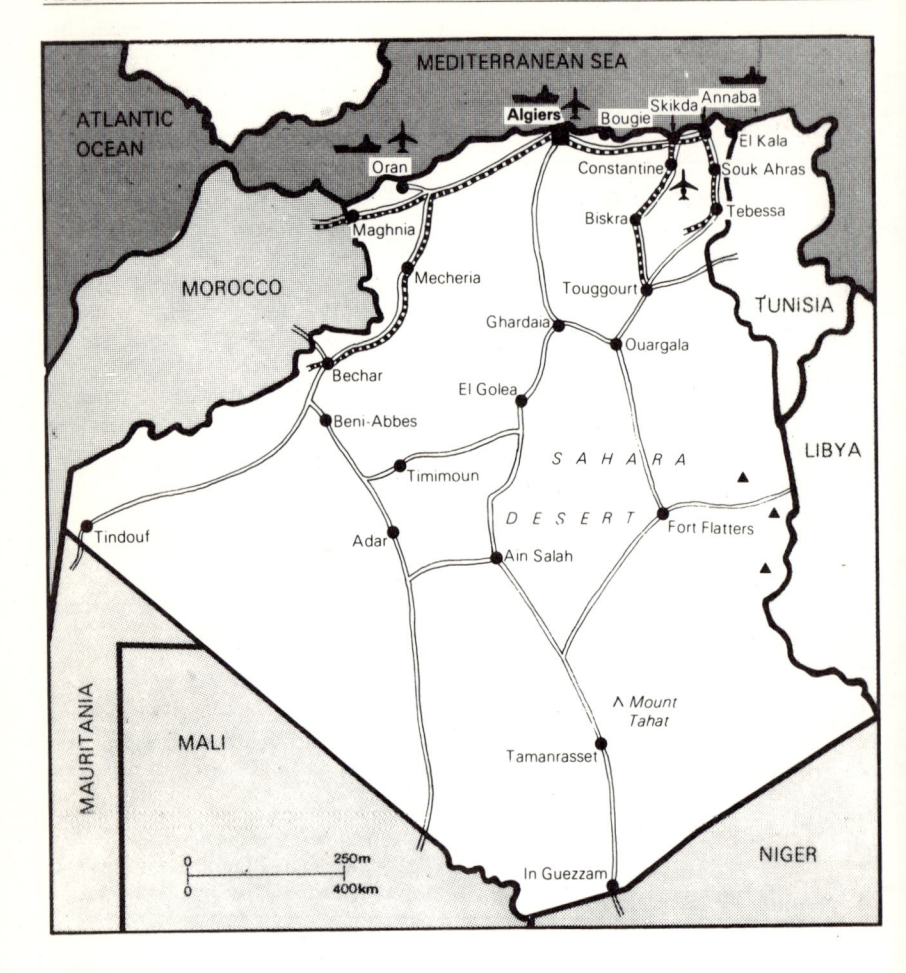

ALGERIA

Climate
Northern Algeria has a Mediterranean-type climate with average temperatures ranging from 13°C/55°F to 24°C/75°F. The temperature in winter rarely drops below 10°C/50°F. Summers are hot and humid with temperatures ranging from 27°C/80°F to 32°C/90°F. Greater variations of temperature occur south of the Saharan atlas, where winter frosts are not uncommon at night. Most of the annual rainfall is during the winter months.

Agriculture
Algeria is a predominantly agricultural country with about 35% of the labour force employed in the agricultural sector. Most of the cultivable land is to be found in the northern coastlands. The former European-owned farms have now been taken over by the state and are managed by workers' committees – these account for about one-third of the total cultivable area and constitute some of the best growing land. A major land

reform programme aims to increase productivity, reduce rural unemployment and increase the wages of agricultural workers.

Main Crops: Wheat, barley, oats, grapes, citrus fruits, vegetables.

Mineral Resources: High-grade iron ore, phosphates, lead, zinc, antimony, uranium, tungsten, oil and gas.

THE ECONOMY

Gross National Product (1976): US$15.3 billion.

Per Capita Income (1976): US$884.

Gross Domestic Product (1978): US$24.6 billion.

Foreign Trade (1978): Total Imports – US$7.29 billion. Total Exports – US$6.34 billion.

Main Trading Partners: Imports – France, West Germany, USA, Italy. Exports – USA, West Germany, France, Italy.

The Algerian economy is heavily centralised with the Government exercising control, through the Sociétés Nationales and Offices Nationales, of the key sectors of the economy such as energy, banking, industry, mines, transport and tourism.

Since independence, the economy has undergone a programme of rapid industrialisation consisting mainly of capital-intensive projects using local raw materials. Major projects include oil refineries, gas liquefaction plants, iron and steel works, and the manufacture of engines, agricultural equipment and electrical goods. The industrial sector was the largest recipient of state investment during the 1970s, although the new Development Plan has shifted the emphasis on to the long-neglected agricultural sector and on to social services such as health and education.

Oil and gas are Algeria's main exports and increasing revenues from these products have enabled the Government to carry out its ambitious economic plans. However, the economy is not without its problems – large foreign debts swallow up a considerable proportion of export revenues, and there is a renewed necessity to find new and lucrative export markets for Algeria's natural gas in particular. The country's enormous reserves of natural gas could make Algeria the world's largest natural gas exporter in the 1980s.

Major Industries: oil and natural gas, food processing, textiles and clothing.

Main Commodities Traded: Imports – machinery, iron and steel, transport equipment, electrical equipment, and foodstuffs. Exports – crude oil and oil products, natural gas, iron and steel, wine, fruit, vegetables, metal ores and concentrates.

Oil Production (1978): 438 million barrels, including condensates.

Gas Production (1978): 14.1 billion cu.metres.

HOW TO GET THERE

Air
There are regular flights to Algiers from most European and Middle Eastern capitals. British Caledonian (Gatwick) and Air Algérie (Heathrow) operate several flights a week between London and Algiers.

Other major airlines flying to Algeria include Aeroflot, Air France, Alitalia, Egypt Air, Iberia, Lufthansa, Sabena, Saudia, Swissair and Tunis Air. There are regular flights from several French cities, Casablanca and Tunis to Annaba, Constantine and Oran.

Flying times to Algiers: from London, 3 hours; from New York, 11 hours; from Sydney, 24 hours.

Algeria's main international airport is Dar el Beida, which is situated about 20km/12½ miles from the centre of Algiers.

Rail
Daily services operate between Oran (Algeria) and Casablanca (Morocco); also between Annaba and Constantine and Tunis. In addition, an overnight rail service operates between Algiers and Tunis.

Road
The main points of entry into Algeria are: from Morocco at Maghnia; from Tunisia at El Kala, Souk Ahras and Tebessa; from Libya at Fort Thiriet; from Niger at In Guezzam; from Mali at Bardj Mokhtar.

ENTRY REGULATIONS

Visas
No visa is required by passport holders of Andorra, Denmark, Egypt, Finland, France, Guinea, Iceland, Iraq, Republic of Ireland, Italy, Jordan, Kuwait, Libya, Liechtenstein, Mali, Mauritania, Monaco, Morocco, Norway, San Marino, Spain, Sudan, Sweden, Switzerland, Syria, Tunisia, United Kingdom and Yugoslavia, for a stay of up to 3 months.

All other nationals require visas obtainable from Algerian diplomatic missions abroad, or (for a maximum stay of 3 months) on arrival at the airport/frontier post. No visa is required for transit passengers. A loading or transit permit, valid for 2 to 5 days, can be obtained on arrival in Algeria.

Visas are not normally granted to passport holders of Chile, South Korea, Malawi, South Africa, Taiwan and Vietnam. Evidence in a passport of a previous or planned visit to Israel may adversely affect the granting of a visa.

Business travellers should support their visa application with a letter from their firm giving details of the business to be undertaken and confirming financial responsibility for the applicant.

Health Regulations
An International Certificate of Vaccination against smallpox is required for entry into Algeria. Valid yellow fever and/or cholera certificates are required by those persons arriving from infected areas.

ALGERIA

Customs
Currency: Any amount of foreign currency may be imported, provided it is declared on the currency declaration form issued on arrival. The import and export of Algerian currency is limited to 50 dinars.

Duty-free articles: 200 cigarettes or 50 cigars or 400g of tobacco. 1 bottle of spirits and 2 bottles of wine. Samples of no commercial value, provided they are not in a saleable condition. Samples of value can be temporarily imported against payment of a deposit which is refunded on re-export of the samples within a given period of time.

Prohibited articles: arms and ammunition, narcotics, pornographic literature, contraceptives, precious metals and stones.

PRACTICAL INFORMATION FOR THE VISITOR

1. Currency
Monetary Unit – Algerian dinar, divided into 100 centimes.
Notes – 5, 10, 50, 100, 500 dinars.
Coins – 1, 10, 20, 50 centimes; 1, 5, dinars.

Visitors should avoid changing large amounts of foreign currency into dinars as they may experience difficulties in reconverting them.

Travellers' cheques may be changed at specified branches of the Banque Nationale d'Algérie, the Banque Extérieure d'Algerie and the Crédit Populaire d'Algérie. In addition, there are exchange facilities at the international airports, the Algiers office of Air Algérie (1 Place Maurice Audin) and the air terminal in Algiers where travellers' cheques can be cashed and foreign bank notes exchanged.

Banking Hours
0800–1500 Saturday to Wednesday.

2. Electricity supply
127 or 220v AC.
A wide variety of plugs are in use in Algeria.

3. Weights and Measures
The metric system is in use.

4. Media
The Government-controlled Radiodiffusion Télévision Algerienne (RTA) operates 3 radio networks broadcasting in Arabic, French and Kabyle, and a national television network. Short daily broadcasts are made in English on the radio. No commercial advertising is accepted on the radio or television.

Newspapers and Journals
Algeria's leading national dailies are *El Moudjahid* and *El Chaab*. Provincial dailies include *El Nasr* (Constantine) and *La Republique* (Oran). *Algérie-Actualités* is a weekly French-language newspaper published in Algiers. An important weekly magazine is *Révolution Africaine*, the organ of the Front de Libération Nationale.

5. Medical Care
Sanitation in many towns is of a poor standard and water is generally unsafe to drink, particularly during the hot summer months. Visitors should drink bottled mineral water which is readily available, or ensure that tap water has been properly boiled and filtered.

6. Telephone, Telex and Postal Services
International telephone calls are often subject to lengthy delays. Telegrams can

33

be sent from any post office between 0800 and 1900 hours. The main post office in Algiers is at 5 Boulevard Mohamed Khémisti and a 24-hour service is maintained there. International telex facilities are available and there is a public call office in the post office at the above address.

All mail to and from Algeria should be despatched by air. All parcels, including those containing sales literature and commercial samples, are likely to be subject to Customs delays. Business travellers are advised to bring such sales material with them personally when visiting Algeria.

7. Public Holidays

1 January	New Year's Day
1 May	Labour Day
19 June	Anniversary of June 19th
5 July	Independence Day
1 November	Anniversary of the Revolution
25–6 December	Christmas

The following Muslim holidays are also observed: *Mouled, Eid el Fitr, Eid el Adha, El Hijra* and *Ashoura*.

8. Time

GMT +1 (+2 March to September).

9. Internal Transport

Air

Air Algérie operates frequent internal services from Algiers to Annaba, Constantine, El Golea, Oran, Ouargala, Tamanrasset, Touggourt and several other smaller centres.

Airline Offices in Algiers

Air Algérie	☎ 642428.
Air France	☎ 631610.
Aeroflot	☎ 605022.
British Caledonian	☎ 614587, 641220.
Lufthansa	☎ 642736.
SAS	☎ 611872.
Swissair	☎ 633367/9.

Rail

Travel by rail tends to be rather slow. Daily services operate from Algiers to Oran, Bougie, Skikda, Annaba and Constantine.

Road

Most main roads, particularly in the north, are of a good standard and a large number of Saharan tracks have been surfaced recently.

Self-drive cars are available for hire in the main cities and towns. An International Driving Licence is required.

Taxis are readily available in the main centres. Meters are in use in Algiers. There is a radio-operated taxi service in Algiers – ☎ 623333.

Car-Hire Firms in Algiers

Africar	☎ 634503.
Algérie Auto Tourisme	☎ 616456.
Altour	☎ 662006, 622600.
Avis	☎ 668527.

10. Tipping

Taxis – 10% of the fare.

Porters – DA2 per bag.

Airport porters – DA5 per bag.

Hotels/restaurants – a service charge is usually included or added to the bill as a separate item.

11. Social Customs

Muslims in Algeria are forbidden by their religion to drink alcohol. However, Algerian law does not prohibit the sale or consumption of alcohol, and in fact many Algerians do drink it.

Most business entertaining takes place in hotels or restaurants, although it is not uncommon for an Algerian to entertain foreign visitors at home. Algerian women do not often participate in business functions outside the home.

ALGERIA

USEFUL ADDRESSES (GENERAL)

Australian Embassy: 60 Boulevard Colonel Bougara, Algiers, ☎ 602804/601965.

British Embassy: Résidence Cassiopée, Bâtiment B, 7 Chemin de Glycines, B.P. 43, Algiers, ☎ 605038/605411/605831.

Canadian Embassy: 27bis Rue d'Anjou, Hydra, B.P. 225, Algiers, ☎ 606611.

Dutch Embassy: 23 Chemin Cheikh Bachir Brahimi, B.P. 72, Algiers, ☎ 782828/9.

French Embassy: Rue Larbi Alik, Hydra, Algiers.

French Consulate: Rue Gouta-Sebti, Annaba; 28 Avenue Benlouizad, Constantine; 3 Square Cayla, Oran.

West German Embassy: 165 Chemin Laperlier, B.P. 664, Algiers, ☎ 634827/634845/6.

Japanese Embassy: 3 Rue du Docteur Lucien Raynaud, Algiers, ☎ 604645/605571.

Swiss Embassy: 27 Boulevard Zirout Youcef, B.P. 482, Algiers, ☎ 633902/638312.

US Embassy: 4 Chemin Cheikh Bachir Brahimi, Algiers, ☎ 601425/601186/601716.

US Consulate: 14 Square de Bamako, Oran, ☎ 355502/352665.

Algerian National Tourist Office: 25–27 Rue Khélifa Boukhalfa, Algiers, ☎ 646864.

Wagons-Lits Tourisme Authorised Representative: Sonatour, 5 Boulevard Ben Boulaid, Algiers.

BUSINESS INFORMATION

Algerian business life is dominated by Government-owned and -controlled organisations. Virtually all imports and exports are handled by state organisations, which usually buy direct from the foreign manufacturer. Government control over foreign trade has resulted in the creation of state monopolies, known locally as *Société Nationale* or *Office National*. Although state-owned, these organisations do not have the automatic guarantee of the Government, and are required to act as ordinary commercial concerns, responsible for their own purchases and debts.

Local commercial agents and distributors are now prevented from operating in Algiers. Foreign firms wishing to do extensive business in Algeria can establish a liaison office under a resident foreign manager to deal with the various state organisations.

Import and Exchange Control Regulations

All goods are subject to import controls of one kind or another, and require an import licence and/or the visa of the state organisation holding the import monopoly. The import of luxury consumer goods is usually prohibited. The holder of an import licence will normally be able to pay for the goods in foreign currency.

Business Hours
Government Offices and State Enterprises
Winter – 0800–1200 Saturday to Wednesday
　　　　 1430–1800
　　　　 0800–1200 Thursday
Summer – 0800–1600 Saturday to Wednesday
　　　　 0800–1200 Thursday

The Muslim week-end (Thursday afternoon and Friday) is observed in Algeria.

Business Events
The Algiers International Trade Fair is held each year in September/October. Enquiries about the fair should be addressed to: Algiers International Trade Fair, Palais des Expositions, Pins Maritimes, B.P. 571, Algiers.

BUSINESS SERVICES

Advertising
Agence Nationale d'Edition et de Publicité (ANEP), 1 Boulevard Pasteur, Algiers – posters, slides and filmlets.

Forwarding/Clearing Agents (State-Owned)
SONATMAG, 1 rue de Cherbourg, Algiers, ☎ 669292.

CNAN (National Shipping Co.), 2 Quai d'Ajaccio, Algiers, ☎ 637413.

Railway
SNTF, 21–31 Boulevard Mohamed V, Algiers, ☎ 630550.

USEFUL ADDRESSES (BUSINESS)

Institut Algérien du Commerce Extérieur (COMEX), Palais Consulaire, 6 Boulevard Amilcar Cabral, Algiers, ☎ 627044/7.

Chambre de Commerce et d'Industrie d'Annaba, Palais Consulaire, 4 Rue du Cenra, Annaba.

Chambre de Commerce et d'Industrie de Constantine, 2 Avenue Zebane, Constantine.

Chambre de Commerce et d'Industrie d'Oran, 8 Boulevard de la Soummam, Oran.

Ministry of Commerce, 44–46, Rue Mohammed Belouizdad, Algiers, ☎ 663366.

Ministry of Foreign Affairs, 6 Rue Ibn Batram el Mouradia, Algiers, ☎ 600585/9.

MAJOR CITIES

Algiers
Algiers is the principal commercial and administrative centre of Algeria, as well as the seat of Government and the focus of much of the country's intellectual and artistic life.

In the heart of the city lies the Kasbah, an enchanting district of narrow, winding streets. The old fortress is to be found here as well as the Grand Mosque and the Sidi-Abderahman Mosque. The area around the Admiralty is the centre of modern Algiers. To the east of the city is the fishing port and fish market, where numerous restaurants specialising in seafood are found.

Higher up out of the city is the district of Mustapha Superieur which overlooks the city and the bay. There are 2 museums situated here: the Bardo Museum is an 18th-century villa and houses extensive collections of clothing, jewellery and musical instruments; and the Stephane Gsell Museum contains examples of Islamic art and archaeology as well as some Roman relics and antiquities.

The National Museum of Fine Arts has an important collection of paintings and sculptures, reputed to be one of the finest in Africa.

Hotels

The Ministry of Tourism hotel classification ranges from 5-star luxury, 4 star, etc., down to 1 star.

ALETTI, Rue Asselah Hocine, ☎ 635040/6.
Modern 4-star hotel on the promenade, near commercial centre.
Rooms: 150.
Facilities: Restaurant, bar and coffee shop. Roof-top terrace. Garden.
Services: TC accepted in payment of bills.

AURASSI, Avenue Frantz Fanon, ☎ 648552.
De luxe 5-star hotel overlooking the Bay of Algiers, 10 minutes from city centre.
Rooms: 455 ♪, ♠, ♎, ☎
Facilities: 3 restaurants, cafeteria, coffee shop and bars. Nightclub. Tennis, swimming, sauna, gym, Turkish baths. Service shops.
Services: TC accepted in payment of bills. ⊟ Amex, Diners Club. Translation bureau.
Conference room – max. capacity 1,100.
Banquet rooms – max. capacity 230.

ST GEORGE, 24 Avenue Souidani Boudjemaa, ☎ 665300.
Traditional Moorish-style 4-star hotel in garden setting, 10 minutes' drive from city centre.
Rooms: 141.
Facilities: Restaurant, bar. Open-air restaurant in summer. Swimming, tennis.
Services: TC accepted in payment of bills. ⊟ Amex, Diners Club.
Banquet room – max. capacity 300.

Restaurants

In addition to the hotel restaurants, others include: *Alhambra*, 29 Rue Ben M'Hidi Larbi; *El Baçour*, 1 Rue Patrice Lumumba, ☎ 635092 – Algerian; *Le Carthage*, 1 Chemin des Glycines, ☎ 602863; *Taverna Romana*, Rue Didouche Mourad, ☎ 602676; *La Pagode*, 27 Rue Victor Hugo, ☎ 664680; *La Roue*, Rue Claude Debussy, ☎ 666652.

Entertainment

The National Theatre at Place Port Said stages colourful productions by Algerian artists and visiting groups from Eastern Europe, China, Cuba and other African countries.

French and English films can be seen in the city's numerous cinemas. The Aletti Hotel has its own nightclub; other popular nightspots are the *Blue Note*, 97 Rue Didouche Mourad, and the *Dar El Alia* with Oriental dancing.

Shopping

There are 2 state-run handicraft centres in Algiers – one at the airport and the other at 2 Boulevard Khemisti. Visitors should check the prices at either of these before purchasing goods in smaller shops. Hand-made goods on sale include pottery, leatherwork, wool and goat's hair carpets and rugs, inlaid silverwork, jewellery and basketwork.

Oran

Oran is Algeria's second largest city and is built on the coastal plateau spilling out over the hills beyond. The old town dates from the 8th century and was further extended by the Andalusian Arabs and the Spaniards who occupied the city from 1509 for almost 300 years.

Historic sights within the city include the 16th-century Santa Cruz Fortress on the Murdjadjo overlooking the city, and the Mosque of the Pasha of Sidi El Houari which dates from the 18th century.

Oran airport is 20km/12½ miles from the city centre.

Hotels
GRAND, 5 Place du Maghreb, ☎ 330181.
Traditional-style 4-star hotel in city centre.
Rooms: 66 🍴, 🛏 on request, ☎, ⛄.
Facilities: Restaurant, bar. Car hire.
Services: 💳 Credit cards not accepted.
Dr. on call. 💲, ♂.
Conference room – max. capacity 20.

LES ANDALOUSES, Oran Les Andalouses, ☎ 04.

ROYAL, 3 Boulevard de la Soummam, ☎ 333152.

WINDSOR, 1 Rue Ben M'hidi, ☎ 333175.

Restaurants
Apart from the hotel restaurants, others in Oran include: *Le Belvedere*, *Le Biarritz*, *La Comette* and *El Gallo*. *The Nahawand*, *El Djazair* and *Nuits du Liban*, all specialising in Arab dishes.

ANGOLA
People's Republic of Angola

    Geography *39*
    The Economy *41*
    How to Get There *41*
    Entry Regulations *42*
    Practical Information for the Visitor *42*
    Useful Addresses (General) *43*
    Business Information *43*
    Business Services *44*
    Useful Addresses (Business) *44*
    Luanda *44*

Size: 1,246,700 sq.km/481,351 sq.miles.

Population 9.9 million (mid-1978).

Distribution: 11% in urban areas.

Density: 5.6 persons per sq.km/14.5 per sq.mile.

Population Growth Rate: 3.0% p.a. (1979 est.).

Ethnic Composition: There are several large ethnic groups, all of Bantu origin. Principal among these are the Ovimbundu, Kimbundu and Bakongo. There are also small mixed and white (mainly Portuguese) minorities.

Capital: Luanda Pop. 600,000.

Major Towns: Huambo Pop. 62,000; Lobito Pop. 60,000; Benguela Pop. 41,000; Lubango Pop. 32,000; Malanje Pop. 31,000.

Language: Portuguese is the official language; the principal African languages are Umbundu, Kimbundu, Kioko and Kongo.

Religion: About 50% are Christian (mainly Roman Catholic), the remainder subscribe to traditional beliefs.

Government: In September 1979 President Jose Eduardo dos Santos succeeded to the Presidency and leadership of the ruling Movimento Popular de Libertacao de Angola-Partido de Trabalho (MPLA-PT), on the death of Dr Agostinho Neto who had been President since independence in 1975. There is continuing friction with guerrillas of the National Union for the Total Independence of Angola (UNITA), who are supported by South Africa.

GEOGRAPHY

Angola consists mainly of a plateau averaging 1,200m/4,000ft in altitude, with mountain ranges reaching over 2,000m/6,500ft. There is a narrow coastal plain, separated

ANGOLA

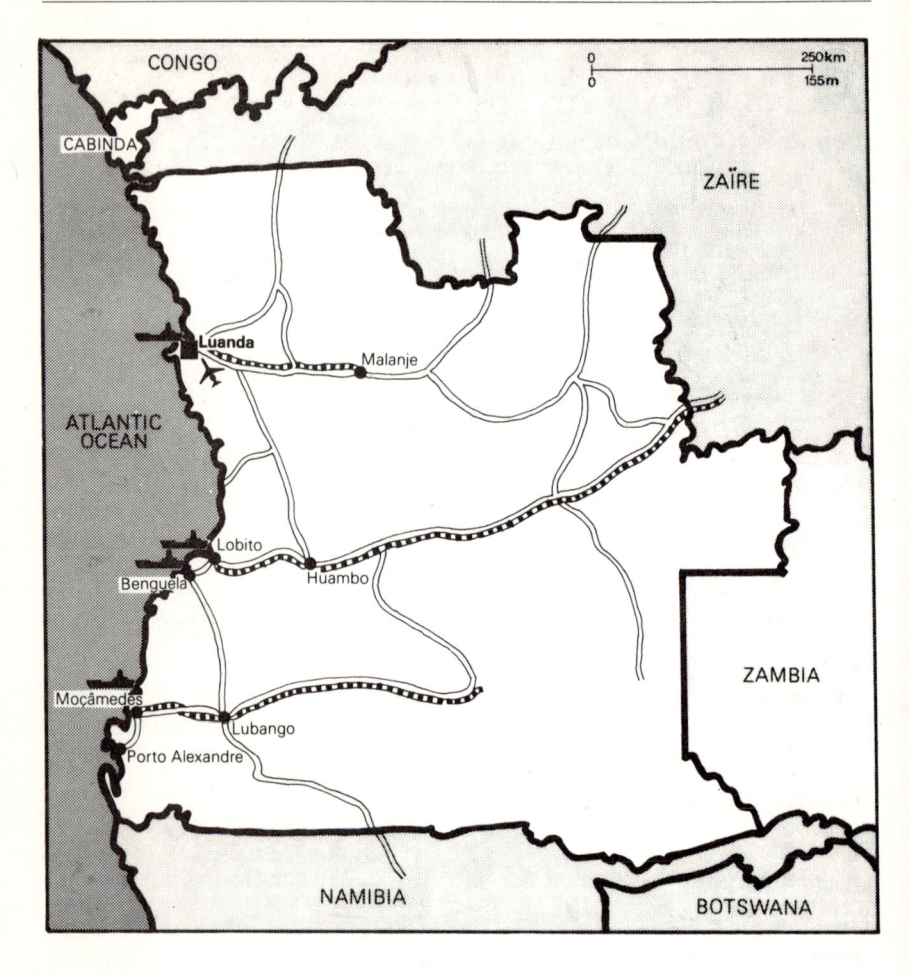

from the plateau by a sub-plateau strip. The south borders on the Namib desert, and the northern plateau and the separated Cabinda enclave are covered in jungle.

Climate
There is a hot, rainy season from October to March with the south generally more temperate and drier than the north. Temperatures on the coast average 24°C/75°F and on the plateau 18°C/64°F.

Agriculture
Of the 90% of the Angolan population believed to be occupied in farming and, in the south, cattle raising, only a small proportion is engaged in commercial agriculture (mainly coffee, cotton and maize growing). Only 2% of arable land is cultivated, and the agricultural economy has yet to return to the pre-1974 production levels. Administration of the estates left idle by the European exodus in 1975 is being reorganised and foreign companies are helping re-establish the sugar and cotton industries.

Main Crops: cassava, coffee, sisal, sugar, maize, cotton, bananas, tobacco, palm oil, vegetables.

Mineral Resources: crude petroleum, diamonds, manganese, salt, phosphates, copper.

THE ECONOMY

Gross National Product (1978 est.): US$2.0 billion.

Per Capita Income (1978): US$300.

Gross Domestic Product (1977 est.): US$1.97 billion.

Foreign Trade (1978): Total Imports – US$780 million. Total Exports – US$1.064 billion.

Main Trading Partners: Imports – Portugal, West Germany, USA, UK, Japan. Exports – USA, Portugal, Canada, Japan, West Germany.

Angola is currently in the process of re-establishing the non-subsistence areas of its economy after almost complete breakdown as a result of its colonial and civil wars. Government plans provide for state, co-operative and private enterprise according to the needs of each economic sector, and a more liberal economic climate, especially with regard to foreign investment, is being encouraged.

The petroleum industry is leading the economic recovery, but like the rest of the mining sector is still experiencing problems. Diamond production has risen recently, but iron ore mining has yet to be resumed. Industry, which is concentrated principally in food-processing and textiles, suffered most severely during the civil war, and its recovery remains dependent on capital investment, more skilled workers and the smooth operation of the reopened Benguela railway, which continues to be troubled by guerrilla activity and inadequate maintenance.

Major Industries: oil refining, food processing, textiles, cement, pulp and paper.

Main Commodities Traded: Imports – machinery, transport equipment, iron and steel, manufactured goods, chemicals, food. Exports – crude petroleum, diamonds, coffee, sisal, fishmeal, cotton, bananas.

International Affiliations: UN, OAU, ADB.

HOW TO GET THERE

Air
Luanda is served by Alitalia, Aeroflot, Cubana, Interflug, DETA (Mozambique), Nigerian Airways, TAP, UTA, and the national airline TAAG, with direct flights from Paris, Rome, Lisbon and several African cities.

Flying time from Paris to Luanda, 9¼ hours.

Belas International Airport is 4km/2½ miles from the city centre.

ANGOLA

ENTRY REGULATIONS

Visas
Visas are required by all visitors and may be obtained from the Angolan diplomatic representative in Lisbon or from the Ministry of Foreign Affairs in Luanda. Exit permits are required by all visitors and must be applied for immediately upon arrival.

Health Regulations
International Certificates of Vaccination are required against cholera and smallpox. Vaccination against yellow fever is required if arriving from an infected area, and is strongly recommended for all visitors.

Customs
Currency: Import of local currency up to 15,000 kwanza is permitted. There is no restriction on importing foreign currency, but it must be sold to customs officials immediately upon arrival. Export of local currency is prohibited. Foreign currency up to the amount imported and sold, less kwanza 500 per day of stay, may be re-exchanged upon departure and exported.

Duty-free articles: A reasonable quantity of tobacco. A reasonable quantity of perfume.

Prohibited articles: Alcoholic beverages. Firearms and ammunition must be surrendered to the authorities who will return them on departure.

PRACTICAL INFORMATION FOR THE VISITOR

1. Currency
Monetary Unit – kwanza (AKZ), divided into 100 lwei.
Notes – 20, 50, 100, 500, 1,000 kwanza.
Coins – 50 lwei; 1, 2, 5, 10 kwanza.

Banking Hours
0800 – 1200 Monday to Friday. All banks were nationalised in 1975.

Principal Banks in Luanda
Banco Nacional de Angola, Avenida 4 de Fevereiro No.151 – central bank and bank of issue.
Banco Popular de Angola – principal commercial bank.
Banco de Crédito Comercial e Industrial, Avenida dos Restauradores de Angola 79–83, Caixa Postal 1395.
Banco Totta-Standard de Angola, Avenida Paulo Dias de Novais 127, Caixa Postal 5554 – associate of Standard Chartered Banking Group.

2. Electricity Supply
220v AC.

3. Weights and Measures
The metric system is in use.

4. Media
The press, radio and television services were nationalised in 1976. The main national daily newspaper is the *Jornal de Angola.*

5. Medical Care
Visitors are strongly advised to take precautions against malaria.

6. Telephone, Telex and Postal Services
Visitors are advised to use airmail for all postage. In Luanda telex facilities are available for guests at the Hotel Continental, and the telephone system is in the process of being re-equipped.

7. Public Holidays

1 January	New Year's Day
4 February	MPLA Day
1 May	Labour Day
11 November	Independence Day
10 December	MPLA Day
25 December	Family Day

8. Time
GMT +1.

9. Internal Transport

Air
The national airline TAAG connects Luanda with other major centres in Angola. There is also a nationalised air-charter company, Empresa de Transportes Aereos de Angola.

Airline Offices in Luanda
TAAG/Angola Airlines ☎ 23523.
Interflug ☎ 38727.
UTA ☎ 35416.

Road
The substantial network of all-weather roads was badly damaged during the civil war, but a repair and construction programme is well under way.

Taxis are available in Luanda and at Belas Airport.

Self-drive and chauffeur-driven cars are available in Luanda.

Traffic travels on the right and an International Driving Licence is required.

Car-Hire Firms in Luanda
Auto Touring, Caixa Postal 3013.
Automoveis de Alugeis de Alameda, Caixa Postal 10152.

10. Tipping
Hotels – a 10% service charge and 3% tourist tax is automatically added to the bill.

USEFUL ADDRESSES (GENERAL)

Luanda
Dutch Embassy: Avenida 4 de Fevereiro 42, Caixa Postal 3624, ☎ 71369.

French Embassy, Avenida Almirante Azevedo Coutinho 26, Caixa Postal 584/C, ☎ 45956.

Swiss Embassy, Avenida 4 de Fevereiro 129, Caixa Postal 3163, ☎ 38314.

Centro de Informação e Turismo de Angola, Caixa Postal 1240, Luanda.

American Express Authorised Representative: Star Travel Service, Caixa Postal 3334, Luanda, ☎ 31901.

Wagons Lits Authorised Representative: Bureau AMI, Caixa Postal 143, Lobito.

BUSINESS INFORMATION

The foreign investment law passed in June 1979 allows for repatriation of profits and guarantees compensation in the case of nationalisation. Foreign investment is not allowed in the fields of banking, telecommunications, insurance and public utilities; and nationalisation is the continuing policy in the fields of transport, shipping and major agricultural enterprises. The Government is considering exempting foreign investors from tax and customs duties.

Business Hours
0800–1200
1400–1800 Monday to Friday
0800–1200 Saturday

BUSINESS SERVICES

Insurance
Cia. de Seguros Angolana, SARL, Caixa Postal 738, Luanda.
Cia. Seguros Garantia Africa, SARL, Caixa Postal 2726, Luanda.
Cia. de Seguros Nacional de Angola, SARL, Caixa Postal 2921, Luanda.

Transport
Servicos do Pôrtos, Caminhos de Ferro e Transportes, Caixa Postal 1250-C, Luanda – rail transport.
Cia. do Caminho de Ferro de Benguela, Caixa Postal 32, Lobito – operates the Benguela railway.
Consorcio Técnico de Aeronáutica, Luanda – air cargo.
Cia. de Navegação Angolana, SARL, Caixa Postal 5953, Luanda – shipping.

USEFUL ADDRESSES (BUSINESS)

Direcção dos Servicos de Comércio (Department of Trade), Caixa Postal 1337, Luanda.

Importang, Luanda – state commission to coordinate imports.

MAJOR CITY

Luanda

Hotels
CONTINENTAL, Rua Duarte Lopes 2, Caixa Postal 5150, ☎ 25231.
Modern hotel overlooking the bay.
Rooms: 80 ♪, ☎. Suites available.
Facilities: Restaurant, bars, some private terraces.

TIUDI, Rua Luis de Camoes 85, ☎ 27661.
Small hotel in city centre.
Rooms: 60. Suites available.

TROPICO, Avenida Luis de Camoes 103, ☎ 31593.
Modern hotel in city centre.
Rooms: 200 ♪, ◉, ◻ (on request), ☎, ♥. Suites available.
Facilities: Restaurant, snack room, bar. Self-service bar in rooms.
Services: A conference room is available.

BENIN
People's Republic of Benin

Geography 45
The Economy 47
How to Get There 48
Entry Regulations 48
Practical Information for the Visitor 49
Useful Addresses (General) 51
Business Information 51
Business Services 52
Useful Addresses (Business) 52
Cotonou 53

Size: 112,622 sq.km/43,483 sq.miles.

Population: 3.38 million (1978 est.).

Distribution: 13.5% in urban areas.

Density: 75 persons per sq.km/129 per sq. mile.

Population Growth Rate: 2.8% p.a.

Ethnic Composition: The major ethnic groups are the Fon, the Aja, the Yoruba, Bariba and Somba. The European community is approximately 5,000.

Capital: Porto Novo Pop. 104,000. (Cotonou, the major port town, is the effective capital.)

Major Cities/Towns: Cotonou Pop. 178,000; Abomey Pop. 50,000; Ouidah Pop. n.a.

Language: French is the official language. The principal African dialects are Fon, Yoruba and Dendi. Some English is spoken in government and business circles, but its usage is limited.

Religion: Approximately 68% of the population adhere to traditional tribal beliefs. 15% are Muslim; the remainder are Christians, mostly Roman Catholic.

Government: The People's Republic of Benin (formerly Dahomey) gained complete independence from France in 1960. Since independence there has been a succession of military coups, with ten changes of government in two decades. The last coup, in 1972, brought to power another military government founded on the principles of Marxist-Leninist Scientific Socialism. The Parti de la Révolution Populaire du Bénin (PRPB) is the ruling political party.

GEOGRAPHY

Benin consists of a long, narrow strip of land stretching northwards from the Gulf of Guinea. The southern coastal plain rises to a forested plateau with areas of fertile land,

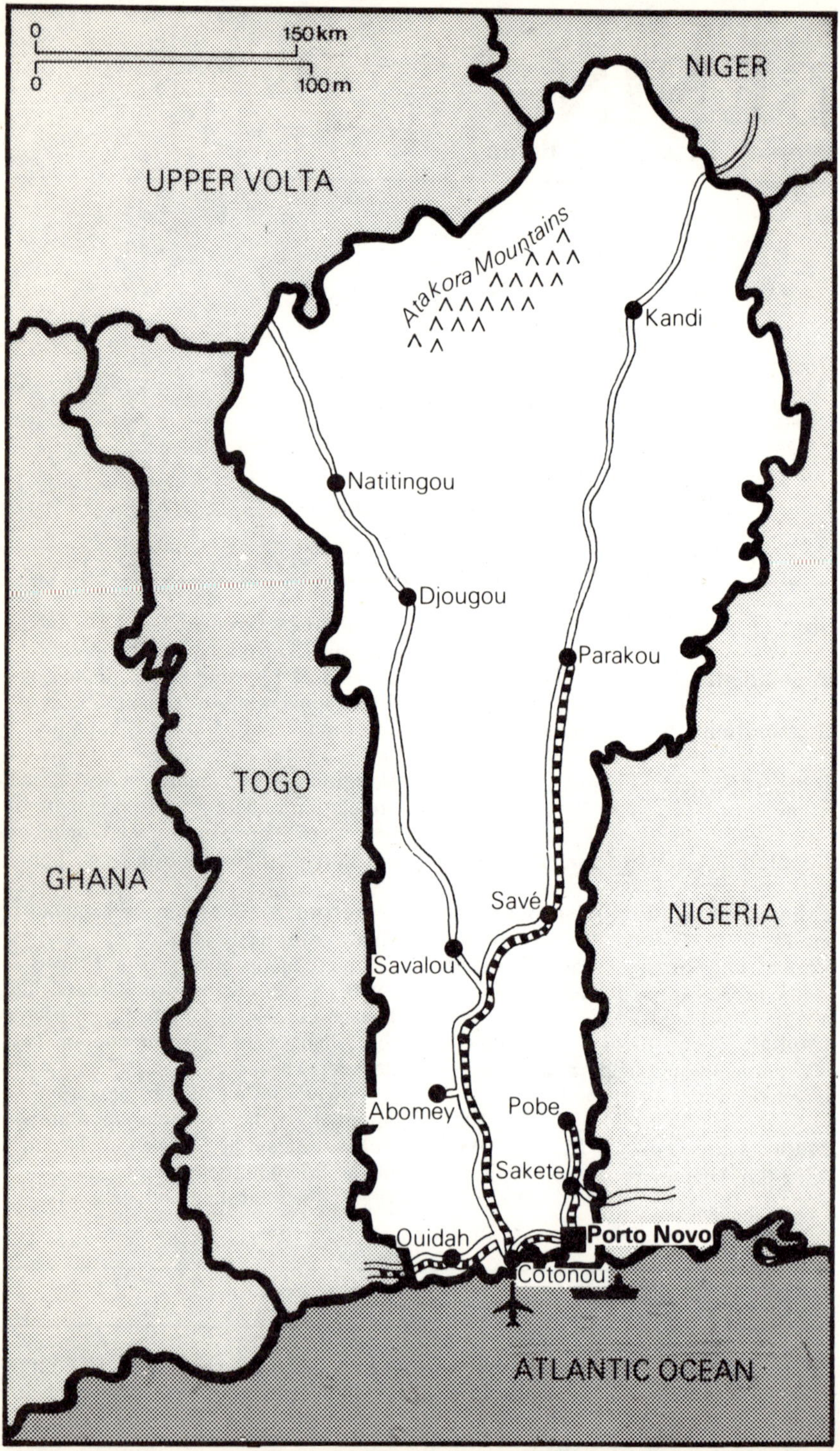

0
150 km
0
100 m
NIGER
UPPER VOLTA
Atakora Mountains
Kandi
Natitingou
Djougou
Parakou
TOGO
GHANA
NIGERIA
Savé
Savalou
Abomey
Pobe
Sakete
Ouidah
Porto Novo
Cotonou
ATLANTIC OCEAN

while to the north-west are the Atakora Mountains, with a maximum height of 457m/1,500 ft.

Climate

The climate in the south is equatorial with high humidity, especially along the coast. The two main rainy seasons are March to mid-July and mid-September to November when temperatures range from 20°c/68°F to 34°c/93°F. The north has a tropical climate with one rainy season from July to October. Temperatures in the hot season (March to April) may be as high as 46°c/115°F, dropping to 10–15°c/50–59°F in December and January.

Agriculture

Agriculture is the mainstay of the economy, employing the majority of the population and producing raw materials for most of Benin's industries.

Palm oil is the principal crop and palm oil products account for about 20% of the country's exports. Other valuable exports are cotton, coffee, shea nuts and copra. Despite the strong emphasis on agriculture, Benin is not wholly self-sufficient in foodstuffs; some staple foods are still imported.

The development plan announced in 1977 accorded a high priority to the development of agriculture.

Main Crops: palm kernels, cotton, coffee, groundnuts.

Mineral Resources: oil, iron ore, limestone.

THE ECONOMY

Gross National Product (1977): US$660 million.

Per Capita Income (1977): US$200.

Gross Domestic Product (1977 est.): 141.9 million CFA francs.

Foreign Trade (1977): Total Imports – US$283 million. Total Exports – US$113 million.

Main Trading Partners: Imports – France, Japan, West Germany, Netherlands, USA, UK. Exports – France, Nigeria, West Germany, UK, Japan.

Benin's agriculture provides the majority of the country's exports and is the principal source of raw materials for the main industries. There has been no large-scale industrial development, but there are a number of sizeable industrial plants, including the sugar works at Savé and the Onigbolo cement works. Secondary industries under development include beer and soft drinks, palm oil products, textiles and bricks.

In recent years, Benin has become increasingly important as an entrepôt, particularly for Nigeria. Substantial revenues are derived from the use of the country's ports and transport facilities by her neighbours as well as from the re-export of consumer and luxury goods to Nigeria. Cotonou's role as a commercial centre is aided by a licensing and tariff system favouring products from the Franc Zone and the European Common Market.

The increase in economic activity during the late 1970s was accompanied by an increase in Benin's balance of payments deficit and a substantial decline in the country's foreign assets. Long-term economic planning involves the restructuring of the agricultural sector together with investment in industrial sector and in the development of the infrastructure. To achieve these aims, substantial private and foreign capital is sought and, in keeping with present Government policy, there is a high degree of state participation in all new major projects.

France is the main supplier of foreign aid to Benin, and the market is dominated by French commercial and industrial firms. Private enterprise is widespread in the commercial sector; however, the export of cement and all agricultural produce and the import of certain essential consumer goods are monopolised by two state firms.

Major Industries: food processing, palm oil products, beverages, textiles, furniture, nails.

Main Commodities Traded: Imports – foodstuffs, machinery, vehicles, iron and steel products. Exports – palm oil.

International Affiliations: UN, IBRD, OAU, ACP, ADB, ECOWAS, Franc Zone, OCAM, NRC.

HOW TO GET THERE

Air
There are regular services to Cotonou from Paris (UTA and Air Afrique). British Caledonian and Nigeria Airways operate daily flights from London to Lagos with connections to Cotonou. (Alternatively there is a good road link between Lagos and Cotonou. The journey takes about 3½ hours by car, allowing for border formalities.) From New York, Air France fly to Paris (Charles de Gaulle), connecting with the UTA/Air Afrique flights to Cotonou.

Regular flights also operate to Cotonou from Abidjan, Accra, Douala, Lagos, Lome and Monrovia.

Flying time to Cotonou from Paris, 10 hours.

Cotonou Airport is 5 km/3 miles from the city centre. Taxis are available at the airport, and fares should be agreed upon before commencing the journey.

Road
There are good-quality tarred roads from Lagos and Accra and visitors may take a taxi to Cotonou from either Lagos or Lomé (122 km/76 miles). The border usually closes at 1900 hours.

ENTRY REGULATIONS

Visas
Visas are required by nationals of all countries except: Cameroon, Central African Republic, Chad, Congo, Denmark, France, Gabon, West Germany, Ghana, Italy, Ivory Coast, Madagascar, Mali, Mauritania, Niger, Rwanda, Senegal, Togo and Upper Volta. Holders of Israeli diplomatic passports also do not require visas.

All other nationals must be in possession of a valid passport and a visa, obtainable from embassies and consulates of the People's Republic of Benin abroad.

Entry is normally refused to white nationals of South Africa.

Business visitors should ensure that the validity of their passport extends for at least 3 months beyond the date of issue of their visa.

The embassy or consulate of the People's Republic of Benin will advise the necessary procedure for obtaining a visa, the supporting documents which are required and the length of time taken to issue a visa.

Health Regulations
International Certificate of Vaccination against smallpox and yellow fever are required by all persons entering or leaving Benin. Visitors are also advised to be in possession of a valid cholera vaccination certificate.

Customs
Currency: There is no limit to the amount of local or foreign currency which may be imported into Benin, but all monies should be declared on entry. Not more than 25,000 CFA francs per person may be taken outside the Franc Zone on departure. Any unused foreign currency can be freely exported. (Banks in France will exchange CFA francs, but visitors will find it difficult to exchange them outside the Franc Zone.)

Duty-free articles: Personal effects. 50 cigarettes, 25 cigars or 100g of tobacco. Samples of no commercial value.

Articles liable to duty: Samples of value should be declared on arrival. Normal duties and taxes will be levied on all samples sold locally.

PRACTICAL INFORMATION FOR THE VISITOR

1. Currency
Monetary Unit – CFA franc.
Notes – 100, 500, 1,000, 5,000, 10,000 CFA francs.
Coins – 1, 2, 5, 10, 25, 50, 100 CFA francs.

Banking Hours
0800–1130
1430–1530 Monday to Friday.

The 3 principal commercial banks in Benin were nationalised between 1974 and 1975. The Banque Internationale pour l'Afrique Occidentale and the Banque Internationale pour le Commerce et l'Industrie du Benin now form part of the Banque Commerciale du Benin through which all Government business is conducted.

Banque Commerciale du Benin, Rue du Révérend Pere Colineau, B.P. 85, Cotonou – branches throughout the country.

2. Electricity Supply
220v AC 50Hz.
Plugs: 2 square or round pins.

3. Weights and Measures
The metric system is in use.

4. Media
There is no television network in Benin. The Government-owned radio station, La Voix de la Revolution, broadcasts in French, English and several African languages. Commercial advertising is accepted on the radio.

Newspapers and Journals
Dailies include: *L'Aube Nouvelle, Bulletin de l'Agence Béninoise de Presse* and *Ehuzu*.

The *Journal Officiel de la République du Bénin* is published fortnightly in Cotonou. The Benin Chamber of Commerce publishes a weekly bulletin which circulates among the local business community and includes announcements from foreign firms seeking representation in Benin.

5. Medical Care
Tap water is not safe to drink in Benin; boil it or drink bottled mineral water. Avoid eating uncooked fruit and vegetables, and keep to the better hotels and restaurants.

Intestinal upsets are common among foreign visitors, so it is advisable to take suitable medicines with you. Antimalarial prophylactics should be taken. TAB (typhoid and paratyphoid) injections are also recommended.

Hospitals in Benin
Cotonou	☎ 312713.
Porto Novo	☎ 2491/4.
Parakou	☎ 2241.

6. Telephone, Telex and Postal Services
There is a direct telephone link between Cotonou and Paris, which connects with other cities in Europe. Services are available to neighbouring countries; connections to French-speaking countries are usually better than those to English-speaking territories. Direct dialling is available between the main cities and towns in Benin. Calls made from a public coin box are more expensive.

Public telex facilities are available from 0700–1900 hours, Monday to Saturday.

All mail to and from Benin should be despatched by air.

7. Public Holidays
1 January	*New Year's Day*
16 January	*Anniversary of Victory against Mercenary Attack*
1 May	*Labour Day*
1 August	*Independence Day*
26 October	*Benin Armed Forces Day*
30 November	*National Day*
25 December	*Christmas*
31 December	*Harvest Day*

The following movable Christian and Muslim holidays are also observed: *Easter Monday, Whit Monday, Eid el Fitr* and *Tabaski*.

When a public holiday falls on a Sunday, it is usually observed the following Monday.

8. Time
GMT + 1.

9. Internal Transport
N.B. The movement of foreign residents is restricted within Benin by law. Although, technically speaking, this does not apply to foreign visitors, it is advisable to clear all travel plans in advance with the appropriate district or provincial authorities.

Air
Escadrille Béninoise operates regular services from Cotonou to Parakou, Natitingou, Kandi and Abomey. 2-seater planes are available for charter from Escadrille Béninoise and the Aeroclub in Cotonou.

An airport tax of 100 CFA francs is payable on all internal flights.

Airline Offices in Cotonou
Air Afrique	☎ 312107/8.
Air France	☎ 312107/8.
UTA	☎ 314513.

Rail
Daily services operate along the coastal line between Porto Novo and Cotonou. There is a good service between Cotonou and Parakou in the north with first-, second-, and third-class coaches.

Road

Most roads in the south of the country are tarred. The coast road between Cotonou and Porto Novo is metalled (this is the principal road linking Accra and Lagos).

Many roads in the north are gravel, and become impassable during the rainy season. Petrol stations are scarce, and drivers should carry extra supplies of water and petrol.

Traffic travels on the right-hand side of the road.

Self-drive and chauffeur-driven cars are available for hire in Cotonou. Visitors must be in possession of a valid International Driving Licence.

Taxis are plentiful in the main cities and towns. In Cotonou taxis can be hired for journeys to Porto Novo and Parakou as well as to Lomé and Lagos.

Car-Hire Firms in Cotonou

Locar Benin	☎ 313837.
Locauto	☎ 313442.
Onatho	☎ 312687.
Soda Locar	☎ 313157.
Sonatrac	☎ 312357.

10. Tipping

Porters: 100–200 CFA francs, depending on the number of cases carried.

Hotels/restaurants: 10% of the bill.

11. Social Customs

Business and social customs in the main cities and towns are based on the French model. Visitors should have a reasonable command of the French language.

In the north, where European influence has been slight, the social system remains predominantly tribal.

USEFUL ADDRESSES (GENERAL)

Cotonou

Dutch Consulate: c/o John Walkden & Co Ltd, Avenue Général Dodds, B.P. 24.

French Embassy: Route de l'Aviation, B.P. 766 et 966.

French Consulate: Avenue du Général de Gaulle, B.P. 605.

US Embassy: Rue Caporal Anani Bernard, B.P. 2012, ☎ 312692.

Onatho (Official Tourist Office): B.P. 89, ☎ 312687/313217.

Wagons-Lits Tourisme Authorised Representative: Transcap Voyages, Boulevard Front de Mer, B.P. 483, ☎ 312838.

BUSINESS INFORMATION

The present licensing and tariff systems in Benin favour products imported from the Franc Zone; imports from EEC countries are also favoured.

The majority of Benin's import trade is in the hands of long-established merchant houses with purchasing organisations abroad, many being in France. These merchant houses act as both wholesalers and retailers.

Various sectors of the economy have been nationalised since 1974, including insurance, forwarding and clearing agents, cement, beer, soft drinks and petrol distribution. The import of alcohol, tobacco and khaki cloth products is soon expected to be brought under state control.

It is difficult to appoint a new agent as many are already committed to representing a large number of firms and various government controls limit the firms which are able to represent foreign manufacturers. Local firms with a head office or buying agency in

France are unlikely to accept a new agency without prior consultation. It is therefore advisable to visit the French headquarters of such firms before embarking on a visit to Benin.

Import and Exchange Control Regulations

Import licences (normally valid for 6 months) are required for all goods except those from France and the Franc Zone. Whilst imports are controlled by global quotas, many goods are on a liberalised list. Licences are issued for a specific type of goods; substitution is strictly prohibited. Import licences are readily available for the import of spare parts for capital equipment and for capital goods deemed necessary for the country's development plans.

Restrictions are placed on the import of alcoholic beverages, livestock, arms and ammunition, pornographic films and literature, drugs, narcotics and living plant seeds.

The 2 basic import duties are fiscal duty and customs duty – goods of EEC origin are subject to the former only.

Exchange control is applicable to all currencies with the exception of the CFA franc and the French franc. Foreign exchange is made available under two separate headings: the European Economic Community and global quotas. These quotas specify the total foreign exchange available for purchases from each of the groups; the available exchange is allocated in groups of commodities.

Business Hours
Government Offices and Business Houses
0800–1230
1500–1830   Monday to Friday
0700–1200   Saturday

BUSINESS SERVICES

Import/Export Firms
John Colt & Co, B.P. 4, Cotonou.
John Walkden & Co (United Africa), B.P. 24, Cotonou.

Insurance
Société Nationale d'Assurances et de Réassurances (SONAR), Cotonou.

Shipping
Cie Béninoise de Navigation Maritime (COBENAM), B.P. 2032, Cotonou.
SOCOPAO-Bénin, B.P. 253, Cotonou – agents for Elder Dempster, Palm Line and United West Africa Service.

USEFUL ADDRESSES (BUSINESS)

Chambre de Commerce et d'Industrie du Bénin, Avenue Général de Gaulle, B.P. 31, Cotonou.

Groupement Interprofessionel des Entreprises du Bénin, B.P. 6, Cotonou.

Syndicat des Commercants Importateurs et Exportateurs du Bénin, B.P. 6, Cotonou.

BENIN

MAJOR TOWN

Cotonou

Cotonou is the effective capital of Benin, although Porto Novo, 29 km/18 miles to the north-west, remains the country's official administrative capital. The majority of Benin's commercial activity is centred in and around Cotonou, which is also the chief port.

Cotonou remains relatively unspoilt with little of the large-scale urban development which characterises other West African capitals. The town centre is lively and colourful with constant activity around the markets, in particular the lagoon market. The most dominant feature of the centre, however, is the futuristic conference hall and office block built for the now defunct Union Africaine et Malgache. The area around the port recalls a typical fishing village.

Cotonou is well placed for short excursions inland: to the lagoon village of Ganvie (17½km/11 miles) where some 10,000 people live in houses which rise on stilts above the waters of the lagoon; and to Abomey-Calavi, another lagoon village.

Hotels

There is no official hotel rating system in Benin.

CROIX DU SUD, B.P. 280, ☎ 312954/8. Modern hotel near Ministerial buildings and President's residence, 3km/2 miles from airport.
Rooms: 55 ♒, ⚭, ⌘.
Facilities: Restaurant, bar. Nightclub. Swimming.
Services: ✉ Amex, Diners Club. Meeting facilities.

HOTEL DU LAC, B.P. 184, ☎ 314970. Modern hotel overlooking sea, just outside city centre.
Rooms: 40, 4 suites. ♒.
Facilities: Restaurant, bar, nightclub. Swimming, water sports.
Services: ✉ Amex, Diners Club.

HOTEL DE LA PLAGE, Boulevard de France, B.P. 36, ☎ 312560/2. Prestigious colonial-style hotel on beach, 5 minutes' walk from city centre, 5km/3 miles from airport.
Rooms: 54 ♒, ⚭, ⌂, ⌘. Suites available.
Facilities: Restaurant, bar, snack bar. Swimming. Car hire.
Services: TC, FC. ✉ Amex, Diners Club. Dr. on call. S, ♂.

HOTEL DU PORT, B.P. 884, ☎ 314243. Modern hotel overlooking harbour, near city centre.
Rooms: 52, 6 bungalows. ♒, ⚭, ⌂, ⌘.
Facilities: Restaurants, bar, nightclub. Swimming. Car hire.
Services: TC, FC. ✉ Amex, Diners Club. Dr. on call. S, ♂.

Restaurants

The Hotel de la Plage has a popular open-air restaurant with music. There is a good restaurant at the Hotel du Port. *Paris Snack* and *Pam Pam* serve French food and wine. *Les Trois Paillottes* on the road to Porto Novo serves traditional African food. Other restaurants are: *Chez Pepita* – Spanish and seafood; *Le Capri* – Italian; and *La Florida* – fondues.

Nightclubs

The Croix du Sud, Hotel du Lac and Hotel du Port each have their own nightclub. Others include *The Cave Club, Cosmos, Rive-Gauche, Playboy, Canne à Sucre,* the *Calebasse* and the *Lido*.

Entertainment

There are swimming pools in all the main hotels and a variety of watersports are available. Swimming in the sea around Cotonou can be dangerous, and only strong swimmers are advised to bathe. Tennis can be played at the *Club du Bénin*. There is also a yacht club in Cotonou.

Shopping
Best buys: engraved bronze figures, patchwork, tapestries, wood carvings.

Handicrafts and souvenirs are sold at the numerous stalls scattered along the Marina. The Dan Tokpa market on the shores of Cotonou Lagoon sells traditional goods as well as imported goods, mainly from Nigeria. A number of souvenir stalls can be found in the Maison du Tourisme on Avenue General LeClerc.

BOTSWANA
Botswana

Geography *55*
The Economy *57*
How to Get There *58*
Entry Regulations *58*
Practical Information for the Visitor *59*
Useful Addresses (General) *60*
Business Information *61*
Business Services *62*
Useful Addresses (Business) *62*
Gaborone *62*
Francistown *63*

Size: 600,732 sq.km/231,804 sq.miles.

Population: 710,000 (1977 est.).

Distribution: 12.3% in urban areas.

Density: 1.2 persons per sq.km/3.1 per sq.mile.

Population Growth Rate: 1.9% p.a. (1970-7).

Ethnic Composition: The majority belong to the 8 Tswana tribes; there are also Bushmen (the aboriginal people), European and Asians.

Capital: Gaborone Pop. 36,900.

Major Towns: Kanye Pop. 40,000; Serowe Pop. 40,000; Molepolole Pop. 31,000; Selebi-Pikwe Pop. 30,000; Francistown Pop. 26,000; Mochudi Pop. 25,000.

Language: English is the official language, Setswana the main African language. The Bushmen speak a dialect of the Khoisan language.

Religion: The majority adhere to traditional beliefs; about 15% are Christians.

Government: Botswana became independent in September 1966. The President and National Assembly are elected for a 5-year term of office with the House of Chiefs acting in an advisory capacity. The principal political parties are the ruling Botswana Democratic Party (BDP), the Botswana People's Party (BPP), the Botswana National Front (BNF) and the Botswana Independence Party (BIP).

GEOGRAPHY

Botswana is a landlocked nation, consisting mainly of dry rolling tableland at an average altitude of 900m/2,953 feet. The Kalahari area in the west is semi-desert;

BOTSWANA

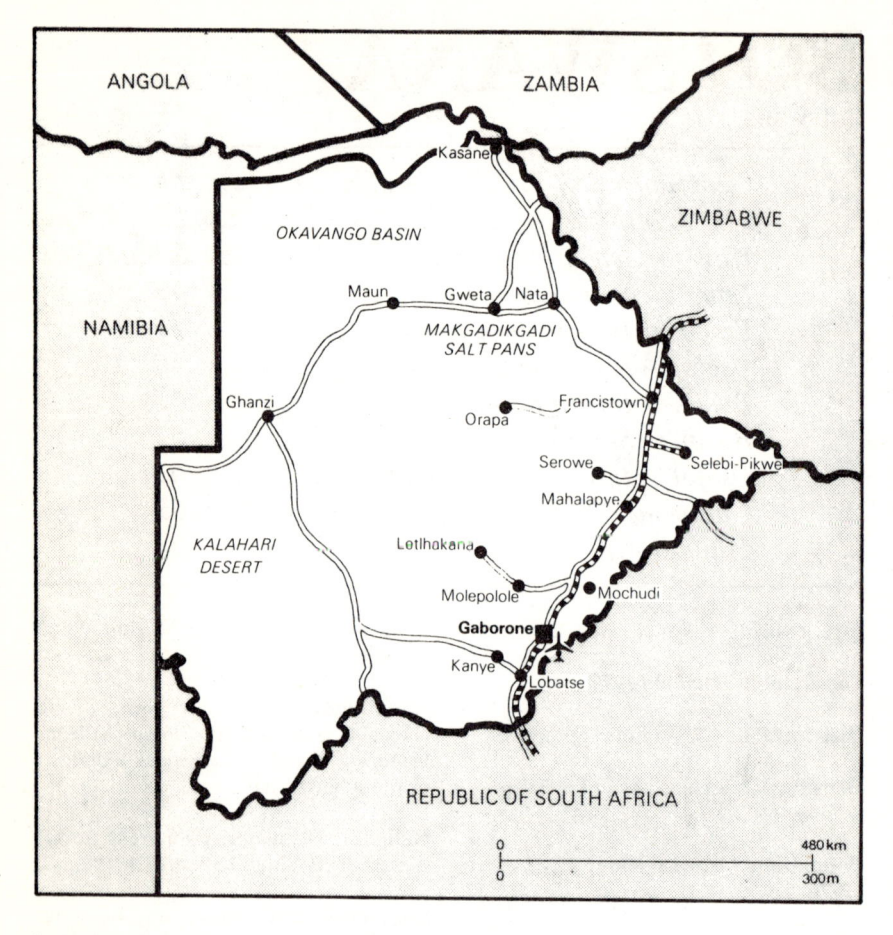

further north are the swamps of the Okavango Basin and the Makgadikgadi Salt Pans. The most fertile and populous area is the strip of land in the east of Botswana, where most economic activity is concentrated.

Climate

Dry-season (May–September) day temperatures average around 25°C/77°F with cold and sometimes frosty nights. The warmer rainy season reaches its height in December and January when temperatures reach 38°C/100°F. Most rain falls in the hilly eastern regions; further to the west rain is infrequent.

Agriculture

Some 90% of the population engage in agriculture, with livestock raising the most important activity. Meat exports are worth about 30% of total exports in a good year, and the agricultural sector as a whole contributes about 20% of the Gross Domestic Product. Most livestock raising is on a subsistence basis; however, the uneven distribution of water resources, transport and abattoir facilities has tended to encourage the concentration of commercial ranching in the hands of a relatively small group of owners around the Lobatse abattoir. The number of cattle in Botswana is around 4 million, of which half are owned by 5% of all households; some 45% of households have no cattle at all. The total number of goats is 1.5 million; sheep number some 500,000.

The major subsistence crops are sorghum, maize, millet and beans, with cotton and oil seeds grown as cash crops. Frequent droughts have severely damaged livestock and crops in recent years, and there is concern that overstocking in the good years will lead to overgrazing and the erosion of vegetation and soil cover with disastrous results in the event of a prolonged drought. The long-term aim of the Government is to achieve self-sufficiency in food production, and to that end poultry, fisheries, dairy, horticulture and forestry industries are being developed. At present, food continues to be imported. European Development Fund grants are being used to develop vaccine for cattle in collaboration with a French company in an attempt to end the outbreaks of disease which in the past have led to bans on the export of meat from Botswana.

Main Crops: sorghum, maize, millet, pulses, groundnuts, sunflower seeds, roots and tubers, cotton.

Mineral Resources: coal, copper, nickel, diamonds, semi-precious stones, small amounts of gold and asbestos. 1977 surveys suggested the presence of lead, zinc, manganese, uranium and mineral fuels.

THE ECONOMY

Gross National Product (1978 est.): US$460 million.

Per Capita Income (1978 est.): US$620.

Gross Domestic Product (1978): 332.2 million pula.

Foreign Trade (1978): Total Imports – US$290.2 million. Total Exports – US$224.4 million.

Main Trading Partners: Imports – SACUA countries, EEC, USA. Exports – SACUA countries, EEC.

The development of mineral resources has been the most important factor in the steady growth of the economy since independence, and mining has now overtaken agriculture as the largest contributor to Gross Domestic Product. Despite some problems, the copper-nickel mines at Selebi-Pikwe and, even more importantly, the diamond mines at Orapa and Letlhakane have significantly increased export earnings in recent years; a new mine is planned at Jwaneng. Coal is produced at Molepolole for domestic consumption in electricity production. There is little manufacturing industry apart from meat and mineral processing. The high cost of water and electricity and the lack of technical and management skills have meant that what domestic market there is has continued to be supplied by South Africa. The expansion of tourism and mining has given some help to the construction industry, and the European Development Fund has cooperated in the establishment of industrial areas in the rural villages.

With economic growth have come various social problems, including rapid urbanisation and increasing disparities in wealth. Industrial development has created very

BOTSWANA

few new jobs and unemployment is growing. However, the long-term economic outlook could still be very favourable, if social and ecological problems can be solved, because Botswana has enough potentially profitable natural resources to ensure continued interest on the part of foreign investors. At present Botswana receives aid from the World Bank, the United Nations and other international agencies as well as bilateral donors. Aid has been stepped up as the number of refugees from neighbouring countries has increased.

Main Industries: meat processing, mineral processing, textiles, construction.

Main Commodities Traded: copper-nickel matte, diamonds, semi-precious stones, meat products, hides and skins, textiles.

International Affiliations: UN, IBRD, OAU, ACP, ADB, World Bank, IMF, Commonwealth, SACU.

HOW TO GET THERE

Air
There are regular flights to Gaborone from Johannesburg. Air Botswana operate a daily service (except Sunday) from Johannesburg to Francistown, and to Selebi-Pikwe 4 times a week. South African Airways fly direct to Gaborone from London once a week. Both Zambia Airways and Air Botswana fly to Gaborone from Lusaka 3 times a week, with some flights stopping in Francistown.

Flying time from London is 13 hours, New York 19.

Road
Botswana has good road connections with South Africa and Zimbabwe. A new road links Francistown with the Kazungula ferry at the Zambian border. There is also a road connection to Namibia.

Rail
The Bulawayo-Cape Town Railway passes through Francistown, Mahalapye, Gaborone and Lobatse.

ENTRY REGULATIONS

Visas
Visas are required by nationals of all countries, except British Commonwealth, EEC countries, Austria, Finland, Greece, Iceland, Liechtenstein, Norway, South Africa, Sweden, Switzerland, Uruguay and the USA – for a stay of up to 7 days. Visitors from these countries who intend to stay longer should apply to the local immigration or police authorities for a permit before the 7-day period expires.

All other nationals require visas obtainable from Botswana diplomatic missions abroad. Visa applications should be supported by letter giving details of the purpose of the visit and accommodation arrangements, and confirming financial responsibility for the applicant. A banker's reference may be required.

All visa applications are referred to Gaborone and can take up to 4 weeks before authorisation. Urgent applications can be referred by telex.

Health Regulations
A valid International Certificate of Vaccination against yellow fever is required by all persons entering Botswana. Those persons arriving from a cholera-infected area must be in possession of a valid cholera vaccination certificate.

Customs
Currency: There are no restrictions on the import of foreign currency, provided it is declared on arrival. Export is allowed up to the amount imported. There is no limit to the amount of Botswana currency that may be imported, but export is limited to BTP 50 per person.

Duty-free articles: Personal effects. 400 cigarettes, 50 cigars or 250 grams of tobacco. 1 litre of wine and 1 litre of spirits. Small amounts of perfume.

Restricted articles: Firearms and ammunition.

PRACTICAL INFORMATION FOR THE VISITOR

1. Currency
Monetary Unit – pula, divided into 100 thebe.
Notes – 1, 2, 5, 10, 20 pula.
Coins – 1, 5, 10, 25, 50 thebe; 1 pula.

Travellers' cheques may be readily exchanged in hotels and at the airport.

Banking Hours
0830–1300   Monday to Friday
0830–1100   Saturday

Currency issue has been controlled by the Bank of Botswana since August 1976, when Botswana left the Rand Monetary Area.

Principal Banks in Gaborone
Barclays Bank of Botswana Ltd, Barclays Bank Building, The Mall, P.O. Box 478, ☎ 52421.
Bank of Botswana, P.O. Box 712.
Botswana Cooperative Bank Ltd, P.O. Box 713.
National Development Bank, Development House, P.O. Box 225.
Standard Bank Botswana Ltd, Standard House, The Mall, P.O. Box 496.

2. Electricity Supply
240v AC 50Hz.

3. Weights and Measures
The metric system is in use.

4. Media
Radio Botswana broadcasts in Setswana and English. There is no television service, although it is possible to receive South African television.

Newspapers and Journals
The *Botswana Daily News* is a Government-sponsored paper in Setswana and English. *Masa, Puo Pha* and *Therisanyo* are the monthly party publications of the BPP, BNP and BDP respectively. South African newspapers are on sale in the larger towns.

5. Medical Care
Outside the main towns all water should be boiled before drinking. Malaria is prevalent in the north of the country, including the wildlife parks, and visitors there are advised to take anti-malarial prophylactics; in years of heavy rainfall, malaria may also be found in other areas of the country. The presence of tsetse fly means that sleeping sickness is a health risk; suitable protective clothing and insect repellent are advisable. Stagnant water should not be used for washing or bathing as there is a risk of bilharzia.

BOTSWANA

6. Telephone, Telex and Postal Services
All international telephone services are via Cape Town.

Telegrams can be sent from all main post offices.

Telex facilities are available at the Post Office, The Mall, Gaborone.

All mail to and from Gaborone should be despatched by air.

7. Public Holidays

1 January	New Year's Day
24 May	President's Day
2nd Friday in June	Commonwealth Day
1st Monday in August	Public Holiday
30 September	Botswana Day
25–6 December	Christmas

The following movable Christian holidays are also observed: *Good Friday, Easter Saturday, Easter Monday, Ascension Day* and *Whit Monday.*

8. Time
GMT + 2.

9. Internal Transport
Air
There are airports at Gaborone, Lobatse, Francistown, Orapa, Selebi and Maun, and numerous airstrips scattered across the country. Air Botswana flights to Maun call at Francistown and Selebi. All other internal flights are operated by charter.

Light aircraft may be hired from Air Botswana (Pty), P.O. Box 92, Gaborone.

Airline Offices in Gaborone
Air Botswana, P.O. Box 92.
British Airways, P.O. Box 92, The Mall, ☎ 51921/3.
South African Airways, Embassy Chambers, The Mall, ☎ 2961.
Zambia Airways, P.O. Box 192, Zambia House, The Mall, ☎ 3150.

Rail
The Government is taking over the Rhodesian railway in Botswana. There is a passenger service on the line which runs from Francistown, via Gaborone, to Lobatse.

Road
There are good all-weather roads linking the following towns: Gaborone – Lobatse – Kanye; Gaborone – Mahalapye – Francistown; Francistown – Gweta – Maun; Francistown – Kazungula.

The Lobatse-Gaborone road is asphalted.

Self-drive and chauffeur-driven cars are available for hire in Gaborone. A number of safari companies hire out trucks and Land-Rovers.

Traffic drives on the left of the road.

Car Hire Firms
Avis, President Hotel, P.O. Box 790, Gaborone, ☎ 2717; (Airport) ☎ 2961.
Botswana Development Corporation, P.O. Box 438, Gaborone.
Botswana Game Industries, Private Bag 30, Francistown.
Cliff Engineering, P.O. Box 282, Gaborone.
Holiday Safaris, Holiday Inn, Private Bag 16, Gaborone.
Leonard Motors, P.O. Box 252, Gaborone.

10. Tipping
Taxis – 10% of the fare.

Hotels/restaurants – 10–15% of the bill.

USEFUL ADDRESSES (GENERAL)

Gaborone
Swedish Embassy: P.O. Box 17.

USSR Embassy: P.O. Box 81.

US Embassy: P.O. Box 90, ☎ 2944/7.

West German Embassy: P.O. Box 315.

Nigerian High Commission: P.O. Box 274.

British High Commission: P.O. Box 23, ☎ 2483/5.

Zambia High Commission: P.O. Box 362.

Dutch Consulate: c/o Holiday Inn, Nyerere Drive North, Private Bag 16, ☎ 2134.

British Council: British High Commission Building, P.O. Box 439, Queens Road, The Mall, ☎ 53602.

Tourist Information Bureau: P.O. Box 131.

BUSINESS INFORMATION

Botswana welcomes the participation of foreign investors in developing industry, particularly where specialist skills and opportunities for local employment and training are offered. Several parastatal organisations exist to guide the potential investor. Botswana offers a stable economic situation, various tax allowances and other fiscal concessions to investors.

Mineral resources are not fully exploited, and this is the area of major interest to foreign companies. Although Botswana has left the Rand Monetary Area, South Africa Customs Union Agreement (SACUA) membership has been retained, which gives preference to member countries in the sale of goods to the domestic market. Because of the Lomé Convention, the EEC is a privileged market for Botswana's exports.

Representatives or agents intending to collect orders must be in possession of a licence obtainable from the Director of Customs and Excise.

Import and Exchange Control Regulations
All goods imported from SACUA member countries are free of import duties; otherwise import regulations follow those of South Africa. This means that import permits are necessary. Since August 1976 exchange control with other countries has been in operation.

Business Hours
Government Offices
April to October –   0800–1300   Monday to Friday
                      1415–1700

November to March – 0730–1245   Monday to Friday
                      1400–1600

Business Houses
0800–1700 Monday to Friday
0800–1300 Saturday

BUSINESS SERVICES

Insurance

Botswana Eagle Insurance Co. Ltd., Botsalano House, P.O. Box 1221, Gaborone.

Botswana Insurance Co., Madirelo House, P.O. Box 336, Gaborone.

ECB Insurance Brokers (Botswana) Ltd., Botsalano House, P.O. Box 1195, Gaborone.

IGI Botswana Ltd., Botsalano House, P.O. Box 715, Gaborone.

Insurance Brokers Botswana Ltd., P.O. Box 1212, Gaborone.

Minet Botswana Ltd., Tswana House, P.O. Box 624, Gaborone.

USEFUL ADDRESSES (BUSINESS)

Botswana Agricultural Marketing Board, Private Bag 35, Gaborone.

Botswana Development Corporation, P.O. Box 438, Madirelo House, Gaborone.

Botswana Enterprises Development Unit (BEDU), Plot No. 1269, Lobatse Road, P.O. Box 14, Gaborone.

Botswana Information Services, P.O. Box 51, Gaborone.

Botswana Livestock Development Corporation (Pty.) Ltd, P.O. Box 455, Gaborone.

Botswana Meat Commission, Private Bag 4, Lobatse.

Botswana Power Corporation, P.O. Box 48, Badiredi House, Gaborone.

Department of Wildlife, National Parks and Tourism, P.O. Box 131, Gaborone, ☏ 2285.

Director of Customs and Excise, Private Bag 41, Gaborone.

Northern Botswana Chamber of Commerce, P.O. Box 2, Palapye. (Others in Francistown, Selebi-Pikwe and Mahalapye.)

MAIN CITY AND TOWN

Gaborone

Since it was selected as the site for the capital of the future independent state of Botswana in 1962, Gaborone has grown rapidly. The arched buildings of the National Assembly are perhaps the best example of Gaborone's modern architecture, most of which was erected since 1964. The city has a central pedestrian area, The Mall, around which are clustered shops, offices and Government buildings. The Mall runs down from the National Assembly to the Town Hall neatly dividing the city in two, and from this central area roads radiate out to the suburbs. The University, National Library, National Archives and several Government training establishments are to be found in the city. The National Museum contains displays of the art, crafts and natural resources of Botswana.

Hotels

There is no official hotel rating system. Reservations are advisable in view of the shortage of hotel accommodation.

HOLIDAY INN, Private Bag 16, Nyerere Drive North, ☎ 2121.
Modern hotel 2km/1 mile from town centre, 1 km/½ mile from international airport.
Rooms: 119 ♨, 🍴, 🛏, ⚐, ♂
(0600–2400). Suites available.
Facilities: Restaurant, bar. Nightclub, casino. Swimming pool, water sports, tennis, squash, golf (18 hole). Car hire. Safaris arranged.
Services: TC, FC. 💳 Access, Amex, Barclaycard, Diners Club, Eurocard, Master Charge. Dr. on call. 🅢
Conference room – max. capacity 120.

PRESIDENT HOTEL, P.O. Box 200, The Mall (South), ☎ 2215/6/8.
Small modern hotel in town centre, 2km/1 mile from airport.
Rooms: 24 ♨, ⚐.
Facilities: Restaurant, bar. Car hire. Safaris arranged.
Services: TC, FC. 💳 Barclaycard, Diners Club. Dr. on call.

GABORONE HOTEL, P.O. Box 5, ☎ 4226/7/8.
Budget hotel near railway station.
Rooms: 17.
Facilities: Restaurant, bar.
Services: TC, FC. 💳 Barclaycard.

Restaurants

The hotels all have restaurants, often serving colonial-style British menus. There is also a Chinese restaurant.

Entertainment

Just outside Gaborone is the Dam, an ideal spot for watersports or relaxing at weekends. Several sports and social clubs serve the expatriate community. There are also a few nightclubs and cinemas.

Francistown

Francistown is the industrial and commercial centre of Botswana, and is still growing rapidly in population and area. Not a particularly attractive town, its appearance is in considerable contrast to Gaborone. Originally settled during the late 19th century by miners, the town bears many reminders of those days. Francistown is on the major road and rail routes and is the place to go before setting out for the northern game parks. Out of town one can visit the ancient ruins to the north or head out for the Game Reserves of the Makgadikgadi Pans.

Hotels

GRAND HOTEL, P.O. Box 30, ☎ 300.
The best hotel in Francistown.
Rooms: 28 ♨, ⚐. Suites available.
Facilities: Restaurant, bar. Car hire.
Services: TC, FC. 💳 Barclaycard.

TATI HOTEL, P.O. Box 15, ☎ 321.
Cheaper hotel.
Rooms: ♨, ⚐.
Facilities: Restaurant, bar, discotheque.
Car hire. Open-air arena.
Services: TC, FC. 💳 Barclaycard.

Shopping

The best buys are animal skins which can be bought from the shop at the factory of *Botswana Game Industries* (P.O. Box 118) in the town. The *Lekgaba Centre* is a notable art workshop where wood and ivory carvings and utensils are exhibited and sold.

BURUNDI
Republic of Burundi

Geography 64
The Economy 66
How to Get There 67
Entry Regulations 67
Practical Information for the Visitor 67
Useful Addresses (General) 69
Business Information 69
Business Services 70
Useful Addresses (Business) 70
Bujumbura 70

Area: 27,834 sq.km/10,747 sq.miles.

Population: 4.2 million (1978 est.).

Distribution: 5% in urban areas.

Density: 143 persons per sq.km/391 per sq.mile.

Population Growth Rate: 2.2% p.a.

Ethnic Composition: 84% are Hutu, about 15% are Tutsi, and less than 1% are Twa pygmies.

Capital: Bujumbura Pop. 160,000 (1976 est.).

Major Town: Gitenga Pop. 25,000.

Language: The official languages are Kirundi and French. Swahili is also spoken.

Religion: About 50% are Christian, mainly Roman Catholic, and some 25,000 are Muslim. The remainder of the population adhere to traditional indigenous beliefs.

Government: Since independence from Belgium in July 1962, Burundi has been ruled by one or another Tutsi faction. Political change has been characterised by coups and purges, often of extreme violence. The single political party is the Union for National Progress (UPRONA), and President Colonel Jean Baptiste Bagaza determines state and party policy with the aid of the Supreme Revolutionary Council. Military rule began in 1966 in response to an Hutu uprising; there are plans to hand over power to a civilian government in 1981.

GEOGRAPHY

Burundi is a small densely populated country situated to the north-east of Lake Tanganyika in central Africa. Burundi and Zaïre are separated by the River Ruzizi which runs southward from Lake Kivu to Lake Tanganyika in the western section of the East African Rift Valley system. East of the valley floor the land rises sharply to form a range of hills at an average altitude of 1,800m/5,900 ft. Further to the east the terrain drops to a plateau at an elevation of between 1,400–1,800m/3,720–5,900 ft.

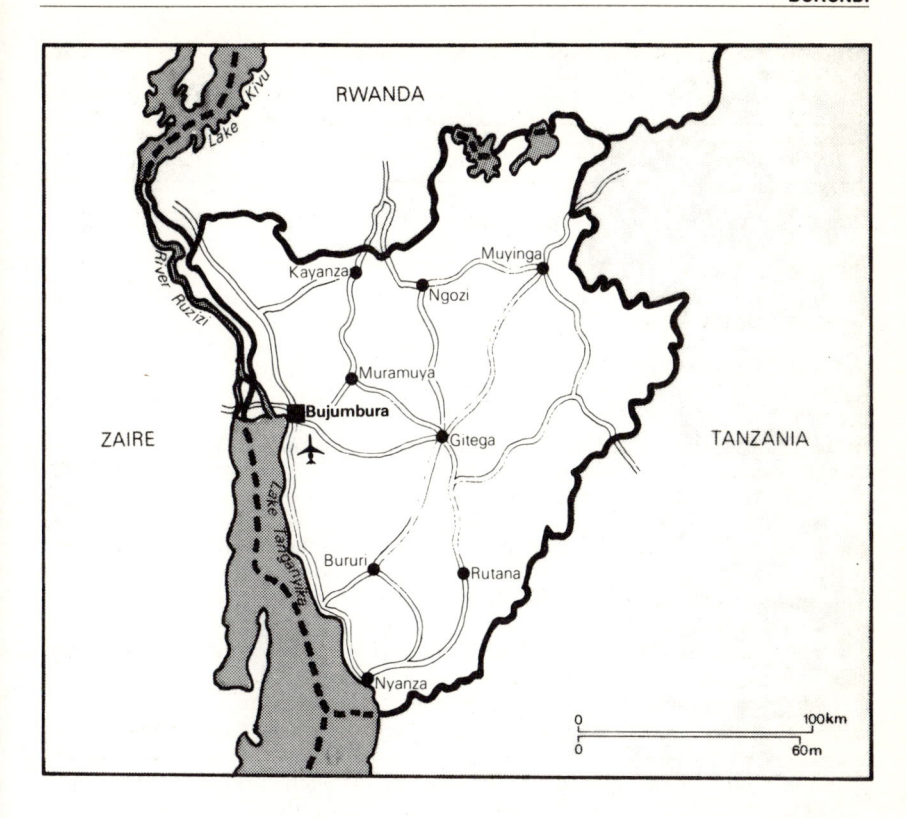

Climate
Average annual temperatures in the Rift Valley are 23°c/73°F and annual rainfall averages 750mm/30ins. On the plateau temperatures average 20°c/68°F, and rainfall 1,200mm/47ins. The dry season lasts from May to August.

Agriculture
Over 90% of the population engage in agriculture, mostly at a subsistence level. Agriculture contributes some 65% of the GDP, and coffee exports alone are worth 90% of total export earnings. The main subsistence crops are bananas, millet, sorghum, cassava, beans and rice. The most important cash crops are coffee, tea, cotton, palm oil, tobacco and pyrethrum. Livestock raising is commonplace, and herds are generally in the hands of the Tutsi minority amongst whom status is measured in head of cattle owned. Fishing is of importance around Lake Tanganyika. The objectives of the 1978–82, 5-Year Plan are to encourage agricultural diversification and to overcome the problems of nutritional deficiencies and soil erosion in the rural areas. To a limited extent, the Government has encouraged cooperatives and has planned a number of agri-villages.

Main Crops Traded: coffee, tea, cotton.

BURUNDI

Mineral Resources: bastaenite, casserite, colombo-tantalite, nickel, oil, uranium, gold, cobalt, copper, platinum.

THE ECONOMY

Gross National Product (1976): US$460 million.

Per Capita Income (1976): US$120.

Gross Domestic Product (1977): US$492.4 million.

Foreign Trade (1977): Total Imports – FRB 6,677.5 million. Total Exports – FRB 8,073.3 million.

Main Trading Partners: Imports – Belgium/Luxembourg, West Germany, France, Kenya, Japan, UK, USA, Netherlands. Exports – USA, West Germany, Italy, UK, France, Belgium/Luxembourg.

Burundi is heavily dependent upon the export of coffee for revenue, and economic performance has been closely tied to the volume of coffee output and world prices. This situation was recognised at the Lomé Convention of 1975 when Burundi was included as one of the 24 poorest countries qualifying for special assistance under the export stabilisation scheme (STABEX). Continuing aid has been necessary to finance capital projects and to counteract budgetary deficiencies.

Apart from the agricultural sector, it is in mineral resources that most potential lies. Although bastaenite and casserite mining is declining as the mines have become only marginally viable, large reserves of nickel and colombo-tantalite and some oil and uranium await exploitation. The manufacturing sector is largely made up of beer and soft drink production and the processing of agricultural products. A textile factory is under construction with Chinese assistance, and tourism is being encouraged around Lake Tanganyika.

The Third (1978–82) Development Plan has accorded priority to agricultural diversification and to infrastructure projects, especially the transport network. Recent rises in the cost of fuel and other imports, declining export revenue from coffee and transportation difficulties have hampered economic development; although as a member of the Great Lakes Economic Community (CEPGL), it is hoped that import substitution may be implemented successfully from the wider economic base and resources provided by the 3 member countries (Rwanda, Burundi and Zaïre). Plans include the development of alternative energy sources.

The principal donors of aid and loans are the World Bank, the African Development Bank, the Arab Bank for Development in Africa, the Kuwait Development Fund, the European Development Fund and the IDA. Technical assistance has been received from Belgium, France, West Germany and China.

Major Industries: food and drink products, textiles, construction materials, insecticides.

Main Commodities Traded: Imports – fuel and lubricants, transport equipment and machinery, chemicals, consumer goods.

International Affiliations: UN, IBRD, OAU, ACP, ADB, CEPGL, KRBO.

BURUNDI

HOW TO GET THERE

Air
The international airport is 15 km/9 miles from Bujumbura town centre. Sabena operates a direct service to Bujumbura Airport from Brussels twice weekly, and several other flights stop over. Air Zaïre fly between Kinshasa and Bujumbura. Air Burundi (STAB) flies to Bukavu (Zaïre), Goma (Zaïre) and Kigali (Rwanda) from Bujumbura.

Road
A good road exists from Zaïre to Burundi, via Bukavu. The road from Bujumbura to Kigali (Rwanda) is reportedly being asphalted.

Lake
Cargo steamers operating on Lake Tanganyika carry some passengers to Bujumbura. The most frequent services are from Kigoma (Tanzania), a journey of about 12 hours.

ENTRY REGULATIONS

Visas
Visas are required by all foreign nationals and are obtainable from representatives of Burundi abroad or by application to the Foreign Office in Bujumbura, giving full details of name, birth date, nationality, passport, reasons for visit and references. In certain circumstances visas may be granted at Bujumbura Airport. White nationals of South Africa are not admitted. An Embarkation Tax is levied on passengers leaving Bujumbura Airport.

Health Regulations
International Certificates of Vaccination against smallpox are required if arriving within 14 days of leaving an infected area, and for yellow fever if arriving within 6 days of leaving an infected area. Cholera, malaria, tetanus, typhoid and paratyphoid protection is recommended.

Customs
Currency: There is no limit to the amount of foreign and local currency which may be imported if declared upon arrival. Not more than 2,000 FRB may be exported. Any unused foreign currency may be exported up to the amount declared.

Duty-free articles: 1,000 cigarettes or 1kg of tobacco. 1 litre of alcoholic beverages.

Articles liable to duty: Samples or personal items of value may require a deposit equal to duty payable until exported. Gifts exceeding 300 FRB may be dutiable.

PRACTICAL INFORMATION FOR THE VISITOR

1. Currency
Monetary Unit – Burundi francs (FRB), divided into 100 centimes.

Notes – FRB 10, 20, 50, 100, 500, 1,000 5,000.
Coins – FRB 1, 5, 10.

BURUNDI

The Burundi franc is theoretically tied to the value of the Belgian franc, although in practice they are not readily convertible outside Burundi. All exchange transactions must be conducted through one of the main banks or at Bujumbura Airport. Dealings on the black market for currency are strictly illegal.

The visitor is advised to exchange only as much currency as is needed for day-to-day requirements.

Banking Hours
0800–1200 Monday to Friday.

The principal banks in Burundi are the *Banque Commerciale du Burundi*, the *Banque de Crédit de Bujumbura*, the *Banque de la République de Burundi* and the *Banque Belgo-Africain Burundi*, all of which are based in Bujumbura.

2. Electricity Supply
220v AC 50Hz.

3. Weights and Measures
The metric system is in use.

4. Media
2 radio stations broadcast in Burundi. Voix de la Révolution, the government station, transmits daily in Kirundi, French and Swahili. Radio Cordac is a missionary station. Burundi has no television service.

All publications in Burundi are government controlled.

Newspapers and Journals
Flash-Infor is the major daily published in French. Others include: *Le Renouveau de Burundi*, a daily paper in French published by the Ministry of Information; *Burundi Chrétien*, a weekly French-language paper issued by the Archbishopric of Chitega; *Ubumwe*, a weekly Kirundi paper, and *Unité et Révolution*, the Ministry of Information French weekly. Agence Burundaise de Presse publish a daily information bulletin.

5. Medical Care
Cholera, tetanus and TAB (typhoid and paratyphoid) vaccinations are recommended if a stay of more than a few days is envisaged; also recommended are anti-malarial prophylactics. Tap water should be boiled before drinking.

Western medical facilities in Bujumbura are limited; they are almost non-existent in the rural areas.

6. Telephone, Telex and Postal Services
Telephone and postal services are sometimes unreliable. Overseas telephone connections are via Brussels. All mail should be despatched by air.

7. Public Holidays

1 January	New Year's Day
1 May	Labour Day
1 July	National Independence Day
18 September	UPRONA Day
13 October	Rwagasore Day
25 December	Christmas Day

In addition, the following movable Christian festivals are also observed: *Easter Monday, Ascension Day, Whit Monday, Assumption* and *All Saints Day*.

8. Time
GMT + 2.

9. Internal Transport

Air
There are no regular internal commercial air services, although aircraft may be chartered.

Airline Offices in Bujumbura
Air Burundi (STAB), B.P. 2460, 2 Blvd. de l'Uprona, ☎ 3460.
Air Zaire, ☎ 6184.
Sabena, B.P. 720, Ave Patrice Lumumba, ☎ 2075.

BURUNDI

Road
There is a fairly extensive network of roads of which only 80km is asphalted. There is no system of public transport, and taxis are very rare.

10. Tipping
Taxi – 10% of the fare.

Hotels/restautants – 10–15% of the bill.

USEFUL ADDRESSES (GENERAL)

Bujumbura

Belgian Embassy: B.P. 1920, 9 Ave de l'Industrie, ☎ 6176.

Chinese Embassy (People's Republic): B.P. 2550, ☎ 4307.

Egyptian Embassy: B.P. 1520, 31 Ave de la Liberté, ☎ 2031.

French Embassy: B.P. 1740, 60 Ave de l'Uprona, ☎ 6464.

North Korean Embassy: B.P. 1620, ☎ 2881.

Libyan Embassy: ☎ 5155.

Rumanian Embassy: ☎ 4139.

Rwandan Embassy: B.P. 400, ☎ 4145.

USSR Embassy: B.P. 1034, 9 Ave de l'Uprona, ☎ 6098.

US Embassy: B.P. 1720, Chaussée Prince L. Rawagasore, ☎ 3454.

West German Embassy: B.P. 480, 22 Rue 18 Septembre, ☎ 3211/2.

Vatican Embassy: B.P. 1068, 46 Chaussée Prince L. Rawagasore, ☎ 2326.

Zaïre Embassy: B.P. 872, 2-4 Ave du Zaïre, ☎ 2276.

British Consulate: B.P. 1750.

Swiss Consulate: B.P. 1284, Blvd du 28 Novembre, ☎ 4129.

Office National du Tourisme: B.P. 902, ☎ 2023.

Université de Bujumbura: B.P. 1550.

Burundi Travel Agency: 7 Ave de la Victoire, ☎ 4161.

Wagon-Lit Tourisme Authorised Representative: Bureau AM1, B.P. 750, ☎ 2665.

BUSINESS INFORMATION

Investment from abroad is welcomed where it accords with Government plans, and enterprise in co-operation with the state is preferred. Foreign property and assets are safeguarded by the Government as long as they do not conflict with national interests. Considerable potential exists for the development of mineral resources, alternative energy supplies, the transport system, agriculture and tourism in particular. Labour-intensive industry is especially acceptable, as full employment is a major aim of Government policy.

Business Hours
Government Offices
0800–1200   Monday to Friday

BURUNDI

Business Houses
0800–1200
1400–1630 Monday to Friday
0800–1200 Saturday

BUSINESS SERVICES

Insurance
Ch. le Jeune Assurance SPRL, 7 Place de l'Independance, B.P. 622, Bujumbura, ☎ 6090.
Societe Nouvelle d'Assurances au Burundi (SONABU), 18 Rue de la Residence, B.P. 171, Bujumbura, ☎ 2817.

Shipping
Societe Burundaise Arnolac, B.P. 2080, Bujumbura, ☎ 6036.
Agence Maritime International SA (AMI), Place de l'Indépendance, B.P. 750, Bujumbura, ☎ 3975.

Import/Clearing Agents
Benalco, 15 Avenue de la Poste, B.P. 390, Bujumbura, ☎ 6089.
Athanassio Plaxitele, B.P. 782, Bujumbura, ☎ 2132.
Anand Narah Patel, Bujumbura, ☎ 2132.
Clearing and Insurance Cie, 7 Avenue de la Victoire, B.P. 703, Bujumbura, ☎ 4161.

USEFUL ADDRESSES (BUSINESS)

Association des Commercants Burundi (ACB) Blvd du 1er Novembre, Bujumbura, ☎ 3977.

Chambre de Commerce et de l'Industrie, B.P. 313, Bujumbura.

MAJOR CITY

Bujumbura
Bujumbura is the administrative capital as well as the main commercial and industrial centre. The city was founded by German colonists in 1899 and has grown to become a large port, its position on the shores of Lake Tanganyika being of vital importance in this inaccessible country. Hills rise up sharply behind Bujumbura to reinforce the impression of remoteness.

The Postmaster's House and the modern Parliament Buildings represent examples of the wide variety of architecture in the city, with early colonial houses providing a marked contrast to the strikingly modern recent constructions.

Hotels
There is no official hotel rating system.

AER HOTEL SOURCE DU NIL, Avenue du Stade, B.P. 2027, ☎ 5222.

Large modern (1977) hotel in large park near lake.
Rooms: 150 ♪, ⌂, ⌶, ⌂, ♂. Suites available.
Facilities: Restaurant, bars. Nightclub.

Cinema, shops. Swimming pool, tennis, golf, riding, watersports.
Services: TC, FC. ⊟ Amex, Barclay Visa, Carte Blanche, Diners Club, Eurocheque. Audiovisual equipment. Conference room – max. capacity 300 persons. Also banquet and reception rooms.

BURUNDI PALACE HOTEL, Avenue de l'Uprona, B.P. 225, ☎ 2920.
Modern hotel in town centre.
Rooms: 29 ♄, ▲, ♆.
Facilities: Restaurant, bar.

PAGUIDAS–HAIDEMOS HOTEL, Avenue du Peuple Burundi, B.P. 2, ☎ 2251/2.
Older hotel in city centre.
Rooms: 77 ♄, ☎, ▲, ♆.
Facilities: Restaurant, bar. Cinema. Tennis.
Services: ⊟ Amex, Diners Club. Meeting and banquet rooms

Others include:
CENTRAL HOTEL, Place de l'Indépendance, ☎ 2658.
HÔTEL GRILLON, Avenue du Zaïre, B.P. 34, ☎ 2519.
HÔTEL RESIDENCE, Avenue de Stanley, B.P. 405, ☎ 2773.

Restaurants
Most of the hotels in and around Bujumbura have restaurants serving European food. In addition to the hotel restaurants other eating establishments include: *La Cremaillerie,* ☎ 2527; *Chez Charles,* ☎ 3283; *Amahovo,* ☎ 4116; *L'Oasis,* ☎ 3116; *La Taverne,* ☎ 5102.

Nightclubs
L'Arlequin, ☎ 2747; *Coco Nut Grove,* ☎ 2846; *Le Scotch Club,* ☎ 3996.

Entertainment
The public beach is 5 km/3 miles west of the city. The *Entente Sportive* offers membership to visitors. The University Museum has collections of zoological, botanical and mineralogical specimens from the region.

Shopping
Best buys: basketware, canes, woven goods, drums and weaponry.
There is an open market in Bujumbura where food and handicrafts are on sale at prices considerably below those in the airport and hotel shops. The *Librairie St Paul* sells books, journals and handicrafts.

CAMEROON
United Republic of Cameroon

Geography	73
The Economy	74
How to Get There	75
Entry Regulations	75
Practical Information for the Visitor	76
Useful Addresses (General)	78
Business Information	78
Business Services	79
Useful Addresses (Business)	79
Douala	80
Yaounde	81

Size: 475,442 sq.km/183,569 sq.miles.

Population: 8.1 million (1978 est.).

Distribution: 25% in urban areas.

Density: 43 persons per sq.km/116.6 per sq.mile. (Population density varies enormously, ranging from 135 persons per sq.km/350 per sq.mile in the coastal area of Wouri to less than 5 persons per sq.km/12 per sq.mile in the north).

Population Growth Rate: 2.3% p.a.

Ethnic Composition: There are an estimated 200 tribal groups. In the south the Bantu peoples predominate; in the north are Hamitic, Negroid, Sudanese and Arab peoples. Small groups of Pygmies are found in the southern forest areas.

Capital: Yaoundé Pop. 274,339.

Major Cities/Towns: Douala Pop. 485,797; Nkongsamba Pop. 71,000; Foumban Pop. 59,701; Kumba Pop. 50,000.

Language: French and English are the official languages, the former being spoken by about three-quarters of the population. In East Cameroon French is used exclusively in Government and business circles. A large number of African languages are also spoken.

Religion: About 30% are Christian, 15% Muslim (mainly in the north) and the remainder Animist.

Government: In 1972 East Cameroon and West Cameroon became a unitary state known as the United Republic of Cameroon. The President and the National Assembly are elected for a 5-year term, although the term of office of the National Assembly can be shortened or lengthened at the insistence of the President. The Union Nationale Camerounaise (UNC) is the sole political party.

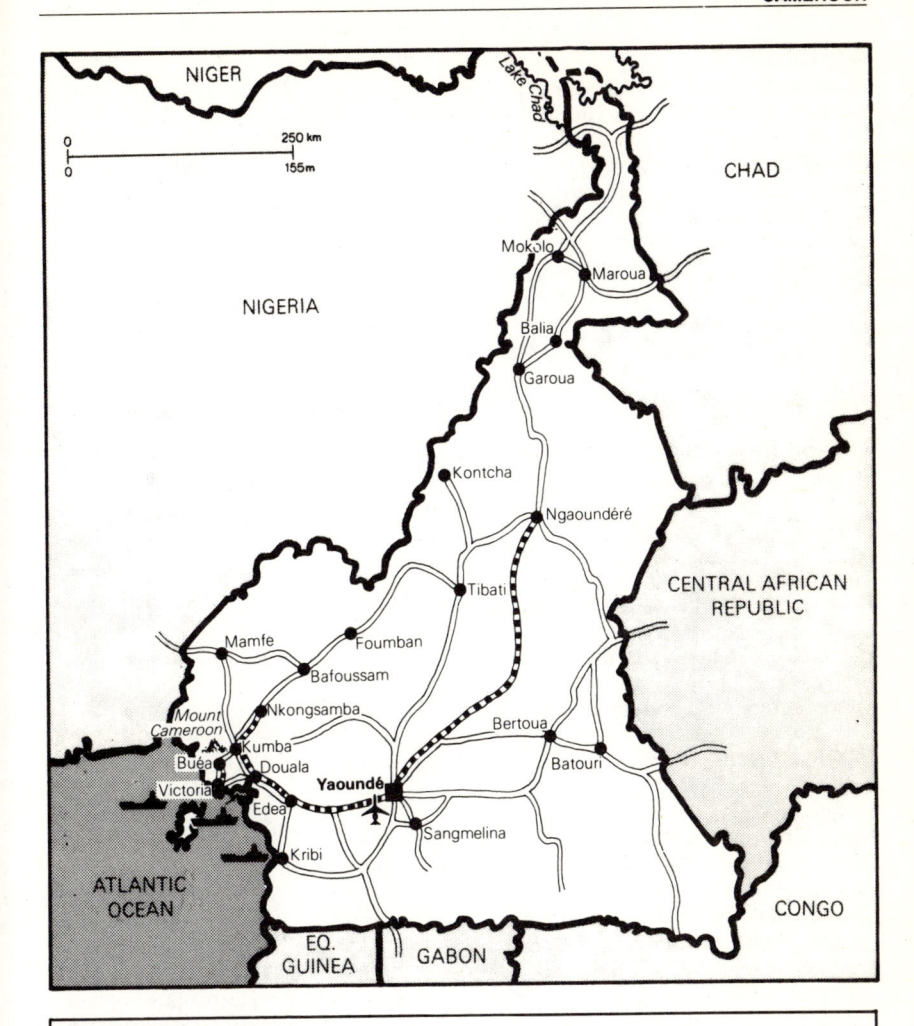

GEOGRAPHY

Cameroon can be divided into 4 distinct geographical regions: the northern region of low-lying savannah; the central plateau region; the range of volcanic hills in the west, where Mount Cameroon (4,070m/13,358ft) is situated; and the southern coastal area of mangrove swamps and dense equatorial forest. The population is concentrated in the west, where the highly fertile volcanic soils are suited to intense cultivation.

Climate
In the west and south the climate is tropical; temperatures in Douala range from 19°C/67°F to 32°C/90°F and the humidity is high. The main rainy season lasts from June to September/October. The north is drier with greater extremes of temperature: as low as 6°C/42°F in January, and as high as 43°C/110°F in July. Temperatures in the mountainous, western region are lower and vary according to altitude.

Agriculture

Agriculture is the principal economic activity, providing employment for 80% of the population and accounting for 70% of all export earnings. Cameroon is the world's fifth largest producer of cocoa and an important producer of coffee. Cocoa contributes around 25% of export revenue and coffee some 30%; other export commodities are cotton, rubber, bananas and considerable quantities of wood. The country's dependence on a small number of commodities for export earnings makes the economy vulnerable to fluctuations in the world markets for these products, and recent world economic trends have hit the economy badly.

Current efforts to strengthen the agricultural sector include increased cultivation of other crops such as bananas, oil palm, rice, sugar and rubber, and the establishment of a nationwide marketing organisation for all agricultural products.

Main Crops: cocoa, coffee, cotton, bananas, groundnuts. rice, palm kernels.

Mineral Resources: oil, bauxite, iron ore, limestone.

THE ECONOMY

Gross National Product (1978 est.): US$3.7 billion.

Per Capita Income (1978 est.): US$460.

Gross Domestic Product (1978 est.): US$4.2 billion.

Foreign Trade (1978): Total Imports – US$1.95 billion. Total Exports – US$1.1 billion.

Main Trading Partners: Imports – France, USA, West Germany, Japan, Italy. Exports – France, Netherlands, West Germany, Italy, USA, USSR.

The economy is still heavily reliant on primary exports and foreign investment to sustain growth. Except for the aluminium plant at Edéa, industry consists mainly of light manufacturing, assembly and processing for the domestic market.

Cameroon has considerable resources including cheap hydro-electric power potential and offshore oil deposits; agricultural expansion is also possible. However, the expansion of markets and industrial capacity, greater domestic input in the manufacturing sector and greater support for the small-scale food grower must all occur if the structurally weak economy is to improve in the long term.

The current Development Plan aims for a greater degree of self-reliance and provides for a free-enterprise economy with a high degree of state participation. Recent industrial projects include an oil refinery, a fertiliser factory, palm oil mills, a pharmaceutical plant, and a pulp and paper factory. Further growth is anticipated in import substitution, industrial fishing, mining, livestock development and tourism.

Major Industries: food processing, textiles, timber processing, aluminium.

Main Commodities Traded: Imports – transport equipment, petroleum products, iron and steel, electrical machinery, foods and beverages, synthetic textiles. Exports – cocoa, coffee, timber, cotton, aluminium, rubber, bananas.

International Affiliations: UN, IBRD, OAU, ACP, ADB, Franc Zone, UDEAC.

HOW TO GET THERE

Air
Cameroon Airlines and UTA operate a daily flight from Paris to Douala with connections to Yaoundé. Cameroon Airlines also fly to Douala from Rome. Sabena fly from Brussels to Douala. There are no direct flights from London to Douala, but British Caledonian fly to Accra and Lagos, from where there are direct flights to Douala.

From the United States, Pan Am fly from New York to Accra, Dakar, Abidjan and Lagos, with connecting flights to Douala.

The following African airlines also fly to Cameroon: Air Afrique, Air Gabon, Air Mali, Air Zaïre, Ethiopian Airlines, Ghana Airways and Nigeria Airways.

The main international airport is at Douala, 4½ km/3 miles from the city centre.

An airport tax of 560 CFA francs is payable for inter-African flights and 3,500 CFA francs for inter-continental flights.

Taxis are plentiful at the airport, and courtesy coaches operate to the Akwa Palace, Falaise, Des Cocotiers, Résidence de Joss, Novotel, De l'Air and Beauséjour Hotels.

ENTRY REGULATIONS

Visas
Visas are required by nationals of all countries and should be obtained, prior to departure, from embassies and consulates of the United Republic of Cameroon abroad.

Visitors should ensure that the validity of their passport extends for at least 3 months beyond the date upon which the visa application is made.

Visa applications should be supported by valid International Certificates of Vaccination against smallpox, cholera and yellow fever, together with a letter (from a travel agent or airline) giving full details of the booking.

Business travellers should accompany visa applications with a letter from their company giving full details of the business to be undertaken and confirming financial responsibility for the applicant.

Visas are valid for 1 month for a stay which can vary according to requirements. Transit visas, valid for up to 48 hours, can be obtained at Douala Airport on arrival.

Nationals of South Africa, and anyone whose passport bears evidence of a previous or planned visit to that country, will be refused entry into Cameroon.

Health Regulations
Valid International Certificates of Vaccination against smallpox, cholera and yellow fever are required for entry.

Customs
Currency: There is no limit to the amount of foreign currency which may be brought in, but the total amount imported should be declared on arrival. Up to 25,000 CFA francs may be exported by visitors going on to a non-Franc Zone country, together with any unspent foreign currency.

Duty-free articles: Personal effects including 1 radio, camera, typewriter, etc., per person. 50 cigarettes or 25 cigars or 100g of tobacco. 1 litre of spirits.

CAMEROON

PRACTICAL INFORMATION FOR THE VISITOR

1. Currency
Monetary Unit – CFA franc.
Notes – 100, 500, 1,000, 5,000, 10,000 CFA francs.
Coins – 1, 2, 5, 10, 25, 50, 100, 500 CFA francs.

Currency is issued by the *Banque des Etats de l'Afrique Centrale*, Rue du Docteur Jamot, B.P. 1917, Yaoundé, and B.P. 5445, Douala.

Cameroon belongs to the Franc Zone and visitors may experience difficulty in exchanging CFA francs outside of this zone. It is advisable to exchange back CFA francs into French francs or another foreign currency before leaving Cameroon.

Banking Hours
East Cameroon –
0800 – 1130
1430 – 1530 Monday to Friday
West Cameroon –
0800 – 1330 Monday to Friday

Domestic Commercial Banks
Banque Internationale pour le Commerce et l'Industrie du Cameroun, Avenue du Président Ahidjo, B.P. 5, Yaoundé, ☎ 222011; Rue Kitchener, B.P. 4070, Douala, ☎ 423231.
Cameroon Bank Ltd, B.P. 48, Victoria.
Société Générale de Banques au Cameroun, Avenue Monseigneur Vogt, B.P. 244, Yaoundé, ☎ 222122/222744; B.P. 4042, Douala, ☎ 421010.

The *Chase Manhattan Bank* has a representative office in Douala, ☎ 425805/425291.

2. Electricity Supply
East Cameroon – 110v and 320v AC 50Hz.
West Cameroon – 220v AC 50Hz.
Plugs – 2 round pins.

3. Weights and Measures
The metric system is in use.

4. Media
There is no television service. Radiodiffusion du Cameroun is the Government-owned radio service, which operates 4 radio stations (Yaoundé, Douala, Garoua and Buéa). Programmes are broadcast in French, English and several African languages.

Newspapers and Journals
There is only 1 daily newspaper, the *Cameroon Tribune*, which is published in French in Yaoundé. A weekly version is published in English.

The *Cameroon Times* (English) is published in Victoria 3 times a week. Other newspapers and periodicals include *Cameroon Panorama* (monthly), *La Gazette* (weekly), *Nleb Bekristen* (fortnightly) and *L'Unité* (weekly), the organ of the Union Nationale Camerounaise.

The Chambre de Commerce, d'Industrie et des Mines publishes a monthly bulletin.

5. Medical Care
Malaria is endemic, and visitors are advised to take anti-malarial prophylactics. TAB (typhoid and paratyphoid) inoculations are also recommended.

Tap water is not safe to drink; all water should be boiled and filtered. Bottled mineral water is readily available in the main centres.

Medical facilities are good, particularly in Yaoundé and Douala, where there are many private doctors. Treatment and medicines are expensive, however.

6. Telephone, Telex and Postal Services
Cameroon has direct telephone links, via satellite, with London, Paris and New York. Internal telephone services are adequate, and most major towns are connected to the automatic dialling system.

CAMEROON

Yaoundé and Douala have a direct telex link with Paris, and Buéa and Victoria are connected via Douala. Telex facilities are available at the Mont Fébé Novotel in Yaoundé.

All mail to and from Cameroon should be despatched by air.

7. Public Holidays

1 January	Independence Day
11 February	Youth Day
1 May	Labour Day
20 May	National Day
1 October	Reunification Day
10 December	Human Rights Day
25–6 December	Christmas

The following Muslim and holidays are also officially observed: *Eid el Kabir, Eid el Fitr, Good Friday, Easter Monday, Whit Monday* and *Assumption*.

8. Time
GMT +1.

9. Internal Transport

Air
Cameroon Airlines operate daily return flights from Douala to Yaoundé (30 minutes). Regular flights link Douala and Yaoundé with Foumban, Ngaoundéré, Garoua, Maroua, Batouri, Koutaba, Dschang, Balia, Mamfé and Tiko.

Charter flights can be arranged through Ardic Aviation or Air Service in Douala.

Douala International Airport is 4½km/3 miles from the city centre. Yaoundé Airport is 4km/2½ miles from the city centre.

Airline Offices in Douala

Air France	☎ 424999.
Cameroon Airlines	☎ 422525.
Iberia	☎ 421450, 426090.
Nigeria Airways	☎ 426234, 421521.
Pan Am	☎ 421924.
Swissair	☎ 422929.
UTA	☎ 422020.

Rail
There is a rail service from Douala to Yaoundé and Ngaoundéré, and from Douala to Kumba and Nkongsamba. The journey from Douala to Yaoundé can take up to 12 hours.

Road
There are a limited number of tarred roads; the main ones connect Douala and Bafoussam, Douala and Buéa, Douala and Edéa and Yaoundé and Sangmelina. Other roads linking main centres are only partially tarred, and many become virtually impassable during the rainy season – this applies to the road between Douala and Yaoundé.

Taxis are plentiful in Douala, Yaoundé, Buéa and Victoria, and prices are fixed by the Government.

Car-hire facilities are available in Douala, Yaoundé and Victoria. An International Driving Licence is required. Traffic travels on the right-hand side of the road.

Car-Hire Firms
Douala – Autolocation; Avis, ☎ 424298; Locamat; Lovoto.
Yaoundé – Autolocation.
Victoria – King; John Holt.

10. Tipping
Taxis – no tip necessary.

Porters – 100 CFA francs.

Hotels/restaurants – a service charge is usually included in the bill.

11. Social Customs
Visitors to East Cameroon should have a good working knowledge of French. Most business people in West Cameroon speak English.

12. Photography
Visitors should exercise discretion when taking photographs and should not attempt to photograph the police, military or any military establishment. It is advisable to seek permission before taking photographs of displays of traditional dancing, tribal ceremonies, etc.

77

USEFUL ADDRESSES (GENERAL)

Yaoundé

Canadian Embassy: Immeuble Soppo Priso, Rue Conrad-Adenauer, B.P. 572, ☎ 220203, 222922.

Dutch Embassy: Le Concorde, 5ème étage (ouest), B.P. 310, ☎ 220544.

French Embassy: Plateau Atemengue, B.P. 1631, ☎ 221822.

Swiss Embassy: Villa Zoga Massy, Quartier Bastos, B.P. 1169, ☎ 222896.

UK Embassy: Le Concorde, Avenue John F. Kennedy, B.P. 547, ☎ 220545, 220796.

US Embassy: Rue Nachtigal, B.P. 817, ☎ 221663.

West German Embassy, Rue Horace Mallet, B.P. 1160, ☎ 220056.

Commissariat General au Tourisme: Avenue du 27 août 1940, B.P. 266, ☎ 224111.

British Council: Les Galeries, Rue de l'Intendance, B.P. 818, ☎ 221696, 223172.

Wagons-Lits Tourisme Authorised Representative: Transcap Voyages, Rue de l'Intendance, B.P. 919.

Douala

British Consulate: Rue Alfred Saker, B.P. 1016, ☎ 422177, 422245.

Dutch Consulate: c/o SOCARTO, 15 Rue Pau, B.P. 5028.

French Consulate, Avenue des Cocotiers, B.P. 869.

US Consulate: 21 Avenue du Général de Gaulle, B.P. 4006, ☎ 423434.

West German Consulate: Boulevard de la Liberté 47, ☎ 423500.

American Express Authorised Representative: Camvoyages, 15 Avenue de la Liberte, B.P. 4070, ☎ 423188.

Wagons-Lits Tourisme Authorised Representative: Transcap Voyages, Immeuble Joss, Rue Ivry, B.P. 4059, ☎ 421128, 421295.

BUSINESS INFORMATION

Generally speaking, foreign commercial or industrial companies wishing to operate must set up branch headquarters and accounts within the country.

There are a few reliable agencies operating only in West Cameroon, but the country is mainly covered by French companies based in East Cameroon. Foreign companies wishing to appoint a local agent will find it advantageous to visit the Paris headquarters of these French firms as well as their branches in Douala.

Commercial law is based on the French system in East Cameroon and the British (Nigerian Code) in West Cameroon; trade literature is published in the corresponding language in each area.

Import and Exchange Control Regulations

An import licence is required for imports from all countries outside the Central African Customs and Economic Union (UDEAC). A few items are totally prohibited or require authorisation to import; most are controlled by an annual import programme.

Foreign exchange may be obtained from an approved bank once an import licence is granted. To obtain such a licence, firms must be registered with the Ministry of Economy and Planning, meet certain financial conditions and occupy premises in the country.

Business Hours

East Cameroon
Government Offices and Business Houses
0800 – 1200 Monday to Friday
1430 – 1730
0800 – 1200 Saturday

West Cameroon
Government Offices
0730 – 1430 Monday to Friday
0730 – 1200 Saturday

Business Houses
0800 – 1200 Monday to Friday
1430 – 1630
0800 – 1200 Saturday

BUSINESS SERVICES

Advertising
Cameroon Public Expansion (CPE), B.P. 1137, Douala, ☎ 424444.

Insurance
Agence Camerounaise d'Assurances, Rue de l'Hippodrome, B.P. 209, Yaoundé.
Caisse Centrale de Coopération Economique, B.P. 46, Yaoundé.
Compagnie Camerounaise d'Assurances et de Réassurances, B.P. 4068, Douala.
Guardian Royal Exchange Assurance (Cameroon) Ltd, 56 Boulevard de la Liberté, B.P. 426, Douala.
Société Camerounaise d'Assurances et de Réassurances, 86 Boulevard de la Liberté, B.P. 280, Douala.

Shipping
Cameroon Shipping Lines, 32 Rue des Ecoles, B.P. 4054, Douala.
SAMOA, Boulevard Leclerc, B.P. 1127, Douala – agents for Lloyd Triestino, Black Star Line, Gold Star Line and Europe Africa Line.
Société Ouest-Africaine d'Entreprises Maritimes (Cameroun), Rue Alfred Saker, Douala.
SOCOPAO (Cameroun), B.P. 215, Douala – agents for Palm Line, Bank Line, CNAN, Nigerian Shipping Line, Polish Ocean Lines, Westwind Africa Line.

USEFUL ADDRESSES (BUSINESS)

Chambre de Commerce, d'Industrie et des Mines du Cameroun, B.P. 4011, Douala, ☎ 422888; B.P. 36, Yaoundé, ☎ 224776; B.P. 50, Victoria, ☎ 334230.

Chambre d'Agriculture, de l'Elevage et des Forêts du Cameroun, Parc Repiquet, B.P. 287, Yaoundé, ☎ 223885, 222844; B.P. 400, Douala, ☎ 425280.

CAMEROON

Cameroon Development Corporation, B.P. 28, Bota, Victoria.

National Produce Marketing Board (ONCPB), B.P. 378, Douala.

Cameroon Co-operative Exporters Ltd, B.P. 19, Kumba.

MAJOR CITIES

Douala

Douala is by far the largest and most energetic city in Cameroon, with a modern port, industrial zones, residential areas and a renovated commercial quarter originally established by the Germans towards the end of the last century.

The residential sections of Bali and New Bell are the centres of recent urban migration, and a walk through these areas with their merchants and craftsmen overflowing into the street is a good introduction to the character of the city. Douala has many interesting museums and monuments, including the pagoda-style palace of the World War I king, Manga Bell, the stone tomb of King Akwa, and several sacred trees.

The city is very hot and humid, but it is easy to visit the cooler slopes of nearby Mount Cameroon or the beaches at Victoria along the coast.

Hotels

There is no official hotel rating system.

AKWA PALACE, 52 Avenue de la Liberté, B.P. 4007, ☎ 422601. Traditional-style hotel in city centre.
Rooms: 89 ♫, ☻ on request, ♍, △, ♆. Suites available.
Facilities: Restaurant, grill, bars. Swimming. Car-hire.
Services: TC, FC. ▤ Amex, Diners Club. Dr. on call. S. Audio-visual equipment. Conference room – max. capacity 200. Banquet room – max. capacity 150.

DES COCOTIERS, Avenue des Cocotiers, B.P. 310, ☎ 425800. Traditional-style 1st-class hotel in residential area, 3km/2 miles from city centre.
Rooms: 56 ♫, △, ♆.
Facilities: Restaurant, bar. Nightclub, casino. Swimming, tennis near by. Car hire.
Services: TC, FC. ▤ Amex, Diners Club. Dr. on call. S, ♂.

Restaurants

In addition to the hotel restaurants, there are several French restaurants including *Le Méditerranée*, Rue Joss, ☎ 428887; *Le Paris*, Avenue de la Liberte, ☎ 421289; *Le Lido*, Rue Joffre, ☎ 421214; *Le Central*, Boulevard Ahmadou-Ahidjo, ☎ 425206. There is also Vietnamese cuisine at *Le Lotus*, Rue Kitchener; Italian cuisine at *Al Vesuvio*, ☎ 424292; and Cameroonian food at the restaurant in the Hotel Beauséjour, ☎ 426322.

Nightclubs

Among the recommended nightclubs are *Le Castel*, opposite the Hotel Beauséjour; *La Jungle*, Rue Sylvani; and *Le Scotch Club* at the Hotel des Cocotiers. There are dozens of other nightclubs which double as restaurants, and a travel agent or taxi driver can usually direct visitors to one serving the preferred style of cuisine.

Entertainment

Douala has several cinemas, libraries, private sports clubs offering temporary membership (tennis, fishing, swimming, water-skiing, sailing), a flying club and a municipal swimming pool.

Shopping

There are several outdoor markets in Douala, including the Lagos market, in the square of the Grand Mosque, selling everything imaginable. There is a wide variety of Nigerian goods on sale at the Deido market, and several fish and fruit markets. Visitors are constantly pursued by street vendors and the haggling is generally good-natured.

Yaoundé

The capital Yaoundé is attractively set 'on seven hills' beneath the spectacular Mount Fébé, with dense jungle only a few miles from the city limits. The green, shady city enjoys a cooler, less humid climate than the coastal area and a more relaxed pace than Douala.

Mount Fébé has a large tourist complex – hotel, nightclub, casino, restaurant and golf course – with spectacular views over the city, and there is a small museum nearby with exhibits from former Cameroon civilisations. The colourful Sunday morning mass in the Ndong Melen district west of the town centre is a striking example of the mixture of European and African culture and religion in this area.

Hotels

NOVOTEL-MOUNT FÉBÉ PALACE, B.P. 4178, ☎ 224224.
Luxury modern hotel on Mount Fébé overlooking city, 10 minutes' drive from city centre; 9km/6 miles from Yaoundé airport.
Rooms: 232 ♪, ♦. Suites availabe.
Facilities: Restaurant, cocktail lounge, bars. Nightclub, discotheque. Swimming, sauna, tennis, golf. Car-hire, free taxi service to town.
Services: TC, FC. ▤ Amex, Bankamericard, Barclay Visa, Diners Club, Eurocard, Master Charge.
Conference facilities – max. capacity 400 persons.

CENTRAL HOTEL, B.P. 6, ☎ 223611.
Small 1st-class hotel, centrally located.
Rooms: 22 ♪. Suites available.
Facilities: Restaurant, bar. Terrace, garden.

Restaurants

All the major hotels have French restaurants, in addition to which there is *Le Cintra*, ☎ 223388; *Les Boukarous*, ☎ 221513; and the *Safari Club* above the Mount Fébe Hotel. Others include: *Les Galeries*, ☎ 224205 – Algerian and French, and *Aux Baguettes d'Or*, ☎ 223929 – Chinese.

Nightclubs

The *Mount Fébé Palace* and the *Safari Club* both have nightclubs orientated towards French business visitors. There are several more modest nightclubs in the city.

Entertainment

Yaoundé is a convenient centre for excursions to such areas as Mbalmayo, 48km/30 miles to the south, where there is an attractive village market, or taking a canoe trip down the Nyong River. There are several cinemas in the city, and sports clubs offering tennis, riding, sailing, golf and flying.

Shopping

The *Marché des Artisans*, selling Cameroonian and other African handiworks, is downtown near the post office. As in Douala, the street vendors are good natured but unrelenting, and tend to offer goods of inferior quality and higher price than in the provinces.

CENTRAL AFRICAN REPUBLIC

Central African Republic

Geography	83
The Economy	84
How to Get There	84
Entry Regulations	85
Practical Information for the Visitor	85
Useful Addresses (General)	86
Business Information	87
Business Services	87
Useful Addresses (Business)	87
Bangui	88

Size: 622,984 sq.km/240,534 sq.miles.

Population: 3.1 million (1977 est.).

Distribution: 20% in urban areas.

Density: 5 persons per sq.km/12 per sq.mile. Population density is much higher in the west as large areas of the east are virtually uninhabited.

Population Growth Rate: 2.2% p.a.

Ethnic Composition: The Banda and the Baya make up about half the population; the Baka and the Zande are the most prominent of the many other ethnic groups.

Capital: Bangui Pop. 350,000.

Major Towns: Berbérati Pop. 38,000; Basangoa Pop. 35,000.

Language: French is the official language, but Sangho, a lingua franca, has been adopted as the national language.

Religion: There are large numbers of Animists and Christians and a small percentage of Muslims.

Government: The country returned to the status of Republic in September 1979 after 3 years as the Central African Empire under Emperor Bokassa.

CENTRAL AFRICAN REPUBLIC

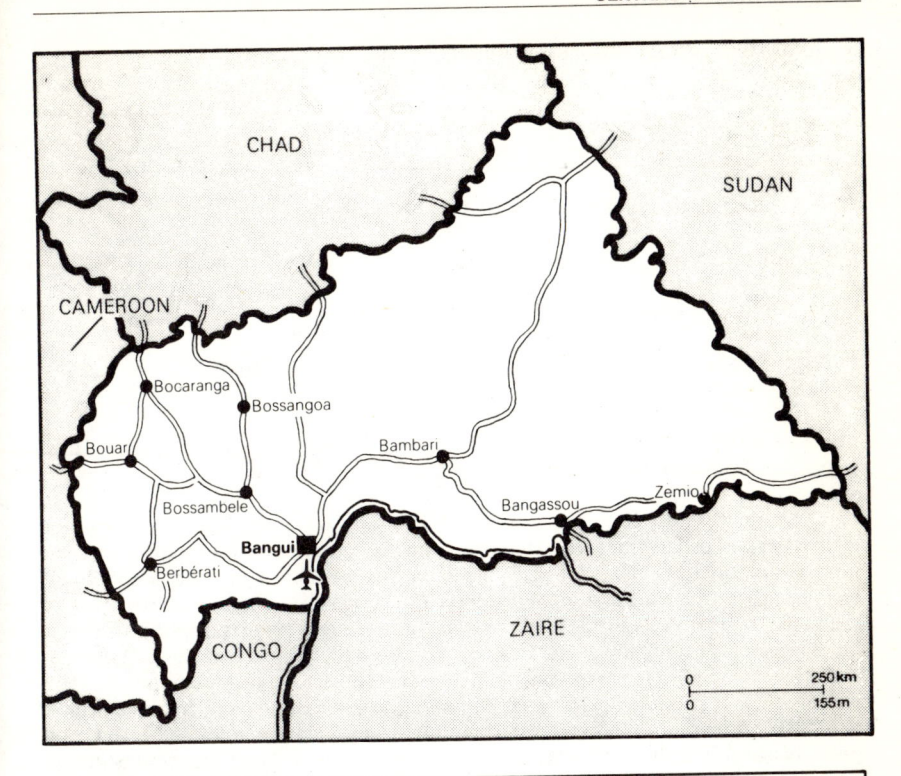

GEOGRAPHY

A land-locked state, the Central African Republic is essentially an enormous, undulating, rocky plateau drained by 2 major river systems, with mountains in the north-east and south-east. The north-east is sub-desert terrain, and in the south-west there is dense tropical rain-forest.

Climate
The climate is generally hot, with the dry season running from December to April and the rainy from May to November (the wet season is shorter in the north). The average temperature in Bangui is 25°C/77°F. The north is somewhat hotter.

Agriculture
Agriculture employs about 85% of the working population and the country is almost self-sufficient in food production. Principal food crops for domestic consumption are cassava, maize, millet and sorghum. Coffee and cotton are the most important cash crops; both are produced mainly on small-scale indigenous farms. Efforts are being made to improve the livestock and fishing industries. There are also large timber resources, but these cannot be properly exploited until an efficient transport infrastructure is established.

Main Crops: cassava, groundnuts, cotton, maize, coffee, millet, sorghum, tobacco, rice, sesame seed, plantain, bananas, sweet potatoes.

Mineral Resources: diamonds, uranium, limestone.

THE ECONOMY

Gross National Product (1978 est.): US$370 million.

Per Capita Income (1978 est.): US$119.

Gross Domestic Product (1978 est.): US$503 million.

Foreign Trade (1978 est.): Total Imports – US$79 million. Total Exports – US$84 million.

Main Trading Partners: Imports – France, West Germany, USA, UK, Netherlands. Exports – France, Belgium, Luxembourg, USA, Israel, Spain.

The Central African Republic is rich in economic reserves. There is scope for increased food production, large untapped mineral reserves, and substantial fish and forestry potential. At present, foreign aid and investment are being sought to rebuild the run-down transport system and exploit the country's estimated 10,000 tons of uranium reserves. There are as yet no railways, most freight being transported by river, but it is planned eventually to link Bangui by rail with the port of Douala (Cameroon). An all-weather road is being constructed to Bakouma to transport uranium when mining begins. The principal exports continue to be diamonds, coffee and cotton.

Industry is limited to the processing of primary products (textiles and leather, oil mills, an abattoir, a flour mill, a brewery and a tobacco factory) and import substitution (car assembly, soap, bicycles, paint, bricks, domestic utensils).

Major Industries: cotton ginning, diamond cutting, processing of leather, tobacco, timber.

Main Commodities Traded: Imports – machinery, transport supplies, iron and steel, chemicals, beverages, textiles. Exports – diamonds, cotton, coffee, timber.

International Affiliations: UN, IBRD, OAU, ACP, ADB, Franc Zone, OCAM, UDEAC.

HOW TO GET THERE

Air

UTA operate thrice-weekly services from Paris to Bangui via N'djaména (Chad) or Tripoli (Libya). Aeroflot operate a weekly service from Moscow to Bangui via Cairo (Egypt). Within Africa, Bangui is connected by Air Afrique, Air Centrafrique, Air Zaïre and Cameroon Airlines with Brazzaville, Kinshasa and Douala.

Flying time from Paris to Bangui 9 hours.

On departure, an airport tax of 1,200 CFA francs is payable (3,500 CFA francs for North American destinations).

Bangui Airport is 4km/2½ miles from the centre of town.

ENTRY REGULATIONS

Visas
Visas are required by all visitors, except nationals of France, West Germany, Israel, Liechtenstein, Romania, Switzerland and Francophone African countries. Visas may be obtained from embassies of the Central African Republic or from French consular representatives.
It is advisable for business travellers to ensure that their passport is valid for at least 3 months from the date of application for a visa.

Health Regulations
Valid International Certificates of Vaccination against smallpox, cholera and yellow fever are required.

Customs
Currency: There is no limit to the amount of foreign currency imported, but it must be declared. Foreign currency up to the amount imported and declared may be exported. Local currency may be freely imported and exported within the Franc Zone, but there is a limit of 75,000 CFA francs on import from and export to countries outside the zone.

Duty-free articles: 1,000 cigarettes or 250 cigars or 2kg of tobacco (N.B.: women may only import cigarettes). A reasonable quantity of alcoholic beverages and perfume. Samples of no commercial value.

PRACTICAL INFORMATION FOR THE VISITOR

1. Currency
Monetary Unit – CFA (Communauté Financière Africaine) franc, divided into 100 centimes.
Notes – 100, 500, 1,000, 5,000, 10,000 CFA francs.
Coins – 1, 2, 5, 10, 25, 50, 100 CFA francs.

Travellers' cheques can be cashed in Bangui, but it is recommended that travellers use French franc cheques which are more easily convertible.
The *Banque des Etats de l'Afrique Centrale*, B.P. 851, Bangui, is the central bank of issue for 5 African states, including the Central African Republic.

Banking Hours
0700–1200 Monday to Saturday

Domestic Banks in Bangui *Union Bancaire en Afrique Centrale*, B.P. 839, Rue de Brazza.
Banque National Centrafricaine de Dépôts, B.P. 801, Place de la République.

Foreign Banks in Bangui *Banque International pour l'Afrique Occidentale*, B.P. 910.
Caisse Centrale de Coopération Economique, B.P. 817.

2. Electricity Supply
220/380v 50Hz.
Plugs: 2 round pins.

3. Weights and Measures
The metric system is in use.

4. Media
The Government-owned radio station in Bangui broadcasts in French, English

CENTRAL AFRICAN REPUBLIC

and Sangho. A limited television service was established in 1974.

Newspapers and Journals
Centrafric Press is the only daily newspaper. *Terre Africaine* is published weekly; the economic *Journal Officiel* fortnightly and *Bangui-Match* monthly.

5. Medical Care
Anti-malarial precautions must be taken. Bilharzia and intestinal upsets are prevalent, so water must be filtered or boiled, and uncooked fruit and vegetables avoided. Bangui has a general hospital, but there are few health facilities outside the capital.

6. Telephones, Telex and Postal Services
Bangui has a post office from which telegrams and mail can be sent, but visitors are advised to post their mail in other countries if possible, as the mail service from Bangui is very slow. Telex and telephone facilities are available at the post office and at major hotels.

7. Public Holidays
1 January	New Year's Day
29 March	Anniversary of the Death of Boganda
1 May	Labour Day
14 May	Anniversary of the First Government
13 August	Independence Day
1 December	National Day
25 December	Christmas Day

The following movable Christian feasts are also observed: *Ascension, Whitsun* and *Assumption*.

8. Time
GMT + 1.

9. Internal Transport

Air
Air Centrafrique operates irregular connections between Bangui, Berbérati, Bouar, Bambari and several smaller towns.

Airline Offices in Bangui
Air Afrique, B.P. 875.
Air Centrafrique, B.P. 1432, Rue du President Boganda.
Aeroflot, ☎ 3249.
UTA/Air France, ☎ 614900.

Road
Few roads have a tarmac surface, but the main routes are currently being upgraded.

Traffic travels on the right.

Unmetered taxis are available in Bangui and it is advisable to settle the fare before starting the journey.

Car-Hire Firms in Bangui
Tsiros Location ☎ 2986
Auto Service ☎ 2257

10. Tipping
Taxi drivers, hotel and restaurant staff: 10% of the bill.

Airport porters: 100 CFA francs.

USEFUL ADDRESSES (GENERAL)

Bangui
Dutch Consulate, c/o Pontéco, Rue du 1er Janvier 1966, B.P. 32, ☎ 614822.

French Embassy, Blvd du Général de Gaulle, B.P. 884, ☎ 613000.

Japanese Embassy, Avenue du Président Nasser, B.P. 1367, ☎ 610668.

US Embassy, Avenue du 1er Janvier 1966, B.P. 924, ☎ 610200.

West German Embassy, Avenue du Président Nasser, B.P. 901, ☎ 2290.

Direction Générale du Tourisme, B.P. 655, ☎ 2375.

Wagons-Lits Authorised Representative, Bangui-Tourisme, B.P. 875, ☎ 3424.

BUSINESS INFORMATION

Foreign investment is encouraged. As much of the trading business is French-owned or operated, contact with parent companies in France is advisable. All correspondence, literature and business negotiations must be in French. The local Chambers of Commerce may be able to assist with the appointment of a local agent, and the Government now insists that for every foreigner employed in the Central African Republic, work must be provided for a Central African citizen.

Import and Exchange Control Regulations

Imports from outside the Franc Zone usually require an import licence and are subject to the common system of customs duties operated by the UDEAC states (Customs and Economic Union of Central Africa).

All payments for imports outside the Franc Zone require the prior authorisation of the Ministry of Finance.

Business Hours
Government Offices and Business Houses
0800–1200 Monday to Saturday
1430–1800 Monday to Friday

BUSINESS SERVICES

Insurance
Agence Centrafricaine d'Assurances, B.P. 512, Bangui.
Entreprise d'Etat d'Assurances et de Réassurances, Bangui.
Société Jeandreau et Cie SARL, B.P. 140, Bangui.

Transport
Agence Centrafricaine des Communications Fluviales, B.P. 822, Bangui – river transport.
Compagnie Nationale des Transports Routiers, B.P. 330, Bangui – road transport.

USEFUL ADDRESSES (BUSINESS)

Chambre d'Agriculture, d'Elevage, des Eaux et Forêts, Chasses et Tourisme, B.P. 850, Bangui.

Chambre de Commerce, B.P. 813, Bangui, ☎ 2094.

Chambre des Industries et de l'Artisanat, B.P. 252, Bangui, ☎ 2176.

CENTRAL AFRICAN REPUBLIC

MAJOR CITY

Bangui

Bangui was established by the French in 1889 on the Oubangui river. The small Boganda Museum has an interesting collection of African artifacts, and there is a workshop of diamond cutters which is open to visitors.

Hotels

There is no official hotel rating system.

Rock Hotel, Blvd Général de Gaulle, B.P. 569, ☎ 2088. Near city centre, overlooking river.
Rooms: 38 ♪, ◉, ✿ Suites available.
Facilities: Garden restaurant, grill room. American bar and nightclub. Parking, car-hire. Golf, tennis, fishing available nearby.
Services: TC, FC. ⊟ Amex, Diners Club. ♂.
Conference room – max. capacity 60.

Safari Hotel, Blvd General de Gaulle, B.P. 1317, ☎ 3020. Modern hotel near city centre, overlooking river.
Rooms: 45 ♪, ◉, ✿. Suites available.
Facilities: Restaurant, snack bar, several bars. Nightclub. Service shops. Parking.
Services: TC, FC. ⊟ not accepted. ♂, 🆂.
Water sports and safaris arranged.

Restaurants

The hotel restaurants are the best, particularly that at the *Rock Hotel*. *The New Palace Hotel* has a pleasant terrace restaurant. Other restaurants are *La Banquise* and *La Portugaise*.

CHAD
Republic of Chad

Geography	*90*
The Economy	*91*
How to Get There	*92*
Entry Regulations	*92*
Practical Information for the Visitor	*93*
Useful Addresses (General)	*95*
Business Information	*95*
Business Services	*96*
Useful Addresses (Business)	*96*
N'djaména	*96*

Size: 1,284,000 sq.km/495,752 sq. miles.

Population: 4.31 million (1978 est.).

Distribution: 14% in urban areas.

Density: 3.5 persons per sq.km/9 per sq.mile.

Population Growth Rate: 2.1% p.a. (1970–6 av.).

Ethnic Composition: The largest ethnic group are the Sara People in the south. The population of the north is largely of Sudanic origin, while in the far north are the nomadic Tuareg and Toubou peoples. There are about 3,000 resident Europeans, mainly French.

Capital: N'djaména Pop. 241,639 (1976).

Major Towns: Moundou Pop. 54,925; Sarh Pop. 54,047; Abéché Pop. 43,125.

Language: French is the official language. Several African languages are spoken in the centre and south, the principal ones being Sara, Massa and Moundang. Arabic is spoken in the north.

Religion: More than half are Muslims; approximately 40%, Animists; and 5%, Christians, mainly Roman Catholic.

Government: Following a coup in 1975, the National Assembly was dissolved and the Government taken over by a 9-member military council. In 1977 the Supreme Military Council was abolished under the terms of the *Charte Fondamentale* and replaced by the Council of Defence and Security. In November 1979 a transitional government of national unity (GUNT) was formed, and efforts continue to establish a unified Government, which will probably entail the distribution of power among the various prefectures of Chad. Although there are no official political parties, a number of influential groups have taken part in the conferences which have been held to discuss the mechanics of unified Government; among these are the Front de Liberation Nationale de Tchad (FROLINAT), the Mouvement Populaire pour la Liberation du Tchad (known as the Third Army) and the

CHAD

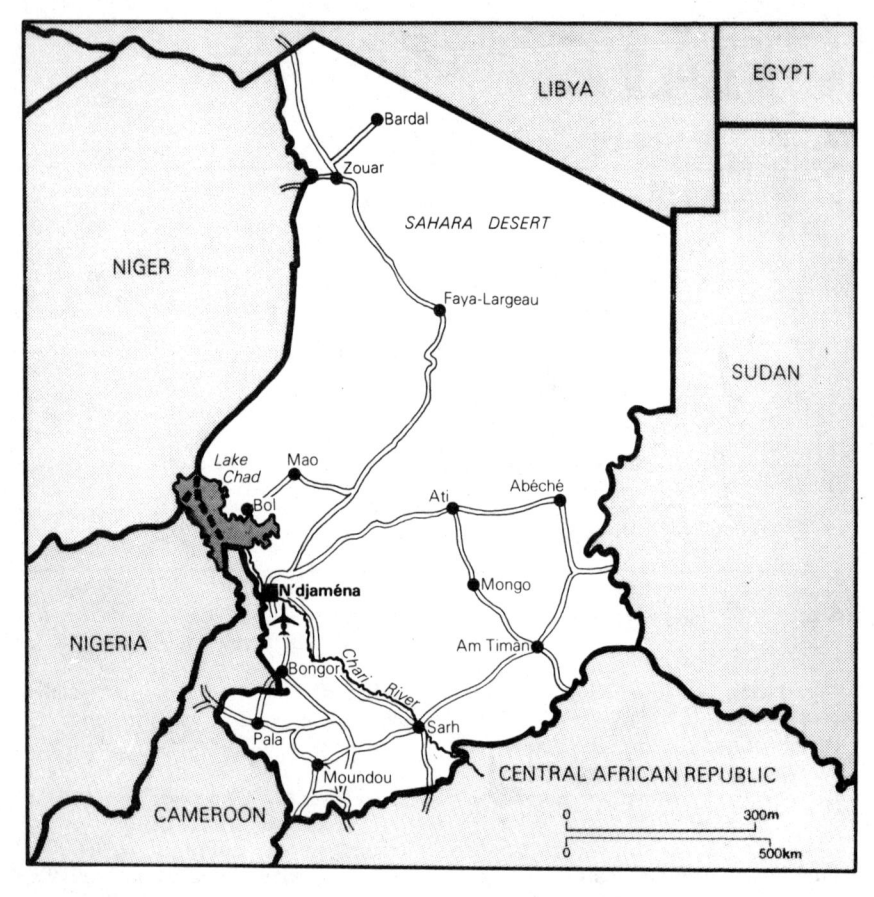

Conseil de Commandement des Forces Armées du Nord (CCFAN). The political situation remains unpredictable as internal conflict escalated to civil war during the early part of 1980.

GEOGRAPHY

Chad is a landlocked country situated in north central Africa. The north consists of desert and semi-desert with frequent outcrops of rock, while the land to the south is more fertile. On the western border lies the vast Lake Chad. The centre and south consist largely of savannah.

Climate
The north is hot and dry with temperatures reaching 38°C/100°F or more in summer and dropping to around freezing point at night in winter. Temperatures in the south are lower, averaging 29°C/85°F around N'djaména.

The main rainy season lasts from June to October. The best months to visit Chad are December and January.

Agriculture

Agriculture is the principal economic activity, employing almost 90% of the working population. The economy centres around the cash crop of cotton, which provides approximately 65% of Chad's total exports. The main subsistence crops are sorghum, millet, groundnuts and rice.

The production of more cotton has been actively encouraged, and greater areas of land have been set aside for this purpose. Rice cultivation is also increasing in the south.

Livestock raising (camels, sheep and cattle) is the second most important activity after agriculture, and this is centred in the Sahelian belt. The severe droughts which plague this region have drastically reduced the herds; in addition, large numbers of animals are believed to be smuggled out of the country each year. Fishing in rivers and in Lake Chad is also an important economic activity.

Main Crops: cotton, rice, sorghum, groundnuts, millet.

Mineral Resources: oil, natron, uranium, tungsten.

THE ECONOMY

Gross National Product (1977 est.): US$540 million.

Per Capita Income (1977 est.): US$130.

Gross Domestic Product (1976): US$279.6 million.

Foreign Trade (1977): Total Imports – US$142.2 million. Total Exports – US$106.6 million.

Main Trading Partners: Imports – France, Nigeria, USA, Cameroon. Exports – Zaïre, Nigeria, Congo (People's Republic), France.

Chad is one of the poorest countries in Africa, if not the world. Its highly disadvantageous landlocked situation is one of the main problems, making transport costs for Chad's foreign trade crippling. Port Harcourt in Nigeria is the nearest port, lying some 1,770 km/1,100 miles away. Chad's internal transport system and communications are also poor and inadequate, further isolating the country's productive regions from the sea.

The economy is virtually dependent on cotton, and production is often affected by severe droughts with a résultant drop in the country's foreign exchange earnings. Until recent years the only industrial activity consisted of cotton gins, but some small-scale industrial development has taken place. A sugar refinery and abattoir have been established in N'djamena, together with a textile complex in Sahr and a brewery in Moundou.

Oil has been discovered, but exploitation to date is minimal; production is concentrated in the small refinery in N'djaména. Conoco and Shell are the principal foreign firms engaged in oil exploitation in partnership with the Chad Government.

Fighting in the north and east of the country is another factor affecting the economy, which now relies heavily on foreign aid, particularly from France. Aid for the rice-growing project at Sategui-Deressia and other development projects has also been forthcoming from the World Bank, the African Development Bank and the International Development Association.

Major Industries: cotton processing, textiles, sugar refining, brewery, meat processing.

Main Commodities Traded: Imports – mineral products, foodstuffs, transport equipment, electrical machinery, textiles. Exports – cotton, beef.

International Affiliations: UN, IBRD, OAU, ACP, ADB, Franc Zone, LCBC.

HOW TO GET THERE

Air
N'djaména International Airport is frequently used as a stopover for flights from Europe to French-speaking Africa, and there are at least 4 flights a week from Paris (Charles de Gaulle Airport) operated by UTA and Air Afrique.

Within Africa, there are regular flights to N'djaména from Bangui, Douala and Kinshasa. Chad is served by Air Afrique, UTA, Aeroflot, Cameroon Airlines and Air Zaïre.

Flying time to N'djaména from Paris, 7 hours.

An airport tax of 3,500 CFA francs is payable on departure by all passengers travelling to Europe.

N'djaména International Airport is 2 km/1 mile from the city centre.

Road
Chad is accessible by road from the Central African Republic, Cameroon and Nigeria. A *carnet de passage* is required, together with an International Driving Licence and a green card (insurance) or all-risks insurance.

ENTRY REGULATIONS

Visas
Visas are required by nationals of all countries except: Andorra, Benin, Cameroon, Central African Republic, Congo (People's Republic), France, Gabon, West Germany, Ivory Coast, Madagascar, Mali, Mauritania, Monaco, Niger, Rwanda, Senegal, Togo, Upper Volta and Zaïre – for a stay of up to 3 months.

Visas should be obtained, in advance, by all other nationals from Chad diplomatic missions or, alternatively, the nearest French embassy or consulate.

Visa applications should be accompanied by valid International Certificates of Vaccination against smallpox, yellow fever and cholera, and proof that the visitor holds an onward or return ticket.

Visitors should ensure that the validity of their passport extends for at least 3 months beyond the date the visa application is made. The validity of a visa is variable and the length of stay can vary up to 3 months. Visas are issued within 24 hours unless referred for authorisation, causing a delay of 6 to 8 weeks. All applications for a stay of more than 3 months will be referred.

Health Regulations
Valid International Certificates of Vaccination against smallpox, yellow fever and cholera are required by all persons entering Chad.

Customs
Currency: There is no limit to the amount of foreign or local currency which may be imported, but all monies must be declared on arrival. Unused foreign currency may be freely exported, but there is a limit of 25,000 CFA francs to the amount of local currency which may be exported.

Duty-free articles: Personal effects. 50 cigarettes or 25 cigars or 100g of tobacco. Samples of no commercial value.

Articles liable to duty: Samples of value may be temporarily imported (except by post) free of duty, provided they are accompanied by an ATA Carnet.

PRACTICAL INFORMATION FOR THE VISITOR

1. Currency
Monetary – CFA franc.
Notes – 100, 500, 1,000, 5,000, 10,000 CFA francs.
Coins – 1, 2, 5, 10, 25, 50, 100 CFA francs.

It is advisable to have French franc travellers' cheques when visiting Chad as these are more easily convertible. However, sterling and US dollar travellers' cheques can be cashed. It is advisable to exchange travellers' cheques only when and as required since it is difficult to exchange CFA francs outside of the Franc Zone.

Banking Hours
0700–1200 Monday to Saturday

The central bank and bank of issue for Chad is the *Banque des Etats de l'Afrique Centrale*, B.P. 50, N'djaména, ☎ 2458. This is the bank of issue for: Cameroon, the Central African Republic, Chad, the Congo (People's Republic) and Gabon.

Principal Domestic Banks
Banque de Développement du Tchad, B.P. 19, N'djaména.
Banque Tchadienne de Crédit et de Dépôts, 6 Rue Robert Lévy, B.P. 461, N'djaména, ☎ 2477.

Foreign Commercial Banks
Banque Internationale pour l'Afrique Occidentale, B.P. 87, N'djaména, ☎ 2373.
Banque Nationale de Paris, 15 Avenue Charles de Gaulle, B.P. 38, N'djaména, ☎ 2391.

2. Electricity Supply
220v AC 50Hz.
Plugs: 2 round pins.

3. Weights and Measures
The metric system is in use.

4. Media
There is no television service in Chad. Radiodiffusion Nationale Tchadienne is the Government-owned radio station, broadcasting in French, Arabic and several local languages.

Newspapers and Journals
Info-Tchad is a daily news bulletin published in French by the Chad Press Agency. *Tchad et Culture* is a Christian perodical published eight times a year in N'djaména. *Informations Economiques* is the weekly publication of the Chambre de Commerce, d'Agriculture et d'Industrie de la République du Tchad.

5. Medical Care

Malaria is prevalent in some parts of Chad and visitors are advised to take malarial prophylactics. Foreigners are often prone to intestinal upsets, and suitable medicines should be carried with you as they may not be available locally.

All drinking water should be boiled and filtered; alternatively, bottled mineral water is readily available. Avoid eating uncooked fruits and vegetables and unwashed salad.

The main hospital in N'djaména is partly staffed by French army doctors. There are hospitals in the towns of Moundou, Sarh and Abéché as well as a number of *centres médicaux* (medical centres) across the country, although these tend to be badly equipped and understaffed.

6. Telephone, Telex and Postal Services

Chad has direct telephone links with Paris, Abidjan, Bangui, Brazzaville, Douala, Khartoum, Kinshasa and Lagos. However, no international calls can be made after 1800 hours.

A public telex facility is available at the Office des Postes et Télécommunications in N'djamena.

Postal services are subject to lengthy delays. All mail, to and from Chad, should be despatched by air.

7. Public Holidays

1 January	New Year's Day
11 January	National Holiday
2 April	Anniversary of the UEAC
13 April	Anniversary of the Revolution
1 May	Labour Day
25 May	African Liberation Day
11 August	Independence Day
15 August	Feast of the Virgin Mary
1 November	All Saints Day
28 November	Proclamation of the Republic
25 December	Christmas Day

The following movable Muslim and Christian holidays are also observed: *Eid el Fitr, Eid el Kabir, Mouled, Easter Sunday and Monday, Ascension Day, Whit Monday.*

When a public holiday falls on a Sunday, it is observed on the following Monday. If a holiday falls on a Friday, the Saturday is often also observed as a holiday. Similarly when a holiday falls on a Tuesday, the Monday is often a public holiday.

8. Time.
GMT + 1.

9. Internal Transport

Air
Air Tchad operate flights from N'djaména to Ati, Am Timan, Abéché, Bol, Bongor, Faya-Largeau, Mongo, Moundou, Mao, Pala, Sarh and Zakouma.

Airline Offices in N'djaména
Air France	☎ 3341/2.
Lufthansa	☎ 2730/1.
UTA	☎ 3341/2.

Road
Road conditions in the southern part of the country are of a reasonable standard, although most of the dirt tracks become impassable during the rainy season (June to October). Road travel outside N'djaména is generally considered to be unsafe as many roads are mined and rebel activity continues across the country.

Taxis are available in the main towns and a minimum fare is in operation. Taxis can be hired by the hour or half-day.

Car-hire facilities are available in N'djaména. An International Driving Licence is required and a sizeable deposit usually has to be paid.

Traffic travels on the right.

Car-Hire Firms in N'djaména
Auto Location ☏ 3008.
Tchad Tourisme ☏ 3410.
Texaco Taxis ☏ 3008.

10. Tipping
Taxis – 10% of the fare.

Airport porters – 100 CFA francs.

Hotels/restaurants – 10% of the bill.

11. Social Customs
Visitors to Chad should have a good working knowledge of French. It is important to remember that more than half of the population are Muslims, living mainly in the northern part of the country. The feast of *Ramadan* is strictly observed and visitors should be careful to observe the ban on eating, drinking and smoking during daylight hours while in public. This does not apply in a number of restaurants which remain open to non-Muslims during *Ramadan*.

Segregation of the sexes is fairly rigid in Chad, particularly in the towns.

USEFUL ADDRESSES (GENERAL)

In N'djamena
Honorary British Consul: Mr. E. V. Dupuy, c/o SOCOPAO, B.P. 751, ☏ 2930.

Dutch Consulate: Sonasut, Route de Farcha N'djaména, B.P. 37, ☏ 3436.

French Embassy: Rue du Lieutenant Franjoux, B.P. 431, ☏ 2576/8.

US Embassy: Rue du Lt-Colonel d'Ornano, B.P. 413, ☏ 3091/4.

West German Embassy: Rue de Marseille 24, B.P. 893, ☏ 2377/8.

Direction du Tourisme: B.P. 86, ☏ 2817.

Wagons-Lits Tourisme Authorised Representative: Agence Touristique du Tchad, B.P. 281.

BUSINESS INFORMATION

The majority of importing firms are branches of French companies, and it is often worthwhile contacting the parent company in France before establishing contact with the local firm.

Companies wishing to appoint an agent in N'djaména are advised to seek the assistance of the local Chamber of Commerce [see Useful Addresses (Business)]. The Chamber will often arrange to insert an advertisement in its weekly publication, *Informations Economiques*.

The principal buying seasons are February–May and September–December.

Import and Exchange Control Regulations
Imports from outside the Franc Zone usually require an import licence. Applications for a licence to import goods for use in one of the country's development sectors will be considered individually.

All payments for imports from outside the Franc Zone require the prior authorisation of the Ministry of Finance.

Business Hours
Government Offices and Business Houses
0800–1200
1500–1800 Monday to Friday
0800–1200 Saturday

BUSINESS SERVICES

Insurance
Assureurs Conseils Tchadiens Faugere, Jutheau & Cie, B.P. 120, N'djaména.
Societe de Représentation d'Assurances et de Reassurances Africaines, B.P. 481, N'djamena.

Road Transport
Cooperative des Transportateurs Tchadiens, B.P. 336, N'djamena.

USEFUL ADDRESSES (BUSINESS)

Chambre de Commerce, d'Agriculture et d'Industrie de la République du Tchad, B.P. 458, N'djaména, ☎ 3657.

Société Nationale de Commercialisation du Tchad, B.P. 630, N'djamena.

Caisse Centrale de Coopération Economique, B.P. 478, N'djaména.

MAJOR CITY

N'djaména
The continuing civil war is reported to be taking its toll on N'djaména, and much of the city is said to be severely damaged.

Formerly called Fort Lamy, N'djaména is a city of striking contrasts, with its more than 100 modern commercial buildings and its residential suburbs sharply juxtaposed against the old quarter of the city with its bustling daily market and traditional, flat-roofed adobe houses. The city has an interesting museum housing collections of fossils, tools, pottery, stone objects and engravings, many of which are relics of the Sao culture of the 9th century.

Hotels
There is no official hotel rating system in Chad.

DU CHARI, B.P. 118, ☎ 3313.
Modern hotel overlooking the Chari River, 1km/½ mile from city centre.
Rooms: 32 ♫, ☎. Suites available.
Facilities: Restaurant, bar. Garden.

GRAND PLACE DE L'INDEPENDANCE, B.P. 108, ☎ 3888.
Traditional-style hotel in city centre.
Rooms: 28 ♫, ☎, ⚹, ⚐. Suites available.
Facilities: Restaurant, bar. Car-hire.
Services: ᵀᶜ, ᶠᶜ. ✉ not accepted. ⚙, ♂.

LA TCHADIENNE, B.P. 109, ☎ 3311.
1st-class hotel in residential district overlooking Chari River, just outside city centre.
Rooms: 104 ✈, ☎.
Facilities: 2 restaurants, bar. Nightclub. Swimming.
Services: ▤ Amex, Diners Club. Conference facilities.

Restaurants
Probably the best restaurant in N'djaména is that of the Hôtel du Chari. All hotel restaurants are open to non-residents.
Restaurant de la Poste – French and Italian; *Chez Cabrini* – Italian; *Dragon d'Or* and *Le Lotus* – Vietnamese; *Naufal Sami* – Lebanese; *Le Weekend* – French.

Nightclubs
Baby Scotch, Hi-Fi Music and *Le Mécreant*.

Entertainment
N'djaména has facilities for swimming, bowls, volleyball and fishing. The *Chari Club* (open to members and guests only) offers tennis, bowls and good dining facilities.

There are several game reserves within easy reach of N'djaména, including the vast Zakouma National Park (open from December to May; accommodation available) which contains a huge and exciting variety of game. Smaller reserves which lie within a short drive of the capital are Douguia (80km/50 miles) and Mandelia (35km/22 miles).

Lake Chad (120km/75 miles) can be reached by dirt track or by air taxi to Bol.

Shopping
Best buys: leatherware, camel-hair rugs, embroidered cotton goods, pottery, brass carvings.

THE CONGO
People's Republic of the Congo

Geography	99
The Economy	100
How to Get There	101
Entry Regulations	101
Practical Information for the Visitor	102
Useful Addresses (General)	104
Business Information	104
Business Services	105
Useful Addresses (Business)	105
Brazzaville	105

Size: 342,000 sq.km/132,046 sq.miles.

Population: 1.46 million (1978 est.).

Distribution: 33% in urban areas.

Density: 4.2 persons per sq.km/11 per sq.mile.

Population Growth Rate: 2.5% p.a. (1970–5 average).

Ethnic Composition: The main ethnic groups are the Vili on the coast, the Kongo who live around Brazzaville, and the Téké, M'Bochi and Sanga in the northern and central areas. There is also a European community of around 10,000 (mainly French) and a large number of Gabonese.

Capital: Brazzaville Pop. 310,000 (1977 est.).

Major Towns: Pointe Noire Pop. 145,000. Kayes Pop. 30,600 (1974); Loubomo Pop. 29,600 (1974).

Language: French is the official language. Lingala and Kokongo are the principal African languages. English is rarely spoken.

Religion: Approximately half are Animists; and the remainder are mainly Roman Catholics with small groups of Protestants and Muslims.

Government: Following the assassination of President Marien Ngouabi in 1977, the Congo was ruled by a provisional Military Committee until March 1979, when it was announced that the country had returned to constitutional rule. The President and head of state is elected for a 5-year term by the congress of the Parti Congolais du Travail (PCT), the sole political party; the President also heads the Council of State. The Central Committee of the PCT includes most of the Government ministers and the head of the armed forces, under the leadership of the President. A People's National Assembly is elected by direct suffrage from a list presented by the PCT.

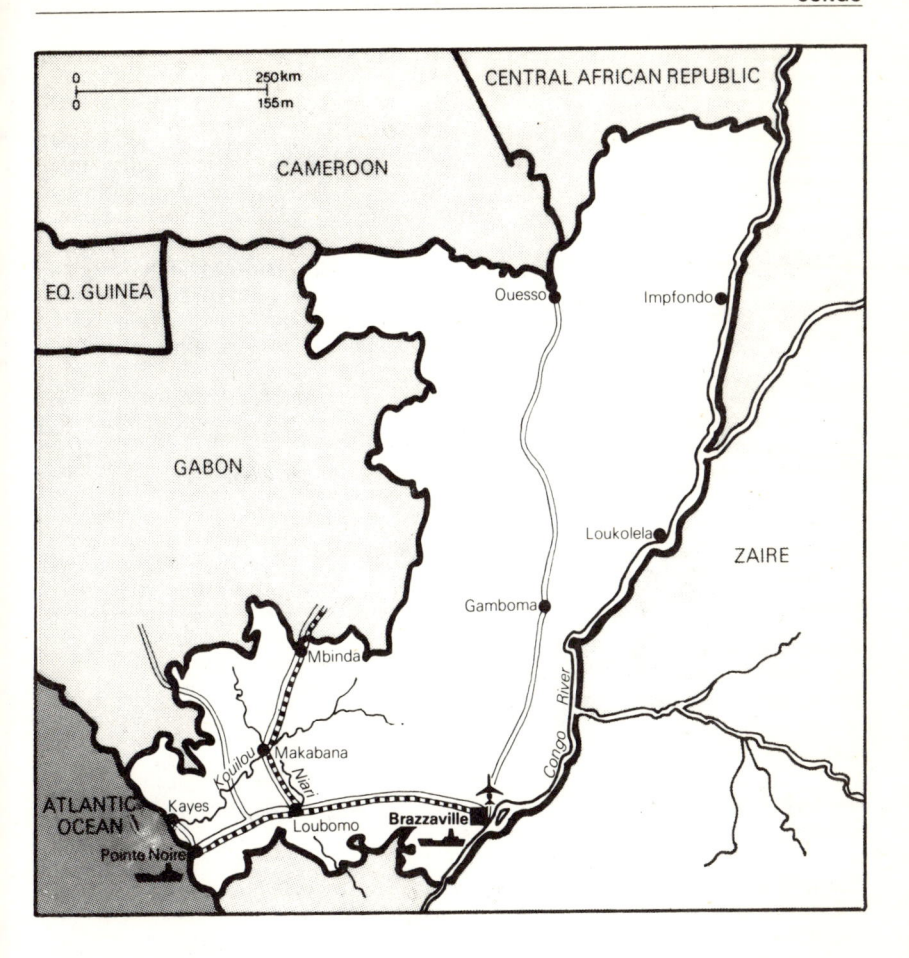

GEOGRAPHY

The Congo is situated across the Equator in west-central Africa. The narrow coastal plain on the Atlantic rises to a mountainous region covered with dense forest. Inland are a succession of plateaux, separated from the mountainous area by the 320km/ 200-mile-wide Niari Valley consisting largely of savannah. Further north are the tropical rain forests of the Congo basin; the far north is heavily forested.

Climate

The Congo has a hot and humid equatorial climate with average temperatures ranging from 21°C/70°F to 27°C/80°F. Humidity is highest in January, when it may reach 90%. There are 2 dry seasons: May to September, and December to mid-January. The main rainy season lasts from mid-January to May, while the short rains fall from October to mid-December. The most pleasant time to visit is from June to September when temperatures and humidity are lowest.

Agriculture

About 70% of the population engage in agriculture although only a very small area is under cultivation, mostly in the south. The main cash crops are sugar cane (the most important export), coffee, cocoa, tobacco and groundnuts. Palm oil is also produced. The major subsistence crops are manioc, rice, yams, potatoes, maize and bananas. Livestock raising is being encouraged by the Government, and a major scheme is under way in the Niari Valley to reorganise existing cattle ranches. The state farms have not been successful; however, the Government intends to persevere with plans to improve productivity, increase the cultivable areas, and diversify agricultural production so that food shortages can be ended and imports replaced by domestic produce. Forestry is an extremely important part of the economy, timber being the major export until 1973. Several new saw mills and processing plants are to be constructed.

Main Crops: sugar cane, tobacco, coffee, cocoa, rice, manioc, timber, palm kernels, groundnuts, maize, sweet potatoes, bananas.

Mineral Resources: oil, potassium, phosphates, iron ore, copper-zinc, lead-zinc, gold.

THE ECONOMY

Gross National Product (1976): US$700 million.

Per Capita Income (1978): US$500.

Gross Domestic Product: N.A.

Foreign Trade (1978): Total Imports – US$267.6 million. Total Exports – US$308.2 million.

Main Trading Partners: Imports – France, Brazil, West Germany, USA, Italy, Japan. Exports – USA, Italy, Brazil, Spain, West Germany, France, UDEAC countries.

Much of the Congolese economy is state controlled and nationalisation seems likely to continue under the current regime, which has reaffirmed its belief in 'scientific socialism' in contrast to the former regime which advocated a 'mixed' economy.

Aside from agriculture, which is the major economic activity, the most important developments over the last 10 years have been in the exploitation of mineral resources. Despite heavy investment during the 1960s, the mining and processing of the large potassium chloride deposits by the Compagnie des Potasse du Congo, in which French concerns held a majority interest, was halted in 1977 as a result of recurrent difficulties in production and sales. Inland oil reserves had been almost exhausted by 1971, but it is hoped that off-shore fields exploited by Agip and Elf-Congo will yield up to 2 million tons annually in the 1980s. Natural gas is extracted at Pointe Indienne. Production of lead, zinc and copper is relatively small, although prospecting for a large range of minerals is continuing.

Manufacturing is fairly well developed, with many enterprises engaged in the processing of agricultural and mineral products. The Office for the Creation and Organisation of State Enterprise is responsible for nationalised industries, of which the most important are a shipyard, a munitions factory, a textile printing works, several breweries and soft drink plants, cigarette manufacturing, fish processing, and oil and flour mills. A major textile complex (SOTEXCO), built with Chinese aid, was closed in 1977. An oil refinery at Pointe Noire is almost complete and a large paper-pulp factory is planned.

Power production is state controlled with most electricity being generated at the Djoue hydro-electric plant and the diesel power station at Pointe Noire. Other hydro-electric and integrated industrial complexes are planned for the Kouilou Dam and Bouenza.

The country's geographical position has long given it an important role in handling trade for the interior countries of Chad, Zaïre and the Central African Republic. Extensions to the railway network are under way to improve cargo handling facilities. Smuggling from neighbouring countries to the Congo is rife and is a substantial, though hidden, part of the economy.

The principal donors of foreign aid are the World Bank, the European Development Fund, France, Canada, China, the African Development Bank, Saudi Arabia and Kuwait. The present Development Plan aims to encourage agricultural, industrial and infrastructure development. However, reductions in oil revenue have forced a number of cuts in the original plans.

Major Industries: sugar production, vegetable oil and flour processing, brewing, soft drinks, shoes and clothing, building materials, cigarettes.

Main Commodities Traded: petroleum, wood, sugar, cocoa, tobacco, coffee.

International Affiliations: UN, IBRD, OAU, ACP, ADB, Franc Zone, UDEAC.

HOW TO GET THERE

Air
UTA and Air Afrique operate 3 flights a week from Paris to Brazzaville.

Aeroflot and Air Algérie fly to Brazzaville from North Africa, and Air Mali and Cameroon Airways fly from West Africa. In addition, Brazzaville has air connections with Cairo, Douala, Khartoum, Lagos, Libreville and Lusaka.

Maya Maya Airport is 4km/2½ miles from the centre of Brazzaville. Taxis are available at the airport. There is no bus service between the airport and Brazzaville.

Road
It is possible to drive from Lambaréné in Gabon to Loubomo and Brazzaville, although the road is not tarred in places.

ENTRY REGULATIONS

Visas
A valid passport and visa are required by all visitors, except for nationals of France and most Francophone African states. West German nationals visiting as tourists need no visa if their stay does not exceed 15 days. Visas should be obtained prior to departure from embassies or consulates of the People's Republic of the Congo. Visas are not issued on arrival in the Congo under any circumstances.

CONGO

Visitors should ensure that the validity of their passport extends for at least 3 months beyond the date for which the visa application is made. Allow several weeks for the visa to be issued.

Except for nationals of Zaïre and Congo, it is forbidden to cross the River Congo.

Health Regulations
Valid International Certificates of Vaccination against smallpox, yellow fever and cholera are required by all persons entering the Congo.

Customs
Currency: There is no limit to the amount of foreign or local currency which may be imported, but all monies must be declared on arrival. A declaration form should be completed, to be presented each time an exchange transaction is completed; this declaration form should then be surrendered on departure from the Congo.

Duty-free articles: Personal effects, including a camera, tape-recorder and binoculars. 50 cigarettes, 25 cigars or 100g of tobacco. A reasonable quantity of perfume. Samples of no commercial value. Personal effects may be imported into the Congo with the duty suspended, provided they are re-exported within 12 months. The duty should be covered by a bond or a deposit.

PRACTICAL INFORMATION FOR THE VISITOR

1. Currency
Monetary Unit – CFA franc.
Notes – 100, 500, 1,000, 5,000, 10,000 CFA francs.
Coins – 1, 2, 5, 10, 25, 50, 100 CFA francs.

Non-franc travellers' cheques can usually be cashed without difficulty, but it is advisable to cash only enough for one's foreseeable requirements during the stay. Visitors will experience difficulty in exchanging CFA francs outside of the Franc Zone.

Banking Hours
0730–1300 Monday to Saturday. Counters close at 1100.

The central bank and bank of issue is the *Banque des Etats de l'Afrique Centrale*, B.P. 126, Brazzaville. (Other member countries of the Banque des Etats de l'Afrique Centrale are Gabon, Central African Republic, Cameroon and Chad.)

Major Commercial Banks
Banque Commerciale Congolaise (BCC), Avenue Amilcar Cabral, B.P. 79, Brazzaville, ☎ 810880/1.
Union Congolaise de Banques (UCB), Avenue Amilcar Cabral, B.P. 147, Brazzaville, ☎ 811066.

2. Electricity Supply
220v AC 50Hz.

3. Weights and Measures
The metric system is in use.

4. Media
Radiodiffusion Télévision Nationale Congolaise transmits programmes in French, Lingala and Kikongo. The national radio station, La Voix de la Révolution Congolaise, broadcasts in French, Lingala and Kikongo from Brazzaville and Pointe Noire. Commercial advertising is not accepted on radio or television.

Newspapers and Journals
Le Courier d'Afrique, *L'Eveil de Pointe Noire*, *Le Journal de Brazzaville* and *Journal Officiel de la République du Congo* – dailies.

La Semaine Africaine is a weekly Catholic newspaper, published in Brazzaville, and circulated in Gabon, Chad and the Central African Republic.

A censorship committee for all the media was set up in 1972.

5. Medical Care
Malaria is prevalent, and visitors are advised to take anti-malarial prophylactics. Dysentery or minor stomach upsets may occur and suitable precautionary medicines can be taken. Avoid uncooked fruit and vegetables and unwashed salads. Tap water is not safe to drink and should be boiled or filtered; alternatively, bottled mineral water can be purchased.

6. Telephone, Telex and Postal Services
Telephone links with neighbouring countries and Europe are relatively good. Telegrams can be sent from the main post offices. There are no public telex facilities in the Congo. All mail, to and from the Congo, should be despatched by air.

7. Public Holidays

1 January	New Year's Day
1 May	Labour Day
22 June	Anniversary of the People's Army
15 August	Assumption
1 November	All Saints' Day
25 December	Christmas Day
31 December	Foundation of the Parti Congolais du Travail

The Anniversary of the Three Glorious Days of 1963 is celebrated from 13–15 August each year, but work is expected to continue during this period. *Easter*, *Ascension Day* and *Whit Monday* are also official public holidays.

When a public holiday falls on a Sunday the following Monday is observed as a holiday. Similarly, when a holiday falls on a Friday or a Tuesday, the following Saturday or preceding Monday respectively are observed as public holidays.

8. Time
GMT + 1.

9. Internal Transport
Air
Lina-Congo operates 2 or 3 flights a day from Brazzaville to Pointe Noire. There are flights from Brazzaville to the main provincial towns of Loubomo, Impfondo, Kayes, Loukolela, Makabana, Ouesso and others. All passengers leaving Brazzaville for destinations in the Congo must pay an airport tax of CFR 500 at the airport.

Aircraft are available for charter from *Aeroservice*, B.P. 774, Brazzaville.

Airline offices in Brazzaville
Aeroflot ☎ 4715, 3230.
Air France ☎ 3636/8.
UTA ☎ 813126/8.

Rail
The Chemin de Fer Congo Ocean operates a daily service between Brazzaville and Pointe Noire (13 hours); dining and sleeping facilities are available. There is a weekly service from Pointe Noire to Mbinda on the Gabonese Border.

Road
Most roads outside Brazzaville and Pointe Noire are earth tracks which become virtually impassable during the rainy season.

Taxis are available in Brazzaville and Pointe Noire.

Self-drive and chauffeur-driven cars are available for hire in these two towns. Most major hotels carry a list of local car hire firms. In Pointe Noire cars are available from Hertz, ☎ 941200/941285.

An International Driving Licence or Licence from the visitor's country of residence is required. Traffic travels on the right-hand side of the road.

10. Tipping
Taxis – no tip necessary.

Hotels/restaurants – a tip of 10% is customary.

11. Social Customs
Visitors should have a good working knowledge of French, as English is rarely understood in business circles.

The correct form of address for a Government minister is *Camarade Ministre*. Similarly, other officials and business contacts should be addressed as *Camarade* rather than simply *Monsieur*.

Visitors experiencing difficulty with the local authorities should contact the nearest embassy of their country of residence. Passports should not be surrendered without first obtaining an official receipt.

USEFUL ADDRESSES (GENERAL)

Brazzaville
Dutch Consulate, Avenue Amilcar Cabral, B.P. 147, ☎ 811067/8.

French Embassy, Rue Alfassa, B.P. 2089, ☎ 811423/4.

West German Embassy, Place de la Mairie, B.P. 2022, ☎ 2770/3568.

US Embassy, B.P. 1015.

Office National Congolais du Tourisme, Plateau, B.P. 456, ☎ 2713.

Syndicat d'Initiative, Avenue du 28 août 1940, B.P. 173, ☎ 3178.

Pointe Noire
Dutch Vice-Consulate, B.P. 717, ☎ 940294, 940754.

French Consulate-General, Angle allée Nicolau et Rue no. 4, B.P. 720, ☎ 940002.

Wagons-Lits Tourisme Authorised Representative: Transcap Voyages, B.P. 1154, ☎ 2160, 2188.

BUSINESS INFORMATION

Although most sectors of the Congolese economy are nationalised the Government welcomes foreign participation in association with the various state organisations. State policy is to move gradually toward a situation whereby the state has a majority holding in all commercial and industrial concerns. At present the state requires at least a 20% share in all mining operations. Most trade is handled by French companies or Greek and Portuguese merchants. The Government-sponsored Office Nationale du Commerce is extending its marketing operations, mainly for Congolese products. It is best to recruit local agents through the Chamber of Commerce, which can also assist in the placing of advertisements and other announcements. All correspondence should be in French; price quotations should be in local currency.

Import and Exchange Control Regulations
Imports from all countries outside the Central African Customs and Economic Union (UDEAC) require an import licence. Some quota restrictions are in force, but these do not apply to imports from the Franc Zone and the EEC. Licences for these imports are usually granted automatically.

CONGO

Foreign exchange is made available for all imports from member countries of the EEC and Organisation Commune Africaine et Mauricienne (OCAM). Foreign exchange payments for imports from other countries are subject to a number of controls.

Business Hours
Government Offices
0800–1300
1430–1700 Monday, Wednesday and Friday
0800–1300 Tuesday, Thursday and Saturday.

Business Houses
0800–1300 Monday and Tuesday
0800–1200
1430–1730 Wednesday and Thursday
0800–1200 Saturday

BUSINESS SERVICES

Insurance
Assurances et Réassurances du Congo, Avenue Amilcar Cabral, B.P. 977, Brazzaville.

Shipping
Société Africaine de Transit et d'Affrètement Congo (SATA-CONGO), B.P. 718, Pointe Noire – inland waterway transport.

Transcap-Congo, B.P. 1154, Pointe Noire – inland waterway transport.

The port of Pointe Noire is served by the following shipping lines: *Société Congolaise de Manutention*, *Société Ouest-Africaine d'Entreprises Maritimes* and *Union Maritime et Commerciale*.

USEFUL ADDRESSES (BUSINESS)

Chambre de Commerce, d'Agriculture et d'Industrie de Brazzaville, B.P. 92, Brazzaville, ☎ 811089.

Chambre de Commerce, d'Agriculture et d'Industrie du Kouilou-Niari, B.P. 665, Pointe Noire, ☎ 940496/940280.

Office Nationale du Commerce, B.P. 2305, Brazzaville.

Office Nationale de Commercialisation des Produits Agricoles, B.P. 144, Brazzaville.

MAJOR TOWN

Brazzaville
Brazzaville is the administrative and commercial capital, stretching for several miles along the banks of the Congo River near the Stanley (Malebo) Pool. The city was founded in 1880 by the French explorer Savorgnan de Brazza and was the capital of French Equatorial Africa from 1910–58. During the Second World War, the Free

105

French Forces in Africa were based in Brazzaville and the Case de Gaulle was built for the General in 1940.

Excellent views of the city, the Pool and Kinshasa over the river are possible from the lighthouse and the Cathedral of St Firmin above the city. Much development has taken place since 1945 in a variety of architectural styles. The Basilica of Ste Anne du Congo, which blends traditional African and European designs, is one of the more interesting buildings. The city has a teaching college, a higher education college and an art school. The National Museum is worth a visit for the rich collection of ethnographical and historical items. The headquarters of the World Health Organisation in Africa is in Brazzaville.

Brazzaville is divided into a number of quarters: administrative (the Plateau); commercial (the Plain); military (the Tchad); residential (l'Aiglon); and an industrial zone (Mpila).

Hotels

There is no official rating system.

Cosmos, Avenue du Beach et Rue Albert 1er, B.P. 2459, ☎ 813380/1.
Modern hotel in town centre, 5km/3 miles from airport.
Rooms: 122 ♪, ⊛, ❐ (suites only), ♨, ♡. Suites available.
Facilities: Restaurant, bar. Nightclub. Tennis, swimming. Car hire.
Services: TC, FC. ⊟ Credit cards not accepted.

Relais de Maya Maya, Boulevard Maréchal Lyautey, B.P. 588, ☎ 810910/2.
Modern hotel overlooking Stanley Pool with chalet-style accommodation.
Rooms: 64 ♪, ☎. Suites available.
Facilities: Restaurant, bar. Nightclub. Swimming, tennis.
Services: ⊟ Amex, Diners Club. Conference room – max. capacity 60.

Other hotels in Brazzaville include:
Olympic Palace, Ravin de la Mission, B.P. 728, ☎ 812502.
Le Mistral, B.P. 494, ☎ 812033.

Restaurants

Ma Campagne, *Le Mistral*, ☎ 812033, *Chez Simone* and *Le Petit Logis*, ☎ 2874 – French; *La Pizzeria* – Italian; *L'Exotique* – Vietnamese; *Chez Colette*; *Les Ambassadeurs*.

Nightclubs

The Cosmos and Relais de Maya Maya Hotels have their own nightclubs. Another popular night spot is *La Saturne*.

Entertainment

Boat trips can be arranged on Stanley Pool with visits to nearby villages and the rapids and falls of the Congo River. The Poto-Poto Art Centre exhibits the work of local artists and has occasional displays of Congolese dance, drama and music. Congolese music is admired all over Africa and there are opportunities to see and hear local groups playing every evening in the bars, while fine singing can be heard on Sundays in the churches and cathedrals.

Sporting opportunities are somewhat limited, although some facilities exist for tennis, fishing, riding and sailing.

Shopping

Best buys: carvings, records, jewellery, basketwork.

In Poto-Poto, just outside Brazzaville, the Moungali and Ouendze markets offer a large range of goods, ranging from snake meat and other local delicacies to local carvings and ritual masks. The arts and crafts centre in Poto-Poto offers paintings and sculptures.

Brazzaville street vendors peddle their wares for locals and visitors, but be prepared to bargain hard.

DJIBOUTI
Republic of Djibouti

Geography	108
The Economy	109
How to Get There	110
Entry Regulations	110
Practical Information for the Visitor	111
Useful Addresses (General)	112
Business Information	112
Business Services	113
Useful Addresses (Business)	113
Djibouti	114

Size: 21,783 sq.km/8,410 sq.miles.

Population: 250,000 (1978 est.).

Distribution: 65% in urban areas.

Density: 11 persons per sq.km/30 per sq.mile.

Population Growth Rate: N.A.

Ethnic Composition: Issas and other Somali, 45%; Afars 40%; the remainder of the population consists of several thousand French and smaller numbers of Arabs, Italians, Greeks, Sudanese and Indians.

Capital: Djibouti Pop. 102,000 (1976 est.).

Major Towns: Tadjoura, Dikhil, Obock and Ali-Sabieh are the largest of a number of settlements.

Language: Arabic is the official language, though French is widely understood. The Somalis and Afars each have their own language of which there are several local dialects.

Religion: Most are Sunni Muslim; there are also Roman Catholic, Protestant and Greek Orthodox churches.

Government: In May 1977, following a number of controversial referenda in the 1960s and '70s, the people of the French Territory of the Afars and Issas voted for independence. The Republic of Djibouti was formally declared independent on 27 June 1977, the last of the French colonies in Africa to become autonomous.

The President of the Republic is Hassan Gouled, elected in 1977. At that time he was the leader of the Somali-dominated African People's League for Independence (LPAI). Since then the Government has attempted to reconcile traditional differences between the Afars and Somalis by emphasising their common Arab identity as Muslims. The Republic of Djibouti joined the Arab League in September 1977. Despite these efforts, however, the political situation remains unstable and the Afar–Issas rivalry has continued, and a large contingent of French soldiers has stayed on to contend with occasional outbreaks of terrorist activity.

DJIBOUTI

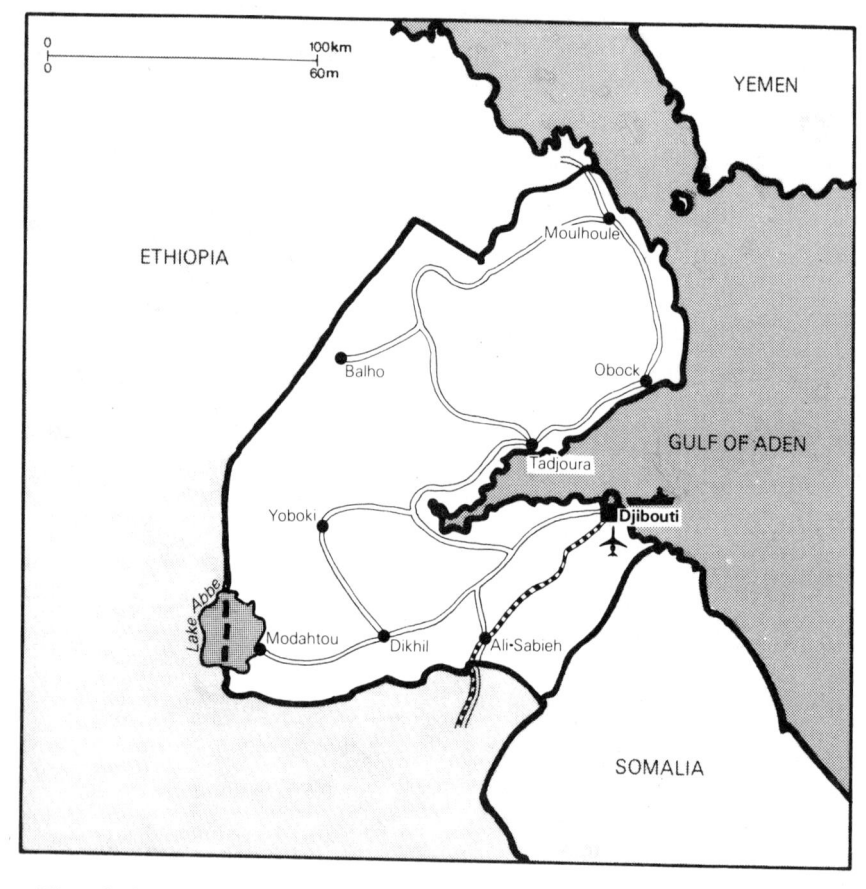

The principal political parties are: the Rassemblement Populaire pour le Progrès, formed in 1979 to replace the LPAI and led by Hassan Gouled; the Union Nationale pour l'Indépendence (UNI), the Afar opposition party; the Mouvement Populaire de Libération (MPL), a Marxist-Leninist Afar party; the Mouvement pour la Libération de Djibouti (MLD) an Afar party based in Dire Dawa (Ethiopia); and the Front de Libération de la Côte des Somalis (FLCS), an Issas party based in Mogadishu (Somalia).

GEOGRAPHY

The Republic of Djibouti lies at the southern end of the Red Sea and to the west of the Gulf of Aden. The country can be divided into 2 contrasting regions: the semi-arid coastal strip around the Gulf of Tadjoura, where there is some irrigated agriculture and a relatively high density of population; and the inland areas which are mostly rocky desert waste, the higher ground enclosing basins and salt lakes. There are occasional arable patches in the inland area, but it is only in the higher regions, where the altitude exceeds 1,200 metres/3,936 ft, that vegetation is perennial.

Climate
Djibouti is generally hot and humid. In the 3 hottest months – June, July and August – temperatures can reach over 45°C/113°F and average between 35°C/95°F and 40°C/104°F. The coolest months are from November to March when temperatures are usually between 20°C/68°F and 30°C/86°F. Temperatures during the months between the warm and cool seasons are transitional and variable. May and September are usually hot and the most humid times of the year. Rain is infrequent and varies considerably from year to year.

Agriculture
The lack of adequate rainfall and virtual absence of any rivers has made crop cultivation very difficult without expensive irrigation schemes. Consequently, little cultivation exists. On the coastal fringe date palms are cultivated, and the products of these are used to fulfil many local needs.

By far the most important agricultural occupation is the herding of livestock. Goats, sheep, cattle, camels and donkeys are the basic livelihood of the nomadic tribesmen who live outside the urban areas, and the skins and hides which they sell constitute a large part of Djibouti's export trade. Traditionally, the camels bred in this area have been highly prized across the Red Sea in Yemen and Saudi Arabia, though this trade is now declining. There is some small scale fishing along the coasts.

Main Crops: dates, some fruit and vegetables.

Mineral Deposits: salt, copper, gypsum.

THE ECONOMY

Gross National Product (1976): US$140 million.

Per Capita Income (1976): US$870.

Gross Domestic Product (1977): FD17,000 million.

Foreign Trade (1976): Total Imports – FD21.28 billion. Total Exports – FD2.92 billion.

Main Trading Partners: Imports – France, Ethiopia, Japan, Belgium, Luxembourg, United Kingdom. Exports – France, United Kingdom, Italy, Ethiopia, South Yemen, West Germany.

The economy is based on trade through the international port of Djibouti. The port, with its easily accessible harbour, modern loading facilities and ample storage area, is well positioned for shipping using the Suez Canal and Red Sea route to the Indian Ocean. The trend towards increased use of the container cargo ships and supertankers taking the route from North America and Europe around the Cape to the Indian Ocean has badly affected Djibouti's trade.

The rail link to Dire Dawa and on to Addis Ababa at one time carried 60% of Ethiopia's imports and 40% of exports. However, the line was closed for just over a year from May 1977, and, although now reopened, it is transporting only a fraction of the previous volume of trade.

DJIBOUTI

The conflict between Ethiopia and Somalia has severely harmed the economy. Refugees from the war in the Ogaden Desert have streamed into Djibouti, adding to the increasing level of unemployment. Despite immediate problems, however, prospects for the long term remain hopeful, particularly with the reopening of the Suez Canal. The large amounts of foreign aid which keep the Republic financially stable are being spent mainly on projects to improve the basic infrastructure of the economy (transport, electricity and water, drainage, education, medical and port services). Aid is provided by the UN, ECDF, the Arab League, France and Saudi Arabia.

Major Industries: port industries, mineral water bottling, construction materials.

Main Commodities Traded: Imports – foodstuffs, machinery, transport equipment, consumer goods, cigarettes, alcohol, petroleum products. Exports – hides and skins.

International Affiliations: UN, OAU, ACP, ADB, AL.

HOW TO GET THERE

Air

Djibouti is not served by direct flights from London, although there are flights from Paris operated by Air France. Air Djibouti flies from Ethiopia, Somalia and both Yemen Republics. Other flights to and from Djibouti are run by Air Madagascar, Yemen Airways, Ethiopian Airways, Somali Airways and Air Mauritius.

The international airport is 5km/3 miles south of the town of Djibouti.

All passengers must pay an airport tax of 600 FD on departure.

ENTRY REGULATIONS

Visas

Entry and exit visas must be obtained from the Embassy of the Republic of Djibouti in Paris, unless visitors are nationals of an EEC country in which case 3- or 10-day visas may be obtained on arrival at Djibouti airport if a ticket for a flight out of Djibouti is held.

The latest information on visa regulations can be obtained from representatives of the Republic and French consulates.

Health Regulations

The following Certificates of Vaccination are required: smallpox, issued not more than 3 years prior to the visit; yellow fever, if travelling from an infected area; and cholera. TAB (typhoid and paratyphoid) injections are recommended; anti-malarial prophylactics are also advisable.

Customs

Currency: There is no limit to the amount of local or foreign currency which may be imported or exported.

Duty-free articles: Personal effects.

PRACTICAL INFORMATION FOR THE VISITOR

1. Currency
Monetary unit – Djibouti franc (FD), divided into 100 centimes.
Notes – 500, 1,000, 5,000 FD.
Coins – 1, 2, 5, 10, 20, 100 FD.

There is no exchange control in the Republic and the Djibouti franc may be freely converted. The Trésor National de la République de Djibouti controls monetary issue. The Djibouti franc is covered by a deposit of US dollars in New York.

No travellers' cheques can be accepted unless endorsed by an external account.

Exchange control regulations should be checked before departure with representatives of the Republic or a French consulate.

Banking Hours
0715 – 1145 Sunday to Thursday

Principal Commercial Banks
British Bank of the Middle East, Place Lagarde, B.P. 2112, Djibouti, ☎ 353291.
Banque de l'Indochine et de Suez, Place Lagarde, B.P. 88, Djibouti, ☎ 353016.
Banque Nationale pour le Commerce et l'Industrie, Place Lagarde, B.P. 2122, Djibouti, ☎ 350857.

2. Electricity Supply
220/380v AC 50Hz.

3. Weights and Measures
The metric system is in use.

4. Media
The radio and television service is Government-controlled. Daily broadcasts are made in French, Arabic and Afar.

Newspapers and Journals
The 3 main newspapers are: *Djibouti Aujourd'hui*, a monthly published in Djibouti; *Carrefour Africain*, published twice monthly by the Roman Catholic Mission in Djibouti; and *Le Réveil de Djibouti*, published weekly by the Information Service of the Ministry of the Interior.

5. Medical Care
Western medical facilities are not good in Djibouti, although there is a French military hospital and a small number of expatriate French doctors remain in the town. Visitors should not drink untreated water and are advised to take precautions against malaria and the heat.

6. Telephone, Telex and Postal Services
The Republic is connected with Europe by an international radio-telephone service.

There is a telex machine available for public use at the main post office in Djibouti.

The telegraph office in Djibouti is open from 0700 – 2000 every day.

All mail sent to and from Djibouti should go by air.

Central Post Office, Blvd de la République, Djibouti, ☎ 352512

7. Public Holidays
1 January	*New Year's Day*
1 May	*Labour Day*
27 June	*Independence Day*
25 December	*Christmas Day*
31 December	*Annual Closing (Banks)*

The following movable Muslim and Christian holidays are also observed: *Mouled, El Nabi, Eid el Fitr, Eid el Adha, El Hijra, Ascension, Pentecost, Assumption* and *All Saints Day*.

Friday is the weekly holiday.

8. Time
GMT + 3.

9. Internal Transport

Air
There are flights between the main towns in the area operated by Air Djibouti and Ethiopian Airlines.

Air Djibouti, B.P. 505, Rue Marchand, Djibouti.
Djibouti Airport, B.P. 204, Djibouti, ☎ 350101.

Rail
The railway connecting Djibouti and Addis Ababa is slow and is not advisable for business travellers.

Road
Only about 10% of the roads are asphalted. There are irregular bus services in and around Djibouti, and taxis operate in the town, charging standard rates. Traffic travels on the right-hand side of the road. Self-drive cars are available in Djibouti.

Car Hire Firms
Hertz, B.P. 1933, ☎ 3015; (airport) ☎ 3013.

10. Tipping
Taxis – No tip.

Porters – 100 FD.

Hotels/restaurants – 10% of the bill.

11. Social Customs
The Republic of Djibouti is a Muslim country and respect for Muslim customs is advisable; however foreigners and expatriates can drink and eat what they like without interference in the bars and restaurants of the city.

Informal entertaining is common among friends in Djibouti. One local custom of note is the habit of chewing Qat, a mildly narcotic leaf.

USEFUL ADDRESSES (GENERAL)

Djibouti
US Embassy: B.P. 85, Villa Plateau du Serpent, Blvd Maréchal Joffre.

Belgian Consulate: B.P. 76.

Dutch and Swedish Consulates: B.P. 89.

Ethiopian Consulate: B.P. 230, Rue Clochette.

Italian Consulate: B.P. 462.

Somalian Consulate: B.P. 549, Rue Bourham-Bey.

West German Consulate: B.P. 519.

Yemen Consulate: B.P. 194, Plateau du Serpent.

Information and Tourist Office: B.P. 1398, Place Ménélik, ☎ 353790.

News Agency – Anglo-France Presse (AFP): B.P. 3537.

BUSINESS INFORMATION

In the past, the importance of Djibouti has been as an entrepôt for goods imported and exported into and out of Ethiopia. Shipping continues to be a major business interest, partly for the reason that as a free port goods in transit attract no duty and there are few exchange and import regulations.

The market for consumer goods is very small as the large French community receive much of their supplies from France, though some of their demand for food and drink is met locally. Many shops and small businesses are run by Greek, Arab and Indian traders who often import wholesale and sell in their own retail outlets.

The biggest business organisations in Djibouti are forwarding and clearing agents, of which a few act as wholesalers to the local market. There is a 22% tax on all consumer goods sold on the local market, and a surtax on cigarettes and alcohol. Petroleum products attract a special surtax.

Foreign investment is welcomed; investors pay no tax for the first 5 years.

Business correspondence should be in French.

Import and Exchange Control Regulations

There are no exchange control regulations, and because Djibouti is basically a free port with no control on imports, import licences are not required.

Port dues are payable on goods loaded or discharged at the port.

Business Hours

Government Offices
0700 – 1200
1500 – 1800 Sunday to Thursday

Business Houses
0730 – 1200
1530 – 1800 Sunday to Thursday
0730 – 1200 Saturday

Shops
0800 – 1200
1600 – 2000 Saturday to Thursday

Banks
0715 – 1145 Sunday to Thursday

BUSINESS SERVICES

Insurance
There are about 10 European insurance companies with agencies in Djibouti.

Forwarding/Clearing Agents in Djibouti
Compagnie Bourbonnaise de Navigation, B.P. 99.
Compagnie Générale Maritime, B.P. 182.
Compagnie Maritime de l'Afrique Orientale, B.P. 89, Rue du Port.
Gellatly Hankey et Cie (Djibouti) SA, B.P. 81, Rue de Genève.
J. J. Kothari and Co Ltd, B.P. 171, Place Lagarde.
Mitchell Cotts & Co (Ethiopia) Ltd, B.P. 85, Blvd de la République.
Société d'Armement et de Manutention de la Mer Rouge (SAMER), B.P. 10.
Société Maritime L. Savon et Ries, B.P. 2125, Avenue St Laurent du Var.

USEFUL ADDRESSES (BUSINESS)

Chambre de Commerce et d'Industrie de Djibouti, B.P. 84, Place Lagarde, Djibouti, ☎ 350826.

Compagnie du Chemin de Fer Franco-Ethiopien, B.P. 2116, Djibouti.

DJIBOUTI

MAJOR TOWN

Djibouti

Djibouti is the only town in the Republic of any significant size and approximately half of the country's population live there. One of the busiest places in town is the colourful market near the Mosque. There are a number of pleasant and interesting walks in and around the town; especially recommended are the Ambouli palm grove and gardens.

Hotels

Hotel accommodation is limited and all visitors should book in advance to ensure rooms and to find out the latest charges. These are some of the larger hotels:

DJIBOUTI PALACE HOTEL, B.P. 166, Blvd de Gaulle, ☎ 350982.

HOTEL DE L'EUROPE, B.P. 83, Place Ménélik, ☎ 350476.

HOTEL CONTINENTAL, B.P. 675, Place Ménélik, ☎ 350146.

HOTEL LA SIESTA, B.P. 508, Plateau du Serpent, ☎ 350592/888.

HOTEL PLEIN CIEL, Blvd Bonhoure, ☎ 3541.

Information on other hotels is obtainable from the Djibouti Tourist Board.

Restaurants and Bars

There are numerous restaurants and bars in the city selling a wide variety of foods from different continents. Among them are: *La Sangria*, Blvd de Gaulle; *Escale*, Letée du Gouvernement, ☎ 352212; *La Palmerier*, Ambouli, ☎ 353990; *La Concorde Bar*, Place Ménélik, ☎ 353152; *La Siesta*, Plateau du Serpent; *Les Tonnelles*, Ambouli Road, ☎ 352689; *Les Relais*, Ambouli Road, ☎ 352494; *Les Tritons*, Ave Maréchal-Foch, ☎ 351672 – beach bar; *Viet-Nam*, Blvd Bonhoure, ☎ 351708 – Chinese and Vietnamese.

Others include: *Le Kintz* and *Palmier en Zinc* – French; *Mickey Restaurant* and *Chez Mama Elena* – Italian; *Chez Thérèse* and *Hotel Bien Venue* – Ethiopian; and *Hanoi* – Vietnamese.

Entertainment

There are a number of clubs and bars whose main custom is with the expatriate French military and civil community. For more information contact the Tourist Development Board.

EGYPT
Arab Republic of Egypt

Geography	116
The Economy	117
How to Get There	118
Entry Regulations	118
Practical Information for the Visitor	119
Useful Addresses (General)	121
Business Information	122
Business Services	123
Useful Addresses (Business)	123
Cairo	123
Alexandria	124
Aswan	125

Size: 1,001,449 sq.km/386,662 sq.miles.

Population: 39.64 million (1978).

Distribution: approx. 45% in urban areas.

Density: Nile Valley/Delta region – 694 per sq.km/1,800 per sq.mile. Cairo: 96,500 per sq.km/250,000 per sq.mile.

Population Growth Rate: 2.3% p.a.

Ethnic Composition: The majority belong to the Mediterranean sub-type exclusive to the Nile Valley. There are some negroid features in the southern populace. The nomads in the Sinai area are related to Arabian tribal groups.

Capital: Cairo Pop. 8.5 million.

Major Cities: Alexandria Pop. 3.2 million; Giza Pop. 712,000; Suez Pop. 315,000; Port Said Pop. 313,000; Mansoura Pop. 212,000; Aswan Pop. 202,000.

Language: Arabic is the official language, but English and French are widely used in business and commerce.

Religion: Islam is the state religion. 90% are Sunni Muslims. The remainder are mostly Christians (especially Coptic) and Jewish. Freedom of worship is allowed.

Government: The Arab Republic of Egypt was founded in 1952. The People's Assembly, elected by universal suffrage, nominates the President, who has extensive powers.

Following the abolition of political parties in 1953, the Arab Socialist Union (founded 1961) was the only recognised political organisation until 1976 when President Sadat lifted the ban.

EGYPT

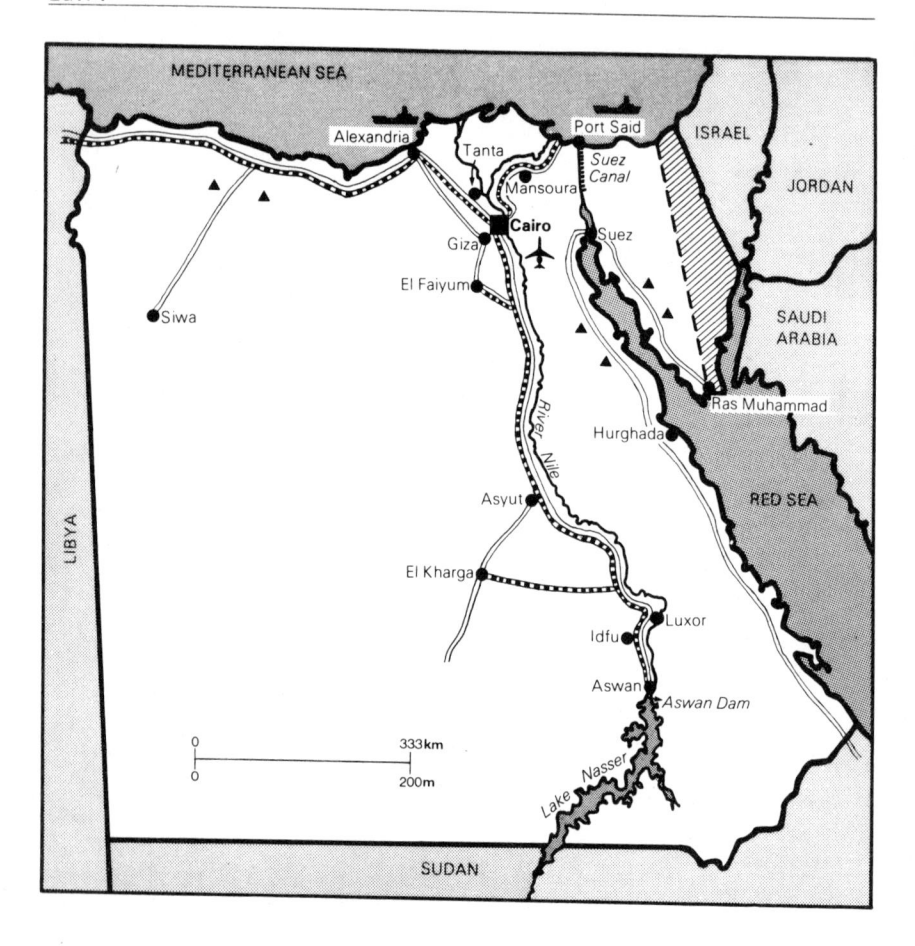

GEOGRAPHY

Egypt is virtually a rainless country except for the Nile Valley and Delta regions (98% of the population live in these areas). The country is favourably located with access to Africa, Asia, the Red Sea and the Mediterranean. The Suez Canal (reopened 1975) provides the shortest route to countries in the Indian and Pacific Oceans from Europe. Apart from the fertile areas around the Nile, the remainder of Egypt consists largely of sparsely inhabited desert lands.

Climate

The climate is dry in summer, and slightly cooler along the coast. Temperatures average 90°F/32°C in summer and 65°F/18°C in winter. Winter rains fall mainly on the Mediterranean coastal area.

A hot, dusty wind – the Khamsin – blows in from the desert during the summer months causing some discomfort.

Agriculture

Agriculture is the main economic activity, contributing 30% of the GNP and employing 47% of the total labour force. Various land reforms have resulted in a redistribution of land, and co-operatives are being established on a large scale in conjunction with the land reform.

Almost all agricultural production takes place in the Nile Valley and Delta. Irrigation is essential to agriculture. The Aswan High Dam has increased the cultivated area by more than a million acres of land. 2 to 3 different crops can be grown in a year in the Delta and central Egypt due to the high level of irrigation.

Main Crops: fodder crops, cotton, rice, fruit and vegetables.

Mineral Resources: phosphates, iron ore, manganese, salt and asbestos.

THE ECONOMY

Gross National Product (1977): US$18.2 billion.

Per Capita Income (1977): US$460.

Gross Domestic Product (1977): £E7,341 million.

Foreign Trade (1978): Total Imports – US$4.82 billion. Total Exports – US$1.98 billion.

Main Trading Partners: Imports – USA, West Germany, France, Italy, Japan. Exports – Italy, USSR, UK, Czechoslovakia, West Germany, Greece.

There has been little growth in the industrial sector over the last decade, despite attempts by the Government to remedy the situation. The state control of the economy was loosened by the 'open door' policy inaugurated in 1974 on the initiative of President Sadat. This policy allowed for tax concessions to foreign investors and the setting up of free zones in Alexandria, Cairo, Port Said and Suez. However, the 'open door' policy has not had the success which was anticipated, partly due to the continuing uncertainty surrounding the Egyptian economy, which has consequently deterred investors.

Over the last few years the Government has incurred vast debts, largely due to its huge military expenditure. With the signing of the peace treaty with Israel in March 1979, and the massive American loan aimed at reviving the economy, there is every hope that Egypt is about to experience a recovery in its economic position. As a result of the peace treaty, however, a number of Arab states have withdrawn investment funds, which could have a damaging effect.

Egypt is also looking to expand its tourist trade and has undertaken an extensive hotel building scheme.

Major Industries: agriculture, iron and steel, chemicals, fertilisers, petroleum, building materials, textiles.

Main Commodities Traded: Imports – cereals, chemicals, machinery, electrical equipment, mineral products. Exports – cotton (raw, yarn and fabrics), rice, crude oil, fruit and vegetables.

Crude Oil Production (1977): 1,753,000 metric tons per average calendar month.

International Affiliations: UN, IBRD, OAU, ADB. Egypt also enjoys a preferential trade agreement with the EEC.

HOW TO GET THERE

Air
Most international airlines have frequent, direct flights to Cairo. Egypt Air operates flights to Cairo from many world capitals.

Cairo International airport is 22km/14 miles from the city centre – transport is readily available.

An airport tax of £E1 is payable on departure from Egypt.

Flying times to Cairo: from London, 4½ hours; from New York, 11½ hours; from Sydney, 24 hours.

ENTRY REGULATIONS

Visas
No visa is required by passport holders of Algeria, Bahrain, Iran, Jordan, Kuwait, Lebanon, Morocco, Oman, Qatar, Southern Yemen, Syria and the Yemen Arab Republic.

All other passport holders require visas obtainable from Egyptian embassies and consulates abroad.

All persons entering Egypt must have the equivalent of £100 sterling in their possession, and passports must be valid for at least 6 months after the proposed date of departure from Egypt.

Business travellers require a supporting letter from their firm, giving details of the business to be undertaken and confirming their financial responsibility.

All visitors must register with the Police or the Ministry of Interior within 1 week of arrival. This can be arranged through hotels or travel agents.

Health Regulations
Smallpox vaccination certificates are required. Visitors from infected areas must have cholera and yellow fever inoculation certificates. TAB (typhoid and paratyphoid) injections are recommended.

Customs
Currency: Egyptian currency may not be taken into or out of the country. Any amount of foreign currency or travellers' cheques may be imported, but the amount taken out should not exceed the amount brought in. Currency declaration forms should be completed with care on arrival and surrendered on departure.

Duty-free articles: Personal effects including cameras, binoculars, jewellery – these must be declared, however. Reasonable quantities of tobacco, wines, spirits and perfumes for personal use. Samples (sent by mail or otherwise) may be brought in, provided their value does not exceed £E40 or if they are not in a saleable condition. Duty paid on samples with a value of £E40 or more is refundable if the samples are re-exported within one year.

Prohibited articles: Narcotics, drugs, cotton.

PRACTICAL INFORMATION FOR THE VISITOR

1. Currency
Monetary Unit – Egyptian pound (£E), divided into 100 piastres (PT) and 1,000 milliemes (mms).
Notes – 1, 5, 10 Egyptian pounds; 5, 10, 25, 50 piastres.
Coins – ½, 1, 2, 5, 10 piastres.

Travellers' cheques may be exchanged through authorised banks and their representatives, and transactions should be recorded on the currency declaration form.
Credit cards are not in general use, but American Express and Diners Club are accepted in the larger hotels, restaurants and shops.

Banking Hours
0830–1230 daily, except Friday and Sunday.
1000–1200 Sunday.

The *Central Bank of Egypt*, 31 Sharia Kasr el Nil, Cairo, ☎ 786681, is the government bank.

Domestic Commercial Banks in Cairo
Arab African Bank, 44 Abdel Khalek Sarwat Street, ☎ 916744.
Arab International Bank, 35 Abdel Khalek Sarwat Street, ☎ 919252, 916120.
Bank of Alexandria, 49 Sharia Kasr el Nil, ☎ 913882, 918245.
Bank Misr, 151 Sharia Mohammed Bey Farid, ☎ 71547, 71753.
Banque du Caire, 22 Sharia Adly Pasha.
National Bank of Egypt, 24 Sharia Sherif, ☎ 75434, 41169, 55563.

These banks have offices in Cairo, Alexandria and other main towns; also at Cairo airport and in major hotels.

International Banks with Offices in Egypt
Bank of America, 15 Brazil Street, Zamalek, P.O. Box 2406, Cairo, ☎ 816722, 813960.
Cairo Barclays International Bank, 12 Midan el Sheikh Youssef, P.O. Box 2335, Garden City, Cairo, ☎ 22195, 27950.
Bank of Credit and Commerce, 1 Ahmed Orabi Street, Manshia Square, Cairo; 9 Talaat Harb Street, Alexandria.
Chase National Bank (Egypt), 12 El Birgas Street, P.O. Box 2430, Garden City, Cairo, ☎ 25263.
American Express International Banking Corporation, 23 Gamal Eldin Aboul, Mahassen Street, Garden City, Cairo, ☎ 25360/26908.
Midland Bank Ltd (Group Representative Office), 3 Ahmed Nessim Street, Giza, Cairo, ☎ 987332.

2. Electricity Supply
220v AC 50Hz.
Plugs: 2-pin round.

3. Weights and Measures
The metric system, together with local systems, is in use.

4. Media
Egypt has a sophisticated TV and radio network, with an extensive foreign radio service broadcasting in some 35 languages (mainly European and African).

Newspapers and Journals
Over 400 newspapers and periodicals are published in Cairo and Alexandria, making Egypt the leading publisher in the Arab world.

Leading dailies are *Al-Ahram* (circulation 780,000) and *Al-Akhbar* (circulation 500,000).

Weekly newspapers include *Akhbar al-Yom* (circulation 1,200,000) and *Asher Sa'a* (circulation 180,000).

The *Egyptian Gazette* is a weekly publication in English.

The *Egyptian Chamber of Commerce Bulletin* and the *Federation of Egyptian Industries Monthly Bulletin* are read in business and industrial circles and represent the trade press as such.

5. Medical Care
In the larger cities, hospitals and clinics offer good medical care. Hospitals in Cairo include:

Anglo-American ☎ 806163/5.
Italian ☎ 821641.

When swimming, keep to pools or the sea to avoid the risk of bilharzia. It is advisable to take supplies of fly and insect repellent as well as medication for gastro-intestinal disorders.

Drinking water in Cairo and Alexandria is safe, but elsewhere bottled water is recommended. Visitors should be cautious about unwashed fruit and vegetables outside of the better hotels and restaurants.

6. Telephone, Telex and Postal Services
International telephone, cable and telegraph services are available. Delays are frequent when telephoning within Egypt from one town to another. The Hilton and Sheraton Hotels in Cairo have public telex facilities open to residents only.

Telephone directories list Egyptians and Egyptian firms under the first letter of the first name. Only non-Egyptians are listed under the first letter of the last name.

Telephone Services in Cairo
Operator ☎ 10.
International calls ☎ 120.
Police ☎ 912644.

Post offices are open daily, except Friday. The Central Post Office, Alaba Square, Cairo offers a 24-hour service.

7. Public Holidays

1 January	New Year's Day
8 March	Syrian Revolution Day
18 June	Evacuation Day
23 July	Anniversary of the Revolution
1 September	Libyan Revolution Day
6 October	Armed Forces Day
24 October	Popular Resistance Day
23 December	Victory Day

The following movable Muslim holidays are also observed: *Mouled, Eid el Fitr, Kurban Bairan (Eid el Adha)* and *El Hijra*.

Christian festivals are observed by Christian businesses in Egypt. Banks are closed on January 1 and on *Coptic Christmas, Coptic Palm Sunday* and *Coptic Easter*.

8. Time
GMT + 2.

9. Internal Transport
Air
Egypt Air operates flights between major cities: Cairo – Alexandria – 45 minutes; Cairo – Luxor – 80 minutes; Cairo – Aswan – 1 hour 45 minutes. For further information, ☎ Cairo 976477, 900554.

Airline Offices in Cairo
Aeroflot ☎ 42132.
Air France ☎ 971848.
Air India ☎ 31877.
British Airways ☎ 971447.
Egypt Air ☎ 985408.
JAL ☎ 817621.

KLM	☎ 971550.
Lufthansa	☎ 28322.
PIA	☎ 49630.
Pan Am	☎ 970444.
Qantas	☎ 971447.
Sabena	☎ 43525.
SAS	☎ 974588/7.
Swissair	☎ 976195.
TWA	☎ 979770.

Rail
Reliable train services operate from Cairo to Luxor, Aswan, Alexandria, Port Said, Suez and other towns. For further information, ☎ Cairo 58458.

Road
Cars may be rented from larger hotels and through Avis. An International Driving Licence is required.
Avis Car Rental
Cairo ☎ 28698;
☎ 811811 (Hilton Hotel);
☎ 963270 (Airport).

Taxis are available in all main towns at a moderate cost. Out-of-town and long-distance trips can be arranged and fares should be negotiated in advance. It may be necessary to enlist the help of hotel staff for this, since few taxi-drivers speak English.

10. Tipping
It is usual to tip for any kind of service in Egypt.
Taxis – 10%.

Porters – 5 piastres per bag.

Hotels/restaurants – 10%–12%.

11. Social Customs
Egypt is one of the more liberal Arab states with few restrictions placed on women. There is no strict segregation of the sexes, and it is legal to drink alcohol.

USEFUL ADDRESSES (GENERAL)

Cairo
Australian Embassy: 1097 Corniche el Nil, Garden City, ☎ 28190, 28663.

British Embassy: Ahmed Raghal Street, Garden City, ☎ 20850/9.

Canadian Embassy: 6 Mohammed Fahmi El-Sayed Street, Garden City, ☎ 23110.

Dutch Embassy: 18 Hassan Sabri Street, Zamelek, ☎ 802024.

French Embassy: 29 El-Giza Street, ☎ 848833.

Japanese Embassy: 14 Ibrahim Naguib Street, Garden City, P.O. Box 281, ☎ 33962.

Swiss Embassy: 10 Abdel Khalek Sariot, P.O. Box 633, ☎ 97871/2.

US Embassy: 5 Latin America Street, Garden City, P.O. Box 10, ☎ 28219.

West German Embassy: 20 Boulos Pacha Hanna Street, Dokki, ☎ 806015/7.

American Express: 15 Kasr el Nil Street, P.O. Box 2160, ☎ 970138/970042.

Thomas Cook Overseas Ltd: 4 Champollion Street, P.O. Box 165, ☎ 46392/5 – also Bureau de Change at Cairo Airport.

Ministry of Information and Culture: ☎ 23529.

Ministry of Tourism: 5 Adly Street, ☎ 923000, 979394.

Wagons-Lits Tourisme: Shepheard's Hotel, Kasr el Ali Street, ☎ 31538.

Alexandria

French Consulate: 2 Place Ahmed-Orabi, P.O. Box 474.

Swiss Consulate: 8 Rue Moukhtar Abdel Halim Khalaf Saba Pacha, P.O. Box 1934, ☎ (03) 50726.

US Consulate-General: 110 Avenue Horreya, ☎ 25306, 25607.

West German Consulate: 14 Rue des Pharaons, ☎ 31587.

Egyptian Tourist Office: Saad Zaghloul Square, Ramleh Station, ☎ 25985.

Thomas Cook Overseas Ltd: 15 Midan Saad Zaghloul, P.O. Box 185, ☎ 27830.

BUSINESS INFORMATION

Despite Egypt's 'open door' economic policy which was introduced in 1974, foreign firms have been slow to invest in Egypt, largely due to problems surrounding foreign exchange. Investments were converted at the wholly unrealistic official exchange rate, making them an unattractive proposition. The introduction of a parallel foreign exchange market together with a number of fiscal reforms have gradually led to an upward trend in investment, although it still remains insufficient for Egyptian needs.

The Egyptian market remains an attractive one, particularly for American exporters. However, a further liberalisation in the financial and economic structure may be necessary before foreign investors are fully convinced of the viability of wide-scale investment.

Individuals may act as agents for foreign firms provided their remuneration is in the form of a fee or salary, and not on a commission basis.

Import and Exchange Control Regulations

Exchange control is carried out through authorised banks under the direction of the Central Exchange Control.

Certain goods are liable to a number of taxes in addition to customs duty, and may attract excise duty, e.g., alcoholic drinks, fuel oil, sugar, coffee.

Major industries and commercial enterprises are state-controlled, and importing is generally in the hands of state trading companies. Import licences are not usually required for smaller shipments.

Free storage for a period of 8 days is granted at all ports.

Business Hours
Government Offices
0800–1400 Saturday to Thursday

Business Houses
0830–1330
1630–1900 Saturday to Thursday

Business Events

An International Book Fair, International Trade Fair and International Festival of Egyptian Fashion are all held annually in Cairo.

BUSINESS SERVICES

Translation
Middle East Observer, 8 Chawarby Street, Cairo.
Haddad Bureau de Traduction et Copie, 39 Sharia Talaat Harb, Cairo.
International Business Associates, 1079 Corniche el Nil, Garden City, Cairo – also secretarial services.
Bureau Technique de Traduction Juridique, Commercial et Littéraire, 28 Sharia Sesostris, Alexandria.

USEFUL ADDRESSES (BUSINESS)

Cairo
Cairo Chamber of Commerce, 4 Midan al-Falaki Street, Bab El-Louk.

Camera di Commercio Italiana per l'Egitto, 33 Sharia Abdel-Khalek Sarwat, P.O. Box 19.

The Federation of Egyptian Industries, 26 Sharia Sherif Pasha.

German-Arab Chamber of Commerce, 2 Sharia Sherif Pasha.

Alexandria
Alexandria Chamber of Commerce, General Post Office.

Egyptian Chamber of Commerce, Al-Ghorfa Eltegareia Street.

MAJOR CITIES AND TOWNS

Cairo
Stretching out along the banks of the Nile, Cairo offers an unusual combination of traditional and modern architecture, with ancient mosques and multi-storey office blocks crowding the city. The city has many fine museums displaying important collections of early Christian, Islamic and Oriental art. Chief among them is the Egyptian Museum in Tahrir Square, containing an extensive collection of Egyptological findings. The Ibn Tulun Mosque can be mounted by an outside staircase and offers a good view of the city, as does the 180m-high tower of Cairo at Gezira.

By far the most famous of all Egypt's offerings from the past are the Pyramids at Giza, together with the many tombs and the Sphinx. These are, in fact, only a small part of a whole series of ancient monuments stretching across the desert over a distance of about 70km/43 miles. From here one can view the entire Nile Valley from west to east. Many of the better hotels are at Giza, 12km/7 miles from the centre of Cairo.

Hotels
The Egyptian Tourist Board grades hotels from 5 star to 1 star.

CAIRO SHERATON, Galae Square, P.O. Box 11, Giza, ☎ 983000.
A modern 5-star de luxe hotel near the Pyramids and Sphinx monument.

Rooms: 369 ♪, ⌂, ⌀, ☖.
Facilities: Restaurants and nightclub, 3 bars. Gambling casino. Swimming. Shopping arcade.
Services: TC, FC, ✉ Amex, Bankamericard, Carte Blanche, Diners Club, Eurocard. S, ♂.
6 conference rooms – max. capacity 400.

EGYPT

MENA HOUSE OBEROI, Pyramids Street, Giza, ☎ 855444.
Traditional 5-star hotel with extensive grounds, 13km/8 miles from city centre.
Rooms: 510 ♒, ⬚, ⬚, ⬚, ⬚, ⬚, ⬚.
Facilities: Restaurant, 24-hr coffee shop, bars. Nightclub. 18-hole golf course, swimming, tennis and riding.
Services: TC, FC. ▤ Amex, Diners Club, Eurocard. Dr. on call. ⬚, ⬚.
Conference room – max. capacity 280.

MERIDIEN LE CAIRE, Corniche el Nil Street, P.O. Box 2288, Rodah, ☎ 845444.
Modern 5-star hotel in city centre.
Rooms: 300 ♒, ⬚, ⬚, ⬚, ⬚, ⬚, ⬚.
Facilities: Oriental and French restaurants, bars. Nightclub. Sauna and swimming.
Services: TC, FC. ▤ Access, Amex, Diners Club, Eurocard, Master Charge. Dr. on call. ⬚.
Conference room – max. capacity 650.

NILE HILTON, Tahrir Square, ☎ 811811/815815.
Modern 5-star hotel overlooking Nile, near city centre.
Rooms: 400 ♒, ⬚, ⬚, ⬚, ⬚, ⬚.
Facilities: 5 restaurants, bars. Nightclub, casino. Shops, hairdressers. Health club, tennis, sauna, swimming.
Services: TC, FC. ▤ Access, Amex, Carte Blanche, Diners Club, Eurocard, Master Charge. Dr. on call. ⬚, ⬚.
Conference room – max. capacity 800.

SHEPHEARD'S, Corniche el Nil Street, Garden City, ☎ 33800.
Rooms: 290 ♒, ⬚, ⬚.
Facilities: Restaurant, banquet hall, 2 bars. Casino. Golf, tennis, swimming at Gezira Sporting Club (5 minutes away) by arrangement.
Services: TC, FC, ⬚, ⬚.

Restaurants

Apart from the hotel restaurants, others include:

Local cuisine: *Versailles*, 30 Mohammed Sakeb Street; *Sofar*, 21 Adly Street, ☎ 54360 – Lebanese; *Abu Shakra*, Kasr el-Aini Street, ☎ 21521; *El-Shimy*, Talaat Harb Street, ☎ 49978; *El-Hatti*, 1 Midan Halim, ☎ 56055.

European and other cuisine: *Estoril*, 12 Talaat Harb Street, ☎ 72009; *Le Grillon*, 8 Kasr el Nil Street, ☎ 41114; *Löwenbrau/München*, 26–31 July Street, ☎ 59877 – German; *Fu Ching*, 39 Talaat Harb Street – Chinese.

Nightclubs

The Saddle Disco, Mena House Hotel, ☎ 855444; *Alhambra*, Cairo Sheraton, ☎ 983000; *Bateau Omar Khayyam*, ☎ 808553; *Sahara City*, beyond the Pyramids, ☎ 850673.

Entertainment

Many of the larger hotels have their own nightclubs, with colourful floor shows and displays of oriental dancing. The Sheraton Hotel has a gambling casino. A *son et lumière* display can be seen at the Pyramids (☎ 852880 for details) and at the Citadel (☎ 53260).

Sporting facilities include swimming, tennis, golf, horse riding, etc. Temporary membership is available from many clubs in the area.

Shopping

Best buys: jewellery, copper and ivory goods, inlaid mother-of-pearl work.

Khan el Khalili is the main shopping area. Some genuine antiquities are for sale, but beware of modern reproductions.

Alexandria

Alexandria is Egypt's principal port and is well known for its beaches, making it a popular holiday resort for many Egyptians. The city was once an important centre of worship for Christians, and the Graeco-Roman Museum and ruins of the Serapium

temple offer a glimpse into bygone ages. The chief Islamic monument – the mosque of Abu al-Abbas al-Mursi – is also worth a visit.
Alexandria airport is 8km/5 miles from the city centre.

Hotels

CECIL, 16 Midan Saad Zaghloul. ☎ 807532. Traditional moderate 1st-class 4-star hotel on seafront, within easy walking distance of city centre.
Rooms: 85 ♪.
Facilities: Restaurant, American bar. Library, games room. Hairdresser. Ballroom.

PALESTINE, (5-star), Montazah Palace. ☎ 66799.
Rooms: 234 ♪, ⚫, ☐, ♆.
Facilities: Restaurant, bar. Garden nightclub and casino. Private beach, sailing and water skiing. Car-hire service.
Services: TC, FC. Credit cards not accepted.

SAN STEPHANO (4-star), El-Geish Avenue, ☎ 63580.

Rooms: 118.
Facilities: Restaurant, cafeteria. Nightclub. Garden, barbecues, solarium. Conference room.

Restaurants

Zafarian, Abu Kir – seafood; *Santa Lucia*, 40 Safeya Zaghloul Street – European; *Elite*, Safeya Zaghloul Street – European; *Pam Pam*, 23 Safeya Zaghloul Street.

Entertainment

Temporary membership is available at several of the town's sporting clubs, offering golf, horse racing, tennis and squash. Alexandria also has yachting, rowing and automobile clubs offering temporary membership to visitors.

Aswan

An attractive town, but temperatures in summer can rise to 40°C/104°F and the intense heat may cause great discomfort to the unacclimatised visitor.
Aswan airport is 18km/11 miles from the town centre.

Hotels

ASWAN OBEROI, Elephantine Island, ☎ 3455.
Deluxe, 5-star hotel built in a picturesque location on an island overlooking the temples of Rameses II and Queen Nefertiti. (New 150-room extension was due to be completed in 1979.)
Rooms: 150 ♪, ⚫, ☐, ♆, △, ☎.
Facilities: Restaurant, bar. Nightclub. Tennis, sauna, swimming, health-club facilities.
Services: TC, FC. ✉ Amex, Diners Club. Dr. on call. S, ♂.

Conference room – max. capacity 150.

CATARACT HOTELS, Abtal el Tahrir Street, ☎ 2233/3222.
Adjacent hotels, one traditional and one modern, in quiet central location near the Nile.
Rooms: 288 ♪, ♆.
Facilities: Restaurant, bars. Dancing. Swimming, boating, tennis.
Services: TC, FC. ✉ Amex, Bankamericard, Diners Club.
Conference facilities.

EQUATORIAL GUINEA
Republic of Equatorial Guinea

Geography	*126*
The Economy	*128*
How to Get There	*128*
Entry Regulations	*128*
Practical Information for the Visitor	*129*
Useful Addresses (General)	*130*
Business Information	*130*
Business Services	*130*
Malabo	*130*

Size: 28,051 sq.km/10,830 sq.miles.

Population: 330,000 (1976 est.).

Distribution: 15% urban.

Density: 11 persons per sq.km/30 per sq.mile.

Population Growth Rate: N.A.

Ethnic Composition: The dominant racial group on the mainland are the Fang, a Bantu people who greatly outnumber the coastal Bantu tribes, the Kombe, Balengue and Bujeba. The Fang are now thought also to outnumber the Bubi, formerly the dominant group on the island of Fernando Po.

Capital: Malabo Pop. 37,000 (1973 est.).

Major Town: Bata Pop. 27,000 (1973 est.).

Language: Spanish is the official language.

Religion: It is estimated that 80% are Roman Catholic; the remainder follow traditional beliefs. In June 1978 all churches were closed and religious practices forbidden. It is not known whether religious freedom has been restored with the change of Government.

Government: In August 1979 Francisco Macias Ngeuma Biyogo was ousted in a coup after 7 years as Life President. The country is now governed by a military junta.

GEOGRAPHY

The island of Fernando Po (formerly renamed Macias Nguema) off the coast of Cameroon and the mainland province of Rio Muni make up Equatorial Guinea, along with several smaller islands. Rio Muni is a jungle enclave with a coastal plain rising to inland mountains. Fernando Po is formed from 3 extinct volcanoes, with the southern area of the island rugged and inaccessible.

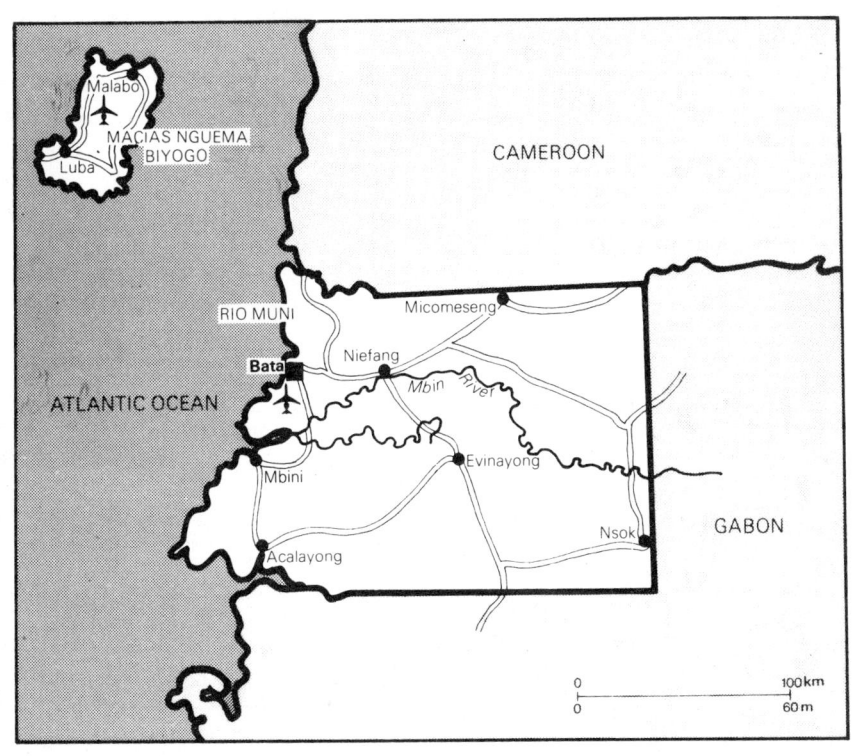

Climate
The country has an equatorial climate with very heavy rainfall. The dry season occurs from January to March. There is a high humidity and temperature throughout the year, with the average temperature in Malabo being 28°C/77°F. Bata is somewhat cooler and drier than Malabo.

Agriculture
Cocoa is Equatorial Guinea's principal export, grown mainly on large plantations on Fernando Po. In 1970 nationalisation of these plantations led to the exodus of the Spanish owners and their Nigerian workers, and both quality and quantity of output declined dramatically in the following decade. The other important agricultural exports are coffee and timber. Coffee production suffered the same fate as cocoa during the 1970s. Timber exports from Rio Muni slumped less severely, with one Swiss/French company working in association with the Government. No current information is available, but it is known that the Nigerian plantation workers began returning to Fernando Po even before the overthrow of the previous Government.

Main Crops: cocoa, coffee, bananas, cassava, palm oil, sweet potatoes.

Mineral Resources: possible offshore oil.

THE ECONOMY

Few reliable statistics have been released on the Equatorial Guinea economy since 1968, but Spain provides most of the country's imports and takes over 90% of its exports.

Equatorial Guinea is almost totally reliant on the agricultural sector, what little industry there is being some local processing of cocoa and coffee. With an inadequate transport and marketing infrastructure, and an uneducated work force, the economy ran steadily downhill during the 1970s: money to buy imports, mainly foodstuffs, ran out, leading to serious shortages, widespread unrest and a large-scale exodus of workers.

Before its overthrow, the former Government was receiving aid from Cuba and in 1978 signed trade agreements with Romania. With the change of Government, Spain has re-established diplomatic contact, and it is expected that the economic breakdown will start to be reversed with the help of foreign aid.

Major Industries: cocoa and coffee processing.

Main Commodities Traded: Imports – food. Exports – cocoa, coffee, timber.

International Affiliations: UN, IBRD, OAU, ACP, ADB.

HOW TO GET THERE

Air
Iberia operates a weekly flight from Madrid to Malabo via Lagos (Nigeria); Aeroflot connects Moscow with Malabo three times a week; Air Cameroon flies regularly between Douala (Cameroon), Malabo and Bata; Transgabon flies between Libreville (Gabon) and Bata.

Flying time from Madrid to Malabo: 5 hrs 50 mins.

There is an airport tax of 100 ekuele on departure.

ENTRY REGULATIONS

Visas
All visitors require visas which may be obtained from diplomatic missions abroad. The principal embassy overseas is *Embajada Republica Guinea Ecuatorial*, Valverde 13, Madrid, Spain. It is advisable to apply well in advance.

Health Regulations
International Certificates of Vaccination against smallpox and cholera are required, and against yellow fever if arriving from an infected area.

Customs
Duty-free articles: 200 cigarettes or 50 cigars or 250 g tobacco. 1 litre of wine and 1 litre of spirits.

PRACTICAL INFORMATION FOR THE VISITOR

1. Currency
Monetary Unit – ekuele, divided into 100 céntimos.
Notes – 1, 5, 25, 50, 100, 500, 1,000 ekuele.
Coins – 5, 10, 50 céntimos; 1, 2½, 5, 25, 50, 100 ekuele.

Travellers' cheques, CFA francs and Spanish pesetas are reported to be negotiable at the larger hotels and banks.

Banking Hours
0900 – 1200 Monday to Friday

The principal bank is *Banco Popular de Guinea Ecuatorial*, which has branches in Malabo and Bata.

2. Electricity Supply
220v AC 50Hz.

3. Weights and Measures
The metric system is in use.

4. Media
There is an irregularly published newspaper, *Unidad de la Guinea Ecuatorial*.
  The 2 Government-operated radio stations, Radio Ecuatorial in Bata and Radio Malabo on Fernando Po, are reported to broadcast intermittently. In addition, a new radio station, The Revolutionary Voice of the National United Workers' Party, was opened in Bata in 1977. A television service has been established in Malabo.

5. Medical Care
Water should be boiled or filtered before being drunk. Anti-malarial precautions must be taken.

6. Telephone, Telex and Postal Services
Visitors are advised to post letters airmail at Douala or Libreville on their return from Equatorial Guinea.

7. Public Holidays
1 January	*New Year's Day*
5 March	*National Day*
1 May	*Labour Day*
25 May	*OAU Day*
7 July	*National Day*
1 November	*All Saints Day*
10 December	*Human Rights Day*
25 December	*Christmas Day*

8. Time
GMT +1.

9. Internal Transport

Air
Lineas Aéreas Ecuatorial (LAGE) operates scheduled flights between Malabo and Bata.
  Malabo airport is 7km/4 miles from the centre of town.
  Flying time between Malabo and Bata is 50 minutes.

Airline Offices in Malabo
LAGE, Avenida Independencia S/N.
Iberia, ☎ 297, 305.

Sea
Fishing boats and small ships occasionally carry passengers between Malabo and Bata.

Road
The only tarred road is around Malabo and between Bata and Rio Benito (Mbini). Other roads have dirt surfaces which are washed out in heavy rain. There is very little traffic, and taxis run only intermittently because of fuel shortages.

USEFUL ADDRESSES (GENERAL)

French Embassy: 13 Calle de Argelia,
P.O.B. 326, Malabo, ☎ 380.

BUSINESS INFORMATION

Before August 1979 foreign firms wishing to operate in Equatorial Guinea had to negotiate special agreements with the former Government. As of mid-1980, no information was yet available on the new Government's policies. Business persons wishing to visit the country are advised to contact either the embassy in Madrid (Embajada Republica Guinea Ecuatorial, Valverde 13, Madrid) or the Spanish Ministry of Foreign Affairs (Oficina Información Diplomática, Ministerio de Asuntos Exteriores, Plaza de la Provincia 1, Madrid 12).

Business Hours
0800 – 1230
1600 – 1830 Monday to Friday
0900 – 1400 Saturday

BUSINESS SERVICES

Shipping
The *Compañía Transmediterránea* sails from Barcelona or Bilbao on a monthly basis and serves Malabo, Luba and Bata.

MAJOR CITY

Malabo
Malabo (formerly Santa Isabel) is situated on Fernando Po. The small town lies on a perfect natural harbour with pleasant beaches and mountain slopes near by. With its Spanish colonial architecture, Malabo was quite attractive, but it has been severely depopulated and run-down during Macias Nguema's 11-year dictatorship.

Hotels
The BAHIA is the only hotel in Malabo known to be open at present.

ETHIOPIA
Ethiopia

Geography	*132*
The Economy	*133*
How to Get There	*134*
Entry Regulations	*134*
Practical Information for the Visitor	*135*
Useful Addresses (General)	*138*
Business Information	*138*
Business Services	*139*
Useful Addresses (Business)	*139*
Addis Ababa	*139*
Asmara	*141*

Size: 1,221,900 sq.km/471,776 sq.miles.

Population: 29.71 million (1978 est.)

Distribution: 11.7% in urban areas.

Density: 23 persons per sq.km/60 per sq.mile.

Population Growth Rate: 2.6% p.a.

Ethnic Composition: The population is mainly composed of peoples of Semitic and Hamitic origin with large numbers of mixed and Negroid groups. The European community, mostly Italian, has decreased since 1974. Minorities include Arabs, Indians, Armenians, Greeks.

Capital: Addis Ababa Pop. 1,327,000.

Major Cities/Towns: Asmara Pop. 317,000; Dire Dawa Pop. 80,890; Harar Pop. 56,360; Dessie Pop. 57,420.

Language: Amharic is the official language and English the second official language, although Italian and French are still widely spoken. Other languages include Galligna, Tigrigna and Ge'ez.

Religion: About 40% are Muslim and 40% Coptic Christians, belonging to the dominant Ethiopian Orthodox Union Church. There are also Animist and Jewish (Falasha) minorities.

Government: Ethiopia has been ruled by a military government since Emperor Haile Selassie was deposed in 1974. The Provisional Military Administrative Council (PMAC), known as the Dergue, is the ruling body which controls all power. The Constitution was abolished by military decree in 1974. Plans announced in 1970 for the promulgation of a new constitution have not yet materialised.

The ban on political parties, imposed by the military government, was lifted in 1976. Since then a number of opposition parties have been suspended and forced to operate underground.

Abyot Seded, a pro-Government Marxist-Leninist party, is now Ethiopia's main political party. The principal opposition parties are Eech-At (suspended, 1978); the Ethiopian Democratic Union and the Ethiopian People's Revolutionary Party (EPRP).

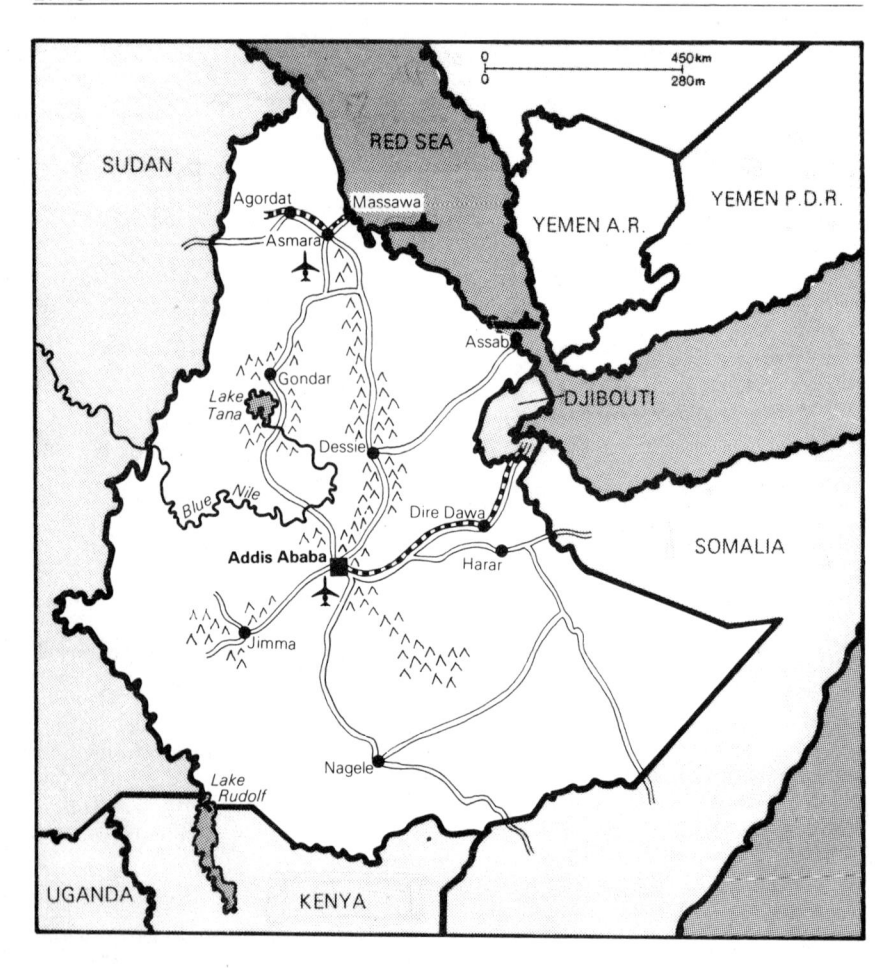

2 main separatist groups are engaged in armed conflict with the Government: the Eritrean Liberation Front and the Eritrean People's Liberation Front.

GEOGRAPHY

The central part consists of a vast, high plateau divided by the rivers of the Blue Nile system. The southern part is bisected by the great Rift Valley which crosses East Africa. The western region consists of lowlands and there is a plains region to the south-east. Ethiopia also has some areas of hot deserts.

Climate
Ethiopia lies within the tropics but climatic conditions vary throughout the country, according to altitude. The climate of the plateau and highlands is temperate, with

average maximum temperatures in Addis Ababa ranging from 20°c/68°F and 26°c/79°F and average minimum temperatures from 6°c/43°F to 11°c/52°F. The main rainfall occurs between July and September. The climate of the lowlands surrounding the plateau region is mainly hot and very dry.

Agriculture

The Ethiopian economy is agricultural and pastoral with about 81% of the population engaged in farming. Agriculture contributes more than 50% of the GDP and produces over 90% of all exports.

The subsistence sector of agriculture provides two-thirds of all agricultural production. The commercial sector remains small and badly neglected by agricultural development planners. Following the nationalisation of all agricultural land in 1975, farming conditions changed dramatically for the tenant-peasants in the south of the country, but the reform had little impact in Northern Ethiopia. Rural backwardness is still one of Ethiopia's major social problems, together with low agricultural productivity due to inefficient, traditional methods and lack of mechanisation.

Coffee is the major agricultural export; sugar, cotton, pulses and oil seeds are also exported. Teff is the most widely grown local crop for local consumption, followed by barley, wheat, maize and sorghum.

Main Crops: coffee, cotton, maize, sugar, teff, wheat, sorghum, oilseeds, pulses, vegetables and fruit.

Mineral Resources: gold, platinum, salt, iron ore, potash, copper and small deposits of other minerals.

THE ECONOMY

Gross National Product (1977): US$3.22 billion.

Per Capita Income (1977): US$110.

Gross Domestic Product (1975–6): 6.0 billion birr.

Foreign Trade (1978): Total Imports – US$439.9 million. Total Exports – US$308.4 million.

Main Trading Partners: Imports – Saudi Arabia, Japan, USA, Italy, West Germany, UK. Exports – USA, Saudi Arabia, Djibouti, Egypt, Japan, West Germany, Italy.

The Ethiopian economy was nationalised in 1974. Development in the agricultural sector has been slow and underexploited, although considerable progress has been made towards diversification. Collection and distribution of agricultural produce have improved under a project financed by the World Bank.

Industry was nationalised at the beginning of 1975, together with financial institutions and insurance companies. Official Government policy envisages a mixed economy with State ownership of industry and resources, while services, small-scale manufacturing and commercial enterprises would belong to the private sector.

Industry at present is largely confined to manufacturing for the domestic market and processing agricultural produce. The food industry accounts for about 40% of total industrial output.

Foreign aid and loans are being used to develop industry, agriculture, education, social services and defence. The lack of adequate communications and trained personnel are severe hindrances to development. The war effort in Eritrea and the Ogaden has seriously depleted Ethiopia's financial reserves, and it is likely to be some time before the economy fully recovers.

Major Industries: food processing, textiles, tobacco, footwear, building materials.

Main Commodities Traded: Imports – machinery and transport equipment, manufactured goods, chemicals, petroleum products, foodstuffs. Exports – coffee, hides and skins, vegetables, oil seeds, pulses, fruit.

International Affiliations: UN, IBRD, OAU, ACP, ADB.

HOW TO GET THERE

Air

Ethiopia has 2 international airports: Bole, which is 8km/5 miles from Addis Ababa; and Yohannes IV, which is 9½km/6 miles from Asmara.

Ethiopian Airlines operate flights to Addis Ababa and/or Asmara from Accra, Athens, Abu Dhabi, Bahrain, Bombay, Cairo, Dar es Salaam, Djibouti, Douala, Entebbe, Frankfurt, Jeddah, Khartoum, Kigali, Kinshasa, Lagos, London, Nairobi, Paris, Rome, Shanghai, Sana'a and the Seychelles.

Alitalia, Air France, Air India, British Airways, Egypt Air, Lufthansa and Saudi Arabian Airlines also fly to Ethiopia.

There are 5 direct flights a week between London and Addis Ababa; 2 of these call at Asmara.

Flying times to Addis Ababa; from London, 9 hours; from New York, 18 hours.

On departure, all passengers for destinations outside Ethiopia must pay an airport tax of 3 birr.

Airline transport and taxis are available at both airports for the journey to the city centres.

ENTRY REGULATIONS

Visas

Visas are required by nationals of all countries and should be obtained from Ethiopian diplomatic missions abroad.

Visa applications should be supported by a letter (usually from a travel agent or airline) confirming that the applicant has outward or return tickets and, for business travellers, a letter from the applicant's firm giving full details of the business to be undertaken and confirming financial responsibility for the applicant.

Business visas are usually valid only for 30 days for a stay of the same length, which can be extended in Addis Ababa for a fee of 5 birr.

Visitors staying more than 30 days must obtain an Exit Visa and Alien's Registration Card from the Immigration Office in Addis Ababa. 2 passport photographs are needed for the Registration Card. (These documents cost 10 birr each.) Exit Visas are issued automatically, free of charge, for visitors staying less than 30 days.

Business visitors should ensure that the validity of their passport extends for at least 3 months from the date the visa applications is made.

Entry or transit visas are not normally granted to nationals of Iraq or Syria, nor to white nationals of Zimbabwe-Rhodesia or South Africa.

Health Regulations

All persons entering and leaving must be in possession of valid International Certificates of Vaccination against smallpox and yellow fever. Vaccinations and immunisation against typhoid, typhus, tetanus and cholera are also advisable.

Customs

Currency: There is no limit to the amount of foreign currency and travellers' cheques which may be taken into Ethiopia, but this must all be declared on arrival and the amount taken out of Ethiopia must not exceed the amount originally imported.

There is a limit of 150 birr on the amount of local currency which may be imported and exported, unless permission from the National Bank is given to exceed this amount.

Duty-free articles: Personal effects – a declaration form must be completed for most valuables. One litre of spirits. 100 cigarettes, 50 cigars or 250g of tobacco.

PRACTICAL INFORMATION FOR THE VISITOR

1. Currency

Monetary Unit – birr, divided into 100 cents.
Notes – 1, 5, 10, 50, 100 birr.
Coins – 1, 5, 10, 25, 50 cents.

Foreign currency can only be changed at branches of the National Bank of Ethiopia. Travellers' cheques can be cashed at any bank, main hotel or large shop.

Banking Hours
0830–1230
1430–1730 Monday to Friday
0830–1230 Saturday

The *National Bank of Ethiopia* is the central bank responsible for exchange control and monetary policy in general. Banks in Ethiopia were nationalised in 1975.

Principal Commercial Banks
Commercial Bank of Ethiopia, National Theatre Square, P.O. Box 255, Addis Ababa, ☎ 447420/9; and Adowa Avenue, P.O. Box 219, Asmara, ☎ 11844.

Addis Bank, Ras Desta Damtew Avenue, P.O. Box 751, Addis Ababa, ☎ 448285.

2. Electricity Supply

220v throughout Ethiopia, except in Eritrea, where the lighting supply is 127v and the power is 220v.
Plugs: 2-pin continental.

3. Weights and Measures

The metric system is in general use, but some local measures still prevail.
1 *frazoula* = 37½ lb = 17 kilos.
1 *gasha* = 98 acres = 40 hectares.

4. Media

The Ethiopian Television Service transmits programmes in Amharic and English in the Addis Ababa area only, although plans exist to extend the service to Asmara and Dessie. Radio Ethiopia provides a commercial broadcasting

ETHIOPIA

service with transmissions in Amharic, English, Arabic, Somali and other languages.

Newspapers and Journals
Addis Ababa
Addis Zemen (Amharic) and *Ethiopian Herald* (English) – daily; *Ethiopia Today/Y'Zareitu Ethiopia* – weekly.

Asmara
Al-Wahda (Arabic) and *Hebret* (Tigrinya and Arabic) – daily; *Ethiopia* (Amharic), weekly.

The *Trade and Development Bulletin*, published monthly by the Eritrea Chamber of Commerce, Industry, Agriculture and Handicraft in Asmara, carries commercial advertising. *Negadras* is published fortnightly by the Chamber of Commerce in Addis Ababa.

5. Medical Care
Malaria is prevalent in most parts of Ethiopia, but not in Addis Ababa and Asmara. It is advisable to take antimalarial prophylactics if journeying out of either of these places.

Only boiled water or bottled mineral water should be drunk to avoid any stomach upset. Raw fruits and vegetables should be carefully washed.

The high altitude of Addis Ababa and Asmara (around 1,400m/8,000ft above sea level) can cause strain on the heart and nervous system. It is advisable to avoid undue exertion during the first few days of any stay, and to eat and drink in moderation. Visitors with a history of heart or lung complaints or high blood pressure should consult their doctor before travelling to Ethiopia.

Care should also be taken to avoid contact with stray dogs or cats, as rabies is prevalent.

6. Telephone, Telex and Postal Services
Telephone links are available from both Addis Ababa and Asmara to the principal countries of Europe, Khartoum, the People's Democratic Republic of Yemen and neighbouring African countries.

A public telex facility is available at the Head Office of the Addis Ababa Region of the Telecommunications Board, Churchill Road (opposite the Ras Hotel) and at Gennet Heroes Square, Asmara.

All mail to and from Ethiopia should be despatched by air.

General Post Office, Churchill Road, P.O. Box 1629, Addis Ababa, ☎ 110421.
General Post Office, Gennet Heroes Square, P.O. Box 229, Asmara, ☎ 111900.
Telecommunications Office, Zeray Derres Square, P.O. Box 234, Asmara, ☎ 112900.

7. Public Holidays
The Ethiopian calendar year is divided into 12 months of 30 days each and one month of 5 days, or 6 days every fourth (leap) year.

By the European (Gregorian) calendar, Ethiopian New Year's Day falls on the 11th September and one day later in the year before each Gregorian leap year. The Gregorian calendar is normally used for business purposes in Ethiopia.

Fixed Holidays
7 January	*Christmas Day*
19 January	*Feast of Epiphany*
2 March	*Commemoration of Battle of Adowa*
6 April	*Victory Day*
1 May	*May Day*
11 September	*New Year's Day*
12 September	*Establishment of the Socialist State of Ethiopia*
27 September	*Mesquel* (Feast of the Finding of the True Cross)

The following movable Muslim and Christian holidays are also observed:

Mouled, Eid el Fitr, Eid el Adha, Good Friday, Easter Sunday. Although not an official holiday, *Christmas Day* is observed by most resident Europeans.

8. Time
GMT + 3.

9. Internal Transport

Air
Ethiopian Airlines operate a network of internal flights linking over 40 cities and towns. There are daily flights between Addis Ababa and Asmara. Business visitors will find air travel the most convenient and often the only viable form of travel in Ethopia.

Airline Offices in Addis Ababa

Air France	☎ 159044.
Air India	☎ 156600.
Alitalia	☎ 154400.
British Airways	☎ 155655.
British Caledonian	☎ 152222*
JAL	☎ 447444*
Lufthansa	☎ 155666.
KLM	☎ 446644.
Swissair	☎ 447444*.
TWA	☎ 447444*.

* c/o Ethiopian Airlines

Road
The all-weather road system now links all provincial capitals and major business and tourist centres.

Travel by road in the province of Eritrea is restricted and subject to police permission in some areas.

Taxis are expensive. Shared taxis in Addis Ababa are comparatively cheaper and operate in the town centre at a fixed rate; these are blue and white and have special green and white number plates. It is useful to carry a map of the city when using these taxis in order to ensure the driver knows your destination.

Car-Hire Firms in Addis Ababa

United Touring Company Hertz)	☎ 151122.
Ras Rental	☎ 155150.
Forship Travel Agency	☎ 112159.
Avis	☎ 444594.

Land-Rovers, VW cars and Microbuses, together with camping equipment, can be hired through the United Touring Company, ☎ 151122.

Visitors should be in possession of a driving licence from their country of residence. If their visit to Ethiopia exceeds 1 month, a temporary licence is required. This is issued on production of a national driving licence and can be obtained from the City Hall in Addis Ababa or Asmara. Traffic travels on the right-hand side of the road.

10. Tipping
Taxis – no tip necessary.

Porters – 1 birr.

Hotels/restaurants – a service charge of around 10% is added to the bill; an additional tip (about 1 birr per head per day) is customary.

11. Social Customs
Many Ethiopians are Muslims and observe the laws of the Islamic faith by refusing alcohol and all forms of pig meat, and by fasting during the month of *Ramadan*. It may be difficult to accomplish much business with Muslim contacts during this month.

Coptic Christians in Ethiopia are not forbidden to drink alcohol, but on certain feast days they refrain from eating animal products.

Entertaining in Addis Ababa and Asmara is generally informal, although semi-formal cocktail parties are not uncommon. Visitors wishing to entertain Ethiopian business contacts could arrange to hold a party at their hotel.

ETHIOPIA

USEFUL ADDRESSES (GENERAL)

British Embassy, Pappasinos Building, 4th floor, Ras Desta Demtew Avenue, P.O. Box 858, Addis Ababa, ☎ 151305/151166.

Canadian Embassy, African Solidarity Insurance Building, Unity Square, P.O. Box 1130, Addis Ababa, ☎ 448385.

Dutch Embassy, Embassy Compound, Old Airport Zone, P.O. Box 1241, Addis Ababa, ☎ 445597.

French Embassy, Quartier Kabana, Omedla Road, P.O. Box 1464, Addis Ababa.

French Consulate, Route de Harar, P.O. Box 12, Dire Dawa.

Japanese Embassy, Finfinne Building, 2nd floor, Maskal Square, P.O. Box 1499, Addis Ababa, ☎ 448215/9.

Swiss Embassy, Near Old Airport, P.O. Box 1106, Addis Ababa, ☎ 447840.

US Embassy, Entoto Street, P.O. Box 1014, Addis Ababa, ☎ 110666.

West German Embassy, Qebena Street, P.O. Box 660, Addis Ababa, ☎ 120433/120540.

Ethiopian Tourist Organisation, Miazia Square 27, Ras Makonnen Avenue, Addis Ababa, ☎ 447470.

British Council, Artistic Building, Adua Avenue, P.O. Box 1043, Addis Ababa, ☎ 110022/4.

Thomas Cook Authorised Representatives: United Touring Company, Churchill Street, P.O. Box 3092, Addis Ababa, ☎ 151122; and Ufficio Viaggi P.L.C., 20–22 Gennet Heroes Square, P.O. Box 877, Asmara, ☎ 11783.

Americal Express Authorised Representatives: ITCO Tourist and Travel Agency, Ras Makonnen & Churchill Streets, P.O. Box 1048, Addis Ababa, ☎ 444334; and Addis Ababa Hilton Hotel Service Desk, ☎ 448400.

BUSINESS INFORMATION

Addis Ababa is the commercial centre of Ethiopia; Asmara and Dire Dawa are also important; although the latter to a much lesser extent.

There are few commissioned agents established in Ethiopia. Foreign manufacturers usually find it necessary to appoint an importer as an agent. Most trading enterprises are run by non-Ethiopians and function jointly as wholesaler, retailer, manufacturer's representative and distributor. Importers fall into two principal categories: smaller importers/retailers, as mentioned above, and foreign trading companies of which there are a dozen or so of considerable importance.

The Ethiopian market is open to manufacturers from all over the world and competition amongst foreign suppliers for the good agents is fierce. Importers are frequently obliged to turn down offers of agencies due to overloading.

There are no clearly defined buying seasons in Ethiopia, but commercial activities tend to decrease during the rainy period from June to September.

Import and Exchange Control Regulations
Imports are controlled by the Ethiopian Import/Export Corporation. Exchange permits are required for all imports for which foreign exchange is to be provided by the National Bank via commercial banks. Permits are granted for most goods.

Business Hours
Government Offices
0900–1300 / 1500–1800 Monday to Friday
0900–1300 Saturday (Addis Ababa only)

Business Houses
Addis Ababa
0900–1300 / 1500–1800 Monday to Friday
0900–1300 Saturday

Asmara
0830–1230 / 1500–1800 Monday to Saturday

BUSINESS SERVICES

Advertising
Publicity and Advertising Inc, P.O. Box 222, Addis Ababa – outdoor advertising (road signs, posters, etc.).

Forwarding/Clearing Agents
Compagnie Maritime Auxilaire d'Outre-Mer (CMAO), Addis Ababa.

Ethiopia Amalgamated PLC, P.O. Box 2090, Addis Ababa.
Gellatly, Hankey & Co (Ethiopia), P.O. Box 482, Addis Ababa.
Messagerie Africaine SC, P.O. Box 5629, Addis Ababa.

USEFUL ADDRESSES (BUSINESS)

Asmara Chamber of Commerce, Ras Makonnen Avenue, P.O. Box 856, Asmara.

Ethiopian Chamber of Commerce, Mexico Square, P.O. Box 517, Addis Ababa, ☎ 448240.

Ministry of Commerce and Tourism, P.O. Box 1769, Addis Ababa, ☎ 448200.

MAJOR CITY AND TOWN

Addis Ababa
Addis Ababa was founded in the late nineteenth century by the Emperor Menelik.

ETHIOPIA

Built on the side of the Int'ot'o mountains, the city has stretched over a large area with no apparent plan for its development.

Addis Ababa is the headquarters of the United Nations Economic Commission for Africa and of the Organisation of African Unity.

The city contains a number of impressive buildings and monuments. The St George Cathedral houses some interesting paintings by Ethiopian artists; the Menelik Mausoleum behind the Old Gyibbi Palace contains the tombs of Emperor Menelik II and Empress T'aytu. Trinity Church was built in 1941, commemorating Ethiopia's liberation from Fascist rule. Addis Ababa university is also worth a visit. The main campus is situated in the grounds of a former palace, where the Institute of Ethiopian Studies museum is also to be found.

Hotels

There is no official hotel rating system in Ethiopia.

ADDIS ABABA HILTON, P.O. Box 1164, ☎ 448400.
Modern deluxe hotel in city centre across from Foreign Office and National Palace.
Rooms: 245 ♪, ⑩, ♨, ☐ on request, ♨, ⌕. Suites available.
Facilities: Restaurant, grill, coffee shop, cocktail lounge, bar. Swimming, tennis, sauna, health club. Shopping arcade. Car hire.
Services: ✉ Amex, Carte Blanche, Diners Club, Eurocard, Master Charge. Dr. on call. **S**, ♂. Audio-visual equipment.
Conference room – max. capacity 750.
Banquet rooms – max. capacity 400.

HOTEL D'AFRIQUE, P.O. Box 1120, ☎ 447485.
Modern hotel near city centre.
Rooms: 74, ♨, ♨.
Facilities: 2 restaurants, cocktail lounges. Discotheque. Golf.
Banquet and conference facilities.

ETHIOPIA, Adwa Square, P.O. Box 1131, ☎ 447400.
Modern 1st-class hotel in business centre.
Rooms: 110 ♨, ☐ on request.
Facilities: Restaurant, cocktail bar. Car hire.
Services: **TC**, **FC**. ✉ Amex, Diners Club. **S**, ♂.

GHION IMPERIAL, Ras Destra Damtew Avenue, P.O. Box 1643, ☎ 447130.
1st-class hotel in extensive gardens next to the Residential Palace.
Rooms: 180 ♨. Accommodation also available in garden pavilions.
Facilities: Restaurant, bars, coffee house. 5 private dining rooms. Nightclub. Tennis, sauna, swimming. Car hire. Conference room.
Services: **TC**, **FC**. ✉ Amex, Diners Club.

WABI SHEBELLE, Ras Abebe Aregay Avenue, P.O. Box 3154, ☎ 447187.
Modern hotel in attractive grounds near Mexico Square.
Rooms: 100 ♨, ☐. Suites available.
Facilities: Restaurants, bar, snack bar, rooftop lounge. Shops. Live folk entertainment. Conference room.
Services: ✉ Amex.

Restaurants

Addis Ababa Restaurant, ☎ 113513, and *Maru Dembia*, ☎ 117701 – Ethiopian; *Au Vieux Logis*, ☎ 118109 – French; *Villa Verde*, ☎ 444760 – Italian; *Hong Kong Bar & Restaurant*, ☎ 444275 and *China Bar & Restaurant*, ☎ 443014 – Chinese; *Omar Khayyam* ☎ 112259 – Middle Eastern; *Cottage*, ☎ 443479 – Austrian and continental.

Nightclubs

The most popular nightclubs are the *Ghion*, *Ras Night*, *Wabi Shebelle* and *Sheba*.

Entertainment

A number of interesting excursions can easily be made from Addis Ababa.

Int'ot'o
The site of the earlier capital of Ethiopia, founded by Emperor Menelik in the 1880s with spectacular views over the city. There are few remains of the town with the exception of two churches, Int'ot'o Mariam and Int'ot'o Raguel.

Debre Zeyt (Bishoftu)
About an hour's drive from the capital are some fascinating volcanic crater lakes with swimming and sailing facilities.

Menagesha National Park
This forest sanctuary for wildlife and birds lies about 35km/22 miles from Addis Ababa.

Shopping
Best buys: gold and silver jewellery, pottery, woven cotton and wool articles.

The Mercato (market) covers a large area on the west side of the city and is divided into sections specialising in various goods, including a section dealing with Ethiopian arts, crafts and antiques. Local gold and silver jewellery is sold by weight. Stall-holders expect some bargaining, but prices in shops are usually fixed.

On the Bole International Airport Road is the *Ethiopian Ceramic Workshop*, where tourists may visit the factory.

Asmara
Asmara is the capital of the province of Eritrea and the second largest city in Ethiopia. Originally a small Coptic village, the town grew rapidly under Italian occupation and still bears many signs of Italian rule. Life in the town has been disrupted by fighting in the province between Ethiopian forces and the Eritrean Liberation Front.

A key place of interest is the Asmara Archaeological Museum, containing a fascinating array of historical objects found in Eritrea and Tigray.

Yohannes IV Airport is 9½km/6 miles from the centre of Asmara.

Hotels
AMBA SOIRA (formerly Asmara Imperial), Deg 30 Hailou Kebbede Street, P.O. Box 181, ☎ 113222.
Modern hotel in quiet central location.
Rooms: 50.
Facilities: Restaurant, bar, private dining rooms. Gardens. Car hire.
Services: TC, FC. 🗐 Amex and Diners Club. 5, ♂.
Conference room.

NYALA, Queen Elizabeth II Avenue, P.O. Box 867, ☎ 113111.
Modern multi-storey hotel near town centre.
Rooms: 70 🛎, ⬜ on request, ☎, △, 📺.
Suites available.
Facilities: Restaurants, grill, pizzeria on top floor, bars, lounge. Nightclub. Shopping arcade. Airline office. Car hire.
Services: TC. 🗐 Amex, Diners Club. Dr. on call. 5, ♂.
Conference room – max. capacity 50.
Banquet rooms – max. capacity 800.

Restaurants
Asmara boasts several good Italian restaurants, including the *Caravel*, *Albergo Italia*, *Esposito*, *Ristorante da Rino* and *Capri*. The *Shoa* and *Sport* specialise in local dishes.

Nightclubs
Nightlife in Asmara is limited to two nightclubs: the *Piccadilly* and *Mocambo*. Dances are occasionally held on Saturdays at the *Caravel* restaurant.

Entertainment
Sporting and leisure facilities are limited. The town has a number of cinemas showing a wide variety of foreign films.

Shopping
The duty-free shop at Asmara Airport sells local handicrafts as well as a good selection of low-priced imported goods including jewellery and hi-fi equipment.

GABON
Gabonese Republic

Geography	*142*
The Economy	*144*
How to Get There	*145*
Entry Regulations	*145*
Practical Information for the Visitor	*146*
Useful Addresses (General)	*147*
Business Information	*148*
Business Services	*148*
Useful Addresses (Business)	*149*
Libreville	*149*

Size: 266,770 sq. km/103,000 sq.miles.

Population: 540,000 (1978 est.) (Some sources estimate the population as high as 1,300,000, but this is not generally considered to be a reliable figure.)

Distribution: 20% in urban areas.

Density: 2.0 persons per sq.km/5.2 per sq.mile.

Population Growth Rate: 1.7% p.a.

Ethnic Composition: The majority are of Bantu origin. The Fang are the largest tribe, followed by the Eshira, Bapounou, Bateke and Okandé. There are approximately 50,000 Europeans (mainly French) and a large number of immigrant workers from neighbouring African countries.

Capital: Libreville Pop. 251,400 (urban agglomeration).

Major Towns: Port Gentil Pop. 77,611; Lambaréné Pop. 22,682.

Language: French is the official language. Several Bantu dialects are also spoken; Fang is widely used in the north.

Religion: About half are Christian. A large proportion of the remainder are Animist, and there is a small Muslim community.

Government: The President is head of state as well as head of the Parti Démocratique Gabonais, the only political party. The President and National Assembly are both elected for 7-year terms.

In 1979 the Parti Démocratique Gabonais proposed a number of constitutional changes affecting the election and term of the President and National Assembly. A referendum to be held in 1979 on these changes was postponed.

GEOGRAPHY

Gabon lies on the Equator and consists of a low-lying coastal strip about 96km/60 miles wide which rises eastwards to a height of over 730m/2,000ft with a high plateau exceeding 1,095m/3,000ft at its highest point. Approximately 85% of Gabon is covered by dense forest.

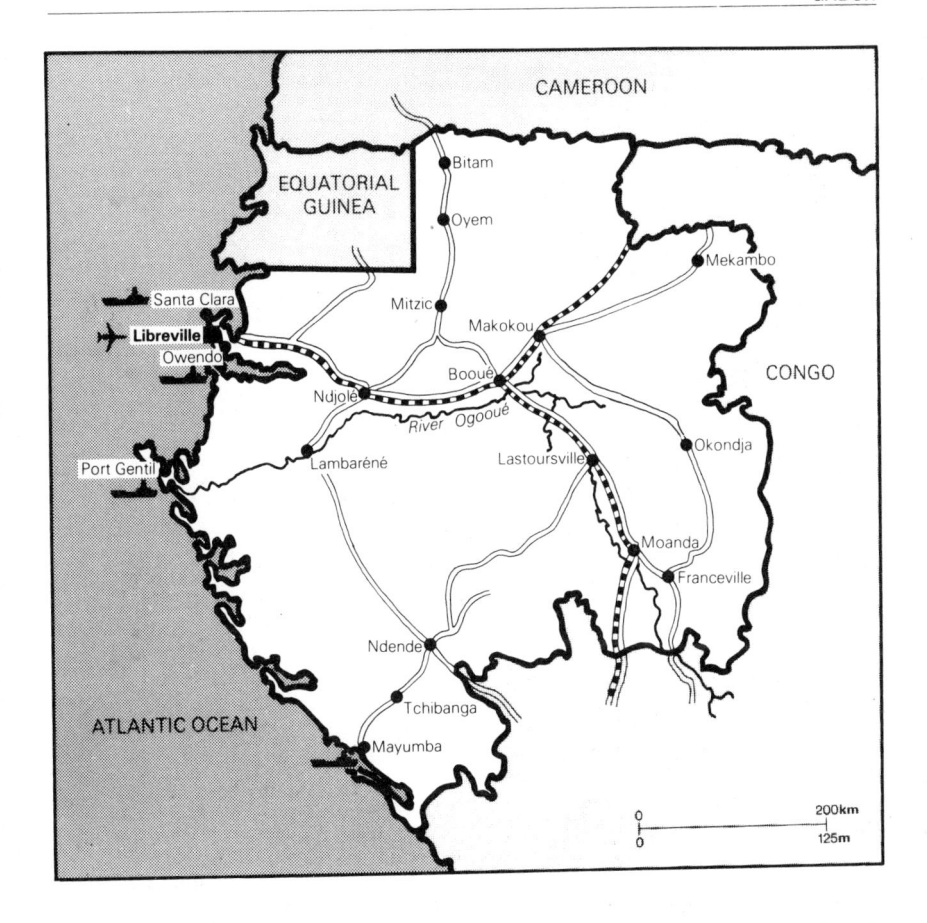

Climate
Gabon has a tropical climate with an average annual temperature of 25°C/77°F. The main rainy season is from mid-January to mid-May, with a shorter season from October to mid-December. The best time to visit is during the cooler, dry season from mid-May to September.

Agriculture
Although agriculture is the main occupation of more than two-thirds of the working population, it is of declining importance within the economy. Less than 1% of Gabon's total area is under cultivation. Local production is thus insufficient to meet domestic demands, necessitating the importation of large quantities of agricultural and dairy products.

Until the commercial exploitation of Gabon's oil and gas reserves, forestry was the mainstay of the economy. The okoumé tree is the most valuable source of wood, and Gabon is the world's largest producer. Other varieties include mahogany, izogo, iroko and tchikola; these go mainly for plywood, pulp and paper manufacture, although more timber is now being processed locally into veneers and furniture.

Main Crops: corn, coffee, cocoa, bananas, rice, yams, cassava.

Mineral Resources: manganese, iron ore, uranium, gold, oil, natural gas.

THE ECONOMY

Gross National Product (1977): US$2,060 million.

Per Capita Income (1977): US$3,730.

Gross Domestic Product (1976): 719.1 billion CFA francs.

Foreign Trade (1977): Total Imports – US$549.5 million. Total Exports – US$1,271.9 million.

Main Trading Partners: Imports – France, West Germany, USA, UK, Netherlands, Belgium, Luxembourg. Exports – France, USA, Spain, Bahamas, UK, West Germany.

Since independence in 1960, Gabon has experienced a high economic growth rate and has one of the highest per capita revenues in Africa. This expansion has largely occurred in the oil and mining sectors, with minerals now accounting for over 80% of total exports. The rise in world oil prices has further contributed to Gabon's increased prosperity, although production fell for the first time in 1977 and the country's known oil reserves are expected to be exhausted by the end of the 1980s.

An increase in mining has necessitated the development of Gabon's infrastructure. The main project in hand is the Trans-Gabon Railway, which will link the principal mining areas, industrial complexes and ports at an estimated cost of 80 billion CFA francs; it will also facilitate greater exploitation of Gabon's timber resources.

Despite substantial economic growth, Gabon introduced an austerity programme in 1977, reducing Government spending and curtailing several development projects.

The Government is keen to develop a diversified economy, which will include an increase in the processing of local raw materials, particularly timber and oil. Among the new industries that have been created or expanded in the light manufacturing sector are soap manufacture, paint, cellulose, textiles, clothing and furniture; there are also plans to expand cocoa and palm oil production.

Major Industries: timber and mineral processing, food processing, oil refining.

Main Commodities Traded: Imports – machinery, foods, transportation equipment, metal products, tobacco, refined petroleum products, industrial chemicals. Exports – wood, petroleum, uranium, manganese.

Oil Production: 76,800 barrels (1978).

International Affiliations: UN, IBRD, OAU, ACP, ADB, OPEC, Franc Zone, OCAM, UDEAC.

HOW TO GET THERE

Air
There are regular flights to Libreville from Paris, Rome and Geneva by Air Afrique, UTA and Swissair. These companies, together with Air Zaïre, operate flights to Libreville from Brazzaville, Douala, Kinshasa and Johannesburg.

Flying times to Libreville: from New York, 14 hours; from London, 13 hours.

The following airport service charges are levied on passengers departing from Gabon to:

Destinations within Gabon –	400 CFA francs.
Nigeria and Zaïre –	800 CFA francs.
All other destinations –	2,000 CFA francs.

Gabon's International Airport is 12km/7½ miles from the centre of Libreville. Taxis and buses operate between the airport and city centre.

ENTRY REGULATIONS

Visas
Visas are required by nationals of all countries except: Andorra, Cameroon, Central African Republic, Chad, Congo, France, West Germany, Ivory Coast, Mauritius, Monaco, Niger, Senegal, Togo, Upper Volta – for a stay of up to 3 months.

Neither entry nor transit is permitted to nationals of Angola, Benin, Cape Verde Islands, Cuba, Ghana, Guinea-Bissau, Haiti and São Tomé and Príncipe, even if they hold a resident's permit.

Visas are obtainable at Gabonese embassies and consulates abroad. Applications for visas by business travellers should be supported by a letter from the applicant's firm giving full details and confirming financial responsibility for the applicant.

Visas are usually valid for 3 months for a stay of varying length. Allow at least 4 weeks for the issue of a visa as all applications are referred to Gabon for authorisation. Urgent applications may be referred via telex at the applicant's expense.

Health Regulations
Valid International Certificates of Vaccination against smallpox, cholera and yellow fever are required by all persons entering Gabon.

Customs
Currency: There is no limit to the amount of Gabonese or foreign currency which may be imported, but all monies must be declared on entry. A limit of 75,000 CFA francs per person is placed on the amount of local currency which may be taken out of the Franc Zone. Any amount of unspent foreign currency may be exported.

Duty-free articles: Personal effects, 200 cigarettes/cigarillos or 50 cigars or 250g of tobacco, 1 litre of spirits and 50g of perfume. Samples of no commercial value are admitted free of duty and taxes. (Other samples may be temporarily imported, except by post, under the ATA Carnet system.)

PRACTICAL INFORMATION FOR THE VISITOR

1. Currency
Monetary Unit – CFA franc.
Notes – 100, 500, 1,000, 5,000, 10,000 CFA francs.
Coins – 1, 2, 5, 10, 25, 50, 100 CFA francs.

French franc travellers' cheques are the most widely accepted in Gabon, although sterling and US dollar cheques can usually be cashed. It is advisable to exchange foreign currency and travellers' ceques into CFA francs only when and as required since these are not easily exchanged in non-Franc Zone territories.

Banking Hours
0730 – 1200 Monday to Friday
1430 – 1600

Domestic Commercial Banks in Libreville
Banque Centrale des Etats de l'Afrique Centrale, B.P. 112.
Banque Internationale pour le Commerce et l'Industrie du Gabon, B.P. 2241, ☎ 722613.
Union Gabonaise de Banque, rue du Colonel Parent, B.P. 315, ☎ 721514/720525.

Foreign Commercial Banks in Libreville
Banque du Gabon et du Luxembourg, B.P. 3879.
Banque de Paris et des Pays Bas, B.P. 2253.
Citibank, Boulevard Quaben and Rue Kringer, B.P. 3940, ☎ 733000/1/2.

2. Electricity Supply
220v AC 50Hz.
Plugs: 2 round pins.

3. Weights and Measures
The metric system is used.

4. Media
Radiodiffusion-Télévision Gabonaise, the Government broadcasting corporation, transmits programmes in French and local African languages. Both radio and television carry advertising.

Newspapers and Journals
L'Union and Gabon-Matin are the principal daily papers. Dialogue is a monthly publication of the Parti Démocratique Gabonais.
A number of French trade journals such as Marchés Tropicaux and Afrique Industrie Infrastructure are available. The Chamber of Commerce, Agriculture and Mines in Libreville issues a monthly newsletter.

5. Medical Care
Malaria is still prevalent in parts; visitors are advised to take the usual prophylactic measures. Uncooked fruit and vegetables and water that has not been boiled and filtered should be avoided. Mineral water is available.

6. Telephone, Telex and Postal Services
Telex facilities are available at the main post office in Libreville and at the Inter-Continental Hotel and the Hotel du Dialogue.
It is advisable to despatch all mail by air. Postal services are often subject to lengthy delays, particularly surface mail and parcels.

7. Public Holidays
1 January	New Year's Day
12 March	Jour de Rénovation
1 May	Labour Day
25 May	Liberation of African Continent Day
15 August	Feast of the Blessed Virgin Mary
18 August	Independence Anniversary

1 November   *All Saints Day*
25 December   *Christmas Day*

The following movable holidays are also observed: *Easter Monday, Youth Day* (2nd Sunday in May), *Ascension Day, Whit Monday, Eid el Fitr.*

When a public holiday falls on a Sunday, the following day is observed as holiday. If a holiday falls on a Friday, then the Saturday too is often observed as a holiday. Monday is often observed as a holiday when Tuesday is a public holiday.

8. Time
GMT + 1.

9. Internal Transport

Air
There are airports at Libreville, Port Gentil, Franceville, Moanda and Lambaréné, as well as a large number of airstrips (private and public) scattered throughout the country.

Air Gabon, the domestic airline, operates regular services between Libreville and Lambaréné, Makokou, Mekambo, Moanda, Franceville, Ndjolé, Port Gentil and Tchibanga.

Airline Offices in Libreville
Air France	☎ 721707.
Pan Am	☎ 722340.
Swissair	☎ 721671/2.
UTA	☎ 721707, 721723.

Road
Many of Gabon's roads are in a poor condition. During the rainy season all attempts at road travel should be abandoned, except on the following routes: Libreville – Lambaréné – Ndende; Libreville – Booué; Libreville – Bitam.

Taxis operate in all the main towns.

Car Hire in Libreville
Self-drive and chauffeur-driven cars are available from many of the leading hotels, and also from:

Autos-Gabon	☎ 722456.
Auto-Service	☎ 720944.
Pierre Bazaille	☎ 722436.
Hertz	☎ 732011.
Europe Cars	☎ 721326.
TVA	☎ 722100.
Avis	☎ 732010, 732513.

A national or International Driving Licence is required; a deposit must be paid for the hire of the car.

10. Tipping
Taxis – 10%.

Porters – 100 CFA francs.

Hotels/restaurants – 10% of the bill.

11. Social Customs
It is essential that business travellers speak reasonable French, as the language is used exclusively in Government and business circles.

USEFUL ADDRESSES (GENERAL)

British Embassy: Bâtiment Sogame, Boulevard de l'Indépendance, B.P. 476.

French Embassy: Boulevard de l'Indépendance, Pont-Pirah, B.P. 2125.

Japanese Embassy: Boulevard Roi Louis Dowe, B.P. 2259, ☎ 732297.

US Embassy: Boulevard de la Mer, B.P. 400, ☎ 722003/4 and 721337.

West German Embassy: Avenue Alfred Mardu, B.P. 299, ☎ 722790.

Dutch Consulate: Gabon Informatique, Avenue du Colonel Parent, B.P. 3946, ☎ 720850/720408.

Ministère du Tourisme: Immeuble Branly, Avenue du Colonel Parent, ☎ 722182.

Ministère de l'Information: B.P. 3127, ☎ 721692.

BUSINESS INFORMATION

Many of the larger trading firms are branches of large French concerns or smaller, privately owned French businesses. The Chamber of Commerce in Libreville may be able to assist in appointing agents and conveying announcements to its members. The Government welcomes foreign investment, especially with Gabonese participation in priority sectors (wood and mineral exports, infrastructure projects). State interests in industry have risen in recent years and a programme to encourage a higher proportion of local managers and promote greater reinvestment in Gabon has been instituted.

Import and Exchange Control Regulations

Import licences have been replaced by a system of 'Prior Authorisation to Import' which applies to all goods, regardless of their origin. 'Prior Authorisation to Import' must be lodged with the Foreign Trade Directorate at least one month before the date of arrival of the goods.

Applications must be accompanied by pro-forma invoices.

Exchange control regulations on payments for imports from countries outside the French Franc Zone stipulate that an authorisation for the transfer abroad of currency must be obtained from the Gabonese Ministry of Finance.

Business Hours

Government Offices
0800 – 1200
1500 – 1800   Monday to Friday
0800 – 1300 Saturday

Business Houses
0730 – 1230
1430 – 1730   Monday to Friday
0730 – 1230 Saturday

BUSINESS SERVICES

Advertising
Havas-Gabon, B.P. 213, Libreville.

Insurance
Assurances Générales Gabonaises, B.P. 2148, Libreville.
Assurances Mutuelles du Gabon, Avenue du Colonel Parent, B.P. 2221, Libreville.
Les Assureurs Conseils Gabonais, Avenue Savorgnan-de-Brazza, B.P. 272, Port Gentil.

Société Nationale Gabonaise d'Assurances et de Réassurances (SONAGAR), B.P. 3082, Libreville.

Shipping
Société Gabonaise de Transport Maritime (SOGATRAM), B.P. 864, Libreville.
Société Maritime Gabonaise (SOMARGA), B.P. 776, Libreville.
Société Ouest Africaine d'Entreprises Maritimes (SOAEM), B.P. 72, Libreville; and B.P. 518, Port Gentil.

GABON

USEFUL ADDRESSES (BUSINESS)

Chambre de Commerce, d'Agriculture, d'Industrie et des Mines du Gabon, B.P. 2234, Libreville, ☎ 722064, 720753.

Syndicat des Commerçants Importateurs et Exportateurs du Gabon (SIMPEX), B.P. 1743, Libreville.

Fonds Européen de Développement (EDF), B.P. 321, Libreville, ☎ 732250.

MAJOR CITY

Libreville

The name Libreville was adopted in the mid-19th century when the town became a refuge for slaves who had been freed by the French. The town had been handed over to the French following treaties with 2 local chiefs.

The development of Libreville has been rapid over the last decade. With its luxury hotels, modern villas, office blocks and sophisticated entertainment and tourist facilities, the city has become one of the most expensive in Africa.

Libreville has a museum with interesting artistic, ethnographical and historical collections. The Nombakele and Mont Bouet are colourful, bustling markets where a variety of local handicrafts are on sale, including wood and stone carvings. On the outskirts of the city a sculptors' village has been established where stone carvers still use traditional carving techniques.

Libreville has a fine beach shaded by coconut trees, and there are other beaches along the coastline with a short driving distance of the city.

Hotels

There is no official hotel rating system in Gabon.

HOTEL DU DIALOGUE, B.P. 3947, ☎ 732470.
Modern 1st-class hotel facing beach, 2km/1 mile outside city centre, 20 minutes' drive from airport.
Rooms: 250 ♪, ⚅, ☐ on request, ♕, ♘, ⌸. Suites available.
Facilities: Restaurant, bars, coffee shop. Nightclub. Swimming, sauna, squash, tennis, golf. Deep-sea fishing, water sports. Private beach. Travel desk. Car hire.
Services: TC, FC, ⊟ Amex, Diners Club. Dr. on call. S, ♂. Audio-visual equipment.
Conference room – max. capacity 200. Banquet rooms – max. capacity 350.

LE GAMBA, Boulevard de Nice, B.P. 10074, ☎ 732267, 732736.
Modern hotel near beach and airport, 12km/7½ miles from city centre.
Rooms: 104, 5 studios, 3 suites. ♪, ⚅, ♘, ⌸.
Facilities: 2 restaurants, bar. Tennis, water sports. Car hire.
Services: TC, FC, ⊟ Amex, Diners Club. Dr. on call. S, ♂.

OKOUME PALACE INTER-CONTINENTAL, B.P. 2254, ☎ 732023.
Modern deluxe hotel in residential area by sea, midway between airport and city centre.
Rooms: 500 ♪, ⚅, ♕, ♘, ⌸. Suites available.
Facilities: Restaurant, rotisserie, 2 cocktail lounges, coffee shop. Nightclub, casino. Swimming, tennis. Beauty salon, barber shop. Car hire. Shops.

149

Services: **TC**, **FC**. ▤ Amex, Diners Club. Dr. on call. ♂, audio-visual equipment. Conference and banquet room – max. capacity 1,000.

Restaurants
Apart from the hotel restaurants, there are a number of other eating houses offering a good standard of cuisine, including *Brasserie de l'Océan, Le Corsaire, Le Surcouf* and *Le Komo. La Paillotte, Le Tropicana* and *Aquarium* are near the sea shore. *La Case Bantoue* and *Kinguélé* serve Gabonese specialities.

Nightclubs
There are few nightspots in Libreville. *La Paillotte* (discotheque) serves food, and live music can be heard at *Le Son des Guitares*. Dances are occasionally held at the *Cercle des Métis.*

Entertainment
Sporting facilities in and around Libreville include the *Barracuda Boat Club* and the *Club Hippique* (riding). Golf, tennis and swimming can all be enjoyed; and surfing is popular, particularly off the Tropicana Beach.

Shopping
Best buys: wood carvings, ivory articles, pottery, postage stamps, stone carvings.

In addition to the handicrafts at the Nombakele and Mont Bouet markets, ivory and ebony carvings can be bought at the Mouila market. There is a small gallery attached to the National Tourist Office, and fine jewellery can be bought from *Masafric* on Avenue du Colonel Parent.

THE GAMBIA
The Gambia

Geography *151*
The Economy *152*
How to Get There *153*
Entry Regulations *153*
Practical Information for the Visitor *154*
Useful Addresses (General) *156*
Business Information *156*
Business Services *157*
Useful Addresses (Business) *157*
Banjul *157*

Size: 11,295 sq.km/4,361 sq.miles.

Population: 570,000 (1978 est.).

Distribution: 10% in urban areas.

Density: 49 persons per sq.km/128 per sq.mile.

Population Growth Rate: 2.6% p.a.

Ethnic Composition: The main groups are the Mandinka, the Wollof, the Fula, the Jola and the Serahuli.

Capital: Banjul Pop. 42,000.

Major Towns: Basse Pop. 86,170; Georgetown/Bausang Pop. 54,232; Kuntaur/Kau'r Pop. 47,669.

Language: English is the official language. Mandinka, Wollof and Fula are widely spoken. A knowledge of French may prove useful.

Religion: About 90% are Muslims; the remainder, Christians and Animists.

Government: The head of state is the executive President who appoints a Cabinet. The House of Representatives is elected for a 5-year term by universal suffrage and includes a number of nominated members. The main political parties are the ruling People's Progressive Party, the National Convention Party and the United Party.

GEOGRAPHY

The Gambia consists of a flat, narrow strip of land (ranging from 48km/30 miles to 24km/15 miles in width) divided in two by the River Gambia. With the exception of its Atlantic coastline, it is flanked on all sides by Senegal.

Climate
The Gambia has a pleasant, sub-tropical climate. The dry, sunny season is from November to April with an average temperature of 24°C/75°F. The period between

GAMBIA

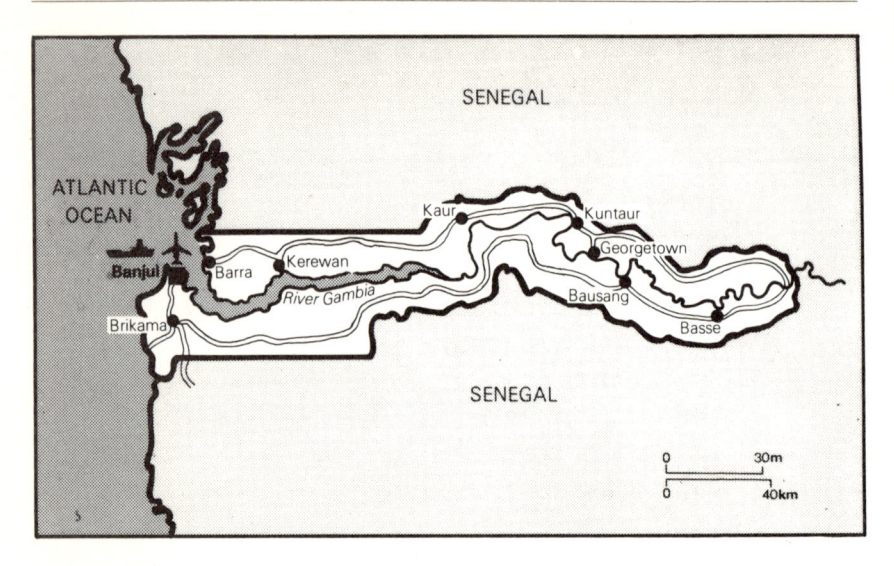

April and October is hotter (particularly inland), with high humidity around the coast. The average temperature for Banjul in these months is 29°c/84°F. The main rainy reason is between July and October.

Agriculture
Agriculture accounts for about 65% of the Gross Domestic Product. The cultivation of groundnuts is the mainstay of The Gambia's economy, but the methods used are primitive with very limited mechanisation. The Gambia depends heavily on the rice crop for domestic food supplies, but is not yet self-sufficient and large quantities of rice are still imported each year.

Main Crops: groundnuts, rice, millet, sorghum, fruit, vegetables, cotton.

Mineral Resources: laterite, stone.

THE ECONOMY

Gross National Product (1977): US$95.3 million.

Per Capita Income (1977): US$200.

Gross Domestic Product (1977): D257.7 million.

Foreign Trade (1978): Total Imports – D209.78 million. Total Exports – D82.89 million.

Main Trading Partners: Imports – UK, China, Netherlands, Japan, France, Burma, West Germany. Exports – UK, Netherlands, France, Italy, Switzerland, Portugal, West Germany.

The Gambia is basically a 1-crop economy. Government expenditure is largely dependent on export tax on groundnuts and groundnut products, and on import duties from the port of Banjul. The steep increase in the price of groundnuts has facilitated economic development, and since independence in 1970 the country has enjoyed a degree of economic growth.

The main area of economic expansion is the tourist industry. As a result of the large-scale Tourism and Infrastructure Project (1975–80), largely financed by the African Development Bank, the World Bank and other international agencies, the Government has begun to develop tourist facilities as well as supporting road, sewerage, water and electricity-supply systems.

The growth of industry is hindered by the largely underdeveloped infrastructure. Industrial activity centres mainly around the processing of groundnuts and the manufacture of lime juice, oil and kaolin. The fishing industry is being aided by the construction of new jetties for the trawlers. Other goods produced locally include candles, cosmetics, soft drinks and cotton clothing.

Major Industries: groundnut processing, cotton, fishing, tourism.

Main Commodities Traded: Imports – food, textiles, clothing, machinery, transport equipment. Exports – groundnuts and groundnut products, palm kernels.

International Affiliations: UN, IBRD, OAU, ACP, ADB, Commonwealth, ECOWAS, GRDO.

HOW TO GET THERE

Air
The international airport of The Gambia is at Yundum, 27km/17 miles from the centre of Banjul.

British Caledonian operate a direct service twice weekly from London (Gatwick) to Banjul. There are several flights a week from Dakar (Senegal) operated by Air Senegal and Ghana Airways and Nigeria Airways.

Banjul is also linked with Freetown (Sierra Leone) by British Caledonian and Nigeria Airways flights.

Flying times to Banjul: from London, 10 hours; from New York, 10 hours.

Road
Banjul can be reached by tarred road from Dakar via the Trans-Gambian Highway (482 km/300 miles) or via the Barra-Banjul ferry service (320 km/200 miles).

ENTRY REGULATIONS

Visas
Visas are required by nationals of all countries except: British Commonwealth and Belgium, Benin, Denmark, Finland, West Germany, Greece, Guinea, Iceland, Republic of Ireland, Italy, Ivory Coast, Luxembourg, Mali, Mauritania, Netherlands, Norway, San Marino, Senegal, Spain, Sweden, Togo, Tunisia and Turkey – for a stay of up to 3 months.

A Visitor's Pass is issued on arrival, valid for one month, but this can be extended on payment of D5.

Visas are valid for 3 months for a stay of up to 3 months. Transit visas are valid for a stay of up to 2 weeks.

Health Regulations

A valid International Certificate of Vaccination against smallpox is required by all persons entering The Gambia. A valid International Certificate of Vaccination against yellow fever is required by those travellers arriving from an infected area. Inoculation against cholera and the enteric group of fevers is recommended.

Customs

Currency: There are no restrictions on the amount of local or foreign currency which may be brought in. Not more than £50 sterling or the equivalent in Gambian currency and not more than £250 in value of any other currency may be exported.

Duty-free articles: Personal effects. 8oz of tobacco or the equivalent in cigarettes or cigars. 2 quarts of wine or beer. 250cl each of perfume and spirits.

Articles liable to duty: Commercial samples are usually admitted free of duty provided they are re-exported within 3 months. However, the amount of duty or security for the payment of duty may have to be deposited, at the discretion of the Collector of Customs. The duty will be refunded or the security cancelled on re-exportation of the samples.

PRACTICAL INFORMATION FOR THE VISITOR

1. Currency
Monetary Unit – dalasi (D), divided into 100 butut (b).
Notes – 1, 5, 10, 25 dalasi.
Coins – 1, 5, 10, 25, 50 butut; 1 dalasi.

Currency is issued by the *Central Bank of The Gambia*, 1-2 Buckle Street, Banjul, ☎ 8103, which is responsible for all central banking operations.

Banking Hours
0800–1300 Monday to Friday
0800–1100 Saturday

Commercial Banks
Gambia Commercial and Development Bank, 78–9 Leman Street, P.O. Box 666, Banjul, ☎ 368, 227, 234.
Banque Internationale pour le Commerce et l'Industrie du Sénégal, 7 Cameron Street, Banjul, ☎ 8145.

Standard Bank Gambia Ltd, 8 Buckle Street, P.O. Box 259, Banjul, ☎ 402, 449.

2. Electricity Supply
240v AC 50Hz.
Plugs: 3 round pins (15 amp) and 3 square pins (13 amp).

3. Weights and Measures
Imperial weights and measures are used, although most importers and merchants are familiar with the metric system.

4. Media
There is no television service in The Gambia. Radio Gambia is a Government-owned, non-commercial network broadcasting in English, Mandinka, Wollof, Fula, Jola and Sarahule. Radio Syd is a commercial station broadcasting mainly music.

Newspapers and Journals
The Gambia News Bulletin is a Government paper published 3 times a week. *Gambia Onward, Gambia Outlook* and *The Gambian* are also published 3 times weekly. There is no established trade press in The Gambia.

5. Medical Care
Malaria is endemic in The Gambia, so visitors should take anti-malarial prophylactics. It is advisable to sleep under a mosquito net, insect repellent may also give added protection.

All drinking water should be boiled, and care should be taken with uncooked vegetables, salads and unwashed fruits.

The main hospital in Banjul is the Royal Victoria Hospital, Independence Drive, ☎ 312.

6. Telephone, Telex and Postal Services
Banjul and the surrounding area have an automatic telephone system which is linked with the Senegalese system. Banjul is linked with several inland towns by radio telephone, which tends to be unreliable.

Telexes can be sent from the General Post Office, Marina Road, Banjul.

All mail to and from The Gambia should be despatched by air.

7. Public Holidays
1 January	New Year's Day
18 February	Independence Day
1 May	Labour Day
25 December	Christmas

The following movable Muslim and Christian holidays are also observed: *Mouled, Eid el Fitr, Eid el Kabir, Good Friday, Easter Monday*.

8. Time
GMT.

9. Internal Transport
Air
There are no internal air services in The Gambia.

Airline Offices in Banjul
British Airways ☎ 778.
British
 Caledonian ☎ 778/9.
Gambia Airways ☎ 778.
Lufthansa ☎ 778.
Nigeria Airways ☎ 438/967.
Swissair ☎ 778.

River
There is a weekly passenger and cargo service from Banjul to Basse, approximately 480 km/300 miles up river. Cabin accommodation is air-conditioned and there are restaurant facilities on the boats. The journey takes about 45 hours. Reservations should be made, in advance, through The Gambia Ports Authority, Banjul.

A ferry service runs every hour between Banjul and Barra (20 minutes).

Road
The majority of roads around Banjul and those linking the main towns are tarred. The principal east/west road across the country runs to the south of the River Gambia linking Banjul and Basse. On the north side of the river, a road connects Barra with Kerewan and Georgetown, although the quality of the surface is poor. The Trans-Gambian Highway linking Dakar and Ziguinchor in Senegal crosses The Gambia, passing through Soma.

Many of the roads in outlying districts are virtually impassable during the rainy season (July to October).

Taxis are available for hire in Banjul but are not fitted with meters, so fares should be agreed upon before commencing the journey.

Self-drive cars are available for hire. A valid driving licence from the visitor's country of residence is acceptable for a short visit. Cars can be hired from the VW Company in Banjul.

10. Tipping
Taxis – not usually necessary unless special service is rendered.

Porters – 25b per bag.

Hotels/restaurants – not necessary if a service charge (usually 10%) has been added to the bill.

11. Social Customs

The majority of the population are Muslims and do not drink alcohol. Strict Muslims will observe all the major festivals of the Muslim calendar, including *Ramadan*, and it may be difficult to accomplish much work during this period if dealing with Muslim business contacts.

Dress throughout The Gambia is generally informal for both daytime and evening occasions.

USEFUL ADDRESSES (GENERAL)

Banjul

British High Commission: 48 Atlantic Road, Fajara, P.O. Box 507, ☎ Serrekunda 2133/4, 2578. (The dialling code from Banjul is 93.)

Dutch Consulate: Shell Company of West Africa Ltd, Dobson Street, P.O. Box 263, ☎ 437.

US Embassy: 16 Buckle Street, P.O. Box 596, ☎ 229.

Government Tourist Board: Bedford Place. (Information office on Marina Parade.)

BUSINESS INFORMATION

The marketing of goods in The Gambia follows a pattern similar to that in other West African countries. Few firms specialise in one particular type of trade or commodity, and the majority act as importer/exporter/wholesaler/retailer/stockist agent dealing in a wide range of goods and services.

The size of the market does not always make the appointment of a local agent viable. Foreign manufacturers will rarely find an exclusive agency to represent them.

Regular visits by overseas representatives are always useful, but these should be carefully planned to fit in with the main buying season, December to May. This period coincides with the main tourist season, which could give an added boost to sales of certain consumer goods.

Import and Exchange Control Regulations

Most goods can be imported into The Gambia under an Open General Licence, although certain goods, including rice and wheat flour, require a specific import licence.

There are no exchange restrictions on transfers to the sterling area. Transfers to all other areas require the authorisation of the Exchange Control Section of the Ministry of Finance and Trade.

Business Hours

Government Offices
0800–1445 Monday to Thursday
0800–1145 Friday and Saturday

Business Houses
0800–1200
1400–1700 Monday to Thursday
0800–1200 Saturday

GAMBIA

BUSINESS SERVICES

Insurance
The Gambia Insurance Co Ltd, Wellington Street, Banjul.

Shipping
Elder Dempster Agencies Ltd, Buckle Street, Banjul, ☎ 432.

The Gambia River Transport Co Ltd, 61 Wellington Street, P.O. Box 215, Banjul.

The *Nigerian National Line* and *Black Star Line* also operate shipping services to The Gambia.

USEFUL ADDRESSES (BUSINESS)

Gambia Chamber of Commerce: 78 Wellington Street, P.O. Box 333, Banjul, ☎ 765.

Gambia Produce Marketing Board: Marina Foreshore, Banjul.

National Trading Corporation of The Gambia: Wellington Street, P.O. Box 61, Banjul.

MAJOR TOWNS

Banjul
Banjul, the capital of The Gambia, was known as Bathurst until 1973. The town was founded in the early nineteenth century as a settlement for freed slaves. Near the ferry landing at Barra stands Fort Bullen, which was built to defend the settlement.

About 24 km/15 miles from the capital is the Abouko Nature Reserve where many different birds can be seen – more than 400 species have been recorded in The Gambia – and crocodiles, hippos, monkeys and pythons.

Hotels
There is no official hotel rating system in The Gambia.
N.B.: Many hotels cater for package holidays and during the main tourist season, November to May, accommodation is usually fully booked well in advance.

City Centre
ADONIS, 23 Wellington Street, P.O. Box 377, ☎ 262/4.
Modern hotel overlooking river.
Rooms: 46, 2 suites. ♪, △, ♡.
Facilities: Restaurant and bar.
Services: TC, FC. ⊟ Amex. Dr. on call. S, ♂.

ATLANTIC, Marina Road, P.O. Box 296, ☎ 8241/2.
Modern hotel on beach, 1 mile from town centre.
Rooms: 80 ♪, ☎, △, ♡. Chalet accommodation available.
Facilities: Restaurant, grill, 2 bars. Tennis, swimming. Car hire.
Services: TC, FC. ⊟ Amex. Dr. on call. S, ♂.
Conference room – max. capacity 100. Banquet rooms – max. capacity 300.

Outside Banjul
FAJARA, Atlantic Road, P.O. Box 489, ☎ (93) 2351, 2339.
Modern hotel consisting of a main hotel block and bungalows.
Rooms: 273 ♪, △.
Facilities: Restaurants, bars. Nightclub.

GAMBIA

Tennis, swimming, volleyball. Golf nearby. Car hire.
Services: TC, FC. ▭ Amex. Dr. on call. S, ♂.

PALM GROVE, Mile 2, ☎ 8119.
Modern hotel situated 3km/2 miles from town centre.
Rooms: 22 ⛌ (in some), ⌂, ⏿.
Facilities: restaurant, bar.
Service: TC, FC. ▭ not accepted. Dr. on call. S, ♂.

SUNWING, Cape Point, Cape St Mary, P.O. Box 638, ☎ (93) 2428, 2435.
Modern hotel near beach, 13km/8 miles from town centre.
Rooms: 200 ⛲, ⌂.
Facilities: Grill, restaurant, bars. Mini-golf, swimming.
Services: TC. ▭ not accepted. Dr. on call. ♂.
Conference room – max. capacity 80.

Restaurants

Most hotel restaurants are open to non-residents; both African and European dishes are served. There are very few other restaurants suitable for business entertaining, the majority being low-cost snack bars.

Those serving European food include the *Adonis, Club 98* and *Uncle Joe's*. Local dishes are served at the *Gambia Restaurant*, Wellington Street; *Nioukabouka*, Peel Street; *Lion's Head*, Hagan Street; and *Super Bird*, just outside the town centre.

Nightclubs

Club 98, Bakau; *Bambooland Club,* Serekunda; *Casuarina Club*, Fajara; *Omar Khayyam*, Fajara.

Entertainment

Banjul lies surrounded by a number of long, sandy beaches such as the Mile 3 Beach, Mile 5 Beach and, further away, the Frufut (26km/16 miles) and Tanji (27 km/17 miles) Beaches. All of these can be reached by taxi from the town centre.

Banjul offers a good selection of sporting facilities. Tennis, cricket and football are popular, as is fishing. The *Bathurst Sailing Club* and *Fajara Golf Club* are both within easy reach of Banjul, and there is riding at Yundum.

Shopping

Best buys: woodcarvings, jewellery, batik cloth, beadwork, snakeskin handbags, belts.

The market in Banjul sells a wide variety of local handicrafts. Of particular note is the gold jewellery and the hand-printed cloth, which can be bought either in lengths or in ready-made garments.

GHANA
Republic of Ghana

Geography	*160*
The Economy	*161*
How to Get There	*162*
Entry Regulations	*162*
Practical Information for the Visitor	*163*
Useful Addresses (General)	*165*
Business Information	*166*
Business Services	*166*
Useful Addresses (Business)	*167*
Accra	*167*

Size: 238,537 sq.km/92,100 sq.miles

Population: 10.97 million (1977 est.).

Distribution: 34% in urban areas.

Density: 42 persons per sq.km/110 per sq.mile.

Population Growth Rate: 2.9% p.a.

Ethnic Composition: The main ethnic groups are the Akan, in the south; the Ashanti, in the forested areas; and the Fanti, around the coast. Others include the Guans, around the plains of the Volta; the Ga- and Ewe-speaking peoples of the south and south-east; and the Mochi-Dagomba in the north.

Capital: Accra Pop. 900,000 (metropolitan area).

Major Cities/Towns: Kumasi Pop. 260,286; Sekondi-Takoradi Pop. 161,000; Tema Pop. 74,000; Tamale Pop. 84,000.

Language: English is the official language. Ghanaian languages include Twi, Fanti, Ga, Ewe, Dagbeni, Hausa and Nzima.

Religion: Approximately 40% are Christians. There is also a large Muslim community, mainly in the north, and a significant Animist population.

Government: After several years of rule by various military factions, the Armed Forces Revolutionary Council (AFRC) supervised a freely contested election in June 1979. In September 1979 Ghana returned to civilian rule with the inauguration of a new Government headed by the President.

The People's National Party is the ruling political party, having gained a majority of seats in Ghana's 140-member National Assembly. Other principal parties are the Action Congress Party, Popular Front Party, Social Democratic Front, Third Force Party and the United National Convention.

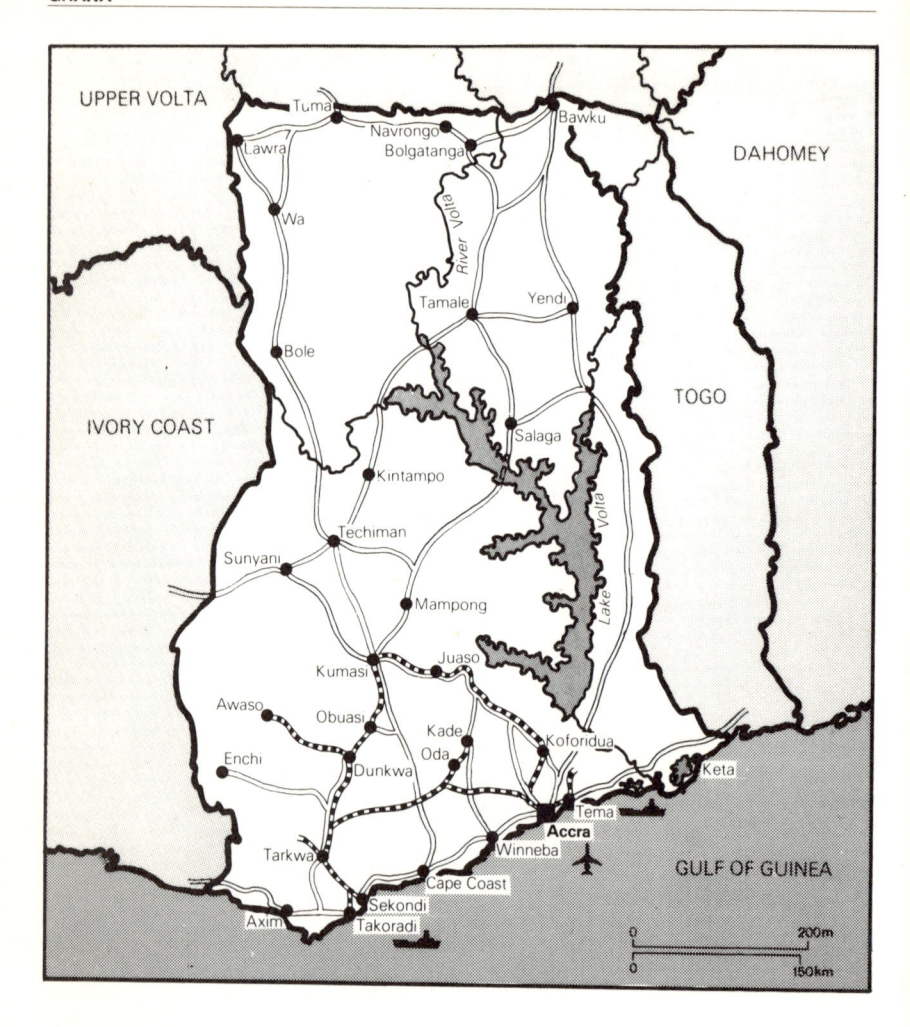

GEOGRAPHY

The coastal region consists mostly of low-lying scrubland and plains, although near to the mouth of the Volta River is a belt of lagoons and swamps forming the Volta Delta. The interior of the country consists mainly of extensive rain forest with savannah and open woodland in the extreme north.

Climate

The climate is tropical, i.e. hot and humid; inland, temperatures rise and humidity levels fall, so that the north is normally hot and dry. The main rainy season is June–July, but rainfall may occur later or earlier than this period. The average minimum and maximum temperatures for Accra are 23°C/73°F and 30°C/86°F.

Agriculture

An estimated 54% of Ghana's labour force is engaged in agriculture, yet agriculture's contribution to the GDP is below 40% as a result of low productivity. Most of the domestic food supply is produced by small-scale peasant farmers, although there are still a number of basic commodities which are imported.

Cocoa is the main export crop, accounting for about 70% of all export earnings. The decline of the cocoa industry over recent years has severely hampered Ghana's development plans.

Main Crops: cocoa, palm oil, palm kernels, coconuts, maize, rice, cassava, yams, groundnuts.

Mineral Resources: gold, bauxite, diamonds, manganese and small deposits of other minerals, including petroleum.

THE ECONOMY

Gross National Product (1977): US$4.08 billion.

Per Capita GNP (1977): US$380.

Gross Domestic Product (1977): 5.16 billion cedis.

Foreign Trade (1978): Total Imports – US$781.9 million. Total Exports – US$958.2 million.

Main Trading Partners: Imports – Nigeria, UK, West Germany, USA. Exports – USA, UK, Japan, West Germany.

The Ghanaian economy has experienced a considerable decline in recent years. Within the cocoa industry, a combination of factors – including ageing trees, unsuitable marketing policy and smuggling – has resulted in a dramatic fall in output, coupled with the fact that world prices are now very weak. Gold production has also fallen despite rising world prices; and, despite expansion, Ghana's timber industry, which produces plywood, furniture and veneers, is running at well under full strength.

In mid-1978 the Government embarked upon a course of action aimed at economic stabilisation – this included devaluing the currency and, in 1979, introducing a comprehensive 'Import Programme' in order to avoid past abuses, such as the over-issue of licences and inefficient resource allocation. Foreign investment is welcomed and the Government receives substantial aid from various world agencies.

The Government plans to maintain a mixed economy, with public and private sectors of industry.

Some corporations within the public sector are wholly Government-owned; others have a small degree of private participation.

In the industrial sector many food-processing industries are already well established. Other products made locally include soap, cigarettes, paint, plastics, motor vehicles, aluminium and sheet metal. There is also a petroleum-refining industry.

Major Industries: cocoa and other food processing, timber processing, aluminium, mining.

Main Commodities Traded: Imports – machinery and transport equipment, cereals, alumina, petroleum, textiles. Exports – cocoa, timber, gold, diamonds, manganese ore, aluminium.

International Affiliations: UN, IBRD, OAU, ACP, ADB, Commonwealth, ECOWAS.

HOW TO GET THERE

Air

Ghana Airways operate regular flights to Accra from London, Paris, Rome, Beirut, and other West African capitals. Other airlines flying to Accra include Alitalia, Aeroflot, British Caledonian, KLM, Lufthansa, MEA, Pan Am and Swissair.

Ghana Airways and Nigerian Airways operate a joint service linking the major towns along the western seaboard. There are also regular services between Accra and Khartoum, Addis Ababa and the Middle East.

Flying times to Accra: from London, 7½ hours; from New York, 11 hours.

Kotoka International Airport is 10 km/6 miles from the centre of Accra. An airport tax of 3 cedis is payable by all passengers on departure from Ghana. Taxis are available at the airport for the journey to Accra.

Road

A good coastal road links Lagos to Accra, passing through Lomé (Togo). There is also access to Ghana by road from Abidjan in the Ivory Coast and from Upper Volta. Long-distance taxis (available mainly in coastal centres) operate between Ghana and these countries.

ENTRY REGULATIONS

Visas

Visas are required by nationals of all countries, except the British Commonwealth, Denmark, West Germany, Togo, Upper Volta – but nationals of these countries must hold entry permits before travelling to Ghana.

Entry permits and visas are available from Ghanaian embassies and diplomatic missions abroad.

Travellers to Ghana are required to purchase cedi vouchers (a form of travellers' cheque) which may be cashed only in Ghana by the purchaser. These vouchers must be obtained prior to departure, and must be signed at the time of purchase. The minimum purchase is ¢140 for the first day and ¢70 for each additional day. Sales of cedi vouchers will be made only against travellers' cheques endorsed throughout the world or against recognised non-sterling convertible currencies, i.e., US dollars, Swiss francs, Deutschmarks, etc.

No entry permits will be issued unless the traveller is in possession of cedi vouchers.

Business travellers require a letter from their firm giving full details of the trip and confirming financial responsibility for the applicant.

Visas are valid for 3 months for a stay of up to 14 days, which may be extended in Ghana.

GHANA

Health Regulations
All visitors to Ghana must be in possession of valid International Certificates of Vaccination against smallpox, cholera and yellow fever. TAB (typhoid and paratyphoid) injections are also recommended.

Customs
Currency: There is no restriction on the amount of foreign currency and travellers' cheques which may be taken into Ghana, but no Ghanaian currency may be imported. All foreign currency should be declared on entry on Form T5 (usually issued on board the aircraft). All exchange transactions must be entered on Form T5, which must be surrendered to the authorities on departure. Any unused imported foreign exchange may be exported, but any unused local currency must be reconverted into foreign currency.

Duty-free articles: Personal effects. 400 cigarettes or the equivalent in cigars or tobacco. Half a bottle of spirits or perfume. Cameras, typewriters, tape recorders, etc., are theoretically subject to duty, but in practice visitors may take 1 of each of these into Ghana, provided it has been owned for at least 6 months. Commercial samples of no value.

Articles liable to duty: Commercial samples of value may be imported without payment of duty provided security for the duty is deposited with the Customs Authorities and the goods are re-exported within 3 months.

PRACTICAL INFORMATION FOR THE VISITOR

1. Currency
Monetary Unit – cedi (¢), divided into 100 pesewas (P).
Notes – 1, 2, 5, 10 cedis.
Coins – ½, 1, 2½, 5, 10, 20 pesewas.
Cedi vouchers (see 'Entry Regulations') can be exchanged for cedis on arrival. Travellers may exchange their foreign currency into local currency at banks.
All exchange transactions must be entered on Form T5 issued on arrival. Visitors who do not use all their cedi vouchers can obtain refunds in Ghana.

Banking Hours
0830–1400 Monday to Thursday
0830–1500 Friday

The central bank and bank of issue is the *Bank of Ghana*, P.O. Box 2674, Accra.

Principal Commercial Banks
Barclays Bank of Ghana Ltd, High Street, P.O. Box 2949, Accra, ☎ 64901.
Ghana Commercial Bank, High Street, P.O. Box 134, Accra, ☎ 64914/7 and 63524.
Ghana Co-operative Bank, Liberty Avenue, P.O. Box 5292, Accra North.
National Savings and Credit Bank, Liberty Avenue, Accra.
Standard Bank Ghana Ltd, High Street, P.O. Box 768, Accra, ☎ 64590/9 – branches in Cape Coast, Kumasi, Legon and Takoradi.
National Investment Bank, Liberty Avenue, P.O. Box 3726, Accra.
Agricultural Development Bank, P.O. Box Box 4191, Accra.

2. Electricity Supply
230/250v AC 50Hz.
Plugs: 3 pin round and flat, ranging from 5 to 15 amps.

3. Weights and Measures
The metric system is in use.

4. Media
The Ghana Broadcasting Corporation is responsible for radio and television broadcasting throughout the country. Radio programmes are transmitted in English and 6 Ghanaian languages, with an external service broadcasting in several languages. Both the television and radio networks accept commercial advertising.

Newspapers and Journals
The 3 dailies circulated throughout Ghana are the *Daily Graphic*, the *Ghanaian Times* and the *People's Evening News*. The main weeklies are the *Mirror*, *Weekly Spectator* and *The Palaver Tribune*.

Local trade journals include *Business Weekly* and the *Ghana Trade Journal*, published monthly. 2 quarterly magazines which circulate in commercial and business circles are *Ghana Enterprise*, published by the Ghana National Chamber of Commerce, and *Ghana Manufacturer*, published by the Ghana Manufacturers' Association.

5. Medical Care
Visitors are advised to take anti-malarial prophylactics. The use of mosquito nets may be recommended in certain areas. Tap water is safe in the main towns, but in more remote areas water should be boiled and filtered.

6. Telephone, Telex and Postal Services
International telephone calls from Ghana are subject to frequent delays, sometimes up to 2 or 3 days. Cables can be sent all over the world via the Posts and Telecommunications Department.

International telex facilities are available, and there is a public call office at Extelcom House, High Street, Accra (open from 0700 to 2100 hours daily, except Sunday).

All mail should be despatched by air. Most post offices are open from 0730 to 1230 and 1400 to 1630 hours (some close at 1500 hours on Saturdays).

7. Public Holidays
1 January	New Year's Day
13 January	National Redemption Day
6 March	Independence Day
1 July	Republic Day
25–6 December	Christmas

In addition to the above, *Good Friday*, *Holy Saturday* and *Easter Monday* are also observed.

8. Time
GMT.

9. Internal Transport

Air
Ghana Airways operate daily services from Accra to Kumasi, Takoradi, Tamale and Sunyani. An airport tax of ¢1 is payable by all passengers on flights within Ghana.

Airline Offices in Accra
Air France	☎ 28328.
British Caledonian	☎ 66222/6.
Ghana Airways	☎ 21921.
KLM	☎ 24030.
Lufthansa	☎ 22423.
Nigeria Airways	☎ 24735.
Pan Am	☎ 21151.
Swissair	☎ 66488, 66571.

Rail
Rail services are generally slow. There is a regular service between Accra, Kumasi and Takoradi.

Road
The main towns are connected by a good all-weather road system. A motorway links Accra and Tema (30 minutes) and there are reasonable roads from Accra to Kumasi (4 hours), Takoradi (3½ hours), and Akosombo (2 hours).

Taxis are available in the main towns but are not metered, so fares should be negotiated before starting the journey.

Self-drive and chauffeur-driven cars are available for hire in Accra, the latter being more commonly used by visitors.

GHANA

Car-Hire Firms in Accra

Allways Travel Agency (Hertz)	☎ 24590.
De Luxe Car Rentals Ltd	☎ 66156.
Speedway Rent-a-Car (Avis)	☎ 28799.

A Ghanaian or International Driving Licence issued outside Ghana and stamped by the Ghanaian Licensing Authorities is required. International Driving Licences are valid only for the period of stay stated by the Immigration Authorities in the visitor's passport, but not exceeding 90 days.

Traffic travels on the right-hand side of the road.

10. Tipping

Tipping is known as 'dash' in Ghana.

Taxis – no tip expected.

Porters – 20P per bag.

Hotels/restaurants – 10% of the bill.

11. Social Customs

A personal approach is highly valued in Ghanaian business circles, and it is important that representatives of foreign companies make regular visits, even though these may not immediately result in new orders. Business entertaining often takes the form of private cocktail parties or dinner parties, which visitors can arrange to hold at their hotel.

USEFUL ADDRESSES (GENERAL)

Accra

Australian High Commission: 2 Milne Close, off Dr Amilcar Cabral Road, Airport Residential Area, P.O. Box 2445, ☎ 77972.

British High Commission:
Commercial Department, 3rd Floor, Barclays Bank Building, High Street, P.O. Box 296, ☎ 64123/9; **Consular Section**, Ring Road, east of city centre, ☎ 64651.

Canadian High Commission: E. 115/3 Independence Avenue, P.O. Box 1639, ☎ 28555, 28502.

Dutch Embassy: 89 Liberation Road, corner Ring Road, P.O. Box 3248, ☎ 21655.

French Embassy: 12th Road, off Liberation Avenue, P.O. Box 187.

Japanese Embassy: 8 Rangoon Avenue, off Switchback Road, P.O. Box 1637, ☎ 75616.

Swiss Embassy: 9 Water Road, North Ridge Area, P.O. Box 359, ☎ 28125, 28185.

US Embassy: Intersection of Liberia and Kinbu Roads, P.O. Box 194, ☎ 66881.

West German Embassy: Valldemosa Lodge, Plot No. 18, North Ridge Residential Area, 7th Avenue Extension, P.O. Box 1757, ☎ 21311.

Ghana Tourist Board: State House, 6th Floor, Bay 2, P.O. Box 3106, ☎ 65461, 28933.

British Council: Liberia Road, P.O. Box 771, Accra, ☎ 21766.

Thomas Cook Authorised Representative: Universal Travel and Tourist Services (Ghana) Ltd, Republic House, Liberty Avenue, P.O. Box M99, ☎ 22813, 28049.

American Express Authorised Representative: Scantravel (Ghana) Ltd, High Street, P.O. Box 1705, ☎ 63134, 64204.

BUSINESS INFORMATION

Since independence, Ghana's trading partners have become more diversified with less emphasis on traditional trading partners such as Britain. Trade has increased with countries who are major suppliers of foreign aid. There are good opportunities for the sale of agricultural and industrial equipment and supplies for development projects.

Within the local trading community there is very little specialisation, either in terms of commodities or the type of trade. One firm may deal with a wide range of unrelated commodities and act as importer/exporter, wholesaler/retailer and stockist-agent.

The largest merchant companies usually have offices in Europe. The state-owned Ghana National Trading Corporation buys supplies from a number of countries. A limited number of the smaller merchant firms are now beginning to specialise.

Most timer and mining enterprises order machinery direct from overseas suppliers; raw materials are normally imported through local agents.

Many Government ministries and corporations buy through the Ghana Supply Commission, although the larger bodies such as the Ghana Industrial Holding Corporation and the State Construction Corporation have, in the past, placed large overseas orders directly on their own behalf.

The Ghanaian Business (Promotion) Act (1970) provides for exclusive agencies to be limited to wholly-owned Ghanaian enterprises.

Import and Exchange Control Regulations

Import licences are required for most goods imported into Ghana. There are four categories of imports: those requiring specific import licences; those for which licences are not normally issued; prohibited goods; and those not requiring licences, e.g., household effects, unsolicited gifts. Import licences are not normally granted for luxury goods.

Exchange control regulations are stringent in view of Ghana's shortage of foreign exchange. The Government insists on sight payment for imports, and credit for imported goods is normally refused to importers. Government imports are also paid on sight. The importation of plant and equipment valued in excess of ¢100,000 requires the approval of the Bank of Ghana.

The period from September to March/April is most favoured for business visits.

Business Hours
Government Offices
0800–1230
1330–1700 Monday to Friday

Business Houses
0800–1200
1400–1630 or 1700 Monday to Friday

Some firms work on Saturday mornings, but most now operate on a 5-day week.

BUSINESS SERVICES

Advertising
Afromedia (Ghana) Ltd, P.O. Box 1262, Accra – printed hoardings and posters.

Apra Services Ltd, P.O. Box 6761, Accra.
Ghana Advertising and Marketing Ltd, P.O. Box 3209, Accra.
Mobile Film Publicity Services Ltd, P.O. Box 2715, Accra.

N.B. The use of mobile vans complete with sales staff, broadcasting equipment, etc., is a popular means of advertising branded products.

Shipping
Alpha (West Africa) Line Ltd, P.O. Box 451, Tema.
Black Star Line Ltd, P.O. Box 2760, Accra.
Holland-West Afrika Lijn NV, P.O. Box 269, Accra.
Liner Agencies (Ghana) Ltd, P.O. Box 66, Accra.
Scanship (Ghana) Ltd, P.O. Box 1705, Accra.

USEFUL ADDRESSES (BUSINESS)

Ghana National Chamber of Commerce: P.O. Box 2325, Accra.

Ghana Supply Commission: Cocoa House, Liberty Avenue, P.O. Box M35, Accra.

Export Promotion Council: P.O. Box M146, Accra.

The Ghana National Trading Corporation: P.O. Box 67, Accra.

Ghana Industrial Holding Corporation: P.O. Box 2784, Accra.

MAJOR CITY

Accra

Accra can be divided into 2 distinct areas: the old, crowded area of Jamestown around the harbour; and the main area to the east, with its spacious roads and open places where the Government offices and most business houses are situated.

The seat of Government is the Osu Castle, built in 1662, and overlooking the sea. Also on the waterfront is the Black Star Square, where all major official ceremonies are staged. The State House in the East Ridge district of the city is an impressive modern building with extensive conference facilities. The National Museum near Castle Road has a collection of both ancient and modern Ghanaian works of art.

East of Accra is a long stretch of beaches, most of which have their own beach clubs.

Hotels

There is no official hotel-rating system in Ghana. The Government-owned hotels of the State Hotel Corporation are usually of a good standard. There are also a number of Government resthouses, which can be booked through the State Hotel Corporation office in the nearest main town.

It is common practice for bills to be paid in advance.

AMBASSADOR, Independence Avenue, P.O. Box 3044, ☎ 64646.
Modern 1st-class hotel set in extensive tropical gardens near city centre, 6½ km/4 miles from airport.
Rooms: 152 ♪, ⬛, ☐ on request, ⟁, ⌾.
Suites available.
Facilities: Main restaurant, Chinese and outdoor restaurants, several bars. Casino with restaurant bar. Swimming, tennis; golf, beach club near by. Car hire.

GHANA

Services: TC, FC. ✉ Amex, Diners Club. Dr. on call. S.
Conference room – max. capacity 900.
Banquet rooms – max. capacity 300.

CONTINENTAL, Liberation Road, P.O. Box 5252, ☏ 75361.
Modern 1st-class hotel on main road to airport, 15 minutes' drive from city centre.
Rooms: 155, 5 suites. ♪.
Facilities: Restaurant, bar; snack terrace. Nightclub, casino. Nightly dancing, entertainment. Service shops. Car hire. Beach club, golf and tennis near by. Conference and banquet facilities.
Services: TC, FC. ✉ Amex, Diners Club.

PANORAMA CLUB, 25 Senchi Street, Airport Residential Area, P.O. Box 9039, ☏ 75356.
Modern hotel near airport, 6 km/4 miles from city centre.
Rooms: 15 ♪, ♨, ⛱, ☕. Suites available.
Facilities: Restaurant, bar. Tennis, swimming, sauna. Car hire.
Limited conference and banquet facilities.
Services: TC, FC. No credit cards. Dr. on call. S, ♂.

STAR, Fourth Circular Road, P.O. Box 652, ☏ 77728.
1st-class hotel on edge of city, mid-way between centre and airport.
Rooms: 60 ♪, ♨, ⛱, ☕. 20 chalets also available.
Facilities: Restaurant, bar. Entertainment, dancing. Golf, tennis, swimming near by. Car hire.
Services: TC, FC. ✉ Amex. Dr. on call. S, ♂.

Restaurants

Among Accra's better known restaurants are: *The Black Pot*, Riviera Beach Club – local dishes; *Le Rêve*, Liberty Avenue – French; *Club 400*, Liberty Avenue; *The Mandarin*, off Ring Road East; *Golden Phoenix*, Ambassador Hotel, and the *Palm Court*, Marine Drive – all Chinese; *Maharajah*, Pagan Road – Indian.

Nightclubs

Nightclubs and discotheques include *Napoleon Keteke*, *Metropole*, *Play Boy* and the *Tip Toe Gardens*.

Entertainment

Orchestral and theatrical performances, including Ghanaian folk operas are staged at the Arts Centre on 28th February Road. Art exhibitions are occasionally held here.

Accra has good sports facilities, including golf courses and polo grounds. There is racing on Saturdays at the Accra race-course, and football is played on Sundays at the stadium near Black Star Square. Swimming and water sports are also popular.

Shopping

Best buys: printed cloth, gold and silver jewellery.

The colourful Makola market in the city centre sells a wide variety of local goods, including native handicrafts from the Ashanti region and northern Ghana.

Modern and traditional African art is sold at stalls near the Community Centre on High Street.

Handicrafts are also on sale at *Africa House*, Castle Road; *Shop One*, Liberation Circle; and *La Boutique Africaine*. Lengths and ready-made garments of Kente cloth can be brought from the *Opoku Kente Weaving Centre*. For a wide selection of West African literature, try *Simpson's* or the *Atlas Book Shop* near the Ambassador Hotel.

GUINEA
Republic of Guinea

Geography	*169*
The Economy	*171*
How to Get There	*172*
Entry Regulations	*172*
Practical Information for the Visitor	*173*
Useful Addresses (General)	*174*
Business Information	*175*
Business Services	*175*
Useful Addresses (Business)	*175*
Conakry	*176*

Size: 245,857 sq.km/94,925 sq.miles.

Population: 5.1 million (1978 est.).

Distribution: 19% in urban areas.

Density: 19.4 persons per sq.km/50 per sq.mile.

Population Growth Rate: 3.0% p.a. (1970–7).

Ethnic Composition: There are more than 15 tribes, including the Fulani, Malinké and Soussou.

Capital: Conakry Pop. 600,000.

Major Town: Kankan Pop. 60,000.

Language: French is the official language; several African languages and dialects are also spoken.

Religion: Approximately 75% are Muslims; the remainder are mostly Animists, and there are about 30,000 Christians, mainly Roman Catholics.

Government: Guinea's only party, the Parti Démocratique de Guinée (PDG), exercises control over all the institutions of Government. The head of state is the President, who is elected for a 7-year term of office. The single-chamber Nationai Assembly is also elected for a 7-year period; the Parti Démocratique de Guinée presents a single list of candidates for election.

The highest authority of the PDG is Congress and the day-to-day running of the party is the responsibility of the Central Committee and the Political Bureau.

GEOGRAPHY

Situated on the west coast of Africa, Guinea is dominated by a mountainous plateau which rises to a height of more than 1,220m/4,000ft above sea level; the northern part is known as the Fouta Djallon, while to the south are the Guinea Highlands. Guinea has a narrow coastal plain with areas of tropical swampland. The south, along the Liberian border, consists of dense tropical forests.

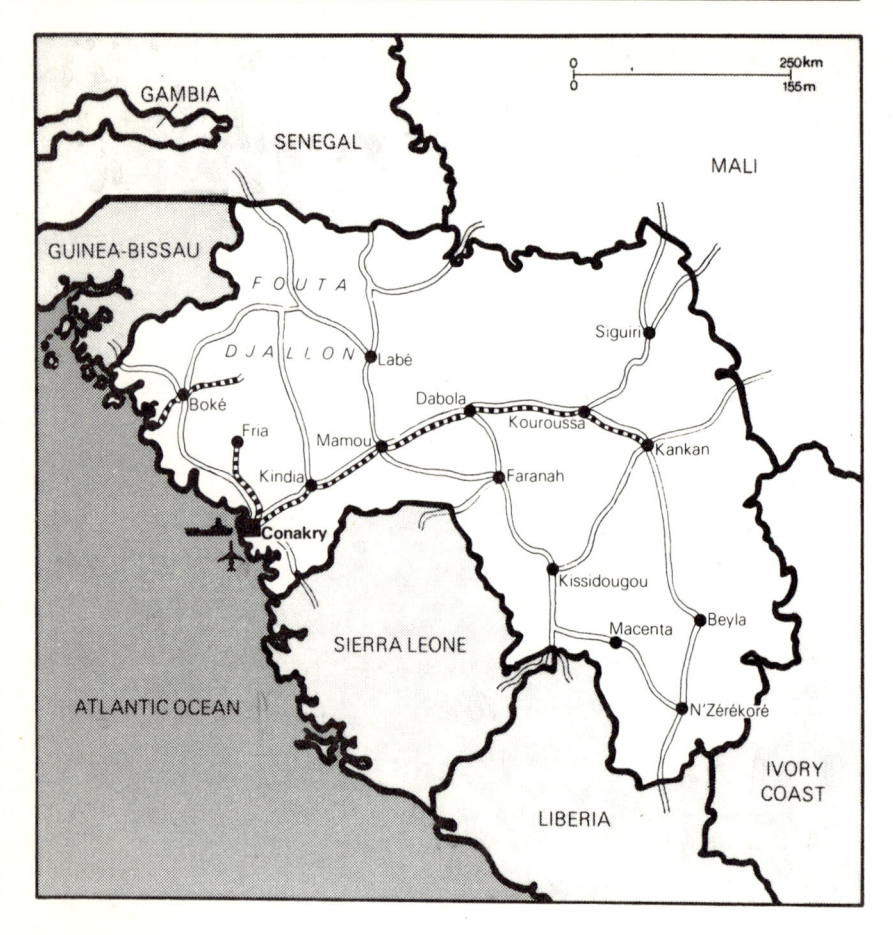

Climate

Guinea has a tropical climate and lies in the monsoon belt of the southwestern part of West Africa. There are 2 main seasons: the dry season from November to May, and the wet season from May to October. Average temperatures along the coast are 32°C/90°F during the dry season and 23°C/73°F during the wet seasons, with slightly lower temperatures inland.

The average annual rainfall is 430cm/169in, almost all of which falls during the wet season.

Agriculture

The main economic activity is agriculture, which employs 80% of the population, mainly on a subsistence basis. Rice, maize, cassava, millet and sweet potatoes are the main subsistence crops; coffee, bananas, palm kernels and pineapples are among the chief cash crops.

Guinea has enormous agricultural potential, with good soil conditions and a climate which would enable it to produce a large variety of produce, but production has fallen drastically since independence, partly due to the break-up of the French-owned plantations. Attempts have been made to modernise production techniques, and since 1973 agricultural planning in the form of rural collectives and price pegging has been in operation. However, there have been continuing problems of drought (1977), overgrazing and soil erosion, and Guinea still has to import food and subsidise exports.

Main Crops: rice, cassava, millet, coffee, bananas, pineapples, palm kernels.

Mineral Resources: bauxite, iron ore, gold, diamonds, uranium and titanium. There is a possibility of oil reserves offshore.

THE ECONOMY

Gross National Product (1978 est.): US$1.07 billion.

Per Capita Income (1978 est.): US$210.

Foreign Trade (1977 est.): Total Imports – 5.66 billion sylis. Total Exports – 6.63 billion sylis.

Main Trading Partners: Imports – France, West Germany, USA, USSR, Belgium, Luxembourg, United Kingdom. Exports – USA, West Germany, USSR, Spain, Canada, France.

There is little doubt that Guinea has sufficient agricultural and mineral resources to provide a secure economic base for further long-term industrial expansion. Though still a poor country, there have been signs in recent years that Guinea is beginning to utilise this potential.

Mining is the fastest growing sector and principal source of export revenue. The high grade bauxite reserves are immense and the state has a 49% share in the Friguia Company which works the mines and processes output. Hydroelectricity has been developed to meet the needs of the industry. There are 2 other mines at Boké and Kindia and output has risen steadily to 11.3 million tonnes in 1976. Future projects are planned with various foreign companies and governments providing technical and financial assistance. Plans are well advanced for the exploitation of the substantial iron ore deposits in partnership with Japanese, French, Romanian and Spanish interests.

The manufacturing sector is small, accounting for only 5% of the GDP. Plants are generally state-controlled and small scale to meet domestic requirements only. The aim is to expand this sector and to reduce imports. Textiles, agricultural processing, construction materials and brewing are the major manufacturing activities.

Visible trade has improved as bauxite production and prices have risen, though Guinea still has large foreign debts. The World Bank resumed loans to the country in 1975, and Arab countries have continued to donate aid. Smuggling, traditionally in diamonds, still forms a considerable part of the economy despite official attempts to prevent it.

Major Industries: mining, mineral processing, textiles, agricultural processing.

Main Commodities Traded: alumina, iron ore, coffee, fruit.

GUINEA

International Affiliations: UN, IBRD, OAU, ACP, ADB, ECOWAS.

HOW TO GET THERE

Air
UTA and Air Afrique operate regular flights from Paris and West African capitals to Conakry. There are 3 flights a week from Dakar and regular services from Rabat (Air Maroc) and Algiers (Air Algérie). Sabena fly to Conakry from Brussels continuing on to Lagos.

Other airlines flying to Conakry include Interflug, Air Mali and CSA (Czechoslovak Airlines). Aeroflot operates a 1-way only service from Conakry to Dakar.

Conakry International Airport is 15km/9 miles from the centre of Conakry. Taxis are the only means of transport between the airport and city centre.

Road
There is access by road into Guinea from Liberia, Sierra Leone, Mali and Senegal, but road conditions are poor and often hazardous; this is not a recommended means of travelling to Guinea.

ENTRY REGULATIONS

Visas
Visas are required by nationals of all countries, with the single exception of Mali, and should be obtained in advance of the proposed visit from Guinean diplomatic missions abroad.

Visitors are likely to experience some difficulty in obtaining a visa, partly due to the small number of Guinean embassies abroad and also to a certain amount of official cautiousness.

There is no Guinean Embassy in the United Kingdom; visas should be obtained from the Ambassade de Guinée, 24 Rue Emile Menier, Paris XVI, ☎ 5537225/8.

Before departure from Guinea, visitors should ensure that their return or onward ticket has been certified by the Département de la Régulation Aérienne et Maritime in Conakry. Without this certification, the airline ticket will be of no use and is valueless.

Health Regulations
Valid International Certificates of Vaccination against smallpox, yellow fever and cholera are required by all persons entering Guinea.

Customs
Currency: The import and export of Guinean currency is strictly forbidden. There is no limit to the amount of foreign currency and travellers' cheques which can be brought in, but all monies must be declared on entry. Visitors must fill in a currency declaration form which should be retained and produced on departure. All currency transactions should be entered on the form by an authorised bank.

Duty-free articles: Personal effects. 400 cigarettes. 2 bottles of spirits. Samples of no commercial value.

PRACTICAL INFORMATION FOR THE VISITOR

1. Currency
Monetary Unit – syli, divided into 100 cauris.
Notes – 10, 25, 50, 100 sylis.
Coins – 50 cauris; 1, 2, 5 sylis.

Sylis are not freely convertible outside Guinea; therefore visitors are advised to exchange foreign currency into sylis only when and as required. It is not possible to exchange excess sylis into foreign currency on departure from Guinea.

Travellers' cheques and foreign currency notes, preferably in US dollars or French francs, can be exchanged for sylis on arrival at the airport, a bank or the Hotel de l'Indépendance. A black market is in operation offering sometimes as much as 5 times the official exchange rate; however, penalties for illegal transactions are heavy and visitors are advised to avoid such dealings.

Banking Hours
0800 – 1230 Monday to Saturday

All banking is under the control of the *Banque Centrale de la République de Guinée*, Boulevard du Commerce, B.P. 692, Conakry, ☎ 41781.

There are 3 other licensed banks:
Banque Guinéenne du Commerce Extérieur, Conakry.
Banque Nationale de Développement Agricole, Avenue de la République, Conakry.
Crédit National pour le Commerce, l'Industrie et l'Habitat, 6ème Avenue, Conakry.

2. Electricity Supply
220v AC 50Hz.

3. Weights and Measures
The metric system is in use.

4. Media
Radio and television broadcasting are state-controlled and carry no commercial advertising. Radiodiffusion Nationale de Guinée transmits programmes in French, English, Arabic, Portuguese and African languages. Black-and-white television broadcasting began in 1977.

Newspapers and Journals
Horoya, the organ of the Parti Démocratique de Guinée, is published 2 or 3 times a month. The *Journal Officiel de Guinée* is a fortnightly publication. *Fonikee* is the official paper of La Jeunesse Démocratique Africaine and *Le Travailleur de Guinée* is published by La Confédération Nationale de Travailleurs Guinéens.

5. Medical Care
TAB (typhoid and paratyphoid) and tetanus injections are recommended for visitors. Malaria is prevalent in some areas, including Conakry, and visitors are advised to take anti-malarial prophylactics. Tap water is not safe to drink; filtered or bottled water only should be drunk.

Hospital facilities are of a very basic nature and virtually non-existent outside Conakry.

6. Telephone, Telex and Postal Services
The communications network is highly underdeveloped, both at the domestic and international level. Visitors may find services unreliable and subject to lengthy delays.

7. Public Holidays

1 January	*New Year's Day*
1 May	*Labour Day*
14 May	*Anniversary of the Founding of the PDG*
2 October	*Independence Day*
1 November	*Army Day*

GUINEA

22 November   *Anniversary of the 1970 Invasion*
25 December   *Christmas Day*

In addition, the major Christian festivals are observed, as well as these Muslim holidays: *Mouled, Eid el Fitr* and *Tabaski*.

8. Time
GMT.

9. Internal Transport

Air
Air Guinée operates regular flights from Conakry to Boké, Kankan, Kissidougou, Labé, Macenta, N'Zérékoré and Siguiri.

Airline Offices in Conakry

Air Afrique	☎ 43495/7.
Air Guinée	☎ 42981 (reservations). 61537 (Airport).
Sabena	☎ 43140.
UTA	☎ 43657/9.

Rail
There are passenger services from Conakry to Kankan via Kindia, Mamou and Dabola.

Road
Roads are of poor standard, many being little more than dirt tracks which become virtually impassable during the rainy season. The main tarmac roads link Conakry with Kissidougou via Kindia, Mamou and Faranah; Mamou with Labé; and Conakry with Kankan.

Buses and taxis operate in Conakry. Taxis are relatively cheap but are not always easy to find, especially in the afternoon and evening. It is sometimes possible to hire taxis by the hour.

Self-drive cars can be hired from the *Agence Charbonneaux* in Conakry. Traffic travels on the right-hand side of the road.

10. Tipping
Taxis – No tip necessary.

Porters – 10 sylis per bag.

Hotels/restaurants – A service charge is included in the bill.

11. Social Customs
Alcohol should not be offered to Muslims, and visitors should show respect for the various religious festivals and fasts which take place. It is unwise for women to wear clothing which might be considered in any way revealing or offensive.

Guineans tend to be sensitive about political issues and are often suspicious of visitors from the West. It is advisable to refrain from making too many comments about the nature of the Government, although an interest in the country and its affairs is usually appreciated.

12. Photography
Visitors should ensure that they obtain permission from the Ministry of Information and Tourism before taking any photographs. It is unadvisable to attempt to photograph anything of an official nature, particularly military personnel or installations and Government buildings.

USEFUL ADDRESSES (GENERAL)

Conakry
Honorary British Consul: c/o Magus Ltd, B.P. 158, ☎ 43705/8.

French Embassy: B.P. 373 and 570, ☎ 41655/41681.

Japanese Embassy: Mafanko Corniche Sud, B.P. 895, ☎ 61438.

Swiss Embassy: Rue de l'Ecole de Santé, B.P. 720, ☎ 61387.

US Embassy: 2ème Boulevard and 9ème Avenue, B.P. 603, ☎ 41520/4.

West German Embassy: B.P. 540.

Office du Tourisme: Place des Martyrs.

BUSINESS INFORMATION

There exists substantial potential for the development of mineral resources, manufacturing and infrastructure projects. Private investment is tolerated if it accords with Government priorities and is conducted in partnership with the state. The Government has a 49% share in all mining developments, takes 65% of profits, and reserves the right to nominate directors in return for providing supporting facilities and services. Contracts and licences are granted if guarantees are made to buy extracted ore and to follow on-site processing plans for a 20-year period. Other areas being encouraged under the current development plan are fisheries, forestry, tourism and social services.

Import Regulations

Import licences are required for all goods. Restrictions or prohibitions apply to imports of the following goods: distilling equipment and some alcoholic drinks and alcohol, matches, arms, ammunition and military equipment, artificial food colourings, tinned fish, saccharin, gramophone records, narcotics, books and newspapers, medals and coins, explosives and poisonous substances.

Business Hours
Government Offices and Business Houses
0730 – 1500 Monday to Thursday
0730 – 1300 Friday
0730 – 1400 Saturday

BUSINESS SERVICES

Insurance
Société Nationale d'Assurances et de Réassurances de la République de Guinée, B.P. 179, Conakry.

Shipping
ENTRAT, B.P. 315, Conakry – state-owned forwarding firm.

Société Navale Guinéenne, B.P. 522, Conakry – agent for Delta Steamship Lines Inc, Elder Dempster Line, Hanseatic Africa Line, Lloyd Triestino, Palm Line, Scandinavian West Africa Line and United West Africa Service.

USEFUL ADDRESSES (BUSINESS)

Importex, B.P. 125, Conakry, ☎ 42809.

Ministère du Commerce Extérieur, Conakry, ☎ 42694.

MAJOR CITY

Conakry

The old town of Conakry lies in a beautiful setting on Tumbo Island off the Kaloum Peninsula, surrounded by blue sea and palm-lined beaches. The island is linked by a causeway to the peninsula where new suburbs have grown up. There is a stark contrast between the town's residential areas with elegant villas dating from the Colonial period and the dismal, crowded suburbs where the majority of the population live.

The administrative and commercial centres of Conakry are situated on the island, which is laid out in symmetrical fashion with long, straight avenues lined with flowering trees. Places of interest include: the Chinese-built People's Palace, seat of Guinea's National Assembly; the Roman Catholic cathedral; the Botanical Gardens in the suburb of Camayenne; and the President's Palace.

A short boat trip from the harbour on Tumbo Island will take you to the Iles de Los, a series of islands between 5–10km/3–6 miles off Tumbo Island. The island of Roume was at one time a centre for the slave trade; Tamara Island has good beaches backed by splendid woodlands.

Hotels

There is no official hotel rating system.

CAMAYENNE, B.P. 578, ☎ 61139.
Modern hotel by the sea, 4km/2½ miles from town centre.
Rooms: 120 (in some). Suites available.
Facilities: Restaurant, bar.

HÔTEL DE L'INDÉPENDANCE, Premier Boulevard, B.P. 287, ☎ 43491.
Situated by sea, within walking distance of town centre.
Rooms: 80 (in some).
Facilities: Restaurant, bar.
Services: not accepted.
N.B. In September 1979 alteration work was started on the Hôtel de l'Indépendance; at the time of writing the hotel was due to re-open at the end of 1980.

GRAND HÔTEL DE L'UNITÉ, B.P. 683, Telex 2139.

HOTEL GBESSIA INTERNATIONAL AIRPORT, Gbessia, B.P. 743, ☎ 61145.
Modern hotel near airport, 13km/8 miles from town centre.
Rooms: 60, 8 suites.
Facilities: Restaurant, bar. Cabaret.
Services: not accepted.

Restaurants

The number of good restaurants is limited; visitors may prefer to eat in the hotel restaurants. Others include *Royal St Germain, Paradis, Le Grillon, L'Oasis* and *Les Petits Bateaux* – local dishes.

Nightclubs

The *Hotel Gbessia* has a cabaret with regular jazz sessions; there is also jazz at the *Eldorado*. Other nightspots include: *Le Jardin de Guinée* and *La Paillotte* – open air dancing.

Entertainment

Theatrical and dance groups from all over the country perform in Conakry and during the last 2 weeks of October the annual cultural festival known as the 'Quinzaine Artistique' is held. The 28 September Stadium in the suburb of Landreah is a popular venue for such occasions.

Sporting facilities are limited. There are some opportunities for water sports along the mainland coast and off the Isle de Los, although this is an area of dangerous currents and is only suitable for strong swimmers.

Shopping

Best buys: wood carvings, embroidery, jewellery, leather rugs, records.

The markets are generally a better place for buying handicrafts than the town's shops, which may be relatively low on stock. Beware of some stall-holders who price their goods in CFA francs or Liberian dollars. This is a highly illegal practice.

There is a duty-free shop at Gbessia Airport.

GUINEA-BISSAU
Republic of Guinea-Bissau

Geography	179
The Economy	180
How to Get There	181
Entry Regulations	182
Practical Information for the Visitor	182
Useful Addresses (General)	183
Business Information	184
Business Services	184
Useful Addresses (Business)	184
Bissau	184

Size: 36,125 sq.km/13,948 sq.miles (at low tide and including the Bijagos Archipelago).

Population: 777,214 (1979 census).

Distribution: in urban areas.

Density: 21.5 persons per sq.km/55.7 per sq.mile.

Population Growth Rate: N.A.

Ethnic Composition: The African population is made up of 15 tribal groups, the main ones being the Balante, Fulani, Mandyako, Malinke and Pepel. There are also mestiços of mixed European and African descent and small numbers of Cape Verdeans, Europeans, Syrians and Lebanese.

Capital: Bissau City pop. 109,486.

Major Towns: Bafata pop. 8,000.

Language: Portuguese is the official language, although *Crioulo*, the Creole lingua franca, is more widely spoken. Balante, Fulani and various other tribal languages are also spoken.

Religion: Most people hold traditional Animist beliefs; some 35% are Muslim and about 1% are Christian, mostly Roman Catholics in urban areas.

Government: Independence from Portugal was proclaimed by PAIGC forces in September 1973 after 10 years of war and was recognised by Lisbon in September 1974. The sole political party is the Partido Africano da Independência da Guiné e Cabo Verde (PAIGC), led by President Luiz Cabral. Voting is by secret ballot for all over 18 years of age, and elections are for candidates on a list standing for regional councils. The regional councils themselves elect representatives to the National People's Assembly. The Council of State Commissioners is engaged in the administration of PAIGC policies and is responsible to the National Assembly. Government association with Cape Verde is strong and the 2 nations plan to integrate their legal and administrative apparatus.

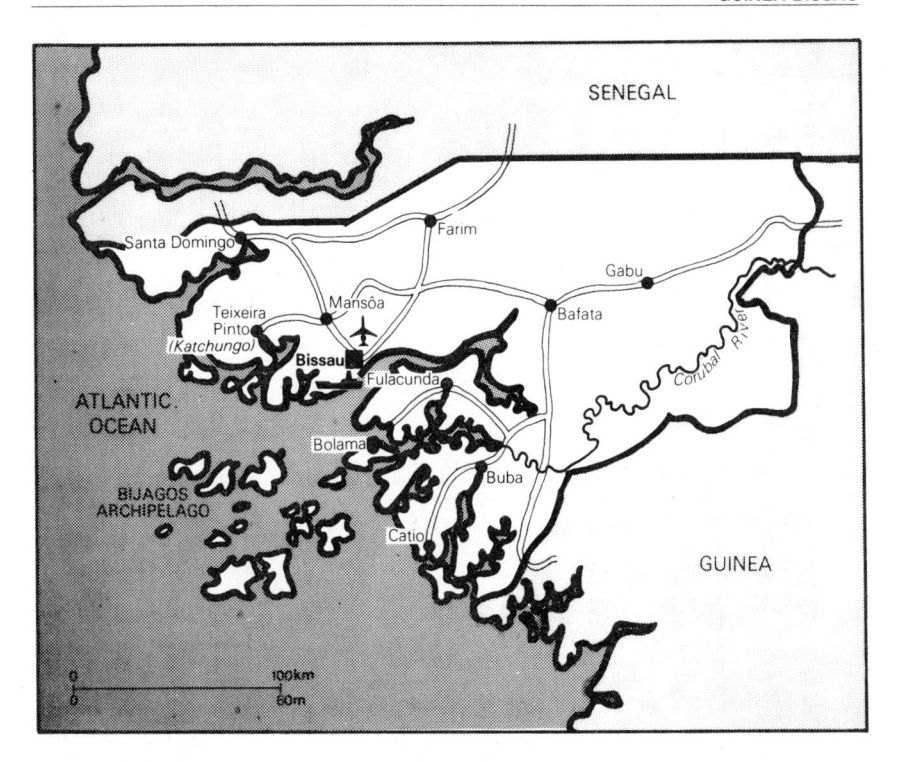

GEOGRAPHY

The coastal areas around the river estuaries where rain forests turn to mangrove and swamp are very low-lying and constitute a considerable part of the country's area. Guinea-Bissau territory includes a number of offshore islands. Inland from the coastal plains are flat wooded savannah plateaux rising to higher hills along the Guinean border.

Climate

Conditions in the tropical climate of Guinea-Bissau are generally hot and wet, with average annual temperature at 20°C/68°F. The hottest months are April and May when average temperatures are 30°C/84°F. the coolest time of year is in December and January, with temperatures averaging about 23°C/73°F. Humidity is especially high from July to September. Dry winds blow out from the Sahel interior from December to April, and rainfall is reduced at this time of year. Rainfall is plentiful and variable with 1,000–2,000mm/39–79ins in the north and in Bissau some 1,778mm/70ins falling annually.

Agriculture

Agriculture is the major economic activity, with rice the staple crop. The damage of the war years is being overcome, and Guinea-Bissau hopes to be self-sufficient in this vital crop soon. In the rural areas rice, maize, beans, cassava and sweet potatoes are the most important food crops. Of the cash crops groundnuts and palm kernels are the major export earners (70% in 1977); coconuts account for some 11% of total export value. Cattle raising is important in the inland regions. Livestock estimates in 1977 were 260,000 cattle, 181,000 goats and 172,000 pigs. Meat production is virtually sufficient to satisfy domestic demand, with some hides and skins being exported. Forestry output is mostly in hardwoods; however an extensive reafforestation programme is under way and felling has been much reduced.

The state has nationalised the land, but private concessions are granted and traditional tilling rights have not been altered. Self-sufficiency is the objective of government plans and crop diversification, new rotation systems and new strains are being adopted to this end. Much work is being done to develop salt- and fresh-water varieties of rice. Other new projects include a projected sugar refinery at Mansôa with irrigated plantations near by to supply cane, a groundnut processing plant at Cumere built with Saudi aid and the development of cotton production with help from the European Development Fund. Other new cash crops being introduced are soya beans and tobacco in state co-operative plantations. It is Government policy to maintain state farms if they can be proved to be efficient or are engaged in experimental work. A programme to boost the fishing industry is under way with the state fishing company Estrelo do Mar, run with Soviet assistance, engaging in co-operation agreements with Algeria, France and Portugal. Fisheries are now the 2nd most important export after groundnuts. The agricultural outlook is improving steadily and, though some food is still imported, the amounts are declining as peasant production improves after the drought year of 1977/8.

Main Crops: subsistence crops – rice, manioc, maize, beans, sweet potatoes, yams, fruits; cash crops – groundnuts, coconuts, palm kernels, sesame seeds, cashew nuts, tobacco, sugar cane, cotton, timber.

Mineral Resources: bauxite. Phosphates, zinc, copper and offshore petroleum are also thought to be present.

THE ECONOMY

Gross National Product (1976 est.): US$100 million.

Per Capita Income (1976): US$140.

Gross Domestic Product: N.A.

Foreign Trade (1977): Total Imports – 1,235.1 million pesos. Total Exports – 428.1 million pesos.

Main Trading Partners: Imports – Portugal, USSR, Sweden, France, West Germany, Belgium/Luxembourg, Italy, Netherlands, Pakistan, USA, UK. Exports – Portugal, Egypt, Senegal, France, Spain, Cape Verde, West Germany, Algeria.

As a Portuguese colony in the years before the guerrilla war and independence, the country relied heavily upon the colonial power for imports and for a large share of the export market. Industry was not developed and little help given to African enterprise. As a consequence the PAIGC Government took over an economy distorted by colonial policies, damaged by the years of war and suffering from massive budgetary deficits. The reconstruction programme has been based primarily on increasing agricultural production to reduce food import bills. The policy of encouraging small-scale and state-farm agriculture has helped absorb unemployment resulting from the return of refugees and the loss of jobs in Portuguese government and businesses. Rapid improvements have been made in a number of areas, particularly in infrastructure projects. Health, education, transport and communications are priority areas. A chain of 'People's Shops' has been set up to take over much of the distributive sector, and a new national currency was introduced in 1976.

In the agricultural sector new developments are planned involving integrated projects with processing facilities. Amongst these schemes are a sugar refinery, a pulp and paper factory and a groundnut oil refinery. Fishing is also to be extended to supply domestic and export markets.

Manufacturing is on a small scale. The domestic market is small and apart from food processing there are some companies involved in making construction materials.

Bauxite exists in the Boe area with mining and an aluminium plant planned for Saltinho, if studies suggest that it is viable.

Tourism is given guarded approval, and some hotels have been reconstructed in recent years.

Other major projects inlcude a thermo-electric power station, the enlargement of Bissau harbour and an extensive improvement in road and ferry connections with the EDF providing assistance for the latter projects. Aid is received from many bilateral and multilateral donors including the USSR, Scandinavian countries, the EEC, the Arab and African development banks. Though a small nation, Guinea-Bissau has a number of valuable resources which, combined with imaginative and pragmatic policies, could rebuild a stronger economy less reliant on the aid now provided.

Major Industries: rice and palm milling, groundnut processing, brewing, soft drinks, wooden floor tiles, foam rubber, bricks, repair work.

Main Commodities Traded: Imports – food and drink, consumer goods, industrial supplies, fuel, machinery and transport equipment. Exports – groundnuts, palm kernels, shellfish, fish, timber, coconuts.

International Affiliations: UN, IBRD, OAU, ACP, ADB, ECOWAS.

HOW TO GET THERE

Air
Air Algérie fly to Bissau from Algiers once weekly; Aeroflot connect Moscow and Bissau once a week; and TAP (Portugal) operate a twice weekly service from Lisbon. Air Senegal and TAGB (Guinea-Bissau) provide scheduled flights to and from Dakar (Senegal). TACV (Cape Verde) and TAGB connect Bissau with Cape Verde. Air Guinea fly to Bissau from Conakry (Guinea).
Bissau International Airport is 11km/7 miles from the city centre.

Road
There are road and ferry connections with Banjul and Ziguinchor (Senegal), but these are not a recommended means of entry into Guinea-Bissau. Main routes are due to be improved as part of the Gambia–Senegal–Guinea-Bissau highway.

ENTRY REGULATIONS

Visas
Visitors require a visa unless officially invited by the Government. Visas can be obtained from representatives of Guinea-Bissau abroad or by applying at least 2 weeks in advance of arrival to the Commissariado de Estado da Seguranca Nacional e Ordem Publica da Republica da Guinea-Bissau (State Directorate of National Security and Public Order of the Republic of Guinea-Bissau). Applications must include 2 passport photos and complete details of the visitor's itinerary and purpose of the visit. A visa will then be available at the airport upon arrival. All visitors without a waiting visa will be immediately deported. Most visitors travel via Dakar (Senegal), where visas may be obtained.

Health Regulations
An International Certificate of Vaccination for smallpox is required if arriving within 14 days of leaving an infected area. All visitors staying in Guinea-Bissau for longer than 2 weeks or who have arrived within 6 days of leaving an infected area require a Certificate of Vaccination for yellow fever. Cholera vaccination is advisable.

Customs
Currency: The import and export of local currency is prohibited. There are no restrictions on the import of foreign currency, provided that it is declared upon arrival. Export of foreign currency is permitted up to the amount of declared.

Duty-free articles: Reasonable quantities of tobacco products. Perfume for personal use.

Restricted articles: Alcoholic beverages. Pets. Firearms.

PRACTICAL INFORMATION FOR THE VISITOR

1. Currency
Monetary Unit – Guinea peso, divided into 100 centavos.
Notes – 50, 100, 500 pesos.
Coins – 5, 10, 20, 50 centavos; 1, 2½, 5, 10, 20 pesos.

The central bank and bank of issue is the *Banco National da Guine-Bissau*.

Domestic Banks in Bissau
Banco National da Guine-Bissau, C.P. 38.
Caixa de Credito da Guine – savings and loan bank.
Caixa Economica Postal – postal savings bank.

2. Electricity Supply
220v AC 50Hz.

3. Weights and Measures
The metric system is in use.

4. Media
Radio-difusao da Republica da Guine-Bissau is the Government radio station broadcasting on several frequencies. The media are government controlled in Guinea-Bissau.

The official government newspaper is *No Pintcha*, published thrice weekly in Portuguese.

5. Medical Care
Malaria is endemic in Guinea-Bissau, and anti-malarial prophylactics should be taken. Tap water should be boiled or filtered before drinking.
  Medical facilities are not good but are improviding steadily. Several new hospitals are under construction.

6. Telephone, Telex and Postal Services
Telephone, telegraph and postal services are satisfactory, but international calls may be delayed. Public telex facilities are available at the central post office in Bissau.

7. Public Holidays
1 January	New Year's Day
20 January	National Heroes Day
8 March	Women's Day
1 May	Workers Day
3 August	Colonialism Martyrs Day
12 September	National Day
24 September	Republic Day
25 December	Christmas Day

8. Time
GMT.

9. Internal Transport
Air
All domestic flights are operated by the national airline, Transportes Aereos da Guine-Bissau (TAGB), who provide services to small field airports at Farim, Bafata, Buba, Catio, Gabu and Santo Domingo.

Airline Offices in Bissau
Transportes Aereos da Guine-Bissau, C.P. 111.
Aeroflot, Rua 19 de Settembro 6, ☎ 2707.
TAP (Portugal), Praca dos Herois Nacionais 14, ☎ 3991/2/3.

Road
The Portuguese-built road system is currently being improved, and some 1,000km/621 miles of road are now asphalted. Buses and taxis operate in Bissau, but are not common outside the capital.

Sea and River
Many towns are accessible by boat, and several scheduled ferry services operate on the rivers. Sea and river links are currently being improved.

USEFUL ADDRESSES (GENERAL)

Bissau
Brazilian Embassy, Avda Pansau Na Isna 30, C.P. 29.

People's Republic of China Embassy, Rua Eduardo Mondlane 31.

Cuban Embassy, Rua Joaquim N'Com 1.

Egyptian Embassy, Rua 12 de Setembro 6-A.

French Embassy, Rua Eduardo Mondlane 67–A, C.P. 195, ☎ 2633/4.

Portuguese Embassy, Rua 16, no. 6.

Swedish Embassy, Rua 13, no. 16.

US Embassy, Avda Domingos Ramos, C.P. 297, ☎ 2816/7.

USSR Embassy, Avda Pansau Na Isna.

Dutch Consulate, Avda 3 de Agosto 44, C.P. 23, ☎ 2841/3.

Hon. British Consul, c/o Magus Ltd, C.P. 307, ☎ 3349.

Centro de Informacãos e Turismo, C.P. 294.

GUINEA-BISSAU

BUSINESS INFORMATION

Government policy is to retain a state majority holding in all major companies; important sectors of the economy are also state controlled and planned. Foreign assistance is welcomed on a limited scale in joint projects with the state. Most opportunities for foreign companies are likely to occur in work connected with one or another of the aid-supported development schemes. Technical help and capital equipment are needed in the reconstruction of agriculture, fishing, transport and communications. There are already a number of foreign companies present from Europe and Africa working with the state; however, policy towards foreign investors remains extremely cautious.

Bissau is the main trade and administrative centre and it is the largest port.

All business literature should be in Portuguese or French.

Import and Exchange Control Regulations

All imports must be given prior approval by state officials. Import licences may be authorised by the Directorate of Foreign Trade and, if granted, the necessary exchange will be made available. A customs fee surcharge of 5% ad valorem is levied on all goods. A Consumption Tax and other duties are payable on selected goods at varying rates.

Business Hours
Government and Business Offices
0800–1200
1500–1800 Monday to Friday

BUSINESS SERVICES

Shipping

Guinemar, Sociedade de Agencias e Transportes da Guine Lda., Rua Guerra Mendes 4–4A, Bissau.

Naguicave – joint Guinea-Bissau/Cape Verde Shipping Co.

USEFUL ADDRESSES (BUSINESS)

Directorate General of Foreign Trade, Ministry of Commerce, Bissau.

MAJOR CITY

Bissau

Bissau, founded in 1687 by the Portuguese, was developed as a fortified port to handle transit trade and in 1942 the city was made the capital of Portuguese Guinea. The colonial past is apparent in the architecture and layout of the city, with its avenues, promenades, cafés and old colonial buildings, many of them several hundreds of years old. However, Bissau is also a modern African city, and new offices, shops and public buildings have recently been constructed. The city is small and easily covered on foot. There is a small open-air market in Bissau. The National Museum is housed in the PAIGC headquarters.

Hotels

There is no official hotel rating system. Accommodation is limited, and reservations should be made well in advance. Information on hotels is scanty but amongst those in the city are: *Hotel 24 de Settembre*, *Grand Hotel*, *Hotel Pidjiguiti*, *Hotel Ancar*.

IVORY COAST
Republic of Ivory Coast

Geography	186
The Economy	188
How to Get There	189
Entry Regulations	189
Practical Information for the Visitor	190
Useful Addresses (General)	192
Business Information	192
Business Services	193
Useful Addresses (Business)	193
Abidjan	194

Size: 322,460 sq.km/124,502 sq.miles.

Population: 7.48 million (1978 est.).

Distribution: 28% in urban areas.

Density: 21 persons per sq.km/54 per sq.mile.

Population Growth Rate: 3.9% p.a.

Ethnic Composition: There are more than 60 tribes forming 6 principal groups: Akans, Krous, Lagunaires, Malinkés, Mandés du Sud and Voltaiques. The most influential tribe are the Baoulés living in the central region. There are large numbers of other Africans – mainly Mossis from Upper Volta and Malians – working in the Ivory Coast, and also French, Lebanese, Syrian and Italian communities.

Capital: Abidjan Pop. 1,389,978.

Major Cities/Towns: Bouaké Pop. 265,875; Korhogo Pop. 45,000; Daloa Pop. 60,000; Grand Bassam Pop. 26,000; San Pedro Pop. 45,000.

Language: French is the official language. A number of African languages are spoken, the principal one being Dioula.

Religion: Approximately 65% are Animists, 23% Muslims, 12% Christians (Roman Catholic and Protestant).

Government: A President, elected every 5 years by direct universal suffrage, heads the Government and appoints the Council of Ministers. The National Assembly, also elected for a 5-year term, is composed of members belonging to the sole political party, the Parti Démocratique de la Côte d'Ivoire (PDCI).

GEOGRAPHY

The country consists of a coastal strip in the south merging with equatorial rain forests, while to the north lies a drier savannah belt.

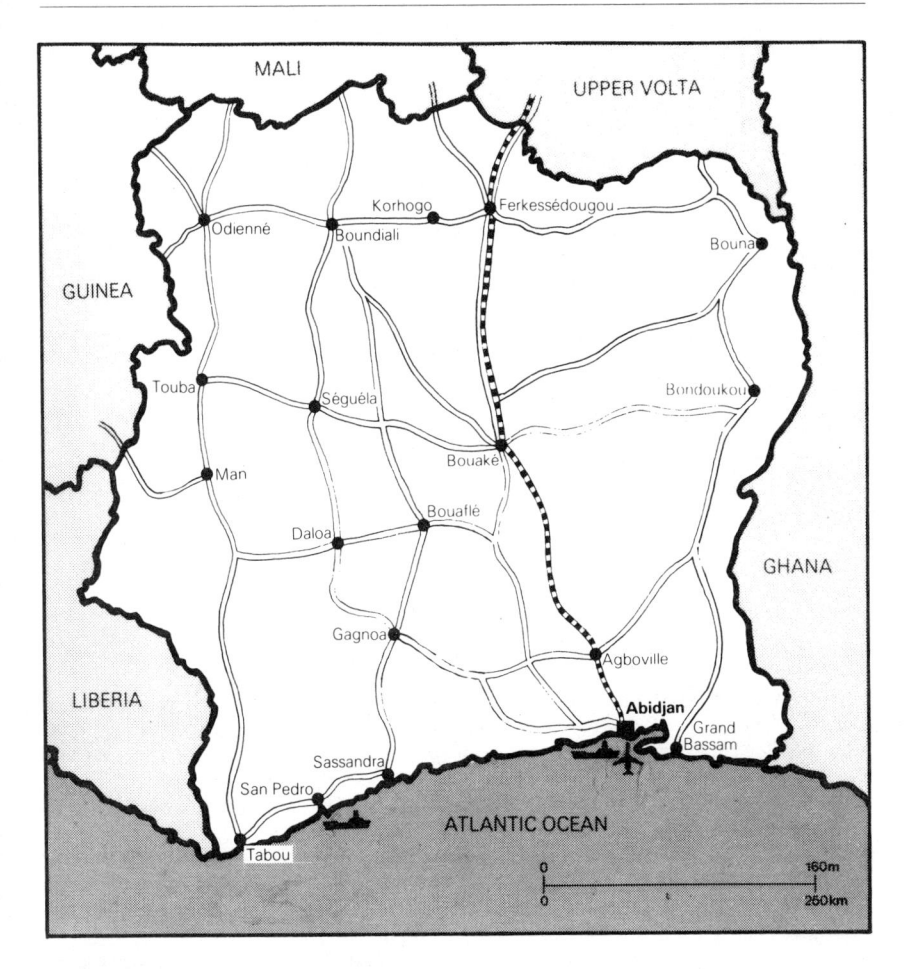

IVORY COAST

Climate
Climatic conditions vary considerably between north and south. In the south, the climate is tropical with a mean humidity of 82%; average temperatures for Abidjan range from 23°C/73°F to 30°C/86°F; the hottest period is from January to April; and the main rainy season is from May to July. In the north, temperatures range from 21°C/69°F to 35°C/95°F and there is little rain, most of it falling between May and October.

Agriculture
The economy is based on agricultural exports, and around 82% of the population is employed in the agricultural sector. The Ivory Coast is the world's largest producer of cocoa and the 3rd largest producer of coffee. Agriculture remains heavily concentrated in coffee, cocoa and timber, which account for over 70% of the value of all exports.

The Ivory Coast is virtually self-sufficient in some foodstuffs such as rice. It imports fish, dairy products and luxury food items.

IVORY COAST

Main Crops: cocoa, coffee, bananas, rice, pineapples, cotton, coconuts, palm oil, sugar, cassava, corn.

Mineral Resources: diamonds, manganese, iron ore.

THE ECONOMY

Gross National Product (1977): US$6.46 billion.

Per Capita Income (1977): US$710.

Gross Domestic Product (1977): 1,590.4 billion CFA francs.

Foreign Trade (1978): Total Imports – 522.5 billion CFA francs. Total Exports – 524.38 billion CFA francs.

Main Trading Partners: Imports – France, USA, West Germany, Japan. Exports – France, Netherlands, USA, West Germany, Italy.

The Ivory Coast experienced something of an economic boom during the 1970s with a real increase in GNP and average per capita income, now one of the highest in black Africa. Agricultural exports are largely responsible for this boom, and the increase in the world price of coffee and cocoa, together with an increase in local output, have made coffee and cocoa major sources of foreign exchange earnings. The Government's programme of agricultural diversification has produced additional crops for export; e.g., palm oil, pineapples, rubber, cotton. Bananas and timber are still important primary commodities.

The industrial sector has expanded rapidly since independence, but still accounts for only around 20% of the GNP. Despite an overt policy of 'Africanisation' by the Government in many economic sectors, a large proportion of commercial and industrial concerns are still concentrated in French hands.

The emphasis of indusrual development has largely been an import substitution together with export-orientated agro-industries. Food processing accounts for about one-third of industrial production and includes coffee powdering, chocolate manufacture, fruit canning and soft drinks, rice milling and sugar refining. The Government is planning to expand the textile and clothing industries, which are concentrated around Bouaké. Mechanical and metallurgical industries include vehicle assembly, chemicals and the manufacture of aluminium sheets, metal parts, car batteries and fertilisers.

Major Industries: food processing, timber, textiles, clothing, vehicle assembly, oil refining.

Main Commodities Traded: Imports – transport equipment, machinery, petroleum products, electrical equipment, luxury foodstuffs. Exports – coffee, cocoa, timber, bananas, pineapples, cotton, petroleum products.

International Affiliations: UN, IBRD, OAU, ACP, ADB, CEAO, ECOWAS, Franc Zone, OCAM.

HOW TO GET THERE

Air
The following major airlines operate regular services to Abidjan: Alitalia, Egypt Air, KLM, MEA, Pan Am, Sabena, Swissair. UTA and Air Afrique fly daily from Paris to Abidjan, the latter operating via Geneva and Rome. British Caledonian have three flights a week.

Flights to Abidjan from the African continent are operated by Air Mali, Air Zaïre, Egypt Air, Ghana Airways and Nigeria Airways.

Flying times to Abidjan: from London, 11 hours; from New York, 12 hours.

Port Bouet Airport is 16km/10 miles from the centre of Abidjan. Taxis are available at the Airport. Some of the larger hotels provide free transport to and from the airport.

ENTRY REGULATIONS

Visas
Visas are required by nationals of all countries except: (i) United Kingdom of Great Britain and Northern Ireland, Jersey, Guernsey and its dependencies, for a stay of up to 3 months; (ii) Denmark, Finland, West Germany, Republic of Ireland, Italy, Norway, Sweden, Tunisia, for a stay of up to 3 months; (iii) Andorra, Benin, Cameroon, Central African Republic, Chad, Congo, France, Gabon, Madagascar, Mali, Mauritania, Monaco, Niger, Senegal, Togo, Upper Volta, for an unlimited stay; (iv) holders of diplomatic or service passports of Belgium, Israel, Luxembourg, Netherlands, for a stay of up to 3 months.

All other nationals require visas, obtainable from embassies of the Ivory Coast abroad.

Business travellers requiring visas should support their application with a letter from their firm giving full details of the business to be undertaken and confirming financial responsibility for the applicant.

Visas are valid for 3 months for a stay of variable length.

Health Regulations
A valid International Certificate of Vaccination against smallpox is required by all persons entering the Ivory Coast. Yellow fever and cholera vaccination certificates are no longer obligatory, but it is advisable to be vaccinated against these diseases.

Customs
Currency: There is no limit to the amount of local or foreign currency which may be imported, provided it is declared on arrival. There is a limit of 125,000 CFA francs to the amount of local currency which may be taken out of the Ivory Coast.

Duty-free articles: Personal effects. 200 cigarettes or 400g of tobacco. 1 bottle of spirits. One camera, portable typewriter, tape recorder, etc., provided they are more than 6 months old. Samples of no commercial value. (Samples of value can be temporarily imported under an ATA Carnet without any duty being paid, although a deposit or guarantee of the deposit must be placed with the issuing Chamber of Commerce.)

PRACTICAL INFORMATION FOR THE VISITOR

1. Currency
Monetary Unit – CFA franc.
Notes – 100, 500, 1,000, 5,000, 10,000 CFA francs.
Coins – 1, 5, 10, 25, 50, 100 CFA francs.

The Ivory Coast is a member of the *Banque Centrale des Etats de l'Afrique de l'Ouest*, B.P. 1769, Abidjan.

Banking Hours
0800–1130
1430–1630 Monday to Friday

Principal Domestic Banks
Banque Internationale pour le Commerce et l'Industrie de la Côte d'Ivoire, Avenue Franchet d'Espérey, B.P. 1298, Abidjan.
Banque Réale de la Côte d'Ivoire, B.P. 4411, Abidjan.
Société Ivoirienne de Banque, 34 Boulevard de la République, B.P. 1300, Abidjan.
Société Générale de Banques en Côte d'Ivoire, 5 Avenue Louis Barthe, B.P. 1355, Abidjan.
Banque Internationale pour l'Afrique Occidentale, B.P. 1274, Abidjan.

Foreign Commercial Banks
Barclays Bank International Ltd, Immeuble Alpha 2000, Rue Gourgas, B.P. 522, Abidjan, ☎ 322804.
Chase Manhattan Bank, B.P. 211977, Abidjan, ☎ 326817.
Citibank, 15 Avenue Louis Barthe, B.P. 20788, Abidjan, ☎ 324610.

2. Electricity Supply
230v AC 50Hz.
Plugs: 2 round pins.

3. Weights and Measures
The metric system is used.

4. Media
Television broadcasts in French are transmitted to approximately one-third of the Ivory Coast. Radiodiffusion Ivoirienne broadcasts in French, English and African languages.

Newspapers and Journals
Fraternité Matin is the only daily paper. *Fraternité Hebdo* is a weekly published by the Parti Démocratique de la Côte d'Ivoire. Both carry advertising. Other publications include *Ivoire Dimanche* (weekly), *Eburnea*, *Le Messager* and *La Semaine d'Abidjan* (weekly).

2 trade journals printed abroad have a small circulation in Abidjan: *Marchés Tropicaux et Méditerranéens* (Paris) and the *Moniteur Africain* (Dakar).

The Chamber of Commerce publishes its own trade bulletins, and the Centre Ivoirien du Commerce Extérieur publishes a quarterly review, *L'Exportateur Ivoirien*.

5. Medical Care
Anti-malarial prophylactics should be taken. Tap water is generally not safe to drink and should be boiled; bottled water is available. Visitors are advised to carry a preventative against stomach upsets and to take care with uncooked fruit and vegetables.

Abidjan offers reasonable medical facilities, and there are a number of European doctors in practice.

6. Telephone, Telex and Postal Services
There is a direct-dial telephone service to France, Italy, Lebanon, Senegal and the USA, linking up with other European countries. For all countries other than these, dial ☎ 16.

A direct automatic exchange links Abidjan and Bobo-Dioulasso (Upper Volta).

There is a public telex office in Abidjan at the main Post Office on the Place de l'Indépendance. Telexes can be sent from most hotels.

The main post office in Abidjan is open from 0800 to 1845 hours, Monday to Saturday. There is no street delivery of mail in the Ivory Coast; all mail should be addressed with the post office box (*boîte postale*) number. All mail to and from the Ivory Coast should be sent by air.

7. Public Holidays

1 January	New Year's Day
1 May	Labour Day
15 August	Assumption of the Virgin Mary
1 November	All Saints Day
7 December	National Day
25 December	Christmas Day

The following movable Christian and Muslim holidays are also observed: *Easter Monday*, *Ascension Day*, *Whit Monday*, *Eid el Fitr* and *Tabaski*.

When a public holiday falls on a Sunday, the following Monday is observed as a holiday. Whenever National Day falls on a Tuesday or a Friday, the preceding Monday or the following Saturday respectively is also observed as a holiday.

8. Time
GMT.

9. Internal Transport

Air
Air Ivoire operates regular flights from Abidjan to Bouaké, Daloa, Man, Korhogo, Sassandra, San Pedro and Tabou. A number of air taxi services are also in operation.

Airline Offices in Abidjan

Air France	☎ 226231.
British Caledonian	☎ 321140.
Iberia	☎ 226991/2.
Lufthansa	☎ 323715.
Pan Am	☎ 349132.
Swissair	☎ 225051/2.
UTA	☎ 332300, 332500.

Rail
The main railway line runs from Abidjan to Bouaké (7¼ hours) and Ferkessedougou and on to Ouagadougou in Upper Volta. For further information apply to *Compagnie des Wagons-Lits*, B.P. 699, Abidjan, ☎ 322066.

Road
Taxis in Abidjan are cheap, but passengers should ensure that the meter is switched on at the start of the journey and that Tariff 1 is used. Tariff 2 is used after midnight and for journeys outside the city limits. Taxis can be hired for a half or whole day; this usually works out cheaper than a hired car.

Self-drive cars are available for hire in the main towns; cars can also be picked up at Port Bouet Airport. An International Driving Licence or licence from the visitor's own country is required.

Car-Hire Firms in Abidjan

Avis	☎ 323034; (airport) 368512
Hertz	☎ 340014; (airport) 368943.
Air Service Ivoirien	☎ 368014.

Other firms are Locauto, Auto Ivoire and Abidjan Location Auto.

10. Tipping
Taxis –10% of the fare.

Porters – 50 CFA francs per bag.

Hotels/restaurants – a service charge of 10–15% is usually added to the bill. It is customary to give a tip of 100 CFA francs to hotel room staff on departure.

11. Social Customs
French is used exclusively in government and business circles; English is rarely understood. French customs and manners predominate in both business and social life in Abidjan and the other main towns.

USEFUL ADDRESSES (GENERAL)

British Embassy: 5th floor, Immeuble Shell, 48 Avenue Lamblin, B.P. 2581, Abidjan, ☎ 226615, 322776.

Canadian Embassy, Immeuble 'Le Général', 4ème et 5ème étages, Avenue Botreau-Roussel, B.P. 21194, Abidjan, ☎ 322009.

Dutch Embassy, Immeuble Shell, 48 Avenue Lamblin, B.P. 1086, Abidjan, ☎ 323110.

French Embassy, Rue Lecoeur, Quartier du Plateau, B.P. 1393, Abidjan, ☎ 226262.

West German Embassy, Immeuble SMCL, 2ème étage, 11 Avenue Barthe, B.P. 1900, Abidjan, ☎ 222676.

Japanese Embassy, Immeuble Alpha 2000, Tour A1, 8ème étage, Avenue Chardy, B.P. 1329, Abidjan, ☎ 332863, 323043.

Swiss Embassy, Immeuble Les Arcades, Avenue Franchet d'Espérey, B.P. 1914, Abidjan, ☎ 321721.

US Embassy, 5 Rue Jesse Owens, B.P. 1712, Abidjan, ☎ 324630, 322581.

Office National du Tourisme, 9 Avenue Barthe, B.P. 1173, Abidjan, ☎ 226035.

Syndicat d'Initiative, 8 Avenue Lamblin, B.P. 1561, Abidjan, ☎ 222948.

Wagons-Lits Tourisme Authorised Representatives, Transcap Voyages, Avenue Houdaille, B.P. 1908, Abidjan, ☎ 228312, 321251; Transcap Voyages, B.P. 20, Sassandra, ☎ 1980; Transcap Voyages, B.P. 382, San Pedro.

American Express Authorised Representative, Socopao – Côte d'Ivoire, 14 Boulevard de la République, B.P. 1297, Abidjan, ☎ 320211, 227632, 228381.

BUSINESS INFORMATION

Foreign investment has been largely responsible for the country's economic transformation since independence. There are few restrictions on investment within the country and on the flow of capital in or out. The majority of foreign investment continues to be French and there are, at present, an estimated 60,000 French nationals in the Ivory Coast. The bulk of foreign trade is carried out by French firms, and there is a natural orientation towards French sources of industrial supply.

Most established French export and import companies have their headquarters and purchasing organisations in Paris. In general, most importers deal with a wide variety of goods and often act in a number of trading capacities. Commercial practice is based on the French commercial code. In addition to visiting the Ivory Coast, foreign suppliers may find it advantageous to visit the headquarters or buying agencies of local firms either in Paris or elsewhere outside of the Ivory Coast.

Import and Exchange Control Regulations

In general, all imports from countries outside the Franc Zone are subject to import

authorisation. Following the signing of the Lomé Convention, there are special regulations for imports into the Ivory Coast from EEC countries.
Exchange control applies to all currencies other than the CFA and French francs. Foreign exchange is made available under three main headings: the EEC, Bilateral Trade Agreements and Global Quotas.

Business Hours
Government Offices
0800–1200
1430–1700 Monday to Friday
0800–1200 Saturday

Business Houses
0800–1200
1430–1730 Monday to Friday
0800–1200 Saturday

Some firms are closed all day Saturday.
The best time to visit the Ivory Coast is between November and May so as to avoid the rainy season. This also coincides with the peak buying period, which falls towards the end of the year and around the beginning of the new year.

BUSINESS SERVICES

Advertising
COMACICO-BENIN, B.P. 51, Abidjan.
SECMA, B.P. 105, Abidjan.
(Both firms service cinemas throughout the country with advertising.)

Insurance
Compagnie Nationale d'Assurance, B.P. 1333, Abidjan.
La Securité Ivoirienne, Immeuble La Pyramide, B.P. 569, Abidjan.
Société Nouvelle d'Assurances de Côte d'Ivoire, 1 Avenue Louis Barthe, B.P. 1041, Abidjan.

Shipping
SAMOA, B.P. 1611, Abidjan – agents for Gold Star Line, Lloyd Triestino and Seven Star Line.
Société Ivoirienne de Transport Maritime (SITRAM), Avenue Lamblin, B.P. 1546, Abidjan.
Société Ouest-Africaine d'Entreprises Maritimes (SOAEM), B.P. 1727, Abidjan – agents for Scandinavian West Africa Line, Société Navale de l'Ouest and Union West Africa Line.
SOCOPAO, Km 1, Boulevard de Marseille, B.P. 1297, Abidjan – agents for Italian West Africa Line, K Line, Palm Line and Splosna Plovba.
Transcap Shipping, B.P. 1908, Abidjan – agents for Elder Dempster Lines, Barber Line, Mitsui-OSK Line, Palm Line, Nautilus Line and Hoegh Line.

USEFUL ADDRESSES (BUSINESS)

Chambre d'Agriculture de la République de Côte d'Ivoire, Avenue Louis Barthe, B.P. 1291, Abidjan.

Chambre de Commerce de la République de Côte d'Ivoire, 6 Avenue Louis Barthe, B.P. 1399, Abidjan, ☎ 324679.

IVORY COAST

Syndicat des Commerçants Importateurs et Exportateurs de la Côte d'Ivoire, B.P. 20882, Abidjan, ☎ 222483.

Syndicat des Entrepreneurs et des Industriels de la Côte d'Ivoire, 18 Avenue Louis Barthe, B.P. 464, Abidjan.

MAJOR CITY

Abidjan

The Plateau is the commercial centre of Abidjan, where most of the business firms and entertainment facilities are concentrated. On its western edge is the Presidential Palace, situated in extensive grounds looking over the Baie du Banco to the forests and lagoons beyond.

East of the Plateau, across the Baie de Cocody, is the residential area of Cocody where the Hotel Ivoire Inter-Continental is situated. Beyond the main embassy district is the African Riviera development, a new garden city with extensive tourist and leisure facilities including villas, apartment blocks and hotels. Another development in the Abidjan area is the new town of Youpougou, past the suburb of Adjamé, which is designed for a future population of 100,000.

The true African character of the city can best be felt in Treichville. The colourful central market is surrounded by many restaurants and, in the evenings, nightclubs throbbing with African music.

Hotels

There is no official hotel rating system in the Ivory Coast.

FORUM GOLF, Boulevard Lagunaire, B.P. 8018, ☎ 348432.
Modern 1st-class hotel on the Ebrié Lagoon, 15 minutes' drive from city centre.
Rooms: 300 ♪,⊛,☐ on request, ⚑, ⚠, ♆.
Facilities: Restaurant, dining terrace, cocktail bars. Swimming, tennis, golf, water sports. Shops. Car hire.
Services: TC, FC, ▤ Amex, Carte Blanche, Diners Club. Dr. on call. ⑤, ⚒.
Conference room – max. capacity 60.
Banquet rooms – max. capacity 450.

IVOIRE INTER-CONTINENTAL, Boulevard de la Corniche, B.P. 8001, ☎ 349480/1.
Modern de luxe hotel set in extensive gardens on Ebrié Lagoon, 10 minutes' drive from city centre, 30 minutes' drive to airport.
Rooms: 750 ♪,⊛,☐ on request, ⚠, ♆.
Facilities: 3 restaurants, pool terrace restaurant, snack bar, tea room, rooftop bar, cocktail bar. Casino. Cinema. Swimming, sailing, water skiing, ice skating, bowling, golf, tennis, sauna, gym. Heliport. Supermarket, shops. Car hire.
Services: TC, FC, ▤ Amex, Carte Blanche, Diners Club. Dr. on call. ⑤, ⚒.
on request. Audio-visual equipment.
Conference room – max. capacity 1,200.
6 meeting rooms.
Banquet rooms – max. capacity 1,000.

DU PARC, Avenue Chardy, B.P. 1775, ☎ 222386/8.
Traditional-style hotel opposite market in city centre.
Rooms: 80, 5 suites. ♪, ⊛, ☐ on request, ⚑, ⚠, ⊠.
Facilities: 2 restaurants, bar. Swimming near by. Car hire. Shop.
Services: TC, FC, ▤ Amex, Diners Club. Dr. on call. ⑤, ⚒.
Meeting and banquet facilities for up to 500 persons.

TIAMA, Avenue de la République, B.P. 4643, ☎ 320822.
Modern 1st-class hotel overlooking the sea in the business district.

Rooms: 145 ☃, ⚫, ☎. Suites available.
Facilities: Restaurants, bar, coffee lounge. Swimming near by. Shops, tour desk.
Services: ▭ Amex, Diners Club. Conference room – max. capacity 120.

Restaurants
There are many French restaurants in Abidjan. The Hotel Ivoire Inter-Continental and Relais de Cocody both have very good ones; *La Vigie* on the ocean front can also be recommended.

Other restaurants include: the *Dragon*, Boulevard Botreau Roussel, ☎ 323415 – Chinese; *Baie d'Along*, 11 Rue des Colibris, Marcory, ☎ 357779 – Vietnamese; *Babouya*, Treichville – Mauritanian; *Petit Auberge*, Rue des Pêcheurs, ☎ 356600; *Maison du Maroc*, Avenue Franchet d'Esperey, ☎ 226960 – Moroccan; *Chez Valentin*, Treichville, ☎ 324716; *La Santa Maria*, Boulevard de Marseille, ☎ 355466 – seafood; *Pizza di Sorrento*, Boulevard de Marseille, ☎ 355775 – Italian; *Attoungblan*, 4 Boulevard Delafosse, Treichville, ☎ 223714 – African.

A special restaurant section in the Blue Pages of the Abidjan telephone directory gives a more comprehensive listing.

Nightclubs
La Boule Noire, *Hi-Fi Club*, *Scotch Club Discotheque*, *King*, *Twenty One* and *In Club* are a few of the many nightclubs and discotheques.

Entertainment
Abidjan has several air-conditioned cinemas, and there is a theatre in the University complex at Cocody. The *French Cultural Centre* on the Plateau presents films and plays and has a reference and lending library.

There is also a wide choice of water sports, with many hotels offering sailing, water skiing, surfing and motor boating. Fishing is excellent along the shores of the lagoon. Some travel agencies organise deep-sea fishing for shark, swordfish, dolphin and marlin.

Shopping
Best buys: woven and printed cloth, sculpture, bead necklaces, basketware, ivory carvings, leatherwork.

Apart from the Treichville market, there is a large food and cloth market at Adjamé and one on the Plateau, opposite the Hotel du Parc. Local handicrafts and souvenirs are sold at *La Rose d'Ivoire* in the Hotel Ivoire Inter-Continental; a second shop is in the Nour al Hayat complex on the Plateau. African art can be bought at *La Galerie Tai*.

KENYA
Republic of Kenya

Geography	*196*
The Economy	*198*
How to Get There	*199*
Entry Regulations	*199*
Practical Information for the Visitor	*200*
Useful Addresses (General)	*203*
Business Information	*203*
Business Services	*205*
Useful Addresses (Business)	*205*
Nairobi	*205*
Mombasa	*207*
National Parks and Game Reserves	*209*

Size: 582,644 sq.km/224,960 sq.miles.

Population: 14.86 million (1978 est.).

Distribution: 10% in urban areas.

Density: 25.4 persons per sq.km/65.8 per sq.mile.

Population Growth Rate: 3.5% p.a.

Ethnic Composition: There are 4 principal linguistic groups: the Bantu, Nilo-Hamitic, Nilotic and Cushitic. The largest tribes are the Kikuyu, Luhya, Luo, Kalenjin and Kamba. There are some 250,000 Europeans, Asians and Arabs.

Capital: Nairobi Pop. 736,000.

Major Towns: Mombasa Pop. 351,000; Kisumu Pop. 35,000. Nakuru Pop. 50,00.

Language: Swahili is the national and most widely spoken language, but English is normally used in business and official circles.

Religion: Approximately 50% are Christians, 40% Animists, and the remainder Muslims or Hindus.

Government: Kenya is an independent republic within the British Commonwealth. The Executive is headed by the President, who is elected by direct popular vote. Legislative power rests with the National Assembly.

Kenya is a de facto one-party state, the ruling party being the Kenya Africa National Union which was headed by Jomo Kenyatta from 1961 until his death in 1978.

GEOGRAPHY

Kenya is a land of contrasting geographical features ranging from arid desert in the north to the rolling savannahs of the south, from the Indian Ocean coast to the shores

KENYA

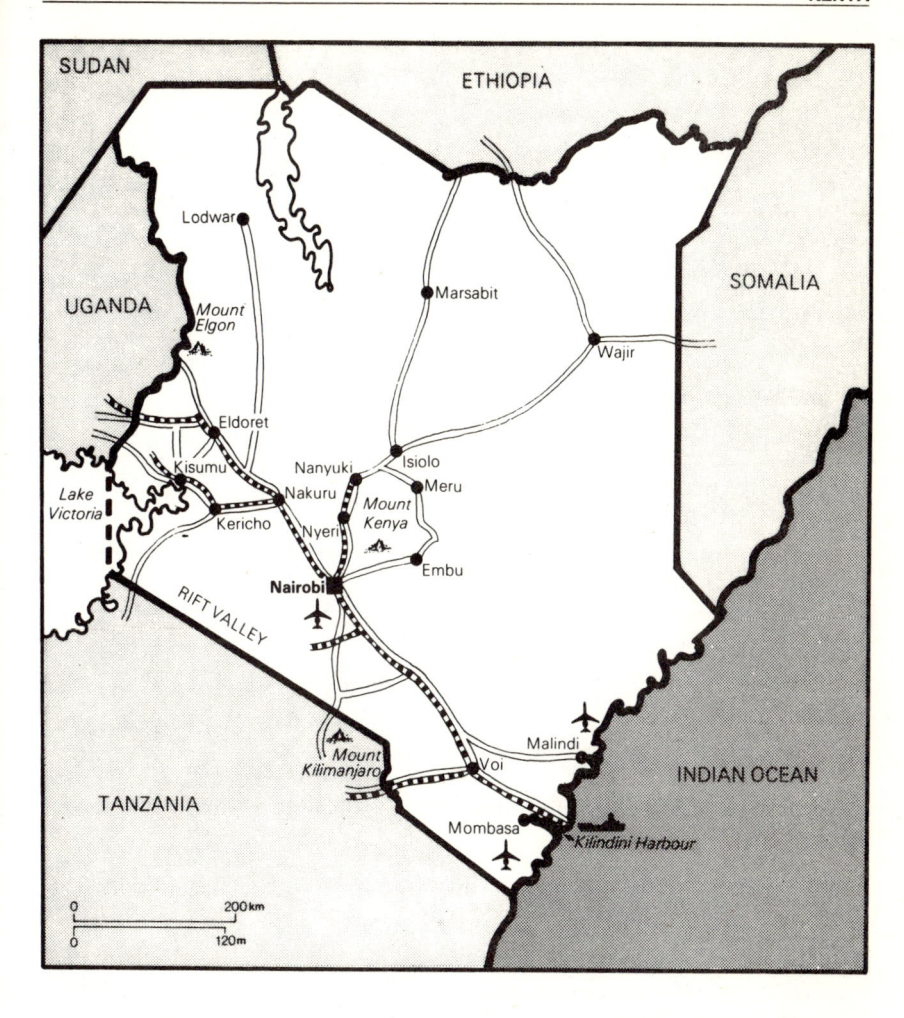

of Lake Victoria in the west, the largest lake in Africa. The country is divided from north to south by the Rift Valley, separating the central highlands (where the fertile arable lands are situated) from the western plateau. The Valley is largely barren and has a low rainfall. The area between the highlands and the coastline is dry bushland inhabited by nomadic, cattle-breeding tribes.

Climate

The climate along the coast and in the low-lying areas is tropical with temperatures ranging from 21°C/69°F to 32°C/89°F. Humidity is high, but this is alleviated by the monsoon winds from January to November. The hottest months are February to March; the coolest, June and July.

The highlands enjoy a more temperate climate, with two rainy seasons: April–June, and October–November. Temperatures in Nairobi range from 10°C/50°F to 28°C/82°F. Temperatures are higher near Lake Victoria (16°C/60°F to 30°C/86°F), and the rainfall in this area is usually greater. The best time to visit is during the drier periods of December–May and July–September.

Agriculture

Agriculture forms the mainstay of the economy and accounts for about 35% of the GDP, while providing a living for almost 80% of the working population. Production is carried out on both large estates and smallholdings with the latter gaining increasing importance, particularly in relation to estates held by foreign firms.

Coffee and tea have been Kenya's main agricultural exports for many years and, together with a number of other products, they constitute 80% of the country's total exports. Horticulture is becoming an important export activity, with exotic flowers, fruits and vegetables exported to Europe outside the normal season there. Development plans include major water-supply and irrigation projects and the expansion of mechanised farming and use of fertilisers.

Main Crops: coffee, tea, sisal, pyrethrum, cashew nuts, maize.

Mineral Resources: soda ash, fluorspar, salt, limestone, lead, gold.

THE ECONOMY

Gross National Product (1978): US$5.55 billion.

Per Capita Income (1977): US$276.

Gross Domestic Product (1978): Sh 42.49 billion.

Foreign Trade (1978): Total Imports – US$1.54 billion. Total Exports – US$985.3 million.

Main Trading Partners: Imports – UK, Iran, Japan, West Germany, USA, Tanzania, Saudi Arabia. Exports – UK, West Germany, Tanzania, Uganda, USA, Netherlands, Zambia.

During the first 10 years of independence (1963–74), Kenya had one of the highest economic growth rates in Africa (average 6.8% p.a.). The start of the world trade recession in 1974 led to economic stagnation, higher inflation and unemployment problems, and the situation was further aggravated by severe droughts in 1974 and 1975.

There are signs that the economy is now recovering; real growth has been achieved together with improvements in the balance of payments and the current account deficit. One of the main contributing factors has been a sharp increase in the world prices of coffee and tea. Tourism is the second largest source of foreign exchange, after coffee, and Kenya is becoming increasingly important as a centre for international business conferences and conventions.

The Government has an important stake in many major industries – power generation, oil refining, cement and others. Food processing is the principal manufacturing industry, followed by textiles and petroleum products. Heavier industries are also being developed; major projects include vehicle assembly plants, textile plants, and fertiliser and pharmaceutical factories. Many of these enterprises consist of joint ventures between overseas and local firms and Government or semi-Government investment institutions.

The 1978–83 Five-Year Development Plan envisages further expansion of the economy with continued emphasis on industries using local raw materials, new export markets for manufactured goods, further development of the tourist industry, the reduction of the inflation rate, and rural development.

Major Industries: food processing, textiles, oil refining, consumer goods, paper, tobacco, rubber.

Main Commodities Traded: Imports – machinery, transport equipment, manufactured goods, lubricants, chemicals. Exports – coffee, tea, sisal, pyrethrum, horticultural products, meat.

International Affiliations: UN, IBRD, OAU, ACP, ADB, Commonwealth. Its link with Tanzania and Uganda in the East African Community (1967) has now been dissolved.

HOW TO GET THERE

Air
Kenya's main international airport is Embakasi, 16 km/10 miles from the centre of Nairobi.

There are regular air services connecting Kenya with Europe, Asia, North America, Australasia and the Far East as well as with most of Africa. Most flights to Embakasi have connections to Mombasa.

Kenya Airways fly to Nairobi from London, Paris, Frankfurt, Zürich, Copenhagen, Cairo, Karachi, Bombay, Mauritius, Seychelles, Mogadishu and Addis Ababa.

Flying times to Nairobi: from London, 9 hours; from New York, 20 hours; from Sydney, 24 hours.

An airport tax of 20 shillings is payable on departure.

Most airlines provide transport between the airport and Nairobi at a reasonable cost. Taxis are available at a higher cost.

Road
Access by road is possible from Uganda, Tanzania and Ethiopia.

A valid driving licence from the visitor's own country is accepted for up to 90 days, provided it is endorsed at a local Kenyan police station. All drivers (with the exception of those driving cars with Ugandan or Tanzanian registration) must acquire an international circulation permit within 7 days of arrival, issued free of charge by the Licensing Officer in Nairobi.

ENTRY REGULATIONS

Visas
Visas are required by nationals of all countries except: citizens of the British Commonwealth other than Australia and Zimbabwe, and persons of Bangladeshi, Indian or Pakistani origin holding British passports; Denmark, Ethiopia, West Germany, Republic of Ireland, Italy, Norway, San Marino, Sweden, Turkey, Uruguay.

KENYA

The Government refuses entry to white nationals of Zimbabwe and South Africa, and to residents of these two countries of Bangladeshi, Indian or Pakistani origin.

Persons of Bangladeshi, Indian or Pakistani origin residing in East Africa must possess the equivalent, in convertible foreign currency, of 120 Kenyan shillings per day for the period of stay required.

Persons of Bangladeshi, Indian or Pakistani origin residing elsewhere and holding passports of any country other than Zimbabwe or South Africa must possess the equivalent, in convertible foreign currency, of 4,000 Kenyan shillings.

Visa applications should be accompanied by a letter (usually from a travel agent or airline office) confirming that return or outward tickets are held and that the traveller has sufficient funds for the stay.

Visas are valid for 3 months for a stay varying in length, depending upon the traveller's requirements.

All travellers require a visitor's pass, issued free on arrival, which can have a validity of up to 6 months, renewable for up to a maximum of one year.

Health Regulations

A valid International Certificate of Vaccination against smallpox is required by all persons entering Kenya. A certificate of vaccination against yellow fever is required on departure (not on entry); visitors are advised to obtain this before departing for Kenya. Cholera and yellow fever certificates are compulsory for all persons travelling to Kenya via infected areas. Typhoid and paratyphoid injections are obligatory for persons arriving from India, Pakistan and other typhoid areas.

Customs

Currency: The import and export of Kenyan currency is strictly prohibited. There is no restriction on the import of foreign currency, but this must be declared on entry and a record kept of all currency transactions during the stay, as this may be required on departure. Tourists may not take out a greater amount of foreign currency than they brought in.

Kenyan currency is not redeemable outside East Africa.

Duty-free articles: Personal effects. 250g of tobacco or the equivalent in cigarettes or cigars. 1 bottle of wine or spirits. 1 pint of toilet water (of which not more than ¼ pint is perfume). Firearms and ammunition require a police permit before they are released from Customs. Samples which have a commercial value should be covered by a bond, obtainable from any bank before departure, in order to avoid the payment of duty deposit on entry.

Prohibited articles: Imports from South Africa and Zimbabwe. Export permits are required for hunting trophies or articles, such as handbags, made from animal skins.

PRACTICAL INFORMATION FOR THE VISITOR

1. Currency
Monetary unit – Kenya shilling (Sh), divided into 100 cents. (20 shillings = Kenya £.)
Notes – 5, 10, 20, 100 shillings.
Coins – 5, 10, 50 cents; 1 shilling.

Banking Hours
0900–1300 Monday to Friday
0900–1100 Saturday

The *Central Bank of Kenya*, Haile Selassi Avenue, P.O. Box 30463, Nairobi, is the bank of issue.

Principal Commercial Banks

Barclays Bank of Kenya Ltd, Queensway House, Mama Ngina Street, P.O. Box 30120, Nairobi, ☎ 337485.

Chase Manhattan Bank, Kencom House, 7th floor, P.O. Box 57051, Nairobi, ☎ 334990, 336587.

Citibank N.A., Cotts House, Wabera Street, P.O. Box 30711, Nairobi, ☎ 333524.

The Commercial Bank of Africa Ltd, Commercial Bank Building, Standard Street, P.O. Box 30437, Nairobi.

First National Bank of Chicago, International life House, Mama Ngina Street, P.O. Box 30691, Nairobi.

Grindlays Bank International (Kenya) Ltd, Kenyatta Avenue, P.O. Box 30550, Nairobi.

The Kenya Commercial Bank Ltd, Government Road, P.O. Box 48400, Nairobi, ☎ 336681.

The National Bank of Kenya Ltd, Harambee Avenue, P.O. Box 41862, Nairobi.

Standard Bank Ltd, P.O. Box 30003, Nairobi, ☎ 331210; Treasury Square, P.O. Box 90170, Mombasa.

2. Electricity Supply

240v AC 50Hz.
Plugs: 2 round pins, 3 square pins. Adaptors are available to suit both types.

3. Weights and Measures

The metric system is used.

4. Media

The Voice of Kenya is the national broadcasting service – television programmes are transmitted in English and Swahili, while radio services are in these 2 languages and 13 others. There are facilities for spot announcements and sponsored programmes on both radio and television; the former is more effective, reaching a wider audience.

Enquiries about radio and television advertising should be sent to the Advertising Manager, Voice of Kenya, P.O. Box 30456, Nairobi.

Newspapers and Journals

Dailies: *The Daily Nation* and *The Standard* (both English); *Taifa Leo* (Swahili).

The main weeklies are *The Sunday Nation* (English), and *Baraza* and *Taifa Weekly,* both Swahili. *Kenya Yetu* is published monthly in Swahili by the Ministry of Information and Broadcasting.

The *East African Report on Trade and Industry* has a wide circulation in business circles. *Kenya Farmer* is an important trade magazine, published in English and Swahili, and is distributed free to members of the Agricultural Society of Kenya.

5. Medical Care

Malaria has been virtually eradicated in many parts, but the risk is higher in the coastal areas. Travellers are advised to consult their doctors about anti-malarial prophylactic tablets if they are entering a malaria area.

Tap water is safe to drink in the main centres, but care should be taken with uncooked vegetables and unwashed fruit and salads. Avoid swimming in rivers and lakes because of the risk of bilharzia.

Health services are relatively limited, with the exception of those in Nairobi and Mombasa where there are both public and private hospitals. Out-patient treatment is available in Nairobi at the Nairobi Hospital, ☎ 21401, and the Aga Khan Hospital, ☎ 742301, and at the Pandya Clinic in Mombasa.

6. Telephone, Telex and Postal Services

Kenya has an extensive international telephone service, and trunk calls can be made throughout the country and to other East African countries. An STD system is in operation in Nairobi and covers most of the large cities and towns in East Africa. In Nairobi and other main centres, dial 999 for emergency services.

Overseas and inland telegrams can be sent from all Post and Telegraph offices

KENYA

(hours: 0800–1700 Monday to Friday; 0800–1300 Saturdays). Nairobi Post Office is open 24 hours a day. Telegrams may also be sent via any call box or private telephone. There are public telex booths in Nairobi and Mombasa.

All mail to and from Kenya should be despatched by air.

7. Public Holidays

1 January	New Year's Day
1 May	Labour Day
1 June	Madaraka Day
20 October	Kenyatta Day
12 December	Independence Day
25–6 December	Christmas

In addition, the following movable Muslim and Christian holidays are also observed: *Eid el Fitr, Eid el Adha, Good Friday* and *Easter Monday*.

8. Time
GMT + 3.

9. Internal Transport

Air
An extensive internal air service is operated by Kenya Airways, including scheduled flights to Mombasa, Malindi, Kisumu and other destinations. There are also a number of private airlines (e.g. Caspair), which fly to small airstrips, and serveral air charter companies.

Airline Offices in Nairobi

Air Canada	☎ 21024.
Air France	☎ 333301/5.
Alitalia	☎ 24361.
British Airways	☎ 334440.
British Caledonian	☎ 336138/9.
JAL	☎ 20591, 333277.
Kenya Airways	☎ 29291.
KLM	☎ 332673/7.
Lufthansa	☎ 26271.
Pan Am	☎ 28379.
Swissair	☎ 331012.
Caspair	☎ 501421.

Aircraft and Helicopter Charter (Nairobi)

Africair	☎ 501210.
Air Kenya	☎ 501601.
Kenya Air Charters	☎ 21064.

Rail
There are daily services between Nairobi and Mombasa with regular connections to Kisumu and through to Uganda; also branch lines to Nyeri, Nanyuki and through Voi to Tanzania. For details, telephone the Chief Traffic Manager in Nairobi, ☎ 21211.

Road
Roads connecting main centres are good standard, but the quality deteriorates away from these trunk roads, especially during the rainy season. Self-drive and chauffeur-driven cars are available for hire.

There are 2 types of taxi in the main towns: the older, yellow band taxis with inoperable meters (it is advisable to negotiate fares in advance for these taxis); and the modern, metered taxis. Long-distance taxis are widely used and carry up to 7 passengers. The *Rift Valley Peugeot Service* operates between Nairobi and Nakuru; the *Mombasa Peugeot Service* operates between Nairobi and Mombasa.

Car-Hire Firms

Nairobi – Avis	☎ 334317, 336703.
Hertz	☎ 331960.
Mombasa – Avis	☎ 23048, 20465.
Hertz	☎ 20741.

10. Tipping

A tip of 10% is usual except when a service charge is added, when a small additional tip is customary.

Taxis – Sh 1.50 on a Sh 10 fare, but not more than Sh 3.50.

Hotel Porters – Sh 2.

11. Social Customs

In business circles, social customs are generally based on the British model. Dress is fairly informal, particularly in the humid coastal region, where it is quite acceptable for men to wear open-necked shirts and shorts when meeting Government officials or business contracts.

USEFUL ADDRESSES (GENERAL)

Nairobi

Australian High Commission: Development House, Government Road, P.O. Box 30360, ☎ 334666.

British High Commission: 13th Floor, Bruce House, Standard Street, P.O. Box 30465, ☎ 335944.

Canadian High Commission: Comcraft House, Haile Selassie Avenue, P.O. Box 30481, ☎ 334033.

Dutch Embassy: 6th Floor, Uchumi House, Nkhrumah Avenue, P.O. Box 41537, ☎ 27111.

French Embassy: Embassy House, Harambee Avenue, P.O. Box 41784.

Japanese Embassy: Wabera Street, P.O. Box 20202, ☎ 332955.

Swiss Embassy: 7th floor, International Life House, Mama Ngina Street, P.O. Box 20008, ☎ 28735/6.

US Embassy: Cotts House, Wabera Street, P.O. Box 30137, ☎ 334141.

West German Embassy: Embassy House, Harambee Avenue, P.O. Box 30180, ☎ 26661.

Visitors Information Centre: ☎ 23285.

Kenya Tourist Development Corporation: Tourist Information Office, opposite Hilton Hotel, ☎ 29751.

British Council: Kenya Cultural Centre, Harry Thuku Road, P.O. Box 40751, ☎ 334855/7.

Thomas Cook Authorised Representative: United Touring Co Ltd, Travel House, Muindi Mbingu Road, P.O. Box 42196, ☎ 31960.

American Express Authorised Representative: Express Kenya Ltd, Consolidated House, Standard Street, P.O. Box 40433, ☎ 334727/28.

Mombasa

Dutch Consulate: Ned Lloyd House, Kilindini Road, P.O. Box 80301, ☎ 25241.

British Council: City House, Nyerere Avenue, P.O. Box 90590. Mombasa, ☎ 23076.

Thomas Cook Authorised Representative: United Touring Co Ltd, Kilindini Road, P.O. Box 84782, ☎ 20741.

American Express Authorised Representative: Express Kenya Ltd, Khrumah Road, P.O. Box 90631, ☎ 24461.

BUSINESS INFORMATION

Although the Government is anxious to attract foreign investment, it is at the same time attempting to ensure that a maximum amount of trade is handled by Kenyan citizens. A number of institutions – such as Industrial and Commercial Development Corporation and the Development Finance Company of Kenya Ltd – have thus been established, with the aid of international agencies, to assist African ventures and enterprises.

The emphasis on rural development in the current Development Plan (1978–83) calls for large-scale supply of machinery and equipment for water-supply and irrigation schemes, as well as for the food-processing, consumer-goods and building-materials industries. The intended development of roads and railways and the expansion of power generation plants and telecommunications will also provide valuable opportunities for foreign suppliers.

Nairobi is the main centre for most business activities; shipping is headquartered in Mombasa. Nakuru is a large agricultural centre. Tea and sugar are based, respectively, in Kericho and Kisumu.

Most foreign firms appoint an agent or distributor in Nairobi or Mombasa. Some agents have stock-holding and servicing facilities; there are also indenting agents and agents importing on their own account.

Stockist-distributors are among the latter and sometimes offer the best means of selling engineering products and equipment and other products requiring spares and servicing facilities.

The Kenya National Trading Corporation was established in 1965 to promote the Africanisation of trade in specified basic commodities. The KNTC trades on its own account as an exclusive buyer and distributor or issues licences enabling selected traders to import for themselves.

Import and Exchange Control Regulations

Specific import licences are required for a variety of goods, although some manufactured goods may be imported under Open General Licence. Some items requiring an import licence can only be imported through the Kenya National Trading Corporation. Imports are classified into 4 schedules, periodically revised, for licensing purposes.

The approval of the Central Bank must be obtained before importation (this is a means of restricting or prohibiting the provision of foreign exchange for goods competing with local products and for some luxury items). Almost all imports are subject to pre-shipment quality and quantity inspections and price comparison by officers of the General Superintendence Company in the country of origin.

Business Hours
Government Offices and Business Houses
0830–1230
1400–1630   Monday to Friday

Business Events

The most important trade event is the Nairobi International Show, held at the end of September or early October each year. The show is organised by the Agricultural Society of Kenya and, although originally an agricultural show, it has now been extended to all sections of the local and overseas business community, with many Government organisations participating.

The New Kenya Exhibition is also held annually in Nairobi.

The Kenyatta Conference Centre in Nairobi, one of the largest and best equipped in Africa, is the venue of many international conventions and conferences.

KENYA

BUSINESS SERVICES

Forwarding/Clearing Agents in Mombasa
ETCO (Mombasa) Ltd, P.O. Box 90390.
General Superintendence Co (EA), P.O. Box 90264.
Kenya Transit and Trading Co, P.O. Box 90192.
Leslie & Anderson (EA) Ltd, P.O. Box 90150.
Nakulines Ltd, P.O. Box 84675.
Neville Owen-Thomas Forwarding Co Ltd, P.O. Box 90262.
Reynolds & Co Ltd, P.O. Box 95026.
Wafco Ltd, P.O. Box 80952.

Finance Houses
Credit Finance Corporation Ltd, P.O. Box 84418, Mombasa.
East African Trust and Investment Company Ltd, P.O. Box 47384, Nairobi.
Jamnadass Ltd, P.O. Box 10439, Nairobi.
National Industrial Credit (EA) Ltd, P.O. Box 44599, Nairobi.
United Dominions Corporation (East Africa) Ltd, P.O. Box 49946, Nairobi.

Shipping
Africa Mercantile Co (Overseas) Ltd, P.O. Box 90110, Mombasa. (Agents for Harrison Line, Oriental African Line and Scandinavian East African Line.)
Eastern Africa National Shipping Line Ltd, P.O. Box 90621, Mombasa.
MacKenzie (Kenya), P.O. Box 90120, Mombasa. (Agents for Farrell Lines and P & O Line.)
Mitchell Cotts Kenya Ltd, Cotts House, Kilindini Road, P.O. Box 90141, Mombasa. (Agents for Lloyd Triestino Line, Compagnie Maritime Belge, Nippon Yusen Kaisha, Lloyd Brasileiro and Compagnie Paulista de Comercio Maritimo)
Nedlloyd (EA) Ltd, P.O. Box 80149, Mombasa.

USEFUL ADDRESSES (BUSINESS)

Chief Purchasing Officer, Ministry of Works, P.O. Box 30260, Nairobi, ☎ 26441.

Industrial and Commercial Development Corporation, P.O. Box 45519, Nairobi.

Kenya Association of Manufacturers, P.O. Box 30225, Nairobi.

Kenya External Trade Authority, P.O. Box 43137, Nairobi.

Kenya National Chamber of Commerce & Industry, Ufanisi House, Haile Selassie Avenue, P.O. Box 47024, Nairobi, ☎ 20866/7; Digo Road, P.O. Box 90271, Mombasa, ☎ 26228.

Kenya National Trading Corporation, P.O. Box 30587, Nairobi.

Law Society of Kenya, P.O. Box 72219, Nairobi, ☎ 25558.

MAJOR CITIES AND TOWNS

Nairobi
The largest city in East Africa, Nairobi has become a highly developed commercial and communications centre. It is also the site of the headquarters of the United Nations Environment Programme Secretariat.

Known as the 'City of Flowers', Nairobi boasts many parks and gardens, and its streets are lined with jacarandas, bougainvillea and other tropical flowers.

The Arboretum and City Park are two of the finest areas within the city. Also worth a visit are the National Museum, housing a large selection of prehistoric exhibits, and Snake Park on Museum Hill, home of some 200 species of snakes.

The National Park is just 8km/5 miles from the centre, and although it is one of the smallest of Kenya's wildlife reserves, visitors will have an opportunity to see a vast range of wild animals in their natural habitat. To the south of the park is the Ngong National Reserve.

Hotels

There is no official hotel rating system.

INTER-CONTINENTAL NAIROBI, City Hall Way, P.O. Box 30353, ☎ 335550.
Modern de luxe hotel in city centre overlooking Uhuru Park.
Rooms: 440 ♪, ●, ❏, ✿, ⚠, ☯. Suites available.
Facilities: French-style restaurant and cocktail lounge, coffee bar, poolside restaurant, bars, English-style pub. Swimming. Barber, beauty shops. Bank, shopping arcade.
Services: TC, FC. ☐ Amex, Barclay Visa, Diners Club. Dr. on call. ⚡, ♂.
Conference room – max. capacity 800.
Banquet rooms – max. capacity 300.

NAIROBI HILTON, Mama Ngina Street and Government Road, P.O. Box 30624, ☎ 334000.
De luxe tower hotel in city centre, 5 minutes from airline terminal and railway station.
Rooms: 339 (64 poolside rooms, 10 suites). ♪, ●, ❏ on request, ✿, ⚠, ☯.
Facilities: Restaurant, grill room, trattoria, supper club with dancing, coffee shop, cocktail bar. Swimming, sun deck, health club. Shops. Car hire.
Services: TC, FC. ☐ Amex, Barclay Visa, Diners Club. Dr. on call. ⚡, ♂.
Conference and banquet facilities – max. capacity 4,000.

NEW STANLEY, Kiniathi Street and Kenyatta Avenue, P.O. Box 30680, ☎ 333233.
Moderate 1st-class hotel in city centre near Kenyatta Conference Centre, 5 minutes' walk from airline terminal.

Rooms: 228 ♪, ●, ❏, ✿, ⚠, ☯. Suites available.
Facilities: Restaurant, grill room, coffee shop, bars. Nightly dancing and cabaret. Shops.
Services: TC. ☐ Amex, Diners Club. ⚡, ♂.
Conference room – max. capacity 300.
Banquet rooms – max. capacity 200.

NORFOLK, Harry Thuku Road, P.O. Box 40064, ☎ 335422.
Colonial-style hotel (built 1904) opposite National Theatre, ½ mile from city centre.
Rooms: 168 ●, ✿, ⚠, ⬡. Suites, private cottage accommodation available.
Facilities: Restaurant, bar, coffee lounge, café. Terraces. Swimming, golf, tennis, squash.
Services: TC. ☐ Amex, Diners Club. ⚡.
Conference room – max. capacity 100.

PANAFRIC, Kenyatta Avenue, P.O. Box 30486, ☎ 335166.
Modern 1st-class hotel in park area, ½ mile from city centre, 12km/7½ miles from airport.
Rooms: 172 ♪, ●, ❏ on request, ⚠, ☯. 6 suites.
Facilities: Grill room, snack bar, dancing, lounge bars. Swimming, Hairdressing, beauty salon. Shop. Car hire.
Services: TC, FC. ☐ Amex, Barclay Visa, Diners Club. ⚡, ♂.
Conference room – max. capacity 200.
Banquet rooms – max. capacity 120.

NAIROBI SERENA, Central Park, P.O. Box 46302, ☎ 337979/331847.
Attractive 1st-class hotel in central loca-

tion, set in gardens overlooking Central Park, ½ mile from business district.
Rooms: 200 🐟, 🛁, 🍴, 🔺, 📺. Suites available.
Facilities: Restaurant, grill room, coffee shop, cocktail lounge, bars. Boutiques, hairdressers. Swimming; golf, tennis, squash near by. Safaris arranged. Car hire.
Services: TC, FC, 🔲 Amex. Dr. on call. **S**, ♂.
Conference room – max. capacity 400. Function rooms for up to 2,000 persons.

SIX EIGHTY, Kenyatta Avenue, P.O. Box 43436, ☎ 332680.
Modern 1st-class hotel in city centre.
Rooms: 340 🐟, 🛁, 🚿 on request, 🍴, 🔺, 📺. Suites available.
Facilities: Restaurant, snack bar, cocktail bar, pub, bars. Shopping arcade. Car hire.
Services: TC, FC, 🔲 Amex, Barclay Visa, Diners Club. Dr. on call. **S**, ♂ on request.
Conference room – max. capacity 200.
Banquet rooms – max. capacity 400.

Restaurants
The better hotels in Nairobi offer a high standard of cuisine, as do many of the pleasantly situated country hotels outside the city. Recommended restaurants include *Alan Bobbe's Bistro*, Koinange Street; *The Lobster Pot*; *Marino Restaurant*, International Life House; *Tamarinda; Lavarini's*, Government Road – Italian; *Mandarin* – Chinese; *Kentmere Club*, Limuru; *Omar Khayyam*, Arwings-Kodhek Road – Indian; *Tina's*, Government Road – local dishes; *Friends' Corner*, Latema Road – African.

Entertainment
Many of the larger hotels have nightly dancing with cabaret and live bands or discotheque. The *Casino* has its own restaurant and bars, and offers a colourful floor show as well as dancing and gambling. The Kenya National Theatre attracts theatre, dancing and musical groups as well as other cultural activities, and there is a residential professional repertory company at the Donovan Maule Theatre on Parliament Road. Nairobi has several large cinemas showing international films and 2 English-language drive-in cinemas.

Sporting facilities are extensive and of a high standard; football, cricket, tennis, golf, hockey and polo are all popular. The *Muthaiga Golf Club* and *Royal Nairobi Club* have resident professionals, and there are several other clubs, including a municipal golf course on the Langata Road. Temporary membership for visitors is available at many of these clubs and at other sports and social clubs.

Tours are available to local villages where displays of Kenyan culture and traditional dancing can be seen. The displays given by the Bomas of Kenya at their theatre near the National Park are highly recommended.

Shopping
Best buys: wood and stone carvings, beadwork, pottery, gold and silver jewellery, handbags, jackets, belts and other articles made from animal and reptile skins (these require export licences obtainable at the place of purchase).

The Municipal Market in Market Street, near Biashara Street, is arranged on two floors: fruit, vegetables and flowers are sold on the ground floor; curios are sold on the upper floor. Saris and other Oriental articles can be purchased from the *Bazaar* near Jevanjee Gardens, and the markets off Pumwani and River Roads are well worth a visit. Local handicrafts are sold at the *Craftsman's Gallery* on Standard Street or the shopping arcades in the Hilton and Inter-Continental Hotels.

Mombasa
Mombasa is the chief port of Kenya and the second largest city. Built on an island, the city has been the scene of stormy battles in the past and was named the 'Island of War'

by the Arabs. Fort Jesus is the most impressive historical monument. Built in the late 16th century by the Portuguese as protection against the Arabs and Turks, it changed hands many times before being abandoned by the Portuguese to the Arabs in 1729. Following an attack by the British Navy in 1875, it became a prison and today houses an excellent museum.

The old harbour of Mombasa is still used by *dhows* carrying their wares between East Africa and Arabia, Persia and India, although the commercial harbour at Kilindini now deals with most of the goods passing through Mombasa.

The Old Town in the south-eastern part of the island has an Oriental charm about it with its maze of narrow streets and mosques. The Hindu Temple on Muragogo Road has a dome covered in pure gold; the temple in Haile Selassie Road is also worth a visit. Other sights of interest are: the Ivory Room off Treasury Square; the Uhuru Fountain, built in the shape of Africa; and the huge elephant tusks which span the Kilindini Road.

Hotels

MOMBASA BEACH, P.O. Box 90414, ☎ 471861.
Modern 1st-class hotel built on cliff overlooking beach, 8km/5 miles from city centre.
Rooms: 100 ♫, ⬤ + ☐ on request, △, ▽. Suites available.
Facilities: Restaurant, bar. Discotheque, Cinema, live entertainment. Swimming, water sports, deep sea fishing. Golf near by. Car hire.
Services: TC, FC. ▤ Amex, Barclay Visa, Diners Club. Dr. on call. S on request. Meeting facilities for up to 40 people. Banquet rooms – max. capacity 100.

NYALI BEACH, P.O. Box 90581, ☎ 471551.
1st-class hotel on beachfront, 6½km/4 miles from Mombasa.
Rooms: 186 ♫, ⬤, ☐ on request, △, ▽.
Facilities: Restaurant, grill room, bars. Swimming, private beach. Deep sea fishing, aqua sports, golf. Car hire. Conference room. Daily transport to Mombasa provided
Services: TC, FC. ▤ Amex, Diners Club. S on request.

OCEANIC HOTEL, Mbuyuni Road, P.O. Box 90371, ☎ 311191.
Resort overlooking Indian Ocean, 1 mile from city centre.
Rooms: 85 ♫ on request, ⬤.
Facilities: Restaurant, lounges, 2 bars, casino. Swimming, golf, water-skiing, Free limited transport to city centre.
Services: ▤ Amex, Bankamericard, Barclay Visa, Diners Club, Master Charge.

Restaurants

Seafood is a speciality of many of Mombasa's restaurants; Arab, Indian, Middle Eastern, Continental and Oriental food are also to be found. Recommended restaurants include *Fontanella*, near Manor Hotel – seafood; *Taj Mahal*, Salim Road – Indian; *Curry Bowl*, Kilindini Road – Indian; *Rooftop Restaurant*, Hotel Splendid – Indian and seafood.

Entertainment

Mombasa has a number of cinemas. The city's nightlife is largely concentrated around the Kilindini Road and there are several lively nightclubs and bars in this area, including the popular *Sunshine Day and Night Club*. There are many fine beaches in Mombasa and the surrounding area and most kinds of watersports are available.

Shopping

Best buys: silver and gold, native cloth, basketwork, wood carvings.
Go to the Old Town for craft goods, silver and gold jewellery and other articles. Biashara Street, parallel to Jomo Kenyatta Street, is the best area for cloth (Kikoni, Kanga, Kitenge), basketwork and local handicrafts.

National Parks and Game Reserves

Kenya has an impressive array of species of wildlife, and certain areas of the country have been designated as parks or game reserves. At present there are 20 major reserves covering a total area of about 34,000 sq.km/13,124 sq.miles.

Visitors may drive around most of the parks in their own vehicles; usually it is only permitted to leave one's car at certain specified viewing places. In parks such as the Aberdare National Park, visitors must use the transport provided. Bookings for the lodges within the camps should be made through travel agents in Nairobi well in advance as accommodation is limited. Full details may be obtained from the Kenya Tourist Development Corporation.

The main national parks and reserves are: *Nairobi National Park* – 8km/5 miles from Nairobi; *Amboseli National Park* – 40km/25 miles north of Mt Kilimanjaro; *Tsavo National Park* – along the Mombasa–Nairobi Road; *Meru National Park* – 110km/68 miles from Meru, north-east of Mt Kenya; *Masai-Mara Game Reserve*; *Aberdare National Park*; and *Kenya National Park* – 160km/100 miles north-east of Nairobi.

LESOTHO
Kingdom of Lesotho

Geography	210
The Economy	212
How to Get There	213
Entry Regulations	213
Practical Information for the Visitor	214
Useful Addresses (General)	215
Business Information	216
Useful Addresses (Business)	216
Maseru	217

Size: 30,355 sq.km/11,720 sq.miles.

Population: 1.3 million (1978 est.).

Distribution: 1% in urban areas.

Density: 40.2 persons per sq.km./104.1 per sq.mile.

Population Growth Rate: 2.4% p.a. (1970–7).

Ethnic Composition: Almost all the people are Basotho, although there are some 3,000 Europeans and Asians.

Capital: Maseru Pop. 45,000.

Major Town: Teyateyaneng Pop. 10,000.

Language: English and Sesotho are the official languages.

Religion: About 70% are Christians, mostly Roman Catholics; there is also a small number of Muslims, and the remainder hold traditional beliefs.

Government: The Kingdom of Lesotho became independent of British administration as one of the 3 'High Commission Territories' in South Africa on 4 October 1966. The Head of State is King Moshoeshoe II, though since returning from exile in 1970 he has lost political power and is now the constitutional monarch. The ruling party since 1965 has been the Basuto National Party (BNP). In a coup d'état in January 1970 the Constitution was suspended and rule was by decree for 3 years. No elections have taken place since then. The major opposition is the Basuto Congress Party. The other political parties are the Marema Tlou Freedom Party and the Lesotho United Democratic Party.

GEOGRAPHY

Lesotho is a small, landlocked mountainous country entirely above 1,000 metres/ 3,280 feet in altitude and surrounded on all sides by the Republic of South Africa, to the east by Natal Province, to the south by Cape Province, and to the north and west by the Orange Free State. The highest peaks are in the Drakensberg mountains in the extreme east, though the Maloti mountains which cover much of the central area also rise to over 3,000 metres/9,840 feet in some places. The many rivers have cut deep valleys and spectacular gorges through these mountainous areas. It is only in the far western quarter, the 'Lowlands', that the altitude drops significantly to between 1,000–2,000 metres/3,280–6,560 feet. This lowland belt averages 50km/30 miles in width and is part of the South African highveld. It is the most densely populated region of Lesotho and, despite its relatively poor soil, is the centre for much agricultural activity.

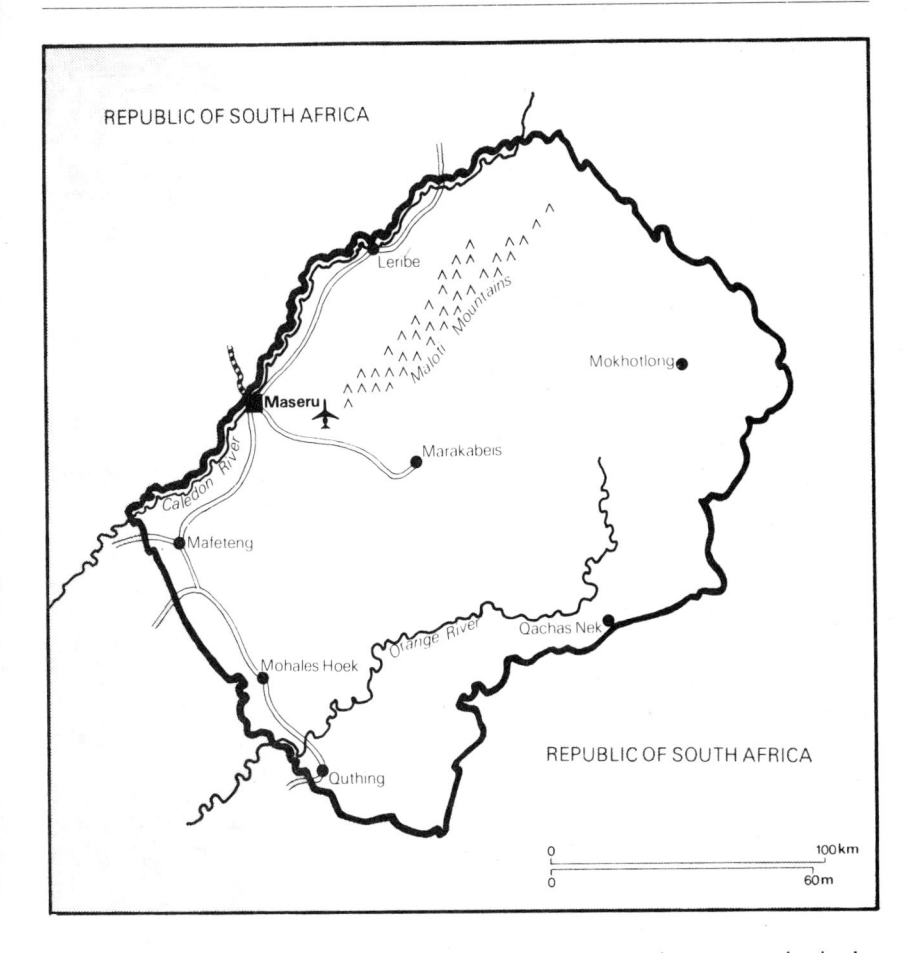

Climate

Day temperatures in the lowlands during the warm summer season (October to April) average 27°c/80°F, falling to a cold season minimum of −7°c/19°F with frequent frosts. At higher altitudes, temperatures are lower and differences between day and night and winter and summer temperatures are greater. Snow is common in the mountains. Average annual rainfall is 700mm/28in in the lowlands, rising to 2,000mm/79in in the highest areas along the eastern borders. Although rainfall and temperatures can be variable and unreliable, prolonged droughts are rare. Most rain falls in the summer months.

Agriculture

Only 13% of the total land area is cultivable, and the intense use of this land has led to soil erosion in many places. 87% of the population engage in agriculture, and some 30% of the GDP is contributed by this sector. There is little 'modern' agriculture although up to 30% of output is marketed, most of which goes to South Africa. The main crop is maize; other crops grown are sorghum, wheat, peas, beans and barley. Livestock raising is widespread, but there is no modern abattoir so cattle are exported on the hoof. Lesotho has a food deficit, with imported food and aid value greater than domestic production.

All land is invested in the Basotho Nation, and 5 large rural development projects undertaken with foreign aid are attempting to reconcile traditional systems of land tenure with modern commercial methods. Government priority is being given to improving agricultural facilities, especially veterinary services, giving instruction in conservation, raising new crops and increasing production for export. Forestry has recently been established under the Lesotho Woodlot Project (1973).

Main Crops: wheat, maize, sorghum, peas.

Mineral Resources: diamonds; oil prospecting is under way.

THE ECONOMY

Gross National Product (1978 est.): US$360 million

Per Capita Income (1977): US$280.

Gross Domestic Product (1977): US$145.5 million.

Foreign Trade: Total Imports – R179.6 million (1976). Total Exports – R12.2 million (1977).

Main Trading Partner: Imports and exports – South Africa.

A poor and economically underdeveloped country with few natural resources, Lesotho is heavily dependent upon the remitted wages of the large proportion of the male labour force working as contract labourers in the Republic of South Africa. Agriculture is the most important sector of the economy though the pressure on land and poor soils have made agriculturalists conservative and development policies hard to implement. The manufacturing sector is very small, contributing about 3% of the GDP, largely as a consequence of South African domination of the small domestic market. However, the Lesotho National Development Corporation (LNDC) has encouraged some small industry, notably in textiles and clothing, diamond processing, tyre retreading and the production of a number of electrical consumer items.

The processing of agricultural products is the most important industry, but has had limited success in import substitution. Mineral production has expanded in recent years with the opening of a new diamond mine at Letseng-La-Terai, which is expected to produce a high yield of large gemstones. Coal, oil and uranium prospecting is to be continued. Tourism is the fastest growing sector with the number of visitors, mostly from South Africa, steadily increasing over the last 10 years. Both manufacturing and tourism are basically capital intensive and are unlikely to increase employment opportunities significantly or to raise the standard of living of most Basotho.

The economic prospects in the short term are not favourable. Lesotho's drastic balance of payments is bearable only because Lesotho is a member of the Rand Monetary Area whose economic survival entails close cooperation with the Republic. Increasing aid from foreign countries and international agencies has helped to alleviate some of the deficiencies of the economy, though it cannot effectively end the economic dominance which South Africa – as employer, supplier and investor – exercises by virtue of Lesotho's geographical position. Major donors of aid are the African Development Bank, the World Bank, the European Development Fund and the UK.

Major Industries: agricultural processing, mineral processing, tourism, electrical assembly, textiles and clothing.

Main Commodities Traded: wool, mohair, cloth, diamonds, hides, skins.

International Affiliations: UN, IBRD, OAU, ACP, ADB, Commonwealth, SACU.

HOW TO GET THERE

Air
There are no direct intercontinental flights to Lesotho. The usual route by air is the thrice-weekly service between Maseru and Johannesburg, operated jointly by Lesotho National Airways and South Africa Airways. A joint service operated by Lesotho National Airways and DETA (Mozambique) connects Maseru to Maputo. Leabua Jonathan Airport is 5km/3 miles from Maseru town centre.

Road
Asphalted roads link Lesotho with South Africa in the south, west and north. Before setting out, it is advisable to check on border-post opening hours. Routes to the South African black 'homeland' of Transkei are formally closed as far as the Lesotho Government is concerned, since it does not recognise the 'Republic of Transkei' and cannot comply with border formalities.

Rail
The South African railway network extends 3km/2 miles into Lesotho to Maseru.

ENTRY REGULATIONS

Visas
Visas are required by all visitors, except for nationals of Commonwealth countries, Belgium, Denmark, Finland, Greece, Iceland, Ireland, Israel, Italy, Japan, Luxembourg, Madagascar, Netherlands, Norway, San Marino, Sweden, South Africa, South Korea, Taiwan and USA.

Visas may be obtained from the Director of Immigration in Maseru, the diplomatic representatives of Lesotho abroad, or, if none exists, from British representatives acting for Lesotho. Make sure that you have a re-entry permit for South Africa if travelling from South Africa to Lesotho and back again.

Health Regulations

An International Certificate of Vaccination for smallpox is required except for children under 13 months. Certificates for cholera and yellow fever are required if arriving within 6 days of leaving an infected area.

Customs

Currency: The import and export of local currency is restricted to R50 in notes. The maximum amount of foreign currency that may be imported in notes is the equivalent to R50. There are no limits to the amount of foreign or local currency that may be brought in as cheques or travellers' cheques, provided that it is declared upon arrival. Unused currency may be subsequently exported. The latest regulations are available from the Commissioner of Financial Institutions in Maseru.

Duty-free articles: Used personal effects. 50 cigars, 400 cigarettes or 250 g of tobacco. 1 litre of alcoholic beverages. 300ml of perfume.

PRACTICAL INFORMATION FOR THE VISITOR

1. Currency

Monetary unit – maloti, divided into 100 lesente; South African rand (R) divided into 100 cents.
Notes – 2, 5, 10, 20 maloti; 1, 2, 5, 10, 20 rand.
Coins – 1, 2, 5, 10, 25, 50 lesente; 1 maloti; ½, 1, 2, 5, 10, 20, 50 cents.

Banking Hours
0830–1300 Monday to Friday
0830–1100 Saturday

As a member country of the Rand Monetary Area (RMA), the local currency is freely convertible and at par with the South African rand. Local currency is controlled by the Lesotho Bank.

Principal Commercial Banks in Maseru
Barclays Bank International Ltd, P.O. Box 115, Kingsway.
Standard Bank Ltd, P.O. Box 1001.
Lesotho National Development Bank, P.O. Box 999.

2. Electricity Supply

220v AC 50Hz.

3. Weights and Measures

The metric system is in use.

4. Media

Radio Lesotho is a commercial station broadcasting in Sesotho and English. It is possible to receive South African television in Lesotho, and there are plans to create a national television service.

Newspapers and Journals
The *Lesotho Weekly* is the major English-language newspaper. *Mochochonono* (Comet) is published weekly in Sesotho by the Department of Information. *Mohlaboni* (Warrior) is published fortnightly in English and Sesotho. South African newspapers are available on the day of issue in the main centres. There are two newspapers issued by churches: *Moeletsi oa Basotho* (The Counsellor of Basotho), a Catholic weekly in Sesotho, and *Leselinyana La*

Lesotho (Light of Lesotho), published fortnightly in Sesotho and English by the Lesotho Evangelical church.

5. Medical Care

Malaria and bilharzia are not present; however, tuberculosis, typhoid and polio do occur. Gastroenteritis and other stomach ailments are common. The water supply is heavily chlorinated, but in general water should be boiled before drinking.

Government and mission hospitals are supplemented by clinics and dispensaries in rural areas. The Lesotho Flying Doctor Service operates in the remotest areas of the country. Dentists and medical specialists are available in Maseru.

6. Telephone, Telex and Postal Services

The telephone service is linked to the South African network, and all international calls are via the Republic. Telegram and telex facilities are available in the main centres and are also routed via South Africa. All overseas post should be dispatched by air.

7. Public Holidays

1 January	New Year
12 March	Moshoeshoe's Day
21 March	National Tree Planting Day
2 May	King's Birthday
13 June	Commonwealth Day
1 October	National Sports Day
4 October	National Independence Day
25/6 December	Christmas Holiday

Good Friday, Easter Monday and the 1st Monday in July, are also observed as public holidays.

8. Time

GMT + 2.

9. Internal Transport

Air

There are over 30 airstrips for light aircraft; scheduled charter, tourist, mail and Government services between Maseru and other main centres are operated by Lesotho Airways Corporation and two private operators.

Airline Offices in Maseru
Lesotho Airways Corporation, P.O. Box 861.

Road

The length of asphalted road in Lesotho has increased rapidly since independence in 1966 to over 200km/124 miles, and most of the main routes are now at least all-weather gravel highways. Other roads range from gravel or dirt surfaces to mountain tracks passable in only the most robust vehicles. The best roads are to be found in the west and south.

Public transport is generally inadequate and taxis are available only in Maseru. Self-drive cars can be hired in Maseru, at the airport and from some hotels. Petrol is occasionally unavailable at the weekends.

Traffic drives on the left.

Car Hire Firms in Maseru
Maluti Travel Agency ☎ 2554.

10. Tipping

Taxis – No tip necessary.

Hotels/restaurants – 10–15% of the bill.

Porters – 10–15% depending upon service.

USEFUL ADDRESSES (GENERAL)

British Council: M. G. Holcroft, P.O. Box 429, Hobson's Square, Maseru.

Uganda High Commission: P.O. Box 1188, Maseru.

UK High Commission: P.O. Box 521, Parliament Road, Maseru, ☎ 3961.

US Embassy: P.O. Box 333, Maseru 100, ☎ 22666/7.

Director of Immigration: P.O. Box 363, Maseru.

Lesotho National Tourist Office: P.O. Box 1378, 209 Kingway Road, Maseru.

National University of Lesotho: P.O. Roma, Lesotho.

BUSINESS INFORMATION

Foreign investment is welcome, but must be coordinated by the Lesotho National Development Corporation. Investment is needed mainly in the industrial, tourist, mining and commercial sectors. The Government offer a 6-year tax holiday under the Pioneer Industries programme, guarantees against nationalisation, profit repatriation, fully serviced industrial sites, state loans and participation; Lesotho has duty-free access to EEC markets and free-trade agreements with South Africa, Swaziland and Botswana. Major industrial areas with serviced estates are at Maseru and Maputo. South Africa dominates the domestic market and has in the past been unwilling to accept rival business ventures in Lesotho; however, a number of European and Taiwanese firms have been successful in establishing commercial and industrial ventures.

Import and Exchange Control Regulations

Lesotho is a member of the South African Customs Union and, as such, goods from South Africa, Swaziland and Botswana pay no duty. Products from other countries are liable to controls similar to those exercised in South Africa. All goods not included on the 'free list' require import permits. There is no exchange control between South Africa, Swaziland and Lesotho, all members of the Rand Monetary Area. Exchange control regulations are otherwise the same as those of South Africa.

Business Hours
Government Offices
0800–1245 Monday to Friday
1400–1630

Business Houses
0800–1300 Monday to Friday
1400–1700
0800–1300 Saturday

USEFUL ADDRESSES (BUSINESS)

Lesotho National Development Corporation (LNDC), P.O. Box 666, Maseru, ☎ 2901. Subsidiary: Basuto Enterprise Development Corporation (BEDCO).

Livestock Marketing Corporation, P.O. Box 800, Maseru.

Lesotho Electricity Corporation, P.O. Box 423, Maseru.

Commissioner of Labour, P.O. Box 2121, Maseru.

Director of Customs and Excise, P.O. Box 891, Maseru.

MAIN CITY AND TOWNS

Maseru

Maseru, the administrative and commercial capital of Lesotho, is situated in the eastern lowlands on the banks of the Caledon River which marks the border with the Republic of South Africa. Although the population of the city has increased rapidly since independence, Maseru retains a peaceful and relaxed atmosphere in contrast to neighbouring South Africa. Increasing numbers of tourists are coming over the border from South Africa, and amenities in Maseru have improved in response to the profitable trade. Maseru was made the capital by Moshoeshoe I in 1869.

Hotels

There is no official hotel rating system. Hotels tend to be particularly crowded at weekends and holiday periods, and advance booking is advisable.

LESOTHO HILTON, Private Bag Hilton, ☎ 3957.
Modern hotel overlooking Maseru.
Rooms: 242 ♪, ⓜ, ⓐ, ❏, ✿, ⚘, ⌼. Suites available.
Facilities: Restaurants, bars. Swimming, sauna, tennis, golf, squash, bowling. Car hire.
Services: TC, FC. ⊟ Amex, Barclay Visa, Diners Club. Dr. on call. S, ♂. Audio-visual equipment.
Conference room – max. capacity 500.
Banquet room – max. capacity 300.

MASERU HOLIDAY INN, 12 Orpen Road, P.O. Box 868, ☎ 2434.
Situated 2km/1 mile from city centre, overlooking Caledon River.
Rooms: 236 ♪, ⓜ, ⓐ, ❏, ⚘, ⌼. Suites available.
Facilities: Restaurants, bars. Casino. Tennis, sauna, swimming, health hydro. Car hire.
Services: TC, FC. ⊟ Access, Amex, Barclaycard, Diners Club, Eurocard, Master Charge. Dr. on call. S, ♂. Audio-visual equipment.
Conference room – max. capacity 500.
Banquet room – max. capacity 350.

VICTORIA HOTEL, P.O. Box 212, ☎ 2002.
Situated in business district; built in a blend of traditional and modern styles.
Rooms: 102 ♪, ⓜ, ⓐ, ❏, ✿, ⚘, ⌼ (0700–2300). Suites available.
Facilities: Restaurants, bars. Nightclub, casino. Cinema. Swimming, sauna, golf, tennis, squash, riding, fishing. Car hire.
Services: TC, FC. ⊟ Access, Amex, Barclaycard, Carte Blanche, Diners Club, Eurocard, Master Charge. Dr. on call. S, ♂. Audio-visual equipment.
Conference room – max. capacity 450.

Other Hotels

Airport Hotel, P.O. Box 1050, ☎ 2081.
Lancers Inn, P.O. Box 30, ☎ 214.
Lakeside Hotel, P.O. Box 602, ☎ 3646.

Restaurants

All hotel restaurants are open to non-residents.

Entertainment

The Holiday Inn complex has a casino which caters for South African tourists. Day excursions to the mountains are provided by tour operators to see the spectacular scenery and to visit Bushman rock paintings. Just out of Maseru is the mountain retreat from which Moshoeshoe the Great led the various Basotho clans against invaders.

Mountaineering, trekking, fishing and riding expéditions are all available from

Maseru, and there are plans to build a ski resort with synthetic snow. To get away from the commercialised entertainments of the tourist companies, visit the National Stadium on Saturday for the soccer match or the Catholic Cathedral on Sunday to hear the hymn singing. At Monja, 40km/25 miles south of Maseru, there is a museum displaying cultural, historical and geological items.

Shopping

Best buys: mohair rugs and blankets, sheepskin goods, and kolonyama pottery. Various items of local craftsmanship are on sale at the *Basuto Hat*, official shop of the Lesotho National Development Corporation. The outdoor market near the National Stadium is good for food, vegetables and crafts.

LIBERIA
Republic of Liberia

Geography	*220*
The Economy	*221*
How to Get There	*222*
Entry Regulations	*222*
Practical Information for the Visitor	*223*
Useful Addresses (General)	*225*
Business Information	*225*
Business Services	*226*
Useful Addresses (Business)	*226*
Monrovia	*226*

Size: 111,370 sq.km/43,000 sq. miles.

Population: 1.72 million (1978).

Distribution: 28% in urban areas.

Density: 15 persons per sq.km/41 per sq.mile.

Population Growth Rate: 3.36% p.a.

Ethnic Composition: Over 90% are indigenous Africans from roughly 16 tribes. A small minority are descendants of black settlers from the United States and West Indies.

Capital: Monrovia Pop. 208,629.

Major Towns: Harbel Pop. 60,000; Buchanan Pop. 25,000.

Language: English is the official language; some 30 African dialects are also spoken.

Religion: At least 80% are Animists; the remainder are Christians (all denominations) and Muslims.

Government: On 12 April 1980 a coup d'état staged by non-commissioned officers and led by Master Sergeant Samuel Doe removed President Tolbert and the True Whig Party from power. Tolbert and many of his Government were executed and the Constitution, originally modelled on the US system of Government, was abandoned. The new Government is to consist of a policy-making body, the People's Redemption Council, and an advisory cabinet. Members of the Council are to be drawn from the parties of opposition under the Tolbert Administration, which has been condemned for corruption, injustice and failing to alleviate poverty and unemployment.

LIBERIA

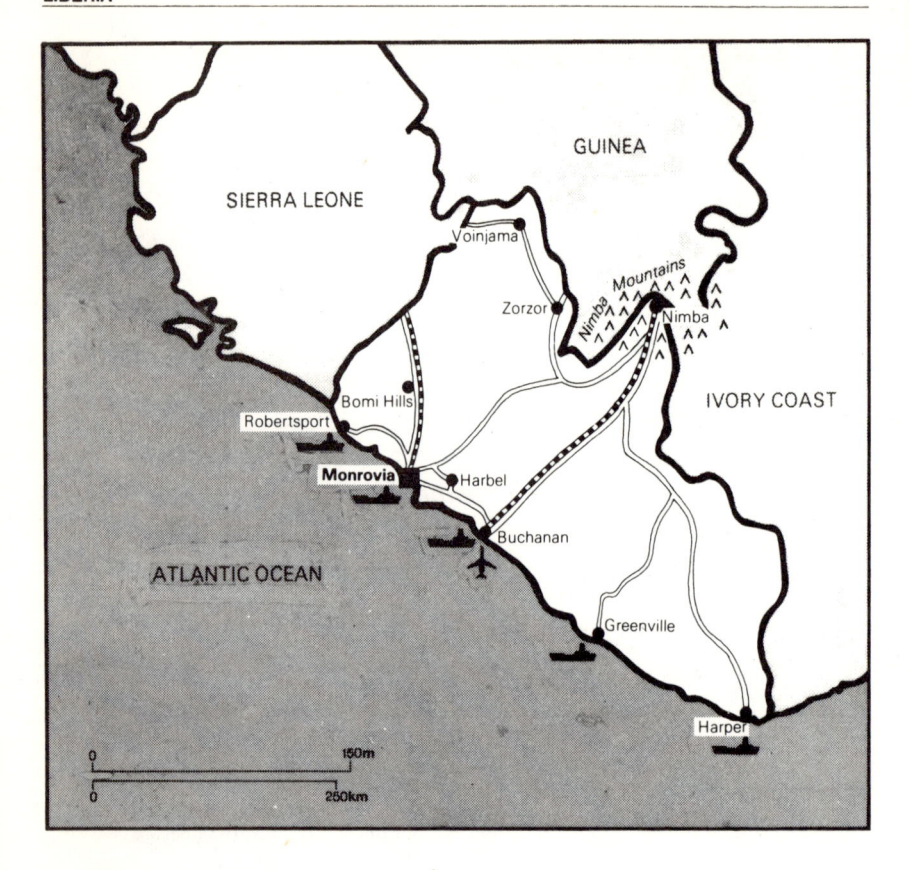

GEOGRAPHY

Liberia lies in the south-west corner of the bulge of Africa. It consists of a narrow coastal plain intersected by marshes, creeks and tidal lagoons; a central region of plateaux and narrow valleys, where the high rain forest is situated; and a mountainous area rising to a height of 1,523m/5,000ft in places, situated alongside the border with Guinea.

Climate
Temperatures range from 21°c/70°F to 32°c/90°F; humidity is high, averaging between 85 and 90%. The rainy season is from May to October.

Agriculture
Approximately two-thirds of the population exist outside the money economy, living by subsistence agriculture; farming contributes some 30% of nominal Gross Domestic Product. Rubber is the most important cash crop, rubber plantations being the largest labour employers. Until 1976 Firestone had a monopoly concession agreement, but several other companies are now involved in the industry.

The agricultural sector is hampered by low productivity and backwardness – Liberia still has to import large quantities of rice, the country's staple food, as production is not high enough to meet local consumption. Substantial aid programmes have been introduced with the United Nations Food and Agricultural Organisation playing a major role in attempting to increase rice production. Coffee, cocoa and palm kernels are important export products; substantial palm oil exports are due to start soon with the establishment of two new processing plants.

Main Crops: rubber, rice, cassava, coffee, cocoa, palm kernels, coconuts.

Mineral Resources: iron ore, diamonds, manganese, gold, bauxite.

THE ECONOMY

Gross National Product (1977): US$710 million.

Per Capita Income (1977): US$430.

Gross Domestic Product (1978): Liberian $744 million.

Foreign Trade (1978): Total Imports – Liberian $480.9 million. Total Exports – Liberian $486.4 million.

Main Trading Partners: Imports – USA, Saudi Arabia, West Germany, UK, Japan. Exports – West Germany, USA, Italy, France, Belgium, Luxembourg, Netherlands, Spain.

Much of the economic activity is in the hands of foreign enterprise as a result of the Government's 'open door' policy encouraging foreign investment and as a result of foreign aid, particularly from the United States. The important industries of iron ore mining, rubber and forestry are largely controlled by foreigners, although the Government now has shares in most concessions.

The current Economic Development Plan places emphasis on economic diversification in order to reduce Liberia's dependence on iron ore exports, and focus on agricultural development and increased productivity, improved communications for the transportation of agricultural products, improved social services and the establishment of light industries.

Iron ore now accounts for almost 75% of Liberia's export earnings, the country being a major world producer of high-grade iron ore. LAMCO, a joint venture of the Liberian Government and American and Swedish interests, accounts for over 60% of total production; due to the continuing world recession in steel production, however, most iron ore mining companies were forced to cut back production in the late 1970s.

Manufacturing is still on a small scale, accounting for only 5% of the GDP in 1976. There is a shortage of skilled workers and managerial staff, despite the encouragement of foreign concerns to help in the training of Liberian workers. An Industrial Free Zone has been established outside Monrovia to attract foreign investment in the manufacturing sector.

Major Industries: rubber, iron ore, timber, diamonds.

Main Commodities Traded: Imports – machinery, transport equipment, manufactured goods, fuels, foodstuffs, chemicals. Exports – iron ore, rubber, diamonds, timber.

International Affiliations: UN, IBRD, OAU, ACP, ADB, ECOWAS, MRU.

HOW TO GET THERE

Air

There are direct services to Monrovia from Amsterdam (KLM), Brussels (Sabena), Geneva and Zürich (Swissair) and London Gatwick (British Caledonian).

There are also direct flights from the United States (New York, Pittsburgh, Philadelphia, San Francisco and Washington, D.C.) provided by Pan American, British Airways, Air Afrique, Nigeria Airways, UTA, British Caledonian and National Airlines; and from Canada (Toronto) by Air Canada. Direct services are also operated from Abidjan, Freetown, Lagos and several other West African cities.

Flying times to Monrovia: from London, 8 hours; from New York, 9 hours.

Monrovia has 2 airports: Roberts International Airport (61km/38 miles from the city centre) and Spriggs Payne Airport, close to the city centre but only suitable for small aircraft. Some of the West African airlines land at Spriggs Payne. Most international flights arrive at Roberts and are met by a coach service. Ordinary and shared taxis also operated between the airport and city centre.

An airport tax of L$5 is payable by all passengers on departure from Liberia.

ENTRY REGULATIONS

Visas

Visas are required by nationals of all countries, except Sierra Leone.

Visas are obtainable from Liberian embassies and consulates abroad. Applications should be accompanied by a doctor's certificate confirming general good health and freedom from infectious diseases. In addition, business travellers require a letter from their firm giving details of the business to be undertaken and the name of the contact in Liberia and confirming financial responsibility for the applicant.

Visas are valid for 60 days for a stay of variable length according to the visitor's requirements. Visas are issued within 48 hours of application, unless referred for authorisation, when the delay can be several weeks.

Health Regulations

Valid International Certificates of Vaccination against smallpox, yellow fever and cholera are required by all persons entering Liberia.

Customs

Currency: No currency regulations are in force. Any amount of foreign and local currency may be imported or exported.

Duty-free articles: Personal effects. 200 cigarettes. 1 bottle of spirits. Commercial samples not intended for sale of a value of less than L$1 (a stamp duty of 25 sents is payable at the port of entry for all samples). Licences are required for the import of firearms, ammunition and some pharmaceuticals.

LIBERIA

Articles liable to duty: Diamonds and precious metals bought in Liberia are subject to export taxes.

Prohibited articles: Sugar. Frozen chicken. Candles. Portland cement. Safety matches. Powdered detergents. Rubber footwear with canvas tops.

PRACTICAL INFORMATION FOR THE VISITOR

1. Currency
Monetary Unit – Liberian dollar (L$), divided into 100 cents.
Notes – 1, 5, 10, 20 Liberian $.
Coins – 1, 5, 10, 25, 50 cents; 1 Liberian dollar.

The Liberian dollar is at par with the US dollar. US notes and coins and Liberian coins are all in circulation. As Liberia is within the Dollar Area, travellers' cheques sould be suitably endorsed.

Banking Hours
0800 – 1200 Monday to Thursday
0800 – 1400 Friday

The *National Bank of Liberia*, Broad Street, P.O. Box 2048, Monrovia, is the central bank.

Principal Domestic Banks in Liberia
Bank of Liberia, Warren and Carey Street, P.O. Box 2031, Monrovia.
International Trust Company of Liberia, 80 Broad Street, P.O. Box 292, Monrovia, ☎ 21600.
Liberian Bank for Development and Investment, Tubman Boulevard, P.O. Box 547, Monrovia.
Liberian Trading and Development Bank Ltd (TRADEVCO), Tradevco Building, 57 Ashmun Street, P.O. Box 293, Monrovia, ☎ 21800.

Foreign Commercial Banks
Chase Manhattan Bank, Ashmun and Randall Streets, P.O. Box 181, Monrovia, ☎ 21500 – branch in Harbel.
Citibank, Ashmun Street, P.O. Box 280, Monrovia.

2. Electricity Supply
110/120v AC 60Hz.
Plugs: 2 round or square pins.

3. Weights and Measures
Imperial weights and measures, as adapted by United States usage, are used in Liberia.

4. Media
Radio and television broadcasting are controlled by the Government-owned Liberian Broadcasting Corporation (LBC). ELTV is the commercial television service of the LBC. Radio Liberia (ELBC) is a commercial radio station which carries general product advertising and provides sponsored programmes and spot advertising. ELWA is a missionary radio station which does not carry advertising. The Lamco Broadcasting Station (ELNR) transmits programmes in English and African languages, and relays the BBC World Service News.

Newspapers
The 3 English-language newspapers circulating in Monrovia are *The Liberian Age* (twice weekly), *The New Liberia* and the *Sunday Express*.
    Liberian Outlook is a monthly magazine, published in Monrovia, which accepts advertising. There is no trade press to speak of in Liberia, but certain Ministries produce news sheets published in English and local languages.

5. Medical Care
Malaria is endemic in some parts of Liberia; visitors should consult their doctor before departure about antimalarial prophylactics. Swimming in

LIBERIA

rivers and inland lakes should be avoided because of the risk of bilharzia, but it is safe to swim in the sea and lagoons.

All drinking water should be boiled and filtered.

Chemists are well stocked with medicines. There are a number of good private doctors as well as public clinics and hospitals.

6. Telephone, Telex and Postal Services

Monrovia has a direct dial telephone system; a microwave system is gradually being extended throughout the country. A satellite system provides international telephone and telex communications.

Telex services are operated by Liberian Radio Telecommunications and by the French Cable Station, providing a link between Monrovia and Europe and North America. Telegrams can be sent and received via LTC and the French Cable Station.

There is no street delivery of letters. All mail is collected from the post office. Letters should be addressed with the post office box number. Business correspondence within Monrovia is often delivered by messenger service.

There are two post offices in Monrovia; most large towns also have a post office.

All mail to and from Liberia should be sent by air.

7. Public Holidays

1 January	*New Year's Day*
7 January	*Pioneers' Day*
11 February	*Armed Forces Day*
15 March	*J. J. Roberts' Birthday*
14 May	*National Unification Day*
25 May	*African Liberation Day*
26 July	*Independence Day*
24 August	*Flag Day*
29 November	*Birthday of President Tubman*
25 December	*Christmas Day*

The following movable holidays are also observed: *Decoration Day* (2nd Wednesday in March); *Palm Sunday*; *Good Friday*; *Easter Monday*; *Fast and Prayer Day* (2nd Friday in April); *Thanksgiving Day*.

3. Time
GMT.

9. Internal Transport

Air
Liberian National Airways operate regular flights between Monrovia (Spriggs Payne Airfield) and major coastal and inland towns, including Harper near the border with the Ivory Coast. There are over 60 small airfields in Liberia. Several air-taxi companies have light aircraft available for charter to these airfields.

Airline Offices in Monrovia
Air Afrique/UTA	☎ 222899, 222900.
Air France	☎ 222900.
British Airways	☎ 222312.
British Caledonian	☎ 222245.
Iberia	☎ 221364.
KLM	☎ 22631/2.
Lufthansa	☎ 222144, 226780 (Air Liberia).
Pan Am	☎ 221133.
Swissair	☎ 222280.

Road
Liberia has a number of good tarred roads connecting many of its major centres. Monrovia is linked to Robertsport and Bomi Hills in the north-west, and Harper in the south-east; just outside the capital a road branches off from the highway and leads to the Harbel Plantations of the Firestone Plantations Company and to Roberts Airport and Buchanan. There is no road linking all the coastal towns. Sierra Leone, Guinea and the Ivory Coast can all be reached by road from Monrovia.

Taxis are plentiful in Monrovia. They are not metered and carry several passengers. Taxis can be hired for several hours; the charge should be negotiated in advance.

Chauffeur-driven and self-drive cars are available for hire in Monrovia. An International Driving Licence is required; holders should register with the Chief of Traffic at the main police station. On production of a foreign driving licence, visitors may obtain a driving permit for periods of up to one month from the Licensing Department of the Ministry of Finance, Monrovia.

Car-Hire Firms in Monrovia
Yes Transport
   Service ☎ 22970
Alfred Mensah
   Travel Bureau ☎ 22807
International
   Automobile Co ☎ 22486.

10. Tipping

Taxis – no tip necessary.

Porters – 25 cents minimum.

Hotels – In addition to the service charge which is added to the bill, a tip of about 50 cents is customary.

11. Social Customs

Dress is relatively formal for a tropical climate, and men are usually expected to wear a suit when making business calls. However, an open-necked shirt and trousers is becoming more acceptable in business circles.

USEFUL ADDRESSES (GENERAL)

British Embassy: Mamba Point, P.O Box 120, Monrovia, ☎ 21055/21107.

Dutch Embassy: United Nations Drive, Mamba Point, P.O. Box 284, Monrovia, ☎ 221155.

French Embassy: 94 United Nations Drive, Mamba Point, P.O. Box 279, Monrovia.

Japanese Embassy: 3rd Floor, Providence Building, Ashmun Street, P.O. Box 2053, Monrovia, ☎ 221227, 221974.

Swiss Embassy: 245 Old Sinkor Road, Congotown, P.O. Box 283, Monrovia, ☎ 261065.

US Embassy: United Nations Drive, P.O. Box 98, Monrovia, ☎ 22991.

West German Embassy: Old Congotown, P.O. Box 34, Monrovia, ☎ 26460.

American Express Authorised Representative: Morgan Travel Agency, 80 Broad Street, P.O. Box 1260, Monrovia, ☎ 22149, 26927.

BUSINESS INFORMATION

Much of Liberia's wholesale and retail distribution network is controlled by foreign concerns, especially Lebanese merchants. Few firms, however, operate specifically on agencies. Several of the large foreign concessionary companies import machinery, equipment and supplies for their own use as well as foodstuffs and consumer goods for the retail stores they run for their employees. The larger merchant companies deal in a wide range of goods which they retail to the public and sell wholesale to smaller merchants.

   Monrovia is Liberia's chief trading centre as well as the country's chief port. Buchanan, about 96km/60 miles south-east of the capital, is the main port for the export of iron ore from the Nimba Mountains; Greenville and Harper also serve as ports.

Business Hours
Government Offices
0800 – 1200
1400 – 1600   Monday to Friday

Business Houses
0800 – 1200
1400 – 1600   Monday to Friday
0800 – 1200 Saturday

Business Events
'The Liberian Chamber of Commerce organises small exhibitions and trade fairs either at its headquarters (see 'Useful Addresses – Business') or at a local football stadium.

BUSINESS SERVICES

Insurance
American International Underwriters, Providence Building, Ashmun Street, P.O. Box 180, Monrovia.

American Life Insurance Company, Providence Building, Ashmun Street, P.O. Box 180, Monrovia.

Insurance Company of Africa, 80 Broad Street, P.O. Box 292, Monrovia, ☎ 221600.

Royal Exchange Assurance, Ashmun and Randall Street, P.O. Box 666, Monrovia.

USEFUL ADDRESSES (BUSINESS)

Liberian Chamber of Commerce, Capitol Hill, P.O. Box 92, Monrovia.

Liberian Development Corporation, National Housing and Savings Bank Building, Water Street, P.O. Box 9043, Monrovia.

Liberian Produce Marketing Corporation, P.O. Box 622, Monrovia.

National Enterprises Corporation, P.O. Box 518, Monrovia.

MAJOR CITY

Monrovia
Founded in 1822 as Christopolis, the city was later renamed after the American President James Monroe. Today it stretches over a large area, divided by lagoons into many peninsulas and islands. The port and the industrial area are situated on Bushrod Island, linked to the mainland by a causeway.

Monrovia presents an unusual sight to the foreign visitor: modern, commercial and residential buildings contrast sharply with traditional African dwellings and large, colonial-style residences reminiscent of the American Deep South.

The National Museum is on Providence Island and houses documents and other historical objects dating back to 1822 when the first freed black slaves arrived from the southern United States. The museum also contains examples of native art and handicraft.

Hotels

There is no official hotel rating system.

CARLTON, Broad Street, P.O. Box 285, ☎ 21245.
Modern hotel in the main business district, near the beach.
Rooms: 68 ♺, ⬤, ☐ on request, ☎, △, ⬥.
Facilities: Restaurants, bar. Nightclub.
Services: TC, FC. ▤ Amex, Diners Club. ⪦, ♂.

DUCOR INTER-CONTINENTAL, Snapper Hill, P.O. Box 86, ☎ 22200.
Modern de luxe hotel set on highest point in Monrovia within walking distance of centre.
Rooms: 200 ♺, ⬤, △, ⚎. Suites available.
Facilities: 3 restaurants, cocktail lounge, bars, coffee shop. Nightclub. Garden. Swimming, tennis, mini-golf. Shopping arcade. Car hire.
Services: TC, FC. ▤ Amex, Carte Blanche, Diners Club. Dr. on call. ⪦, ♂ on request.
Conference room – max. capacity 400.
Banquet rooms – max. capacity 350.

HOLIDAY INN, 100 Carey Street, ☎ 22337/21847.
Centrally located hotel within walking distance of business district (not affiliated with International Holiday Inn group).
Rooms: 42 ♺. Suites available with ☐.
Facilities: Restaurant, 24-hour snack bar, discotheque.

TRAVELLER'S ROOST, Broad Street, P.O. Box 1439, ☎ 22522.
Centrally situated hotel comprising 2/3-room service apartments with modern fully equipped kitchens.

Restaurants

Julia's, Gurley Street – French; *Salvatore's* – American and Italian; *Atlantic Restaurant* – French, German and Russian; *Oscar's* – French and Swiss; *Diana's* – Middle Eastern and Indian; *Roseline's* – Liberian dishes.

Entertainment

Monrovia has a thriving nightlife, with many nightclubs and discotheques open until the early hours of the morning.

Performances of African music and dance are held in the Amphitheatre on the island.

Along the coast outside Monrovia are several fine sandy beaches – Bernard's, Elwa, Kenema, Kendaje, Cedar and Caesar's – with facilities for a wide variety of watersports.

Shopping

Best buys: wood (sapwood, ebony, mahogany), stone carvings, ivory, metal figurines and jewellery.

Handicrafts are on sale in the gift shop at the National Cultural Centre. *Safari International Crafts and Designs* and *Afri-Craft*, both in the shopping arcade at Broad and Gurley Streets, have a selection of unusual fabrics, including tie-dye, available in lengths and ready-made garments.

LIBYA
Socialist People's Libyan Arab Jamahiriya

Geography	*228*
The Economy	*230*
How to Get There	*230*
Entry Regulations	*231*
Practical Information for the Visitor	*232*
Useful Addresses (General)	*234*
Business Information	*234*
Business Services	*235*
Useful Addresses (Business)	*235*
Tripoli	*236*
Benghazi	*237*

Size: 1,759,540 sq.km/697,360 sq.miles.

Population: 2.75 million (1978 est.).

Distribution: 95% of the population live in the coastal region, mainly concentrated around Tripoli and Benghazi.

Density: 1.4 persons per sq.km/3.6 per sq.mile.

Population Growth Rate: 4.2% p.a.

Ethnic Composition: The majority are Arabs with large numbers of Berbers; in the south the population is predominantly black.

Capital: Tripoli (Western Province) Pop. 709,167.

Major Towns: Benghazi (Eastern Province) Pop. 331,180; Sebha (Southern Province) Pop. 112,318.

Language: Arabic is the official language, and its exclusive use is encouraged by the Government. Some English and Italian are spoken in business circles.

Religion: Most Libyans are Sunni Muslims; the small Christian and Jewish minorities live mainly in Tripoli.

Government: The General People's Congress is the supreme legislative body in Libya, and has replaced the Revolutionary Command Council which emerged in 1969, following the abolition of the monarchy. Islamic socialism forms the basis of the Constitution, with an emphasis on popular power. Political power is exercised by People's Congresses, Committees, trade unions, etc. and the General People's Congress.

The Arab Socialist Union (founded 1971) is the only official political party, but has been virtually non-existent since the Constitution was changed in 1977.

GEOGRAPHY

With the exception of a range of hills in the north-west known as the Jebel, Libya has few areas of high land. 90% of the country consists of sand and rock deserts, and the only fertile land is the northern coastal fringe and a series of oases scattered across the country. Libya has no permanent rivers, and sporadic rainfall causes frequent crop failure.

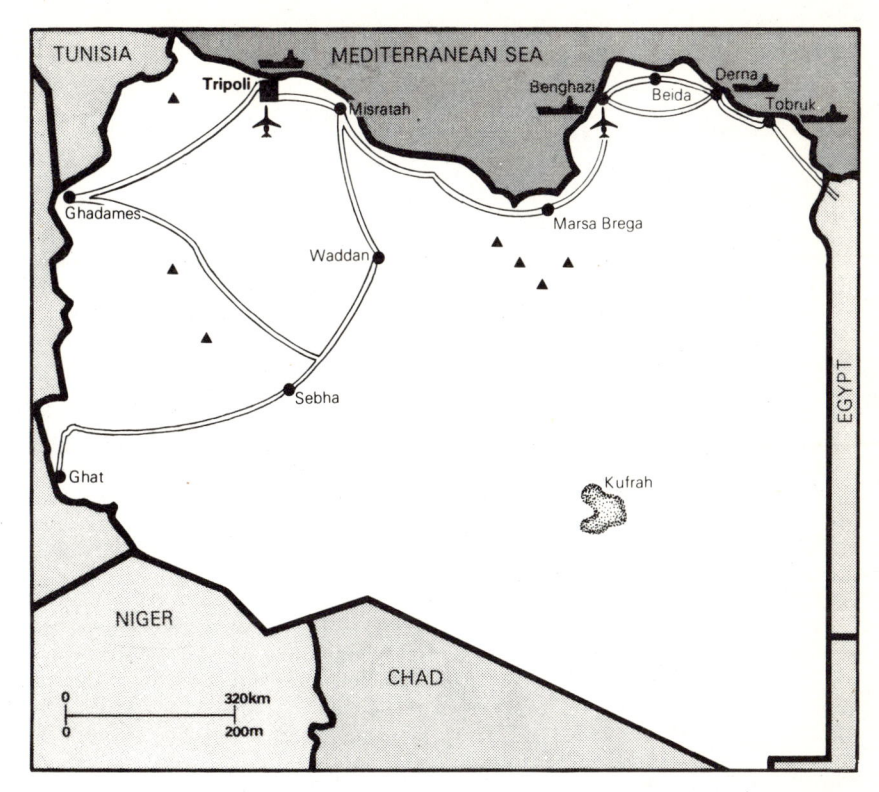

Climate
Most parts of Libya have a hot and arid desert climate, with no rainfall during the summer months. The climate along the coast is more temperate with temperatures of about 38°C/100°F in summer – humidity can exceed 90%. A hot, dry wind known as the *ghibli* blows in from the south, causing a dramatic rise in temperature and some discomfort. Winters are cool, with temperatures occasionally around freezing, particularly in the northern areas.

Agriculture
The discovery of oil in Libya resulted in a rural exodus and a decline in agricultural production which the Government is now anxious to reverse. A large percentage of development finance is being spent on various forms of agricultural development including land reclamation, irrigation and experimental farms. Subsidies are given to the farming community, and Libya aims to achieve self-sufficiency in meat and cereals by the 1980s.

Main Crops: barley, olives, citrus fruits, dates, almonds, tobacco.

Mineral Resources: oil, natural gas, iron ore, gypsum, potassium.

THE ECONOMY

Gross National Product (1977): US$17.6 billion.

Per Capita Income (1976 est.): US$5,583.

Gross Domestic Product (1977): 5,732 million Libyan dinars.

Foreign Trade (1978): Total Imports – US$5,624 million. Total Exports – US$9,856 million.

Main Trading Partners: Imports – Italy, West Germany, France, USA, UK. Exports – USA, Italy, West Germany, Spain, France, Virgin Islands.

Libya is the world's 10th largest oil exporter, and the majority of the country's income comes from oil revenues. Substantial oil reserves together with increased production and higher oil prices are enabling Libya to pursue a policy of economic diversification which will hopefully give the economy a more balanced structure.

Progress is slow and at times uncertain, however, due in part to a shortage of skilled labour and a certain unwillingness on the part of both foreign and domestic private investors to invest on a large scale.

Libya has a separate development budget with the main emphases being on industrialisation, housing and the infrastructure. Heavy industries such as iron and steel are still in their infancy. Manufacturing is largely confined to the processing of agricultural produce; other important light industries are tobacco, furniture, and textiles and clothing. Growth in this sector should eventually reduce Libya's dependence on imported goods, especially on consumer items.

Major Industries: oil, natural gas, food processing, tobacco, building materials.

Main Commodities Traded: Imports – machinery, iron and steel pipes, manufactured goods, food products. Exports – crude oil, barley, olives, citrus fruits, hides and skins, tobacco.

Crude Oil Production (1976): 92 million tonnes.

International Affiliations: UN, IBRD, OAU, ADB, AL, OPEC, OAPEC.

HOW TO GET THERE

Air

Major airlines flying to Tripoli and Benghazi (Benina Airport) are: Aeroflot, Alitalia, British Caledonian, KLM, Lufthansa, Swissair, TWA and UTA.

There are regular flights to Libya from Rome, London, Frankfurt, Athens, Cairo, Paris, Tunis, Algiers and Zürich. British Caledonian operate 6 direct flights a week to Tripoli from London and a weekly flight to Benghazi.

Flying times to Tripoli: from London, 3 hours; from New York, 15 hours.

An airport tax of 500 dirhams is payable on departure from Libya. This does not apply to Libyan nationals or transit passengers.

Foreign business travellers may be charged income tax at Benina Airport, Benghazi, based on the number of days spent in Libya over the previous 12 months. This does not apply at Tripoli Airport, so travellers are advised to use this route into Libya.

A bus service operates between Tripoli Airport and the main hotels in the city.

Tripoli International Airport is 35km/21 miles from Tripoli.

Benina Airport is 29km/18 miles from Benghazi.

Road

The road which runs along the North African coast for some 1,830km/1,140 miles provides a through route from Cairo via Libya to Tunis and on to Algiers and Casablanca. Persons wishing to cross the border into or out of Libya to Tunisia or Egypt should enquire if the border is open.

ENTRY REGULATIONS

Visas

Nationals from the following countries do not require visas: Algeria, Bahrain, Jordan, Kuwait, Mauritania, Morocco, Oman, Qatar, Saudi Arabia, Somalia, Sudan, UAE, Yemen Arab Republic and the People's Democratic Republic of Yemen.

All other nationals require visas, obtainable from Libyan embassies and consulates abroad.

Libyan Government regulations require that a passport holder's particulars must be in Arabic before a visa can be issued. An 'open stamp' which must then be completed in Arabic is necessary; the visa form must also be completed in Arabic. Arrangements for the stamp are usually made by the passport-issuing authority.

British passport holders can obtain the appropriate stamp at all United Kingdom passport offices and at selected British embassies and high commissions abroad. Arrangements for translations into Arabic can be made through the Thomas Cook Passports, Visas and Reservations Department, 45 Berkeley Street, London.

Visas are normally valid for entry within 90 days of issue, for a stay of up to 1 month. Business travellers are advised to plan their visit so that they leave Libya within the period of validity of their visa. The validity of passports should extend for at least 3 months from the date of issue of visas.

Business travellers require a letter from their firm giving details of the business to be undertaken in Libya and the names of business contacts there.

Evidence in a passport of a previous or planned visit to Israel may adversely affect the granting of a visa.

All visitors must register with the immigration authorities within 7 days of arrival in Libya.

Health Regulations

An International Certificate of Vaccination against smallpox is required; also yellow fever and/or cholera certificates if entering from an African country. TAB (typhoid and paratyphoid) injections are recommended.

Customs

Currency: No more than 20 Libyan dinars in bank notes may be taken into or out of the country. There are no restrictions on the amount of other currencies or travellers' cheques. All monies must be declared on entry and departure on a currency declaration form issued on most flights to Libya.

LIBYA

Duty-free articles: 200 cigarettes or 500g tobacco. 250ml perfume. Personal effects. Accompanied samples, providing the business traveller can prove the existence of a Libyan agent – a deposit equivalent to the amount of duty payable may be charged and this is refunded on departure.

Prohibited articles: alcohol.

PRACTICAL INFORMATION FOR THE VISITOR

1. Currency
Monetary Unit – Libyan dinar (LD), divided into 1,000 dirhams.
Notes – 250, 500 dirhams; 1, 5, 10 Libyan dinars.
Coins – 1, 5, 10, 20, 50, 100 dirhams.

Travellers' cheques should be cashed only at banks or hotels and visitors should ensure that their currency declaration form is stamped by the cashing authority. Credit cards are not normally accepted in Libya.

Banking Hours
Winter
0900–1300 Saturday to Thursday
Summer
0800–1230 Saturday to Thursday
1600–1700 Saturday and Wednesday

The *Central Bank of Libya* is the bank of issue and operates the exchange control. Its Commercial Banking Division has branches throughout the country.

Major Banks
The Central Bank of Libya, Sharia Gamal Abdul Nasser, P.O. Box 1103, Tripoli, ☎ 33591; Sharia Omar Mukhtar, P.O. Box 249, Benghazi.
Masraf al Jumhouriya, Sharia Magarief, P.O. Box 396, Tripoli, ☎ 33553; Sharia Gamal Abdul Nasser, P.O. Box 1291, Benghazi.
Masraf al Wahda, Sharia Magarief, P.O. Box 374, Tripoli, ☎ 34016; Sharia Gamal Abdul Nasser, P.O. Box 1320, Benghazi, ☎ 94527.
National Commercial Bank, Maidan Al-Shuhada, P.O. Box 2553, Tripoli, ☎ 37191, Municipality Square Branch, P.O. Box 1279, Benghazi.
Umma Bank, 1 Sharia Omar Mukhtar, P.O. Box 685, Tripoli, ☎ 34031; P.O. Box 221, Benghazi, ☎ 93377.
Sahara Bank, Sharia 1 September, P.O. Box 270, Tripoli, ☎ 32771; Sharia Omar Mukhtar, P.O. Box 2151, Benghazi, ☎ 92766.

2. Electricity Supply
125v AC 50Hz (Western Province) and 220v AC 50Hz (Eastern Province).
Plugs: 2-pin round Continental.

3. Weights and Measures
The metric system is in use.

4. Media
Radio broadcasts are transmitted in Arabic and English from Tripoli and Benghazi. Libya has a colour television network. There are no commercial radio or television programmes.

Newspapers and Journals
El Fajr Al Jadid (daily) and *Al Johad* (3 times a week) both have circulations ranging from 16,000 to 25,000. The *Libyan Press Review* is a daily newssheet in English published in Tripoli. *Arab Oil* is a monthly publication in Arabic and English.

5. Medical Care
There has been a sharp decline in the number of European doctors and dentists working in Libya since the Revolution. The main towns have a high standard of cleanliness and there are no great health hazards. Tap water is safe to drink in the larger towns.

Tripoli –	Government Hospital Emergencies	☎ 30585 ☎ 34682
Benghazi –	Government Hospital Emergencies	☎ 92131 ☎ 89666

6. Telephone, Telex and Postal Services

Direct dialling is available from Libya to most European countries. Delays can be expected with trunk calls, especially during the mornings.

Useful Telephone Numbers

Tripoli – Emergency, Police, Fire, First Aid ☎ 41471.
Benghazi – Police ☎ 99. Fire ☎ 95555.

Libya has limited telex facilities.

Daily international and internal air mail services operate from Tripoli and Benghazi. Post offices are open 7 days a week with restricted services on Fridays.

7. Public Holidays

8 March	Syrian Revolution Day
28 March	Evacuation Day (UK)
25 May	Sudan National Day
11 June	Evacuation Day (US)
23 July	Egyptian National Day
1 September	Libyan Revolution Day
7 October	Evacuation Day (Italian)

The following movable Muslim holidays are also observed: *Mouled*, *El Nabi*, *Eid el Fitr*, *Eid el Adha* and *El Hijra*.

Friday is the official weekday holiday. Banks, Government offices, business houses, etc., are closed on Fridays and work on Sundays. Most oil companies are closed on Saturdays.

8. Time

GMT + 2.

9. Internal Transport

Air

Libyan Arab Airlines operate hourly services between Tripoli and Benghazi. There are also regular services to Ghadames, Sebha, Marsa Brega, Beida, Tobruk and Kufrah.

Airline Offices in Tripoli

Aeroflot	☎ 41257.
Air France	☎ 34362.
British Airways	☎ 33518.
British Caledonian	☎ 33516/7.
KLM	☎ 34348.
Libyan Arab Airlines	☎ 44206.
Lufthansa	☎ 32990, 44488.
PIA	☎ 46229.
SAS	☎ 38048, 37407.
Swissair	☎ 36046/7.
TWA	☎ 35840/1.

Road

International Driving Licences are not required. Self-drive cars are available for hire in Tripoli and Benghazi; also chauffeur-driven cars, but these are very expensive. Driving is on the right-hand side of the road. All traffic signs and signposts are in Arabic script.

Taxis in Libya are expensive with a minimum charge of LD1 for a single journey within Tripoli or Benghazi. Visitors are advised to negotiate all fares on a time basis before engaging a taxi.

Car-Hire Firms in Tripoli

Alta Rentacar, 124 Sharia Imgarief.
El Rahila, Sharia Omar Mukhtar.
Otal, 10–16 Sharia Ikbal.

10. Tipping

Taxis – no tip necessary.

Porters – 50 dirhams per bag.

Hotels and restaurants – 10% service charge is usually included in the bill.

11. Social Customs
Strict observance of traditional Islamic customs is adhered to by most of the Muslim population in this predominantly Muslim nation. The sale and consumption of alcohol are prohibited. There is also strict segregation of the sexes.

USEFUL ADDRESSES (GENERAL)

Tripoli

British Embassy, 30 Sharia Gamal Abdul Nasser, ☎ 31191/5.

Dutch Embassy, 20 Sharia Gelal Bayar, P.O. Box 3801, ☎ 41549/41550.

French Embassy, Omar Lofti Saad Street, Quartier Garden City, P.O. Box 312.

Japanese Embassy, 37 Sharia Abi Ben Kaab, Garden City, P.O. Box 3265, ☎ 46090, 46381.

Swiss Embassy, Jeraba, P.O. Box 439, ☎ 32416.

US Embassy, Sharia Mohammad Thabit, P.O. Box 289, ☎ 34021/6.

West German Embassy, Sharia Hassan el Mashai, P.O. Box 302, ☎ 33827.

Tourist Department, Sharia Adrian Pelt, Tripoli.

North African Maritime and Travel Enterprises, 73/75 Sharia Baladia, P.O. Box 253, Tripoli, ☎ 40565, 40562.

Secretariat for Information and Culture, Sharia Baladia, Tripoli, ☎ 34081.

Benghazi

American Express Authorised Representatives, The Libyan Travel Bureau, Reufeh El Ansari Street, Tourist Building, P.O. Box 306, ☎ 3083, 2565.

BUSINESS INFORMATION

In accordance with Libya's Development Plans, about 17% of total investment has been allocated to agricultural development and some 15% to the industrial sector. Agricultural expansion should mean an increased demand for fertilisers and agricultural machinery. Industrial diversification, while aiming to reduce Libya's dependence on imported consumer goods, will necessitate an increase in the amount of imported capital goods as well as the need for technical advice and consultancy services.

Opportunities for direct foreign investment in Libya are limited and until now have been mainly confined to the petroleum industry and related areas. The Libyan Government tends to engage foreign contractors on a particular project which, on completion, is then handed back to Libyan operators. Foreign firms offering technical advice or working in a consultative capacity may be allowed to operate in Libya through wholly foreign-owned branches.

Agents must be Libyan nationals or, in the case of a company, wholly owned by Libyans. Because of the distance separating Benghazi and Tripoli, it is usually necessary to appoint separate agents for each market.

It is important to remember that all trade literature and correspondence with Government officials should be written in Arabic.

Import and Exchange Control Regulations

A permit is necessary for the transfer of foreign exchange from Libya. Prior approval from the Central Bank of Libya is required for the issue of exchange permits.

Certain goods, particularly those for use in the petroleum industry, are exempt from import duties.

A licence is required to import all goods – this may be an open general licence or, in the case of a wide range of items including some foodstuffs, precious metals, gems and furniture, a specific licence is required. The import of alcohol is strictly forbidden, and there is a ban on imports from South Africa and Israel.

Business Hours

Government Offices
Winter   0800–1400 Saturday to Thursday
Summer   0700–1300 Saturday to Thursday
(In addition, Government employees may work voluntarily from 1530–1730, except on Thursdays.)

Oil Companies
0730–1230
1400–1630 Sunday to Thursday

Business Houses
0900–1300
1600–1930 Saturday to Thursday

Business Events

Tripoli International Trade Fair is held annually in March. For further information contact: Fairs General Board, P.O. Box 891, Tripoli.

BUSINESS SERVICES

Translation Services

Tripoli
Ibrahim Hafez Translation Bureau, 31 Giaddat Omar Mukhtar, ☎ 33885.
Bakkush Services Agency, 39 Beirut Street, P.O. Box 2463, ☎ 44659, 44038.

United Agents, Khweldi Building, Entrance B, 1st Floor, Khaled Ben Waled Street, P.O. Box 3791, ☎ 39633, 40320.

Benghazi
Abdul Majid Ben Sa'oud, Sharia Gzeir, P.O. Box 126, ☎ 92597.

USEFUL ADDRESSES (BUSINESS)

Chamber of Commerce, Industry and Agriculture for the Western Province, Sharia Al Jumhouriya, P.O. Box 2321, Tripoli, ☎ 34539, 36855.

Chamber of Commerce, Industry and Agriculture for the Eastern Province, Sharia Gamal Abdul Nasser, P.O. Box 208, Benghazi, ☎ 92490, 94526.

LIBYA

Secretariat for Agriculture and
   Agrarian Reform, Sidi Masri, Tripoli,
   ☎ 37338.

Secretariat for Industry and
   Minerals, Alfath Road, Tripoli,
   ☎ 40150.

Secretariat for Petroleum, Sadoon
   Swehli Street, Tripoli, ☎ 33195.

MAJOR CITIES AND TOWNS

Tripoli
The history of Tripoli dates back to Phoenician and Roman times, although few ancient traces remain with the exception of the arch of Marcus Aurelius in the old city.

Modern Tripoli, with its wide streets and spacious open areas, is more a product of the period of Italian occupation. The old city is of most interest to visitors, with the 16th-century castle overlooking the harbour and port and the maze of narrow winding alleys and traditional *souks* or markets. The castle houses a museum containing sections on the archaeology, ethnography, epigraphy and natural history of Libya.

N.B. Visitors are advised not to photograph the port.

Hotels
The Department of Tourism classifies hotels as de luxe, 1st class, 2nd class, etc.

LIBYA PALACE, Sharia Sidi Issa, P.O. Box 727, ☎ 31181.
1st-class hotel in city centre.
Rooms: 400 ♪, ▥, ▲, ☎, ◻ on request, △.
Facilities: American bar, international restaurant and bar, roof garden. Swimming pool. Hairdresser. Car hire.
Services: TC, FC. ▤ Amex, Diners Club. Dr. on call. ♂.
Conference room – max. capacity 500.
Banquet room – max. capacity 500.

MEDITERRANEAN, off Sharia Omar Mukhtar, P.O. Box 6207, ☎ 43016.
Modern 1st-class hotel beside sea, ½ mile from city centre.
Rooms: 290 ♪, ▲, ☎. Suites available.
Facilities: Restaurant, bar. Hairdresser. Bank. Swimming.

UADDAN, Sharia Sidi Issa, P.O. Box 337, ☎ 30041.
Modern de luxe hotel near city centre, overlooking sea.
Rooms: 96 ♪, ▲, ☎, ◻ on request.

Facilities: Restaurant, bars. Nightclub, casino. Cinema, theatre. Swimming pool. Beauty parlour.
Services: TC, FC.
Conference room – max. capacity 400.

Restaurants
Apart from the hotel restaurants, others include: *Excelsior*, *Caravan*, *Le Paris* and several *Wadi al-Rabee* restaurants.
N.B. Alcohol is forbidden by law and is not served in Libyan hotels and restaurants.

Entertainment
Tripoli has several cinemas, but no regular theatre or concert hall. There are a number of municipal beaches around the town, but swimming is generally better further outside Tripoli. Sporting activities available include football, golf, horse-racing, ten-pin bowling and tennis.

Shopping
Weavers, coppersmiths, goldsmiths and leatherworkers can be seen at work in the *souks*, and their goods are on display for sale.

Benghazi
Benghazi is the main town in Libya's Eastern Province. Part of the modern town is built on top of the ancient city of Berenice, formerly inhabited by both the Greeks and the Romans.

Benghazi was severely damaged during World War II and many of the buildings dating from the periods of Turkish and Italian rule were destroyed.

Hotels
GEZIRA PALACE, Ali Wouraieth Street, P.O. Box 285, ☎ 96001.
De luxe hotel overlooking sea.
Rooms: 150 ♪, ⬤, ☎, ◻ on request.
Facilities: Restaurant, bar. Swimming pool.

OMAR KHAYYAM, Sharia Gamal Abdul Nasser, P.O. Box 2148, ☎ 95100.
De luxe hotel near city centre, overlooking sea.
Rooms: 186 ♪, ⦿, ⬤, ☎, ◻, △, ⌖.
Facilities: Restaurant, bar. Swimming pool. Car hire.

Services: ⊟ Amex. Dr. on call. **S**, ♂.
Conference room – max. capacity 200.
Banquet room – max. capacity 500.

Restaurants
Apart from the hotel restaurants, the 2 main restaurants in Benghazi are the *Palace* and the *Vienna*.

Entertainment
2 cinemas, the *Berenice* and the *Rex*, show foreign films. There is no theatre or concert hall in Benghazi.

MADAGASCAR
Democratic Republic of Madagascar

Geography	239
The Economy	240
How to Get There	241
Entry Regulations	241
Practical Information for the Visitor	242
Useful Addresses (General)	244
Business Information	245
Business Services	245
Useful Addresses (Business)	246
Antananarivo	246

Size: 587,041 sq.km/226,657 sq.miles.

Population: 8.29 million (1978 est.).

Distribution: 14% in urban areas.

Density: 14.9 persons per sq.km/38.6 per sq.mile.

Population Growth Rate: 2.8% p.a.

Ethnic Composition: There are 18 major tribal groups, mainly of Malayan-Indonesian origin. The largest group comprises the Merina (1.9 million) and the Betsileo living on the high plateaus; the east is dominated by the Betsimisaraka; others include the Antandroy, Tsimihely and Sakalava.
  There is also a small population of Europeans (mainly French), Indians and Chinese.

Capital: Antananarivo Pop. 520,000 (1976 est.).

Major Towns: Toamasina (Tamatave) Pop. 62,500; Mahajanga (Majunga) Pop. 70,000; Antseranana (Diégo-Suarez) Pop. 45,480.

Language: Malagasy and French are the official languages. A number of dialects are also widely spoken.

Religion: About 50% are Animists; 40% Christians (Protestant and Roman Catholic); the remainder Muslims.

Government: Following the assassination of the President in 1975, the Government was taken over by the Supreme Revolutionary Council. The President of the Republic, elected for a 7-year term, is Head of State and President of the Supreme Revolutionary Council.
  In 1977 elections were held for the National Assembly; all candidates belonged to Madagascar's sole political party, the Front National pour la Défense de la Révolution Socialiste Malgache (FNDR), a new party made up of parties banned in 1975, including Avant-Garde de la Révolution Malgache (AREMA), Parti du Congrès de l'Indépendance de Madagascar (AKFM) and Elan Populaire par l'Unité Nationale (VONJY).

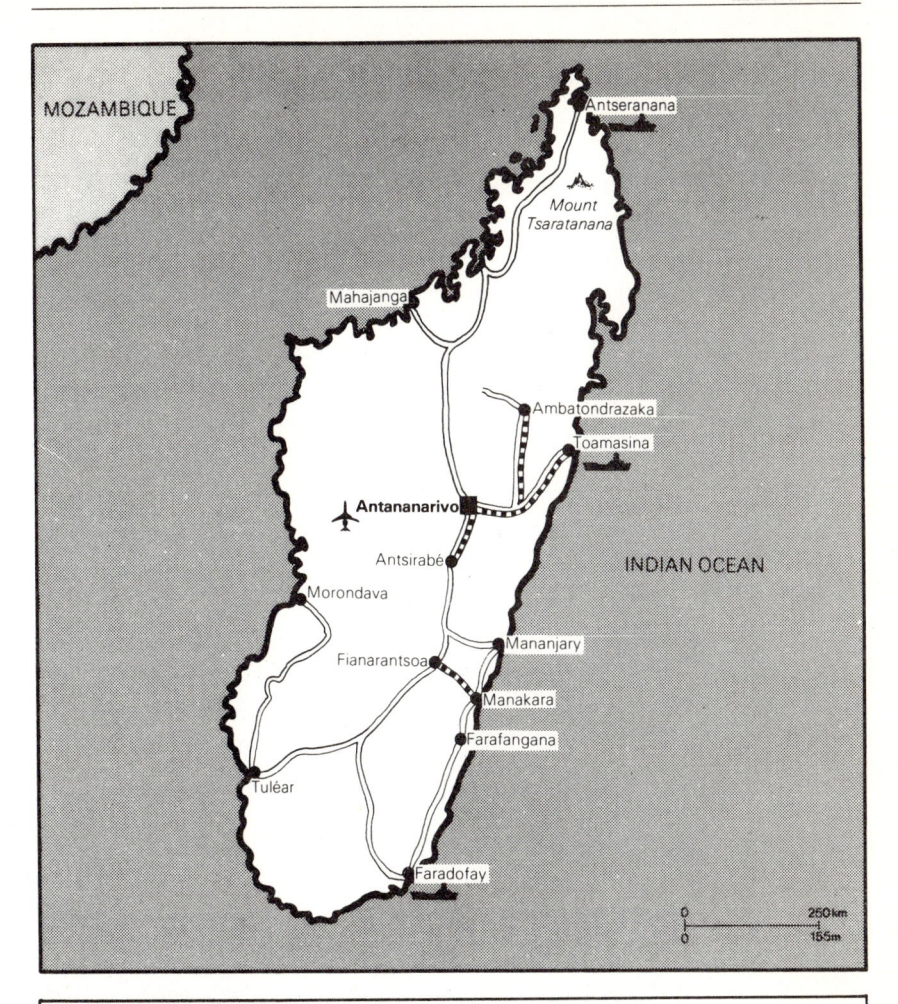

GEOGRAPHY

Madagascar lies in the Indian Ocean, some 450km/280 miles off the coast of East Africa. The island is the 4th largest in the world, being 1,600km/994 miles in length and 570km/354 miles at its widest point.

The central area is dominated by a high plateau region, rising to 2,800m/9,190ft at Mt Tsaratanana. To the east lies the narrow, swampy coastal strip, while in the west and south-west is an area of savannah and forest land where there is much agricultural activity along the coastal plains.

Climate
The climate is tropical along the east and north-west coasts; hot and dry on the west coast; and arid in the south. The central region is more temperate, with temperatures rarely rising above 30°c/85°F.

The dry season lasts from April to October. The rainy season is from November to March when temperatures are at their highest. The monsoon season runs from December to March.

Agriculture

Agriculture is the mainstay of the economy and is given top priority in the Government's development plans. It accounts for approximately 40% of the Gross Domestic Product, and more than 80% of the population are in this sector, the majority living at subsistence level.

Coffee is the principal cash crop, followed by vanilla, spices, sugar, cloves and pepper. Rice is the staple diet of Madagascar and the Government is making extensive efforts to increase rice production by extending the area under cultivation while at the same time encouraging the cultivation of substitute food crops.

Agricultural reform programmes include the expansion of land under cultivation and the nationalisation of large plantations formerly owned by colonialists; farms owned by individual Malagasy farmers will remain in their hands. Increased administrative authority and economic responsibility are being vested in the local village councils (*fokonolona*).

Plans also exist for the development of the meat industry, with state farms being created to organise commercial beef production.

Main Crops: rice, coffee, vanilla, cloves, sugar-cane, sisal, cassava, tobacco, pepper.

Mineral Resources: chromite, graphite, mica, bauxite, industrial beryl.

THE ECONOMY

Gross National Product (1977): US$1.96 billion.

Per Capita Income (1977): US$210.

Gross Domestic Product in Purchasers' Values (1977): 456.3 billion Malagasy francs.

Foreign Trade (1977): Total Imports – US$326 million. Total Exports – US$367 million.

Main Trading Partners: Imports – France, Qatar, China, West Germany, USA. Exports – France, USA, Réunion, Japan, West Germany.

After several years of Government policy aimed at increasing state control of the economy, 1978 saw a marked shift in emphasis. For the time being there will be no further nationalisations, and a concerted drive to expand both agricultural and industrial production is under way. Known as 'Horizon 2000', this programme has resulted in a marked increase in capital investment and renewed efforts to encourage private and foreign investment.

At present, the industrial sector is largely confined to the processing of agricultural products, and accounts for approximately 20% of the GDP. The textile and clothing industry is also important.

Major industrial developments since independence include the establishment of an oil refinery at Toamasina, vehicle assembly plants, cotton mills and fertiliser manufacture. The island's extensive mineral deposits of chromite, bauxite, coal, graphite and mica make mining an area of enormous potential growth.

Other development projects currently in hand include the building of a hydro-electric power plant with financial aid from the International Development Association and the growth of the ferro-chrome, pulp, cement, and steel-manufacturing industries. As an associate member of the European Economic Community, Madagascar receives financial aid from the European Community Fund for Overseas Development and from other international organisations such as the United Nations.

Major Industries: food processing, paper, textiles, mining, agricultural products, fertilisers, car assembly.

Main Commodities Traded: Imports – transport equipment, machinery, foodstuffs, electrical appliances, raw materials, crude petroleum. Exports – coffee, cloves, vanilla, sugar, sisal, petroleum products.

International Affiliations: UN, IBRD, OAU, ACP, ADB.

HOW TO GET THERE

Air

Air France and Air Madagascar operate direct services from Paris to Antananarivo, and Alitalia and Air Madagascar fly direct from Rome.

From London, Air France and British Airways fly to Paris with transfer connections to Madagascar. British Airways also fly to Mauritius via Rome and Nairobi, with connections to Madagascar available to Nairobi and Mauritius.

Air Madagascar fly twice weekly to Antananarivo from Nairobi and once a week from Dar es Salaam. Air Tanzania operate a weekly service from Dar es Salaam.

Flights are also available from Maputo, Djibouti, Réunion and the Comoro Islands.

Flying times to Antananarivo: from London, 9 hours (no direct flights); from New York, 20 hours.

The International Airport is at Ivato, 16km/10 miles from the centre of Antananarivo.

An airport tax of 1,500 Malagasy francs is payable by all passengers on flights from Madagascar.

Air Route Services/ATO operate a bus service between the airport and Antananarivo.

ENTRY REGULATIONS

Visas

A valid passport and visa are required by all visitors. Visas should be obtained in advance from embassies and consulates of the Democratic Republic of Madagascar. French embassies and consulates no longer issue visas for Madagascar.

There is no Malagasy diplomatic mission in the United Kingdom. Visas can be obtained from the Malagasy Embassy in France (1 Boulevard Suchet, Paris 16ème, ☎ 5041816) or in Belgium (276 Avenue de Tervueren, Brussels 15).

Visa applications should be made well in advance of the proposed visit as they may be referred for authorisation causing some delay. Business visitors should ensure that the validity of their passport extends for at least 3 months beyond the visa's date of issue.

Health Regulations

A valid International Certificate of Vaccination against smallpox is required by all persons entering Madagascar. International Certificates of Vaccination against cholera and yellow fever are required by persons arriving from an infected area.

Customs

Currency: There is no limit to the amount of foreign currency which may be taken in. A limit of 5,000 Malagasy francs is placed on the amount of local currency which may be imported or exported.

Duty-free articles: Personal effects. 500 cigarettes or 25 cigars or 500g of tobacco. 1 bottle of wine or spirits. Samples of no commercial value. The import of duty-free perfume is not permitted.

Articles liable to duty: Commercial samples of value are admitted temporarily, provided a bond or deposit is given to cover the amount of duty payable. The bond is cancelled or the deposit returned if the samples are re-exported within 6 months.

PRACTICAL INFORMATION FOR THE VISITOR

1. Currency

Monetary Unit – Malagasy franc (FMG), divided into 100 centimes.
Notes – 50, 100, 500, 1,000, 2,000 Malagasy francs.
Coins – 1, 2, 5, 10, 20 Malagasy francs.

Visitors to Madagascar are advised to cash their travellers' cheques only when and as required as reconversion of Malagasy francs is impossible.

Banking Hours

0800 – 1100
1400 – 1600 Monday to Friday

Banks are closed in the afternoon on the day before a public holiday.
All commercial banks in Madagascar were nationalised in 1975.
The central bank of issue is the *Banque Centrale de la République Malgache*, Avenue Le-Myre-de-Vilers, B.P. 550, Antananarivo, ☎ 21751.

Domestic Commercial Banks

Bankin'ny Indostria, 74 Rue du 26 juin 1960, B.P. 174, Antananarivo.
Bankin'ny Tantsaha Mpamokatra, Place de l'Indépendance, B.P. 183, Antananarivo.
Banky Fampandrosoana ny Varotra, 14 Làlana Jeneraly Rabehevitra, B.P. 196, Antananarivo, ☎ 20691/20043.
Banque Malgache d'Escompte et de Crédit, Place de l'Indépendance, B.P. 183, Antananarivo.

2. Electricity Supply

110/220v AC 50Hz (380v AC 50Hz is also available).
Plugs: 2 round pins.

3. Weights and Measures

The metric system is in use.

4. Media

All broadcasting is under the control of the government-owned service, Radio Télévision Malagasy.

Television programmes are transmitted in Malagasy and French by Télévision Malagasy. Commercial advertising is not accepted on television.

Radiodiffusion Nationale Malgache, the government radio network, broadcasts in Malagasy and French and carries commercial advertising. For further details contact the radio publicity service: Radio-Publicité, Maison de la Radio, B.P. 442, Antananarivo.

Newspapers and Journals

Dailies: *Madagascar - Matin, Madagasikara Mahaleotena, Maresaka, Hehy.*

Vaovao is a weekly paper published by the Government. *Fanilo* and *Lakroan'i Madagasikara* are weekly publications in Malagasy.

The Antananarivo Chamber of Commerce, Industry and Agriculture publishes a monthly bulletin giving details of recent developments in the import and export trade and of new business opportunities.

5. Medical Care

Tap water is generally unsafe to drink and should be boiled and filtered; alternatively, bottled water is available.

Malaria is prevalent, except in the central plateau region, including Antananarivo; anti-malarial prophylactics should be taken before, during and after the visit by anyone intending to visit the coastal regions. TAB (typhoid and paratyphoid) injections are also recommended.

Hospital facilities are limited and generally of a poor standard with very little modern equipment. Apart from the General Hospital in Antananarivo, there is a French military hospital, the Catholic-run Clinique des Soeurs and the University Medical Centre.

6. Telephone, Telex and Postal Services

International telephone and telegraph communications are available between Madagascar and the African mainland and Europe. Telegrams should be sent via the PTT Telegraph Office.

Internationla telex facilities are available, but there are no public telex offices. Residents at the Colbert and Hilton Hotels can make use of the telex facilities there.

All mail to and from Madagascar should be despatched by air.

7. Public Holidays

1 January	New Year's Day
29 March	Memorial Day
1 May	Labour Day
26 June	Independence Day
1 November	All Saints Day
25 December	Christmas Day
30 December	Anniversary of the Democratic Republic of Madagascar

Good Friday, Easter Monday, Ascension Day and *Whit Monday* are also officially observed.

The main annual holiday period in Madagascar is from mid-July to the end of September.

8. Time

GMT + 3.

9. Internal Transport

Air

All principal towns are linked by the services of the national airline, Air Madagascar. There are more than 100 airfields across the country.

Airline Offices in Antananarivo

Air France/UTA ☎ 22321.
Air Madagascar ☎ 26300, 22222.
Lufthansa ☎ 22027.
Swissair ☎ 22222.

Rail

Rail services connect Antananarivo with Toamasina to the north and Antsirabé to the south.

There are also rail links between the capital and Ambatondrazaka, and further south between Fianarantsoa and Manakara on the east coast.

Road
An adequate road system connects Antananarivo with the main towns in the south. Most main roads remain open throughout the year; however, roads west of Fianarantsoa and the main road linking the capital and the port of Toamasina become virtually impassable during the rainy season.

The most common form of land transport between main towns is by bush taxi (*taxi-brousse*).

Taxis are plentiful in Antananarivo. They are not fitted with meters but operate on a fixed rate below a certain mileage; fares for longer distances must be negotiated with the driver. Fares double after 2000 hours.

Self-drive and chauffeur-driven cars are available for hire. An International Driving Licence is required.

Traffic travels on the right-hand side of the road.

Car-Hire Firms in Antananarivo
Hertz ☎ 23336.
Madagascar Air-tours (Avis), Hilton Hotel ☎ 265-15.

10. Tipping
Taxis – no tip necessary except for trips outside of the towns.

Porters – FMG50 per bag.

Hotel/restaurant staff – from FMG200.

11. Social Customs
It is essential that business visitors have a good working knowledge of French; English is rarely spoken or understood.

Much business entertaining is done in the home; visitors may reciprocate by entertaining in one of the better restaurants.

12. Photography
Visitors should note that it is forbidden to photograph public buildings, although there are no notices warning of this ban.

USEFUL ADDRESSES (GENERAL)

Antananarivo
British Consulate: 5 Rue Robert Ducrocq, B.P. 167, ☎ 25151.

Dutch Consulate: c/o Radio Nederland, Lotissament Bonnet-Ivandry, B.P. 404, ☎ 42222.

French Embassy: 3 Rue Jean-Jaurès, B.P. 204, ☎ 23700.

French Consulate General: Avenue Hubert-Garbit, ☎ 21488.

Japanese Embassy: 8 Rue Docteur Villette Isoraka, B.P. 3863, ☎ 26102.

Swiss Embassy: Immeuble de la Préservatrice, Solombavambahoaka Frantsay 77, B.P. 118, ☎ 22846.

US Embassy: 14/16 Rue Rainitovo, B.P. 620, ☎ 21257.

West German Embassy: 2 Rue du Pasteur Rabeony, B.P. 516, ☎ 23802/3, 21691.

Others
Office National du Tourisme de Madagascar: Place d'Ambotijatovo, B.P. 610, Antananarivo.

French Consulate: Boulevard Labourdonnais, B.P. 155, Toamasina, ☎ 32721.

French Consulate General: Rue Benyowski, B.P. 220, Antseranana, ☎ 21339, 21043.

BUSINESS INFORMATION

There is a growing market for consumer and domestic goods; the market for industrial equipment and machinery remains constant, with the possibility of future growth as economic development is realised.

Foreign suppliers may find it necessary to be represented by one of the local importing firms, which are becoming increasingly interested in acquiring foreign agencies. If local representation proves inadequate, however, it is advisable to make direct contact with the purchasing body in Madagascar.

Government purchases and those of other official bodies are made through importers by way of calls for tender, which are published in the official weekly gazette. Purchases made for projects sponsored by the European Community Fund for Overseas Development are normally limited to companies within the EEC and associated countries.

Import and Exchange Control Regulations

All imports are subject to exchange control and import licensing on an annual quota basis. Import licences are only granted to importers on the agreed list of the Ministry of Commerce.

Applications for import licences should be accompanied by detailed *pro forma* invoices (5 copies); these should be in French – alternatively translations may be supplied. Import licences are endorsed by the Directorate of Commerce and are lodged with a bank – this guarantees that the necessary foreign exchange will be made available for payment.

Foreign exchange control is strict, and it should be noted that most payments for Madagascar are subject to lengthy administrative delays.

Business Hours
Government Offices and Business Houses
0800 – 1200
1400 – 1730 Monday to Friday
0800 – 1200 Saturday

BUSINESS SERVICES

Advertising
Publimad, B.P. 1251, Antananarivo.
Radio-Publicité, Maison de la Radio, B.P. 442, Antananarivo.
Société Malgache de Publicité, B.P. 1650, Antananarivo.

Insurance
Assurance France – Madagascar, B.P. 710, Antananarivo.
Compagnie Malgache d'Assurances et de Réassurances 'Ny Havana', B.P. 3881, Antananarivo.
Société Malgache d'Assurances, Faugère, Jutheau et Cie, 13 Rue Patrice Lumumba, B.P. 673, Antananarivo.

Shipping
Compagnie Générale Maritime, B.P. 1185, Antananarivo.
Compagnie Malgache de Navigation, Rue Rabearivelo, B.P. 1021, Antsahavola, Antananarivo.
S. A. M. Darrieux et Cie, B.P. 1248, Antananarivo – agents for Nedlloyd Lines.

MADAGASCAR

Société Malgache des Transports Maritimes, 6 Rue de Nice, B.P. 4077, Antananarivo.

Solitany Malagasy, Avenue Grandidier, B.P. 140, Antananarivo.

USEFUL ADDRESSES (BUSINESS)

Fédération des Chambres de Commerce, d'Industrie et d'Agriculture du Madagascar, 20 Rue Colbert, B.P. 166, Antananarivo, ☎ 21567.

Société d'Intérêt National des Produits Agricoles, B.P. 754, Antananarivo – purchase and distribution of food and cash crops.

Société Nationale de Commerce, B.P. 3187, Antananarivo – state import and export organisation.

Bureau de Développement et de Promotion Industriels, 43 Rue Rabezavana, B.P. 31, Antananarivo.

Office Militaire National pour les Industries Stratégiques, 21 Làlana Razanakombana, Antananarivo.

MAJOR CITY

Antananarivo

Antananarivo, which for many years was known as Tananarive, is now called by its original name meaning 'the town of a thousand men'. The capital is the centre of Madagascar's commercial and cultural life and the focal point of the country's communications network.

Antananarivo is built on a number of levels on the sides of a horseshoe-shaped hill. On the sacred hilltop is the *Rova* or royal village, site of the palaces of the Merina kings and queens.

Coming down from the peak, one passes through the winding stairways and alleys of the old town, with its closely packed earthen houses. At the foot of the hill lies Lake Anosy, the central Place de l'Indépendance and the town's various markets.

The Queen's Palace on the sacred peak is now a national museum and contains some beautiful and intricate panelling. The King's Palace is built in the Italian style; several other palaces are strongly reminiscent of Indonesian architecture.

The Zoo and Botanical Gardens are at the southern end of the city at Tsimbazaza, where there is also a fabulous collection of butterflies housed in the Orstom Building of the Franco-Malagasy Orstom Ethnographic Research Centre (open from 1400–1700 hours on Tuesday, Thursday, Sunday).

Hotels

There is no official hotel rating system.

Colbert, 29 Rue Printsy Ratsimamanga, B.P. 341, ☎ 20202.
Modern 1st-class hotel in city centre.
Rooms: 52 ☎.
Facilities: Restaurant, bar. Tennis, golf. Conference facilities.

Hôtel de France, 34 Avenue de l'Indépendance, B.P. 607, ☎ 20293, 21304.
Traditional-style hotel in city centre.
Rooms: 39 ♪, ☎, ♨, ♡.
Facilities: Restaurant, pizzeria, snack bar, bars.
Services: TC, FC, ✉ not accepted. Dr. on call.

MADAGASCAR

MADAGASCAR HILTON, Lac Anosy, B.P. 959, ☎ 26060.
Modern 1st-class hotel on outskirts of city overlooking Lake Anosy, 5 minutes' drive from city centre.
Rooms: 189 ♪, ⑭, ◉, ☐ on request, ⚠, ⌂. Suites available.
Facilities: Restaurant, grill room, bars, coffee shop, snack bar. Casino. Swimming, bowling alley. Tennis near by. Car hire.
Services: TC, FC, ⊟ Amex, Bankamericard, Carte Blanche, Diners Club, Eurocard, Hilton International, Master Charge. Dr. on call. S, ♂. Audio-visual equipment.
Conference room – max. capacity 500.
Banquet rooms – max. capacity 500.

Restaurants

French cuisine is available in the hotel restaurants, which are open to non-residents. Other French restaurants are the *Café de Paris*, Avenue de l'Indépendance; *Chez Audier*, Rue Colbert; *Relais Normand* and *Le Cellier*. There are also numerous Vietnamese restaurants, including: *Le Pavillon de Jade*; *Kim Son*; and *Doan Van Bien*. Malagasy dishes are served at: *La Rotonde*; *Restogasy*, Route No. 7; and the *Tantely*.

Nightclubs

La Baladin – live music; *Papillon Bar*, Hilton Hotel – piano music; *Le Caveau*; *Le Casino*, Avenue Foumbeyrolles; *Le Cannibale*; *Tantely*.

Entertainment

Theatre productions are staged infrequently, at the vast Tranom'pokonolona in the district of Isotry. There are several European-run sports clubs offering tennis and golf; temporary membership is usually available to foreign business visitors. Horse racing takes place on Sundays.

Shopping

Best buys: straw and bamboo goods, embroidered cloth, silk, silver jewellery, semi-precious stones.
The Zoma is the main market, operating every day with dozens of additional stalls on Fridays; bargaining is essential for every purchase. There are also markets in the district of Andravoahangy (Wednesdays) and in Isotry (Saturdays).
The *Taillerie de la Grande Ile* boutiques in the Hilton Hotel and on Rue Auguste Ranarivelo have a good selection of precious and semi-precious stones and jewellery.

MALAWI
Republic of Malawi

Geography	248
The Economy	250
How to Get There	251
Entry Regulations	251
Practical Information for the Visitor	252
Useful Addresses (General)	254
Business Information	255
Business Services	255
Useful Addresses (Business)	256
Blantyre	256

Size: 118,484 sq.km/45,747 sq.miles.

Population: 5.78 million (1978).

Distribution: 10% in urban areas.

Density: 43 persons per sq.km/111 per sq.mile.

Population Growth Rate: 3.1% p.a.

Ethnic Composition: The majority are descended from Bantu tribes and belong to the following ethnic groups: Chewa, Yao, Tonga, Tumbuka, Lonwe, Ngonde, Chipoka and Sena.

Capital: Lilongwe Pop. 102,924.

Major Towns: Blantyre Pop. 228,520; Zomba Pop. 20,000.

Language: English and Chichewa are the official languages. After these, Tumbuka and Yao are the most important of the several African languages and dialects spoken. English is used exclusively for business purposes.

Religion: About 50% are Christians; the remainder are Muslims and Animists.

Government: Malawi became a Republic within the Commonwealth in 1966. Executive power rests with the President who acts as Prime Minister. The National Assembly consists of a majority of elected members, with up to 15 members nominated by the President. The Malawi Congress Party is the sole legal political party.

GEOGRAPHY

A landlocked country, Malawi is dominated by Lake Malawi which lies in the great Rift Valley running from north to south throughout most of Malawi. The lake covers an area of approximately 24,000 sq.km/9,266 sq.miles and is 580km/360 miles long.

There are 3 main regions: the mountainous Northern Region with altitudes rising to 2,735m/7,500 ft; the Central Region, consisting of high plateaux which rise from the lake shore; and the Southern Region of low-lying plains and scattered mountain areas, including Mt Mulanje and Mt Zomba.

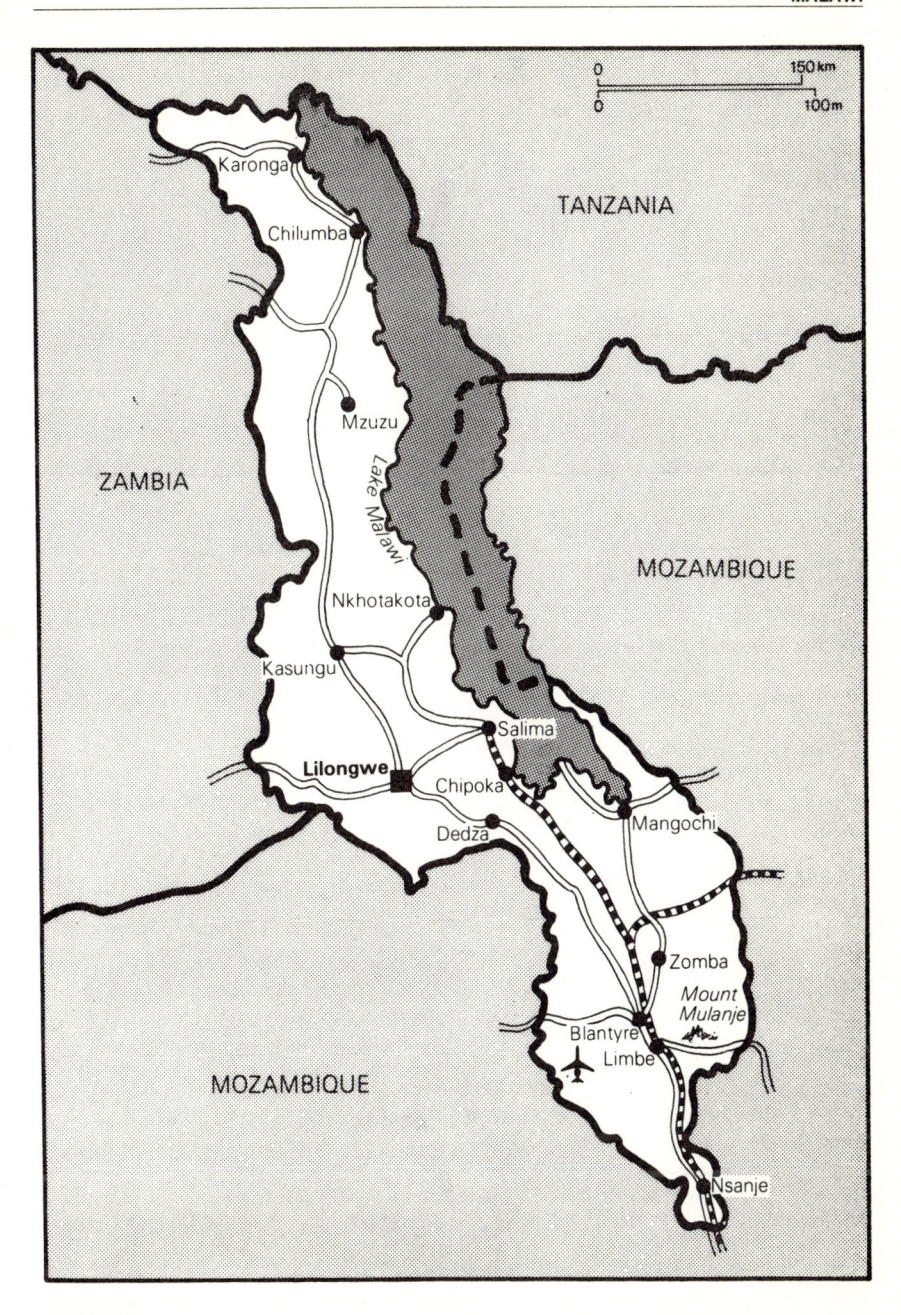

Climate
Malawi lies within the tropics and has a high annual rainfall. Summers (September to April) are hot, with temperatures averaging 27°c/80°F, and rainy; the main period of

rain is from December to March, and thunderstorms occur frequently. Winters are warm and dry with an average temperature of 20°c/68°F, although ground frosts are not uncommon in highland areas.

Agriculture

Some 90% of the population depend upon agriculture for a living, and agricultural products account for approximately 95% of Malawi's export earnings. Although much of the farming is subsistence, the cash crop sector has increased considerably and is largely the reason for the success of Malawi's agriculture-based economy since independence.

Tobacco and tea are the chief export crops and are mainly grown on large estates. There is some smallholder cultivation of these crops, but productivity remains low. Maize is the chief food crop grown for domestic consumption.

Main Crops: tea, tobacco, maize, cotton, groundnuts, rice.

Mineral Resources: bauxite, asbestos, graphite and coal. Deposits are small and not commercially viable at present.

THE ECONOMY

Gross National Product (1978): US$1.1 billion.

Per Capita Income (1978): US$180.

Gross Domestic Product (1978): K897.2 million.

Foreign Trade (1978): Total Imports – US$263.0 million. Total Exports – US$186.5 million.

Main Trading Partners: Imports – South Africa, UK, Japan, Zimbabwe. Exports – UK, USA, Netherlands, South Africa.

Economic performance since independence has been impressive, with a steady economic growth of about 6.5% p.a. The value of domestic exports has increased steadily and the budget deficit inherited at the time of independence was completely wiped out in the early 1970s, partially with the help of substantial Western aid. Malawi is a recipient of aid from several development agencies and individual countries, in particular South Africa, Israel and Taiwan. The present Government's virulent anti-Communism eliminates the possibility of aid from the Soviet Union, Eastern Europe and China.

Great emphasis is placed on the private sector as the driving force of economic growth. The main area of private enterprise is estate agriculture, particularly tea, tobacco and sugar estates, which together produce over 80% of Malawi's export earnings.

Since independence the industrial sector has developed at a rate of 13% p.a., although it has been seriously affected by rising oil prices since 1974 and must import all its petroleum.

Manufacturing is aimed mainly at import substitution, producing consumer goods such as textiles, matches, cigarettes, beer, spirits and shoes. Small quantities of these goods are now exported. Although the Government often maintains a shareholding interest in foreign ventures through the Malawi Development Corporation, it continues to attract foreign capital with its advantageous financial policy (tariff protection; free, unlimited repatriation of profits; etc.).

Major Industries: food processing, textiles, matches, cigarettes, consumer goods.

Main Commodities Traded: Imports – motor vehicles, iron and steel, petroleum products, machinery, medical and pharmaceutical goods, foodstuffs. Exports – tea, tobacco, groundnuts, maize, cotton.

International Affiliations: UN, IBRD, OAU, ACP, ADB, Commonwealth.

HOW TO GET THERE

Air

The main airport is Chileka, situated 17½ km/11 miles from the centre of Blantyre.

There are regular flights to Blantyre from many European capitals. British Airways and Air Malawi operate 3 direct flights a week from London (Heathrow and Gatwick Airports respectively). From the United States there are direct flights to Nairobi in Kenya with connections to Blantyre.

Air Malawi and South African Airways operate 7 flights a week from South Africa to Blantyre. There are also frequent flights from Maputo (Mozambique), Nairobi (Kenya), Lusaka (Zambia), Dar es Salaam (Tanzania), Entebbe (Uganda), Addis Ababa (Ethiopia) and Port Louis (Mauritius), as well as from Nicosia, Aden, Bombay and Beira.

Flying times to Blantyre: from London, 13½ hours; from New York, 23 hours; from Sydney, 30 hours.

Taxis and buses connect Chileka Airport with Blantyre.

A passenger service charge of K2 is payable by all passengers departing on international flights from Chileka Airport. This charge must be paid in Malawian currency.

ENTRY REGULATIONS

Visas

Visas are required by nationals of all countries except: (i) British Commonwealth, Belgium, Denmark, Finland, West Germany, Iceland, Republic of Ireland, Italy, Luxembourg, Madagascar, Netherlands, Norway, Portugal, San Marino, South Africa and Sweden; (ii) USA – for a stay of less than 12 months; and (iii) Mozambique, with Portuguese passports, entering from Mozambique – for a stay of up to 2 months.

All other nationals require visas obtainable from Malawi diplomatic missions abroad.

Travellers not requiring visas (as listed above) must obtain entry permits on arrival. They must be in possession of onward or return tickets and have sufficient funds for their stay.

Visa applications should be accompanied by a letter (from travel agent or airline) confirming that onward or return tickets have been issued and by a letter from the applicant's firm giving details of the business to be undertaken and confirming financial responsibility for the applicant.

Visas are valid for 3 months for a stay of variable length, according to requirements. Allow 2/3 weeks for visas to be issued unless the application is referred for authorisation, when the delay can be several weeks longer.

Health Regulations
International Certificates of Vaccination against smallpox and cholera are required by all persons entering Malawi. Visitors arriving from an area where yellow fever is endemic must be in possession of a valid yellow fever vaccination certificate.

Customs
Currency: There is no limit to the amount of foreign currency which may be taken in, but visitors should obtain a receipt from the Customs Authorities at the point of entry as they will be asked to declare the balance on departure. The amount of local currency which can be imported or exported is limited to K20. Malawi currency is not convertible abroad, so visitors should ensure that they do not leave the country with any local currency.

Duty-free articles: Personal effects. 200 cigarettes or 250g of tobacco. 1 bottle of wine and 1 bottle of spirits. Samples of no commercial value. A guarantee is required to cover the import duty on other samples; this is cancelled when the samples are re-exported.

PRACTICAL INFORMATION FOR THE VISITOR

1. Currency
Monetary Unit – kwacha (K), divided into 100 tambala (t).
Notes – 50 tambala and 1, 5, 10 kwacha.
Coins – 1, 2, 5, 10, 20 tambala.

Travellers' cheques in dollars, sterling and other acceptable currencies are freely convertible, but visitors may experience difficulty in exchanging lesser known currencies. Travellers' cheques are accepted at PTL stores and Oilcom petrol stations throughout the country and at Kandolo stores in Blantyre, Zomba and Lilongwe.

Banking Hours
0800–1230 Monday, Tuesday, Thursday, Friday
0800–1130 Wednesday
0800–1030 Saturday

The *Reserve Bank of Malawi*, Victoria Avenue, P.O. Box 565, Blantyre, is the central bank of issue.

Principal Commercial Banks
National Bank of Malawi, Henderson Street, P.O. Box 945, Blantyre, ☎ 633211.
Commercial Bank of Malawi Ltd, Victoria Avenue, P.O. Box 1111, Blantyre, ☎ 633144.

2. Electricity Supply
230–240v AC 50Hz.
Plugs: 3 square pins; 2 or 3 round-pin plugs may be found in older systems.

3. Weights and Measures
Imperial weights and measures are in general use, except for pharmaceuticals, petrol and petroleum products for which metric measures are used.

4. Media
There is no television service in Malawi. The Malawi Broadcasting Corporation transmits radio programmes in English and Chichewa, and accepts commercial advertising. For further details, contact

the Director of Commercial Services, Malawi Broadcasting Corporation, P.O. Box 30133, Chichiri, Blantyre 3.

Newspapers and Journals
The Daily Times (Monday to Friday) and *The Malawi News* (Saturday) are the only regularly published English-language newspapers. Advertisements for both can be sent to Private Bag 39, Blantyre, ☎ 31066.

2 monthly publications are *Boma Lathu* (Chichewa), published by the Department of Information and *Moni* (Chichewa and English), published in Limbe.

5. Medical Care
Tap water is safe to drink in the main towns, except where labelled to the contrary. Elsewhere it should be boiled and filtered, or bottled water should be drunk. Visitors are advised to take anti-malarial prophylactics. Mosquito nets are supplied by hotels where necessary.

Lake Malawi is free from bilharzia and is safe for bathing, but visitors should avoid swimming in pools and slow-moving rivers.

There are adequate medical and dental services in Blantyre, Lilongwe, Zomba and Limbe.

Main Hospitals in Malawi
General Hospital, Livingstone Road, Lilongwe, ☎ 2215.
Queen Elizabeth Central Hospital, P.O. Box 95, Blantyre, ☎ 30333.
General Hospital, Salisbury Road Section, Zomba, ☎ 289.

6. Telephone, Telex and Postal Services
There are no public telex offices, although private telex facilities exist.

International telephone and telegram services are limited.

Post offices are open from 0730–1200 and 1330–1630 Monday to Friday, and from 0730–1200 on Saturday.

All mail to and from Malawi should be despatched by air; surface mail is subject to lengthy delays.

7. Public Holidays
1 January	New Year's Day
3 March	Martyrs' Day
14 May	Kamuzu Day
6 July	Republic Day
1st Monday in August	August Day
17 October	Mothers' Day
25–6 December	Christmas

Good Friday, *Easter Saturday* and *Easter Monday* are also public holidays.

If a public holiday falls on a Sunday it is observed on the following Monday; if the Monday is also a public holiday then it is observed on the following Tuesday.

8. Time
GMT + 2.

9. Internal Transport
Air
Air Malawi operates daily flights from Blantyre to Lilongwe; it also connects Blantyre with Zomba, Mangochi, Salima, Nkhotakota, Kasungu, Mzuzu, Karonga and Chilumba.

In addition, aircraft are available for charter from Air Malawi, Capital Air Services Ltd and Leopard Air Ltd. Air Malawi also operates all-inclusive 'Skylake' package tours from neighbouring countries.

Airline Offices in Blantyre
Air India	☎ 32454.
Air Malawi	☎ 33111, 33177.
British Airways	☎ 34002.
British Caledonian	☎ 33111.
JAL	☎ 2314.
Lufthansa	☎ 2001, 2314.
Swissair	☎ 2314.

Rail
Malawi's 2 railway lines run from Salima to Lilongwe and from Salima to Nsanje via Blantyre-Limbe. The latter continues on through Mozambique to the

port of Beira. South of Salima, at Chipoka, trains connect with the passenger and cargo service operating on Lake Malawi.

Road
The main towns in the Central and Southern Regions are linked by good, tarred roads. Driving conditions during the rainy season can be hazardous, particularly on secondary roads.

Taxis are not very plentiful and cannot be hailed in the street. For taxi services in Blantyre, telephone ☎ 34514, 30918, 30948, 50025, 30812.

Self-drive and chauffeur-driven cars can be hired in the main towns. An additional daily charge is added to the hire cost for the services of a chauffeur; overtime is payable after 1600 hours.

Most national driving licences are valid, but visitors are advised to obtain an International Driving Licence.

Principal Car-Hire Firms in Blantyre
Automotive
  Products Ltd   ☎ 30161, 31555.
Hall's Garage
  Ltd   ☎ 34833, 2356.
Mandala Motors
  Ltd   ☎ 31011, 33837.
United Touring
  Company   ☎ 30122, 31055.

10. Tipping
Taxis – 20t per journey.

Porters – 5t per bag.

Hotels – a 10% service charge is added to the bill.

Restaurant staff – 5% of the bill.

11. Social Customs
Business customs and practices are similar to those of Western Europe. However, as in many other African countries, offices open much earlier – around 0730 – and most people retire around 2100 hours during the week.

According to Malawian law, it is an offence for men to have long hair (the length of hair should not fall below an imaginary line drawn horizontally around the head at the level of the mouth) or to wear bell-bottom trousers. anyone contravening this law is likely to be refused entry into the country and is liable to arrest and prosecution.

Women are not permitted to wear skirts and dresses which do not cover the whole knee when standing upright. It is also an offence for women to wear shorts or trousers in public places. These restrictions do not usually apply within Blantyre and Lilongwe Airports, the Lakeshore hotels and most national parks and forest reserves. In general, exceptions are also made when engaged in a sporting activity or when wearing national costume.

USEFUL ADDRESSES (GENERAL)

Blantyre
Australian Honorary Consul, Mr A. Sattar Sacranie, P.O. Box 5133, Limbe, ☎ 50844.

Dutch Consulate, Delamere House, Victoria Avenue, P.O. Box 390, ☎ 33609.

West German Embassy, Kamuzu Highway, P.O. Box 5695, Limbe, ☎ 50860.

Honorary Consul of the Republic of Ireland, Mr R. F. Fitzsimmons, P.O. Box 462, ☎ 34851.

Department of Tourism Delamere House, P.O. Box 402, ☎ 36811.

MALAWI

Chief Information Officer,
Information Department, P.O. Box 494, ☎ 35977.

Lilongwe
British Council, Taurus House, Area 40/4, P.O. Box 30222, ☎ 30484, 30266.

British High Commission, Lingadzi House, P.O. Box 30042, ☎ 31544.

French Embassy, Area 40, Road No.3, P.O. Box 30054, ☎ 30377.

South African Embassy, Mpico Building, City Centre, P.O. Box 30043, ☎ 30888.

US Embassy, Area 40, Flat No.18, P.O. Box 30016, ☎ 30396.

BUSINESS INFORMATION

Increasing economic activity and high investment have created a strong demand for imported goods and services, particularly of capital goods and materials for industry and building.

Representation of foreign suppliers is dominated by several large firms, but increasing numbers of Malawian agents are seeking to represent foreign firms, particularly for consumer goods. Import & Export Co Ltd (a subsidiary of the Malawi Development Corporation) and the Press Group are amongst the largest trading firms.

Business travellers who intend to solicit orders personally or to offer goods for sale on their own account or on behalf of other enterprises should note that by law they must be in possession of a commercial travellers' licence. These are obtainable from the District Commissioner, P.O. Box 97, Blantyre, and are issued subject to the approval of the Ministry of Trade, Industry and Tourism. Licences are valid for one year and cost approximately £50 sterling.

Import and Exchange Control Regulations
Import licences are required for only a few specified goods. Foreign exchange in payment for imports will only be remitted by banks on production of a Customs Bill of Entry as evidence that the goods have arrived in Malawi.

Business Hours
Government Offices
0730–1630 Monday to Friday (1½ hours for lunch).
Some offices are closed to the public in the afternoon.
0730–1200 Saturday

Business Houses
0730–1600 Monday to Friday (1½ hours for lunch).
0730–1200 Saturday

BUSINESS SERVICES

Advertising
Graphic Advertising Ltd, Private Bag 39, Blantyre, ☎ 33803.

Debt Collection
The following firms of solicitors will undertake debt collection:

MALAWI

Wilson and Morgan, Victoria Avenue, P.O. Box 9, Blantyre, ☎ 34988.

Sacranie, Gow & Co, Churchill Road, P.O. Box 5133, Limbe, ☎ 50844.

Insurance
National Insurance Co Ltd, P.O. Box 501, Blantyre.

Shipping
Manica Mann George (Malawi) Ltd, Manica House, Victoria Avenue, P.O. Box 460, Blantyre, ☎ 34533 – airfreight, shipping and forwarding agents with offices throughout Malawi.

USEFUL ADDRESSES (BUSINESS)

The Chamber of Commerce and Industry of Malawi, Livingstone Avenue, P.O. Box 258, Blantyre, ☎ 634150.

Malawi Development Corporation, Development House, Victoria Avenue, P.O. Box 566, Blantyre, ☎ 636100.

Agricultural Development and Marketing Corporation, P.O. Box 5052, Limbe.

Ministry of Trade, Industry and Tourism, P.O. Box 30366, Lilongwe.

MAJOR TOWNS

Blantyre

Although Lilongwe has been the capital of Malawi since 1975, Blantyre is the largest town and the centre of commerce and industry. It was founded in 1895 and was named after Livingstone's birthplace in Scotland.

Built in an attractive setting surrounded by hills and mountains, the city covers a large area encompassing the neighbouring centre of Limbe about 8km/5 miles away. In between is the main industrial area and the Government complex at Chichiri.

A number of places in Blantyre are of interest to the foreign visitor. St Michael's Church on the Chileka Road is a reminder of the Scottish missionaries who wielded considerable influence and power here in the late 19th century.

The Independence Arch and Museum of Malawi, both in Chichiri, are also worth a visit.

Just off the Limbe-Midima Road on Mikolongwe Hill is the Mwalawolemba ('Rock of Writing') Rock Shelter, which has some unusual rock paintings and offers a view of Mulanje, the highest mountain in Malawi.

Hotels
There is no official hotel rating system.

Blantyre
MOUNT SOCHE, Glyn Jones Road, P.O. Box 284, ☎ 35588.
Modern 1st-class hotel set in terraced gardens in city centre.
Rooms: 98 ♫, ⚓, ☎, ♨, 🅿. Suites available.
Facilities: Restaurant, cocktail bar, coffee shop, bars. Discotheque. Poolside bar, snack service. Swimming. Golf, tennis, squash near by. Car hire.
Services: TC, FC, ✉ Amex, Bankamericard, Barclaycard, Diners Club. Dr. on call. Telex facility. 💲, ♂.
Conference and banquet facilities for up to 300 persons.

RYALL'S, Hannover Avenue, P.O. Box 21, ☎ 35955.

Traditional-style hotel (modernised, 1973) in town centre.
Rooms: 65 ♄, ♨, ⛨, ⚠, ⌘. Suites available.
Facilities: Restaurant, grill, snack bar, poolside and other bars. Swimming. Car hire. Airport bus available. Bookshop.
Services: TC, FC, ☏ Amex, Bankamericard, Diners Club. Dr. on call. Conference and banquet rooms for up to 300 persons.

Limbe

CHISAKALIME, Tsiranana Road, P.O. Box 5249, ☎ 52266, 50670.
Small, recently modernised hotel, conveniently situated for both Blantyre and Limbe.
Rooms: 24.
Facilities: Restaurant, bar. Nightclub. Taxi service available.

SHIRE HIGHLANDS, Churchill Road, P.O. Box 5204, ☎ 50055.
Colonial-style hotel situated in the centre of Limbe, close to the tobacco auction halls.
Rooms: 40.
Facilities: Restaurant, 2 bars, lounges. Swimming. Shop. Banquet rooms.

Restaurants

Amongst the hotel restaurants in Blantyre, the *Ndirande* at the Mount Soche Hotel (dancing nightly), the *21 Grill* at Ryall's Hotel and the *Balmoral* at the Shire Highlands Hotel are popular eating places, open to non-residents.

Other restaurants in Blantyre include: *Maxim's*, St. Andrews Street, ☎ 35073 – Continental; *Safari*, Haile Selassie Road, ☎ 34454; the *Café Capri*, Haile Selassie Road, ☎ 35975 – Portuguese; *Hong Kong*, Glyn Jones Road, ☎ 34395, and *China Bar and Restaurant*, Glyn Jones Road, ☎ 35448 – Chinese. Restaurants in Limbe include: the *Riviera* – Indian; and *El Paso*, Churchill Road, ☎ 51039.

Entertainment

There are several cinemas in Blantyre, including a drive-in on Chikawa Road. Dancing is held nightly at many of the larger hotels.

Blantyre has a number of sports and social clubs, including the popular *Blantyre Sports Club*. There is also a small 'crazy golf' course on Victoria Avenue.

One of the highlights of the year is Republic Day (July 6), when there is a colourful display of traditional dancing at Kamazu Stadium.

Shopping

Best buys: wood and ivory carvings, basketwork, beadwork, pottery.

The main shopping area of Blantyre is around Victoria Avenue. Nearby, in Glyn Jones Street, is the *Malawi Arts and Crafts Centre*, which stocks a wide range of local handicrafts. Street vendors selling traditional curios are numerous.

The market in Limbe is also worth a visit. The stalls are packed with colourful, attractive goods, including the brightly coloured *chirundu* cotton lengths, and reed- and raffia-woven goods (baskets, hats, mats, etc.).

MALI
Republic of Mali

Geography	258
The Economy	260
How to Get There	261
Entry Regulations	261
Practical Information for the Visitor	262
Useful Addresses (General)	264
Business Information	264
Business Services	265
Useful Addresses (Business)	265
Bamako	265

Size: 1,240,000 sq.km/478,766 sq.miles.

Population: 6.33 million (mid-1978 est.).

Distribution: 11% in urban areas.

Density: 4.9 persons per sq.km/12.8 per sq.mile.

Population Growth Rate: 2.5% p.a. (1970–77 avg.).

Ethnic Composition: There are more than 20 tribes, the principal one being the Bambara, followed by the Fulani, Songhai, Malinké, Touareg, Sénoufo, Marka and Dogon.

Capital: Bamako Pop. 400,000.

Major Towns: Mopti Pop. 35,000; Ségou Pop. 31,000; Kayes Pop. 29,000.

Language: French is the official language. The most widely spoken African languages are Bambara and Malinké; Arabic is understood in the north.

Religion: Approximately 65% Muslim, 30% Animist, and the remainder mainly Roman Catholic.

Government: Since the overthrow of the Government in 1968 and the abolition of the National Assembly, Mali has been governed by the Military Committee of National Liberation (CMLN), which has ruled by decree. The President of the CMLN is also the national President and Head of State.

In June 1979 elections were held for the Presidency and for a new National Assembly to serve for a 4 year term of office. The Union Démocratique du Peuple Malien (UDPM) is the sole political party.

GEOGRAPHY

Mali is a landlocked country situated in central West Africa. Its northern half is mostly desert, and in the north-east the Adrar des Iforas Massif rises to a height of 800m/2,626ft. Much of the country is covered with loose sand, with the exception of the area around the River Niger which waters the arid grazing lands of the Sahel. The south is mainly savannah and is the most populated area.

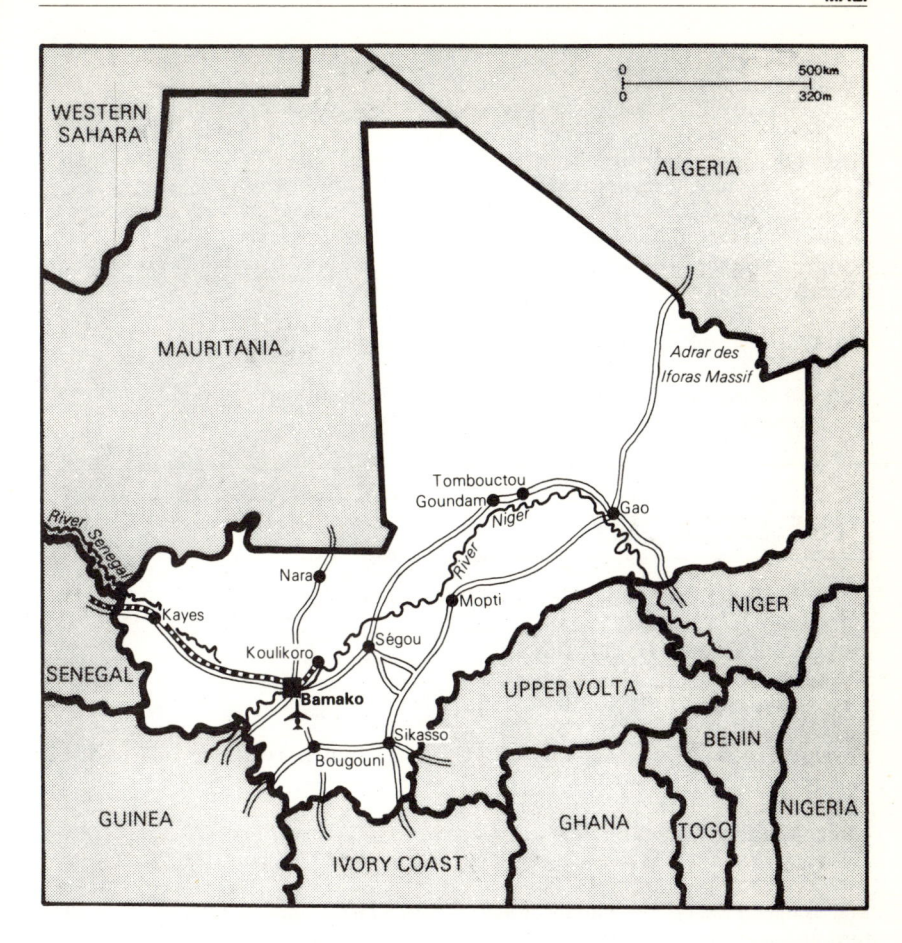

Climate
Mali has a harsh climate and suffers from severe droughts in the central and northern areas. There are 3 main seasons: the cool, dry season from November to February; the hot, dry season from February to May with temperatures between 46°c/115°F and 49°c/120°F (the average for Bamako is 35°c/95°F); and the rainy season from June to October when temperatures drop and humidity rises to around 80%.

Agriculture
The majority of Mali's population live in rural areas and are engaged in agriculture, largely at the subsistence level. The major subsistence crops are sorghum, millet, rice and maize; cotton and groundnuts are cultivated as cash crops. Livestock rearing is another important agricultural activity and is the main livelihood of Mali's nomad population.

The effects of the Sahelian drought (1972–6) were catastrophic for Mali. Large numbers of livestock died and huge quantities of foodstuffs had to be imported to feed the starving population.

High priority is now being accorded to the building of two dams which, it is hoped, will avert similar crises: the Selingué Dam on the River Niger (begun 1976) and the Manantali Dam on the River Senegal – both of which are backed by large amounts of foreign aid from international agencies and individual countries.

Another major development project is the 'Mali-Sud' scheme involving the resettlement of thousands of people and substantial increases in the production of rice, cotton and cereals. The scheme also involves the control of river-blindness which, in the past, has caused severe health problems in this area.

Main Crops: rice, cotton, groundnuts, maize, sorghum, millet.

Mineral Resources: salt, limestone, bauxite, gold, iron, copper, nickel, manganese, phosphates.

THE ECONOMY

Gross National Product (1978): US$760 million.

Per Capita Income (1978): US$120.

Gross Domestic Product (1976): 278.3 billion Mali francs.

Foreign Trade (1978): Total Imports – US$148.7 million. Total Exports – US$94.2 million.

Main Trading Partners: Imports – France, Ivory Coast, Senegal, China, West Germany. Exports – France, China, Ivory Coast, West Germany, UK.

Mali is one of the poorest nations in Africa with a highly underdeveloped infrastructure and industrial sector and an agricultural sector that remains at the mercy of drought and disease. Since 1976, Mali has suffered from a chronic deficit in its balance of payments. As a result, the country relies heavily on foreign aid to overcome this deficit and to finance the development projects which are the key to future economic prosperity. France is the largest single donor, while several international agencies have also provided funds, including the International Development Agency and the African Development Bank. The continuing deterioration of the country's trade balance, resulting in a sharp increase in prices, and the need to increase foreign exchange earnings led the Government to introduce an austerity programme in 1977.

Industrial activity is largely on a small scale; about 80% is aimed at import substitution, while the remainder consists of agricultural processing for export. 60% of the industrial sector is state-owned, although in recent years there has been a move back towards a mixed economy with both private and state participation.

After food processing, textiles is the most important industry, while the manufacturing of leather, cigarettes and cement has risen steadily.

Mining is at present limited to the extraction of salt and limestone. Sizeable deposits of several other minerals have been located, but commercial exploitation depends on financial aid and future improvements in Mali's communications network.

MALI

Major Industries: food processing, textiles, leather, cement.

Main Commodities Traded: Imports – machinery, transport equipment, petroleum products, foodstuffs, iron, steel, chemicals, pharmaceuticals. Exports – cotton, livestock, groundnuts, fish products.

International Affiliations: VN, IBRD, OAU, ACP, ADB, CEAO, ECOWAS, Franc Zone, NRC, OMVS.

HOW TO GET THERE

Air
There are regular services to Bamako from Paris, Marseilles, Bordeaux, Algiers, Casablanca, and most North and West African capitals.

Major airlines flying to Bamako include Air Afrique, UTA, Aeroflot, Interflug, Air Guinée and Air Mali.

Flying times to Bamako: from Paris, 7 hours; from Dakar, 1½ hours.

Bamako International Airport is 5km/3 miles from the town centre. Buses run between the airport and town centre.

An airport tax of 3,000 Mali francs is payable on departure from Mali.

Rail
A twice-weekly passenger service connects Dakar in Senegal and Bamako. The journey takes approximately 27 hours. Sleeping accommodation and dining facilities are available on the train.

Road
Mali is accessible by road from Upper Volta and the Ivory Coast, although some roads may not be passable during the rainy season. The road from Senegal to Kayes is of a poor standard.

ENTRY REGULATIONS

Visas
Visas are required by nationals of all countries except France and former French territories. Visas should be obtained in advance from Malian embassies and consulates abroad.

There is no Malian diplomatic mission in the United Kingdom, but visas can be obtained from the Malian Embassy in Paris, 89 Rue du Cherche-Midi, Paris 6, ☎ 5485843; or in Brussels, 112 Rue Camille Lemmonier, B-1060 Brussels, ☎ 3457432.

All visitors must be in possession of a return or onward ticket or proof of intended departure.

Visa applications should be made well in advance of the proposed visit. In an emergency only, a visa can be obtained on arrival provided that prior application for a visa has been made. This can be done via telex to the Head of Immigration Services, Senou Airport, Bamako.

Health Regulations
International Certificates of Vaccination against smallpox, cholera and yellow fever are required by all persons entering Mali.

Customs
Currency: There is no limit to the amount of foreign or local currency which may be taken into Mali, but all monies must be declared on entry. There is a limit of 50,000 Mali francs to the amount of local currency which may be exported.

Duty-free articles: Personal effects; 50 cigarettes or the equivalent in cigars or tobacco; samples of no commercial value, provided their gross weight is less than 3 kilos/6.6 lbs. Cameras and film should be declared on entry.

PRACTICAL INFORMATION FOR THE VISITOR

1. Currency
Monetary Unit – franc malien (Mali franc), divided into 100 centimes.
Notes – 50, 100, 500, 1,000, 5,000, 10,000 Mali francs.
Coins – 5, 10, 25 Mali francs.

The Mali franc has a fixed rate against the CFA franc of MF2 = CFA 1 and against the French franc of MF100 = FF1.
Travellers' cheques and certain foreign currencies can be exchanged at the major banks in Bamako. CFA franc notes are usually acceptable as payment in Mali; French franc notes are also occasionally acceptable.

Banking Hours
0800–1100 Monday to Friday

The *Banque Centrale du Mali*, B.P. 206, Bamako, ☎ 23756, is the central bank of issue.

Domestic Commercial Banks
Banque de Développement du Mali, B.P. 94, Bamako.

Banque Malienne de Crédit et de Dépôts, Avenue Modibo Keita, B.P. 45, Bamako, ☎ 25336.

Foreign Commercial Banks
Banque Internationale pour l'Afrique Occidentale, Avenue Mohamed V, B.P. 15, Bamako, ☎ 25601/2.

Caisse Centrale de Coopération Economique, Rue Testard, B.P. 32, Bamako.

2. Electricity Supply
220v AC 50Hz.

3. Weights and Measures
The metric system is in use.

4. Media
There is no television service at present in Mali. Radio Mali, the Government station, broadcasts programmes in French, English, Bambara and several other African languages.

Newspapers and Journals
L'Essor, published by the Military Committee for National Liberation, is the only daily newspaper.
Podium is a weekly periodical. *Sunjata*, published monthly, covers social and political affairs. *Kibaru* is a monthly publication for rural areas.
There is no trade press in Mali.

5. Medical Care
Tap water in Bamako is generally safe to drink; elsewhere visitors should drink bottled mineral water which is readily available.
Malaria is endemic and anti-malarial

MALI

prophylactics should be taken. It is advisable to be vaccinated against cholera and TAB (typhoid and paratyphoid); tetanus injections are also recommended.

The Government Hospital in Bamako deals with emergency cases. There are also a number of doctors in private practice in Bamako.

6. Telephone, Telex and Postal Services

International telephone communications from Mali are poor and subject to long delays. The domestic telephone service is adequate.

Telexes can be sent from the Central Telex Office, Office des Postes et Télécommunications, Bamako, ☎ 23199.

Postal services to and from Mali are irregular, and even airmail letters may take up to 2 weeks. All mail should be despatched by air.

7. Public Holidays

1 January	New Year's Day
20 January	Fête de l'Armée
1 May	Labour Day
25 May	Africa Day
22 September	Independence Day
19 November	Revolution Day
25 December	Christmas Day

The following movable Muslim and Christian holidays are also publicly observed: *Mouled*, *Eid el Fitr*, *Eid el Kâbor* and *Easter Minday*.

8. Time

GMT.

9. Internal Transport

Air

Internal air services are operated by Air Mali, linking Bamako with Gao, Goundam, Kayes, Mopti, Nara, Nioro du Sahel and Tombouctou.

Airline Offices in Bamako

Aeroflot ☎ 22693, 22097.
UTA/Air France ☎ 22212.

Rail

There are main services from Bamako to Koulikoro (twice daily) and from Bamako to Kayes (6 times a week).

River

Regular weekly services operate between Koulikoro and Gao from July to December (a distance of 1,300km/807 miles). From December to March, journeys by river are only possible from Gao to Mopti.

Road

The main tarred roads in Mali link Bamako with Sikasso in the south via Bougouni, and with Mopti and Gao in the northwest, via Ségou. A tarred road links Bamako with Koulikoro.

Taxis are readily available in Bamako. They are not fitted with meters, but prices are very reasonable.

Self-drive cars are available for hire in Bamako. An International Driving Licence is required. Traffic travels on the right-hand side of the road.

Car-Hire Firms in Bamako

Bamby Auto	☎ 25446.
Jacquard et Cie	☎ 22547.
Smert	☎ 25942.

10. Tipping

Taxis – no tip necessary.

Airport Porters – 100 Mali francs per bag.

Hotel/restaurant staff – a service charge is included in the bill; any additional tip is optional.

11. Social Customs

Visitors to Mali should have a good working knowledge of French. There are no commercial interpreting or translating services in Mali.

It is worth taking note of the correct forms of address to use when meeting local business contacts. These forms of address are the same as in France, thus a company director should be addressed as *Monsieur le Directeur*; a government minister as *Monsieur le Ministre*, etc.

USEFUL ADDRESSES (GENERAL)

Bamako
British Consulate: B.P. 1708, ☎ 22064.

Dutch Consulate: c/o Sehoma S.A., Immeuble Bathily, Rue Mohamed V, B.P. 1523, ☎ 25389.

French Embassy: Square Patrice Lumumba, B.P. 17, ☎ 22951.

US Embassy: Rue Testard and Rue Mohamed V, B.P. 34, ☎ 25663/4 and 25834/24835.

West German Embassy: Badalabougou Zone Est, Lotissement A6, B.P. 100, ☎ 23299, 23715.

Commissariat du Tourisme: Hôtel de l'Amitié, ☎ 24673.

Wagons-Lits Authorised Representative: Office Malien de Tourisme, B.P. 222.

BUSINESS INFORMATION

The demand for consumer and consumer durable goods in Mali over the next few years is likely to be low following the introduction of the Government's austerity programme. The majority of trade opportunities for foreign supplies are likely to arise out of the development projects, with demands for industrial equipment and machinery, spares, raw materials and even skilled personnel. The bulk of other purchases will most probably be made by the Government-owned commercial and industrial organisations. Where a contract has been placed for the supply of plant or machinery, suppliers are expected to provide the specialists necessary for the installation of the plant.

Few transactions between Malian officials and foreign suppliers are ever concluded by letter; thus the importance of a tour by a company representative cannot be overstressed.

A high value is placed on personal contact in Mali, visitors should be prepared for protracted negotiations and the leisurely rate at which business is conducted.

Import Regulations
Import licences are required for all imported goods.

Business Hours
Government Offices and Business Houses
0800 or 0900–1200
1500–1800 } Monday to Friday
0800 or 0900–1200 Saturday

During the month of *Ramadan* the continuous working day is in force: 0800–1600 Monday to Friday and 0800–1200 on Saturday.

BUSINESS SERVICES

Insurance
Caisse Nationale d'Assurance et de Réassurance, Rue Combes, B.P. 568, Bamako.

Transport
Compagnie Malienne de Navigation B.P. 150, Bamako – river transport.

Compagnie Malienne de Transports Routiers rue du Commandant-Riault, B.P. 208, Bamako – road transport.

USEFUL ADDRESSES (BUSINESS)

Chambre de Commerce et d'Industrie du Mali, B.P. 46, Bamako.

Chambre de Commerce de Kayes, B.P. 81, Kayes.

Société Malienne d'Importation et d'Exportation, B.P. 182, Bamako.

AFRIMEX, 1 Avenue Mohamed V, B.P. 1284, Bamako – import/export agency.

MAJOR CITY

Bamako

Bamako is situated in the broad valley of the River Niger which flows through the city centre. In comparison with the capitals of neighbouring countries, Bamako is relatively modern with spacious tree-lined avenues and squares and several towering office blocks and hotels.

The Great Mosque is one of the city's most impressive landmarks. Nearby is the Centre Artisanal, where local artisans work with gold, silver, ivory, leather and ebony. The Ethnological Museum, zoo and botanical gardens are also worth a visit.

Hotels
There is no official hotel rating system.

HÔTEL DE L'AMITIÉ, B.P. 1720, ☎ 25362. Modern luxury hotel in city centre overlooking River Niger.
Rooms: 185 ♪, 🎨, ♊, ♋, ⚐. Suites available.
Facilities: 2 restaurants, bars. Nightclub. Cinema. Swimming, tennis. Shops. Car hire.
Services: TC, FC. ⊟ Amex, Diners Club. Dr. on call. ♫, ⚥. Translation bureau, audio-visual equipment.
Conference room – max. capacity 300.
Banquet room – max. capacity 300.

LE GRAND, Avenue Van Vollenhoven, B.P. 104, ☎ 22481/3.
Moderate 1st-class, colonial-style hotel situated in residential area outside city centre.
Rooms: 68 ♪ (in some), ♊, ♋. Suites available.
Facilities: Restaurant, bar. Nightclub. Banquet room. Car hire.
Services: TC, FC. ⊟ Not accepted. Dr. on call. ♫, ⚥.

LE MOTEL, B.P. 911, ☎ 23622/4.
Modern motel 2km/1½ miles from city centre, and 5km/3 miles from airport.
Rooms: 52 ♪.
Facilities: Restaurant, bar. Nightclub, dancing.
Services: ⊟ Major credit cards accepted.

Restaurants
The restaurants of the Hôtel de l'Amitié and the Grand Hotel are open to non-

residents. Other restaurants in and around Bamako include *L'Aquarium* – French; *Le Berry* – French; *Les Trois Caïmans* – in an attractive setting overlooking the river with its own nightclub; *Le Lido*, outside the city centre; *La Gondole*.

Nightclubs

There is dancing at *Les Trois Caïmans* and *Le Village*. *Les Daltons* at the Lido is also popular for dancing and occasional live entertainment. The Hôtel de l'Amitié and the Grand Hotel both have nightclubs.

Entertainment

Mali boasts a fine National Dance Troupe, which spends much of its time abroad with occasional productions staged in Bamako.

Football is a popular sport, and the River Niger provides plenty of scope for sailing, fishing, water skiing and other water sports. Swimming is not recommended because of the risk of bilharzia. Bamako also has a private tennis club.

Approximately 120km/75 miles from Bamako is the National Park of La Boucle de Baoulé which contains a large variety of game.

Shopping

Best buys: wood carvings, gold and silver jewellery, leatherwork, pottery, embroidered cloth.

The *Centre Artisanal* near the Grand Mosque has the largest selection of traditional handicrafts and is especially good for gold and silver jewellery and artefacts. Visitors wishing to purchase an article of gold should ensure that it bears the official stamp of the Service des Mines.

MAURITANIA
Islamic Republic of Mauritania

> Geography 267
> The Economy 269
> How to Get There 270
> Entry Regulations 270
> Practical Information for the Visitor 271
> Useful Addresses (General) 272
> Business Information 272
> Business Services 273
> Useful Addresses (Business) 273
> Nouakchott 273

Size: 1,030,700 sq.km/397,953 sq.miles.

Population: 1.54 million (1978 est.).

Distribution: 22% in urban areas.

Density: 1.5 persons per sq.km/3.8 per sq.mile.

Population Growth Rate: 2.6% p.a.

Ethnic Composition: Three-quarters are Arab/Berber Moors, nomads divided along social lines into 'white' and 'black' groups. The remainder are Negroes, who are mainly sedentary cultivators along the Senegal River.

Capital: Nouakchott Pop. 135,000 (1976).

Major Towns: Nouadhibou Pop. 22,000; Kaédi Pop. 21,000; Zouérate Pop. 17,500.

Language: Arabic and French are the official languages. The Moors speak an Arabic dialect, Hassaniyya; the Senegal Valley Negroes speak native dialects.

Religion: Islam of the Malekite sect.

Government: The civilian Government of President Ould Daddah was overthrown in a bloodless military coup in July 1978; the current President heads a 13-member Military Committee for National Salvation.

GEOGRAPHY

Mauritania is essentially a vast plain of sand, scrub and rock. In parts of the country the land rises in rocky plateaux with deeply eroded ravines. In the south is the fertile Senegal River Valley.

In 1976 Mauritania annexed the southern half of Western Sahara, and the area remains a centre of dispute between Mauritania, Morocco and the Polisario guerrillas who seek independence.

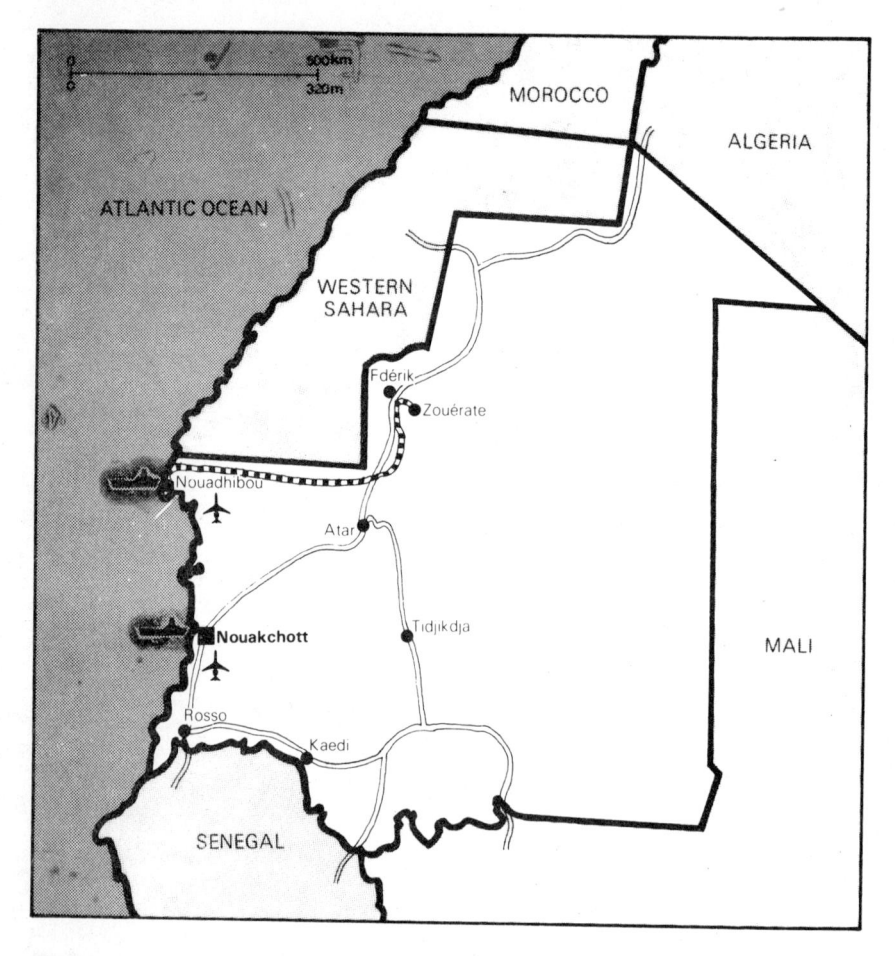

MAURITANIA

Climate
Two-thirds of the country is Saharan with negligible rainfall but the south has a rainy season from July to October. The coastal area has milder temperatures except for the hotter Nouakchott region, and hot sandy desert winds blow in March and April. Best time to visit is December to February; the maximum temperature at this time is between 18°C/65°F and 29°C/85°F.

Agriculture
Although agriculture now contributes only about one-third of the Gross Domestic Product, the vast majority of the population is still dependent on it for their livelihood. Fishing makes the most important agricultural contribution to exports, and the annexation of southern Western Sahara in 1976 contributed a rich new fishing area. Over 60% of the population live off stock-raising, and a programme of reconstitution is now returning the herds of goats, cattle, camels and sheep to their former levels after the devastation of the Sahel drought of the early 1970s which drastically reduced the animal population. Crops, principally millet and sorghum, are grown mainly in the

Senegal River region in the south, and both crop and livestock development is expected to benefit from the planned irrigation programme based on 2 dams to be constructed on the river by the Organisation for the Development of the River Senegal (backed by Mauritania, Mali and Senegal).

Main Crops: millet, sorghum, dates, cow peas, maize, rice, vegetables, groundnuts.

Mineral Resources: iron ore, copper, gypsum, tungsten, petroleum, chromium, phosphates, uranium.

THE ECONOMY

Gross National Product (1978 est.): US$420 million.

Per Capita Income (1978 est.): US$273.

Gross Domestic Product (1978 est.): US$539 million.

Foreign Trade (1978): Total Imports – US$181 million. Total Exports – US$122 million.

Main Trading Partners: Imports – France, US, West Germany, UK, Senegal. Exports – France, UK, Italy, Japan, Spain.

Although most of the population is still dependent on agriculture for a living, Mauritania's economy is largely centred on the vast iron ore resources around Zouérate. Revenue from this area has fluctuated in the last few years because of falling world demand and guerrilla attacks on the railway which carries the ore to Nouadhibou for export. Plans are being pursued, with finance from Arab and Western sources, to develop fresh iron ore deposits north of the present mines, which are expected to be exhausted within 10 years. Copper has been mined since 1967 at Akjoujt, but production ceased in 1978 because of the low grade of the deposit and so far has not been restarted. In addition, SNIM, the partially nationalised mining company, is prospecting for tungsten, petroleum, phosphates and uranium.

Outside the mining sector, industrial development is limited to processing agricultural products (fish processing at Nouadhibou, sugar refining, flour milling, meat and dairy products) and some import substitution (textiles, paint, industrial gas). A petroleum refinery at Nouakchott began production in 1978, but has since ceased operation.

The increase in revenue from mining has been matched by expenditure on the guerrilla war and the administration of the annexed portion of Western Sahara. This, together with recurrent drought problems, has resulted in a trade deficit which leaves Mauritania reliant on aid from abroad. Emphasis in the current recovery programme is being placed on the neglected rural sector (food currently accounts for over one-fifth of total imports).

Major Industries: mining, food processing (principally fish), textiles, plaster and cement production, bricks, paints, industrial gas.

MAURITANIA

Main Commodities Traded: Imports – mechanical equipment, transport equipment, foodstuffs, petroleum products, iron and steel, electrical machinery. Exports – iron ore, fish products, gypsum, gum arabic, dates.

International Affiliations: UN, IBRD, OAU, ACP, ADB, AL, BADEA, CFAO, ECOWAS, OMUS.

HOW TO GET THERE

Air
UTA connects Paris with Nouakchott and with Nouadhibou once a week. Iberia and Air Mauritanie connect Madrid with Nouadhibou thrice weekly via Las Palmas. In addition, Air Afrique, Air Mauritanie, Royal Air Maroc and Air Senegal operate daily return flights between Dakar (Senegal) and Nouakchott, and there are direct connections from Dakar to New York and London.

Nouakchott Airport is 4km/2½ miles from the city centre.

A departure tax of MOG 220 is charged for African destinations and MOG 560 for destinations outside Africa.

Flying times to Nouakchott: from Paris, 6½ hours; from New York via Dakar, 8½ hours; from London via Dakar, 6½ hours; from Dakar to Nouakchott, 45 minutes.

ENTRY REGULATIONS

Visas
Visas are required by all visitors, except those from France, Italy, Romania, Liberia, the Gambia and former French territories in Africa.

Visitors intending to fly return from Dakar to Mauritania also require a multiple-entry Senegalese visa.

Business visitors should ensure that their passport is valid for at least 3 months beyond the date of application for their visa.

Health Regulations
International Certificates of Vaccination against smallpox and yellow fever are required, and vaccinations against tetanus and cholera are advisable.

Customs
Currency: Import of local and foreign currency is unlimited, but foreign currency must be declared. Local currency up to MOG 1,000 may be exported. Foreign currency up to the amount imported and declared may be exported, and the import declaration must be produced.

Duty-free articles: 200 cigarettes or 25 cigars or 454g of tobacco. 1 litre of spirits or 2 litres of wine. A small amount of perfume. 1 still camera. 1 cine camera. 1 wireless set. Samples of no commercial value.

Restricted articles: A gun licence and an import licence must be obtained before arrival from the Home Ministry in order to import sporting guns.

MAURITANIA

PRACTICAL INFORMATION FOR THE VISITOR

1. Currency
Monetary Unit – Ouguiya (MOG), divided into 5 khoums.
Notes – 100, 200, 1,000 ouguiya.
Coins – 1 khoum; 1, 5, 10, 20 ouguiya.

Travellers' cheques can be exchanged at banks and at major hotels.

Banking Hours
0800–1115 Monday to Friday
1430–1630

The central bank of issue in Nouakchott is *Banque Centrale de Mauritanie*, B.P. 623, Avenue de l'Indépendance.

Commercial Banks in Nouakchott
Banque Internationale pour la Mauritanie, Avenue Gamal Abdul Nasser, B.P. 210 – branches in several smaller towns.
Société Mauritanienne de Banque, Avenue Gamal Abdul Masser, B.P. 614.
Banque Arabe Libyenne – Mauritanienne, B.P. 626.
Banque Arabe Africaine en Mauritanie, Rue Amadou Konate, B.P. 622.

Foreign Bank in Nouakchott
Caisse Centrale de Coopération Economique, Immeuble de Brakna, B.P. 217.

2. Electricity Supply
220v AC 50Hz.
Plugs: 2 round pins.

3. Weights and Measures
The metric system is in use.

4. Media
Radiodiffusion Nationale de Mauritanie is a commercial service and broadcasts in French, Arabic and several Negro dialects.
Agence Mauritanienne de Télévision et de Cinema operates a limited television service in Arabic and French.
There is a Government daily newspaper, *Ach-Chaab*, printed in French and Arabic. *Le Peuple* is a bi-monthly, also printed in French and Arabic. In addition, the Ministry of Justice produces the *Journal Officiel* twice monthly and the Société Nationale de Presse produces the *Nouakchott Information* bulletin.

5. Medical Care
Visitors should take anti-malarial precautions. Water should be boiled or filtered, and uncooked fruit and vegetables avoided.
Medical facilities in Nouakchott are rudimentary and expensive.

6. Telephone, Telex and Postal Services
Visitors are advised to post all mail by air. Telephone services are being consolidated and improved under the current 5-year plan, and international telex facilities are available at the main Office des Postes et Télécommunications in Nouakchott.

7. Public Holidays
1 January — New Year's Day
1 May — Labour Day
25 May — OAU Day
28 November — National Day

In addition, the following Muslim feasts are observed: *Mouled*, *Eid el Fitr* and *Eid-el Adha*.

8. Time
GMT.

9. Internal Transport
Air
Air Mauritanie regularly connects Nouakchott and Nouadhibou with

271

MAURITANIA

several smaller towns. Light aircraft are available for hire from the Nouakchott Aero Club.

Airline Offices in Nouakchott
Air Mauritanie ☎ 2211, 2681
UTA/Air Afrique ☎ 2084

Road
There are tarred roads from Nouakchott to Rosso on the Senegal border and to Akjoujt, but as yet no road between Nouakchott and Nouadhibou. Most of the roads are sand tracks, but a programme of improvement is under way.

There is a good taxi service in both Nouakchott and Nouadhibou, but taxis are unmetered and very expensive.

10. Tipping
Hotels/restaurants – 10–15% of the bill.
Tips for other services are appreciated.

USEFUL ADDRESSES (GENERAL)

Nouakchott

Dutch Consulate: Avenue du Général de Gaulle, B.P. 318, ☎ 52240.

French Embassy: Rue Ahmed Ould M'Hamed, B.P. 231, ☎ 51740.

US Embassy, B.P. 222, ☎ 52660.

West German Embassy, B.P. 372, ☎ 52032.

Secrétariat Général à l'Artisanat et au Tourisme, B.P. 246.

Société Mauritanienne de Tourisme et d'Hôtellerie, B.P. 552.

Socopao Travel Agency, B.P. 361.

BUSINESS INFORMATION

Agents are generally based in Dakar in Senegal, which is the centre of trade for this part of Africa. However, Mauritanian authorities favour Mauritanian agents, so it may be advantageous to appoint an agent in Nouakchott. Most of the established trading firms are based in France, and all business must be conducted in French. Close personal contact with the agent must be maintained.

Import and Exchange Control Regulations
Mauritania imposes both fiscal and customs duties on imports, with additional taxes at varying rates. Certain organic products require health and sanitation certificates.
　　The Government encourages foreign investment. The 1976 Investment Code protects such investment and guarantees the repatriation of profits.

Business Hours
Government Offices and Business Houses
0800–1200 Monday to Friday
1430–1800
During *Ramadan*, Government offices work 0730–1430.

MAURITANIA

BUSINESS SERVICES

Insurance
Société Mauritanienne d'Assurances et de Réassurances, 12 Avenue Gamal Abdul Nasser, B.P. 163, Nouakchott.

Road Transport
Société Nouvelle des Etablissements Lacombe, B.P. 204, Nouakchott.

Shipping
Société Ouest Africaine d'Entreprises Maritimes (Mauritanie), B.P. 351, Nouakchott.
Compagnie Mauritanienne de Navigation Maritime, B.P. 587, Nouakchott.

USEFUL ADDRESSES (BUSINESS)

Bureau d'Achats pour la République Islamique de Mauritanie, B.P. 272, Nouakchott – import organisation.

Chambre de Commerce, d'Agriculture et d'Industrie de la République Islamique de Mauritanie, B.P. 215, Nouakchott.

Société Nationale d'Importation et d'Exportation, B.P. 290, Nouakchott.

MAJOR CITY

Nouakchott
The capital and administrative centre, Nouakchott was founded on independence in 1960. It lies near the old Moorish settlement, the Ksar, on the Atlantic coast and all modern buildings in the town are in the traditional Berber style. A deep-water port is being developed near Nouakchott by the Chinese. Worth visiting is the camel market and the crafts centre. There are excellent beaches near by; deep-sea fishing is available.

Hotels
There is no official hotel rating system.

MARHABA, B.P. 135, ☎ 52094.
Modern hotel near city centre.
Rooms: 64 ♪, △, ⌘. Suites available.
Facilities: 2 restaurants, snack bar, bars. Nightclub. Parking, car hire. Swimming.
Services: TC, FC. 🖃 Not accepted. ♂, S.

PARC, B.P. 150, ☎ 52144.
Modern hotel in city centre.
Rooms: 17 ♪, ⊛, △, ⌘. Suite available.
Facilities: Restaurant, bars. Nightclub. Parking, car hire.
Services: 🖃 Not accepted. Dr. on call. ♂, S.
Conference room – max. capacity 200.
Banquet room – max. capacity 200.

SABAH, B.P. 452, ☎ 51552.
New hotel 6km/3.5 miles from city centre, on beach front.
Rooms: 40 ♪.
Facilities: Restaurant, bars. Swimming.

Restaurants
In addition to the hotel restaurants, there are *l'Atlantide*, *Café Oriental*, *Nezha* and *Chantal*.

Shopping
Best buys: woven wool rugs, silver and copper jewellery, dyed leather, daggers, tooled leather saddles.
The *Crafts Centre* has an excellent variety of silver jewellery, woodcraft, daggers and carpets.

MAURITIUS
Mauritius

Geography	275
The Economy	276
How to Get There	277
Entry Regulations	278
Practical Information for the Visitor	279
Useful Addresses (General)	281
Business Information	281
Business Services	282
Useful Addresses (Business)	282
Port Louis	283
Curepipe and the Central Plateau	284

Size: 2,045 sq.km/790 sq. miles (including Roderigues, Agalega and St Brandon islands, which Mauritius administers).

Population: 918,000 (1978 est.).

Distribution: 44% in urban areas.

Density: 445 persons per sq.km./1,152 per sq.mile.

Population Growth Rate: 1.5% p.a.

Ethnic Composition: Mauritians of Indian descent 69%, Creoles 29%; the remainder Sino-Mauritians, Franco-Mauritians or expatriates.

Capital: Port Louis Pop. 150,000.

Major Towns: Beau-Bassin/Rose Hill Pop. 84,000; Curepipe Pop. 55,000; Quatre-Bornes Pop. 54,000; Vacoas/Phoenix Pop. 52,000.

Languages: English is the official language, however many speak a Creole patois based on French with elements of African and Asian languages. French is widely understood; Chinese, Hindi and Urdu are also spoken.

Religion: Some 51% of Mauritians are Hindu, 17% are Muslim, and 31% are Christian, mostly Roman Catholic.

Government: 3 centuries of intermittent colonial rule ended on 12 March 1968 when Mauritius gained its independence from Britain. Members are elected to seats in the Legislative Assembly by universal suffrage. The Government is elected for a maximum period of 5 years in office.

The present government is a civilian coalition formed in 1976 in which the Labour Party and the Parti Mauricien Social Démocrate are the main partners under the leadership of Sir Seewoosaur Ramgoolam. The major opposition party is the Mouvement Militant Mauricien (MMM), others include the Comité d'Action Musulman, the Independent Forward Bloc, the Mauritian People's Progressive Party, the Parti du Centre Républicain and the Union Démocratique Mauricienne.

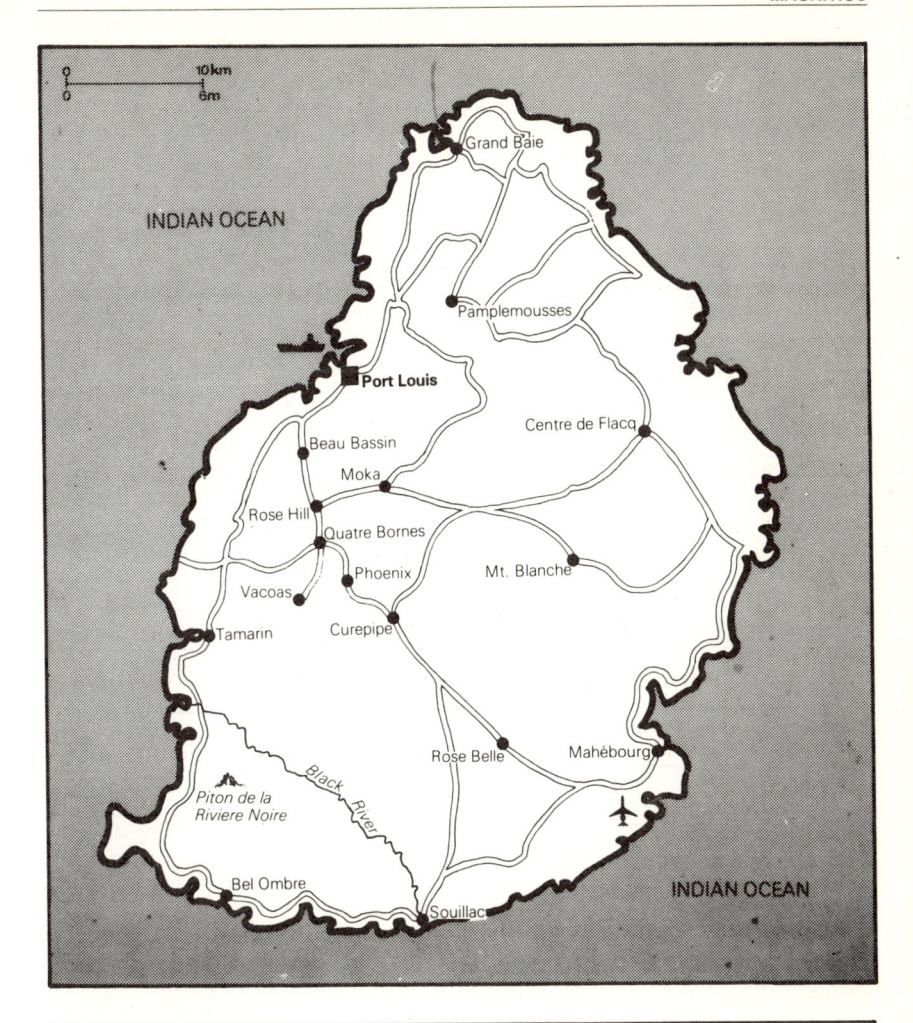

GEOGRAPHY

One of the islands in the Mascarene archipelago, lying about 800km/500 miles to the east of Madagascar, Mauritius was originally formed by a now-inactive volcano. The island's coast is virtually surrounded by a coral reef, from which the land rises up to the inland plateau that slopes from the highest points in the south-west to the lower north-east. The highest peak is the Piton de la Rivière Noire (825 metres/2,711 feet) in the Black River range.

Climate

The Mauritian climate is sub-tropical maritime, giving warm temperatures on the coast all year round. There is a general climatic distinction between the warmer, drier coast and the cool, rainy inland areas. Extremes of temperature are not experienced, although it is hotter between November and April when humidity also tends to increase. Rainfall is fairly evenly spread throughout the year with a tendency for it to be slightly drier between September and December when the occasional heavy rainstorms are less frequent. Cyclones are most likely between December and March.

Agriculture

Sugar is by far the most important single product. The cane fields cover almost half the island, being particularly concentrated on the central plateau where cane is grown on almost all of the cultivable land.

Attempts are now being made to diversify the crops grown in Mauritius in order to develop a greater measure of self-sufficiency in such basic foodstuffs as maize, milk, meat and vegetables which have in the past been imported. The good soil and, for the most part, favourable, climate could support a wide variety of other agricultural crops which would provide additional work in a nation determined to achieve full employment for its inhabitants.

The production of tea has recently increased after several years of declining output; in 1977, 4,727 tonnes were produced, of which 3,429 tonnes were exported. The tobacco fields produce about 650 tonnes per year, satisfying most of the local demand.

Main Crops: sugar-cane, molasses, tea, tobacco.

Mineral Resources: There are no known mineral deposits. Explorations for oil are still being made in the Indian Ocean, although it is doubtful that any finds will be of sufficient size to be commercially viable.

THE ECONOMY

Gross National Product (1978 est.): US$760 million.

Per Capita Income (1978 est.): US$830.

Gross Domestic Product (1977 est.): Rs 4.17 billion.

Foreign Trade (1978): Total Imports – US$424 million. Total Exports – US $325.8 million.

Main Trading Partners: Imports – UK, France, South Africa, Japan, West Germany, Australia. Exports – EEC countries, Canada, USA, South Africa, Seychelles and Comoro Islands, USSR.

Mauritius has relied heavily upon the production of sugar for its economic well being since the 18th century, and, as a classic example of a 1-crop economy, it has prospered or suffered as the price of sugar has moved up and down in the world markets. A degree of stability for the agricultural production and prices paid to developing countries by the importing nations was envisaged in the Lomé Conventions of 1975 and 1980. Under these agreements, Mauritius is guaranteed an export quota of EEC countries at a fixed price, which, in recent years, has been considerably higher than the prevailing world market price. The dramatic rises in sugar prices during 1973, 1974 and 1975 gave a short-lived boost to the economy, although subsequently the trend has been toward lower prices on the open market. The loss of preferential markets in

Britain and severe damage to the cane crop caused by cyclones in 1975 and late 1979 have caused additional problems for the sugar industry in recent years. Peak production was achieved in 1973 when 718,000 tonnes were produced.

An important development has been the growth of manufacturing industries, both for the home market and export. Clothing, footwear, foodstuffs, drinks, building materials and household goods are among the items produced and sold locally. The export industries have concentrated on producing labour-intensive goods that require a skilled work force. Materials are usually imported; sophisticated products are often exported. The Government has sought to actively promote this sector of the economy by creating Export Processing Zones (EPZs), within which local and foreign investors receive considerable incentives in the way of tax exemption, freedom from import duties and various other services at reduced rates. The EPZ companies (see 'Economy') have grown rapidly in number from 5 in 1970, to 43 in 1974, to 91 in 1977, and their exports have risen from Rs3.9 million in 1971 to Rs430 million in 1977. The fastest-growing industries within the EPZs have been textiles, electronic components, diamond cutting and polishing and other precision-engineering trades. Chemical, tyre-manufacturing and toy industries are also present.

The aim is now for a mixed economy in which private enterprise is encouraged, while the public sector plays an important role in developing the economic infrastructure.

Tourism is the third largest foreign exchange earner for Mauritius and has served to stimulate a number of local craft industries which supply traditional products and gifts for tourist consumption. The modern facilities offered by the hotels combined with the natural beauty and magnificent beaches of the island have attracted increasing numbers of tourists from South Africa, the USA and Europe. Mauritius has become a successful resort, catering mainly for the luxury market.

At 1970 prices, the growth rate of the economy has been around 5.5% per annum (1970). The active commercial and industrial community and positive attitude of the Government towards problems of industrialisation have helped to make Mauritius increasingly attractive for the foreign investor.

Commercial fishing has grown to the extent that there is now a small, but established, export trade in canned fish.

Major Industries: sugar products, tea, clothing, precision engineering, craft industries, tourism.

Major Commodities Traded: Imports – machinery and transport equipment, rice, wheat flour, vegetables, livestock, milk, fuels and lubricants, chemicals, pharmaceuticals. Exports – sugar products, tea, textiles, various electronic and consumer goods.

International Affiliations: UN, IBRD, OAU, ACP, ADB, Commonwealth, OCAM.

HOW TO GET THERE

Air

Air France operate a daily service from Paris; British Airways fly direct from London once a week. Air Mauritius also operates a direct service to London and, in conjunction with Air France, provides a daily flight to Réunion from Plaisance Airport. Both

Air Mauritius and Air India maintain a service between Mauritius and Bombay once a week. Alitalia and Lufthansa operate 1 flight a week each way between Mauritius and Rome, and Mauritius and Frankfurt, respectively. Several other services link Mauritius to Africa and Australia via Zambia Airways, Qantas, South African Airways and other African airlines.

A tax of 10% is payable on all airline tickets bought in Mauritius. An airport tax of Rs20 must be paid by all passengers leaving Mauritius.

Plaisance Airport is situated in the south-east of the island about 48 km/30 miles from Port Louis and 24 km/15 miles from Curepipe.

Sea
Many shipping lines call at Port Louis, the only port on the island.

ENTRY REGULATIONS

Visas
Visas are required by nationals of all countries, except those belonging to the British Commonwealth, the European Economic Community or Finland, Greece, Iceland, Norway, Pakistan, South Africa, Sweden, Tunisia and Turkey for visits of up to 6 months. All visitors must be in possession of a return or onward ticket when they arrive. Entry visas valid for up to 6 months may be extended upon application when in Mauritius. British consulates issue visas wherever there is no Mauritian representative. It usually takes between 2 and 7 days to issue a visa unless the application is referred, in which case the delay may be several weeks.

Health Regulations
Vaccination certificates against Cholera and Yellow Fever are required by all visitors arriving from infected areas, and smallpox vaccination certificates by visitors from all countries.

Customs
Currency: The importation of foreign currency in the form of banking instruments – drafting, letters of credit, travellers' cheques etc. – is unrestricted. Visitors may take in any amount of foreign currency in notes and up to Rs 700 in Mauritian currency. Only Rs 350 may be exported. Unused imported foreign currency may be taken out of the country.

Duty-free articles: Personal baggage. 250 grammes of tobacco, including cigars and cigarettes. 2 litres of wine, ale or beer. 75cl of spirits. Commercial samples liable to duty of less than Rs1 can be imported duty-free. Samples liable to a duty of more than Rs1 may be imported temporarily if a deposit equal to the amount of duty payable is made and the sample re-exported within 6 months.

A free Listener's Licence valid for 2 months is granted to visitors arriving with radio sets on the understanding that the equipment will be exported when the visitor leaves.

Articles liable to duty: A permit from the Exchange Control is required for the export of any articles made wholly or mainly from gold, platinum, silver, diamonds or other precious or semi-precious stones, pearls, and articles mounted or set with precious or semi-precious metals and stone.

Permits are needed from the Controller of Supplies for the exportation of articles exceeding Rs1,000 in value, exclusive of personal effects and clothing.

Prohibited articles: Live animals can only be imported if a permit has been obtained from the Department of Agriculture. A maximum of 6 seashells can be exported from Mauritius. Plant material – sugar cane in particular – cannot be introduced to Mauritius unless a Plant Import Permit previously obtained from the Department of Agriculture is held along with the relevant certificates from the country of origin.

PRACTICAL INFORMATION FOR THE VISITOR

1. Currency
Monetary unit – Mauritius rupee (Rs), divided into 100 cents.
Notes – 5, 10, 25, 50 Rs.
Coins – 1, 2, 5, 10, 25, 50 cents; 1 R.

Mauritius rupees are not worth much outside the island. Visitors are advised to use travellers' cheques or sterling wherever possible and to exchange only at the major banks for day-to-day needs. All major international and sterling credit cards are acceptable.

Banking Hours
1000 – 1400 Monday–Friday
0930 – 1130 Saturday

Domestic Banks
Bank of Mauritius, Sir William Newton Street, Port Louis.
Development Bank of Mauritius, P.O. Box 157, Chaussée Street, Port Louis.
Mauritius Co-Operative Central Bank, Co-operative House, Dumat Street, Port Louis.
Mauritius Commercial Bank Ltd, 11 Sir William Newton Street, Port Louis.
The State Commercial Bank Ltd, Intendance Street, Port Louis.

Major Foreign Commercial Banks
Barclays Bank International Ltd (UK), Sir William Newton Street, Port Louis.
Bank of Baroda (India), Sir William Newton Street, Port Louis.
Bank of Credit and Commerce International SA, Desforges Street, Port Louis.
Banque National pour le Commerce et l'Industrie (Ocean Indien), Duc d'Edimbourg Street, Port Louis.
Citibank NA (USA), 4 Léoville l'Homme Street, Port Louis.
Habib Bank AG, Sir William Newton Street, Port Louis.
Habib Bank Ltd (Pakistan), Sir William Newton Street, Port Louis.
Mercantile Bank Ltd, Place des Armes, Port Louis.

2. Electricity Supply
220v AC 50Hz
Plugs: 13 amp flat pin.

3. Weights and Measures
The metric system is in general use.

4. Media
A monopoly on radio and television broadcasting is held by the Mauritius Broadcasting Corporation, who run a commercial service that accepts advertising.

Newspapers and Journals
The dailies, published in French and English, are: *Advance*; *Libération*; *Le Mauricien*; *Le Militant*; *L'Express*; *The Nation*; *Star*; and *Le Populaire*. Others include: *Le Lernéen*, with the information on the sugar industry; and *China Times* and the *Chinese Daily News* in Chinese. *Janata*, in Hindi, is published twice weekly. The weeklies, in French

and English, are: *Le Dimanche*; *Mauritius Times*; *Weekend*; *La Vie Catholique*.

Amongst the periodicals are *The Indian Cultural Review*, in English, issued quarterly; *PROSI*, organ of the Public Relations Office of the Sugar Industry, in French and English; and *Revue Agricole et Sucrière d'Ile Maurice*, in French and English.

Cinema
The island has 38 cinemas in which English, French, American and Indian films are shown.

5. Medical Care
Malaria has now been eradicated, and there are no endemic tropical diseases on the island. Water and food is generally safe.

Hospitals
Civil Hospital, Voley Pougnet Street, Port Louis, ☎ 23201.
Sir Seewoosagur Ramgoolam National Hospital, Pamplemousses, ☎ 33561.

6. Telephone, Telex and Postal Services
Radio and cable connections link the island's telephone network to the rest of the world; the service is run by Cable and Wireless Ltd, who also operate a telex service for visitors at their office in Chaussée Street, Port Louis. Credit facilities are available for telegrams, telex and telephone services.

There are few public telephones, though an automatic service links all areas.

Post is sent by air mail to other parts of the world.

7. Public Holidays
1 January	New Year
12 March	Independence Day
1 May	Labour Day
25 December	Christmas Day

Various Hindu, Muslim, Chinese and Christian religious holidays are observed by the island's respective communities.

8. Time
GMT + 4.

9. Internal Transport

Air
No internal service is operated on the island.

Airline Offices and Representatives in Port Louis
Air Mauritius (MK), P.O. Box 60, 1 Sir William Newton Street, ☎ 21281.
Hotel Mallac & Co Ltd, Edith Cavell Street, ☎ 20861 – agents for Lufthansa and Zambia Airways.
Rogers & Co Ltd, Sir William Newton Street, ☎ 21281 – agents for Air France, Air India, British Airways, South African Airways and Qantas.
Scott & Co, Place Foch, ☎ 24101 – agents for Alitalia.

Road
Roads are of a good general standard. Many of them are asphalted, and there is a 15km/9 mile length of dual carriageway between Port Louis and Curepipe.

Bus services connect most parts of the island, and taxis can be hired in the larger towns. Self-drive cars are available in Port Louis, Curepipe and from some of the larger hotels. Cars may also be chartered.

Traffic travels on the right-hand side of the road. The French rule of priority to the left is observed at roundabouts and crossroads.

Car-Hire Firms in Port Louis
Avis, Al Madina Rd., P.O. Box 740, ☎ 26031/2, 21624.
White Sands Tours, Chaussée Street, ☎ 23712, 25535.
Hertz Trans Maurice Ltd, Queen Street, ☎ 24841.
VIP Car Hire, 18 Geoffrey Street, ☎ 20821.
Central Motors Ltd, 17 Brabant Street, ☎ 21749.
Pop Tours, Place Foch, ☎ 25134.

Car Hire Firms in Curepipe
Hertz Trans Maurice Ltd, Royal Rd., ☎ Curepipe 789.
Concorde Tourist Guide Agency, Arcades Lurinjee, P.O. Box 44, ☎ Curepipe 65.

10. Tipping
Taxis – No tip.

Hotels/restaurants – 10% of the bill.

USEFUL ADDRESSES (GENERAL)

Port Louis
Central African Republic Embassy: 50 Rue Remy Oliver, ☎ 24861.

Egyptian: 12 F. Felix de Valois Street.

French Embassy: 14 St Georges Street, ☎ 23755/6.

Indian Embassy: Baroda Buildings, Sir William Newton Street, ☎ 23775/6.

Madagascar Embassy: Sir William Newton Street, ☎ 22843/4.

Pakistan Embassy: Anglo-Mauritius Building, Intendance Street, ☎ 21862.

UK High Commission: Lerné House, Chaussée Street, ☎ 20201/5.

US Embassy: Anglo-Mauritius Building, Intendance Street, ☎ 23218/9.

Danish Consulate: c/o Scott & Co, 1 Corderie Street, ☎ 23291.

Belgian Consulate: c/o Blyth Bros., New Quay Street, ☎ 21241.

Dutch Consulate: c/o Blyth Bros., New Quay Street, P.O. Box 56, ☎ 21241.

Finnish Consulate: c/o Rogers & Co, Sir William Newton Street, ☎ 21286.

Japanese Consulate: c/o Blyth Bros., New Quay Street, ☎ 21241.

Portuguese Consulate: c/o Ireland Blyth, 10 Dr Ferrière Street, ☎ 22811.

Spanish Consulate: Queen Street, ☎ 22325.

Swiss Consulate: c/o Poncine & Fils, 2 Jules Koenig Street, ☎ 20819.

West German Consulate: 60 Desforges Street, ☎ 20666.

Automobile Association of Mauritius: 2 Queen Street, ☎ 21104.

Government Tourist Office: Lerné House, Chaussée Street, ☎ 21846/7.

Police Headquarters: Line Barracks, ☎ 21212.

Others
British Council: H. F. Grant, Royal Road, P.O. Box 111, Rose Hill, ☎ 42034/5.

USSR Embassy: Queen Mary Avenue, Floreal, Curepipe, ☎ 426, 1545.

BUSINESS INFORMATION

Mauritius offers the investor a skilled and adaptable labour force with a standard of education comparable to that of many European countries. Industrial rents here are relatively low, as are transport costs, and foreign investment in the EPZs is encouraged.

Most of the import trade is conducted through local agents and import merchants, and it is best to appoint one. There are several commission agents, most of whom also import. Importers generally prefer to deal with specialist producers and exporters.

Commercial law covering agency agreements in Mauritius is based on the French Code of Commerce of 1805, though changes have been made.

Import and Export Control Regulations

Licensed traders need no import licences, especially if the goods are for a manufacturer holding a valid Export Enterprise Certificate. Licences are required for some goods, amongst which are precious stones and metals, motor vehicles, refrigerators, TV and radio sets, industrial machinery, and some foodstuffs and plants.

Travelling agents, defined as persons taking orders for goods and wares to be imported from firms trading outside the state, must take out a licence costing Rs120 quarterly.

Permits are needed from the Controller of Supplies for the exportation of articles exceeding Rs1,000, exclusive of personal effects and clothing.

Business Hours
Government Offices
0900 – 1200
1230 – 1530 Monday to Friday

Business Houses
0830 – 1630 Monday to Friday
0900 – 1130 Saturday

BUSINESS SERVICES

Insurance
Albatross Insurance Co. Ltd, Laboma House, 35 Sir William Newton Street, Port Louis.
Anglo-Mauritius Assurance Society Ltd, Anglo-Mauritius House, Intendance Street, Port Louis.

Birger & Co. (Insurance) Ltd, Anglo-Mauritius House, Intendance Street, Port Louis.

In addition, there are 10 foreign insurance companies in Mauritius.

USEFUL ADDRESSES (BUSINESS)

Mauritius Agricultural Federation, Dumat Street, Port Louis.
Mauritius Chamber of Commerce and Industry, Anglo-Mauritius House, Intendance Street, Port Louis.
Mauritius Co-operative Union Ltd, Co-operative House, Dumat Street, Port Louis.

Australian Trade Correspondent, Anglo-Mauritius House, Intendance Street, Port Louis, ☎ 21700.
Canadian Commercial Commissioner, c/o Blanche Birger & Co., 18 Jules Koenig Street, Port Louis, ☎ 20821.

Chinese Chamber of Commerce,
5 Joseph Rivière Street, Port Louis.
Indian Trades Association, Sir William Newton Street, Port Louis.

South African Trade Commission, c/o Emmanuel Cadet & Co, Port Louis, ☎ 22817.

MAJOR CITY AND TOWNS

Port Louis

The capital city lies at sea level within a semi-circle of mountains on the north-western coast. It is the oldest town in Mauritius and has been the centre of its trade and industry since the 18th century. Most of the business activity is concentrated in the port area and the neighbouring commercial centre. The port was named after King Louis XIV of France, in whose name the East India Company took possession of the island in 1715.

The architecture ranges from the elegant mansions of the plantation owners in the hilly suburbs to the Chinese and Indian temples. The city was founded by the French Governor Maté de Labourdonnais and the gridiron layout of the town is characteristic of French town planning. Amongst the most interesting streets is Pope Hennessey Street, where some old wooden houses still stand from the days when Port Louis was the main residential centre. The Place des Armes is a beautiful esplanade leading down from the French-built Government House to the port; it is surrounded by most of the major offices, banks and Government buildings. The nearby Mauritius Institute houses the National Archives and the Natural History Museum, both dedicated to the history, flora and fauna of the Indian Ocean.

Huge crowds turn out for many of the religious festivals that take place in Port Louis; amongst the most spectacular are the Hindu festival of Maha Shivaratree and the Tamil Ceremony of the Lavadee.

Other places of interest are the Anglican and Roman Catholic cathedrals, the Jummah Mosque, the Chinese Pagoda, the Town Hall, the old theatre and the city's numerous gardens. Horse racing takes place at the Champ de Mars Hippodrome on weekends between May and October. Port Louis also has a lively and colourful nightlife with many interesting Chinese, Arab, Indian and African goods on sale.

Hotels

There is no hotel rating system.

AMBASSADOR HOTEL, corner of Sir William Newton Street and Desforges Street, ☎ 24105.
De luxe hotel.
Rooms: 96 ♙, ⊛, ☎, ⚲, ⌫.
Facilities: Restaurants, bars. Parking.
Services: TC, FC. ▤ Amex, Diners Club. Dr. on call.
Conference room – max. capacity 100.
Banquet room – max. capacity 100.

Restaurants

Most hotels have restaurants open to non-residents. Others include: *La Flore Mauricienne,* ☎ 22200 – European; *Lai Min Restaurant,* ☎ 20042 – Chinese; *Café Snow White,* ☎ 22356 – local, European and Chinese; *Café de la Cité,* ☎ 24475 – local and European; *La Bonne Marmite,* ☎ 22403 – local and European; and *Caripoule,* ☎ 21295 – Indian.

Nightclubs

Many of the restaurants have nightclubs and discotheques.

Shopping

Local handicrafts can be bought in the market, or in one of the specialist stores in Port Louis, including: *Mauritius Boutique*, Jardin de la Compagnie; *K. Sunasee*, Sir William Newton Street; and the *Cottage Industries Showroom*, Desforges Street.

Curepipe and the Central Plateau

Curepipe is centrally positioned on the island plateau and, together with the nearby residential towns of Beau Bassin, Rose Hill, Vacoas, Phoenix and Quatre-Bornes serves principally as a dormitory for the sugar industry and Port Louis. Curepipe has a business district, several public buildings, schools, theatres, arcades and gardens and is linked to Port Louis by a dual carriageway, making travel to the capital easy. Places of interest include the botanical gardens, City Hall and the spectacular Trou aux Cerfs, crater of an extinct volcano above the town, from which there is an extensive view of the island.

At Moka the Governor General's residence has fine lawns and excellent views of the sea. The many waterfalls and mountain paths are added attractions in this area for the more energetic. It is possible to view the sugar mills in action, an experience offering an insight into the way of life which for many Mauritians has remained basically unchanged for centuries.

Curepipe has a number of handicraft shops where traditional products in jade, basketwork, ivory and cloth may be purchased.

Hotels

CONTINENTAL HOTEL, 256 Royal Road, Curepipe, ☎ Curepipe 2036/7.
Centrally located, moderately priced 1st-class hotel, simply furnished.
Rooms: 52 ♪, ⊛, ⊠, ⊿, ☍. Suites available.
Facilities: Restaurants, bars. Parking. Shopping arcade. Table tennis.
Services: TC, FC. ⊟ Amex, Diners Club. Dr. on call. ♂.
Conference room – max. capacity 200.

BELLE VUE HOTEL, Royal Road, Eau Coutée, Curepipe, ☎ Curepipe 2044.
Traditional-style hotel.
Rooms: 42. ♪, ⊠, ⊿, ▽ (0700–2300). Suites available.
Facilities: Restaurants, bars. Parking.
Services: TC, FC. ⊟ Amex, Diners Club. Dr. on call.
Conference room – max. capacity 30.

Restaurants
Curepipe: *La Pontinière,* ☎ Curepipe 648 – local, European; *Le Provencal,* ☎ Curepipe 2201 – European; *Casino de Maurice,* ☎ Curepipe 12 – European; *El Cimarron,* ☎ Curepipe 1318 – European; *Maharajah Restaurant,* ☎ Curepipe 532 – Indian; *Pot de Terre,* ☎ Curepipe 2204 – local, European.

Rose Hill: *Café de Chine,* ☎ 42740 – Chinese, local and European; *Magic Lantern* – Chinese, European; *Flower Pub* – Chinese, European and local food in an English pub atmosphere; *Café de France,* ☎ 41431 – Chinese; *Riverside,* ☎ 44957 – Chinese, local, European and Indian; *Talk of the Town,* ☎ 42740 – Chinese, European and local; and *Blue Mauritius,* ☎ 44097 – Chinese, European and local.

Quatre-Bornes: *Dragon Vert,* ☎ 44564 – Chinese, local; *Pavilion* – Chinese, local and European.

Vacoas: *Mandarin* – Chinese, local and European.

Nightclubs
There is a casino in Curepipe.

Shopping
Local craftwork and other souvenirs may be bought as *Ma Cabane,* Royal Road, Curepipe; *S.P.E.S. Boutique,* Arcades, Curepipe; *Lorinne,* Royal Road, Curepipe; *Women's Self-Help Boutique,* Royal Road, Rose Hill; and *Arts Métiers,* Commercial Centre, Rose Hill.

MOROCCO
Kingdom of Morocco

Geography	*286*
The Economy	*287*
How to Get There	*288*
Entry Regulations	*288*
Practical Information for the Visitor	*289*
Useful Addresses (General)	*291*
Business Information	*292*
Business Services	*293*
Useful Addresses (Business)	*293*
Rabat	*294*
Casablanca	*295*
Tangier	*296*

Size: 458,730 sq.km/177,069 sq.miles.

Population: 18.9 million (1978 est.).

Distribution: 35% in urban areas.

Population Growth Rate: 2.9% p.a.

Ethnic Composition: The majority are Arab, although 35% are of Berber origin.

Capital: Rabat Pop. 900,000.

Major Cities: Casablanca Pop. 1,900,000; Fez Pop. 399,000; Marrakech Pop. 407,000; Meknes Pop. 376,000; Tangier Pop. 189,000.

Language: Arabic is the official language, with certain Berber tribes having their own dialects. Most Moroccan Government officials and business people speak French, with some Spanish spoken in the north. English is rarely used.

Religion: The majority are Muslims. The majority of Europeans (French and Spanish) are Roman Catholics, and there is a sizeable Jewish community.

Government: Morocco is an independent hereditary monarchy. The King presides over the Cabinet and appoints its members, including the Prime Minister. The House of Representatives is the legislative body, and two-thirds of its members are elected by direct, universal suffrage. All legislation must have the approval of the King.

The main political parties are the Istiqlal, the Rassemblement National des Indépendants, the Union National des Forces Populaires (UNFP), the Union Socialiste des Forces Populaires (USFP) and the Mouvement Populaire. Increasing control by the monarchy over the Government has weakened the political parties, and until recently the Istiqlal and the UNFP refused to participate in government for this reason. The former is now one of four opposition parties whose leaders are Cabinet members.

MOROCCO

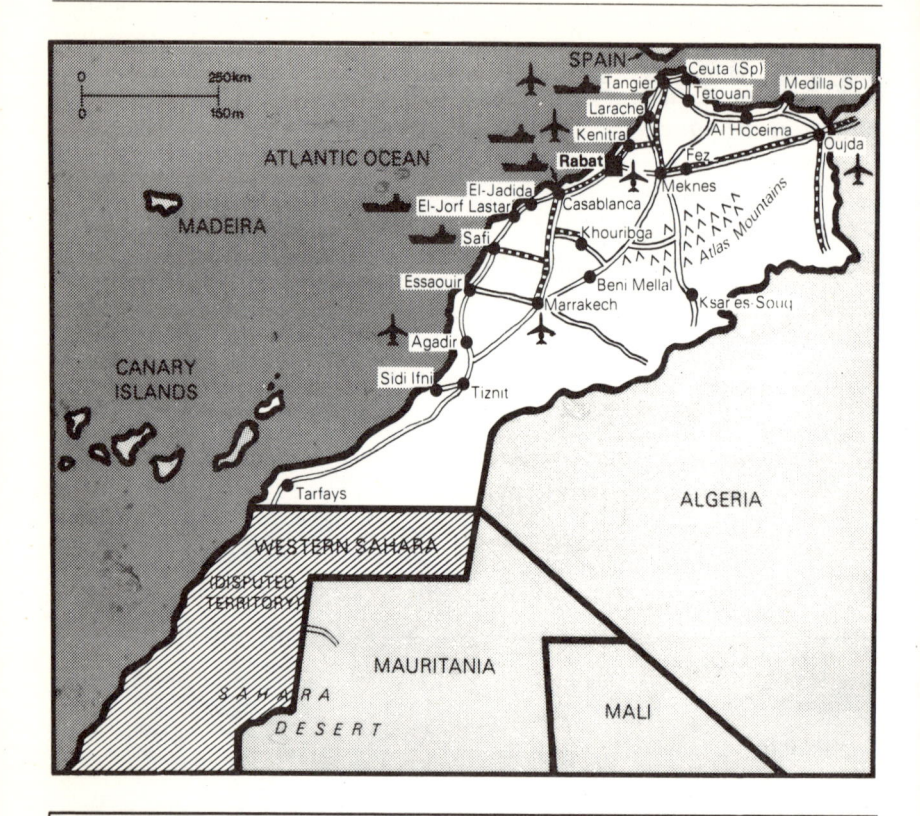

GEOGRAPHY

The landscape is one of great contrast with the dominant feature being the Atlas Mountain range – the High Atlas to the south reaches a height of more than 4,000m/13,130ft. Between these mountains and the Atlantic stretch the fertile plains where the majority of the population is concentrated, while to the south and east lie the dry steppes, eventually merging into the Sahara desert.

The partition of the Spanish Sahara was agreed between Mauritania and Morocco in 1976 when the new frontier was established. The Moroccan annexation of the Western Sahara is not recognised by Algeria, which is actively backing the Polisario Front, who claim independence for the entire area and are engaged in guerrilla activities against the occupying Moroccan troops.

Climate
The Moroccan climate is essentially Mediterranean, although inland temperatures are more extreme. Summer temperatures around the coast average 22°c/72°F, while inland they may rise to 38°c/100°F and over. Winters are mild, with average temperatures of 10°c/50°F in the coastal regions and below 5°c/41°F in the mountain areas.

Agriculture
Just over half the working population are engaged in agriculture, which accounts for

about 21% of the GDP. Agriculture is sharply divided into the modern and traditional sectors – the majority of Moroccan farms are small with crops grown for local consumption, while the larger farms, established by European settlers, concentrate on production for market and export purposes. This situation is gradually changing. Land formerly owned by foreigners is now being redistributed and cooperatives have been established.

Main Crops: cereals, citrus fruits and vegetables. The cultivation of sugar beet, cotton and sunflowers is expanding rapidly.

Mineral Resources: phosphates, iron ore, lead, zinc, copper.

THE ECONOMY

Gross National Product (1978): US$53.45 billion.

Per Capita Income (1978): US$670.

Foreign Trade (1978): Total Imports – US$2.63 billion. Total Exports – US$1.49 billion.

Main Trading Partners: Imports – France, USA, West Germany, Spain, Italy, Iraq, UK. Exports – France, West Germany, Italy, UK, Spain, Poland.

Morocco is the world's largest exporter of phosphates. World phosphate prices have fallen sharply from their 1974 peak, and in 1978 phosphates accounted for only about 32% of total exports by value.

The 1973–7 5-Year Plan concentrated on the development of phosphate mining and food-processing industries as well as general industrial expansion and the development of tourism. Manufacturing industries have grown rapidly, particularly in the fields of textiles, construction materials, chemicals and food processing (mainly for export).

Morocco's traditional visible trade deficit is offset to some extent by receipts from tourism and remittances from Moroccan workers overseas.

Future development plans are expected to concentrate on the expansion of light manufacturing industries and agricultural and social development, with less emphasis on large industrial projects.

A trade agreement between the EEC and Morocco was concluded in 1976, and the EEC is now Morocco's major trading partner. Morocco also has growing economic links with the major Arab oil producers, especially Saudi Arabia and Kuwait, and an important trade agreement was signed with the USSR in 1978.

Major Industries: phosphates, sugar refining, textiles, chemicals, food and tobacco processing.

Main Commodities Traded: Exports – phosphates, fruits and vegetables, canned fish. Imports – sugar, wheat, crude oil, machinery, chemicals.

International Affiliations: UN, IBRD, OAU, ADB, AL, BADEA.

MOROCCO

HOW TO GET THERE

Air
There are international airports at Agadir, Casablanca, Fez, Marrakech, Rabat and Tangier; all are linked by direct flights to many European cities.

Royal Air Maroc flies from Algiers, Brussels, Cairo, Dakar, Frankfurt, Geneva, Las Palmas, Lisbon, London, Madrid, Marseille, Milan, Montreal, New York, Paris and Tunis.

Major airlines flying to Morocco are Aeroflot, Air France, Alitalia, British Airways, British Caledonian, Iberia, Pan Am and Sabena.

Flying times to Casablanca: from London, 3¼ hours; from New York, 8 hours.

Distances of airport from city centres: Agadir – 8km/5 miles; Casablanca – 30km/18 miles; Fez/Sais – 10km/6 miles; Marrakech/Menara – 3½km/2 miles; Meknes/Mezergues – 2km/1 mile; Rabat/Sale – 2km/1 mile; Tangier/Boukhaf – 12km/7 miles.

Sea
Frequent passenger and car ferries operate from Gibraltar, Algeciras and Malaga to Tangier.

Road
The ferry services mentioned above carry cars – alternatively there is access to Morocco from Algeria at Oujda.

The following documents are needed to take a car into Morocco: International Certificate of Motor Insurance (green card) or Moroccan Insurance Certificate, International Driving Licence, car registration book.

Rail
There is a direct connection from Paris via Bordeaux, Madrid, Algeciras and ferry to Tangier, and on to Casablanca. Regular services to Morocco run from Oran in Algeria.

ENTRY REGULATIONS

Visas
Nationals from the following countries do not require visas: Andorra, Argentina, Australia, Austria, Bahrain, Belgium, Brazil, Canada, Chile, Congo, Denmark, Egypt, Finland, France, Greece, Guinea, Iceland, Indonesia, Iran, Iraq, Ireland, Italy, Ivory Coast, Japan, Kuwait, Lebanon, Liberia, Liechtenstein, Luxembourg, Mali, Mexico, Monaco, Netherlands, New Zealand, Niger, Norway, Oman, Pakistan, Peru, Philippines, Puerto Rico, Qatar, Romania, San Marino, Saudi Arabia, Senegal, Spain, Sudan, Sweden, Switzerland, Tunisia, Turkey, United Kingdom (including the Channel Islands), USA, Venezuela and Yugoslavia.

Visitors from all these countries may stay for a period of up to 3 months, after which they must register with the police if an extension of their stay is required.

Nationals from all other countries require visas, obtainable from Moroccan Embassies abroad. Applications from holders of Indian, Jordanian, Libyan, Palestinian and Syrian passports are always referred at additional cost to the applicant. Visitors arriving without the necessary visa can obtain a permit for a 72-hour stay, provided they hold an outward ticket.

Nationals of Israel and South Africa are not usually permitted to enter Morocco.

Evidence in a passport of a previous or planned visit to Israel may adversely affect the granting of a visa.

Health Regulations
International Certificates of Vaccination against smallpox, cholera and yellow fever are only required if arriving from infected areas. However, all visitors are advised to have smallpox and TAB inoculations.

Customs
Currency: No Moroccan currency may be imported or exported by travellers. There are no restrictions on the amount of foreign currency which may be brought into Morocco. It is sometimes difficult to re-exchange Moroccan currency on departure, so it is advisable to change only small amounts of foreign currency at a time while staying in Morocco.

Duty-free articles: 400g tobacco, 200 cigarettes or 50 cigars. 1 bottle of wine or spirits. Personal effects such as cameras, tape recorders, typewriters, etc., limited to 1 of each item per person.

Commercial samples may be temporarily imported on payment of a deposit, which is refundable if the samples are re-exported within 12 months.

PRACTICAL INFORMATION FOR THE VISITOR

1. Currency
Monetary Unit – dirham (DH), divided into 100 centimes.
Notes – 5, 10, 50, 100 dirhams.
Coins – 1, 2, 5, 10, 20, 50 centimes; 1 dirham.

Banking Hours
Winter – 0815–1130
            1415–1630 Monday to Friday
Summer – 0830–1130
             1500–1700 Monday to Friday

The *Banque du Maroc*, 22 Avenue Mohammed V, B.P. 45, Rabat, ☎ 20531/30026, is the national central bank of issue. All banks formerly under foreign control are now at least 50% Moroccan-owned.

The *Banque Marocaine du Commerce Extérieur*, 174 Boulevard Mohammed V, Casablanca, is the leading commercial bank.

Other Banks
Arab Bank Ltd, 174 Boulevard Mohammed V, Casablanca.

Banque Marocaine pour l'Afrique et l'Orient (formerly British Bank of the Middle East), 80 Avenue Lallar Yacout, Casablanca, ☎ 72401, 67441, 26887.

All of the major banks have branches in the cities and main towns.

2. Electricity Supply
Casablanca, Rabat, Tangier – 110/220v AC 50Hz.
Marrakech – 115v AC 50Hz.
Fez – 110v AC 50Hz.
Plugs: 2-pin round.

3. Weights and Measures
The metric system is in use.

4. Media
Radiodiffusion Télévision Marocaine broadcasts in Arabic, French, Berber, Spanish and English. Television programmes are in both French and Arabic. A foreign radio service from Morocco is broadcast in Arabic, French and English.

Newspapers and Journals
Le Matin, Maroc Soir, Al-Bayane – Casablanca, *L'Opinion, Al Alam, Al Anba* – Rabat.

A wide range of weekly and monthly periodicals are also published. There is no regular trade press.

5. Medical Care
The better health facilities are located in Casablanca and Rabat.

It is not advisable to drink tap water, and care should be taken with fresh fruit and vegetables. Typhoid and paratyphoid are endemic and TAB inoculations are recommended.

6. Telephone, Telex and Postal Services
International telex facilities are available. The following hotels have telex facilities available to non-residents:

Rabat – Hilton Hotel, Tour Hassan Hotel.

Casablanca – El Mansour Hotel, Marhaba Hotel.

7. Public Holidays
1 January	New Year's Day
3 March	Fête du Trône
1 May	Labour Day
9 July	King Hassan's Birthday
18 November	Independence Day

The following Muslim holidays are also observed: *Mouled, Eid el Fitr, Eid el Adha, el Hijra.*

Local festivals, or *moussems*, are held in different parts of Morocco throughout the year. Times vary according to the Muslim calendar.

Sunday is the weekly holiday in Morocco, although many companies and government offices work only a half day on Fridays.

8. Time
GMT.

9. Internal Transport
Air
Internal air services connect Casablanca, Rabat, Tangier, Marrakech, Agadir, Fez, Tetouan, Oujda and Al Hoceima.

Airline Offices in Casablanca
Air France	☎ 274242.
Air India	☎ 271122.
British Caledonian	☎ 278079, 260958.
Iberia	☎ 279600.
KLM	☎ 272729.
Lufthansa	☎ 223027, 223210.
Pan Am	☎ 271122.
PIA	☎ 221018, 269273.
Royal Maroc	☎ 271122.
SAS	☎ 224184.
Swissair	☎ 271234.

Rail
A daily service operates from Casablanca to Tangier (6 hours). Also, services operate from Casablanca to Marrakech, Rabat, Fez, Meknes and onwards to Oujda and the Algerian border.

Road
Good bus services to all parts of the country are run by the Compagnie des Transports Marocains.

There are two kinds of taxis: the *petit* taxis, normally painted red, offer the cheapest service but do not carry baggage as do the larger taxis.

Car Hire Firms

Avis
Agadir	☎ 2755.
Casablanca	☎ 272424.
Marrakech	☎ 30745.
Rabat	☎ 20888.
Tangier	☎ 33031.

Hertz
Agadir	☎ 3939.
Casablanca	☎ 223220.
Fez	☎ 22812.
Marrakech	☎ 31680.
Rabat	☎ 34475.
Tangier	☎ 33322.

Locoto
  Casablanca ☎ 270500.

An International Driving Licence is required.

10. Tipping
Taxis – large: 10%.
  small: 50 centimes to DH 1.

Hotels/restaurants – a service charge of 10–15% is usually added to the bill. A small tip of DH 2–3 is usual for hotel porters.

Porters – DH 1 to DH 1.50 per bag, depending on weight.

11. Social Customs
The customs and mores of the people living in Morocco's cities and large towns basically centre around the Arab culture, while in rural areas Berber traditions still prevail. However, both cultures are unified in their observance of the Islamic fatih.

Alcohol is not prohibited in Morocco, although its availability is likely to be restricted during the month of Ramadan.

Within the business community the Muslim code of practice is less strictly adhered to and, under the influence of the French and Spanish communities, social customs tend to be more along European lines.

USEFUL ADDRESSES (GENERAL)

Rabat
British Embassy: 17 Boulevard de la Tour Hassan, B.P. 45, ☎ 20905/6.

Canadian Embassy: 13 Bis Rue Jaafar es Sadiq, Rabat-Agdal, B.P. 709, ☎ 71375/6.

Dutch Embassy: 40 Rue de Tunis, B.P. 329, ☎ 33512/3.

French Embassy: 6 Avenue Mohamed V, ☎ 20421/6.

Japanese Embassy: 19 Avenue Tarik Ibn Ziad, ☎ 22159, 30146.

Swiss Embassy: Square de Berkane, B.P. 169, ☎ 24695, 31024.

US Embassy: 2 Avenue de Marrakech, B.P. 99, ☎ 30361/2.

West German Embassy: 7 Rue Mohammed el Fatih, B.P. 235, ☎ 32532.

National Office of Tourism: 22 Avenue d'Alger, ☎ 21252.

Syndicat d'Initiative: Rue Patrice Lumumba, ☎ 23272.

Wagons-Lits Tourisme: 1 Avenue Al Amir Moulay Abdallah, ☎ 22645/6.

Casablanca
British Consulate-General: 60 Boulevard d'Anfa, B.P. 762, ☎ 261440.

Dutch Consulate-General: Algemene Bank Marokko S.A., Place du 16 Novembre, Immeuble des Habous, Passage du Grand Socco, B.P. 478, ☎ 221712, 221820.

French Consulate: Avenue du Prince-Moulay Abdallah, B.P. 36.

Swiss Consulate: 79 Mahaj Al-Hassan At Tani (Avenue Hassan II), B.P. 5, ☎ 260211/12.

US Consulate-General: 8 Boulevard Moulay Youssef, B.P. 80, ☎ 260521/23.

West German Consulate: 42 Avenue de l'Armée Royale, B.P. 165, ☎ 264872/3.

Wagons-Lits Tourisme: 60 Rue de Foucauld, ☎ 261211/4.

American Express Authorised Representative: Voyages Schwartz, 112 Avenue du Prince Moulay Abdallah, ☎ 222946/273133.

Tangier

British Consulate-General: 52 Rue d'Angleterre, B.P. 2033, ☎ 35895/7.

French Consulate: 2 Place de France, B.P. 401.

Dutch Consulate: Immeuble 'Miramonte', 47 Avenue Hassan II, ☎ 31245.

West German Consulate: 47 Avenue Hassan II, ☎ 21600.

US Consulate-General: Chemin des Amoureux, ☎ 35904.

Syndicat d'Initiative: Rue Velazquez, ☎ 35486.

National Office of Tourism: 29 Boulevard Pasteur, ☎ 32996.

Wagon-Lits Tourisme: 86 Rue de la Liberté, ☎ 31640.

American Express Authorised Representative: Voyages Schwartz, 76 Avenue Mohammed V, 33459/33471.

Other American Express Authorised Representatives
Voyages Schwartz, Rue de Hôtel Deville, Immeuble 'Freres', Agadir.
Voyages Schwartz, Rue Mauritania, Immeuble 'Mouataouakil' 1, Marrakech, ☎ 33321.

Other Wagons-Lits Tourisme Offices
26 Avenue des Forces Armées Royales, Agadir, ☎ 3528. Immeuble du Grand Hotel, Boulevard Mohammed V, Fez, ☎ 22958. 122 Avenue Mohammed V, Marrakech, ☎ 31687. Immeuble Sifiche, 1 Zenkat Ghana, Meknes, ☎ 21995/6. Place Mohammed V, Oujda, ☎ 2520.

BUSINESS INFORMATION

Development plans in Morocco are relatively ambitious and are likely to suffer without a recovery in phosphate earnings – there are optimistic signs that the export demand for phosphates will increase while there is a general recovery in world trade and an increased demand for fertilisers. Imports will be reduced wherever possible to improve the country's trade deficit.

State participation in industry is high and is increasingly being carried out in conjunction with local private enterprise and foreign companies. At the same time, strict measures have been introduced to control speculation and reduce inflation.

The majority of agents importing foreign goods are based in Casablanca. Agency agreements are governed by the general rules on liabilities and contracts under Moroccan law.

Import and Exchange Control Regulations

Although Morocco is in the Franc Zone, exchange control measures apply to transactions within that area as well as with the rest of the world.

Certain restrictions regarding import licences have been relaxed, and for some imported goods an *engagement d'importation* is sufficient to clear goods through Customs. A *certificat d'importation* issued by the Ministry of Commerce may be necessary for certain specified goods.

Business Hours
Government Offices
Winter – 0830–1200
1430–1800 Monday to Friday
0800–1300 Saturday
Summer – 0830–1200
1600–1900 Monday to Friday
0800–1300 Saturday
During Ramadan – 0900–1400 Monday to Friday

Business Houses
0900–1200
1500–1800/1900 Monday to Friday
Most business houses are open on Saturday morning.

Many business people and government officials are on holiday from mid-July to mid-August, when some businesses virtually close down. Visitors are advised to avoid a trip to Morocco during this period, and also during the period of Ramadan.

Business Events
An International Trade Fair is held every other year (1981, 1983, etc.) in Casablanca, usually during the spring. For further information contact: International Fair, 11 Rue Jules Mauran, Casablanca.

BUSINESS SERVICES

Publicity Agencies
Agence Marocaine de Publicité, 88 Boulevard Mohammed, Casablanca.
Havas Maroc, 61 Avenue de l'Armée Royale, Casablanca.
Publivente, 71 Rue Allal ben Abdullah, Casablanca.
Luri, 18 Rue Sanlucar, Tangier.

Translation
Assimil, 71 Rue Allal ben Abdullah, Casablanca ☎ 267567.
Ecole Berlitz, 10 Avenue de l'Armée Royale, Casablanca, ☎ 268932.

USEFUL ADDRESSES (BUSINESS)

British Chamber of Commerce for Morocco: 291 Boulevard Mohammed V, Casablanca.

Chambre de Commerce et d'Industrie de Casablanca, 98 Boulevard Mohammed V, B.P. 423, Casablanca.

MOROCCO

Chambre Française de Commerce et d'Industrie du Maroc, 15 Avenue Mers Sultan, B.P. 73, Casablanca.

Confédération Générale Economique Marocaine (CGEM), 23 Boulevard Mohammed Abdouh, Casablanca.

La Fédération des Chambres de Commerce et d'Industrie du Maroc, 11 Avenue Allal ben Abdullah, B.P. 218, Rabat.

Ministry of Finance, Rabat, ☎ 27171, 30552.

Ministry of Information, Rabat, ☎ 31705, 32016.

Ministry of Trade, Industry, Mines & Merchant Shipping, Rabat, ☎ 51073, 27511.

Office de Commercialisation et d'Exportation, 45 Avenue des Forces Armées Royales, Casablanca.

MAJOR CITIES AND TOWNS

Rabat

Rabat was founded in the 12th century but only regained its former importance when the French established the city as the administrative capital of Morocco at the beginning of this century. The modern aspect of Rabat, with its broad avenues and luxurious homes and office blocks, dates from this period, yet blends in well with the old city. The ancient city of Chellah to the east is one of Rabat's most interesting sights, although only the ruined mosque and ancient tombs remain to be seen today.

The Kasbah of the Oudaias has many fascinating attractions including a small carpet factory open to visitors, and various craftsmen working out in the open street. The Museum of Moroccan Arts is also here. The Royal Palace and Mosque and other government offices occupy the centre of the city in an enclosed area called the Mechouar.

Hotels

The Ministry of Tourism hotel classification ranges from 5 star to 1 star.

RABAT-HILTON, Aviation-Souissi, B.P. 450, ☎ 72151.
A de luxe (5-star) hotel built in extensive grounds, 5 minutes' drive from the city centre.
Rooms: 259 ♪, ⅏, 🍎, ⛉, △, 🕾. Suites available.
Facilities: International and Moroccan cuisine. Coffee shop, cocktail lounge, bar. Nightclub. Shops. Swimming, tennis, golf. Hairdresser, boutique. Car hire.
Services: TC, FC. 🖃 Amex, Carte Blanche, Diners Club, Eurocard. Dr. on call. 🛎, ♂.
Conference rooms – max. capacity 1,000.
Banquet rooms – max. capacity 900.

DE LA TOUR HASSAN, 26 Avenue Abderrahman Annega, B.P. 14, ☎ 21401.
Modern de luxe (5-star) hotel in heart of city, luxuriously decorated in Moorish style.
Rooms: 150.
Facilities: Restaurant, dining room, roof-top supper club with international and Moroccan cuisine. Swimming, sauna. Hairdresser, boutique, Golf. Conference and banquet rooms.

RABAT CHELLAH, 2 Rue d'Ifni, ☎ 24052.
Modern 1st-class (4-star) hotel in city centre.
Rooms: 100 ♪, ⅏, △, 🕾.
Facilities: Restaurant, grill, bar. Boutique.
Services: TC, FC. 🖃 Amex, Diners Club. Dr. on call. 🛎, ♂.
No conference facilities.

Restaurants

The restaurants in the larger hotels offer both international and Moroccan cuisine. Other include: *L'Oasis*, 7 Rue al Osgofia, ☎ 22185 – French and Moroccan; *Kabbaj Palace*, Rue Mokhtar el Souissi, ☎ 34241 – Moroccan; *Koutoubia*, 10 Rue Pierre Parent, ☎ 26125 – Moroccan; *Chez Pierre*, Avenue Mohammed V, ☎ 23090 – French; *Le Capri*, Place des Alaouites, ☎ 33281 – Italian; *Hong Kong*, 261 Avenue Mohammed V, ☎ 23594 – Chinese; *Le Mandarin*, Avenue Soumaya, ☎ 24699 – Chinese.

Nightclubs

Aquarium, Boulevard Mohammed V; *El Farah,* Hotel de la Tour Hassan, ☎ 21401; *Hilton Hotel Night Club,* ☎ 72243; *La Cage,* Place Bremond, ☎ 20334; *L'Entonnoir,* Place Bremond, ☎ 34132.

Entertainment

Sports

Tennis – *Olympique Marocain*, ☎ 22351. Riding – *Club Equestre*, Route du Zaers ☎ 50294. Golf – *Dar Es Salaam Royal Club* (18 holes) ☎ 20205. *Souissi Royal Golf Club* (9 holes) ☎ 40359. Sailing – *Royal Yacht Club* ☎ 20264.

Shopping

The main shopping area is concentrated around Avenue Mohammed V and Avenue Allal ben Abdullah. Traditional Moroccan wares are sold in the Medina, where visitors will find a fine selection of carpets, leather work, pottery, jewellery and embroidered goods.

Casablanca

Casablanca is Morocco's main port and, as the principal commercial and industrial centre of the country, has developed into a modern, bustling, European-style city. In contrast, the city is skirted by a mass of *bidonvilles*, or shanty towns, with severe problems of overcrowding and poverty.

Unlike Fez or Marrakech, Casablanca does not abound with buildings and places of great historic interest. The *souks* in the Medina are notably tourist-orientated. The new Medina in the eastern part of the city houses the Royal Palace, Great Mosque and Mahakma (law courts) – the latter are open to non-Muslims and constitute a fine example of modern Moorish architecture.

Hotels

EL MANSOUR, 27 Avenue de l'Armée Royale, ☎ 265011. De luxe (5-star) hotel in heart of business centre.
Rooms: 250 ♫, ⌂, ♃, ⎕, ♁. Suites available.
Facilities: International and Moroccan restaurants, coffee shop, bar. Sauna, massage. Boutique, hairdresser.
Services: TC, FC. ✉ Amex, Diners Club. Dr. on call. Airline, car hire, travel agency. S, ♂.
Conference rooms – max. capacity 1,200.
Banquet rooms – max. capacity 800.

MARHABA, 63 Avenue de l'Armée Royale, ☎ 224199.
Modern 5-star hotel in heart of business district.
Rooms: 135 ♫, ⅏, ⌂, ♃, ♁, ☍. Suites available.
Facilities: Restaurants, cocktail lounge. Roof terrace. Sauna, massage. Boutique, hairdresser. Travel agency, car hire.
Services: TC, FC. ✉ Amex and Diners Club. Dr. on call. S, ♂.
Conference and banquet rooms – max. capacity 300.

ANFA PLAGE, Boulevard de la Corniche, ☎ 58242.
Modern 4-star hotel in residential centre, near sea.
Rooms: 130 ♫, ⅏, ⌂, ♃, ☍. Suites available.

Facilities: 2 restaurants, 3 bars. Swimming, tennis. Nightclub. Hairdresser.
Services: TC, FC, ☐ Amex, Diners Club. Dr. on call. S, ♂.
Conference room – max. capacity 30.
Banquet rooms – max. capacity 200.

TRANSATLANTIQUE, 79 Rue Colbert, ☎ 60761/2. 1st class (4-star) hotel in heart of business centre.
Rooms: 60 ☎.
Facilities: Restaurant, cocktail lounge.

Restaurants
Seafood: *La Mer,* El Hank, ☎ 21084; *Le Petit Rocher,* El Hank, ☎ 21195; *Le Cabestan,* El Hank, ☎ 21060; *A Ma Bretagne,* Ain Diab, ☎ 52111; *Le Clapotis,* Ain Diab, ☎ 58144.

Moroccan: *Al Mounia,* 111 Rue du Prince Moulay Abdullah, ☎ 22686; *Sijilmassa,* Ain Diab, ☎ 58233; *L'Etoile Marocaine,* 107 Rue Allal ben Abdullah, ☎ 64781.

Spanish: *La Corrida,* Rue Gay-Lussac, ☎ 78155; *Tio Pepe,* Boulevard de la Corniche, ☎ 58189.

Others: *Don Camillo,* 13 Rue de Verdun, ☎ 61644 – Italian; *Viking,* 22 Rue Ferhat Hachad, ☎ 78266 – Scandinavian; *La Pagode,* 95 Rue Ferhat Hachad, ☎ 77185 – Chinese.

Nightclubs
Don Quichotte, 44 Place Mohammed V, ☎ 22051; *Embassy,* 2 Boulevard Mohammed V, ☎ 65707; *Le Bahia,* Boulevard de la Corniche, ☎ 58242; *La Notte,* Boulevard de la Corniche, ☎ 58361; *La Rose Orientale,* 4 Rue Nolly, ☎ 75589; *Puerta del Sol,* 7 Avenue Hassan II, ☎ 22772.

Entertainment
Sports
Tennis – *Tennis Romandie,* ☎ 51640. Golf – *Golf Club d'Anfa* (9 holes) ☎ 51026.

Shopping
Along the Boulevard Mohammed V are many fine shops, mainly filled with French imported goods which tend to be very expensive. The government-controlled *Maison de l'Artisanat,* opposite the Hotel Marhaba, sells goods at fixed prices and will arrange shipment abroad.

Tangier
Tangier's proximity to Europe has established it as a city with an international flavour, and yet it has retained much of the traditional Moroccan charm. The old city overlooking the port is of the most interest and adjoins the Gran Socco, believed to be the original site of the Forum in the Roman city of Tinghis. This is the heart of Old Tangier where the Kasbah is to be found, containing many fine buildings, the Museums of Moroccan Art and Antiquities and the 300-year-old Royal Palace. The Great Mosque which dates from the late 17th century stands in the old town.

Hotels
LES ALMOHADES, Avenue des Forces Armées Royales, B.P. 311, ☎ 36025. De luxe (5-star) hotel facing sea, about 1 mile from city centre.
Rooms: 150 🍴, 🍽, 🛁, ☎, ⛱, 📺. Suites available.
Facilities: International and Moroccan restaurants, bars. Discotheque. Sauna, swimming, tennis. Shops, hairdressers. Car hire.
Services: TC, FC, ☐ Amex, Diners Club. Dr. on call. S, ♂.

Conference room – max. capacity 300.
Banquet room – max. capacity 220.

EL MINZAH, 85 Rue de la Liberté, ☎ 35885.
De luxe (5-star) hotel in traditional Moorish style, 12km/7½ miles from airport.
Rooms: 100 ☎. Suites available.
Facilities: Restaurant with French and Moroccan cuisine, bar, coffee shop. Evening entertainment. Swimming, tennis, golf.

Services: ✉ Amex, Diners Club. Conference and banquet rooms.

INTER-CONTINENTAL, Boulevard de Paris, ☎ 36053.
Modern de luxe (5-star) hotel near city centre.
Rooms: 130 ♪ (in some rooms), ⚌, ⚭, ⚏, ⚎. Suites available.
Facilities: 2 restaurants (European and Moroccan). Oriental nightclub, discotheque. Roof terrace. Sauna, swimming. Boutique. Car hire.
Services: TC, FC. ✉ Amex, Bankamericard, Carte Blanche, Diners Club, Eurocard, Master Charge. Dr. on call. $, ♂.
Conference room – max. capacity 100.
Banquet rooms – max. capacity 200.

CHELLAH, 47–49 Rue Allal ben Abdullah, ☎ 36388.
1st-class (4-star) hotel near city centre, 500 yards from beach.
Rooms: 180 ♪, ⚌, ⚭, ⚏, ⚎, ⚐, ⚑.
Facilities: Restaurant, lounge bar. Nightclub. Heated swimming pool. Boutique. Car hire.
Services: TC, FC. ✉ Amex cards. Dr. on call. $, ♂.
Conference and banquet rooms – max. capacity 350.

GRAND HOTEL VILLA DE FRANCE, 143 Rue de Hollande. ☎ 31475.
Traditional style 1st-class (4-star) hotel overlooking the Kasbah and the Straits of Gibraltar.
Rooms: 60.
Facilities: Restaurant (Moroccan and French cuisine), bars and patio. Swimming. Boutique.

Restaurants
Moroccan: *Damascus,* 2 Avenue Prince Moulay Abdullah, ☎ 34730; *Hammadi,* Rue d'Italie, ☎ 34514; *Marhaba,* Kasbah, ☎ 37643.
French: *La Grenouille,* Rue Rembrandt, ☎ 39042; *Guittas,* Rue San Francisco, ☎ 37333; *Alhambra,* Rue Docteur Fumey, ☎ 21021; *La Clairière,* Route du Cap Spartel, ☎ 33885.
Spanish: *Manila,* Boulevard Pasteur, ☎ 34632; *Montero,* Rue Belgique, ☎ 39114; *Pilo,* Rue de Fez, ☎ 34569; *Romero,* Avenue Prince Moulay Abdullah. ☎ 32277.
Others: *Les Ambassadeurs,* Avenue Prince Moulay Abdullah, ☎ 35704 – Italian; *La Pagode,* Rue Balmes, ☎ 38086 – Vietnamese, Chinese.

Nightclubs
African Rhythms, Avenue Prince Heritier, ☎ 33439; *Churchill Club,* 11 Rue Sanlucar, ☎ 26662; *Koutoubia Palace,* 7 Rue Sanlucar, ☎ 39525; *Morocco Palace,* Avenue Prince Moulay Abdullah, ☎ 39814.

Entertainment
Sports
Tennis – *Tennis Emsallah,* ☎ 38026; *Tennis Municipal Club,* ☎ 37324. Golf – *Country Club,* Boubanah (9 holes), ☎ 38925. Sailing and sea fishing – *Yacht Club,* ☎ 39939.

Shopping
Every variety of bazaar and shop can be found in the Medina where gold, silver, brass, copper, silk and wool goods are on sale. Bargaining is an integral part of any sale.

MOZAMBIQUE
People's Republic of Mozambique

Geography *299*
The Economy *300*
How to Get There *301*
Entry Regulations *302*
Practical Information for the Visitor *302*
Useful Addresses (General) *304*
Business Information *304*
Business Services *305*
Useful Addresses (Business) *305*
Maputo *305*
Beira *306*

Size: 783,030 sq.km/302,329 sq.miles.

Population: 11.75 million (1979 est.).

Distribution: 8% in urban areas.

Density: 15 persons per sq.km/38.9 per sq.mile.

Population Growth Rate: 4.6% p.a. (1970–80).

Ethnic Composition: The main ethnic groups are the Makua-Lomwe, Thonga and Shona. Other sub-groups and tribes include the Chopi, Tonga, Makonde, Yas, Chewa, Nyanja, Shangona, Ronga, Tswa, Hlengere, Tere, Ndan and Manyika. There are also small communities of Asians and Europeans.

Capital: Maputo Pop. 384,000.

Major Towns: Beira Pop. 140,000; Nampula Pop. 50,000.

Language: Portuguese is the official language. The wide variety of African languages correspond to the ethnic divisions, with smaller groups speaking their respective local dialects. Some English is spoken in business and Government circles. Swahili is spoken in the northern coastal areas.

Religion: Most people uphold traditional African beliefs, although there are some Muslims and Roman Catholics.

Government: Full independence from Portugal was gained on 25th June 1975. FRELIMO is now the sole political party; its President is also head of state. The first elections after independence, held in late 1977, elected representatives to Local Assemblies by universal suffrage. The Local Assemblies themselves elect members of the City and District Assemblies, who in turn elect representatives to the 10 Provincial Assemblies. The Provincial Assemblies return delegates to the National Popular Assembly.

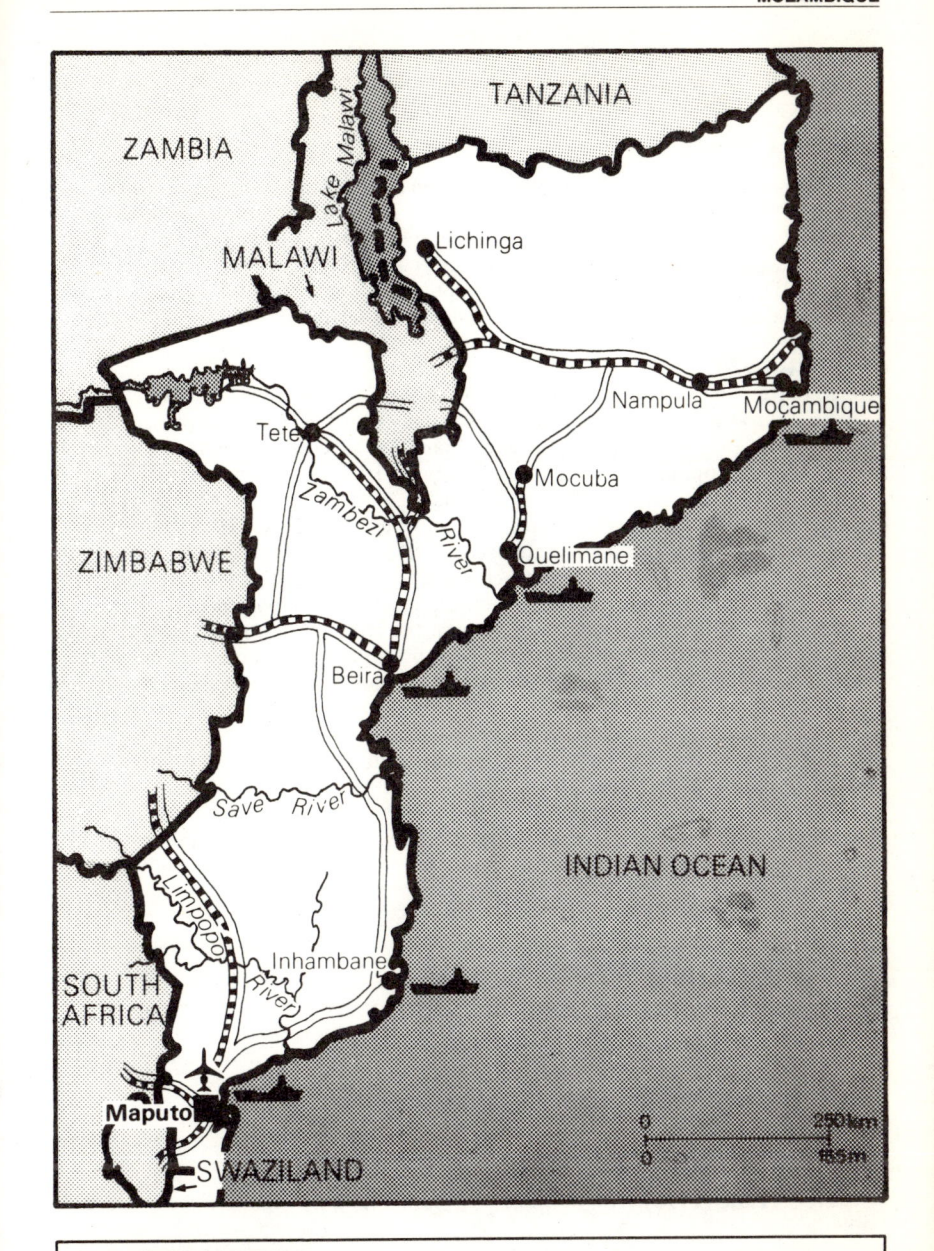

GEOGRAPHY

Mozambique lies in the south-east of continental Africa. Its eastern coastline on the Indian Ocean is 2,470km/1,545 miles long. There are 3 major geographical regions: the eastern coastal plain; the broad upland areas gently sloping to the sea; and the higher hills and mountains to the east of the country. The Limpopo, Zambezi and Save rivers are the largest flowing through Mozambique to the Indian Ocean. A significant part of Lake Malawi is Mozambiquan territory.

Climate

The 2 main seasons are the hot wet season from October to March and the cooler dry season between April and September. Both rainfall and temperature depend upon the direction of the winds, which cause considerable variation from year to year. Wet-season temperatures average between 27°C/80°F and 29°C/85°F, becoming cooler in the uplands. Dry-season temperatures in Maputo are some 8°C/15°F cooler than the wet-season averages, with the difference lessening further north.

Agriculture

Restructuring the agricultural sector is one of the Government's principal economic objectives, as there are large areas of potentially productive land at present under-utilised. Agriculture is the biggest contributor to the Gross National Product and 80–90% of the population live in rural areas. Since 1978 agriculture has been based on communal villages and state farms. The major export crops are cashew nuts, tea, cotton sugar cane, copra, sisal, groundnuts and fruit. Domestic crops of most importance are maize, rice cassava and tobacco. Forestry and livestock raising are also of some importance, although the presence of the tsetse fly over the northern part of the country has limited production, necessitating meat to be imported.

Favourable soils and climate, especially in the river valleys, encourage optimism about long-term agricultural potential, and substantial investments are now planned to develop integrated irrigation projects with complementary processing facilities in the next few years.

Main Crops: maize, rice, potatoes, groundnuts, cassava, cotton, cashew nuts, copra, tobacco, sugar cane, tea, sisal, fruits.

Mineral Resources: coal, columbo-tantalite, beryl, tourmaline, bismutite, gold, iron ore, mica, quartz, euxenite, ilmenite, tepidolite, microlite, monozite, pollucite.

THE ECONOMY

Gross National Product (1976 est.): US$1.6 billion

Per Capita Income (1976 est.): US$170

Gross Domestic Product: N.A.

Foreign Trade (1976): Total Imports – US $303 million. Total Exports – US $334 million

Main Trading Partners (1978): Imports – Zimbabwe, Iraq, South Africa, UK, France. Exports – Japan, USA, UK, Singapore, Portugal.

Upon independence the FRELIMO Government inherited an economy ruined by the destruction and sabotage caused during the years of war and the actions of some of the

MOZAMBIQUE

departing Portuguese. A pragmatic programme of economic reconstruction on socialist lines has been adopted, and Mozambique has continued to trade with South Africa. The situation in Zimbabwe led to the closure of the border and hence the loss of railway traffic to the Indian Ocean port of Beira, but hopes of trade with independent Zimbabwe are high. The loss of tourist revenue since 1975 has brought an end to another lucrative sector of the economy. The major concern of the Government is to encourage self-sufficiency in food production by substituting domestic produce for imported items. It is hoped that communal and state-organised production units will end the continuing occasional food shortages.

Although industry has been under 'state intervention' since 1976, there are some private concerns, especially in the manufacturing sector. The main manufactured products are footwear, tanned products, drinks, trucks, bicycles, tyres, cotton textiles, cement and cigarettes.

There are plans to develop the fishing industry and to expand the already successful export of shrimps. Mining potential is relatively undeveloped. There are known to be large coal reserves sufficient for export income, and columbo-tantalite extraction is already well established. Mozambique also has large iron ore deposits, important beryl mines, tourmaline, gold, bismutite, bauxite, manganese, diamonds, uranium and asbestos. Natural gas has been discovered; however, despite continuing explorations no oil has yet been found.

Infrastructure projects are being given a high priority by the government. Transport services are being improved and power-generating capacity expanded. The Cabora Bassa dam is the largest of a number of dams producing hydro-electric power and is the biggest hydro-electric scheme in Africa, exporting power to South Africa. The development of heavy industry is regarded as an essential part of the future economy. There is a state-owned oil refinery.

Mozambique has traditionally had a trade deficit, and continues to receive aid from a number of countries including Norway, Sweden and the UK. The long-term prospects are good as integrated projects encouraging energy production, mining, industrial developments and supporting agricultural production come into operation, but at present industrial production is running below capacity. The solution to the Zimbabwe conflict should greatly help the economy of Mozambique. Recent heavy flooding has damaged the economy.

Major Industries: building materials, drink, cigarettes, sugar, clothing, agricultural processing, oil refining.

Main Commodities Traded: Imports – machines and electrical equipment, transport equipment, textiles, crude oil, paper, wheat, machinery, chemicals, foodstuffs. Exports – sugar, cashew nuts, molasses, cotton, tea, sisal, shrimps, coal, textiles, timber, vegetable oils, copra, beans, cement, petroleum.

International Affiliations: UN, OAU, ADB.

HOW TO GET THERE

Air
The International airport at Mavalane (8km/5 miles from Maputo) is served by flights from London and Luanda by DETA (Mozambique Airlines); from Johannesburg and Durban by DETA and South African Airways; from Manzini (Swaziland) by DETA

and Air Swazi; from Tananarive (Madagascar) by DETA and Air Madagascar; from Lusaka by DETA and Zambian Airways; from Mtwara, Dar es Salaam and Nairobi by DETA; and from Moscow by Aeroflot. Many flights call at Beira Airport, and DETA and Air Malawi operate flights to Beira from Blantyre (Malawi). Other airlines operating to Mozambique include Interflug (GDR), TAAG (Angola) and TAP (Portugal).

Sea
There are no regular passenger services, although cargo and passenger-carrying ships occasionally call at Maputo and Beira.

Rail
A good railway service links Johannesburg with Maputo and Blantyre with Beira. It is hoped that rail links with Zimbabwe will soon be resumed.

Road
Roads link Mozambique with all neighbouring countries. The roads in the south of the country tend to be better than those in the north.

ENTRY REGULATIONS

Visas
Visas are required by all visitors, except Mozambique nationals or returning residents. Visas are obtainable from the Ministry of Foreign Affairs or from diplomatic representatives abroad. Information relating to the purpose of the visit, travel and accommodation arrangements, the length of stay and full supporting documentation is needed before a visa will be granted. All businessmen should have a letter from their company accepting financial responsibility for the visitor.

Health Regulations
International Certificates of Vaccination against smallpox, cholera and yellow fever are required. Typhoid and para-typhoid (TAB) injections are recommended.

Customs
Currency: There are no restrictions on the import of foreign currency including travellers' cheques and cheques provided they are declared on arrival. The import and export of local currency is forbidden. All foreign passport holders must change the equivalent of ESM 500 on arrival at the airport, upon departure one may change back again, less an amount deemed appropriate for the expenses of the visitor's stay.

Duty-free articles: 200 cigarettes or 50 cigars or 250 grams of tobacco. 1 litre of wine. 250cc of spirits. 250cc of toilet water. Photographic equipment and films and samples of no commercial value may be imported if they comply with local customs regulations. Small consignments of goods for personal use are exempt from duty.

Restricted articles: Drink. Drugs. Arms and amunition.

PRACTICAL INFORMATION FOR THE VISITOR

1. Currency
Monetary Unit – Mozambique escudo (ESM), divided into 100 centavos.

Notes – ESM 50, 100, 500, 1,000.
Coins – 10, 20, 50 centavos. ESM 1, 2.5, 5, 10, 20.

MOZAMBIQUE

Banking Hours
0800–1100 Monday to Friday.

All banks were nationalised and re-organised in 1978 under laws which forced closures and takeovers of various foreign and Mozambiquan banks. The Bank of Mozambique took over all liabilities and assets, with the single exception of the Banco Standard Totta de Moca. The Bank of Mozambique is responsible for currency issue.

Banco de Mozambique, Av. 25 de Setembro, Maputo.
Banco Standard Totta de Mozambique, Praca 25 de Jumbro, P.O. Box 1119, Maputo.

2. Electricity Supply
220v AC 50Hz. Various plugs are in use.

3. Weights and Measures
The metric system is in use.

4. Media
All broadcasting is state controlled. Radio Mozambique is a commercial station which transmits programmes in Portuguese and other local languages. There is no television service.

Newspapers and Journals
There are 2 daily papers: the Government-sponsored *Noticias*, published in Maputo; and *Noticias da Beira*.

Boletim da Republica de Mozambique is published 3 times weekly and contains official announcements.

Weeklies include *Brado Africans*, *Renovocas* and *Tempo*, all published in Maputo.

Monthlies of interest to businessmen include the *Monthly Digest of Statistics* and *Economia de Mozambique*.

5. Medical Care
Precautions against malaria are advisable as general protection. Water should be boiled. Bilharzia and sleeping sickness are endemic in some rural areas. Western medical facilities are very limited.

6. Telephone, Telex and Postal Services
International lines linking Mozambique to neighbouring countries are available at any time. European calls should be made between 0900 and 2300; other places in the world can be reached at other times. Calls between telephones in Mozambique may only be made during certain hours of the day.

A telex service is available in Maputo and Beira.

All correspondence to or from Mozambique should be sent by air mail.

7. Public Holidays
1 January	New Year's Day
3 February	Heroes Day
7 April	Women's Day
1 May	Labour Day
25 June	Independence Day
25 September	Armed Forces Day

The Muslim and Roman Catholic communities observe their respective festivities.

8. Time
GMT + 2.

9. Internal Transport

Air
DETA fly between Maputo and Beira, Quilimane, Angoche, Ceutimbo, Tete, Lichinga, Nampula and several other towns.

Air taxi services are available and are operated by COMAG (General Aviation Company of Mozambique). There are many small airstrips.

Mavalane Airport is 8km/5 miles from Maputo.

Beira Airport is 13km/8 miles from Beira town centre.

Airline Offices
DETA, C.P. 2060, Mavalane Airport, Maputo.

10. Tipping
Taxis – 10% of the fare.

Porters – ESM 10.

Hotels/restaurants –10% of the bill.

11. Social Customs
Many Portuguese courtesies are still observed and '*o senhor*' is the correct form of address for people who are not FRELIMO party members. Party members should be addressed as '*camarada*.'

USEFUL ADDRESSES (GENERAL)

Embassies in Maputo
France, C.P. 4781, Avenida Julius Nyerere 2361, ☎ 743444.

Germany (Federal Republic), C.P. 1595, Rua Pero de Alenque 214, ☎ 22400.

Netherlands, C.P. 1163, Rua de Antonio Bocarra 193, ☎ 74421.

Pakistan, C.P. 4745.

Switzerland, C.P. 135, Avenida Julius Nyerere 1213, ☎ 742432.

USA, C.P. 783, Rua de Mesquita 35 (3rd floor), ☎ 26051/2/3.

UK, C. P. 55, Avenida V. I. Lenine, 310, ☎ 26011.

Centro de Informaçao e Turismo, C.P. 1179, Avenida de Republica, ☎ 25011.

BUSINESS INFORMATION

From February 1976 provisions were made for the transfer of private commercial companies to state ownership. Most important industrial and agricultural enterprises are now under the control of the state. However, the Government have reaffirmed that investment from overseas is accepted as long as it concurs with their plans. The areas in which most investment potential lies are in the exploitation of mineral, oil and gas reserves, and in infrastructure and social service projects. When making tenders for contracts in Mozambique it is particularly important that full details should be given to comply with the strict conditions governing tenders. However, once permission to export to Mozambique has been granted and an import licence obtained, Government help should be available to speed payments which have in the past been delayed. All foreign trade is dealt with by ENACOMO, the import and export board.

Trade correspondence is better received if in Portuguese or Spanish than if in English. Translation facilities in Mozambique are hard to find.

The Agricultural, Commercial and Agricultural Fair (FACIM) is held in Maputo around August/September every year.

Import and Exchange Control Regulations
A General Customs Surcharge is payable on most imported goods, with additional taxes levied on luxury items including tobacco, petrol, motor vehicles, cameras and other consumer goods. Import licences are required for all goods, with priority given to certain specified items – particularly those designated as essential (e.g., foodstuffs, fuels, chemicals, raw materials, some capital goods). The lowest priority is accorded to goods competing with local produce.

Importers may purchase foreign exchange on production of an import licence. Goods of less than 2,500 ESM in value are not subject to licensing except if described as luxury goods in the current priority list. Importers must be registered and licensed with local import services before goods are ordered. Samples may be temporarily imported on payment of a deposit equal to the amount of duty payable, if they are re-exported within 1 year; the deposit will be refunded. Live animals and animal products, food and drink for resale are all subject to import and export restrictions.

Business Hours
0830–1130 Monday to Friday
1400–1700
0800–1100 Saturday
From November to April in the hotter areas:
0700–1300 Monday to Friday
0700–1100 Saturday

Business Event
An International Trade Fair (FACIM) is held annually in Maputo during September.

BUSINESS SERVICES

Clearing Agency
Agencia Nacional de Depacho is the national clearing agency.

Shipping
Agencia Nacional de Frete e Navegacao (ANFRENA), Rua de Bapamoyo 296, Maputo.
Companhia Mozambique de Navegacao, C.P. 786, Rua Joaquim Lapa 22, Maputo.
Companhia Nacional de Navegacao, C.P. 2694, Maputo.
Companhia Portuguesa de Transportes Maritimos, C.P. 2, Avenida Samora Machel 239, Maputo.

Insurance
Empresa Mozambicana de Siguros (EMOSE) is the only state-run insurance enterprise.

USEFUL ADDRESSES (BUSINESS)

Direccao Nacional de Comercio Interno, Praca 25 de Junho, Maputo.

Direccao Nacional de Comercio Externo, Praca 25 de Junho, Maputo.

Empresa das Cojas de Povo (People's Shops Organisation), C.P. 806, Maputo.

Direccao Nacional de Economica e Comercializacas Agraria, C.P. 806, Maputo.

Empresa Nacional Comercializacao (ENACOMO), C.P. 1831, Maputo.

Dirrecao Nacional Portose Caminhos de Ferro, C.P. 276, Maputo.

MAJOR CITY AND TOWN

Maputo
Maputo, formerly known as Lourenço Marques, has been the capital since 1948 and is

also the administrative capital of Maputo province. It is a busy and growing port in the south of the country on the rail route from Swaziland. The new post-independence buildings have added to the variety of architectural styles in the city, the old colonial residences and administrative buildings contrasting with those of the renowned Mozambiquan designer Pancho Guides.

Hotels

Since independence, hotels have been under state intervention. Hotel accommodation is limited, so bookings should be made well in advance. Full details of hotels and facilities available for visitors can be obtained from the Tourist Information Centre in Maputo.

HOTEL POLONA, Avenida Julius Nyerere, C.P. 1151, ☎ 741001.

HOTEL CARDOSO, Avenida Brito Camanche, C.P. 35, ☎ 741071.

HOTEL GIRASSOL, Avenida Brito Camanche, C.P. 2172, ☎ 4001/3.

Restaurants

Most hotels in Maputo have restaurants open to non-residents. Amongst the many restaurants serving local and foreign dishes are the *Another*, *Bussola*, *El Greco*, *Grelha*, *Kava Kahina*, *Macau*, *Mini Golf*, *Pekim*, *Piri-Piri*, *Ponto Final*, *Princesa*, *Vela Azul*, and *Zambi*.

Entertainment

In pre-independence days Lourenço Marques was much visited by South African tourists on account of its night-clubs, brothels, casinos and other entertainments, illegal in South Africa. This tourist trade has now ceased, though a number of restaurants have evening music and dancing. Of cultural interest are the art galleries and museums in which are displayed the work of local artists and items of historical interest; chief among these are the National History Museum, the National Arts Museum and the Museum of the Revolution. The Government is attempting to recover and encourage traditional culture in music, dance and other arts.

Shopping

Best buys: wood and ivory carvings, animal hides, woodwork, marble and bone items.

The lively municipal covered market in the town centre is good for food and craft produce. Other outdoor markets are set up in the outskirts of Maputo. Street vendors are ready to sell their wares to the visitor at any opportunity.

Beira

Once a tourist destination for visitors from Rhodesia, Beira is the 2nd city of Mozambique, although the closure of the railway line to Zimbabwe during the war years has meant that the economic significance of the town as a port has declined. It is hoped that its future will be more secure now that Zimbabwe is an independent nation.

Hotels

HOTEL EMBAIXADOR, C.P. 1249, ☎ 23121.
HOTEL DOM CARLOS, C.P. 139, ☎ 711158.
HOTEL MOÇAMBIQUE, C.P. 1690, ☎ 25011.

Restaurants

Local and Portuguese dishes are available in the *Campino*, *Arcadia*, *Jockey-Bar*, *Kanimambo*, *Piquenique*, *Luso* and *Veleiro* restaurants. Seafood and chicken dishes are particularly good.

NAMIBIA
Namibia

Geography	308
The Economy	309
How to Get There	310
Entry Regulations	310
Practical Information for the Visitor	311
Useful Addresses (General)	312
Business Information	312
Business Services	313
Useful Addresses (Business)	313
Windhoek (Otjomuise)	313

Size: 824,292 sq.km/318,250 sq.miles.

Population: 1.25 million (1977 est., including Walvis Bay).

Distribution: N.A.

Density: 1.5 persons per sq.km/3.9 per sq.mile.

Population Growth Rate: 8% p.a.

Ethnic Composition: The largest single group are the Ovambo; others include Kavango, Damara, Herero, Nama and the aboriginal San Bushmen. About 8% are of European descent.

Capital: Windhoek (Otjomuise) Pop. 75,000.

Major Towns: Walvis Bay Pop. 25,000; Keetmanshoop Pop. 17,000; Swakopmund Pop. 14,000; Luderitz Pop. 8,000.

Language: English, German and Afrikaans are the official languages, of which Afrikaans is the most widely used. African languages fall into two groups: Khoisan, of which different dialects are spoken by the San Bushman, Damara and Nama, and the various Bantu languages used by Ovambo, Kavango and Herero. There are also Tswana and Lozi speakers in eastern Namibia.

Religion: Some 80% are Christians, mostly Lutheran. Traditional beliefs are more strongly held in the north.

Government: Namibia is at present governed by a South African Administrator General, in defiance of UN General Assembly resolutions since 1966, resulting in the cancellation of the South African mandate to administer the territory and an International Court of Justice decision in 1971. In 1969 Namibia was reduced to the status of the fifth province of the Republic by the South African Government with areas having since been designated as Bantustans in accordance with South African apartheid policy. South West Africa People's Organisation of Namibia (SWAPO) guerrillas have been fighting the large numbers of South African troops in the territory since 1966. The general level of opposition, both armed and peaceful, to the South African presence has

NAMIBIA

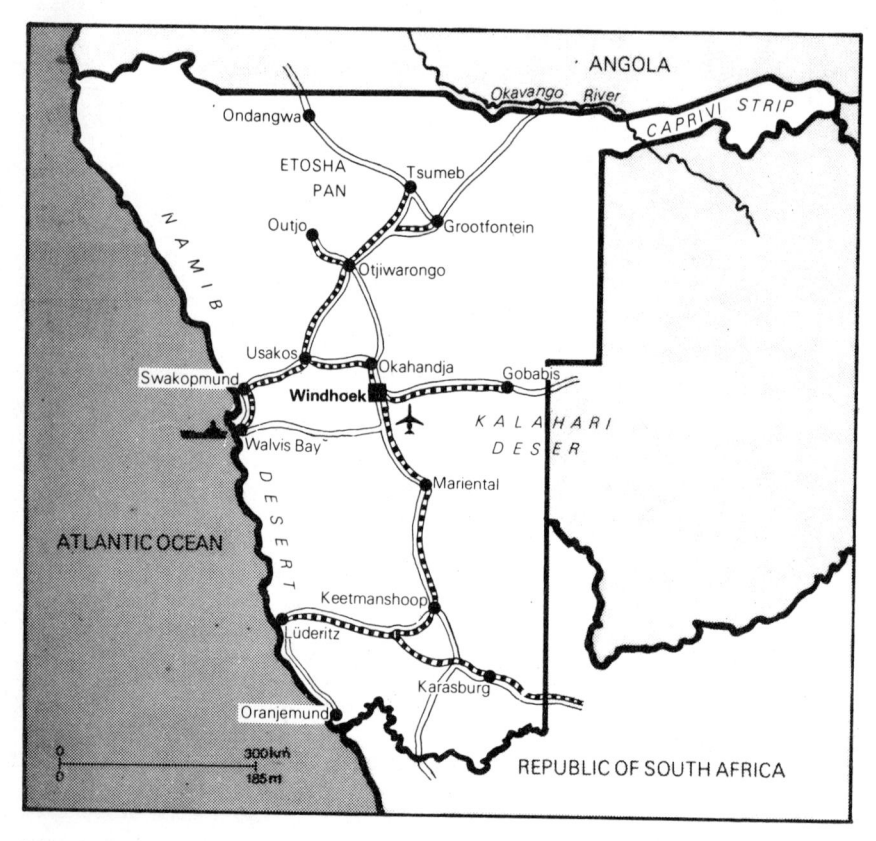

increased through the 1970s with the MPLA victory in Angola over South African-backed UNITA forces, bringing increased support for SWAPO policies inside Namibia. In 1967 the UN established the council for Namibia to administer the territory; however South Africa has continued to impede all attempts by the UN to initiate free elections. South Africa has attempted to set up an independence constitution worked out at the Turnhalle Conference and backed by the Democratic Turnhalle Alliance (OTA). In the wake of the Zimbabwe settlement, pressure on South Africa to relinquish control is likely to increase as international attention focuses on Namibia.

GEOGRAPHY

Sandwiched between the Namib Desert, which runs down the western Atlantic coastline, and the Kalahari Desert inland is the plateau which forms most of Namibia at an average altitude of 1,100 metres/3,600 feet rising to above 2,000 metres/6,560 feet in the centre of the country. In the far north is the low-lying and swampy Etosha Pan. There are few rivers, none of which are perennial within the country, and much of the drainage is into the inland basins of the Kalahari region.

Climate
The cool Benguela current keeps coastal temperatures low and it becomes cooler as the land rises inland. The hottest areas are the northern inland regions. Both the Namib and the Kalahari Deserts are arid, with low annual rainfall. On the plateau average rainfall increases from under 100 mm/3.9 inches in the south to over 500 mm/19.7 inches in the north-east. Most rain falls in the warmer summer season, though rainfall cannot be relied upon and droughts are frequent.

Agriculture
Livestock raising for meat, dairy and wool products is the most important agricultural activity. Soils are generally poor, though maize, millet, sorghum, wheat, beans and potatoes are grown. Agriculture contributes about 20% of the GDP; about 30% of the white settlers and nearly all Africans not working as contract labourers engage in agriculture. Traditional herding patterns have been destroyed with the development of commercial cattle and sheep ranching by white settlers on the best grazing land. In 1976 there were some 2.8 million cattle, 5 million sheep, 2 million goats and 40,000 pigs in Namibia. Cattle are exported on the hoof to South Africa, and sheep provide additional income from the export of valuable Karakul pelts (Persian lamb) – up to 50% of world supplies are from Namibia. Other hides and skins are also exported.

Main Crops: maize, sorghum, millet, pulses, potatoes, wheat.

Mineral Resources: diamonds, uranium, copper, cadmium, lead, zinc, lithium ores, silver, vanadium, tin, other precious and semi-precious stones. Oil prospecting continues and methane gas has been found. Deposits of coal are also reported.

THE ECONOMY

Gross National Product (1977 est.): R 700 million.

Per Capita Income (1975 est.): US$980.

Gross Domestic Product (1977 est.): R 1,135 million.

Foreign Trade (1977 est.): Total Imports – R 400 million. Total Exports – R 700 million.

Main Trading Partners: Imports – SACUA countries, West Germany, UK, USA, Japan. Exports – SACUA countries, West Germany USA, UK, Japan.

The major cause of economic growth has been the continuing expansion of the mining sector. It is the export of mineral and other primary products which makes the occupation of the territory by South Africa extremely rewarding in budgetary surpluses generated and which has yielded large profits to foreign investors prepared to defy UN sanctions under the decree of 1975. Although no economic statistics on Namibia have been issued by the South African administration since 1959, estimates made by the UN Council for Namibia and others indicate continuing increases in the volume and value of export production as large-scale industry has expanded.

Mineral production accounts for some 60% of the GDP and is the principal source of export earnings and government revenue. Diamond output is particularly valuable,

NAMIBIA

the volume of production being low but with a high gemstone proportion of good quality and extensive reserves. Copper is extracted for processing into blister by a number of companies, among which the Tsumeb Corporation is the largest. Namibia has quickly become a major producer of uranium with the opening of the Rössing mine, and a number of companies are now involved in extraction and concentration processes and in developing fresh deposits. It is possible that the rising export value of uranium will make this Namibia's major economic asset.

Agriculture is the 2nd most important contributor to the GDP (20%), with export production of livestock, fish, skins and hides being the most valuable.

Manufacturing, which constitutes about 10% of the GDP, is concerned with producing domestic consumer items, construction materials, and goods for the assembly and transport industries. The domestic market for consumer items is small and largely confined to the wealthy white population. The distribution of incomes is extremely uneven, and development of the African economy has never been encouraged enough to promote sufficient demand for this sector.

The processing of agricultural and fish products is also of importance, with the production of frozen and canned seafoods, fish meal and fish oil on the rise in recent years.

Tourism is a small-scale industry attracting visitors from South Africa to the game parks and beaches.

Major Industries: mineral and agricultural processing, brewing, paint and construction industries, transport repairs, printing, assembly and engineering.

Main Commodities Traded: diamonds, copper, uranium, other minerals, fish products, hides and skins, livestock.

International Affiliations: Namibia is administered as a part of the Republic of South Africa and as such is a part of SACU.

HOW TO GET THERE

Air
There are regular services from Johannesburg and Cape Town to J.G. Strydom Airport, 40km/25 miles from Windhoek town centre, provided by South African Airways. Lufthansa operate direct flights between Windhoek, Frankfurt and Zürich.

Rail
The South African railway network extends to the main centres in Namibia from the Republic.

Road
Good roads enter the south of Namibia from South Africa and extend to Windhoek and the north via Keetmanshoop. There are also roads into Namibia from Angola and Botswana.

ENTRY REGULATIONS

Visa, health and customs regulations are the same as for the Republic of South Africa.

PRACTICAL INFORMATION FOR THE VISITOR

1. Currency
South African currency is in use.
Monetary Unit – South African rand (R), divided into 100 cents.
Notes – 1, 2, 5, 10, 20 rand.
Coins – ½, 1, 2, 5, 10, 20, 50 cents.

Banking Hours
0900 – 1530 Monday, Tuesday, Thursday, Friday
0900 – 1300 Wednesday
0830 – 1100 Saturday

Principal Commercial Banks in Windhoek
Bank of South West Africa Ltd, Bulow Street, P.O. Box 1, Windhoek 9100.
Barclays National Bank Ltd, P.O. Box 195, Kaiser Street.
Barclays Western Bank Ltd, P.O. Box 2941.
French Bank of Southern Africa.
Nedbank Ltd, P.O. Box 370.
Standard Bank SWA Ltd, P.O. Box 3327, 4th Floor, Standard Bank Chambers, Kaiser Street.
Trust Bank of Africa Ltd.
Volkskas Ltd, P.O. Box 2121.

2. Electricity Supply
220/230v AC 50Hz.

3. Weights and Measures
The metric system is in use.

4. Media
The South West Africa Broadcasting Corporation relays radio broadcasts from South Africa and also transmits local programmes in English, Afrikaans, German and the main African languages. The Voice of Namibia is the radio station operated by SWAPO from Lusaka, Luanda and Brazzaville, broadcasting in English and the main African languages. There is no television service in Namibia.

Newspapers and Journals
Allgemeine Zeitung – a German language daily; *Namib Times* – published twice weekly in English, Afrikaans and German; *Suidwes – Afrikaner* – twice weekly in Afrikaans; *Die Republikein* – the weekly organ of the Republic Party in Afrikaans; *Die Swaarthack* – a monthly in English, Afrikaans and German; *Die Suidwester* – twice-weekly paper of the National Party. The *Windhoek Advertiser* is the evening paper of Windhoek, published in English.
The Government publish an *Official Gazette of the Territory of South West Africa* fortnightly.
Namibia Today, published from Lusaka every two months, and *Ombuze ya Namibia* are the only journals to support SWAPO and to openly oppose the South African occupation of Namibia.

5. Medical Care
Anti-malarial prophylactics are recommended for any visitor intending to visit the game parks, which are sometimes swampy. Inland waters may be dangerous on account of bilharzia. Snakes and scorpions are common and can be dangerous to the traveller. All water should be boiled outside the main towns. Medical facilities for whites are generally good, with hospitals in most of the main centres.

6. Telephone, Telex and Postal Services
The telephone service is operated as part of the South African system, and many telephones are automatic. The major centres are linked by direct lines. Telex facilities are available at the larger hotels in the main towns. All mail should be despatched by air.

7. Public Holidays
As in South Africa:
1 January   New Year's Day

31 May	*Republic Day*
10 October	*Kruger Day*
16 December	*Day of the Covenant*
25 December	*Christmas Day*
26 December	*Boxing Day*

The 1st Monday in September, *Good Friday, Easter Monday* and *Ascension* are also observed.

8. Time
GMT + 2.

9. Internal Transport

Air
Daily flights connect Windhoek, Walvis Bay, Swakopmund, Okahanda, Otjiwarongo, Outjo, Tsumeb, Grootfontein and Keetmanshoop. There are many other airstrips and charter flights can be arranged.

Airline Offices in Windhoek
Namib Air (Pty) Ltd, Svidwes Lugdiens, P.O. Box 731, Eros Airport, ☎ 24451.

Road
Roads are good though the long distances involved in travelling between the major towns make car journeys impractical for the business traveller. Coach services connect South Africa with towns in Namibia.

Taxis and car-hire firms operate in the main centres.

Car-Hire Firms in Windhoek
Avis, corner J. Meinert and Tal Sts, ☎ 34411.
Hertz, 43 Strubel St, ☎ 27103.

Rail
Passenger services are available between main towns. Railways are operated as part of the South African network.

Visitors must obtain permits to visit the 'homeland' areas and some of the game parks.

10. Tipping
Taxis – 10% of the fare.

Hotels/restaurants – 10% of the bill.

USEFUL ADDRESSES (GENERAL)

Division of Nature Conservation and Tourism, Post Bag 13186, Windhoek.

The Director of Nature Conservation and Tourism (Reservations), Private Bag 13267, Windhoek.

South African Railway Travel Bureau, French Bank Centre, Kaiser Street, P.O. Box 415, Windhoek 9100, ☎ 2982561/3.

Tourist Office, c/o Kaiser Wilhelm and Bismarck Street, Swaropmund.

BUSINESS INFORMATION

Import and Exchange Control Regulations
Import and exchange control regulations are the same as those of South Africa, Namibia being an intergral part of South Africa for the purpose of tariffs, trade, and exchange control agreements. As such it is also part of the Rand Monetary Area and the South African Customs Union.

Business Hours
Government Offices
0800 – 1630 Monday to Friday

NAMIBIA

Business Houses
0800 – 1300
1400 – 1700 Monday to Friday
0800 – 1300 Saturday

BUSINESS SERVICES

Insurance
African Eagle Life Assurance Society Ltd, Windhoek.
Mutual and Federal Insurance Co. Ltd., P.O. Box 151, Mutual Building, Kaiser St., Windhoek 1900.

Protea Assurance Co. Ltd, Windhoek.
Prudential Assurance Co., P.O. Box 365, Windhoek.

USEFUL ADDRESSES (BUSINESS)

Chamber of Commerce, P.O. Box 191, Windhoek 9100.

Mines Department, Private Bag 13195, Windhoek.

MAIN CITY

Windhoek (Otjomuise)
The capital city is situated in the Khomas-Hochland highlands and is the territory's economic and communications centre. The city is segregated and ringed with African townships. Windhoek became the seat of administration after the 1885 occupation by German forces, and the city retains something of the German atmosphere of the pre-1919 colonial period, as is apparent in the cafés, restaurants, shops, delicatessens and architecture. There are several parks and gardens, in which monuments commemorating German war dead still stand; in one there is a rockery made up of meteorites collected from around the country. Windhoek is surrounded by hills, 3 of which have Gothic style forts built upon them. One of these forts, the Alte Feste, is now a historical museum.

Hotels
Hotel accommodation is limited, and it is advisable to book in advance. Classification of hotels is on a scale of 1–5 stars.

GRAND HOTEL, P.O. Box 2190, Koerner Street, ☎ 15471.
3 star traditional-style hotel near town centre.
Rooms: 90 ♒, ⌘, ⌨, ⚠, 0600–2400 ☎.
Facilities: Restaurant, bar, nightclub.
Services: TC, FC. ✉ Access, Amex, Barclaycard, Diners Club, Eurocard, Master

Charge, Dr. on call, ♂. Audio-visual equipment.
Conference room – max. capacity 120.
Banquet room – max. capicity 130.

KALOHA SANDS HOTEL, P.O. Box 2254, French Bank Centre, Kaiser Street, Windhoek 9100, ☎ 15511.
Rooms: 187 ♒, ⌘, ⌨, ⚠, ☎.
Facilities: Restaurants, bars. Nightclub. Swimming, sauna, health club, tennis, boules, riding, shooting, fishing. Car hire.

313

Services: **TC**, **FC**. ▣ Access, Amex, Barclaycard, Diners Club, Eurocard, Master Charge, Dr. on call. ♂, **S**.
Conference room – max. capacity 100.
Banquet room – max. capacity 65.

HOTEL THURINGER HOF, P.O. Box 112, Kaiser Street, ☎ 6031.
2 star modern hotel in downtown Windhoek.
Rooms: 45 ♪, ⌂, ⊓, △, ○.
Facilities: Restaurant, bars.
Services: **TC**, **FC**. ▣ Amex, Barclaycard, Diners Club.

SAFARI MOTEL, P.O. Box 3900, Republic Road, ☎ 26541.
Resort motel situated near airport.
Rooms: 108 ♪, ⌂, ⊓, △, ○.
Facilities: Restaurants, bars. Swimming, playground. Parking, free transport to city and airport.
Services: **TC**, **FC**. ▣ Barclaycard.
Conference and banquet rooms – max. capacity 1120.

Restaurants

The hotel restaurants tend to offer somewhat heavy fare, but the seafood is good. In the city there are a number of German-style restaurants and bars, but the trend is now towards 'instant' food and takeaways at the expense of the better restaurants.

NIGER
Republic of Niger

Geography	315
The Economy	317
How to Get There	317
Entry Regulations	318
Practical Information for the Visitor	318
Useful Addresses (General)	320
Business Informatiom	320
Business Services	321
Useful Addresses (Business)	321
Niamey	321

Size: 1,267,000 sq.km/489,191 sq.miles.

Population: 5.0 million (1978 est.).

Distribution: 8% in urban areas.

Density: 4 persons per sq.km/10 per sq.mile.

Population Growth Rate: 2.8% p.a.

Ethnic Composition: The settled population in the south and south-west are mainly Hausa (50% of the population) and Djerma-Songhai. There are several nomadic and semi-nomadic tribes to the north, the largest being the Fulani and the Tuaregs.

Capital: Niamey Pop. ·150,000.

Major Towns: Maradi Pop. 42,000; Zinder Pop. 40,000; Tahoua Pop. 31,000.

Language: French is the official language. The principal spoken tongues are Hausa, Songhai, Manga and Arabic.

Religion: 85% are Muslim, a small percentage Christian and the remainder follow traditional beliefs.

Government: In 1974, Lt. Colonel Seyni Kountché came to power in a military coup, suspended the Constitution and abolished the National Assembly, banning the ruling party. President Kountché heads the Supreme Military Council with a cabinet of both military and civilians.

GEOGRAPHY

The largest state in West Africa, Niger is a land-locked country. The Niger River in the south-west flows through the only fertile region. The rest of the country is semi-arid, with the north mainly uninhabitable desert and the south mostly savannah. In the northern central region is the partly volcanic Air Massif.

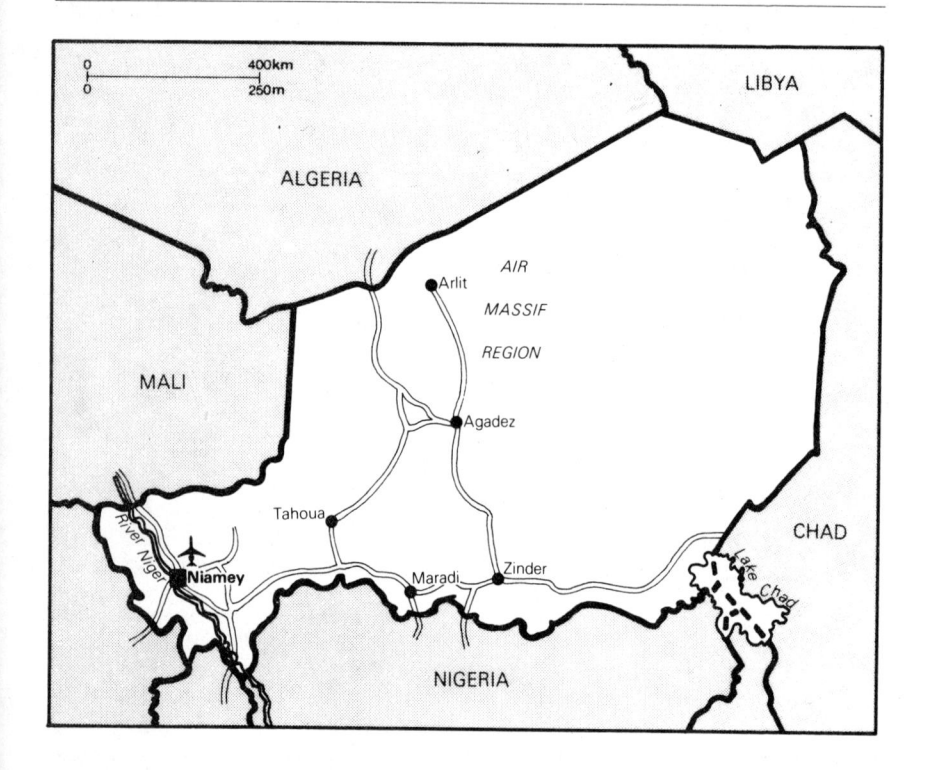

Climate
It is hot and mostly dry, except for the rainy season in July and August. In the dry season (October to May), day temperatures average 28°c/83°F but drop noticeably at night. From November to January the cool but dusty *harmattan* blows from the east, and during the rainy season the south is often subject to tornadoes.

Agriculture
Along with forestry and fishing, agriculture generates half the Gross Domestic Product and engages over 90% of the population. Subsistence crops, specifically millet and sorghum, have returned to normal production after the devasting Sahelian drought of the early 1970s, but the principal cash crop, groundnuts, is still recovering. Cotton, the other main cash crop, has had several good harvests.

The current National Development Plan aims at building up food stocks, reducing cereal imports and completing the reconstitution of livestock herds (cattle, goats, sheep, asses, camels, poultry) which were severely reduced during the drought. The Government is also promoting a longer-term reform programme to set up agricultural co-operatives in all rural areas.

Main Crops: millet, sorghum, cassava, groundnuts, niebe beans, cotton, tobacco, rice, sugar cane.

Mineral Resources: uranium, cassiterite, phosphates, iron ore, coal, gypsum, petroleum, copper, tin, molybdenum.

THE ECONOMY

Gross National Product (1978): US$1.11 billion.

Per Capita Income (1978): US$220.

Gross Domestic Product (1976): 123.9 billion CFA francs.

Foreign Trade (1978): Total Imports – US$198.3 million. Total Exports – US$171.6 million.

Main Trading Partners: Imports – France, Ivory Coast, West Germany, USA, Algeria. Exports – France, Nigeria, Italy, West Germany.

The country's almost total lack of arable land and access to the coast has left it, until recently, completely at the mercy of weather conditions, crop diseases and insects. Niger is thought to have been the country hardest hit by the Sahelian drought, although agriculture is now recovering. The increasing exploitation of its mineral resources, specifically uranium, is transforming the economy. Niger is poised to join the US as the 2 principal world exporters of uranium. Processing at the Arlit uranium mine began in 1971 under SOMAIR, a multinational company formed by French, West German, Italian and Nigerian interests, in which Niger now holds a 33% share. Another mine is in production at nearby Akouta and further exploration is under way. Coal, oil and other minerals are all being explored and power generation has risen rapidly in recent years despite the limited industrial demand.

Industry is devoted mainly to processing agricultural products for export (cotton ginneries, rice and flour mills, tanneries and an abattoir) and import substitution (textiles, cement, soap, beer and soft drinks, plastics, bricks, etc.). Foreign investment is encouraged, but industrial development is slow due to the lack of an adequate transport infrastructure.

Further development of the economy is completely dependent on the drastic improvement of transport facilities. A road and rail network is being planned with Togo and Upper Volta, in the hope that Niger will eventually be able to export its mineral wealth more efficiently via Abidjan on the Ivory Coast.

Major Industries: food processing, cotton ginning, textiles, tanning, ceramics, cement, agricultural implements.

Main Commodities Traded: Imports – transport equipment, petroleum products, mechanical and electrical machinery, iron and steel, textiles, foodstuffs. Exports – uranium concentrates, livestock products, groundnut products, cotton, vegetables.

International Affiliations: UN, IBRD, OAU, ACP, ADB, CEAO, ECOWAS, Franc Zone, OCAM, LCBC, NRC, International Atomic Energy Agency.

HOW TO GET THERE

Air
UTA and Air Afrique operate regular flights to Niamey from Paris, both direct and via Bordeaux or Marseilles.

NIGER

Flights to Niamey from the African Continent are operated by Air Afrique, Air Algérie, Air Mali, Air Niger and Libyan Airlines.

Flying time to Niamey from Paris: 5 hours.

Niamey Airport is 10km/7½ miles from the city centre. Taxis are not available at the airport, but some hotels provide transport.

ENTRY REGULATIONS

Visas

Visas are required by nationals of all countries except: Andorra, Belgium, Denmark, Finland, France, West Germany, Italy, Luxembourg, Monaco, Netherlands, Norway, Sweden, French-speaking African countries and holders of a U.K. passport.

All other nationals require visas, obtainable from Niger embassies or French consulates.

Business visitors should ensure that their passport is valid for a least 3 months beyond the date of issue of their visa.

Health Regulations

A valid International Certificate of Vaccination against smallpox is required by all persons entering Niger. Yellow fever and cholera vaccination certificates are no longer obligatory, but it is advisable to be vaccinated against these diseases.

Customs

Currency: There is no limit to the amount of local or foreign currency which may be imported, nor to the amount of foreign currency which may be exported. Local currency not exceeding 25,000 CFA francs may be exported.

Duty-free articles: Personal effects. 200 cigarettes or 250g of tobacco. 1 bottle of wine. 1 bottle of spirits. A small amount of perfume. Samples of no commercial value. Samples of commercial value should be declared on arrival and will be checked on departure.

PRACTICAL INFORMATION FOR THE VISITOR

1. Currency

Monetary Unit – CFA franc.
Notes – 50, 100, 500, 1,000 and 5,000 CFA francs.
Coins – 1, 2, 5, 10, 25, 50 and 100 CFA francs.

Niger, together with Benin, Ivory Coast, Senegal, Togo and Upper Volta, is a member of the *Banque Centrale des États de l'Afrique de l'Ouest*, B.P. 487, Rond-Point de la Poste, Niamey.

Banking Hours

0800–1200 Monday to Friday.

Domestic Commercial Banks

Banque Internationale pour l'Afrique Occidentale, B.P. 10350, Niamey.
Banque de Développement de la République du Niger, B.P. 227, Niamey.

2. Electricity Supply

220/380v AC 50Hz.
Plugs: 2-pin round.

3. Weights and Measures

The metric system is used.

4. Media

The Government radio station, *La Voix*

du Sahel, broadcasts in French, English, Arabic and several vernacular languages. Television is in operation, but is limited to Saturday evenings and special events.

The Government Information Bureau issues a mimeographed daily news bulletin, *Le Sahel*, and the weekly *Sahel Hebdo*. In addition, there is the monthly *Journal Officiel de la Republique du Niger* and the quarterly *Nigerama*.

5. Medical Care

Anti-malarial prophylactics should be taken, on the advice of a doctor. Typhoid vaccination is also recommended.

Tap water is generally not safe to drink and should be boiled, or bottled water only should be drunk. Visitors are advised to carry a preventative against stomach upset and to take care with uncooked fruit and vegetables. Niamey and Zinder both have reasonably good hospitals.

6. Telephone, Telex and Postal Services

Telecommunications facilities are inadequate, but are being drastically improved under the current development plan. There is a direct telephone connection with Paris from Niamey.

The Grand Hotel du Niger and the Hotel le Sahel offer telex facilities for their guests.

The Post Office in Niamey is open between 0730–1230 and 1530–1730, Monday to Saturday. There is no local delivery of mail, and all mail must be addressed with a post office box (boîte postale) number. All mail, to and from Niger, should be sent by air.

7. Public Holidays

1 January	*New Year's Day*
3 August	*Independence Day*
15 August	*Assumption*
1 November	*All Saints Day*
18 December	*Republic Day*
25 December	*Christmas Day*

In addition, the following movable Muslim and Christian are observed: *Mouled, Good Friday, Easter Monday, Whit Monday, Eid el Fitr* and *Eid el Kabir*.

8. Time

GMT + 1.

9. Internal Transport

Air

Air Niger operates regular flights from Niamey to Tahoua, Agadez, Arlit, Maradi, Zinder. Air taxi services are also available.

Airline Offices in Niamey
Air Afrique ☎ 2711/2.
Air France ☎ 722121/2.
UTA ☎ 733161.

Road

Self-drive cars are available for hire in Niamey. A foreign licence or International Driving Licence is required.

Car-Hire Firms in Niamey
Hertz ☎ 732331.
Agence Transcap ☎ 323436.

10. Tipping

Taxis – 10% of the fare.

Porters – 50 CFA francs per bag.

Hotels/restaurants – A service charge of 10–15% is usually added to the bill. It is customary to give a tip of 100 CFA francs to hotel room staff on departure.

11. Social Customs

It is essential to have a good working knowledge of the French language, as French is used exclusively in Government and business circles and English is rarely understood. French customs and manners predominate in the business and social life of the major towns.

USEFUL ADDRESSES (GENERAL)

Many foreign embassies accredited to Niger are situated in either Lagos (Nigeria) or Abidjan (Ivory Coast).

Office of the Canadian Embassy: B.P. 362, Niamey, ☎ 723686/7.

Dutch Consulate: B.P. 685, Niamey, ☎ 732352.

French Embassy: B.P. 240, Route de Yantala, Niamey, ☎ 722431.

US Embassy: B.P. 201, Niamey, ☎ 722661.

West German Embassy: B.P. 629, Niamey, ☎ 253410.

Office du Tourisme du Niger: B.P. 612, Niamey.

Wagons-Lits Tourisme Authorised Representative: Transcap Voyages, B.P. 522, Niamey, ☎ 323436.

BUSINESS INFORMATION

The Government encourages joint ventures between the state (51% interest) and foreign investors, but the private sector remains limited despite the Investment Code passed in 1974 to encourage enterprises with 80% Nigerian involvement. Most foreign investment continues to be French, but the mining sector in particular is attracting multinational investment. The greater part of foreign trade is conducted by French firms, and there is a natural orientation towards French sources of industrial supply.

Most of the established French export and import companies have their headquarters and purchasing organisations in Paris. In general, most importers deal with a wide variety of goods and often act in a number of trading capacities. Commercial practice is based on the French commercial code. In addition to a visit to Niger, foreign suppliers may find it advantageous to visit the headquarters or buying agencies of local firms either in Paris or elsewhere outside Niger.

Import and Exchange Control Regulations

In general, all imports from countries outside the Franc Zone are subject to import authorisation. Following the signing of the Lomé Convention, there are special regulations for imports into Niger from EEC countries.

Exchange control applies to all currencies other than the CFA franc and the French franc. Foreign exchange is made available under 3 main headings: the EEC, Bilateral Trade Agreements and Global Quotas.

Business Hours

Government Offices
0800–1200
1500–1830 Monday to Friday
0800–1200 Saturday

Business Houses
0800–1200
1500–1830 Monday to Saturday

The best time to visit Niger is between November and May so as to avoid the rainy season. This also coincides with the peak buying period, which falls towards the end of the year and around the beginning of the new year.

NIGER

BUSINESS SERVICES

Insurance
La Leyma, B.P. 14, Niamey. Several French insurance companies are also represented in Niger.

Shipping
Société Nationale des Transports Nigériens, B.P. 135, Niamey – road haulage.
Société Nigérienne des Transports Fluviaux et Maritimes (SNTFM), B.P. 802, Niamey – river transport – the river Niger is navigable from September to March between Niamey and Port Harcourt on the Nigerian Coast.

USEFUL ADDRESSES (BUSINESS)

Société Nationale de Commerce et de Production du Niger (COPRO-Niger) B.P. 615, Niamey.

Chambre de Commerce, d'Agriculture et d'Industrie de la République du Niger, B.P. 209, Niamey.

Syndicat des Commerçants Importateurs et Exportateurs du Niger, B.P. 535, Naimey.

Syndicat Patronal des Entreprises et Industries du Niger, B.P. 415, Niamey.

MAJOR CITY

Niamey
Niamey is a modern city on the banks of the River Niger. The green belt along the river contains the National Museum, an outdoor display of Niger's cultural heritage, with rock paintings, traditional housing and a zoo.

There are 2 markets in the commercial area, the Small Market selling food, and the Great Market selling cloth and craft products. The Great Mosque, a modern building in traditional style, is near by.

Hotels
There is no official hotel rating system.

GRAND HOTEL DU NIGER, B.P. 471, ☎ 2641.
Modern central hotel overlooking the river Niger.
Rooms: 71 ♪, ☎. Suites and separate bungalows available.
Facilities: Restaurant, snack bar, bar. Parking, car hire. Swimming, exotic gardens.
Serivces: TC, FC, ◨ Diners Club.

HÔTEL LE SAHEL, B.P. 627, ☎ 3031.
Niamey's most luxurious hotel, opened in 1965, with air-conditioning and swimming.

Restaurants
Aside from the hotel restaurants, there are the *Viet Nam* (oriental), *Baie d'Along, Flotille, Kasbah* and others.

Nightclubs
The *Hi-Fi* is the most popular nightclub.

Shopping
Best buys at the markets are craftwork, leather goods, jewellery, knives and swords, and blankets. High-quality artifacts are sold at the Museum.

NIGERIA
Federal Republic of Nigeria

Geography	323
The Economy	324
How to Get There	325
Entry Regulations	326
Practical Information for the Visitor	327
Useful Addresses (General)	330
Business Information	331
Business Services	332
Useful Addresses (Business)	332
Lagos	333
Ibadan	335

Size: 923,773 sq.km/356,669 sq.miles.

Population: 85 million (1978 est.). (The United Nations and similar sources continue to give the population of Nigeria as 66.63 million in 1977, but this is now considered unrealistic.)

Distribution: 23% in urban areas.

Density: 71 persons per sq.km/186 per sq.mile.

Population Growth Rate: 2.5% p.a.

Ethnic Composition: There are more than 200 ethnic groups, of which the 4 largest are the Hausa, Yoruba, Ibo and Fulani. The European population is relatively small.

Capital: Lagos Pop. 1.06 million (1975 est.). (The unofficial estimate is around 3 million.)

Major Cities: Kano Pop. 2 million; Ibadan Pop. 2 million; Kaduna Pop. 700,000; Ilorin Pop. 282,000; Port Harcourt Pop. 500,000; Abeokuta Pop. 253,000. (All figures are unofficial estimates for 1979.)

Language: English is the official language. The main African languages are Hausa, Yoruba, Ibo and Edo.

Religion: Approximately 45% Muslim, 30% Christian (varying denominations), and the remainder Animist, adhering to ancient tribal cults and faiths.

Government: Nigeria is under military rule and is governed by the Supreme Military Council whose President is also the Head of State and Chief of the Armed Forces. Nigeria is a federation of 19 states, each with its own military administrator and state ministries.

Elections for the National Assembly, consisting of a Senate and House of Representatives, the State Legislatures and Governorships and the Presidency were due to be held in August 1979 as part of the planned transition to democratic civilian rule. The elections were postponed and no future date was announced.

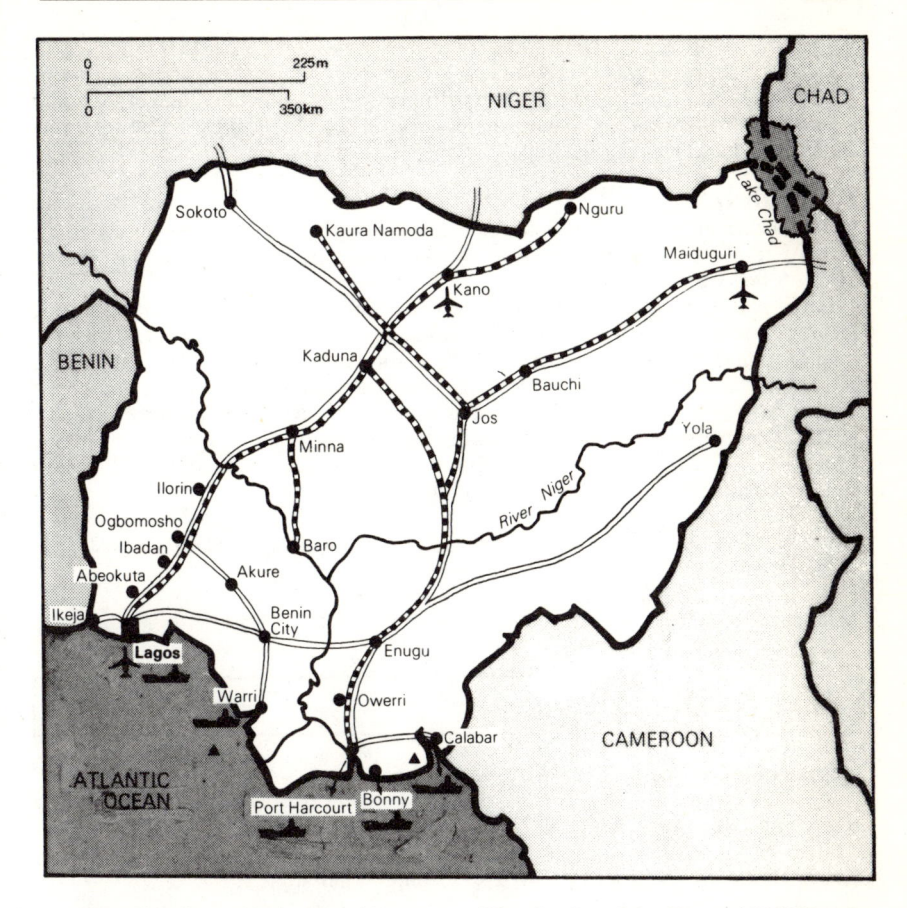

All political parties in Nigeria were banned in 1966; when the ban was lifted in 1978, only 5 parties qualified for registration under the rules of the Federal Electoral Commission: the Greater Nigeria People's Party (GNPP), the National Party of Nigeria (NPN), the Nigerian People's Party (NPP), the People's Redemption Party (PRP) and the Unity Party of Nigeria (UPN).

GEOGRAPHY

Geographical conditions across the country vary considerably. The long coastline consists of sandy bays, lagoons and swamps; the southern region with its swamps and tropical rain forests merges with woodland and savannah in the north, rising to the Central Plateau which is 2,000m/6,560ft above sea level. The extreme north borders the Sahara Desert.

Climate

The climate is tropical, although conditions vary between the north and the south. In the south and particularly along the coast, it is hot and very humid with an average temperature of 29°c/84°F. Daytime temperatures in the north are higher, often reaching 43°c/109°F, but nights are cooler and in December and January may be as low as 4°c/39°F. The rainy season in the north is from April to September, and in the south from March to November. During the dry season the *harmattan* wind blows across from the Sahara, keeping humidity low.

Agriculture

Before the development of the petroleum industry, agriculture was the main economic activity; it still occupies over 50% of the working population, contributing around 20% of the Gross Domestic Product.

Large-scale agricultural development schemes involve the improvement of farming facilities and the introduction of food-processing industries in many areas, with the help of foreign aid and investment. The Government plans to stimulate agricultural production in order to reach self-sufficiency in most basic foodstuffs, and credit incentives and the supply of machinery and fertilisers are designed to achieve this aim.

The economies of the northern states are largely dependent on agriculture where a wide variety of subsistence crops are grown; these are more limited in the southern states, but more cash crops are cultivated there.

Main Crops: cocoa, palm kernels and oil, groundnuts, cotton, yams, cassava, rice, sugar-cane.

Mineral Resources: oil, tin, coal, limestone.

THE ECONOMY

Gross National Product (1978): US$45,720 million.

Per Capita Income (1976): US$414.

Gross Domestic Product (1978): 20,791 million naira.

Foreign Trade (1978): Total Imports – US$11,386 million. Total Exports – US$10,508 million.

Main Trading Partners: Imports – UK, West Germany, USA, Japan, France. Exports – USA, UK, Netherlands, West Germany, France.

Until the oil boom of recent years, the economy was basically agricultural, with agricultural products providing much of Nigeria's foreign exchange earnings. More than half of the work force are still employed in the agricultural sector, but its importance as a source of external revenue has declined. The Government is now looking towards the oil industry to provide the finance needed to stimulate the agricultural sector.

Commercial oil production began in the late 1950s, and the Nigerian National Petroleum Company (NNPC) has widespread control over much of the industry, including the refining and distribution sectors, although the level of foreign participation in Nigeria's oil industry is still high. Following the boom in oil prices in 1974, the Government was hopeful that oil revenues would provide the bulk of the finance needed for all the country's development projects. (Oil now provides about 90% of

Nigeria's foreign exchange earnings.) However, a fall in actual oil production together with the ensuing loss of revenue has altered this situation and led to a cutback in Government spending and the disruption of many development projects. Apart from oil, Nigeria has other mineral deposits and extensive iron ore deposits are expected to supply the new iron and steel industry.

Top priorities for development are communications, power and the expansion of the infrastructure related to the oil industry. Despite Government cutbacks and other financial measures taken, Nigeria still has a balance of payments problem and is now seeking foreign aid to cover her debts and avoid further disruption of development plans. A considerable rise in exports is forecast, but at the same time present development commitments are expected to lead to a rise in imports.

Nigeria's manufacturing sector is small and is dominated by low-technology light industries producing mainly consumer goods. The expansion of the sugar, timber, and pulp and paper industries is in hand and the establishment and development of the iron and steel, vehicle assembly, cement and petrochemicals industries will further diversify the industrial sector. The fastest-growing industries include vehicle assembly, pharmaceuticals, beer and refined petroleum products.

The future for the economy looks promising, with increased oil revenues, the continuing development of the infrastructure and the stimulation of the agricultural sector which still has enormous potential. Real economic growth can be expected in the forthcoming years together with a reduction of Nigeria's budget deficit.

Major Industries: oil, mining, food processing, pulp and paper, textiles, rubber.

Main Commodities Traded: Imports – machinery and transport equipment, manufactured goods, foodstuffs and livestock, chemicals. Exports – crude petroleum, cocoa, palm kernels, cotton, rubber.

Oil Production (1977): 765.5 million barrels.

International Affiliations: UN, IBRD, OAU, ACP, ADB, Commonwealth, OPEC, ECOWAS, LCBC, NRC.

HOW TO GET THERE

Air

The main international airports are Murtala Mohammed Airport at Ikeja, 22 km/13½ miles from the centre of Lagos, and Kano Airport which is 8km/5 miles from the centre of Kano.

There are frequent services to Lagos from Amsterdam, Frankfurt, London, Paris, Rome and Zürich operated by KLM, Lufthansa, British Caledonian and Nigeria Airways, UTA, Alitalia and Swissair.

From London, British Caledonian fly 3 times a week from Gatwick. British Caledonian (Gatwick) and Nigeria Airways (Heathrow) fly directly from London to Kano several times a week. Nigeria Airways 5 times a week from Heathrow.

Pan Am operate regular flights from New York to Lagos, and MEA fly from Beirut to Lagos.

There are direct flights to Lagos from Abidjan, Accra, Banjul, Dakar, Douala, Freetown, Monrovia and Kinshasa.

Flying times to Lagos: from London, 6 hours; from New York, 14 hours; from

Sydney 30 hours. An airport tax of 5 nairas is payable by all passengers on departure from Nigeria.

Taxis are available at Murtala Mohammed Airport, but fares should be fixed in advance as taxi drivers may try to overcharge (cost to Lagos should not exceed 15 nairas). Nigeria Airways operate a bus service from the airport to the major hotels in Lagos at a reasonable cost.

ENTRY REGULATIONS

Visas

Visas are required by nationals of all countries, except the British Commonwealth and Republic of Ireland, although the latter need entry permits.

Entry permits and visas are obtainable at Nigerian high commissions and embassies abroad. Applications should be accompanied by a return air ticket and a letter, in duplicate, from the applicant's firm giving full details of the business to be conducted, including the names and addresses of business contacts and confirming financial responsibility for the applicant. In addition, a letter of invitation (not a telex) from a Nigerian firm or government department, or alternatively copies of any correspondence relevant to the visit are also required.

Business travellers visiting Nigeria for working purposes, such as to install or repair machinery, plant, etc., should supply a copy of the contract or a quota number as well as an official invitation from Nigeria.

Entry permits and visas are usually valid for 3 months for a stay of variable length. The time taken to issue these is normally 3 weeks, but there can be a delay of up to 3 months if the application is referred for authorisation. Intending visitors should therefore allow plenty of time for the permit or visa to be issued and applications should be submitted well in advance of the intended visit.

Entry permits cannot be obtained on arrival. Business travellers should not travel to Nigeria until they have a valid entry permit or visa.

Evidence in a passport of a visit to South Africa may adversely affect the issue of an entry permit or visa. Intending visitors should contact their local passport issuing authority for further details.

Visitors should ensure that they carry passports and travel documents at all times during their stay to certify that they are *bona fide* visitors or travellers in transit.

Business travellers are advised to endorse Nigerian Immigration Department landing cards (issued on the aircraft) with the words 'business visitor' and indicate the length of their stay.

Health Regulations

Valid International Certificates of Vaccination against smallpox, yellow fever and cholera are required by all persons entering Nigeria.

Customs

Currency: All visitors must fill out a currency declaration form, in duplicate, on arrival and on departure. The import or export of Nigerian currency in excess of N50 is prohibited. Currency regulations are strict; visitors should adhere to these and be prepared to account for all monies on departure.

Duty-free articles: Personal baggage, including a camera, typewriter and similar articles for the visitor's personal use. 200 cigarettes, 50 cigars or 8oz of tobacco.

Commercial samples of negligible value, provided they are to be used solely for soliciting orders. A customs declaration form must be completed and handed to the examining officer at the point of entry.

Articles liable to duty: Samples of commercial value are admitted free of duty provided the appropriate duty is deposited or secured by bond, and the samples are re-exported within 6 months.

Prohibited articles: Arms and ammunition. Drugs and narcotics. Visitors wishing to export curios should obtain a clearance permit from the Director of Antiquities. Any curio which the Customs Authorities suspect to be an antiquity may be seized at the airport, and the possession of such a permit will avoid any confusion.

PRACTICAL INFORMATION FOR THE VISITOR

1. Currency
Monetary Unit – naira (N), divided into 100 kobo (K).
Notes – 50 kobo and 1, 5, 10, 20 naira.
Coins – ½, 1, 5, 10, 25 kobo.

It is not possible for foreign visitors to exchange Nigerian currency back into foreign exchange at hotels or commercial banks in Nigeria. A maximum of N5 may be converted on departure at the airport bank, subject to the availability of foreign currency. Avoid foreign exchange transactions with currency touts at the airport.

Banking Hours
0800–1500 Monday
0800–1300 Tuesday to Friday

The *Central Bank of Nigeria*, Tinubu Square, P.M.B. 12194, Lagos, ☎ 53700, is the bank of issue.

Principal Domestic Banks
African Continental Bank Ltd,
   148 Broad Street, P.M.B. 2466, Lagos, ☎ 26365.
Bank of the North Ltd, 5a–6a Lagos Street, P.O. Box 211, Kano, ☎ 2895.
Co-operative Bank Ltd, Co-operative Buildings, New Court Road, P.M.B. 5137, Ibadan.
Mercantile Bank of Nigeria Ltd, 1 Barracks Road, P.M.B. 1084, Calabar.

National Bank of Nigeria Ltd,
   82–6 Broad Street, P.M.B. 12123, Lagos, ☎ 22131/9.
New Nigeria Bank Ltd, Ring Road, P.M.B. 1193, Benin City, ☎ 6512.
Pan African Bank Ltd, 5 Azikiwe Road, P.M.B. 5239, Port Harcourt, ☎ 22286.

There are several foreign commercial banks with offices and branches in Nigeria, as well as a number of locally incorporated foreign banks:

Arab Bank (Nigeria) Ltd, 36 Balogun Square, P.O. Box 1114, Lagos.
Bank of America (Nigeria) Ltd,
   136 Broad Street, Lagos.
Bank of India (Nigeria) Ltd,
   47–8 Breadfruit Street, P.O. Box 1252, Lagos.
Chase Merchant Bank Nigeria Ltd,
   23 Awolowo Road, S.W. Ikoyi, P.M.B. 12035, Lagos, ☎ 21388/53176. (Branch in Kano.)
International Bank for West Africa Ltd,
   94 Broad Street, P.O. Box 12021, Lagos.
First Bank of Nigeria Ltd, Unity House, 37 Marina, P.O. Box 5216, Lagos, ☎ 27312/3.
Union Bank of Nigeria Ltd (formerly Barclays Bank of Nigeria Ltd),
   40 Marina, P.M.B. 2027, Lagos ☎ 21751.

NIGERIA

United Bank of Africa (Nigeria) Ltd, 97/105 Broad Street, P.O. Box 2406, Lagos.

2. Electricity Supply
230v AC 50Hz.
Plugs: 3 flat or round pins.

3. Weights and Measures
The metric system is used.

4. Media
Radio and television are both Government-owned. The Federal Radio Corporation broadcasts in English and several Nigerian languages and has an external service ('Voice of Nigeria') transmitting programmes to Europe, Africa and the Middle East. There are broadcasting stations in each of the states, and these carry commercial advertising. Television is controlled by the Nigerian Television Authority.

Newspapers and Journals
The main English-language dailies are: *Daily Times* (Lagos); *New Nigerian* (Kaduna and Lagos); *Nigerian Observer* (Benin City); *Daily Sketch* (Ibadan); *Daily Express* (Lagos); *Nigerian Tribune* (Ibadan); *West African Pilot*; *Daily Star* (Enugu); *Nigerian Herald* (Ilorin); *Nigerian Chronicle* (Calabar); *Evening Times* (Lagos); *Nigerian Standard* (Jos); *Nigerian Tide* (Port Harcourt); *The Punch* (Ikeja).

The *Sunday Observer* (Benin City); *Sunday Punch* (Ikeja) and the *Sunday Times* (Lagos) are the principal Sunday newspapers.

There are also numerous English-language weekly papers as well as weeklies published in Yoruba and Hausa and sold respectively in the western and northern parts of the country.

Some of the more important trade publications are *Nigerian Trade Journal* (quarterly); *Management in Nigeria* (monthly); *Farmstock*; *Building Construction*; *Nigerian Business Guardian*; *Investors' Digest*; *Business Times*; *Food and Agriculture Magazine*; *Marketing in Nigeria* (every two months); *Nigerian Eurolink*; *Banking and Insurance*; *Nigerian Businessman's Magazine* (monthly); *Commerce in Nigeria*.

Trade magazines which are published in the United Kingdom and have a wide circulation in Nigeria include *African Development*, *West African Technical Review* and *West African Construction*.

5. Medical Care
TAB (typhoid and paratyphoid) injections are recommended. Visitors should also seek advice from their doctor about anti-malarial tablets. Mosquito nets are widely used, especially in the south, and visitors should make proper use of them.

Tap water should be avoided if possible, especially outside of the main towns. Visitors should also avoid eating uncooked fruit and vegetables.

There are both Government and private hospitals in Nigeria – charges at the former are usually the most reasonable.

6. Telephone, Telex and Postal Services
Telephone services tend to be erratic and long delays are frequent, especially with calls made through the operator. Direct dialling is possible in the major towns.

Telegrams can be sent to all parts of the world through the offices of Nigerian External Telecommunications Ltd (NET). Internal telex facilities are available in most cities and major towns.

International telephone, telegram and telex facilities are available at: the head office of NET, NECOM House, 14 Marina, Lagos; the Falomo Shopping Centre, Ikoyi Island, Lagos; and at any of NET's office throughout the country.

All mail to and from Nigeria should be sent by air.

7. Public Holidays
1 January   New Year's Day
1 October   National Day
25–6 December   Christmas
The following Muslim and Christian holidays are also officially observed:

Mouled, Eid el Fitr (3–4 days), *Eid el Kabir*, *Good Friday* and *Easter Monday*.

8. Time
GMT + 1.

9. Internal Transport

Air
Nigeria Airways operate internal air services linking Lagos and Ibadan, Benin, Port Harcourt, Enugu, Calabar, Kaduna, Kano, Jos, Sokoto, Maiduguri and Yola.

It is often difficult to obtain seats on domestic flights at short notice; if possible, visitors should make bookings before arriving in Nigeria.

A number of air charter companies are also in operation.

An airport tax of N2 is payable by all passengers on domestic flights.

Airline Offices in Lagos

Aeroflot	☎ 21233.
Air France/UTA	☎ 23808/9.
Air India	☎ 25787.
British Airways	☎ 20812.
British Caledonian	☎ 25975.
KLM	☎ 630576.
Lufthansa	☎ 26361.
Nigeria Airways	☎ 24811, 31031.
Pan Am	☎ 26191.
Swissair	☎ 632046, 636077.

Air Charter Companies
Aero Contractors ☎ 24347. (Lagos)
Delta Air Charter ☎ 33579. (Ikeja)
Pan-African Airlines (Ikeja) ☎ 33098.

Rail
Rail travel is slow and bookings should be made at least a week in advance. The 2 main lines are Lagos to Kano and Port Harcourt to Kano with branch lines to Kaura Namoda, Nguru, Baro, Jos and Maiduguri.

Road
The main towns are connected by good all-weather roads, but many of the secondary roads are impassable during the rainy season.

Taxi fares should be agreed in advance with the driver even if the taxi is fitted with a meter. Taxis are expensive in Lagos.

Self-drive and chauffeur-driven cars are available for hire in the main towns. An International Driving Licence or valid driving licence from the visitor's country of residence is required.

Traffic travels on the right-hand side of the road.

Car-Hire Firms in Lagos

UTC Motors Division	☎ 56230.
Hertz	☎ 52520, 53846.
Gateway Car Services	☎ 41101.
Nigeria Rent-a-Car (Avis)	☎ 46336.

Hire cars can also be obtained through the main hotels.

10. Tipping
Taxis – 10% of the fare (where fares are agreed in advance, no tip is necessary).

Porters – 10K per bag.

Hotels/restaurants – 10% of the bill, if no service charge is included.

11. Social Customs
Dress is generally informal, but men should wear a suit when visiting Government officials or senior company executives.

Visitors are advised to take note of the various Muslim customs and practices, in particular observance of the laws concerning alcohol and the feast of *Ramadan*. During this month it may be difficult to meet regularly with Muslim business contacts.

The restrictions placed on women in Nigeria are far fewer than in more conservative Muslim countries. Outside of the strict Muslim communities, women are fairly well integrated into business and social life.

USEFUL ADDRESSES (GENERAL)

Lagos

Australian High Commission, 4th Floor, Investment House, 21–5 Broad Street, P.O. Box 2427, ☎ 25981.

British Council, Western House, 8–10 Broad Street, P.O. Box 3702, ☎ 656990/1.

British High Commission, Eleke Crescent, Victoria Island, P.M.B. 12136, ☎ 611842, 611654, 611934, 611789.

Canadian High Commission, New Niger House, Tinubu Street, P.O. Box 851, ☎ 53630.

Dutch Embassy, 24 Ozumba Mbadiwe Avenue, Victoria Island, Private Mail Bag 2426, ☎ 52791, 52790 – Dutch Consulates at Kano and Port Harcourt.

French Embassy, 1 Queen's Drive, Ikoyi, P.O. Box 567.

Embassy of the Republic of Ireland, 31 Marina, P.O. Box 2421.

Japanese Embassy, 24–5 Apese Street, Victoria Island, P.M.B. 2111, ☎ 613797, 614929.

Swiss Embassy, 11 Anifowashe Street, Victoria Island, P.O. Box 536, ☎ 25277.

US Embassy, 1 King's College Road, P.O. Box 554, ☎ 57320.

West German Embassy, 15 Eleke Crescent, Victoria Island, P.O. Box 728, ☎ 58430/33.

The Nigerian Tourist Association, 47 Marina, P.O. Box 2944, ☎ 26129, 26120.

Wagons-Lits Authorised Representative, Transcap Voyages, 20/21 Marina, Wesley House, P.O. Box 2326, ☎ 23840, 24330, 21416, 22331.

American Express Authorised Representative, Scantravel Ltd, Unity House, 37 Marina, P.O. Box 1897, ☎ 50635, 21469.

Ibadan

British Council, Dugbe, P.M.B. 5103, ☎ 410604, 410645.

British Deputy High Commission, Finance Corporation Building, Lebanon Street, P.M.B. 5010, ☎ 21551.

Kaduna

British Council, Hospital Road, P.O. Box 81, ☎ 243484, 212002.

British Deputy High Commission, United Bank of Africa Building, Hospital Road, P.M.B. 2096, ☎ 212178/9, 243080.

US Consulate, 5 Ahmadu Bello Way, ☎ 23373/7.

West German Consulate, Ahmadu Bello Way 22, P.O. Box 430, ☎ 23696.

Wagons-Lits Authorised Representative, Transcap Voyages, 4 Ahmadu Bellow Way, P.O. Box 272, ☎ 3082.

Other Wagons-Lits Authorised Representative Offices: 28 Burma Road, P.O. Box 1095, Apapa, ☎ 21272; P.O. Box 291, Ikeja; 12 Hadeija Road, P.O. Box 3065, Ikeja, ☎ 4707, 4744; 8 Azikiwe Road, P.O. Box 429, Port Harcourt, ☎ 8393.

BUSINESS INFORMATION

The planned development of the Nigerian infrastructure calls for equipment and supplies from overseas suppliers for the defence, social services, educational, housing and communications sectors. The emphasis on agricultural modernisation and expansion will require substantial quantities of fertiliser, seeds, farm machinery, pesticides and service machinery.

Industrial development plans call for the supply of capital goods, particularly in the textile, pulp and paper and cement industries, and expansion of the petroleum industry including new plant and pipelines for 2 new refineries at Warri and Kaduna.

Transport, communications and hydro-electric schemes also provide valuable opportunities for foreign suppliers, and although there is a small demand for consumer durables, there is a significant need for capital goods.

It is generally advisable to appoint agents for the Nigerian market. The most efficient means of representation is to appoint agents in different centres, as the size of the country and relatively poor communications make it virtually impossible for a single agent effectively to cover the whole of Nigeria. Another method is to trade through the large merchant and agency houses which usually offer good after-sales and servicing facilities. A large proportion of trade is handled by indent and commission agents who are often in a position to serve as travelling sales representatives.

It is the stated policy of the Government to concentrate the distributive trades in the hands of Nigerians and although there are few large indigenous agencies at present, they are increasing in number. Departments and corporations of the Federal Government are now increasingly trading through the newly created Nigeria National Supply Company, while several of the State Governments have established their own bulk purchasing organisations.

Import Regulations
Most goods can be imported under Open General Licence, although a number of specific items require special licences. All imports from South Africa and Namibia are prohibited.

Business Hours
Federal and State Government Offices
0730–1530 Monday to Friday
0800–1300 Saturday (state offices only)
Government office hours vary slightly between the different states, so the hours above are only an approximate guide.

Business Houses
0800–1230
1400–1630 Monday to Friday
0800–1230 Saturday (northern states only)

Most large companies work a 5-day week with the exception of those in Lagos which are often open on Saturday mornings.

Business Events
An International Trade Fair is held each year in February in Kaduna and also in Port Harcourt.

BUSINESS SERVICES

Advertising
Afromedia (Nigeria) Ltd, 17b Creek Road, Apapa, P.O. Box 2377, Lagos.
Nigerian Railway Advertising Services, Railway Compound, Ebutte Metta.
Pearl & Dean Ltd, 25 Thorburn Avenue, Yaba – cinema advertising.
Wilmer Publicity, 268 Herbert Macaulay Street, Yaba.

Other major advertising agencies include *Lintas*, *Overseas and General Advertising*, *Ogilvy Benson and Mather*, *ROD Publicity*, *Intermark Associates* and *Cosmos*.

Insurance
Great Nigeria Insurance Co Ltd, 39/41 Martins Street, Lagos, ☎ 20591/2, 56645.
National Insurance Corporation of Nigeria Ltd, 96/102 Broad Street, P.O. Box 1100, Lagos, ☎ 25311/3 – branches in Kaduna, Enugu, Ibadan, Kano, Aba, Jos, Maiduguri and Benin City.

Phoenix of Nigeria Assurance Co Ltd, Mandilas House, 96/102 Broad Street, P.O. Box 2893, Lagos, ☎ 23651/2 – branches in Warri, Port Harcourt, Ibadan and Kano.
Royal Exchange Assurance (Nigeria) Group, 31 Marina, P.O. Box 112, Lagos – 6 branches.
Sun Insurance Office (Nigeria) Ltd, Unity House, 37 Marina, P.O. Box 2694, Lagos, ☎ 631138/653986 – branches in Yaba, Ibadan, Kano and Owerri.

Shipping
Nigerian Green Lines Ltd, Unity House, 13th Floor, 37 Marina, P.O. Box 2288, Lagos.
Nigerian National Shipping Line Ltd, Development House, 21 Wharf Road, P.O. Box 326, Apapa.
Nigerian Ports Authority, 26–8 Marina, P.M.B. 12588, Lagos.
Nigeria Shipping Federation, NPA Commercial Offices Block 'A', Wharf Road, P.O. Box 107, Apapa.

USEFUL ADDRESSES (BUSINESS)

The Nigerian Association of Chambers of Commerce, Industry, Mines and Agriculture, 3rd Floor, Barclays Bank Building, 131 Broad Street, P.O. Box 109, Lagos, ☎ 21910.

Ibadan Chamber of Commerce & Industry, Barclays Bank Building, Bank Road, P.M.B. 5168, Ibadan.

Kano Chamber of Commerce & Industry, P.O. Box 10, Kano.

Lagos Chamber of Commerce & Industry, 131 Broad Street, P.O. Box 109, Lagos.

Manufacturers' Association of Nigeria, 12th Floor, Unity House, 37 Marina, P.O. Box 3835, Lagos.

Nigerian Chamber of Mines, P.O. Box 454, Jos.

Nigerian National Petroleum Corporation, Broad Street, P.M.B. 12701, Lagos.

Port Harcourt Chamber of Commerce, P.O. Box 71, Port Harcourt.

MAJOR CITIES AND TOWNS

Lagos

The history of Lagos dates back to the 15th century when Lagos Island was inhabited by the Yoruba civilisation. It subsequently became a centre for trade between the Kingdom of Benin and Portuguese settlers. In 1862 Lagos became a British Crown Colony until the Colony and Protectorate of Nigeria was declared in 1914.

Lagos is a noisy, bustling, cosmopolitan city reflecting the modern and powerful status of Nigeria in modern Africa. The city is overcrowded with a conglomeration of buildings ranging from shacks and traditional huts to modern, towering skyscrapers.

Lagos can be divided into several distinct areas: Lagos Island, where most of the government and commercial offices are situated; Ikoyi Island and Victoria Island, residential areas where most of the city's better hotels are to be found; and the Brazilian Quarter, which originated as a settlement for freed South American slaves.

Some of the city's more interesting sights include the National Museum at Onikan on Lagos Island, the Palace of the Oba (King) of Lagos, which houses several traditional shrines, and the National Hall which is the city's main conference centre.

Hotels

There is no official hotel rating system.

BRISTOL, 6–8 Martins Street, P.O. Box 1088, ☎ 25901.
Modern 1st-class hotel in commercial centre.
Rooms: 82 ♪, ♨, ♍, ♄. Suites available.
Facilities: Restaurant, bar. Car hire.
Services: TC, FC. ▤ Credit cards not accepted. **S**.
Conference facilities – max. capacity 150.

EKO HOLIDAY INN, Victoria Island, P.O. Box 12724, ☎ 52365.
Modern luxury hotel, 5km/3 miles from city centre.
Rooms: 470 ♪,♨,♍, ♫, ♄, ⛴. Suites available.
Facilities: Restaurants, bars, coffee shop, outdoor café, nightclub. Sauna, swimming. Car hire.
Services: TC, FC. ▤ Amex, Bankamericard, Diners Club, Master Charge.

Dr. on call. **S**, ♂. Audio-visual equipment.
Conference rooms – max. capacity 1,000.
Banquet rooms – max. capacity 1,000.

EXCELSIOR, 3–15 Ede Street, P.O. Box 1167, Apapa, ☎ 41694.
Modern 1st-class hotel in the suburbs.
Rooms: 92 ♪, ♨, ♫.
Facilities: Restaurant, bars, snack bar. Nightclub with floorshows and casino. Boutiques. Barber shop, beauty salon. Swimming. Car hire.
Services: TC, FC. ▤ Credit cards not accepted. ♂.
Conference room – max. capacity 50.
Banquet rooms – max. capacity 150.

FEDERAL PALACE, Ahmadu Bello Way, Victoria Island, P.O. Box 1000, ☎ 26691/9.
Modern 1st-class hotel complex comprising Federal Palace Hotel and Federal Palace Suites Hotel, in residential area overlooking Lagos Harbour.

333

NIGERIA

Rooms: 200, 72 suites ♪, ⏻, ◉, ⬜, ⛉, ⏃, ⚐.
Facilities: Restaurant, grill room, cocktail lounge, bars. Nightclub and casino. Tennis, swimming, sauna, massage room. Car hire. Shopping arcade.
Services: TC, FC. ☐ Amex. Dr. on call. S.
Banquet rooms – max. capacity 450.

IKOYI, Kingsway Road, P.O. Box 895, Ikoyi, ☏ 22181, 24075/7.
Modern 1st-class hotel in quiet, residential surroundings, 15 minutes' drive from city centre.
Rooms: 300 ♪, ◉, ⬜, ⛉, ⏃, ⛝. Suites available.
Facilities: Restaurant, grill room, cocktail lounge, bars. Swimming, golf. Tennis and squash near by. Car hire.
Services: TC, FC. ☐ Credit cards not accepted. Dr. on call. S, ♂.
Conference rooms – max. capacity 500.
Banquet rooms – max. capacity 200.

MAINLAND, 2–4 Murtala Mohammed Way, P.O. Box 2158, ☏ 41101/9.
Modern commercial hotel in city centre.
Rooms: 191, 16 suites ♪, ◉, ⬜ on request, ⛉ (in some), ⏃, ⛝.
Facilities: Restaurants, bars, tea room. Nightclub. Car hire. Private dining rooms.
Services: TC, FC. ☐ Amex. Dr. on call. S, ♂. Translation bureau.
Conference room – max. capacity 500.

Murtala Mohammed International Airport
LAGOS AIRPORT, Ikeja Village, P.O. Box 3, ☏ 32051.
Modern 1st-class hotel, 1 mile from airport, 25km/15½ miles from centre of Lagos.
Rooms: 250 ♪, ◉, ⬜, ⛉. Suites available.
Facilities: Restaurant, grill, bar, snack bar, casino. Swimming. Barber shop and beauty salon. Car hire. Hotel car connecting with all flights.
Services: TC, FC. ☐ Amex, Diners Club. S, ♂.

Conference room – max. capacity 700.
Banquet rooms – max. capacity 400.

Restaurants
There are good restaurants open to non-residents in the larger hotels. Other restaurants of a comparable standard within the city include: *Chez Antoine*, Broad Street, ☏ 25342; *Cathay Restaurant* – Chinese; *Phoenicia*; *Maharini* – Indian; *Bagatelle*, Broad Street, ☏ 22345 – live music and dancing.

Nightclubs
Lagos has a colourful and varied night life. Many nightclubs are in the open air, and live bands appear every night. Some of the more popular ones are: *Caban Bamboo*; *El Morocco*, Excelsior Hotel, ☏ 41694; *Gondola*; *Crystal Gardens*; *Mexico*, *Bacchus* and *Barakoto*.

Entertainment
Lagos offers a wide variety of sporting facilities. There are some good beaches just outside the city, including the Bar Beach on Victoria Island and the Tarkwa Beach which can be reached by ferry from the Federal Palace Hotel.

A number of sports and social clubs offer swimming, tennis, squash, golf, polo and sailing, including the *Island Club*, *Ebute Metta Club*, *Yacht Club* and *Ikoyi Club*.

Many arts and music festivals take place in Nigeria each year, at both national and state level. A guide to these is available from the Nigerian Tourist Association, 47 Marina, P.O. Box 2944, Lagos, ☏ 26129, 26120.

Shopping
Best buys: wood carvings, leatherwork, jewellery, handwoven cloth, metal work.

A selection of handicrafts is on sale in the *Craft Centre* at the National Museum on Lagos Island. Many locally made goods can be purchased in the Jankara Market on Lagos Island. Other markets in and around Lagos are the Oyinbo Market and the Agege Market.

Ibadan

Ibadan, the 2nd largest city in Nigeria, is the capital of Oyo State and, as Nigeria's leading university, is the intellectual centre of the country. Ibadan is situated in the middle of the cocoa-producing area and agricultural processing comprises a large part of the city's industry. The city was founded in the 1830s at the time of the Yoruba civil wars and became the most powerful of the city-states in the region, the British forces eventually taking control in 1893. Ibadan is now a sprawling city which has spread over the surrounding hills in a mixture of old and new architectural styles. The best place from which to see Ibadan is the top of Cocoa House, the cocoa industry administration building, the tallest in the city.

Hotels

GREEN SPRINGS, Ife Road, P.O.B. 159, ☎ 413796.
Modern hotel near airport, 6km/4 miles from city centre.
Rooms: 48 ♪, ●, ◻, ☎, ♨, ♡. Suites available.
Facilities: Restaurants, bars. Swimming.
Services: T₵, F₵. ⊟ Credit cards not accepted. Dr. on call.
Conference room – max. capacity 250.
Banquet room – max. capacity 250.

PREMIER, Mokola Hill, P.O. Box 1206, ☎ 62340.
Modern commercial hotel in town centre near Government and business districts.
Rooms: 87 ♪, ☎. Suites available.
Facilities: Restaurant, bar, cocktail lounge, coffee shop, nightclub, casino. Swimming. Shopping arcade. Car hire.
Services: T₵, F₵.
Conference and banqueting rooms.

Restaurants

Recommended restaurants include the *West End Restaurant*, off Lebanon Street – Lebanese; *Yesmina*, New Court Road – Lebanese; *Mudah Restaurant*, Lebanon Street; and *The Koko-Dome*, Cocoa House.

Nightclubs

The *Grotto*, *Mokola Roundabout* and the *Paradise Club* offer live music. Other nightclubs include the *Club Apollo*, *Oke Ado*, *Mudah Nightclub* on Lebanon Street and the *Grandstand* near the Premier Hotel.

Entertainment

In keeping with its status as the intellectual capital of Nigeria, Ibadan offers a wide variety of cultural activities throughout the year centred on the University of Ibadan. The Mbari Mbayo Club puts on art exhibitions, plays, poetry readings and musical productions. The city is also the home of many dance troupes specialising in performances based on Yoruba folklore. Exhibitions are often held at the university's Institute of African Studies.

Ibadan also has a number of sports and social clubs offering tennis, badminton, swimming, golf, squash and cricket to members and their guests.

Shopping

Best buys: adire cloth, handicrafts, especially carvings and beadwork. Ibadan has about a dozen markets of which the main ones are the Oje, Dugbe, Oja-Iba and Mokola markets.

RWANDA
Republic of Rwanda

Geography	*337*
The Economy	*338*
How to Get There	*339*
Entry Regulations	*339*
Practical Information for the Visitor	*340*
Useful Addresses (General)	*341*
Business Information	*342*
Useful Addresses (Business)	*343*
Kigali	*343*

Size: 26,388 sq.km/10,169 sq.miles.

Population: 4.82 million (August 1978).

Distribution: 5% in urban areas.

Density: 183 person per sq.km/474 per sq.mile.

Population Growth Rate: 2.7% p.a. (1970–75).

Ethnic Composition: The vast majority are Hutu, some 14% are Tutsi and about 1% are Twa pygmies. Ethnic groupings, never mutually exclusive, are now of less importance than formerly.

Capital: Kigali Pop. 90,000 (1978 est.).

Major Towns: Butare Pop. 20,000.

Language: French and Kinyarwanda are the official languages. Some Swahili is also spoken, particularly in commercial circles.

Religion: Over 60% are Christian, mostly Roman Catholic. There is a small Muslim minority, and the remainder uphold traditional beliefs.

Government: Rwanda became independent of Belgium on 1st July 1962. Since the Second Republic was established after a bloodless coup on 5th July 1973 the political leader has been President Juvenal Habyarimana, Commander of the Armed Forces and leader of the Mouvement Révolutionnaire National pour le Développement (MNRD), the sole legal political party since its formation in July 1975. At elections in December 1978 Habyarimana was elected President for a further 5 years by universal adult suffrage; a referendum held at the same time resulted in an overwhelming vote of approval for a return to civilian rule under a new constitution. The Government is composed of an elected legislative body, the National Development Council, with authority to censure the President and his Council of Ministers, who retain supreme executive power.

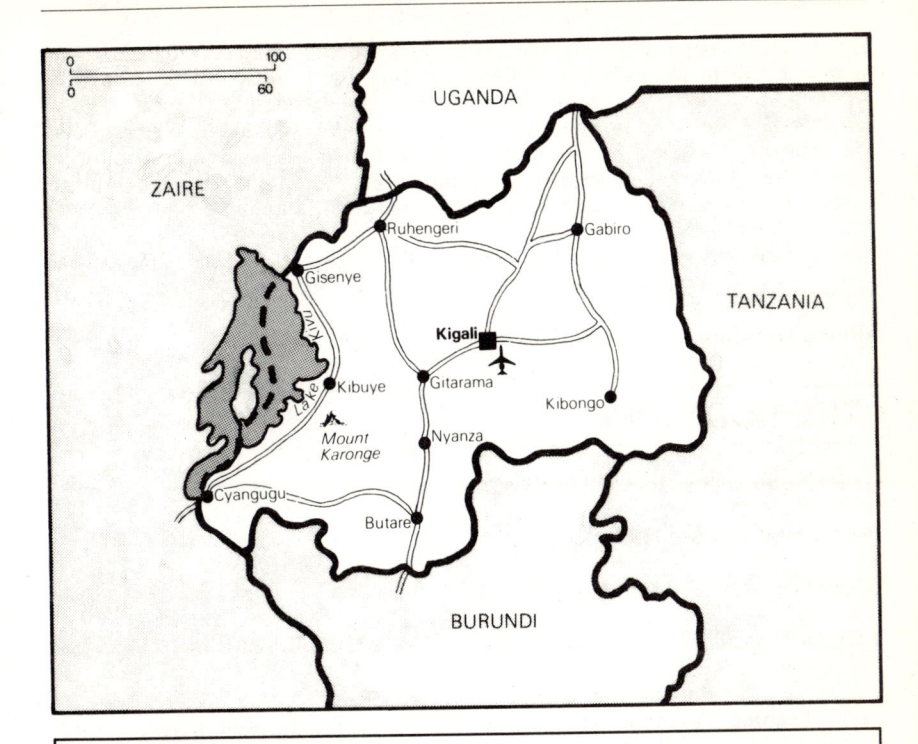

GEOGRAPHY

Rwanda is a small country of hills and deep valleys situated in the remote heart of Africa to the north of Lake Tanganyika. In the north of the country are the Virunga, a chain of dormant volcanoes, the highest of which is Karisimbi at 4,519m/14,826 feet. The average altitude of Rwanda is 1,500m/4,920 feet. Soils are mostly poor, being thin on the slopes and marshy in the valley bottoms.

Climate
Altitude moderates temperatures and the wide diurnal range may be up to 14°C/57°F. The average annual temperature in Kigali is 19°C/67°F. There are 2 rainy seasons, January – May and October – December; the other months are comparatively dry.

Agriculture
Agriculture is the major economic activity, accounting for over 60% of the GDP and employing some 95% of the population. Most people engage in subsistence farming, with a traditional division between Hutu cultivators and Tutsi pastoralists. Poor soils and a fast rising population have encouraged farmers to bring every available piece of cultivable land into use for the production of a variety of food and cash crops. The main food crops produced are beans and peas, sweet potatoes, manioc, sorghum, bananas, maize, millet and rice. The most important cash crops are coffee, tea, cotton, quinquina (cinchona bark for the production of quinine), pyrethrum and tobacco. Livestock raising is also of importance, the Ankole cattle being the traditional measure of wealth, and under the current 5-Year Development Plan livestock production is to be

promoted with increased meat and hides and skins exports envisaged. Other Government aims are to diversify both subsistence and commercial crops, especially to encourage a reduced reliance upon coffee earnings, improve the general level of nutrition of the population, educate farmers about soil conservation, to raise yields and expand the co-operative farming enterprises. This ambitious plan for improving agricultural productivity with minimal disturbance to traditional rural patterns of farming is supported by a number of aid-donating countries and agencies.

Main Crops: beans, sweet potatoes, maize, millet, sorghum, rice, plantain bananas, coffee, tea, cotton, pyrethrum, tobacco, quinquina, timber.

Mineral Resources: cassiterite, wolfram, methane gas, gold.

THE ECONOMY

Gross National Product (1976): US$462 million.

Per Capital Income (1978): US$178.

Gross Domestic Product (1974): FRR 28.7 billion.

Foreign Trade (1977): Total Imports – FRR 10.58 billion. Total Exports – FRR 8.54 billion.

Main Trading Partners: Imports – Belgium/Luxembourg, Kenya, Japan, West Germany. Exports – Belgium/Luxembourg, USA, UK, Zaïre, Netherlands.

One of the poorest states in Africa, Rwanda has had its economic growth restricted by transportation difficulties and rapid population growth. In the current 5-Year Development Plan (1977–81), the emphasis continues to be upon improving agricultural output to feed the growing population. Only some 5% of total agricultural production is exported, with coffee, the major export earner, worth over 10 times as much as any other exported commodity in 1976. However, the output and value of all export crops varies considerably with weather and transport conditions and is also dependent upon price levels in the world markets.

After agriculture, mining is the second most important export industry, accounting for about 30% of export value. Belgian companies dominate mineral production and most exports are to the USA and EEC countries. Cassiterite is extracted and production of tin concentrates averages some 2,000 tons per annum. Wolfram, a tungsten ore, is another important exported mineral and about 1,000 tons are produced each year; production is to be increased in response to the rising value of the ores and a projected foundry will process tin ore near Kigali. Large reserves of methane gas have been discovered underneath Lake Kivu and exploitation of this valuable energy source is planned as part of the CEPGL development programme. Prospecting for uranium, copper, lead and zinc has been carried out recently.

Manufacturing industry is primarily concerned with production for domestic consumption, particularly foodstuffs, drinks and agricultural processing (coffee, tea, cotton, sugar, etc.). There are 2 textile mills, soap, paint and other chemical industries, and a number of small engineering, assembly, construction materials and printing enterprises.

Tourism is to be developed as part of the 5-Year Development Plan and a programme of hotel building is under way, with Kagera National Park in the north-east a big attraction.

Energy production has been made a major priority in the Development Plan, and the completion of the Kitimba Dam will make Rwanda self-sufficient in electricity. Infrastructure development has, with the exception of the road system, been relatively retarded, but education, health, communications and other domestic and industrial services are being expanded in order that Rwanda may become less reliant upon neighbouring and other countries for those skills and facilities needed to realise the country's economic potential.

The current Development Plan is going to be expensive, with 70% of the total US$600 million allocated coming from 5 bilateral donor countries (including Belgium, China, France and West Germany) and the rest from multilateral agencies (EDF, FAO, World Bank) and revenue from coffee sales.

Major Industries: Processing of agricultural produce, textile milling, brewing, repairs and assembly industries, soap, paint, printing, construction materials.

Main Commodities Traded: Coffee, cassiterite, wolfram, tea, cotton, pyrethrum.

International Affiliations: UN, IBRD, OAU, ACP, ADB, OCAM, CEPGL, KRBO.

HOW TO GET THERE

Air

Sabena fly to Kigali from Brussels 4 times weekly, with 3 flights calling at Bujumbura, 2 at Nairobi, 1 at Athens and 1 at Entebbe. Air France operate a service once weekly from Paris. Air Zaïre fly from Kinshasa to Kigali once a week and also operate a service from Goma once weekly. STAB (Burundi) have scheduled flights from Bujumbura and Air Tanzania fly to Kigali from Dar es Salaam once weekly. Ethiopia Airways operate 1 flight a week to Kigali from Addis Ababa. KLM, Iberia, Yugoslavian Airways, Scandinavian Airlines, Air Inter, Czechoslovakian Airlines, Lufthansa, Alitalia, Austrian Airlines and Swissair also have scheduled services to and from Kigali.

Road

There are main roads into Rwanda from Zaïre and Uganda; existing routes from Tanzania and Burundi to Kigali are being improved.

ENTRY REGULATIONS

Visas

All visitors require a visa, except for nationals of Tanzania, Uganda, West Germany and Zaïre.

Visas are obtainable from Rwanda representatives abroad or, if none exists, at Kigali Airport. Direct applications for visas should be sent to Ministère de l'Intérieur, Service de l'Immigration, B.P.63, Kigali, at least 6 weeks in advance with full details of the proposed visit.

Health Regulations
International Certificates of Vaccination for smallpox are required of all visitors. Cholera and yellow fever certificates are necessary for those arriving from infected areas.

Customs
Currency: The import and export of local currency up to FRR5,000 is permitted. There are no limits on the import of foreign currency, provided it is declared upon arrival; visitors may export amounts up to the sum declared.

Duty-free articles: Personal effects. 2 cartons of cigarettes. 2 litres of alcoholic drink.

Articles liable for duty: Ivory goods. The export of game trophy is controlled by the Game Department.

PRACTICAL INFORMATION FOR THE VISITOR

1. Currency
Monetary Unit – Rwanda franc (FRR), divided into 100 centimes.
Notes – 20, 50, 100, 500, 1,000 FRR.
Coins – 1, 2, 5, 10, 20, 50 FRR.

The *Banque Nationale du Rwanda* is the central bank and the bank of issue.

Domestic Banks
Banque Nationale du Rwanda, B.P. 531, Kigali.
Banque Rwandaise de Développement, B.P. 1341, Kigali.

Principal Commercial Banks
Banque Commerciale du Rwanda, Blvd. de la Révolution, B.P. 354, Kigali, ☎ 5591.
Banque de Kigali, Rue des Republicains, B.P. 175, Kigali, ☎ 5493.

Banking Hours
0830 – 1200 Monday to Friday

2. Electricity Supply
120/220v AC 50/60 Hz.

3. Weights and Measures
The metric system is in use.

4. Media
The official radio station is Radiodiffusion de la République Rwandaise broadcasting daily in French, Kinyarwanda and Swahili. There is no television service.

Newspapers and Journals
There is no daily newspaper and the main news sources are the Information Office publications *Imhavo* and *La Relève*. In addition there are a number of Christian and University journals, and some agricultural and trade periodicals. The *Bulletin Agricole du Rwanda* is issued by the Ministry of Agriculture and Livestock. *Cooperative Trafipro Umunyamulyango*, a trade monthly, is published in French and Kinyarwanda.

5. Medical Care
A risk of malaria exists all year round in parts of Rwanda and anti-malarial prophylactics should be taken before, during and after a visit. TAB (typhoid and paratyphoid) and cholera vaccinations are also advisable. Bilharzia may be contracted from some lakes and rivers. Tap water should be boiled or filtered before drinking except in the main centres.

6. Telephone, Telex and Postal Services
The domestic telephone system operates

satisfactorily, but there may be delays for international calls.
Telex facilities are limited.
All mail to and from Rwanda should be dispatched by air.

7. Public Holidays

1 January	*New Year*
1 May	*Labour Day*
1 July	*Independence Day*
26 October	*Government Holiday*
25 December	*Christmas Day*

In addition the Christian festivals of Easter (Thursday, Friday and Monday), *Whit Monday, Assumption* and *All Saints Day* are observed as public holidays.

8. Time
GMT +2.

9. Internal Transport

Air
Air Rwanda operate scheduled flights between Kigali, Kamembe and Butare. It is possible to charter light aircraft and there are small airports at a number of small towns and settlements, including Ruhengeri and Gisenye.
An embarkation tax is payable on all domestic flights.

Air Charter Firms
Star, B.P. 177, Kigali, ☎ 5238.

Taxis Aeriens de Bry, B.P. 352, Kigali, ☎ 5318.
Transafricair, B.P. 383, Kigali, ☎ 5287.

Airline Offices in Kigali
Air Rwanda
Sabena, B.P. 96 ☎ 5294
Air France,
 B.P. 411 ☎ 5566.
Air Tanzania,
 B.P. 385 ☎ 5045.

Road
There are some 6,000km/3,730 miles of major and secondary roads linking all the main centres. Most roads are unpaved and may be impassable in bad weather. The main north-south route between Kigali and Butare is being asphalted.
Modern green buses link many towns, but services are infrequent. Taxis are available in the larger towns.
Cars may be hired in Kigali and drivers need a foreign or International driving licence. Traffic travels on the right-hand side.

Car-Hire Firms in Kigali
Agence Solliard, B.P. 335, ☎ 5660.
Rwanda Links, B.P. 573.
Rwanda Motor, B.P. 448, ☎ 5294.

10. Tipping
Taxis – No tip necessary.

Hotel/restaurant – 10–15% of the bill.

USEFUL ADDRESSES (GENERAL)

Kigali
Belgian Embassy: Blvd. de la Révolution, B.P. 81.

Burundi Embassy: Blvd. de la Révolution, B.P. 714.

Chinese Embassy: Ave. Député Kayuku, B.P. 1345.

French Embassy: Ave. Député Kamuzini, B.P. 53, ☎ 5225.

North Korean Embassy: B.P. 646.

Libyan Embassy: B.P. 1152.

Swiss Embassy: Blvd. de la Révolution 21, Bâtiment Amirwanda, B.P. 597, ☎ 5534.

Ugandan Embassy: B.P. 656.

Soviet Embassy: Ave. de la Paix, B.P. 40.

US Embassy: Blvd. de la Révolution, B.P. 28, ☎ 5601.

Vatican Embassy: Ave. Paul VI, B.P. 261.

West German Embassy: Ave. de la Jeunesse, B.P. 355, ☎ 5222.

Zaïre Embassy: Ave. Député Kamuzini, B.P. 169.

British Consulate: Ave. Paul VI, B.P. 356, ☎ 5905.

Dutch Consulate: c/o NAHU, Ave. de L'Indépendance, B.P. 626, ☎ 5655.

Office Rwandaise du Tourisme et des Parcs Nationaux (ORTPN): B.P. 906, ☎ 6512.

Université Nationale de Rwanda: B.P. 117, Butare.

Travel Agencies in Kigali
AMI, B.P. 262, Kigali, ☎ 5395.

Transintra-Transafricair, B.P. 383, Kigali, ☎ 5287.

Rwanda Travel Service, B.P. 140, Kigali, ☎ 6512 – public transport.

Agence Solliard, B.P. 335, Kigali, ☎ 5660.

BUSINESS INFORMATION

Foreign investment and assistance is encouraged, and a number of European and American based companies have interests in Rwanda. Enterprises must accord with Government plans, and projects with state participation are particularly welcome in this mixed economy. Sectors earmarked for development are agriculture, mining, tourism, energy, education, transport and communications. Rwanda offers the investor relative political stability and cheap labour, although inflationary pressures are mounting due to rising commodity prices and increased aid (now 50% of public expenditure) and increasing fuel and transport costs. Many exports and imports are now transported by air to Mombasa due to the upheavals in Uganda. The domestic market is small and, apart from the expatriate community and urban elites, income levels are very low and the populace scattered. Kigali is the commercial centre of the country.

Import and Exchange Control Regulations
Import licences are needed for all goods and foreign exchange payments will only be authorised when a licence has been granted.

Business Hours
Government Offices and Business Houses
0800 – 1200
1400 – 1700 Monday to Friday

USEFUL ADDRESSES (BUSINESS)

Chambre de Commerce et d'Industrie du Rwanda, B.P. 319, Kigali.

Office des Cultures Industrielles du Rwanda (OCIR), B.P. 104, Kigali.

L'Institute des Sciences Agronomiques du Rwanda (ISAR), B.P. 138, Butare – agricultural development organisation.

MAIN CITY

Kigali

Kigali, the main commercial and industrial centre in Rwanda, is a small city surrounded by terraced hillsides and forests. The city retains a distinctive African atmosphere and European-style development is limited; it is Government policy to stem the drift to the towns apparent in recent years. There is a small outdoor market in Kigali, but little in the way of tourist attractions as such. Butare and the lake resort towns of Gisenye and Shangugu offer more to the visitor in the way of leisure facilities.

Hotels

There is no official hotel rating system. Advance booking is recommended as there are few hotels in Kigali.

HOTEL DES DIPLOMATES, B.P. 269, ☎ 5579.
HOTEL KIVOYU, B.P. 1331, ☎ 5106.
HOTEL DES MILLES COLLINES, B.P. 1332, ☎ 6530.
MOTEL, B.P. 276, ☎ 5673.

Restaurants

All the main hotels have good restaurants open to non-residents, and amongst those in town are *Chez John, Le Picket* and *La Sierra*. There are a number of small bar-restaurants, some with live music and dancing in the evening, including *Aux Délices, La Bonne Source, Café de Kigali, Come Back, Lumière, Panorama, Terminus* and *Venus*.

Shopping

Best buys: woven and bead items, basket ware, sticks and canes, pipes, pottery and traditional wooden spears.

Locally grown coffee is available in large bags for export. A variety of relatively cheap craft goods are on sale in the market.

SENEGAL
Republic of Senegal

Geography *344*
The Economy *346*
How to Get There *346*
Entry Regulations *347*
Practical Information for the Visitor *348*
Useful Addresses (General) *349*
Business Information *350*
Business Services *351*
Useful Addresses (Business) *351*
Dakar *351*

Size: 196,192 sq.km/75,750 sq.miles.

Population: 5.38 million (1978 est.).

Distribution: 20% in urban areas.

Density: 26 persons per sq.km/67 per sq.mile.

Population Growth Rate: 2.6% p.a.

Ethnic Composition: The Wollof consititute about 36% of the population. Other major groups are the Fulani, Serere, Diola, Mandinka and Tukulor. A small, non-African population, mainly French, is centred in Dakar.

Capital: Dakar Pop. 798,800.

Major Towns: Thiès Pop. 117,350; Kaolack Pop. 106,900; Saint Louis Pop. 88,400; Ziguinchor Pop. 72,726.

Language: French is the official language. Wollof is the most widely spoken Senegalese language.

Religion: Over 80% are Muslims; 10%, Christians; the remainder, Animists.

Government: Senegal became an independent Republic in 1960. The President and National Assembly are elected every 5 years. The ruling political party is the Parti Socialiste Sénégalais. The 3 main opposition parties are the Parti Démocratique Sénégalais, Parti Africain de l'Indépendance and the Mouvement Républicain Sénégalais.

GEOGRAPHY

Senegal lies on the west coast of Africa, enclosing the long narrow territory of The Gambia on 3 sides. It is mostly low-lying and dry, with some highland areas in the south-east. The north is semi-desert; the south-west mostly covered by forest.

Climate
Senegal has a tropical climate with a hot and humid season from June to November,

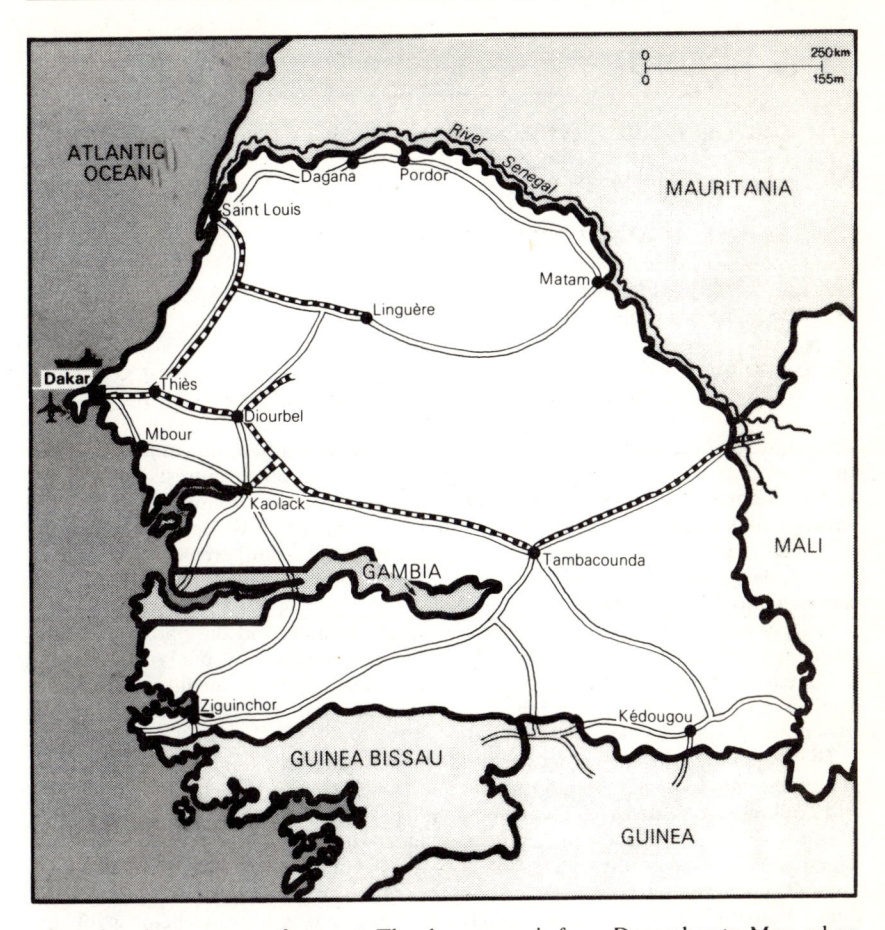

when thunderstorms are frequent. The dry season is from December to May, when maximum temperatures range from 18°C/65°F to 29°C/85°F.

Business travellers are advised to avoid a visit between June and November because of the unpleasant climatic conditions; this is also the main holiday period.

Agriculture
Senegal has an agricultural economy, with groundnuts accounting for some 60% of all exports. Attempts at diversification have led to some success in the cultivation of rice, sugar, bananas and cotton; however large quantities of staples are still imported at considerable cost to the balance of payments.

The development of food crops in general has been slow with production levels constantly falling, particularly when compared to groundnuts.

There is a well-organised fishing industry, and increasing quantities of fish are now available for export.

Main Crops: groundnuts, millet, sorghum, rice, cotton, maize.

Mineral Resources: lime and aluminium phosphates, limestone, titanium, salt.

THE ECONOMY

Gross National Product (1978): US$1,830 million.

Per Capita Income (1978): US$340.

Gross Domestic Product (1977): 487.5 billion CFA francs.

Foreign Trade (1977): Total Imports – 167.46 billion CFA francs. Total Exports – 152.92 billion CFA francs.

Main Trading Partners: Imports – France, USA, Netherlands, West Germany, Nigeria. Exports – France, UK, Netherlands, Ivory Coast, Mauritania, Italy.

Almost 80% of the capital of the main Senegalese companies in the mining, energy, industrial and banking sectors belongs to private or public French interests. Oil mills as well as the phosphates, textiles and chemical industries are all dominated by French interests, as is much of the agricultural sector. Recently, other EEC countries, particularly West Germany, have invested considerable sums of money here. Senegal has also received large amounts of aid from France, the European Development Fund and several United Nations agencies.

Senegal relies heavily on the production of groundnuts and the phosphates and fishing industries. Industrial activity is limited and expansion slow, but both are likely to increase as a result of the country's liberal investment code encouraging foreign participation in major development projects. Most small- and medium-scale industries are controlled by Senegalese nationals.

The main industries are centred around Dakar and include food processing, phosphates, textiles, footwear, oil refining, chemicals, vehicle assembly, building materials and shipbuilding. Major projects currently in hand which have attracted considerable amounts of foreign aid and investment include: the building of a repair yard for supertankers at Dakar; the establishment of the Cayor Complex, which will include a mineral and petroleum port, a refinery and the creation of a new town with a projected population of 150,000; and the Senegal River Valley agro-industrial scheme involving the construction of two dams to provide extensive irrigation.

Major Industries: food processing, phosphates, textiles, chemicals, cement, footwear.

Main Commodities Traded: Imports – foodstuffs, machinery, chemical and petroleum products. Exports – groundnuts, phosphates, canned fish.

International Affiliations: UN, IBRD, OAU, ACP, ADB, CEAO, ECOWAS, Franc Zone, OCAM, GRDO, OMUS.

HOW TO GET THERE

Air
There are direct flights to Dakar from London (Gatwick) operated by British Caledonian, and also from Brussels, Frankfurt, Geneva, Paris, Rome and Las Palmas.

SENEGAL

Pan Am and Air Afrique fly from New York to Dakar. Air France, Lufthansa and Swissair operate flights from Santiago (Chile) to Dakar. Lufthansa and Swissair fly from Rio de Janeiro to Dakar.

Air Canada, Alitalia and Aeroflot also fly to Dakar as well as the following African airlines: Air Afrique, Air Guinée, Air Mauritanie, Air Zaïre, Ghana Airways, Nigerian Airways and Royal Air Maroc.

Flying times to Dakar: from London, 5¾ hours; from New York, 7¾ hours; from Sydney, 24 hours.

The main international airport is Yoff, 15 km/9 miles from the centre of Dakar. A bus service and taxis operate between the airport and city centre. Where applicable, an airport tax is added to the price of an air ticket.

Rail

There is a twice-weekly passenger service from Bamako (Mali) to Dakar with air-conditioned carriages, couchettes and dining car. Further information can be obtained from Fer Tourisme, 38 Boulevard de la République, B.P. 2099, Dakar, ☎ 31747 and 34783.

ENTRY REGULATIONS

Visas

Visas are required by nationals of all countries except: Belgium, Benin, Burundi, Cameroon, Central African Empire, Chad, Congo, France, Gabon, Gambia, West Germany, Italy, Ivory Coast, Luxembourg, Madagascar, Mali, Mauritania, Morocco, Netherlands, Niger, Rwanda, Togo, Tunisia, Upper Volta, Zaïre.

Visas should be obtained from Senegalese diplomatic missions abroad before departing. Visa applications submitted by business travellers should be accompanied by a letter from the applicant's firm detailing the business to be undertaken and confirming financial responsibility for the applicant. Visitors should ensure that the validity of their passport extends for at least 3 months from the date of their visa application.

Visas are valid for 3 months for a stay of up to 3 months. Transit visas are valid for 72 hours.

Applications from nationals of Eastern Europe who intend to stay more than 15 days and from white nationals of South Africa are likely to be referred to Dakar at the applicant's expense; there may be a delay of several weeks before a visa is issued.

Health Regulations

Valid International Certificates of Vaccination against smallpox, yellow fever and cholera are required by all persons entering Senegal. TAB (typhoid and paratyphoid) injections are recommended.

Customs

Currency: There is no limit to the amount of foreign currency which may be taken into or out of Senegal, provided that it is declared on entry and departure and that the amount taken out does not exceed the amount brought in. Not more than 25,000 CFA francs may be imported or exported.

Duty-free articles: Personal effects including one camera, tape-recorder, portable typewriter, etc., per person. 200 cigarettes or 25 cigars or 250g of tobacco. A reasonable amount of perfume. Samples of no commercial value weighing less than 3 kilos gross. There is no free import of alcoholic drink.

PRACTICAL INFORMATION FOR THE VISITOR

1. Currency
Monetary Unit – CFA franc.
Notes – 50, 100, 500, 1,000, 5,000 CFA francs.
Coins – 1, 2, 5, 10, 25, 50, 100 CFA francs.

Travellers' cheques can be cashed at banks and the larger hotels in Senegal.

Banking Hours
0800–1115
1430–1630 Monday to Friday

The *Banque Centrale des Etats de l'Afrique de l'Ouest*, 3 Avenue W-Ponty, B.P. 1398, Dakar, is the central bank.

Commercial Banks
Banque Internationale pour le Commerce et l'Industrie Sénégalaise, 2 Avenue Roume, B.P. 392, Dakar, ☎ 23010.
Banque Internationale pour l'Afrique Occidentale, Place de l'Indépendance, B.P. 129, Dakar.
Société Générale de Banques au Sénégal, 19 Avenue Roume, B.P. 323, Dakar, ☎ 26975.
Union Sénégalaise de Banque pour le Commerce et l'Industrie, 17 Boulevard Pinet-Laprade, B.P. 56, Dakar, ☎ 51188.
Citibank NA, 2 Place de l'Indépendance, B.P. 3391, Dakar, ☎ 34850, 50588.

2. Electricity Supply
127v AC 50Hz (lighting); 220v AC 50Hz (power).
Plugs: 2 round pins.

3. Weights and Measures
The metric system is used.

4. Media
The Government-owned Office de Radiodiffusion-Télévision du Sénégal is responsible for radio and television broadcasting. Radio Senegal broadcasts in French and 6 local dialects and languages.

Newspapers and Journals
Le Soleil is the only daily newspaper, and accepts advertising.

A number of periodicals are also published, including *Afrique Nouvelle*, *Bingo* and *Sénégal d'Aujourd'hui*. A monthly commercial newspaper, *Le Moniteur Africain*, covers trade and industrial developments throughout French-speaking West Africa. *Africa*, an economic review of West and Equatorial Africa, is published 10 times a year. *Sénégal Industrie* is published monthly.

5. Medical Care
Malaria is prevalent in many parts of Senegal, and visitors are advised to take anti-malarial prophylactics. It is advisable to consult a doctor about this before arriving. Visitors should also ensure that drinking water has been boiled and filtered; uncooked fruit and vegetables should be avoided.

Reasonable medical and hospital facilities are available in Dakar and the main towns, but all medical treatment and medicines are expensive. The main hospitals in Dakar are the Hôpital Principal and the Hôpital Dantec.

6. Telephone, Telex and Postal Services
International telex facilities are available; there are public telex facilities at the Hotel Teranga in Dakar.

Telegrams can be sent between 0700 and 2300 hours from the main post office in Dakar.

All mail to and from Senegal should

SENEGAL

be sent by air. There may be some delay and expense incurred in clearing air mail parcels from the Senegal post office.

7. Public Holidays

1 January	New Year's Day
4 April	National Day
1 May	Labour Day
14 July	French National Day
15 August	Feast of Assumption
1 November	All Saints Day
25 December	Christmas Day

The following movable Muslim and Christian holidays are also publicly observed: *Mouled, Kouté* (end of *Ramadan*), *Tabaski, Easter Monday, Ascension Day* and *Whit Monday*.

8. Time
GMT.

9. Internal Transport

Air
Air Senegal flights link Dakar with Saint Louis, Tambacounda, Ziguinchor and other main towns. Private aircraft can be chartered.

Airline Offices in Dakar
Air Afrique	☎ 20370.
Aeroflot	☎ 224815.
Air France	☎ 22941.
British Caledonian	☎ 22292/3.

Iberia	☎ 33870.
Lufthansa	☎ 26505.
Pan Am	☎ 26586/8.
Swissair	☎ 23880/2.

Road
Senegal has a good road network, particularly in the coastal region. Many roads in the interior are earth tracks which become impassable during the rainy season.

Taxis are readily available in Dakar and are usually fitted with meters. Fares double between midnight and 0500 hours. *Taxis de brousse* and *cars rapides* operate between main towns.

There are a number of car hire firms in Dakar and other main towns.

Car-Hire Firms in Dakar
Avis ☎ 33010, 34590; (Yoff Airport) 32790 Ext. 475. Hertz ☎ 26387; (Yoff Airport) 32790.

10. Tipping
Taxis – no tip necessary.

Hotels/restaurants – a service charge of 10–15% is usually included.

11. Social Customs
It is essential that business visitors have a good command of the French language as few people in Senegal either speak or understand English and there are only a limited number of interpreters.

USEFUL ADDRESSES (GENERAL)

British Council: 38 Boulevard de la République, B.P. 6025, Dakar, ☎ 216974/212056.

British Embassy: 20 Rue du Docteur Guillet, B.P. 6025, Dakar, ☎ 27051.

Canadian Embassy: Immeuble Daniel Sorano, 45 Avenue de la République, B.P. 3373, Dakar, ☎ 20270.

Dutch Embassy: 5 Avenue Carde, B.P. 3262, Dakar, ☎ 34083.

French Embassy: 1 Rue Thiers, B.P. 4035, Dakar; Avenue Jean-Mermoz, B.P. 183, Saint Louis.

Japanese Embassy: Immeuble Electra, 2 Rue Malan, B.P. 3140, Dakar, ☎ 20101.

SENEGAL

Swiss Embassy: 1 Rue Victor Hugo, B.P. 1772, Dakar, ☎ 26348/9.

US Embassy: Avenue Jean XXIII, B.P. 49, Dakar, ☎ 20206.

West German Embassy: 43 Avenue Albert Sarraut, B.P. 2100, Dakar, ☎ 26163/4.

American Express Authorised Representative: Socopao-Sénégal, 1 Place de l'Indépendance, B.P. 233, Dakar, ☎ 50124/51026.

Délégation Générale au Tourisme: Place de l'Indépendance, B.P. 2018, Dakar, ☎ 23950.

Wagons-Lits Tourisme Authorised Representative: Transcap Voyages, 20 Boulevard Pinet Laprade, B.P. 58, Dakar, ☎ 22540/22578.

BUSINESS INFORMATION

Dakar is the principal commercial centre of Senegal and an important West African port. Kaolack, another major port, is the centre of the richest groundnut production area and has several groundnut oil mills. Ziguinchor is also important for groundnut production.

There are few technically qualified agents in Senegal and competition for their services is fierce. Agents should preferably be based in Dakar; close contact with the agent is important, especially when competing with established French products. Alternatively, as many of the larger trading firms have their headquarters in France, it may also be possible to make inroads into the Senegalese market through an agent in France.

Import and Exchange Control Regulation

Import licences are required for certain, specified goods although goods originating in the EEC and Franc Zone are exempt from import licences. Exchange authorisation is required for imports from other sources.

Business Hours
Government Offices
0800–1200
1430–1800 Monday to Friday

Business Houses
0800 or 0900–1200
1500–1800 Monday to Friday
0800 or 0900–1200 Saturday

Sunday is the weekly holiday. During the month of *Ramadan*, ending with the *Korité* holiday, some Government offices and other organisations may work a continuous day from 0730–1430.

Business Events

An international trade fair is held in Dakar every two years (1982, 1984, etc.). For further information contact the Foire Internationale de Dakar, Sofidak, Route de Yoff, B.P. 3329, Dakar.

SENEGAL

BUSINESS SERVICES

Advertising
Agence Havas Afrique, 29 Boulevard Pinet–Laprade, B.P. 503, Dakar – radio and cinema advertising.

Forwarding/Clearing Agents
CATA, B.P. 298, Dakar.
SATA R. J., B.P. 1865, Dakar.
SOCOPAO Sénégal, B.P. 233, Dakar.
Transcap, B.P. 58, Dakar.

Shipping
Compagnie Sénégalaise de Navigation (COSENA), 11–13 rue Malenfant, B.P. 3315, Dakar.
Société Sénégalaise de Navigation Maritime (SENAM), 13–14 rue Jules Ferry, B.P. 4032, Dakar.
Union Sénégalaise d'Industries Maritimes (USIMA), 8–10 allées Canard, B.P. 164, Dakar – agents for Cie Générale Transatlantique, Elder Dempster Lines, Deutsche Afrika Line of Hamburg, Gulf West Africa Line of Oslo, SITRAM, Compagnie Maritime Belge and Woermann Line.

USEFUL ADDRESSES (BUSINESS)

Chambre de Commerce, d'Industrie et d'Artisanant de la Région du Cap Vert, B.P. 118, Dakar.

Chambre de Commerce, d'Industrie et d'Artisanat de la Région de Casamance, B.P. 26, Ziguinchor.

Chambre de Commerce, d'Industrie et d'Artisanat de la Région de Sine Saloum, B.P. 203, Kaolack.

Office National de Coopération et d'Assistance pour le Développement, (ONCAD), B.P. 29, Dakar.

MAJOR CITY

Dakar
Dakar lies on the Cape Verde peninsula on a rocky area of land jutting out into the Atlantic. The city was founded in 1857 on the site of a small fishing village and subsequently became the capital of French West Africa in 1902; it became the capital of Senegal in 1958.

The focal point of the modern city is the Place de l'Indépendance, but the true African side of Dakar is best seen around its colourful, bustling markets – the Kermel, Sandaga and Medina markets are the main ones.

The IFAN Ethnographical Museum in the Place Tascher houses treasures and antique curios from Senegal, the Ivory Coast, Benin and Upper Volta. From the top of the minaret of the Great Mosque (67m/220ft) there is a panoramic view over the Dakar peninsula.

2 short excursions from Dakar may also be of interest to the visitor:

The Island of Gorée: A 25-minute boat trip from the port of Dakar, the island was at one time a Dutch naval base and later a major centre for the slave trade. Of note are the 18th-century houses with their decorative wrought-iron balconies, the Governor's Palace, and the ruins of Fort Nassau, Fort Orange and the old slave dungeons. The Island also has three museums: the Maison des Esclaves, the Historical Museum and the Marine Museum.

SENEGAL

Cape Verde: The Cape boasts many fine white sandy beaches, with a variety of water-sport facilities available. Also in the area are the reconstructed village of Soumbedioune and the Musée Dynamique, built for the first Festival of Negro Art in 1966. The Pointe des Alamadies at the end of the Cape is the most westerly point of Africa.

Hotels

The Tourist Board classifies hotels from 4-star down to 1-star.

CROIX DU SUD, 20 Avenue Albert Sarraut, B.P. 232, ☎ 22917.
1st-class (4-star) hotel in city centre, near Government buildings and business district.
Rooms: 63 ♄, ♙, ☎, ⚐, ⚑. Suites available.
Facilities: Restaurant, bar. Car hire.
Services: TC, FC. ▤ Amex, Diners Club. Dr. on call. S.
Conference room.
Banquet rooms – max. capacity 100.

HOTELS MERIDIEN DAKAR, B.P. 8092, Dakar – Yoff.
Modern hotel complex set in a 28-acre park by N'gor Bay, 3½ km/2 miles from airport and 16 km/10 miles from city centre. The 3 hotels in the complex are the Meridien Diarama, the Meridien N'Gor, and the N'Gor Resort Village.
The combined facilities of the complex include 4 restaurants, bars, discotheque, private beach, 2 swimming pools, a commercial centre, car-hire facilities and a variety of sporting activities, together with the facilities and services listed below under the individual hotels:

Meridien Diarama, B.P. 8092, Dakar – Yoff, ☎ 50122.
Modern, superior 1st-class hotel by the sea.
Rooms: 205 ♄, ♙, ☎.
Facilities: Restaurant, cocktail bar, snack bar. Swimming, tennis.
Services: ▤ Amex, Carte Blanche, Diners Club.

Meridien N'Gor, B.P. 8092, Dakar – Yoff, ☎ 45535.
1st-class hotel overlooking the sea.

Rooms: 159 ♄, ♙, ☎.
Facilities: 2 restaurants, cocktail lounge. Shopping arcade. Beauty salon. Conference and banquet facilities.
Services: ▤ Amex, Carte Blanche, Diners Club.

Village de N'Gor, B.P. 8092, Dakar – Yoff, ☎ 45615.
1st-class resort village with native-style bungalows.
Rooms: 157 ♄, ☎.
Facilities: Restaurant, cocktail bars, snack bar. Discotheque. Swimming, volleyball, tennis, riding, sailing.
Services: ▤ Amex, Carte Blanche, Diners Club.

LAGON, Route de la Corniche, ☎ 22215.
Modern 4-star hotel in city centre, overlooking sea.
Rooms: 56 ♄, ♙, ⧠ on request, ☎, ⚐, ⚑. Suites available.
Facilities: Restaurant, bar. Water skiing, fishing. Car hire.
Services: TC, FC. ▤ Diners Club. Dr. on call. S, ♂.
Conference rooms – max. capacity 45.
Banquet rooms – max. capacity 130.

TERANGA, Rue Colbert, B.P. 3380, ☎ 51144.
Modern 4-star hotel in city centre, overlooking sea.
Rooms: 260 ♄, ♙, ⧠, ☎, ⚐, ▥. Suites available.
Facilities: 3 restaurants and bars, tea room. Nightclub with dancing. Tennis, sauna, swimming. Deep-sea fishing, sailing, water skiing. Car hire.
Services: TC, FC. ▤ Amex, Diners Club. S, ♂.
Conference room – max. capacity 350.

Restaurants

There are many restaurants in Dakar; the following is only a small selection.

Le Baobab, Le Tam Tam, Le Ramatou, Le Saint Louis – Senegalese; Le Lagon, L'Esterel, Le Virage – French, Kim Son – Vietnamese; Le Farid – Lebanese. Le Chevalier de Boufflers and the Taverne des Boucaniers are on the Island of Gorée.

Nightclubs
Among Dakar's more popular nightclubs are the Niani, Hugo, Miami, L'Oeil, Le Taverne du Port and Kings. The Casino is on the Route de N'Gor just outside the city centre.

Entertainment
Dakar's long white sandy beaches along Cape Verde and the Petite Côte are ideal for watersports, including sailing and skin diving. Equipment can be hired from Le Lagon, Route de la Petite Corniche; Le Marinas, Route de Bel-Air; Cercle de la Voile, Plage de Hann; and the Hôtel de N'Gor.

Dakar has a number of riding clubs, and all-day rides in the forest of Malika can be arranged through the Ranch du Sagittaire on the Route de Rufisque. Tennis is available through most of the larger hotels and a number of clubs; there is a 9-hole golf course on the Route de Camberene.

Fishing is an extremely popular sport off Cape Verde; from June to October big fish such as tuna, barracuda and blue marlin are caught. The Centre de Pêche Sportive on the Island of Gorée rents out boats and equipment; and Air Afrique run an angling centre in Dakar.

Shopping
Best buys: wood carvings, cloth, gold and silver jewellery, carved ivory, leatherwork, pottery, basketwork.

The Kermel Market, near the port area, is best for flowers and basketwork; the Medina Market in Avenue Blaise Diagne specialises in food, textiles and pottery; and the Place des Maures in fine jewellery. Visitors can see craftspeople at work and buy their wares at the village of Soumbedioune on the Corniche de Fann.

SEYCHELLES
Republic of Seychelles

> Geography *354*
> The Economy *356*
> How to Get There *357*
> Entry Regulations *357*
> Practical Information for the Visitor *358*
> Useful Addresses (General) *360*
> Business Information *360*
> Business Services *361*
> Useful Addresses (Business) *361*
> Victoria *361*

Size: 433 sq.km/171 sq.miles (Mahé – 148 sq.km/57sq.miles; Praslin – 41sq.km/16sq.miles; Silhouette – 16sq.km/6sq.miles; La Digue – 10sq.km/4sq.miles).

Population: 61,900 (1977).

Distribution: 26% in urban areas.

Density: 140 persons per sq.km/361 per sq.mile.

Population Growth Rate: 2% p.a. (1970–7).

Ethnic Composition: Most are Creole descendants of French settlers and African slaves. There are also Indians, Chinese and Europeans.

Capital: Victoria Pop. 23,000.

Major Towns: None.

Language: English and French are the official languages, although most of the population speak the Creole patois.

Religion: Over 90% Roman Catholic and about 8% Anglican.

Government: Independence was formally declared on 28 June 1976. Almost one year later President Mancham was deposed in a coup and Albert René, his Prime Minister in the Coalition Government and leader of the Socialist party, was sworn in as the second President. The new Constitution, effective from June 1977, provides for elections every 5 years to decide by direct popular vote the members of the People's Assembly and the President. The sole political party is the Seychelles People's Progressive Front (SPPF).

GEOGRAPHY

The Seychelles are a group of islands in the western Indian Ocean. Mahé, the main island, lies 1,100km/680 miles north-east of Madagascar, 1,800 km/1,200 miles due east of Mombasa, and 3,300 km/2,050 miles south-west of Bombay.

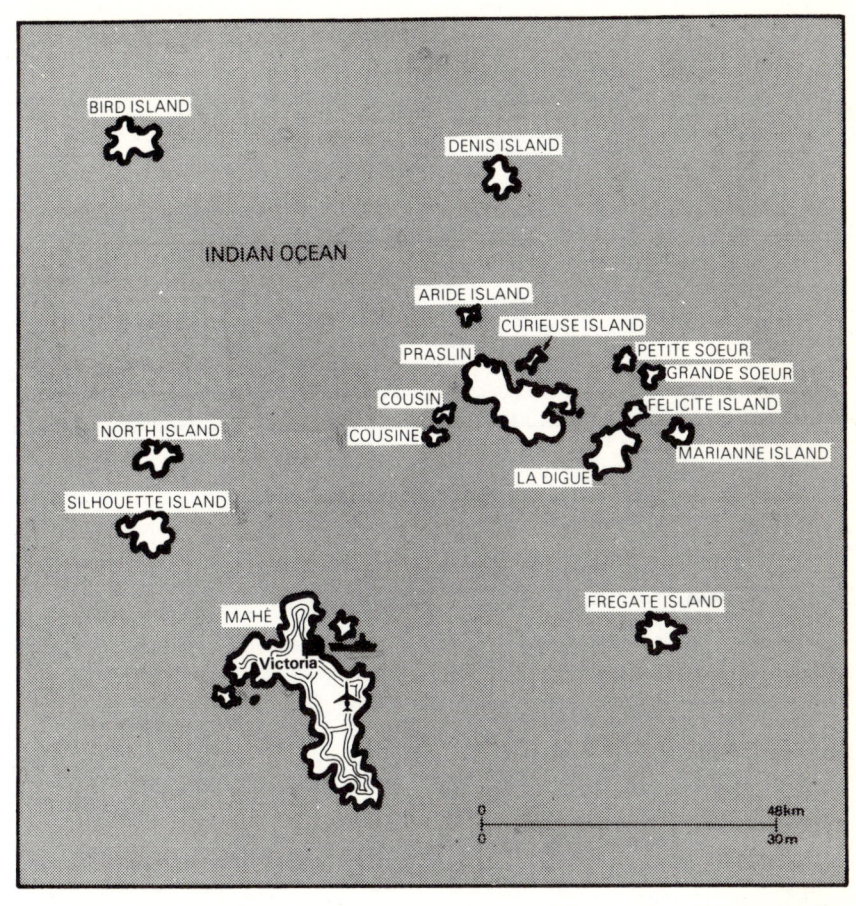

The archipelago consists of 37 granitic and 52 coralline islands. All of the granite islands are situated within 56km/35 miles of Mahé and, in contrast to the coral islands, rise sharply out of the sea. The coral islands are reefs in various stages of development, some with well established vegetation, others only just emerging above the sea. The highest point is Morne Seychelloise standing at 912 metres/2,993 feet on Mahé.

Climate
From November to April the north-east trade winds blow over the Seychelles, making these months hotter and more humid than the rest of the year. When the south-east trade winds blow over the islands from May to October temperatures drop and the wind causes rough seas. The climate is in general very pleasant for there are no extremes of temperature, and high winds or thunderstorms are rare since the islands lie outside the cyclone belt. Mean average temperature at sea level is around 27°C/80°F; mean annual rainfall in Victoria is 2,360mm/93 inches. Temperatures are lower and rainfall greater at higher altitudes.

Agriculture
Poor soils and the small area of cultivable land are contributing factors in the declining

importance of agriculture. The Government hopes to encourage a greater degree of self-sufficiency in agricultural products and to relieve some of the pressure on land with the introduction of a Land Resettlement Scheme which will provide agricultural employment for farmers on 5-acre plots. The programme of agricultural reforms is to concentrate on establishing intensive meat and dairy production, improving existing pig and poultry output, and increasing efficiency in the marketing and distribution of fruit and vegetables grown on the islands.

Traditionally the islands have relied on large amounts of imported food, chiefly rice, to supplement local produce. In recent years, however, rising prices coupled with increased demands from the tourist trade have made the problem of increasing home agricultural production ever more pressing.

Main Crops: copra, cinnamon, tea, limes, coconuts, vanilla, patchouli, peppers, fruit.

Mineral Resources: guano has been extracted on some of the outer coral islands, though this is in decline. Exploration for oil has been undertaken recently within the Seychelles' territorial waters.

THE ECONOMY

Gross National Product (1974 est.): US$31 million.

Per Capita Income (1978 est.): US$1,060.

Gross Domestic Product (1977 est.): SRs 385 million.

Foreign Trade (1977): Total Imports – SRs 340 million. Total Exports – SRs 64 million.

Main Trading Partners (1977): Imports – UK, Kenya, South Africa, Japan, Singapore, Australia, USA. Exports – Pakistan, Mauritius, Greece, Netherlands, UK, USA.

Continuing balance-of-payments difficulties in the wake of oil price rises reflect the vulnerability of the economy to international developments. The rising prices of the many imported foodstuffs and the slackening off of the tourist trade have been important factors in influencing the Government to encourage economic diversification.

Tourism, originally fostered by the British and taken up by President Mancham, has proved to be a successful foreign exchange earner and is now the largest single contributor to Gross Domestic Product. Marketing improvements are planned to lead to a 10% growth in tourist numbers each year, though the Government has pledged to protect the islands from excessive tourist development.

Fishing is the sector with most development potential, and a major effort is being made to establish a modern fishing industry with harbour improvements and processing facilities nearing completion.

Manufacturing is on a small scale. Successful enterprises include a plastics factory, a brewery and agricultural crop processing.

Infrastructure projects are another Government priority with a programme of improvements in housing, health, education and transport. Water and electricity supply projects are also under way.

The Seychelles' economy is still in urgent need of foreign capital to develop new industry and to revitalise older sectors. The current National Development Plan is heavily reliant upon foreign aid from France, the UK, the EEC, China, Canada, India, Norway and the African Development Bank. Oil surveys carried out in the seas around the Seychelles have been unsuccessful to date.

Major Industries: plastics, building materials, beer, cigarettes, construction, agricultural and fisheries processing, some guano mining.

Main Commodities Traded: Imports – foodstuffs, motor vehicles, petroleum products, machinery, chemicals, tobacco. Exports – copra, cinnamon, fish, coconuts, tea, limes, cloves, vanilla, patchouli, guano.

International Affiliations: UN, OAU, ACP, ADB, Commonwealth, OCAM.

HOW TO GET THERE

Air
Direct services to Mahé are provided by British Airways from London, Air France from Paris, Ethiopian Airlines from Addis Ababa, South African Airways from Johannesburg, Air India from Bombay, Air Tanzania from Dar es Salaam, Kenya Airways from Nairobi, Somali Airlines from Mogadishu and Air Madagascar.

The international airport on Mahé is situated 10km/6 miles south of Victoria.

The transfer charge from Seychelles International Airport to the main hotels is SRs50.

Sea
Several cruise ships and passenger-carrying cargo vessels call at Mahé, but there is no regular schedule.

ENTRY REGULATIONS

Visas
Entry visas are not normally required, exceptions being nationals of certain specified countries outside the British Commonwealth. Visas are obtainable upon arrival or from British Consulates. All visitors to the Republic should be in possession of outward or return tickets, or have sufficient funds to deposit up to SRs4,000 with the Principal Immigration Officer and have proof of accommodation for their stay. Visitors' Passes are granted upon arrival for an initial period of 1 month with the possibility of further extension.

Health Regulations
No certificates are required unless travelling from an infected area.

Customs
Currency: There are no restrictions on the import of foreign currency. When departing, visitors may take out up to SRs100 in notes and SRs20 in coins. Exchange only what is needed for day to day expenditure as rupees are valueless outside the Republic.

Duty-free articles: Used personal and household goods brought in within 6 months of entry will be exempted from duty if declared. Up to 125cc of perfume. 250cc of toilet water. 200 cigarettes or 50 cigars or 250 gramms of tobacco. 1 litre of spirits and 1 litre of wine.

Prohibited articles: Narcotics. Firearms. Spear-fishing guns.

Restricted articles: Tea. Seeds. Plants. Meat products. There are also controls on the export of coco-de-mer, shells, live fish and tortoises.

PRACTICAL INFORMATION FOR THE VISITOR

1. Currency
Monetary Unit – Seychelles rupee (SRs), divided into 100 cents.
Notes – 5, 10, 20, 50, 100SRs.
Coins – 1, 5, 25, 50 cents; 1, 5, 10SRs.

Currency is controlled by a Monetary Authority, part of the Department of Finance.

Domestic Banks
Government Savings Bank branches in Victoria and on Grand Anse and Praslin.
Seychelles Development Bank, P.O. Box 217, Victoria.

Foreign currency and travellers' cheques are best exchanged in Victoria.

Principal Foreign Commercial Banks
Bank of Baroda (India), P.O. Box 124, Victoria – open 0830–1300, Monday–Friday.
Bank of Credit and Commerce International S.A., P.O. Box 579, Victoria – open 0830–1230, 1430–1630 Monday–Friday; 0830–1100 Saturday.
Banque Française Commerciale, P.O. Box 122, Victoria – open 0830–1500 Monday–Friday; 0900–1130 Saturday.
Barclays Bank International Ltd, P.O. Box 167, Victoria; also a part-time branch on Praslin – open 0830–1300 Monday–Friday.
Habib Bank Ltd., P.O. Box 702, Victoria – open 0830–1300 Monday–Friday.

Standard Bank Ltd., P.O. Box 241, Victoria – open 0830–1300 Monday to Friday.

2. Electricity Supply
220/240v AC 50Hz.

3. Weights and Measures
The metric system is in use.

4. Media
Radio Seychelles transmits for 12 hours daily in English, French and Creole. The Far East Broadcasting Association transmits religious programmes in a wide variety of European, Asian and African languages.

There is no television service; however, there is a video service which is received in hotels and private homes.

Newspapers and Journals
The 2 daily papers are: *The Nation*, published by the Information Department; and *Le Seychellois*, published in English and French on alternate days, the organ of the Seychelles Farmers' Association. *Weekend Life* is a weekly paper. *L'Echo des Iles* is issued fortnightly by the Roman Catholic Mission in French and Creole.

5. Medical Care
Medical and dental facilities are available with English-speaking doctors and dentists. There are no endemic diseases, and most common ailments suffered by visitors are sunburn and seasickness.

The heat and humidity can be uncomfortable at times, and it is advisable that anyone likely to encounter difficulty with the heat (or with special problems) should bring their own supply of medicines. Water is uncontaminated, and no special health precautions are necessary.

6. Telephone, Telex and Postal Services

There is a 24-hour radio-telephone link from the Seychelles to Nairobi, extendable for world wide connections from there. The service is operated by Cable and Wireless Ltd, who also maintain the local telephone services and radio links with the other islands; the company also provide telegram and telex facilities.

All post being sent abroad goes by airmail. The collections are usually at noon on the day of international flight departures from the main post office in Victoria.

Opening hours of the main post office are: 0800 – 1200, 1300 – 1600 Monday to Friday, and 0800 – 1200 Saturday.

7. Public Holidays

1–2 January	New Year
1 May	Labour Day
5 June	Liberation Day
29 June	Independence Day
15 August	Assumption
1 November	All Saints Day
8 December	The Feast of the Immaculate Conception
25 December	Christmas Day

Easter and *Corpus Christi* are also public holidays.

8. Time

GMT + 4.

9. Internal Transport

Air

Air Mahé and Inter Islands Airways operate several flights a day between Mahé and Praslin, there are also services from Mahé to Bird and Denis Islands. Seychelles International Airport, ☎ 76414/37 or 76815.

Airlines Offices in Victoria

Air France, c/o Travel Services, Victoria House, ☎ 22137.
Air India, represented by SITA, ☎ 22146.
Air Madagascar, SITA, Le Chantier, ☎ 22416
Air Tanzania, represented by Mason's Travel, Michel Building, ☎ 22670.
British Airways, Kingsgate House, ☎ 22001.
Ethiopian Airlines, SITA, Le Chantier, P.O. Box 176, ☎ 23045.
Kenya Airways, represented by Premier Travel, Temooljee Building, ☎ 23591.
Somali Airlines, represented by Blue Safari, Ocean Gate House, P.O. Box 549, ☎ 22768.
South African Airways, represented by British Airways, ☎ 22001.

Sea

Lady Esme, the Government ferry, sails between Mahé, Praslin and La Digue. Various other craft operate services between the islands and can be hired for use.

Road

Roads are good in the Seychelles. Mahé has 137km/82 miles of asphalted roads and 36km/21 miles of earth roads; Praslin has 10km/6 miles of asphalt road and 23 km/15 miles of earth roads; La Digue has 12 km/8 miles of earth roads.

Taxis are available; licensed cabs are identified by a coloured band on the side of the vehicle. Standard rates are laid down by law.

Buses are frequent on Mahé and Praslin. Traditional *camions* decorated with flowers and palm fronds and with open sides also serve as public transport and are specially enjoyed by tourists. For the more intrepid bicycles and even ox-carts are available on some islands.

Traffic travels on the left-hand side of the road.

Self-drive and chauffeur-driven cars are readily available, but the demand is such that advance reservations at peak periods are recommended. Deposits, insurance cover and current driving licence are required.

Car Hire Firms in Victoria
Avis (HQ), P.O. Box 224, ☎ 22542
Hertz, Premier Building, corner of Royal and Albert St, ☎ 22358
Mahé Beach Hotel, ☎ 22711
Seychelles International Airport, ☎ 76445
Victoria Car Hire, ☎ 76314

Addresses of other car hire firms are available from the Visitor Information Office or from the Car Hire Operators Association, P.O. Box 224, Mahé.

10. Tipping
Taxi – Tip for good service.

Porters – Tip according to service.

Hotels/restaurants – 10% of the bill.

11. Social Customs
No special social customs are observed. In general, life here is characterised by an easy-going informality. Formal attire is rarely expected, except if the visitor is on official business when meeting Government representatives. Entertaining is common.

USEFUL ADDRESSES (GENERAL)

Mahé
People's Republic of China Embassy: Cemetery Estate, Mount Fleuris.

French Embassy: Argent Vert, Mount Fleuris, P.O. Box 478, ☎ 22123.

USSR Embassy: Sans Souci, Mahé.

British High Commission: Victoria House, Victoria.

US High Commission: Victoria House, Victoria, P.O. Box 148. ☎ 23921/2.

Tourist Offices and Information:
Visitor Information Office: Kingsgate House, Victoria, ☎ 22655.

Thomas Cook Authorised Representative: Coralline United Touring Company, Premier Building, Victoria, P.O. Box 115, ☎ 2358.

American Express Authorised Representative: Travel Services (Seychelles) Ltd., Pirates Arms Building, Victoria, P.O. Box 356, ☎ 2414.

BUSINESS INFORMATION

Investment is welcomed, and there are no plans to restrict the repatriation of capital. Expatriates may work in jobs where no Seychellois are available. Opportunities exist for the sale of capital equipment in the tourist and fishing industries particularly. The principal sectors in which investments are being encouraged are tourism, fishing, infrastructure and social service projects, and agriculture.

Import Regulations
Import licences are needed for certain goods including many fruits and vegetables, animal feeds, industrial alcohol, chicken, tea and milk. The Seychelles have a preferen-

tial rate agreed for imports originating in EEC and Commonwealth countries. An additional duty of 25 cents per package is levied on all imports.

Government and Business Hours
0800 – 1600 Monday to Friday

BUSINESS SERVICES

Shipping
The Shipping Corporation of India Ltd, Agents — Jurin Jetha and Co., P.O. Box 16, Mahé.

The Union Lighterage Company Ltd, P.O. Box 38, Mahé – agents for Shell Company of the Islands, Shaw Savill and Farrell Lines.

USEFUL ADDRESSES (BUSINESS)

Chamber of Commerce and Industry, Victoria.

Seychelles Copra Association, P.O. Box 32, Victoria.

Seychelles Farmers' Association, c/o P.O. Box 32, Victoria.

Tourism Division, National House, P.O. Box 56, Victoria.

MAJOR TOWN

Victoria
The capital and port of Mahé, by far the largest town in Seychelles, contains the business and administrative centres of the Republic. Victoria is situated on the north-east coast of Mahé island, facing the smaller islands of Ste Anne, Moyenne and Cerf. It is a slightly 'old-fashioned' town with numerous reminders of its colonial past. In the centre is a statue of Queen Victoria and a small-scale replica of the Big Ben clocktower. State House, the seat of Government, is a large colonial mansion away from the town centre with lawns and gardens on view to the public. As is characteristic of ports on the Indian Ocean, many of the streets contain Indian and Chinese shops and restaurants selling local and imported crafts and food; many exotic items can be bought at reasonable prices. There is also a museum and a lively market.

The town is a perfect point of departure for touring the rest of Mahé, the Seychelles' largest and most sophisticated island which is the home of 90% of the Republic's population. Ringed with sandy beaches and coves, Mahé is ideal for relaxing in the sea and sun. Away from the coast the island rises up, and on the higher ground bush forests grow interspersed with tea and cinnamon gardens and fruit groves until one reaches the Morne Seychelloise National Park in the highest parts of the island.

Hotels
There is no official hotel rating system. Many other hotels, guest houses and self-catering accommodation are found on Mahé and the other islands. Information is available from the Tourist Office.

BEAU VALLON BAY HOTEL, Beau Vallon, P.O. Box 550, ☎ 22141.
Spacious modern hotel on beach front, 5km/3 miles from Victoria.
Rooms: 180 ♪, ♫, ♄, ♿. Suites available.

SEYCHELLES

Facilities: TC, FC. Amex, Barclaycard, Visa, Diners Club. Dr. on call, S.
Conference room – max. capacity 80

CORAL STRAND HOTEL, Beau Vallon, P.O. Box 400, ☎ 22036.
Modern hotel, 5km/3 miles from Victoria, in centre of beach at Beau Vallon.
Rooms: 103 ♫, ⚜, ♨, ♦, ☎. Suites available.
Facilities: Restaurants, bars. Nightclub. Parking, car hire. Swimming pool, golf, water sports. Shops.
Services: TC. Amex, Barclaycard, Visa, Diners Club. Dr. on call. S, ♂.
Conference room – max. capacity 80.
Banquet room – max. capacity 180.

FISHERMAN'S COVE, Bel Ombre, P.O. Box 35, ☎ 22552.
Traditional beach-front hotel made in local granite and palm thatch, 5km/3 miles from Victoria.
Rooms: 38 ♫, ▯, ⚜, ▫, ♨, ♦, ☎. Suites available.
Facilities: Restaurants, bars. Parking, car hire. Swimming pool.
Services: TC, FC. Amex, Barclaycard, Visa, Diners Club. Dr. on call. S, ♂.
Conference room – max. capacity 30.

MAHÉ BEACH HOTEL, Port Glaud, P.O. Box 540, ☎ 78451.
Modern luxury hotel built into a granite cliff-face and set in landscaped gardens, 15km/10 miles from Victoria.
Rooms: 177 ♫, ⚜, ♨, ♦, ☎. Suites available.
Facilities: Restaurants, bars. Nightclub. Parking, car hire. Tennis, squash, croquet, bowls, mini-golf, swimming pool, badminton, volley-ball.
Services: TC, FC. Access, Amex, Barclaycard, Carte Blanche, Diners Club, Eurocard, Master Charge. Dr. on call. S, ♂.
Conference room – max. capacity 100 persons.
Banquet room – max. capacity 100.

REEF HOTEL, Anse aux Pins, P.O. Box 388, ☎ 76254.
Luxurious beach-front 5km/3 miles south of airport.
Rooms: 150 ♫, ♨, ♦, ☎. Suites available.
Facilities: Restaurants, bars. Parking, car hire. Tennis, golf, water sports, swimming pool.
Services: TC, FC. Amex, Barclaycard, Diners Club, Visa. Dr. on call. S, ♂.
Conference room – max. capacity 180.

Restaurants
Victoria
Most hotels have restaurants open to non-residents.
Local cuisine: *La Cambuise*, Oceangate House, ☎ 22772 (also European); *La Marmite*, Revolution Avenue, ☎ 22932 (also Chinese and European); *La Mer*, Revolution Avenue, ☎ 22169; *Rocco*, Mount Fleuris, ☎ 22251; *La Tartaruga Felice*, Mount Fleuris, ☎ 22676.
Foreign cuisine: *King Wah*, Benezet Street, ☎ 23658 and *Mandarin*, Revolution Avenue, ☎ 22818 – Chinese; *Continental*, Revolution Avenue, ☎ 22603 – Italian.

Elsewhere on Mahé
Local cuisine: *Auberge Louie XVII*, La Louise, ☎ 22611; *Beachcomber*, Port Lauray, ☎ 78211; *Eden Roc*, Bel Ombre, ☎ 23901; *Isle of Farquhar*, Les Mamelles, ☎ 22030 (also European); *Izlette*, Port Glaud, ☎ 78352; *Oceanic*, Anse à la Mouche, ☎ 76444; *La Rocca*, Baie Ternay, ☎ 76425; *Sundown*, Port Glaud, ☎ 78352.
Foreign cuisine: *Hoi Tin*, Ans Forbans – Chinese; *La Charette*, La Misère, ☎ 78334 – European; *Wayn's Wagon Wheel*, La Louise, ☎ 22841 – steaks.

Entertainment
Facilities exist for the pursuit of many sports and leisure activities, including swimming, diving, yachting, fishing and water-skiing.

Shopping
Local handicrafts are the best buys as souvenirs and gifts. Specialities are basketware, jewellery, hats, worked shells.

SIERRA LEONE
Republic of Sierra Leone

Geography *363*
The Economy *365*
How to Get There *365*
Entry Regulations *366*
Practical Information for the Visitor *367*
Useful Addresses (General) *368*
Business Information *369*
Business Services *369*
Useful Addresses (Business) *370*
Freetown *370*

Size: 71,740 sq.km/27,698 sq.miles.

Population: 3.3 million (1978 est.).

Distribution: 18% in urban areas.

Density: 44 persons per sq.km/114 per sq.mile.

Population Growth Rate: 2.5% p.a.

Ethnic Composition: About 30% are from the Mende and Temne tribal groups; others include the Lokko, Sherbo, Limba, Susu, Fulani and Kono. There is also a small European, Indian and Lebanese population.

Capital: Freetown Pop. 400,000.

Major Towns: Bo Pop. 80,000; Makeni Pop. 70,000; Kenema Pop. 65,000.

Language: English is the official language. Local languages include Krio, Mende and Temne.

Religion: The majority are Animists, and about 25% are Muslims. The Christian minority is mainly in the Freetown peninsula.

Government: Sierra Leone gained independence in 1961 and was declared a Republic in 1971. The President is elected for a 5-year term and heads the appointed cabinet. Parliament consists of a majority of elected representatives and of members appointed by the President. The All People's Congress is the only authorised political party in Sierra Leone.

GEOGRAPHY

Situated on the west coast of Africa, Sierra Leone is mountainous, particularly in the east, and has large, richly forested areas and many rivers. There is a flat coastal plain (with the exception of the hilly Freetown peninsula) and mangrove swamps along the coast.

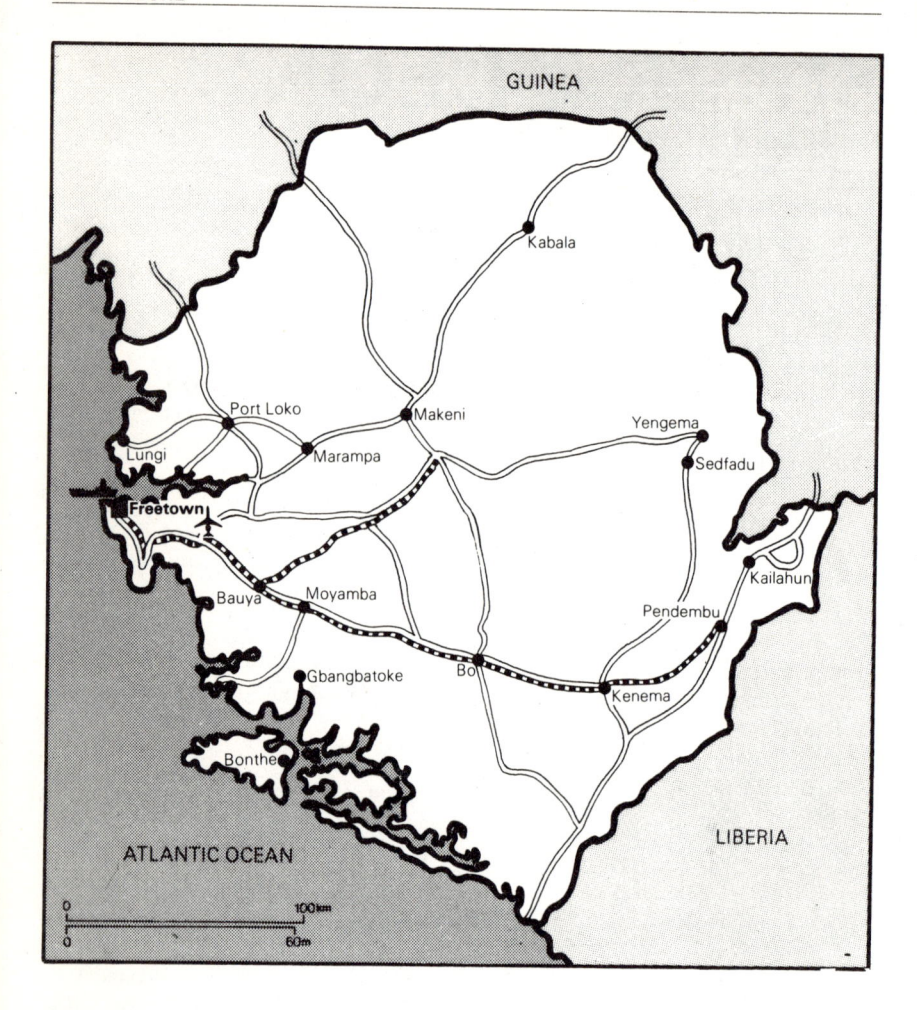

SIERRA LEONE

Climate
The climate is tropical and humid with heavy rainfall, especially along the coast. The rainy season lasts from mid-April to mid-November; rainfall is heaviest from July to September. Temperatures in Freetown range from 24°C/75°F to 30°C/85°F.

Agriculture
Over 70% of the population are engaged in agriculture, with a large proportion living at subsistence level. Agricultural growth is hindered by the system of land tenure in the provinces where much of the land is owned by tribal chiefs.

Most agricultural products destined for export are purchased by the Sierra Leone Market Board, with the notable exception of piassava. Agricultural export earnings have risen in recent years, mainly due to the increased price of coffee and cocoa on the world market, but in general Sierra Leone is a long way from achieving self-sufficiency in many foodstuffs.

Main Crops: rice, coffee, cocoa, ginger, palm kernels, piassava, cassava, cola nuts, citrus fruits.

Mineral Resources: diamonds, iron ore, bauxite, rutile.

THE ECONOMY

Gross National Product (1978): US$760.3 million.

Per Capita Income (1978): US$210.

Gross Domestic Product (1978): 814.7 million leones.

Foreign Trade (1978): Total Imports –US$246.5 million. Total Exports – US$184.4 million.

Main Trading Partners: Imports – UK, Japan, West Germany, Nigeria, China, France, Netherlands. Exports – UK, Netherlands, USA, Japan, West Germany.

Diamonds are the mainstay of the economy providing in excess of 60% of exports; the country's rich mineral deposits are the main sources of foreign exchange. Attempts to establish an agrarian-based economy following independence in 1961 failed due in part to the tribal system of land ownership and the lack of policy co-ordination on agricultural matters.

The majority of diamond mining operations are carried out by DIMINCO in which the Government has a 51% interest. Despite high prices on the world market, the industry is suffering, with large-scale illicit mining and smuggling seriously depleting reserves. The large iron ore mines at Marampa (closed down in 1975 due to unprofitability) have yet to be re-opened, although an estimated 200 million tons of high-grade iron ore is waiting to be mined there. Extensive deposits of rutile (used in making paint pigments) are now being exploited, and the mineral is expected to become a more valuable export than iron ore.

The small domestic market accounts for the limited industrial sector. The Government is anxious to encourage the growth of industries using local raw materials, e.g., furniture, soap, soft drinks, cigarettes and sugar.

Major Industries: mining, food processing, soap, furniture.

Main Commodities Traded: Imports – machinery, vehicles, manufactured goods, electrical equipment, foodstuffs, mineral fuels. Exports – diamonds, bauxite, coffee, cocoa, palm kernels.

International Affiliations: UN, IBRD, OAU, ACP, ADB, Commonwealth, ECOWAS, MRU.

HOW TO GET THERE

Air
International airlines flying to Sierra Leone include: Air Afrique, British Caledonian, CSA, Egypt Air, Ghana Airways, Interflug, KLM, Lufthansa, MEA and Nigeria Airways.

SIERRA LEONE

Sierra Leone Airways, in conjunction with British Caledonian, operate several flights a week from London to Freetown. Together with a number of other airlines, Sierre Leone Airways also operate services connecting Freetown with major cities in West Africa.

Flying times to Freetown: from London, 6¼ hours; from New York, 10 hours; from Sydney, 24 hours.

Lungi Airport lies across the harbour from Freetown. The journey from the airport to the city centre (32km/20 miles) involves a ferry journey and a road journey at either end, and can take up to 2 hours. The airport bus takes passengers to the Paramount Hotel in the city centre.

Passengers should confirm return or onward bookings as soon as possible after arrival in Freetown.

ENTRY REGULATIONS

Visas

Visas are required by nationals of all countries except: British Commonwealth and Republic of Ireland, but an entry permit must be obtained before travelling. Entry permits are available from Sierre Leone high commissions and embassies abroad.

Applications by nationals other than British and Commonwealth passport holders are referred. The applicant must send a reply-paid cable to the Principal Immigration Officer, Immigration Headquarters, 15 Siaka Stevens Street, Freetown, requesting permission to visit and giving the following details: name, nationality, occupation, purpose of travel, length of stay, and date of departure for Sierra Leone.

Alternatively, the applicant's contact in Sierra Leone may request the Principal Immigration Officer to cable such permission to the Sierra Leone diplomatic mission in the applicant's country of residence.

Business travellers require a letter from their firm giving details of the business to be undertaken and the applicant's status, and confirming financial responsibility for the applicant.

Visas and entry permits are usually valid for 3 months for a stay of up to 30 days which may be extended, on application, to a maximum of 3 months.

Health Regulations

Valid International Certificates of Vaccination against smallpox and yellow fever are required. Vaccination certificates against cholera are required by all persons arriving from infected areas; in view of recent reported outbreaks of cholera in Sierra Leone, all travellers to Sierra Leone and advised to be vaccinated against cholera. TAB injections are also recommended.

Customs

Currency: There is no limit to the amount of foreign currency which may be taken in, provided it is declared on arrival (Form M). Any unused part of the amount declared may be taken out on departure, provided the currency declaration Form M is produced. Visitors are not allowed to acquire foreign currency (except leones) during their stay.

Duty-free articles: Personal baggage including a camera and portable typewriter. 1 bottle of spirits. 1 bottle of wine. ½ pint of perfume. 200 cigarettes or the equivalent in cigars or tobacco. A special permit is required for arms and ammunition. Samples of no commercial value. (Other samples may be imported duty-free temporarily, provided they are re-exported within 6 months and the amount of duty or security is deposited.) A customs declaration form must be completed on arrival.

PRACTICAL INFORMATION FOR THE VISITOR

1. Currency
Monetary Unit – leone (Le), divided into 100 cents.
Notes – 50 cents and 1, 2, 5 leones.
Coins – ½, 1. 5. 10. 20, 50 cents.

Banking Hours
0800–1300 Monday to Friday
0800–1100 Saturday

Principal Commercial Banks
Barclays Bank of Sierra Leone Ltd, Siaka Stevens Street, P.O. Box 12, Freetown, ☎ 22501.
Sierra Leone Commercial Bank Ltd, 30 Walpole Street, Freetown, ☎ 25264. (Branches in Kailahun, Kono, Kenema, Njala)
Sierra Leone Development Bank Ltd., Leone House, 21–3 Siaka Stevens Street, Freetown, ☎ 26791.
Standard Bank Sierra Leone Ltd, 12 Lightfoot Boston Street, P.O. Box 1155, Freetown, ☎ 25760. (Branch in Koidu.)

2. Electricity Supply
230/240v AC 50Hz.
Plugs: 2 round pins, 3 square pins.

3. Weights and Measures
The imperial system is used, although the metric system is being considered.

4. Media
Both radio and television are under the control of the Sierra Leone Broadcasting Service and accept commercial advertising.

Newspapers and Journals
The principal daily is the Government-owned *Daily Mail. We Yon* and *Sunday Flash* are published on Sundays. The *Sierra Leone Outlook* is a quarterly publication.
The Sierra Leone Trade Journal is published quarterly by the Ministry of Trade and Industry. The *Sierra Leone Chamber of Commerce Journal* is published every month.

5. Medical Care
Sierra Leone is in a malaria zone, and visitors should take anti-malarial tablets, on the advice of a doctor. Avoid drinking water that has not been filtered and boiled; caution should be taken with raw fruit and vegetables.

Medical facilities are of a poor standard compared to those in other West African countries. Freetown and Bo are the only towns with specialised hospitals carrying relatively modern equipment. There is a private hospital in Freetown at Hill Station.

6. Telephone, Telex and Postal Services
Cablegram, telephone and telex services direct to many parts of the world are offered by Sierra Leone External Telecommunications (SLET). The main SLET office in Freetown is at Lower Lightfoot Boston Street (open daily from 0800–1900).

There is a public telex booth at Mercury House, 7 Water Street, Freetown.

The main post office in Freetown is open from 0800–1630, Monday to Saturday. All mail to and from Sierra Leone should be despatched by air.

7. Public Holidays
1 January	*New Year's Day*
19 April	*Republic Day*
27 April	*Independence Day*

SIERRA LEONE

24 August — President's Birthday
24–5 December — Christmas

The following Muslim and Christian holidays are also observed: *Mouled, Eid el Fitr, Eid el Adha, Good Friday, Easter Monday* and *Whit Monday*.

8. Time
GMT.

9. Internal Transport

Air
Sierra Leone Airways operate internal flights on weekdays from Hastings Airport (22 km/14 miles from Freetown) to Bo, Kenema, Yengema, Bonthe, Gbangbatoke and Kabala.

Airline Offices in Freetown

Air France	☎ 22295.
British Caledonian	☎ 22075.
British Airways/Swissair	☎ 22075.
KLM	☎ 24444/25254.
Lufthansa	☎ 3881/2.
Nigeria Airways	☎ 5103/6347.
Sierra Leone Airways	☎ 22075.
UTA	☎ 26057/26438.

Road
There are a limited number of good all-weather roads; many secondary roads are laterite and are dusty or pot-holed and impassable during the rainy season. The two main roads connect Freetown to Kenema and Lungi to Kabala.

Taxis are readily available in Freetown; they are not fitted with meters so fares should be agreed upon before starting a journey. Taxis may be hired for a whole day.

Self-drive cars may be hired, but these tend to be expensive. An International Driving Licence is required.

Car-Hire Firms in Freetown
Blue Bird Transport Company ☎ 3893.
Sierra Tours, 26 Water Street.

10. Tipping
Taxis – no tip.

Porters – 20 cents.

Hotels/restaurants – a 10% service charge is added to the bill; no extra tip is necessary.

11. Social Customs
Visitors should remember that Government offices work on alternate Saturdays only.

USEFUL ADDRESSES (GENERAL)

British Council: Tower Hill, P.O. Box 124, Freetown, ☎ 22223/7.

British High Commission: 3rd Floor, Standard Bank Sierra Leone Building, Lightfoot Boston Street, P.M.B. c/o GPO, ☎ 23961/5.

Dutch Consulate: B.P. Building (At the Cotton Tree), P.O. Box 1348, Freetown, ☎ 24444.

French Embassy: 13 Lamina Sankoh Street, P.O. Box 510, Freetown.

Swiss Consulate: 14 Howe Street, P.O. Box 451, Freetown, ☎ 23322.

US Embassy: Corner Walpole and Siaka Stevens Streets, Freetown, ☎ 26481.

West German Embassy: Santanno House, Howe Street, P.O. Box 728, Freetown, ☎ 22511/12.

Ministry of Tourism, Arts and Crafts Centre: Government Wharf, Freetown, ☎ 3716.

Thomas Cook Authorised Representative: A. Yazbeck & Sons Agencies, P.O. Box 485, Freetown, ☎ 2063, 4423.

Tourist and Hotel Board: 28 Siaka Stevens Street, Freetown.

BUSINESS INFORMATION

The Government is anxious to encourage foreign investment in the public and private sectors, either in partnership with the Government or independently. Foreign investment is largely governed by the Sierra Leone Development Act, which is currently under revision.

Much of the country's distributive trades are in the hands of Europeans, Indians and Lebanese, as in other parts of West Africa. One firm may act as importer, exporter, wholesaler and retailer dealing in a whole range of commodities. The large merchant houses are usually better equipped to deal with technical or specialist items. The use of manufacturers' representatives is widespread, although firms undertaking this kind of work are usually very heavily committed.

Freetown is the main commercial centre and has one of the finest natural harbours in the world. The Wellington Estate is a recently established industrial estate outside the city which offers good support services and has already attracted a number of small industries.

Import and Exchange Control Regulations

Most goods can be imported under Open General Licences with the exception of some foodstuffs, raw materials and manufactured items requiring specific import licences.

The transfer of funds in payment for imports requires the approval of the Bank of Sierra Leone.

Business Hours

Government Offices
0800–1230 Monday to Friday
1400–1545
0800–1200 on alternate Saturdays

Business Houses
0800–1200 or 1230 Monday to Friday
1400–1630 or 1700
0800–1230 Saturday

BUSINESS SERVICES

Advertising

Lintas (West Africa) Ltd, G.B. Ollivant Building, Rawdon Street, Freetown.

Pearl and Dean, 49 Wilkinson Road, Freetown.

Insurance

National Insurance Company Ltd, 18/20 Walpole Street, P.M.B. 84, Freetown, ☎ 24328/24338. (Branches in Bo and Kenema)

Forwarding/Clearing Agents

Freetown Travel Agencies, P.O. Box 950, Freetown.

International Clearing and Forwarding Agencies Ltd, P.O. Box 717, Freetown.

Sierra Leone Airways, P.O. Box 285, Freetown – air freight only.

Sierra Leone National Shipping Company, 1 College Road, P.O. Box 935, Freetown, ☎ 50221.

SIERRA LEONE

USEFUL ADDRESSES (BUSINESS)

Chamber of Commerce of Sierra Leone: Guma Building, Lamina Sankoh Street, P.O. Box 502, Freetown, ☎ 6305.

The Sierra Leone Produce Marketing Board: Queen Elizabeth II Quay, Cline Town, P.O. Box 508, Freetown, ☎ 50431.

Sierra Leone Ports Authority: P.M.B. Cline Town, Freetown, telex 3262.

MAJOR CITY

Freetown

The original name of Freetown was Romaron, meaning place of the mountain. The British bought the natural harbour and surrounding land from tribal chiefs in 1787 in order to settle freed slaves, hence the capital's modern-day name. The city has retained much of its traditional charm and old-world character although the 18th-century timber houses situated along the waterfront are now rapidly being replaced by modern office blocks and other buildings. Lumley Beach (5km/3 miles from Freetown) is currently being developed as a tourist resort.

In the hills behind the city is the campus of Fourah Bay, West Africa's oldest university, established as a school in 1827. The old slave fort and trading factories at Bunce Island are popular sightseeing attractions.

Hotels

There is no official hotel rating system. Accommodation is limited. Reservations should be made well in advance.

BINTUMANI, Aberdeen Hill, ☎ 31970.
Modern hotel built on a hilltop site overlooking beaches and the bay, 14½km/9 miles from the city centre.
Rooms: 150 ♪, ⬤, ⛱, ⚐, ⛽.
Facilities: Restaurant, bars, coffee shop. Live entertainment. Swimming, tennis, golf, water skiing. Car hire.
Services: TC, FC. ⊟ Major credit cards accepted. Dr. on call. S, ♂.
Adjoining conference centre for up to 600 persons.

CAPE SIERRA, P.O. Box 610, Lumley Beach, ☎ 024266.
Modern beach-resort hotel, 14½km/9 miles from city centre.
Rooms: 75 ♪.
Facilities: Restaurant, bar, nightclub. Casino near by. Entertainment, dancing. Swimming, golf, tennis, squash, deep-sea fishing. Transport to city centre. Conference centre.
Services: ⊟ Amex, Diners Club.

PARAMOUNT, Independence Avenue, Tower Hill, P.O. Box 574, ☎ 22021, 24531.
Modern 1st-class hotel in city centre, opposite State House.
Rooms: 71 ♪, ⬤ on request, ⛱, ⚐, ⛽. Suites available.
Facilities: Restaurant, outdoor dining terrace, cocktail bar, lounge. Airline booking office, pharmacy, shops, hairdresser. 20 minutes' drive to golf, tennis, beaches. Car hire. Conference room.
Services: TC, FC. ⊟ Amex. Dr. on call. S.

Lungi Airport

LUNGI INTERNATIONAL AIRPORT HOTEL/MOTEL, ☎ 025411, 025345.
Situated next to airport, adjacent to beach. All rooms are air-conditioned, and the hotel offers good facilities.

Restaurants

Atlantic, Lumley Beach, ☎ 024300 – part open-air nightclub and restaurant, French and Lebanese food; *La Tropicana,* Roxy Buildings, Walpole Street, ☎ 24041 – nightclub and restaurant; *Cape Club,* Lumley Beach, ☎ 024246 – nightclub and restaurant, weekday evenings only; *Casino Leone,* Lumley Beach, ☎ 024330 – casino with restaurant; *Chung Hwa,* 112 Wilkinson Road, ☎ 30204 – Chinese; *Lighthouse,* near Cape Sierra Hotel – Armenian specialities; *Omar Khayyam,* Pultney Street; *Chez Miramil,* Charlotte Street.

Entertainment

The world-famous Sierra Leone Dance Troupe gives regular performances in Freetown and other parts of the country. There are a number of good sporting clubs including the *Freetown Golf Club,* the *Aqua Sports Club* and the *Young Sportsmen Club.*

Shopping

Freetown is especially noted for its colourful *gara* materials and traditional costumes. The best selection of curios and handicrafts is to be found at the covered market at King Jimmy Wharf and at the East Street markets.

Other shops include: *Alie & Ashimi Co,* Siaka Stevens Street; *Bai Bundu,* 26 Howe Street; *C.A.S.C. Contemporary Arts & Crafts Shop,* 3a Charlotte Street; *Fancy Gara Shop,* opposite Standard Bank, Wallace Johnson Street.

SOMALIA
Somali Democratic Republic

Geography *372*
The Economy *374*
How to Get There *375*
Entry Regulations *375*
Practical Information for the Visitor *376*
Useful Addresses (General) *377*
Business Information *378*
Business Services *378*
Useful Addresses (Business) *379*
Mogadishu *379*

Size: 637,657 sq.km/246,200 sq.miles.

Population: 3.74 million (1978 est.).

Distribution: 19% in urban areas.

Density: 5.4 persons per sq.km/14 per sq.mile.

Population Growth Rate: 2.3% p.a.

Ethnic Composition: The Somali population is mainly Hamitic; among the other larger ethnic groups are the Dir, Isaq and Digil. Other minority groups are Arabs, Indians, Pakistanis and Italians.

Capital: Mogadishu Pop. 350,000.

Major Towns: Hargeisa Pop. 100,000; Berbera Pop. 50,000.

Language: Somali is the language of the country – the written form, using a latin script, was introduced in 1972. English, Arabic and Italian are widely used, and Swahili is spoken in the southern coastal towns.

Religion: Islam is the official religion of Somalia, and most Somalis are Sunni Muslims. There is a small Christian community, mainly Roman Catholic.

Government: The Government is composed of the Central Committee of the ruling Somali Socialist Revolutionary Party and the Council of Ministers. The SSRP is the only legal political party in the Somali Democratic Republic.

The National Assembly was dissolved in 1969 following the overthrow of the Government, and the existing constitution was suspended. A draft Constitution has been drawn up providing for the creation of a People's Parliament and the election of the President by popular vote, but this has still to be approved.

GEOGRAPHY

Somalia lies in the Horn of Africa and has a long coastline along the Gulf of Aden and the Indian Ocean. Most of the country consists of savannah plains covered by semi-arid bush although there is a mountainous region in the north-east rising to a height of 1,220–1,520m/4–5,000ft above sea level. The main cultivated areas lie around Somalia's two permanent rivers, the Juba and Shebelli.

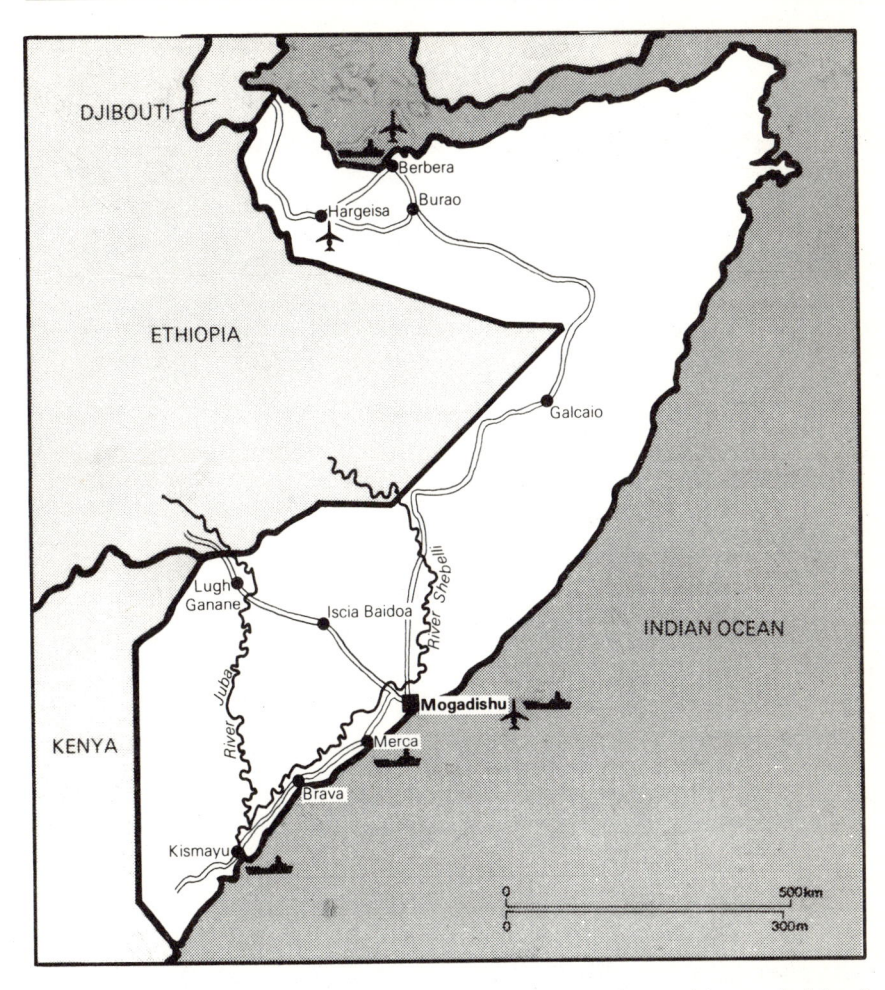

Climate
The climate is hot and arid, although the coastal areas are humid. The southern part lies on the Equator. Average temperatures throughout the year range from 27°C/80°F to 32°C/90°F; in Berbera on the Gulf of Aden summer temperatures may exceed 38°C/100°F. In general the north is cooler due to its altitude. The main rainy season is from June to September.

Agriculture
Over 70% of the population are nomads who depend on the rearing of livestock (cattle, camels, sheep and goats) for a living. The severe drought of 1974 accounted for the loss of more than a million animals, apart from the considerable loss of human life,

and large numbers of the pastoralists who were resettled after the drought have been encouraged to develop fishing.

Exports of livestock (mainly to Saudi Arabia) and of hides and skins constitute about two-thirds of Somalia's export earnings.

Much of Somalia is infertile and suffers from inadequate rainfall, making it suitable only for livestock rearing. The main cultivated areas are along the Juba and Shebelli river valleys, and, as part of a drive towards self-sufficiency, the Government is developing this region with extensive irrigation.

Somalia is a major producer of bananas, and although many of the plantations are still privately owned, the marketing of bananas is handled by an autonomous Government agency. Sugar cane is grown on a large scale, and domestic sugar requirements are largely fulfilled by a nationalised sugar estate and refinery on the Shebelli river at Johar.

Main Crops: bananas, sugar, spices, cotton, maize, oilseeds, sorghum, rice, tobacco, citrus fruits.

Mineral Resources: radioactive ores, including uranium, gypsum, iron, manganese.

THE ECONOMY

Gross National Product (1978): US$470 million.

Per Capita Income (1976): US$130.

Foreign Trade (1978): Total Imports – US$239.4 million. Total Exports – US$109.4 million.

Main Trading Partners: Imports – Italy, USSR, China, Kenya; Exports – Saudi Arabia, Italy, USSR, Kuwait.

Following independence, Somalia received large amounts of foreign aid. Despite subsequent attempts at self-reliance, more than 60% of Somalia's development budget continues to originate from foreign sources.

Development has been slow, initially hampered by the closure of the Suez Canal and more recently by Somalia's war with Ethiopia in the Ogaden. There has been some modernisation of the infrastructure, however, and an increased emphasis on industrialisation and self-sufficiency in foodstuffs.

Industrial concerns are run by both the public and private sectors. The private sector consists largely of small-scale industries supplying a small proportion of domestic needs. Even within the public sector there are no large industrial concerns. Textiles, dairy and meat products are produced locally, as are cigarettes and packaging materials; there is also a fruit juice canning factory.

A new deep-water port has been opened at Mogadishu with World Bank financial assistance; utilisation of smaller ports at Kismayu and Berbera has resulted in a considerable improvement to Somalia's transport situation.

Aid has been forthcoming from many European countries, international agencies and China – the Soviet Union no longer gives aid to Somalia following its decision to support the Ethiopian forces in the Ogaden. A number of development projects are currently being initiated by the Agency for International Development, but progress is

SOMALIA

likely to be slow with a greater emphasis on the development of agriculture and livestock than on industrialisation.

Major Industries: sugar refining, textiles, meat packing, fish and fruit canning, dairy products.

Main Commodities Traded: Imports – manufactured goods, cereals, transport and non-electrical equipment, chemicals, paper products. Exports – livestock, bananas, hides and skins, spices, fish and meat products.

International Affiliations: UN, IBRD, OAU, ACP, ADB, AL, BADEA.

HOW TO GET THERE

Air

There are direct flights to Mogadishu from Aden, Addis Ababa, Asmara, Cairo, Djibouti, Jeddah, Khartoum, Moscow, Nairobi and Rome. The 2 main air routes from London to Mogadishu are via Rome or Nairobi.

There are direct flights to Hargeisa and Berbera from Aden and to Hargeisa from Djibouti.

Major airlines flying to Somalia include Aeroflot, Alitalia, Egypt Air and Somali Airlines.

An embarkation fee of 20 Somali shillings is payable by all passengers departing from Somalia.

Flying times to Mogadishu: from London, 12½ hours; from New York, 20 hours; from Sydney, 24 hours.

Mogadishu International Airport is 6km/3½ miles from the city centre. There is no airport bus service but taxis are readily available at the airport.

ENTRY REGULATIONS

Visas

Visas are required by nationals of all countries and must be obtained from Somali diplomatic missions abroad before departing for Somalia. Visas are not normally granted to nationals of Israel, Taiwan, Portugal and white nationals of South Africa.

Visa applications by business travellers should be accompanied by a letter from their firm giving details of the business to be undertaken and confirming financial responsibility for the applicant.

All visa applications are referred for authorisation with a delay of up to 2 months, so applications should be submitted well in advance. The issue of a visa can sometimes be speeded up if business travellers are able to give as a sponsor the name of the Government agency or commercial contact in Somalia whom they intend to visit.

Visas are usually valid for 3 months for a stay of up to 3 months. Transit visas are valid for 48 hours.

Health Regulations

International Certificates of Vaccination against smallpox, yellow fever and cholera are required by all persons entering Somalia. Immunisation against typhus, typhoid and tetanus is also advisable, although not obligatory.

Customs

Currency: Visitors may bring in and take out any amount of foreign currency and travellers' cheques provided these are declared on a Currency Declaration form (a charge of 2 Somali shillings is made for this) on arrival and departure. All exchange transactions must be recorded on this form. The import and export of East African and Somali shillings are restricted.

Duty-free articles: Personal effects. 200 cigarettes or 200g of tobacco. 1 bottle of wine or spirits. A reasonable amount of perfume. Commercial samples are normally admitted without difficulty.

PRACTICAL INFORMATION FOR THE VISITOR

1. Currency
Monetary Unit – Somali shilling, divided into 100 centesimi.
Notes – 5, 10, 20, 100 Somali shillings.
Coins -- 1, 5, 10, 50 centesimi and 1 Somali shilling.

Foreign currency and travellers' cheques may only be exchanged at banks and authorised hotels. All transactions must be recorded on the currency declaration form issued on arrival. Banks offer better exchange rates than the hotels.

Banking Hours
0830–1130 Saturday to Thursday

All banks were nationalised in 1970. The 3 banks which now make up Somalia's banking system are:

Central Bank of Somalia, Corso Somalia 55, P.O. Box 11, Mogadishu, ☎ 3111, 4121.
Commercial and Savings Bank of Somalia, P.O. Box 203, Mogadishu, ☎ 2641, 2978.
Somali Development Bank, P.O. Box 79, Mogadishu, ☎ 3228, 3800.

2. Electricity Supply
220v AC 50Hz.

3. Weights and Measures
The metric system is in official use but avoirdupois weights and measures are still used, particularly in the north.

4. Media
The Government runs Somalia's 2 radio stations, Radio Mogadishu and Radio Hargeisa, and commercial advertising is widely used on radio. There is no television service at present, although plans exist for the introduction of a network.

Newspapers and Journals
The Xiddigta Octobar (*October Star*) published in Somali is the only daily newspaper. The number of foreign-language publications has decreased since the introduction of the Somali script in 1972. The chief remaining ones are *New Era*, a monthly magazine in English, and *Horseed*, a weekly paper in Italian and Arabic.

5. Medical Care
Malaria is endemic in some parts; visitors should consult their doctor about anti-malarial prophylactics before leaving for Somalia.
   Piped water is available in Mogadishu but visitors should ensure that all water has been boiled and filtered. Locally manufactured mineral water is available.

6. Telephone, Telex and Postal Services
International telephone services from Somalia are limited and connections are usually very poor. Calls to Europe are routed through Rome and should be booked 24 hours in advance. The link from Mogadishu to Kenya is of a better standard.

There is a public telex booth in Mogadishu at the main Post Office opposite the Hotel Juba.

All mail to and from Somalia should be sent by air. Street names are rarely used in Somali addresses, so it is essential to include the P.O. box number.

7. Public Holidays

1 January	New Year's Day
1 May	Labour Day
26 June	Independence Day of the former British Somaliland Protectorate
1 July	Independence Day for the Somali Republic
21–2 October	Anniversary of the Revolution

The following Muslim holidays are also observed: *Mouled*, *Eid el Fitr*, *Eid el Arifa* and *El Hijra*.

8. Time
GMT + 3.

9. Internal Transport
Business travellers should ascertain from the immigration authorities on arrival in Mogadishu that there is no objection if they wish to travel outside of Mogadishu. The declaration in a visa application of intention to travel in Somalia is no guarantee that permission will be granted in Somalia itself.

Air
Somali Airlines operate scheduled flights between Mogadishu, Kismayu, Hargeisa, Berbera and other centres.

Road
The network of paved all-weather roads is limited. Because of restrictions on travel outside Mogadishu it is adivsable to check with the authorities on arrival about road travel.

Self-drive cars are available for hire in Mogadishu. An International Driving Licence is required. Traffic travels on the right-hand side of the road.

Taxis are plentiful in the main town. There is a fixed tariff in Mogadishu, and taxis there can also be hired by the half hour at a reasonable cost. It is advisable to agree upon the charge before starting the journey.

There is no airport bus service between Mogadishu and the airport but taxis are readily available. The official tariff from the airport to the city centre is 10 Somali shillings, although drivers may try to overcharge.

10. Tipping
Taxis – no tip.

Porters – 2 Somali shillings per bag.

Restaurants – 10% of the bill.

Hotels –1 Somali shilling for small personal services.

11. Social Customs
Informality is the key note in Somalia's business and social life. Much business entertaining takes place in private houses although it is also quite common to entertain in restaurants; foreign business visitors will find this the most convenient way of repaying local business contacts for their hospitality.

It is important to remember that the majority of Somalis are Muslims; it is considered an offence to offer them an alcoholic drink.

USEFUL ADDRESSES (GENERAL)

British Embassy, Via Londra, P.O. Box 1036, Mogadishu, ☎ 2288/9.

Dutch Consulate, Corso Primo Luglio, P.O. Box 10, Mogadishu, ☎ 2411/2281.

French Embassy, Corso Primo Luglio, P.O. Box 13, Mogadishu.

US Embassy, Corso Primo Luglio, Mogadishu, ☎ 2811.

West German Embassy, Via Mohammed Harbi, P.O. Box 17, ☎ 2547/8.

National Agency for Tourism, P.O. Box 533, Mogadishu, ☎ 2031.

BUSINESS INFORMATION

A continuing balance of payments problem has resulted in restrictions on the import of many consumer goods, so prospects for foreign suppliers in this sector are limited. Nevertheless, there is a continuing demand for suppliers and consultants in the industrial sector and more particularly in the agricultural sector.

The import of most products is restricted to Government departments and autonomous Government agencies. Commission agents were banned in 1975 and replaced by a single state organisation which operates principally as a buying agent for Government departments: *State Commercial Agencies Department*, P.O. Box 1749, Mogadishu.

Mogadishu is the main commercial centre and the principal port for imports. The port of Berbera deals mainly with the export of livestock and Kismayu with the export of bananas.

Import and Exchange Control Regulations

Import licences are required for certain goods and state agencies have a monopoly over the import of some products. The granting of an import licence carries with it authority for the issue of foreign exchange.

Somalia is a signatory to the Lomé Convention but in general does not give preference to products of EEC countries.

Business Hours
Government Offices
0700–1400 Saturday to Thursday

Business Houses
0800–1230
1630–1900 Saturday to Thursday
Friday is the Muslim Sabbath. Sunday is a normal working day.

Business Events
The International Somali Trade Fair is held in Mogadishu in September/October every second year.

BUSINESS SERVICES

Forwarding/Clearing Agents
Mohamed Ahmed S. Dola & Sons, P.O. Box 526, Mogadishu, ☎ 2277.
Somali Express Forwarding Agency, P.O. Box 82, Mogadishu, ☎ 3218.
Tropical Business Enterprise Ltd, Z-A1/1638 Via Corso Somalia, P.O. Box 1009, Mogadishu.

SOMALIA

Insurance
Cassa per le Assicurazioni Sociali della Somalia, P.O. Box 123, Mogadishu.

State Insurance Company of Somalia, P.O. Box 992, Mogadishu.

USEFUL ADDRESSES (BUSINESS)

Chamber of Commerce, Industry and Agriculture, Via Asha, P.O. Box 27, Mogadishu.

National Agency of Foreign Trade, P.O. Box 602, Mogadishu.

MAJOR CITY

Mogadishu
Both Somali and Italian influences can be clearly seen in the capital. Arabic influence is particularly evident in the old quarter of Hammar Wein, which bears signs of the city's earlier importance as a major trading port; the mosque of Fakhr-Din dates from the 13th century. In the quarter's narrow winding alleys visitors can see craftworkers making objects in gold, silver and cloth using traditional techniques.

Places of interest in Mogadishu include the National Museum of Somalia, housed in the former palace of the Sultan of Zanzibar. The museum has a fine decorative interior with exquisitely carved doors, as well as an extensive collection of silverwork and a maritime section. The mosque of Sheikh Abdul Aziz is also worth a visit.

Hotels
There is no official hotel rating system.

The main hotels of international standard in Mogadishu are the *Juba Hotel*, the *Croce del Sud*, the *Shebelli* and the *Rugta Taleh* (motel suites). With the exception of the Croce del Sud which is Italian-owned, these hotels are run by the Ministry of Tourism.

CROCE DEL SUD, P.O. Box 91, ☎ 22050/23001.
Traditional colonial-style hotel in city centre.
Rooms: 35 ♒, △, ▥.
Facilities: Restaurant, bar. Car hire.
Services: TC, FC. ▤ No credit cards. Dr. on call. ⚕.

Restaurants
There are a number of restaurants offering an adequate standard of cuisine, mainly specialising in local (particularly seafood) and Italian dishes: *Azan's*, near the Shebelli Hotel – Italian; *Trocadero*, Hotel Croce del Sud; *Capuccetto Nero*, near the Croce del Sud – Italian; *Ming Sing*, near the Fiat Circle – Chinese.

Entertainment
The *Lido* and *Azan's* are popular nightclubs with local bands playing both European and African music. The *American Club* offers temporary membership to foreign visitors and has a swimming pool and good dining facilities. The *Golf Club* is another popular meeting place. The long beaches around Mogadishu are unspoilt and very beautiful in places.

Shopping
Best buys: gold and silver jewellery, cloth, basketware and wood carvings.

There are dozens of cloth shops on Via Roma, and in the narrow alleys near by visitors can have gold and silver jewellery made up to their own design here at comparatively low prices. Traditional handicrafts are on sale in the market – be prepared to bargain with the stallholders as they generally ask a far higher price than the one they finally expect to receive.

SOUTH AFRICA
Republic of South Africa

Geography	382
The Economy	382
How to Get There	384
Entry Regulations	384
Practical Information for the Visitor	385
Useful Addresses (General)	389
Business Information	391
Business Services	392
Useful Addresses (Business)	392
Cape Town	393
Durban	395
Johannesburg	397
Port Elizabeth	399
Pretoria	399

Size: 1,223,409 sq.km/472,359 sq.miles.

Population: 23.55 million (1978 est.), excluding Transkei and Bophuthatswana.

Distribution: 48% in urban areas.

Density: 21 persons per sq.km/55 per sq.mile.

Population Growth Rate: 2.7% p.a. (1970-7).

Ethnic Composition: Africans constitute over 70% of the total, the main ethnic groups being Zulu, Xhosa, Tswana, Sotho, Shangaa, Swazi, Ndebele and Venda. Two-thirds of the white population are Afrikaners and one-third are English-speaking. The remainder consist of 'coloureds' (9%) and Asians, mainly Indians (3%).

Capitals: Cape Town (legislative) Pop. 843,000; Pretoria (administrative) Pop. 634,000; Bloemfontein (judicial) Pop. 183,000.

Major Cities: Johannesburg Pop. 1,441,000; Durban Pop. 851,000; Port Elizabeth Pop. 476,000.

Language: English and Afrikaans are the official languages. The most widely spoken African languages are Zulu and Xhosa.

Religion: The majority are Christians of various denominations. Of the remain-

SOUTH AFRICA

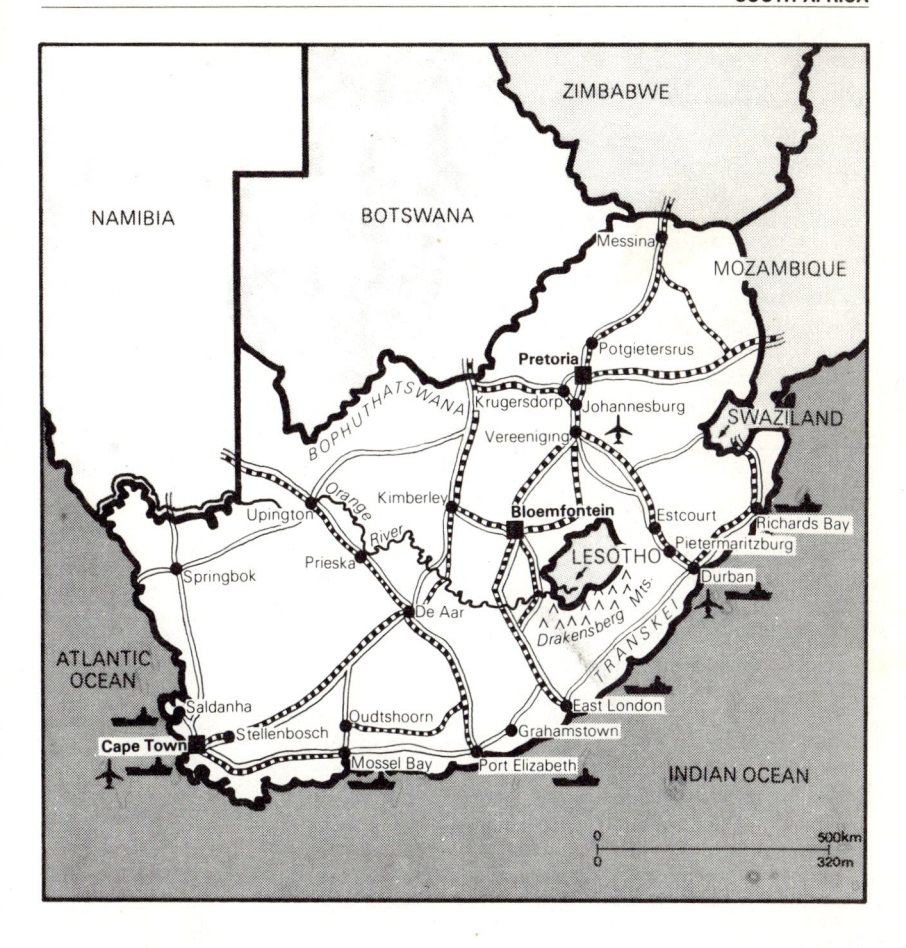

der, some hold traditional beliefs, some are Hindu or Muslim.

Government: The President and members of the Senate and House of Assembly are elected for 7-year and 5-year terms respectively. Only whites may stand for election and only the white population may vote in parliamentary elections. Seven bantustans, or black homelands, have been created under the Government policy of apartheid with unicameral legislatures elected by black voters – this is the only legal form of representation permitted to the African population. The coloured and Asian populations are represented by a Coloured People's Representative Council and a South Africa Indian Council. The homelands of Transkei, Bophuthatswana and Venda were granted independence in 1976, 1977 and 1979 respectively, but remain economically dependent on South Africa.

The ruling political party is the Afrikaner-dominated National Party; the Progressive Federal Party is its chief opposition. The African National Congress, the Pan-Africanist Congress and other black-consciousness organisations are officially banned.

SOUTH AFRICA

GEOGRAPHY

The country consists of a narrow coastal belt framing a high plateau in the interior rising to a height of 1,828m/6,000ft above sea level in places. On the eastern edge of the plateau are the Drakensberg mountains (Mont-aux-Sources, 3,482m/11,428ft, is the highest peak). The interior plateau consists mainly of undulating country featuring sharp escarpments which rise above the flat plains or *veld*.

Climate

In general, South Africa has a sub-tropical climate, although the Western Cape has more of a Mediterranean-type climate with dry summers (October to March) and average temperatures of 20°c/68°F. Temperatures in the east are higher, over 38°c/100°F in summer, with humidity approaching 100% in Durban and parts of Natal and the Transvaal. On the high veld (Johannesburg and Pretoria) summers are hot with frequent torrential thunderstorms. There is a great variation between day and night temperatures in winter, with dry, sunny days often followed by cool, crisp nights. The most pleasant months to visit are between September and May.

Agriculture

Agriculture is an important sector of the economy although today it contributes only 8.7% of the GDP. The country's geographical and climatic differences enable a wide variety of crops to be grown and South Africa is virtually self-sufficient in food supplies – with the exception of imports such as tea and coffee, and wheat following a poor harvest.

South Africa is a major exporter of fruits (fresh and preserved), sugar, fish and maize. Sheep and cattle raising are also important occupations and much of the country is pastoral land. Despite a high level of mechanisation in the farming sector, the level of crop production can vary sharply from one year to the next according to the rainfall. Harvest are often seriously damaged by flooding or drought.

South Africa has a large fishing industry centred around the Western Cape. The main fish products for export are tinned pilchards and rock lobster tails, and there are sizeable whaling operations off the coast of Natal.

Main Crops: maize, sugar, tobacco, fruits, wheat.

Mineral Resources: gold, diamonds, copper, coal, platinum, chrome, manganese, antimony, iron ore, uranium.

THE ECONOMY

Gross National Product (1978): US$43.83 billion.

Per Capita Income (1978 est.): US$1,480.

Gross Domestic Product (1978): 39.76 billion rand.

Foreign Trade (1978): Total Imports – 9.2 billion rand. Total Exports – 12.92 billion rand. (Figures refer to the Rand Monetary Area, excluding Lesotho and Swaziland.)

SOUTH AFRICA

Main Trading Partners: Imports – US, West Germany, UK, Japan, France. Exports – UK, US, Japan, West Germany, Belgium, Luxembourg, France.

South Africa's extensive mineral resources, together with its sophisticated and diversified manufacturing sector, have resulted in enormous economic prosperity. South Africa is the world's largest producer of gold, supplying approximately 75% of the Western world's requirements. The exploitation of other minerals, together with the strengthening of the country's financial structure and economic infrastructure all contributed to considerable growth from the end of World War II to the early 1970s, and South Africa enjoyed an economic prosperity shared by relatively few nations in the industrialised West.

However, following the recession in the world commodity markets after 1974 and with the increased cost of oil (South Africa has no petroleum resources) and military imports, the growth rate of the economy fell back sharply and a recession set in between 1975 and 1977.

The subsequent dramatic rise in the price of gold put the economy back on its feet during 1978 and, by 1979, there was a substantial surplus on the trade balance. Restrictions on capital movements were relaxed considerably in an effort to attract foreign investment, consumer spending has been encouraged by cuts in taxation and the economy is expanding once more.

Nonetheless, a fairly high growth rate must be maintained consistently in order to accommodate the rapid expansion of population and to prevent growing unemployment, and many of South Africa's economic problems remain without any short-term solution. The level of black resistance within the country still runs high and is likely to escalate with the establishment of majority rule in Zimbabwe. Foreign investment is still substantial, but investors are coming under increasing pressure from anti-apartheid groups and, given the political uncertainties within all of southern Africa, there is a greater awareness of the risks involved in investment.

Mining exports account for over half of South Africa's total export earnings. Growth in iron ore and coal mining has been impressive and diamond production has risen. Major investment plans include the increased exploitation of uranium, copper, iron ore and coal deposits. A uranium enrichment plant is expected to be fully operational by the early 1980s. Improved facilities at Saldanha Bay and Richards Bay have resulted in a large increase in iron ore and coal exports.

Manufacturing accounts for 21.5% of the GDP and is an important source of export earnings. Food, drinks and tobacco, paper and paper products, machinery and transport equipment are all expanding industries. The large-scale production of consumer goods includes textiles, clothing, footwear and processed foodstuffs.

Heavy industries have also experienced growth. The expansion programme of the South African Iron and Steel Corporation has led to increased steel production resulting, in turn, in the establishment of associated industries such as mechanical and electrical engineering and the chemical industry.

Major Industries: mining, food processing, iron and steel, textiles, chemicals, vehicle assembly, electrical and non-electrical machinery and equipment.

Main Commodities Traded: Imports – industrial machinery and equipment, transport equipment, petroleum products, arms and defence equipment. Exports – gold, diamonds, iron and steel, coal, wool, copper, fruit.

International Affiliations: UN, SACU.

SOUTH AFRICA

HOW TO GET THERE

Air
The main international airport, serving Pretoria and Johannesburg, is Jan Smuts Airport, 24km/15 miles from the centre of Johannesburg.
  South African Airways and a number of international airlines operate frequent services to South Africa from Europe, North and South America, and Australia.
  South African Airways fly to Johannesburg from many European capitals, Australia, Hong Kong, the United States and South America.
  British Airways and SAA operate daily flights between London and Johannesburg calling at Frankfurt, Zürich or Nairobi and there is a non-stop flight from London to Cape Town once a week, taking approximately 13 hours.
  Flying times to Johannesburg: from London, 12 hours (non-stop); from New York, 18 hours; from Sydney, 18 hours.
  Direct flights to South Africa from within the African continent are available only from Zimbabwe, Malawi, Kenya, Lesotho, Botswana, Swaziland, Mauritius and Zambia.
  An airport bus service connects Jan Smuts Airport with the airline terminals in both Johannesburg and Pretoria, with similar services in Cape Town and Durban.

Rail
South Africa has rail links with Mozambique, Botswana, Zimbabwe and Malawi.

ENTRY REGULATIONS

Visas
Visas are required by nationals of all countries, except: (i) United Kingdom and colonies holding a British Passport (except Malta); (ii) Botswana, Lesotho, Zimbabwe, Swaziland, Republic of Ireland, Liechtenstein and Switzerland – as temporary visitors.
  Visas are obtainable from South African embassies and consulates abroad.
  The visa exemptions specified above do not apply to the following groups of people who must obtain an 'Authorisation to Enter': religious workers, concert performers, stage artistes, musicians, etc., taking up temporary employment, whether paid or unpaid; journalists, photographers, radio, film and television reporters and other persons connected with publicity media.
  Visa applications by business travellers must be accompanied by a letter from the applicant's firm giving details of the business to be undertaken, and confirming financial responsibility for the applicant. If the applicant has been invited to South Africa by an official body, organisation, institution, etc., then the letter of invitation must also be submitted.
  Visas are valid for varying lengths of time up to 1 year; the length of stay will be decided by authorities on arrival.
  Visitors requiring visas should ensure that their passports are valid for at least 12 months beyond the proposed stay. Applicants should allow plenty of time for the visa to be issued, espcially in the case of applications for 'Authorisation to Enter' which are referred to Pretoria.
  On arrival, visitors are issued with a temporary residence permit, valid for 90 days.

Any person wishing to stay longer than 90 days should apply for an extended temporary residence permit.

Some visas are valid for single entry only – visitors wishing to make a trip from South Africa to an adjacent country such as Swaziland and then return to South Africa must obtain a re-entry visa.

Health Regulations

An International Certificate of Vaccination against smallpox is required by all persons entering South Africa. International Certificates of Vaccination against cholera and/or yellow fever are required by all persons arriving from areas where these diseases are endemic.

Customs

Currency: There is no limit to the amount of foreign currency which may be imported. On arrival, all visitors must complete a special customs form listing all their holdings of currency and should retain a stamped copy of the declaration. On departure visitors may take out as much foreign currency as is shown on the customs form.

There is a limit of R50 per person to the amount of local currency which may be imported or exported in bank notes.

Duty-free articles: Personal effects. 400 cigarettes or 50 cigars or 250g of tobacco. 1 litre of wine and 1 litre of spirits. 300ml of perfume.

Articles liable to duty: Samples temporarily imported under an ATA Carnet are exempt from duty. Other samples carried by business visitors for use in taking orders are subject to sales and customs duties, but refunds are normally made on the re-export of the samples. Business visitors travelling by air are advised to ensure that samples being re-exported are cleared at Jan Smuts Airport, the main airport for inter-continental flights. Lengthy delays may occur when samples are imported at one port of entry and exported from another.

Prohibited articles: Narcotics and drugs. Pornographic and politically sensitive literature. *(still true)* *(no longer true)*

PRACTICAL INFORMATION FOR THE VISITOR

1. Currency

Monetary Unit – rand (R), divided into 100 cents.
Notes – 1, 2, 5, 10 rand.
Coins – ½, 1, 2, 5, 10, 20, 50 cents; 1 rand.
The *South African Reserve Bank* is the central bank of issue.

Banking Hours

0900–1530 Monday, Tuesday,
　　　　　　Thursday, Friday
0900–1300 Wednesday
0830–1100 Saturday

Major Commercial Banks

Barclays National Bank Ltd, 84 Market Street, P.O. Box 1153, Johannesburg 2000, ☎ 836-1971.
Chase Manhattan Bank, Life Centre Building, 27th Floor, 45 Commissioner Street, P.O. Box 9606, Johannesburg 2001, ☎ 834-7581/3 (representative office).
Citibank, 45 Commissioner Street, P.O. Box 9773, Johannesburg 2001, ☎ 834-2461; Broadway Industries Centre, Foreshore, P.O. Box 6002, Cape Town, ☎ 47-1670; 2 Durban

SOUTH AFRICA

Club Place, Smith Street, P.O. Box 3427, Durban, ☎ 31-3242.

Midland Bank Ltd, 12th Floor, Exchange Square, 69 President Street, P.O. Box 7780, Johannesburg 2000, ☎ 836-4816 (representative office).

Nedbank Ltd, P.O. Box 1144, Johannesburg 2000.

The Trust Accepting Bank Ltd and the Trust Bank of Africa Ltd, P.O. Box 9597, Johannesburg.

Standard Bank of South Africa Ltd, 88 Commissioner Street, P.O. Box 1031, Johannesburg, ☎ 838-8181; 57 Adderley Street, P.O. Box 57, Cape Town, ☎ 45-8211; Corner Smith & Gardiner Streets, P.O. Box 946, Durban, ☎ 32-0281; 12 Church Square, P.O. Box 802, Pretoria, ☎ 3-9971.

Volkskas Beperk, 229 Van der Walt Street, Pretoria 0002.

All these banks, with the exception of the Chase Manhattan and Midland Banks, have branches throughout South Africa.

2. Electricity Supply

Pretoria: 415–240v.
Port Elizabeth: 433–250 and 380–220v.
Elsewhere the supply is 380–220v AC 50Hz.
Plugs: 3 round pins.

3. Weights and Measures

The metric system is used.

4. Media

Radio and television are under the control of the South African Broadcasting Corporation (SABC). Commercial television was introduced in January 1978.

SABC's main commercial services are Springbok Radio, Radio Highveld, Radio Good Hope and Radio Port Natal broadcasting in both English and Afrikaans. These services carry considerable commercial advertising; radio space should be booked well in advance.

Bantu Radio (SABC) transmits programmes in 7 African languages.

Newspapers and Journals

There are no national daily newspapers circulating throughout the whole of South Africa. However, the main Sundays papers do circulate in the major population centres.

The principal daily, Sunday and weekly papers are:

Morning: *Rand Daily Mail, Citizen, Die Transvaler* and *Die Beeld* – Johannesburg; *Cape Times* and *Die Burger* – Cape Town; *Natal Mercury* – Durban; *Eastern Province Herald* – Port Elizabeth; *East London Daily Dispatch* – East London.

Evening: *The Star* and *Die Vaderland* – Johannesburg; *Cape Argus* – Cape Town; *Daily News* – Durban; *Evening Post* – Port Elizabeth; *Pretoria News* and *Die Hoofstad* – Pretoria.

Sunday: *Sunday Times*; *Rapport* (Afrikaans); *Sunday Express*; *Sunday Tribune.*

Weekly: *To the Point, Financial Mail, S.A. Financial Gazette* and *Business Week* – Johannesburg. (The last 3 financial papers specialise more in industrial advertising than in consumer goods and services advertising.)

A large number of magazines and periodicals are published in English, Afrikaans and some African languages. There are many high-quality trade and technical magazines which carry advertising and have a wide circulation. This is the principal means of advertising for producers of capital goods and manufacturing materials, and full advantage should be taken of the trade press. There are also a number of specialist agricultural publications, as well as 2 magazines of general agricultural interest: *Farmer's Weekly* and *Landbou Weekblad.*

5. Medical Care

Tap water is safe to drink throughout South Africa. Many rivers and lakes are unsuitable for bathing because of the risk of bilharzia.

Visitors should take note of all safety notices when swimming in the sea and

SOUTH AFRICA

should always swim within the shark nets.

Visitors to Zululand and the Eastern Transvaal should seek advice regarding anti-malarial prophylactics. Tablets are readily available from local chemists.

The altitude of Johannesburg (2,000m/5,480ft above sea level) and other cities on the high plateau may cause some discomfort to visitors with a history of heart or lung complaints: it is wise to avoid any undue exertion in these places.

Emergency hospital service –
Johannesburg ☎ 724-1121.
Cape Town ☎ 69-8721.

6. Telephone, Telex and Postal Services

Direct trunk lines link all major South African cities and towns; over 80% of the telephones are operated on the automatic system. Direct dialling is available to many European capitals and to North America.

Public telephone boxes accept 20c, 10c and 5c coins, with a minimum charge of 5c per call.

Public telex facilities are available at the main Johannesburg, Cape Town and Durban post offices.

All mail to and from South Africa should be despatched by air. There are all-night mailing and postage stamp facilities at the Central Post Office, Parliament Square, Cape Town, and at the main post office in Jeppe Street, Johannesburg – the telegraph counter is open until 1800 hours.

7. Public Holidays

1 January	New Year's Day
31 May	Republic Day
1st Monday in September	Settlers' Day
10 October	Kruger Day
16 December	Day of the Covenant
25–6 December	Christmas

The following movable holidays are also observed: *Good Friday, Easter Monday* and *Ascension Day.*

If a holiday falls on a Sunday, the following Monday is observed as a public holiday.

Jewish religious holidays are observed by the Jewish community, which is especially large in Johannesburg and Cape Town, and a number of offices and shops close down on major Jewish religious holidays.

Business travellers should avoid visiting between mid-December and the end of January, as this is the peak annual holiday period.

8. Time

GMT + 2.

9. Internal Transport

Air

South African Airways operate several flights a day linking Cape Town, Johannesburg, Durban, Port Elizabeth, East London, Kimberley and Bloemfontein. Other internal services are operated by Air Cape, Commercial Airways and Namakwaland Air Services.

Airline Offices

	Johannesburg	Cape Town	Durban
Air Canada	☎ 8344049	—	—
Air France/UTA	☎ 219252	☎ 453902	☎ 65228
Alitalia	☎ 8343121	—	—
British Airways	☎ 210011	☎ 227131	☎ 324741
British Caledonian	☎ 285261	—	—
Iberia	☎ 213315	☎ 452528	☎ 31787
JAL	☎ 291815/7	—	—
KLM	☎ 236991	☎ 211870	☎ 325701
Lufthansa	☎ 8363747	☎ 226761	☎ 311126

SOUTH AFRICA

	Johannesburg	Cape Town	Durban
Pan Am	☎ 219391	—	—
Qantas	☎ 281728	—	—
SAA	☎ 237255	☎ 437992	—
SAS	☎ 215201	☎ 430315	☎ 312422
Swissair	☎ 8369941/5	☎ 222784/5	☎ 317706
TWA	☎ 234028/9	—	—

Aircraft and Helicopter Charter

Johannesburg –
- Avex Air ☎ 348890.
- Rennies Air ☎ 8053147.
- Astra Helicopters ☎ 7247377.

Cape Town –
- Air Cape ☎ 932281.
- Namakwaland ☎ 932653.
- Court Helicopters ☎ 932288.

Rail

Modern express trains with air-conditioned dining cars and lounge cars operate along the main line routes; most other train services are slow.

The rail journey from Johannesburg/Pretoria to Cape Town on the luxury Blue Train is spectacular, provided one has plenty of time to spare. The express is air-conditioned and has excellent facilities – including comfortable sleeping accommodation, showers and a high standard of cuisine, all for a relatively reasonable price. Reservations for the Blue Train and other long-distance trains should be made well in advance.

Bedding and meal tickets are obtainable on board express trains.

Road

Driving can be hazardous especially within major cities and along the multi-lane freeways heading out of the urban areas. South Africa has one of the highest accident rates in the world.

Maximum speed limits of 60kph/30mph in urban areas and 80kph/50mph elsewhere should be strictly adhered to, especially on rural dirt roads and the soft-edged highways. Traffic police are allowed to levy on-the-spot fines. Traffic travels on the left-hand side of the road.

Visitors hiring cars should allow for high fuel costs and distance charges which soon mount up in a country the size of South Africa. Petrol filling stations are open from 0800–1800, Mondays to Saturdays, and are closed on Sundays, so long journeys should be carefully planned.

Road distances between the major cities are:

Cape Town – Johannesburg	1,450 km/902 miles.
Cape Town – Durban	1,782 km/1,108 miles.
Johannesburg – Pretoria	58 km/36 miles.
Johannesburg – Durban	645 km/401 miles.
Johannesburg – Port Elizabeth	1,115 km/693 miles.
Johannesburg – East London	998 km/620 miles.

Self-drive or chauffeur-driven cars may be hired in the main centres. Regulations concerning the validity of driving licences differ between the provinces; visitors should be in possession of an International Driving Licence which is valid throughout South Africa.

Taxi charges vary from one city to

SOUTH AFRICA

another. Taxis should be ordered in advance, as it is not possible to hail one in the street. An extra charge is normally made for luggage.

Car-Hire Firms

Johannesburg –	Avis	☎ 218631; (airport) 9753354.
	Budget	☎ 213691.
	Hertz	☎ 8337174; (airport) 9755154.
Cape Town –	Avis	☎ 228329; (airport) 931778.
	Budget	☎ 493126.
	Hertz	☎ 223344; (airport) 934255.
Durban –	Avis	☎ 373541; (airport) 423282.
	Hertz	☎ 373731; (airport) 424648.
Pretoria –	Avis	☎ 30871/2.
	Hertz	☎ 23560.
Port Elizabeth –	Avis	☎ 514271; (airport) 511306.
	Hertz	☎ 514214/5; (airport) 511268.
East London –	Avis	☎ 462215; (airport) 461344.
	Hertz	☎ 29051; (airport) 461064.

10. Tipping

Taxis – 10% of the fare.

Porters – 10–20c per bag.

Hotels/restaurants – a service charge of 10% is usually added to the bill. If not, then a tip of 10% is customary.

USEFUL ADDRESSES (GENERAL)

Cape Town

Australian Consulate: 10th Floor, 1001 Colonial Mutual Building, 106 Adderley Street, ☎ 221576.

British Embassy: 91 Parliament Street, ☎ 227583 (summer only).

British Consulate-General: 11th floor, African Eagle Centre, 2 St George's Street, P.O. Box 1346, ☎ 411466/8.

Canadian Consulate: 16th Floor, Reserve Bank Building, 30 Hout Street, P.O. Box 683, ☎ 225134.

Dutch Consulate: Strandstraat 100, P.O. Box 346, ☎ 431261.

French Consulate: Capetown Centre, 1003 Main Tower, Heerengracht, P.O. Box 1072.

Japanese Consulate: 1410 African Eagle Centre, 2 St George's Street, ☎ 430122.

Swiss Consulate: 634 South African Mutual Building, 14 Darling Street, P.O. Box 37, ☎ 221594/5.

US Consulate: Broadway Industries Centre, Heerengracht, Foreshore, ☎ 471280.

West German Consulate: 825 St Martini Gardens, Queen Victoria Road, ☎ 411421.

Tourist Information Bureau: Upper Ground Floor, Capetown Centre, Heerengracht, P.O. Box 863.

British Council: 91 Parliament Street, ☎ 227583/225803.

SOUTH AFRICA

Thomas Cook Ltd: African Eagle Centre, 2 St George's Street, P.O. Box 12, ☎ 221311, and Cavendish Square, Claremont 7700, Cape Province, ☎ 691108.

American Express International: Greenmarket Place, Greenmarket Square, P.O. Box 2337, ☎ 228581.

Durban

British Consulate-General: 7th Floor, Barclays Bank Building, Field Street, P.O. Box 1404, ☎ 313131.

US Consulate: Durban Bay House, 29th Floor, 333 Smith Street, ☎ 324737.

West German Consulate: 15th Floor, 320 West Street, P.O. Box 80, ☎ 27178.

Thomas Cook Ltd: 57 Gardiner Street, P.O. Box 33, ☎ 68321; and Bhoola Centre, 72 Prince Edward Street, P.O. Box 48227, ☎ 316878,

American Express International: Denor House, 1st Floor, corner Smith and Field Streets, P.O. Box 2558, ☎ 323491.

Johannesburg

British Consulate General: Nedbank Mall, 145 Commissioner Street, P.O. Box 10101, ☎ 218161.

Dutch Consulate: Nedbank Building, 81 Main Street, P.O. Box 3159, ☎ 8348401/2.

French Consulate: Kine Centre, 135 Commissioner Street, P.O. Box 11278.

German National Tourist Office: Loveday Corner, Plein Street, Room No. 407/8, P.O. Box 10883, ☎ 8385334.

Swiss Consulate: corner Main and Simmonds Streets, P.O. Box 3364.

US Consulate: 11th Floor, Kine Centre, Commissioner and Kruis Streets, P.O. Box 2155, ☎ 211684/7.

West German Consulate: corner Bree and Rissik Streets, P.O. Box 4551, ☎ 236166/8.

Johannesburg Visitors' Bureau: Upper Tower Mall, Carlton Centre, Commissioner Street, P.O. Box 4580, ☎ 215971.

Thomas Cook Ltd: 36A Rissik Street, nr. Commissioner Street, P.O. Box 4569, ☎ 230363; and The Firs, Oxford Road, Rosebank, P.O. Box 52261, ☎ 472379.

American Express International: Merbrook, 123 Commissioner Street, P.O. Box 9395, ☎ 374000.

Pretoria

Australian Embassy: 302 Standard Bank Chambers, Church Square, ☎ 37051.

British Embassy: 6 Hill Street, ☎ 743121.

British Consulate: 18/20 Polley's Arcade, 231 Pretorius Street, P.O. Box 1550, ☎ 483020.

Canadian Embassy: Nedbank Plaza, corner Church and Beatrix Streets, Arcadia, P.O. Box 26006, ☎ 487062.

Dutch Embassy: Nedbank Building, corner Church and Andries Streets, P.O. Box 117, ☎ 36451.

French Embassy: 807 George Avenue, Arcadia (winter only).

Japanese Consulate-General:
Prudential Assurance Building, 28 Church Square, P.O. Box 1782, ☎ 486733/4.

Swiss Embassy: 818 George Avenue, Arcadia, P.O. Box 2089, ☎ 747788/9.

US Embassy: Thibault House, 225 Pretorius Street, ☎ 484226.

West German Embassy: 180 Blackwood Street, P.O. Box 2023, ☎ 745931/33.

South African Tourist Corporation:
10th Floor, Arcadia Centre, 130 Beatrix Street, P.O. Box 164, ☎ 25201/5.

Thomas Cook Ltd: Volkskas Centre, 230 Van der Walt Street, P.O. Box 1550, ☎ 483020.

American Express International Inc: SAAU Building, 308 Andries Street, P.O. 3592, ☎ 29182.

British Council: 170 Pine Street, Arcadia, ☎ 746325/6.

BUSINESS INFORMATION

The South African market is highly competitive with great opportunities for suppliers of all types of consumer goods and a large range of capital goods. Success within this market depends largely on the efficiency of local representation or, where manufacturers are supplying direct, on a sound knowledge of the market, frequent visits and efficient after-sales service.

Marketing methods vary according to commodity but, in general, most foreign companies sell through local agents while some operate through a local subsidiary or associated South African company. Local representatives or agents usually hold the exclusive right to market the manufacturer's products across the whole country, although it is not uncommon for agents to be appointed on a regional basis.

In the case of consumer goods, the larger merchant houses tend to buy direct from the manufacturer who supplies goods against indents obtained by the local representative. Some agents carry stocks for distribution. Capital goods are normally sold through the manufacturer's associated or subsidiary organisation in South Africa or, alternatively, through a local agent who will stock any equipment or machinery in heavy demand, and will carry spares and ensure adequate after-sales service is available. Where raw materials are concerned, these are imported either through commission agents or sometimes by agents importing on their own account.

Government purchases and those of other official bodies and organisations, including some of the mining companies, are usually made by tender. Most calls for tender are posted in the Commercial Exchange of Southern Africa in Johannesburg (branch at Welkom in the Orange Free State).

Import and Exchange Control Regulations

All goods imported require an import permit, except for those goods on the Free List (mainly those goods for which local supply is inadequate).

Exchange control regulations are administered by the South African Reserve Bank. Exchange to cover the cost of imports is made available by the importer's bank, provided such imports comply with existing import control regulations.

Restrictions are placed on the repatriation of certain funds held by the subsidiaries and associates of overseas companies.

SOUTH AFRICA

Business Hours
Government Offices
0800–1630 or
0730–1600 Monday to Friday
(The lunch break is usually taken between 1215 and 1330.)

Business Houses
0800–1630 or
0830–1700 Monday to Friday
(Lunch hours vary, but most offices are closed from 1300 to 1400 hours.)

BUSINESS SERVICES

Insurance
African Eagle Life Assurance Society Ltd, Life Centre, 45 Commissioner Street, P.O. Box 1114, Johannesburg.

Commercial Union Assurance Company of South Africa Ltd, Commercial Union House, corner Rissik and Main Streets, P.O. Box 222, Johannesburg.

Guardian Assurance Company South Africa Ltd, Guardian Liberty Centre, 39 Wolmarans Street, Braamfontein, P.O. Box 8777, Johannesburg.

Marine and Trade Insurance Co Ltd, Nedbank Mall, 145 Commissioner Street, P.O. Box 10509, Johannesburg.

Phoenix of South Africa Assurance Co Ltd, Bank of Lisbon Building, 37 Sauer Street, Johannesburg.

Royal Insurance Company of South Africa Ltd, Standard Bank Centre, 78 Fox Street, P.O. Box 1120, Johannesburg.

South African Eagle Insurance Co Ltd, Eagle Star House, 70 Fox Street, P.O. Box 61489, Marshalltown 2107, Transvaal.

Standard General Insurance Co Ltd, Standard General House, 12 Harrison Street, P.O. Box 4352, Johannesburg.

Shipping
South African Marine Corporation Ltd, B.P. Centre, Thibault Square, P.O. Box 27 and 2171, Cape Town 8000, ☎ 453611.

USEFUL ADDRESSES (BUSINESS)

Cape Town
Cape Town Chamber of Commerce: Union Castle Building, St George's Street, P.O. Box 204.

Cape Chamber of Industries: Broadway Industries Centre, 5th Floor, Hertzog Boulevard, Foreshore, P.O. Box 1536.

Durban
Durban Chamber of Commerce: 3rd Floor, Commerce House, Field Street, P.O. Box 1506.

Natal Chamber of Industries: 5th Floor, Metal Industries House, 15 Ordnance Road, P.O. Box 1300.

East London
Border Chamber of Industries: 304 Carmel House, 7 Gladstone Street, P.O. Box 7156.

East London Chamber of Commerce: 14th Floor, Murray & Stewart Centre, Cambridge Street, P.O. Box 93.

SOUTH AFRICA

Johannesburg

Association of Chambers of Commerce of South Africa: 1st Floor, Allied Buildings, corner Rissik and Bree Streets, P.O. Box 694.

British Manufacturers' Representatives' Association: 405 Commissioner Street, Fairview, P.O. Box 3264.

Chamber of Mines of South Africa: 5 Hollard Street, P.O. Box 809.

Johannesburg Chamber of Commerce: P.O. Box 687.

Industrial Development Corporation of South Africa Ltd: Van Eck House, 19 Rissik Street.

South African–Britain Trade Association: P.O. Box 10329.

Transvaal Chamber of Industries: 8th Floor, Allied Buildings, corner Rissik and Bree Streets, P.O. Box 4581.

Port Elizabeth

Chamber of Commerce: SA Wool Board Building, Grahamstown Road, P.O. Box 48.

Midland Chamber of Industries: 1st Floor, SA Wool Board Building, Grahamstown Road, P.O. Box 2221.

Pretoria

Department of Commerce: Legal and General Building, corner Prinsloo and Pretorius Streets, Private Bag X84.

Department of Industries: Civitas Building, corner Struben and Andries Streets, Private Bag X342.

Department of Customs and Excise: Franz du Toit Building, corner Paul Kruger and Schoeman Streets, Private Bag X47.

Directorate of Imports and Exports: Legal and General Building, corner Prinsloo and Pretorius Streets, Private Bag X192.

Pretoria Chamber of Commerce: 307 NBS Building, 259 Pretorius Street, P.O. Box 72.

South African Federated Chamber of Industries: 4th Floor, Nedbank Plaza, Church Street, P.O. Box 4516.

South African Iron and Steel Corporation Ltd (ISCOR): Wagon Wheel Circle, P.O. Box 450.

MAJOR CITIES

Cape Town

Cape Town is situated in the Cape Province on the southernmost tip of Africa. The city was founded in 1652 and is the oldest white settlement in South Africa. Cape Town is the seat of South Africa's legislature, and Parliament meets here from December to June.

Although much of the traditional Cape Dutch architecture has given way to commercial buildings and skyscraper blocks, a number of landmarks still remain to remind the visitors of Cape Town's early history, including the State Rooms of the Cape Town Castle (1666), which contain period furniture and paintings, Koopmans De Wet Museum and the Old Town House.

The famous port lies in the shadow of the magnificent Table Mountain and Lion's Head. A cable-car ride to the top of Table Mountain from the station off Kloof Nek offers a panoramic view of the city and bay. In Newlands, on the slopes of Table

Mountain, are the Kirstenbosch National Botanic Gardens, open daily from sunrise till sunset.

The Mediterranean-like climate of the Western Cape makes it ideal for fruit growing, and the area abounds with orchards and vineyards. Typical of the Province is the town of Paerl, set amongst orchards and vineyards against the backcloth of the Hottentots Holland Mountains. The town of Stellenbosch, seat of the principal Afrikaans University, is the centre of the South African wine industry, and many of the larger companies offer tours around their vineyards with opportunities for wine-tasting as well as sherry and brandy sampling.

There are numerous beaches around the Cape Peninsular coast – Clifton and Llandudno are on the cold Atlantic side, while the popular resorts of Muizenberg, St James and Simonstown lie along the warm Indian Ocean coast.

D. F. Malan Airport is 13km/8 miles from the centre of Cape Town.

Hotels

HEERENGRACHT, St George's Street, P.O. Box 2936, ☎ 413151.
Modern 5-star, de luxe hotel in the Trust Bank Centre in the heart of Cape Town, opposite the air terminal.
Rooms: 210 ♌, ⚫, ☐, ⌑, ⚠, ▥. Suites and duplex suites available.
Facilities: 3 restaurants, grill room, cocktail lounges, bars, coffee shop. Nightclub on 32nd floor. Swimming, massage, sauna. Shopping arcade, service shops. Airport courtesy bus. Car hire.
Services: ТС, ЃС. ⊟ Amex, Barclay Visa, Diners Club, Master Charge. Dr. on call. 𝕾, ♂.
Conference room – max. capacity 500.
Banquet rooms – max. capacity 550.

HOLIDAY INN, 61 Melbourne Road, P.O. Box 2979, ☎ 474067.
Modern 1st-class (3-star) hotel, 3km/2 miles from city centre.
Rooms: 220 ♌, ⚫, ☐, ⚠.
Facilities: Restaurant, 2 bars. Live entertainment. Swimming. Car hire.
Services: ТС, ЃС. ⊟ Amex, Barclay Visa, Diners Club, Standard Bank. 𝕾, ♂.
Conference room – max. capacity 400.

MOUNT NELSON, Orange Street, P.O. Box 2608, ☎ 220012.
Famous traditional-style 5-star de luxe hotel set in extensive landscaped gardens within 10 minutes' walk of city centre.
Rooms: 140 ♌, ☐, ⌑, ⚠, ▥. Suites available.
Facilities: Restaurant, grill room, cocktail lounge, bars. Swimming, tennis. Car hire.
Services: ТС, ЃС. ⊟ Amex. Dr. on call. 𝕾, ♂. Audio-visual equipment.
Conference and banquet rooms – max. capacity 500.

PRESIDENT, Beach Road, Sun Point, P.O. Box 62, ☎ 441121.
5-star de luxe hotel in beautiful setting on sea front, 10 minutes' drive from city centre.
Rooms: 152 ♌, ⚫, ☐, ⌑, ⚠, ▥. Suites available.
Facilities: 3 restaurants, bars. Swimming, sauna, massage. Car hire.
Services: ТС, ЃС. ⊟ Amex, Barclay Visa, Diners Club, Standard Bank, Wesbank. Dr. on call. 𝕾, ♂.
Conference and banquet rooms – max. capacity 250.

DE WAAL, Mill Street Gardens, P.O. Box 2793, ☎ 451311.
Modern 1st-class (4-star) hotel at the foot of Table Mountain, within walking distance of city centre.
Rooms: 134 ♌, ⚫, ☐, ⌑, ⚠, ▥. Suites available.
Facilities: Restaurant, steakhouse, bars. Swimming. Golf, tennis near by. Car hire.
Services: ТС. ⊟ Amex, Barclay Visa, Diners Club, Wesbank. Dr. on call. 𝕾, ♂.
Conference room – max. capacity 180.
Banquet rooms – max. capacity 200.

Restaurants
International: *Grill Room,* Mount Nelson Hotel, ☎ 220012; *Nelson's Eye* – steakhouse; *Pickwick Tavern*; *The Copper Kettle,* Sea Point, ☎ 442822; *The Geneva,* Main Road, Claremount, ☎ 616611; *Hunting Pot,* Long Street, ☎ 435166; *Kronendal,* Hout Bay, ☎ 705172; *Wyldes,* Barnet Street, ☎ 454909.

Seafood: *Café Royal,* Church Street, ☎ 228924; *Harbour Café,* ☎ 436432; *La Perla,* Sea Point, ☎ 442471; *Hildebrand Tavern.*

Italian: *Fracarlo,* Sea Point, ☎ 445521.

Chinese: *Bamboo Inn,* Bree Street, ☎ 433964; *Pagoda Inn,* Bree Street, ☎ 226620.

Entertainment
There are several theatres of which the modern Nico Malan Theatre is the best known. Two of the most popular nightspots are the *Crazy Horse* at the Century Hotel, Sea Point, with a live cabaret, and the *Van Donck* nightclub at the top of the Heerengracht Hotel on St George's Street.

Sporting facilities are plentiful, and there are racecourses at Kenilworth and Milnerton. There are ample opportunities for surfing, scuba diving and fishing, and Cape Town has several good golf clubs.

Durban
Durban is South Africa's major port and also the country's principal resort offering year-round swimming in the warm Indian Ocean and long sandy beaches, including the famous Golden Mile Beach, along the Natal coast. Durban suffers from very high humidity in summer which can cause considerable discomfort to the unacclimatised visitor.

Durban is the centre of the sugar industry and to the north of the city for mile after mile stretch the sugar-cane plantations as well as pineapple and banana plantations. The sugar industry explains the existence of a large Indian population in Durban, and the Eastern influence on the city is apparent. There are several Hindu temples and mosques and an Indian market full of Oriental curios, tropical fruits and spices, and the exotic atmosphere of a genuine Eastern bazaar.

One of Durban's most renowned sights are the Zulu *ricksha* pullers in their colourful costumes decorated with beads and ornaments. Ngoma dances are performed by the Zulus most weekends on the African recreation grounds off Somtseu Road.

Louis Botha International Airport is 11km/7 miles from the centre of Durban.

Hotels
BEVERLEY HILLS, Lighthouse Road, P.O. Box 71, Umhlanga Rocks, ☎ 512211.
5-star resort hotel on Umhlanga Rocks beach, 15 minutes' drive from city centre.
Rooms: 90 ♪, ⌀, ⎕, ⚠, ⬢. Suites available.
Facilities: 3 restaurants, bars. Nightclub. Swimming. Turkish baths. Hairdressing salon. Car hire.
Services: TC, FC. ✉ Major credit cards accepted. Telex. S.
Conference room – max. capacity 100.

BLUE WATERS, 175 Snell Parade, P.O. Box 10201, ☎ 333781.
4-star hotel on the beachfront, 2km/1½ miles from city centre.
Rooms: 264 ♪, ⌀, ⎕, ⚠, ⬢. Suites available.
Facilities: Restaurants, bars. Nightclub. Swimming, sauna, solarium. Golf, tennis, squash. Transport from air terminal and railway station.
Services: TC, FC. ✉ Amex, Barclay Visa, Diners Club. Dr. on call. S, ♂.
Conference room – max. capacity 300.
Banquet rooms – max. capacity 220.

CABANA BEACH, 10 Lagoon Drive, P.O. Box 10, Umhlanga Rocks, ☎ 512371.
Modern, 4-star resort complex set in large park area on beach, 15 minutes' drive from city centre.
Rooms: 215 suites and duplex cabanas ♌, ⌀, ⬜ on request.
Facilities: Restaurant, bistro, grill room, coffee shop, bars. Zulu dancing (Sundays). Swimming, squash, tennis, horse riding, sailing, fishing. Golf near by. Shopping arcade. Tours, safaris arranged. Shuttle bus to city centre.
Services: ⊟ Amex, Barclay Visa, Diners Club. Audio-visual equipment.
Conference room – max. capacity 165.

EDWARD, Marine Parade, P.O. Box 10800, ☎ 373681.
Traditional-style 5-star hotel along beachfront, 5 minutes' drive from city centre.
Rooms: 101 ♌, ⌀, ⬜, ⌶, ⚐, ⌕. Suites available.
Facilities: 2 restaurants, coffee shop, bars. International cabaret. Car hire.
Services: TC, FC. ⊟ Amex, Barclay Visa, Diners Club, Standard Bank. Dr. on call. S, ♂.
Conference and banquet room – max. capacity 150.

ELANGENI, 63 Snell Parade, P.O. Box 4094, ☎ 371321.
Modern 4-star hotel above Golden Mile Beach.
Rooms: 460 ♌, ⌀, ⬜, ⌶, ⚐, ⌕. Suites available.
Facilities: Several restaurants, bars, nightclub. Swimming, sauna, massage. Shops. Car hire.
Services: TC. ⊟ Amex, Barclay Visa, Diners Club, Wesbank. Dr. on call. S, ♂.
Conference rooms – max. capacity 1,100.
Banquet rooms – max. capacity 540.

MAHARANI, 83/91 Snell Parade, P.O. Box 10592, ☎ 327361.
Ultra-modern 5-star tower hotel on Golden Mile opposite North Beach.

Rooms: 270 ♌, ⌀, ⬜, ⌶, ⚐, ⌕. Suites available.
Facilities: Restaurants, bars, coffee shop, Nightclub with restaurant. Swimming, sauna, massage, gym. Beauty shop. Golf, tennis near by. Theatre bookings. Car hire.
Services: TC. ⊟ Amex, Barclay Visa, Diners Club. Dr. on call. S, ♂.
Conference and banquet rooms – max. capacity 350.

ROYAL, 267 Smith Street, P.O. Box 1041, ☎ 320331.
4-star hotel (built 1877, recently modernised), in city centre about 1 mile from beaches.
Rooms: 67 ♌, ⌀, ⬜, ⌶, ⚐, ⌕. Suites available.
Facilities: 2 restaurants, bars. Car hire.
Services: TC, FC. ⊟ Amex, Barclay Visa, Diners Club. Dr. on call. S, ♂.
Conference rooms – max. capacity 220.

Restaurants

Roma Revolving Restaurant; Bali Hai, Elangeni Hotel, ☎ 371321; *Copacabana,* Beverley Hills Hotel, Umhlanga Rocks, ☎ 512211; *Le Beaujolais; Saltori's; The '67'; The Oyster Box,* Umhlanga Rocks, ☎ 512233; *The Causerie,* Edward Hotel, ☎ 373681.

Entertainment

Durban offers safe bathing (within the restricted areas protected by shark nets) and excellent surfing. All kinds of water sports are available, particularly around the resort area of Umhlanga Rocks where many hotels are situated.

The Botanical Gardens are worth visiting, particularly to view the Japanese garden. Durban's Marineland has a large aquarium and a snake park. The city is an important horse-racing centre, and the Durban Turf Club is the scene of South Africa's premier horse race, the July Handicap (first Saturday in July each year).

Johannesburg

Johannesburg has grown from its beginning as a gold town in the 1880s to become the largest city in the Republic and the centre of South Africa's industrial heartland, the mining belt known as the Witwaterstrand or, simply, the Rand. At an altitude of 2,000 metres/6,560 feet, Johannesburg has generally good weather, although it can be cold at nights, especially in winter.

Johannesburg is the centre of real economic and political power in the Republic, and opportunities for industrial and service employment have attracted large numbers of workers from all over Southern Africa to the townships which surround the city. The city in many respects typifies the contradictions of much of South African life, with the members of the affluent white society with their modern buildings, homes and luxurious lifestyles leading a life sharply in contrast to those in the segregated black and coloured areas.

Things to see include the Post Office Tower, the Afrikaaner Museum, the Geology Museum, the Art Gallery, the zoo and parks, the University Planetarium and various mining exhibitions.

Hotels

CARLTON, Main Street, Carlton Centre, P.O. Box 7709, ☎ 218911.
Ultra-modern 5-star de luxe hotel within the Carlton Centre complex in city centre.
Rooms: 600 ♪, ⚫, ☐, ✕, △, ⌨. Suites available.
Facilities: Several restaurants, cocktail lounges, coffee shop. Live entertainment in the 'Top of the Carlton' club. Rooftop pool and garden. Sauna, gym, ice rink. Car hire. Airport transfers.
Services: TC, FC. ✉ Access, Amex, Bankamericard, Barclay Visa, Diners Club, Eurocard, Master Charge, Standard Bank. Dr. on call. S, ♂.
Conference and banquet rooms – max. capacity 1,200.
12 equipped function rooms.

LANDDROST, 88 Plein Street, Joubert Park, P.O. Box 11026, ☎ 281770.
De luxe 5-star high-rise hotel in city centre.
Rooms: 270 ♪, ⚫, ☐, ✕, △, ⌨. Suites available.
Facilities: 4 restaurants, 3 bars. Swimming, gym, sauna, massage. Airline office. Shops. Car hire.
Services: TC. ✉ Amex, Barclay Visa, Diners Club, Standard Bank, Wesbank. Dr. on call. S.
Conference and banquet rooms – max. capacity 200.

PRESIDENT, Corner Eloff and Plein Streets, P.O. Box 7702, ☎ 281414.
Modern 5-star hotel in city centre.
Rooms: 250 ♪, ⚫, ☐, ✕, △, ⌨.
Facilities: Restaurant, grill room, coffee shop, bars. Swimming. Health, beauty centre. Shopping arcade. Tour arrangements, airline booking office. Transport to airport. Car hire.
Services: TC, FC. ✉ Access, Amex, Bankamericard, Barclay Visa, Carte Blanche, Diners Club, Eurocard, Master Charge, Standard Bank. Dr. on call. S, ♂.
Conference rooms – max. capacity 850.
Banquet rooms – max. capacity 550.

RAND INTERNATIONAL, 290 Bree Street, P.O. Box 4235, ☎ 8367911.
4-star multistorey hotel in city centre near Joubert Park.
Rooms: 145 ♪, ⚫, ☐, ✕, △, ⌨. Soundproofing.
Facilities: Restaurant, grill room, cocktail bar. Car hire.
Services: TC. ✉ Amex, Barclay Visa, Diners Club, Standard Bank. Dr. on call. S.

ROSEBANK, Tyrwhitt Avenue, P.O. Box 52025, ☎ 7881820.
Modern 4-star hotel in quiet residential suburb, 7km/4½ miles outside city.
Rooms: 140 ♪, ⚫, ☐, ✕, △, ⌨. Suites available.

SOUTH AFRICA

Facilities: Restaurant, bars, coffee shop. Nightclub. Swimming, tennis, golf. Hairdresser. Rosebank Shopping Centre near by. Car hire.
Services: TC, FC. ■ Amex, Barclay Visa, Diners Club, Standard Bank. S.
4 conference rooms – max. capacity 400. Banquet rooms – max. capacity 280.

SUNNYSIDE PARK, 2 York Road, Parktown, ☎ 6433011.
3-star elegant country mansion set in beautiful garden in residential suburb of Parktown, 3km/2 miles from city centre.
Rooms: 82 ♒, ●, ◻, ☎.
Facilities: 4 restaurants, bars, cocktail lounges. Swimming. Golf, tennis near by. Banquet, meeting rooms.
Services: ■ Amex, Bankamericard, Barclay Visa, Diners Club.

THE TOWERS, corner Kerk and Von Wieilligh Streets, P.O. Box 535, ☎ 372200.
Modern 5-star de luxe hotel near city centre. Accommodation consists of suite units.
Rooms: 135 ♒, ●, ◻, ☎, △, ⌘.
Facilities: Restaurants, bars, lounges, Sauna, massage. Shopping arcade. Car hire.
Services: TC, FC. ■ Amex, Barclay Visa, Diners Club. Dr. on call. S, ♂.
3 conference rooms – max. capacity 200. Banquet rooms – max. capacity 150.

Jan Smuts International Airport

HOLIDAY INN – JAN SMUTS, P.O. Box 388, Kempton Park.
Modern 3-star hotel close to airport.
Rooms: 272 ♒, ☎, ◻.
Facilities: Restaurant, lounge, bar, coffee shops. Live entertainment. Boutiques, service shops. Transport to airport, Johannesburg, Pretoria.
Services: ■ Amex, Barclay Visa, Diners Club. Convention facilities for 300 persons.

SOUTHERN SUN AIRPORT HOTEL, Hully Road, Isando, ☎ 366911.

Modern, Spanish-style 3-star hotel, 1km from airport.
Rooms: 250 ♒, ●, ◻.
Facilities: Restaurants, bars. Swimming, gym. Courtesy coach service to airport. Conference facilities for 300 persons.

Restaurants

Many of the better restaurants are found in the main hotels and are open to non-residents. These have been included in the list below, together with a selection of other restaurants offering a variety of types of cuisine.

International: *Café Royal*; *Heinrich's*, J. G. Strydom Tower; *Three Ships*, Carlton Hotel; *Transvaal Room*, President Hotel; *Mirabelle*, Casa Mia Hotel; *The Prospect*, Sunnyside Park Hotel.

French: *Chez André*, ☎ 233662; *Chez Zimmerli*, ☎ 424815.

Italian: *Franco's*, ☎ 237007; *Rugantino's*, ☎ 235231; *Sardi's*, ☎ 232116; *Villa Borghesa*.

Chinese: *Bamboo Inn*, ☎ 227194; *Pung Ching*, ☎ 235421; *Sai Woo*, ☎ 472917.

Greek: *Athens by Night*, ☎ 6423517; *Plaka*, ☎ 428620.

Seafood: *Lobster Hole*, ☎ 403451; *Norman's Grill*, ☎ 6181320.

Portuguese: *Alfama*, ☎ 222222.

Oriental: *The Perfumed Garden*, ☎ 7246517; *The Curry Tavern*, ☎ 216342.

Nightclubs

Live entertainment, with frequent visits by international stars, is a feature of the *Top of the Carlton* at the Carlton Hotel. Another popular nightspot is the *Top of the Town* at the Holiday Inn, Milner Park. Jazz is usually featured on Sunday nights at the President Hotel.

SOUTH AFRICA

Port Elizabeth

Port Elizabeth is the 2nd city and port of the Cape Province, situated some 1,200km/750 miles east of Cape Town. The city is the centre of the South African car industry and a major wool-exporting centre.

Attractions for the visitor include the Campanile Monument in memory of the town's original British settlers; the Oceanarium complex consisting of a museum, oceanarium, snake park and tropical house; the ancient fortification of Fort Frederick; and Settler's Park, a 130-acre nature reserve right in the heart of the city.

H. F. Verwoerd Airport is 5km/3 miles from the city centre.

Hotels

BEACH, Marine Drive, Summerstrand, ☎ 532161.
3-star hotel overlooking sea, 5km/3 miles from city centre.
Rooms: 63 🛁, ☎, ♨, 📺. Suites available.
Facilities: Restaurant, bars, lounges. Verandah. Car hire.
Services: 🍴, 🅿. 🖃 Amex, Barclay Visa, Diners Club, Standard Bank. 💲, ♂.
Conference and banquet rooms – max. capacity 100.

ELIZABETH, La Roche Drive, Humewood, P.O. Box 13100, ☎ 27321.
Modern 5-star hotel on Kings Beach overlooking Algoa Bay, 3km/2 miles from city centre.
Rooms: 200 ♨, 🛁, 🚿, ☎, ♨, 📺. Suites available.
Facilities: 2 restaurants, coffee shop, cocktail bars. Discotheque, nightclub with cabaret. Swimming, sauna. Cinema, shops. Golf, tennis near by. Car hire.
Services: 🍴. 🖃 Amex, Barclay Visa, Diners Club, Standard Bank. Dr. on call. 💲, ♂.
Conference room – max. capacity 700.
Banquet rooms – max. capacity 600.

HOLIDAY INN, Marine Drive, Summerstrand, P.O. Box 204, ☎ 533131.
3-star hotel on beachfront, 2½km/1½ miles from city centre.
Rooms: 160 ♨. Suites available.
Facilities: Restaurant, bar, lounge. Live entertainment. Swimming. Free transport to and from airport. Golf, water sports near by.
Services: 🖃 Amex, Diners Club.
Conference rooms – max. capacity 250.

Restaurants

The following hotel restaurants are open to non-residents: *The Bell* and *Tudor Room*, Beach Hotel, ☎ 532161; *The Skyroof*, Marine Hotel; *Room at the Top*, Elizabeth Hotel, ☎ 27321.

Pretoria

Pretoria is the administrative capital, situated 48km/30 miles north of Johannesburg. The city has retained much of its old-world atmosphere which is further enhanced by its beautiful jacaranda-lined avenues, at their most picturesque during October and November.

Many landmarks commemorating events in Afrikaner history are situated here. The huge Voortrekker Monument, visible for many miles around, is greatly revered by the Afrikaner population as a national shrine. The home of President Paul Kruger in Church Street is now an Afrikaner museum. Other museums of note are the Transvaal Museum with its extensive collection of geological, archaeological and zoological specimens dating from the Stone Age period; and the Old Museum, which houses a unique exhibition of San (Bushman) art as well as art of many African tribes, and Voortrekker memorabilia.

Other points of interest are the massive Union Buildings of the Government which

SOUTH AFRICA

dominate the city centre, and the Skanskop and Klapperkop forts, built at the beginning of the century to defend the city from British attacks.

Jan Smuts Airport is 40km/25 miles from the centre of Pretoria.

Hotels

BOULEVARD, 186 Struben Street, ☎ 24806.
3-star hotel in the city centre.
Rooms: 75 ♌, ⊛, ☐ on request, ♋, ♒, ♐. Suites available.
Facilities: Several restaurants (including Chinese), bars, cocktail lounges, nightclubs. Car hire.
Services: TC, FC. ▤ Amex, Barclay Visa, Bankamericard, Diners Club, Eurocard, Master Charge. Dr. on call. $, ♂.
Conference room – max. capacity 500.
Banquet rooms – max. capacity 500.

BURGERS PARK, corner Van der Walt and Minnaar Streets, P.O. Box 2301, ☎ 486570.
Modern 3-star, hotel in quiet location overlooking Burgers Park, ½ mile from city centre.
Rooms: 252 ♌, ⊛, ☐ on request, ♋, ♒, ♐. Suites available.
Facilities: 3 restaurants, 2 bars. Swimming, sauna. Golf, tennis, bowls near by. Car hire.
Services: TC, FC. ▤ Amex, Barclay Visa, Diners Club, Standard Bank, Wesbank. Dr. on call. $, ♂.
Conference room – max. capacity 350.
Banquet rooms – max. capacity 250.

PALMS, 682 Pretoria Road, Silverton, ☎ 861014.
Modern 3-star hotel outside city centre, near the Silverton and Ross Lyn industrial centres.
Rooms: 94 ♌, ⊛, ☐ on request, ♋, ♒, ♐. Suites available.
Facilities: Restaurants, bars. Swimming. Car hire.
Services: TC, FC. ▤ Amex, Barclay Visa, Diners Club, Standard Bank. Dr. on call. ♂.
Conference and banquet rooms – max. capacity 700.

Restaurants

Some of the better restaurants include: *The Elite*; *La Provence*; *Ambassador's*, Burgers Park Hotel, ☎ 486570; *Protea Room*, Union Hotel, ☎ 486671; *Janina*; *Waterfalls*; *Flamingo Room*, Boulevard Hotel, ☎ 24806.

SUDAN
Democratic Republic of the Sudan

Geography	402
The Economy	403
How to Get There	404
Entry Regulations	404
Practical Information for the Visitor	405
Useful Addresses (General)	407
Business Information	408
Business Services	409
Useful Addresses (Business)	409
Khartoum	409

Size: 2,502,673 sq.km/966,283 sq.miles.

Population: 17.4 million (1978).

Distribution: Over 60% of the population live in the central area of Sudan, around Khartoum and the Nile River.

Density: 6.2 persons per sq.km/16 per sq.mile (40 per sq.km/104 per sq.mile in Khartoum Province).

Population Growth Rate: 2.6% p.a. (1970–7).

Ethnic Composition: Sudan has many different ethnic groups. A large percentage of the population are Muslim Arabs living in the northern and central areas, together with the Nubians. Black peoples occupy much of the western part of the country, where there has been mixing with migrants from West Africa. The south is inhabited by many different tribes with the Nilotic groups predominating.

Capital: Khartoum Pop. 333,920.

Major Cities/Towns: Omdurman Pop. 299,400; Khartoum North Pop. 150,990; Port Sudan Pop. 127,120; Wad Medani Pop. 106,776; El Obeid Pop. 90,060; Atbara Pop. 66,116; Juba Pop. 56,737.

Language: Arabic is the official language, spoken by about half of the population. Of the more than 100 other languages spoken throughout the Sudan, Nilotic and Nilo-Hamitic tongues are spoken by approximately 23% of the population. English is the most widely spoken foreign language.

Religion: The population is predominantly Muslim, with 80% belonging to the Sunni Sect. There are small Christian communities, and Animism is widespread amongst the southern tribes.

Government: The head of state of the Sudan is the President, who is responsible for maintaining the Constitution and appointing the Prime Minister and other Government ministers. A 250-member People's Assembly is formally vested with legislative power.

In 1972 the Southern Region of Sudan gained regional autonomy within a

SUDAN

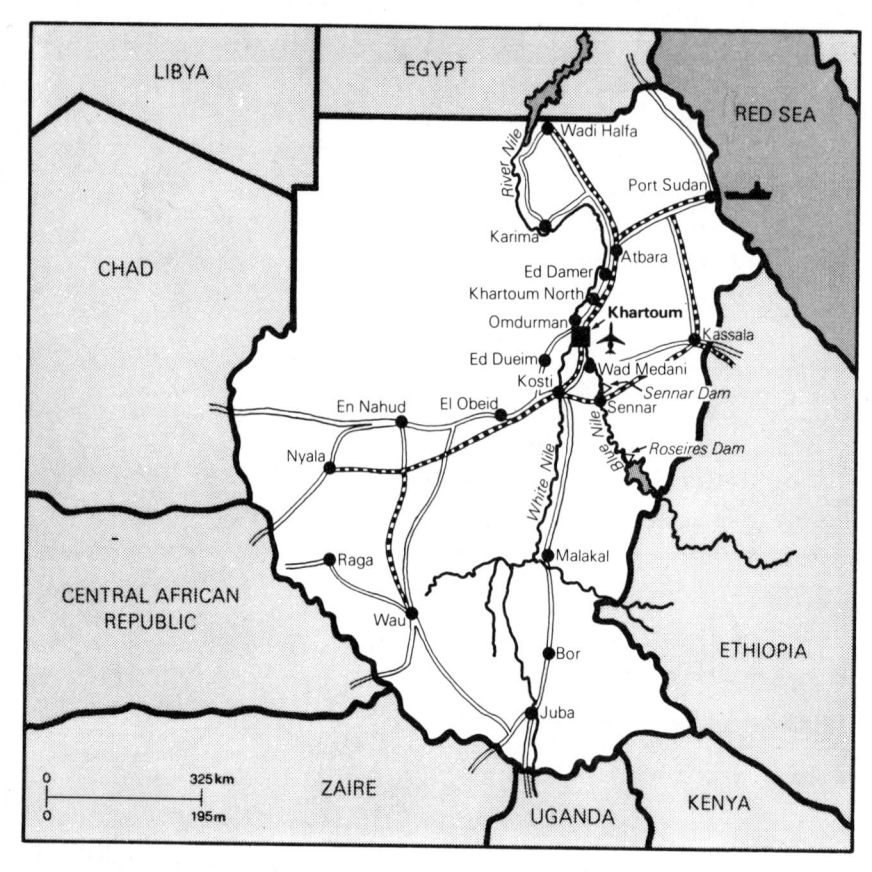

federal structure and is governed by a High Executive Council.
The Sudanese Socialist Union is the only legal political party.

GEOGRAPHY

Sudan is the largest country in Africa, with an area almost equal to that of Western Europe. The country is very varied with desert, savannah and tropical rain forest. The White and Blue Niles flow through southern Sudan, joining the Khartoum to form the main Nile River.

The greatest part of the country consists of an immense plateau, which is separated from the Red Sea coast to the east by a range of hills. Much of southern Sudan consists of savannah and tropical rain forest with large areas of swampland, while the north is a desert region through which the Nile flows, providing the chief means of communication.

Climate

Sudan has a tropical climate, although conditions differ considerably in the various regions. Rainfall is highest in the south, but over much of Sudan it is unreliable and severe crop failures are not uncommon.

From mid-April to June the weather is extremely hot and dry with increasing humidity from July to September. Temperatures in Khartoum range from 32°c/90°F in December to 42°c/108°F in June. The southern provinces are cooler, but have greater humidity in summer. The period from October to mid-April is the most pleasant time to visit.

Agriculture

Sudan is predominantly an agricultural country and depends heavily on agriculture for export earnings and employment. Irrigation is widespread, and several large dams have been built – the Sennar Dam on the Blue Nile irrigates about 1.8 million acres, known as the Managil Extension, and the Roseires Dam will eventually provide year-round irrigation for 3 million acres of land.

Commercial farming is largely confined to the north, while traditional methods of agriculture and livestock rearing prevail in the south. Cotton is the chief cash crop, accounting for approximately 55% of Sudan's total exports by value. The Gezira cotton-growing scheme in the triangle formed by the White and Blue Niles is one of the largest single agricultural enterprises in Africa.

Attempts are being made to increase the cultivation of other cash crops such as sugar, groundnuts and castor seed in order to reduce the country's dependence on cotton. With the development of large-scale irrigation, Sudan's agricultural potential is enormous. Some of the new schemes are being financed with the help of Arab oil-producing nations.

Main Crops: cotton, sugar, groundnuts, gum arabic, oil seeds, sorghum (dura), millet, dates.

Mineral Resources: Various mineral deposits have been located, but exploitation to date is very limited. Known deposits include copper, iron ore, chromite, manganese, gold, salt. Small quantities of oil have recently been discovered in the remote south-west of the country.

THE ECONOMY

Gross National Product (1978 provisional): US$5.5 billion.

Per Capita Income (1978): US$320.

Gross Domestic Product (1976): £S1.78 billion.

Foreign Trade (1978): Total Imports – US$624.1 million. Total Exports – US$562.9 million.

Main Trading Partners: Imports – Iran, India, UK, China, USA, West Germany. Exports – Italy, France, China, West Germany, USA, Saudi Arabia.

The Sudanese economy is primarily based on agriculture, with trade being mainly concerned with the export of primary or processed agricultural products and the import of both capital and consumer goods needed by a developing country.

Sudan is almost self-sufficient in its major food items; current agricultural development plans are aimed at reaching total self-sufficiency in foodstuffs. Cotton still remains Sudan's chief means of earning foreign exchange, which leaves the country in a vulnerable position where balance of payments is concerned.

Agriculture and irrigation are the chief beneficiaries of Government development funds, together with associated food-processing industries. New sugar factories are being built, and a major development of the cotton spinning and weaving industry is envisaged. On a smaller scale, there has been a recent expansion in light manufacturing industries – mainly in the production of basic consumer goods such as soap, shoes, soft drinks and beer. The exploitation of Sudan's various mineral deposits is also to be stepped up.

The 6-Year Development Plan (1977/8 to 1982/3) should go a long way towards solving many of the Sudan's problems related to underdevelopment. Transport and communications, health, education and welfare are all scheduled to benefit from increased investment.

Major Industries: light manufacturing (e.g., foodstuffs, soap, textiles, footwear) paper products, sugar, cement.

Main Commodities Traded: Imports – machinery and equipment, vehicles, manufactured goods and foodstuffs, chemical and petroleum products. Exports – cotton, groundnuts, sesame, gum arabic.

International Affiliations: UN, IBRD, OAU, ACP, ADB, AL, BADEA.

HOW TO GET THERE

Air

Major airlines flying to the Sudan are Aeroflot, Alitalia, British Airways, Egypt Air, Lufthansa, MEA, SAS, Saudi Arabian Airlines and TWA. Sudan Airways operate between Khartoum and Bahrain, Egypt, Ethiopia, West Germany, Greece, Kenya, Italy, Iraq, Lebanon, Libya, Saudi Arabia and the United Kingdom.

Flying times to Khartoum: from London 8 hours; from New York 15½ hours.

Khartoum Civil Airport is the main international airport, located 5 km/3 miles from the city centre. An airport charge of £S1 is payable by all passengers embarking on international flights from Khartoum Airport.

Taxis are available at the airport and, on request, airlines will arrange for transport from hotels to the airport.

ENTRY REGULATIONS

Visas

Nationals of all countries require visas which should be obtained in advance from Sudanese embassies and consulates abroad.

Business travellers require a letter from their firm giving the fullest details of the business to be undertaken in Sudan, the full names and addresses of contacts and the actual amount of funds available to the applicant.

N.B. When filling out the visa application form, applicants should ensure that the information regarding the details of their trip is as precise and complete as possible.

Visas are valid for 3 months from the date of issue for a stay of up to 1 month. Travellers should ensure that the validity of their passport extends for 3 months beyond the date of issue of the visa.

Visitors staying for more than 3 days in the Sudan must register on arrival with the Aliens Department of the Ministry of the Interior. Visitors intending to travel outside of the Three Towns district of Khartoum, Khartoum North and Omdurman should first notify the Ministry of the Interior of their destination.

Evidence in a passport of a previous or planned visit to Israel may adversely affect the granting of a visa.

Health Regulations

All visitors must have valid International Certificates of Vaccination against smallpox and cholera. Visitors wishing to travel to the south of Sudan should also have a valid certificate of vaccination against yellow fever.

Travellers entering Egypt or the UK from Sudan are required to have a yellow fever certificate or a 'location certificate' certifying that they have not been in a yellow fever area. These can be obtained from the offices of the Khartoum Municipality 24 hours or less before departure.

Customs

Currency: There is no limit to the amount of foreign currency which may be taken into the Sudan. All currency, including travellers' cheques and letters of credit, must be declared on entry and exit. The import and export of Sudanese currency are prohibited.

Visitors should exchange their travellers' cheques and foreign currency at authorised exchange points only, and the currency declaration form must be endorsed. This has to be shown to the Customs authorities on departure.

Duty-free articles: Personal effects. 250g tobacco or 200 cigarettes or 50 cigars. 2 pints of spirits.

Articles liable to duty: All commercial samples are subject to the usual import regulations. When dutiable samples accompany a traveller and are re-exported within 12 months, the Customs duty is refunded.

PRACTICAL INFORMATION FOR THE VISITOR

1. Currency

Monetary Unit – Sudanese pound (£S), divided into 100 piastres (PT) and 1,000 milliemes (mms).
Notes – 25, 50 piastres; 1, 5, 10 Sudanese pounds.
Coins – ½, 1, 2, 5, 10 piastres.

Several major hotels and airline offices in Khartoum now accept internationally recognised credit cards, but their use is not widespread throughout the Sudan.

Banking Hours
0830 – 1200 Saturday to Thursday

All commercial banks in the Sudan were nationalised in 1970. The banking system now consists of the Bank of Sudan, which is the central bank, 5 commercial banks and 3 specialised banks. A number of foreign banks have recently been allowed to open branches in Khartoum.

Bank of Sudan, Sharia Gamaa, P.O. Box 313, Khartoum, ☎ 70761/5.

Commercial Banks in Khartoum
Bank of Khartoum, 8 Sharia Gamhouria, P.O. Box 1008, ☎ 81071/2, 70666.
El Nilein Bank, Sharia Khalifa, P.O. Box 466, ☎ 73939.
People's Co-operative Bank, Sharia Qasr, P.O. Box 992, ☎ 73555.
Sudan Commercial Bank, P.O. Box 1116, ☎ 71468.
Unity Bank, Sharia Barlaman, P.O. Box 408, ☎ 74200/6.

Specialised Banks in Khartoum
Agricultural Bank of Sudan, Sharia Gamhouria, P.O. Box 1363, ☎ 77424/5, 77466.
Industrial Bank of Sudan, UN Square, P.O. Box 1722, ☎ 71223.
Sudanese Estates Bank, Sharia Baladia, P.O. Box 309, ☎ 81061/2, 78062.

Foreign Commercial Banks in Khartoum
Bank of Credit and Commerce International, P.O. Box 5, ☎ 73970.
Chase Manhattan Bank, P.O. Box 2679, ☎ 78740, 78703.
Citibank, P.O. Box 2743, ☎ 76623, 76654.
Faisal Islamic Bank, P.O. Box 2415, ☎ 75367.
National Bank of Abu Dhabi, P.O. Box 2463, ☎ 74892.

2. Electricity Supply
240v AC single phase.
Plugs: 2 round pins.

3. Weights and Measures
The metric system is used in commercial circles and imperial measures are also used. Important local measures to be notes are:
kantar (100 *rotls*) = 315lb seed cotton or 100lb lint cotton.
feddan = 1.038 acres.

4. Media
The Sudanese Broadcasting Service transmits radio programmes in Arabic, English, Somali and 8 Sudanese languages. Both television and radio carry advertising. Enquiries should be addressed to: El Gorashi Advertising and Printing Corporation, P.O. Box 536, Khartoum.

Newspapers and Journals
The press was nationalised in 1970. Dailies include *Al Ayam* and *Al Sahafa*. The Ministry of Information and Culture sponsors a number of publications including the *Nile Mirror* and *Sudanow* (both in English).

2 Arabic journals printed in England – *Anglo-Arab Trade* and *Middle East Trade* – both circulate in Sudan, together with a number of other foreign trade publications. The *Journal of the Engineering Society* is published biannually; the Sudan Chamber of Commerce publishes its own journal.

5. Medical Care
Malaria is endemic in many parts of Sudan and visitors should take antimalarial measures as recommended by their doctor. Gastro-enteritis, hepatitis and bilharzia are additional health risks, often resulting from poor sanitation.

Although the water supply in Khartoum and other large towns is safe to drink, visitors are advised to drink boiled or filtered water. Visitors should take extra salt, in tablet or solution form, during the hot summer months.

6. Telephone, Telex and Postal Services
Telegrams may be sent from the main Khartoum Post Office 24 hours a day. International telephone and telex communications have improved considerably since the Satellite Tracking Station came into use.

All mail to and from Sudan should be despatched by air.

7. Public Holidays

1 January	*Anniversary of Sudan Independence*
3 March	*Unity Day*
25 May	*Revolution Day*
12 October	*Republic Day*
25 December	*Christmas*

The following Muslim holidays are also observed: *Mouled, Ascension of the Prophet, Eid el Fitr, Kurban Bairam, El Hijra, Ashoura.*

Easter is a public holiday for all Christians in the Sudan.

8. Time
GMT + 2.

9. Internal Transport
Official permits are required for most journeys within the Sudan. Visitors spending the night in a town outside of the Three Towns district must register with the local police.

Air
Sudan Airways operate regular, internal services to Atbara, Juba, El Obeid, Port Sudan, Wad Medani and other towns. The provincial airport charge is PT 50.

Airline Offices in Khartoum

Aeroflot	☎ 71150.
Air France	☎ 74479.
Air India	☎ 74583.
British Airways	☎ 74577/9.
Lufthansa	☎ 71322.
MEA	☎ 80968.
Pan Am	☎ 80971.
SAS	☎ 81011, 81015.
Sudan Airways	☎ 76411, 76414.
Swissair	☎ 80196, 80229.
TWA	☎ 76413.

Rail
Trains in the Sudan are generally clean and comfortable but tend to be very slow. There are trains from Khartoum to Port Sudan, Wadi Halfa, El Obeid, Nyala, Wau, Kosti and Kassala. Sleeping cars and catering facilities are available on the main routes.

Road
Motorists should enquire about road conditions and administrative restrictions before commencing a journey through the country. Sudan has few tarred roads and conditions during the rainy season (July–September) are bad.

Self-drive cars are available for hire. Traffic drives on the right-hand side of the road.

Taxis are not metered and fares should be arranged before starting a journey. Collective taxis can be found in the Khartoum market place.

10. Tipping
Taxis – No tip expected.

Porters – 5 piastres per bag.

Hotels/restaurants – 10% of the bill.

11. Social Customs
More than three-quarters of the population are Muslims and most Muslim customs are observed. Alcohol, however, is not prohibited. Segregation of the sexes is generally practised, and women rarely attend social and business functions.

USEFUL ADDRESSES (GENERAL)

Khartoum

British Embassy: New Aboulela Building, Sharia Barlaman, P.O. Box 801, ☎ 70760, 70766/9.

Dutch Embassy: Sharia El Mahdi, corner Gama'a Avenue, P.O. Box 391, ☎ 77788/9.

French Embassy: 6H East Plot 2, 19th Street, P.O. Box 377.

Japanese Embassy: House No. 24, Block 10 A.E., 3rd Street, New Extension, P.O. Box 1649, ☎ 44549, 44554.

Swiss Embassy: New Aboulela Building, P.O. Box 1707, ☎ 71161, 72365.

US Embassy: Gamhouria Avenue, P.O. Box 699, ☎ 74611, 74700.

West German Embassy: 53 Baladia Street, Block No. 8 D.E., Plot No. 2, ☎ 77990, 77995.

Sudan Tourist Corporation, P.O. Box 2424, Khartoum, ☎ 70230.

Ministry of Culture and Information, Khartoum, ☎ 74949, 74955.

Thomas Cook Authorised Representatives: Sudan Travel and Tourist Agency, P.O. Box 769, Khartoum, ☎ 72119, 70919; Tigani World Wide Travel Organisation, 76 Sharia Gamhouria, P.O. Box 936, Khartoum, ☎ 76996.

BUSINESS INFORMATION

In 1970 most of the foreign interests operating in the Sudan were nationalised and replaced by Government-owned trading companies. However, a large proportion of the nationalised companies have now been handed back to their original owners, and this has given rise to renewed activity in the private sector. The Development and Promotion of Industrial Investment Act (1972) and the Act to Organise and Encourage Investment in Economic Services (1973) were both designed to attract foreign investment.

About 75% of the country's industrial activity is located in the Khartoum area, although a number of important Government organisations are outside this region. Of particular importance are Sudan Railways at Atbara, the Sudan Gezira Board near Wad Medani and the Ministry of Irrigation and Hydro-Electric Power also at Wad Medani.

Firms wishing to trade in the Sudanese market generally require a local agent who must be registered with the Ministry of Commerce and Supply, and have a current licence to operate.

Personal contact is highly valued in the Sudan; visits by representatives of foreign companies are very important and also facilitate the choice of a good local agent.

Import and Exchange Control Regulations

Import regulations are strict and most goods require a Specific Import Licence, although some goods can be imported under an Open General Licence. The importation of goods from Israel and South Africa is prohibited.

Sudan operates its own exchange control under the supervision of the Bank of Sudan. All payments must be made through banks authorised to deal in foreign exchange. All advance payments require the prior approval of the Exchange Control Authorities.

Business Hours
Government Offices
Khartoum – 0800 – 1400 Saturday to Thursday
Other centres – 0630 – 1400 Saturday to Thursday (with interval for breakfast)

Business Houses
0830 – 1330
1700 – 2000 Saturday to Thursday

Friday is the weekly holiday in the Sudan.

Business Events

In 1978 Khartoum staged its first International Trade Fair and this has become an annual event, taking place in January/February of each year on a permanent site by the Blue Nile. Further details can be obtained from the Director General, Sudan Exhibitions and Fairs Corporation, P.O. Box 2366, Khartoum.

BUSINESS SERVICES

Agents who will arrange collection/despatch of samples include:

Commercial & Shipping Company, P.O. Box 308, Khartoum; Forwarding Department, P.O. Box 74, Port Sudan.

Ezzel din Ali Osman, P.O. Box 544, Port Sudan.

May Trading & Services Ltd, P.O. Box 215, Khartoum; Forwarding Department, P.O. Box 17, Port Sudan.

Palestine Trading Company, P.O. Box 251, Khartoum; P.O. Box 6, Port Sudan.

Sudan Shipping Line Ltd, P.O. Box 1731, Khartoum; Forwarding Department, P.O. Box 426, Port Sudan.

USEFUL ADDRESSES (BUSINESS)

Ministry of Commerce & Supply, P.O. Box 194, Khartoum.

Ministry of Finance, Planning and National Economy, Sharia Gama'a, P.O. Box 194, Khartoum, ☎ 70288.

Sudan Chamber of Commerce, P.O. Box 81, Khartoum, ☎ 72346, 76518.

Sudan Development Corporation, P.O. Box 710, Khartoum.

Sudanese Industries Association, P.O. Box 2563, Khartoum.

MAJOR CITY

Khartoum

Khartoum is the capital of the Three Towns (Khartoum, Khartoum North, Omdurman) which lie at the junction of the Blue and White Niles. Omdurman is considered to be the national capital, Khartoum the commercial and administrative capital, and Khartoum North the industrial capital. All 3 towns are joined together by a series of bridges which span the 2 rivers.

The modern city of Khartoum is built with wide avenues, spacious open areas and large, white colonial-style buildings, but one can still find the old narrow streets and colourful marketplaces tucked away behind the main area of the city.

The People's Palace has a fine collection of antique field guns, swords and other military equipment dating from the time of General Gordon.

Omdurman was built in the 19th century by the Mahdi when he laid siege to Khartoum and General Gordon's forces. It subsequently became the capital of the Mahdi's empire until it was captured in 1898 by the British and Egyptian armies under Lord Kitchener. The Mahdi's tomb can be visited, and adjacent to it stands the Khalifa's Museum, named after the Mahdi's successor Khalifa Abd Ullahi.

The flat-roofed, baked mud houses in Omdurman are good examples of Sudanese architecture. In the shaded, narrow streets visitors will find many small shops and stalls and the bazaar where traditional Sudanese handicrafts are sold – ivory and ebony carved goods, silverware, beadwork and slippers, bags, wallets and belts made from leopard and lizard skins.

Hotels

There is no official hotel rating system in Sudan.

KHARTOUM HILTON, P.O. Box 1910, ☎ 74100/78930.
Modern luxury hotel built at the junction of the Blue and White Niles, 2½ km/1½ miles from centre of Khartoum.
Rooms: 274 ♫, ●, ☐, ☎, ♦, ⌘.
Facilities: Restaurant, grill room. Coffee shop, bar. Nightclub. Airline office, shops, barber shop. Tennis, sauna, swimming, bowling alley, billiards, health club.
Services: TC, FC. ▤ Amex. Dr. on call. S, ♂.
Conference room – max. capacity 434.
Banquet rooms – max. capacity 324.

KHARTOUM MERIDIEN, P.O. Box 1716, ☎ 75970.
Modern 1st-class hotel in city centre, 10 minutes drive from airport.
Rooms: 150 ♫, ●, ☐ on request, ☎, ♦, ⌘.
Facilities: Restaurant, bar. Sauna, swimming. Garden.
Services: TC, FC. ▤ Amex. Dr. on call.
Banquet room – max. capacity 150.

SUDAN, Sharia el Nil, P.O. Box 1845, ☎ 80811.
Modern hotel in the city centre.
Rooms: 80 ♫, ⫿, ●, ☎, ♦, ⌘. Suites available.
Facilities: Restaurant, bar. Gift shop, hairdresser. Squash.
Services: TC, FC. ▤ Amex. Dr. on call. S, ♂.

Restaurants

Good international cuisine can be found in the restaurants of the Hilton, Grand, Sudan and Sahara Hotels. Other restaurants in Khartoum include: *St James*, Sharia Gamhouria; *Blue Nile Casino*, Khartoum North; *The Gordon Cabaret* – dinner and dancing, 72045; *Shish Kebab Restaurant.*

Nightclubs

Hilton Hotel, ☎ 74100 – open-air; *Hamad Floating Casino*, Sharia el Nil, Khartoum; *Blue Nile Cafeteria*, Sharia el Nil, Khartoum; *Jimmy's Night Club*, Khartoum.

Entertainment

Khartoum has several cabarets and cinemas. The National Theatre, Sharia el Nil, Omdurman, ☎ 51549, stages productions from October to June.

A number of sporting clubs offer swimming, tennis, golf, polo, cricket, and hockey. Race meetings are held regularly in Khartoum on Fridays during the winter. Khartoum also has a zoo.

A number of cruises operate along the Nile; launches for up to 15 persons can be hired at 24 hours' notice.

The *Sudan Club*, P.O. Box 322, Khartoum, is an exclusively British club offering limited accommodation for men and women; the club has a restaurant, bar and library facilities, as well as swimming, badminton, volleyball, snooker, billiards, squash and tennis for residents. Visiting business travellers can obtain temporary membership on application to the Secretary.

Shopping

Best buys: hides and skins, jewellery, ivory and ebony carved goods.

Sudan Folklore House, 67 Sharia El Qasr, ☎ 71729 – ivory and skins; *Sudan Crafts*, Sharia El Qasr, ☎ 77367 – souvenirs; *Khartoum Tannery*, P.O. Box 134, Khartoum South – hides, skins, chamois.

SWAZILAND
Kingdom of Swaziland

Geography	411
The Economy	413
How to Get There	414
Entry Regulations	414
Practical Information for the Visitor	415
Useful Addresses (General)	416
Business Information	417
Business Services	417
Useful Addresses (Business)	418
Mbabane	418

Size: 17,373 sq.km/6,704 sq.miles.

Population: 526,000 including over 30,000 absentee workers (1978).

Distribution: 15% in urban areas.

Density: 30.1 persons per sq.km/77.9 per sq.mile.

Population Growth Rate: 2.5% per annum (1970–7).

Ethnic Composition: Some 90% are Swazi; other groups are Zulu, Tonga, Shangaan, Europeans (2.3%) and Asians (1%).

Capital: Mbabane Pop. 22,260 (1976).

Major Towns: Manzini urban district Pop. 29,500; Big Bend Pop. 2,900; Nhlangano Pop. 1,700; Piggs Peak Pop. 1,400; Siteki Pop. 1,400.

Language: Siswati and English are the official languages.

Religion: About 60% are Christians, mainly Baptist and Roman Catholic; most of the remainder adhere to traditional indigenous beliefs.

Government: Swaziland has been an independent monarchy since 6 September 1968. In 1973, in the wake of civil unrest and electoral setbacks, King Sobhuza II abandoned the Constitution and dissolved all political parties. The King now heads the Liblandla, an administrative body made up of representatives of forty *tinkuhandlas*, a traditional tribal system of government, established in January 1979 following elections in the tribal assemblies. The sole legal political party is the Imbokodvo National Movement. The Ngwane National Liberatory Congress (NNLC), the major opposition party, is in exile based in Mozambique.

GEOGRAPHY

Swaziland is a small landlocked country. The four main geographical regions run north–south and are, from west to east, the highveld at an elevation of over 1,000 metres/3,300 feet, the middle veld at an average altitude of 600 metres/1,300 feet, the almost tropical lowveld and the Lubombo uplands, an escarpment in the extreme east of the country.

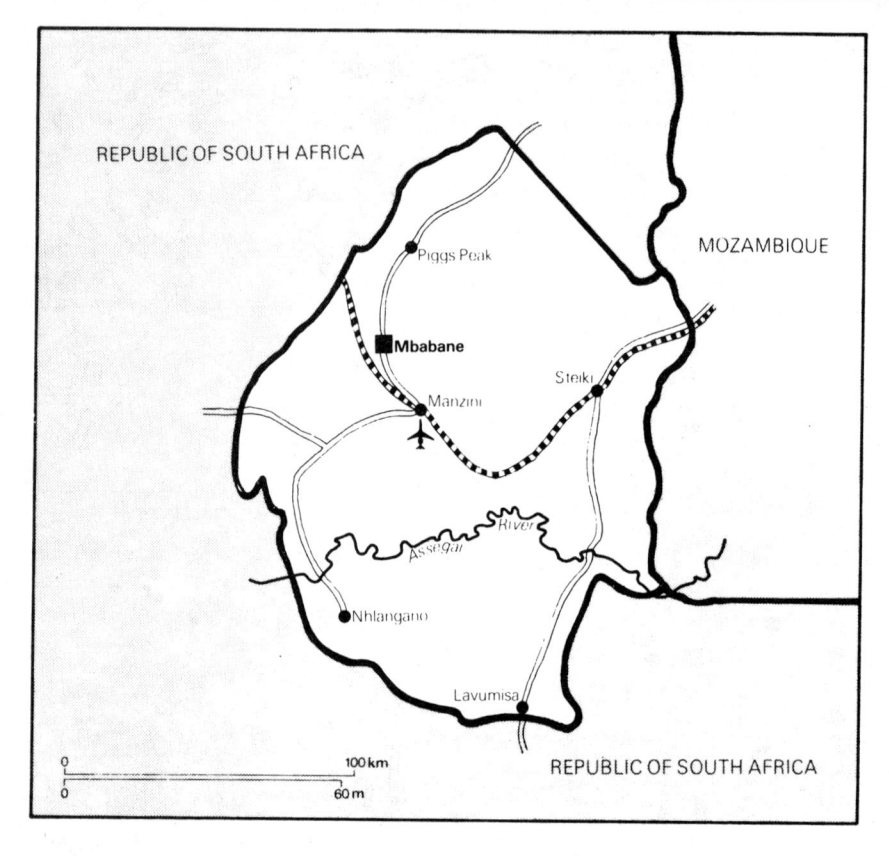

Climate
Rainfall and temperatures vary according to altitude, ranging from humid tropical conditions in the lowveld during the summer months of October to March to sharp frosty nights in the highveld winter. Annual rainfall averages between 1,000–2,000mm/40–80in in the highveld, falling to 500–850mm/20–30in in the lowveld where frequent droughts occur. Average temperature is 16°C/60°F in the highveld, and 22°C/72°F in the lowveld.

Agriculture
Agriculture is the most important sector of the economy and is responsible for one-third of Gross Domestic Product (1963–73) and 77% of total exports (1976). 70% of the population engage in agriculture, which provides just under half of all wage employment. Major subsistence crops are maize, groundnuts, beans, sorghum and sweet potatoes. Peasant cash crops include cotton, tobacco, pineapples, rice and sugar cane. Livestock raising is also widespread. Most of this activity is carried out on the 54% of the total land area which is held in trust for the Swazi Nation by the King.

Much of the remainder of the land is owned by non-resident non-Swazis, and this constitutes the modern commercial sector. The main commercial crop is sugar cane; also grown are citrus fruits, cotton and pineapples. Cattle and sheep ranching is also common, as is forestry. The Government plans to improve productivity by expanding beef and forestry production and by continuing irrigation schemes with the aid of grants, loans and technical assistance from a number of agencies. Prevention of soil erosion, disease control and the acquisition of unused freehold land for the Swazi nation are amongst Government priorities.

Main crops: sugar cane, maize, citrus fruits, cotton, other fruits, sweet potatoes, potatoes, rice, beans, tobacco.

Mineral Resources: coal, iron ore, asbestos. Recent surveys report possible reserves of diamonds, gold and uranium.

THE ECONOMY

Gross National Product (1978): US$340 million.

Per Capita Income (1978): US$634.

Gross Domestic Product (1977 est.): 272.5 million emalangeni.

Foreign Trade (1977 prov. est.): Total Imports – US$142 million. Total Exports – US$157 million.

Main Trading Partners: Imports – South Africa, UK, Japan, USA. Exports – South Africa, UK, Japan, EEC, Mozambique.

The economy is characterised by the marked contrast between 2 divergent patterns of development. On the one hand is the vast majority of the population who engage in subsistence agriculture or work as contract labour abroad, and, on the other hand, the modern commercial and industrial sector employing about a third of the labour force but contributing a steadily rising proportion of the GDP.

The sugar industry is the largest single foreign exchange earner with 2 mills at present producing about 230,000 tons a year. A 3rd mill is planned to be operated by a British company with investment from the Nigerian Government, the German Development Company (DEB), Coca-Cola, Mitsui of Japan, the Commonwealth Development Corporation (CDC) and the World Bank through the IDF. Under the Lomé Convention, much of Swaziland's sugar exports go to the EEC. The CDC is also involved in pulp processing with the Swazi nation as shareholders in Usuti Pulp. Usuti also manage the large commercial forestry sector. Production of asbestos and iron ore is declining, although coal production is being expanded for domestic consumption.

The manufacturing sector is relatively large, providing over one-third of Gross Domestic Product. Wood and sugar processing predominate with other activities including cotton ginning, beer and soft drinks, confectionery, textiles, electrical assembly and building material production. Tourism is expanding rapidly, with uncensored cinemas, shows and gambling providing attractions for many South African visitors.

Transportation facilities are good, with the rail link to Mozambique traditionally the

SWAZILAND

route for exports. The recent completion of an alternative rail route to Richard's Bay near Durban has eased transport problems, and another rail route is planned from Mpaka into the Transvaal.

Gross National Product has grown by 15% p.a. (1971–5) and at an estimated 11% p.a. since then. Swaziland has consistently had balance of trade surpluses in recent years, with boom years in 1974 and 1975 on account of high world sugar prices.

Major Industries: sugar production, pulp processing, cotton spinning, fruit and juice canning, beef production, brewing, fertilisers, craft industries, mining, tourism.

Main Commodities Traded: sugar, fruit, beef, cotton, wood pulp, asbestos, fertilisers.

International Affiliations: UN, IBRD, OAU, ACP, ADB, Commonwealth, SACU.

HOW TO GET THERE

Air
Royal Swazi Airlines fly between Matsapa Airport and Johannesburg 5 days per week, and South African Airways operate a twice-weekly return service between the same destinations. Royal Swazi Airlines also fly to Durban. DETA (Mozambique) operate a service to Matsapa from Maputo. There is a service to Lusaka (Zambia) and one flight a week from Mauritius, also operated by Royal Swazi Airlines.

Matsapa Airport is 8km/5 miles from Manzini.

Road
Bus services connect Johannesburg with Mbabane and Maputo with Manzini. There are several road routes to Swaziland from South Africa and Mozambique. Most of them are asphalted. Visitors intending to travel by road should check on the border post opening hours before setting off.

ENTRY REGULATIONS

Visas
Visas are required except for nationals of British Commonwealth countries, Belgium, Denmark, Finland, Gambia, Greece, Iceland, Republic of Ireland, Israel, Italy, Liechtenstein, Luxembourg, Netherlands, Norway, Portugal, South Africa, Sweden, Uruguay and USA, provided the visit does not exceed 2 months.

Visas are available from the Chief Immigration Officer, P.O. Box 372, Mbabane, or from Swaziland representatives abroad. Persons intending to stay longer than 2 months need a Temporary Residence Permit, also available from the Chief Immigration Officer. Visitors must have proof of sufficient funds to purchase an outward ticket if they are not in possession of such a ticket.

Health Regulations
International Certificates of Vaccination against smallpox, yellow fever and cholera are required if arriving from infected areas.

Customs

Currency: There are no restrictions on the transport of funds between member countries of the Rand Monetary Area (RMA) – South Africa, Lesotho and Swaziland. A maximum of R50 per person or equivalent in Swaziland currency may be imported into or exported out of the RMA. There is no limit to imports or exports of foreign currency. Unused imported currency may be exported on departure.

Duty-free articles: Personal effects. 400 cigarettes, 50 cigars or 250g of tobacco. 0.75 litres of alcoholic beverages. ½ pint perfume. Married couples travelling together receive free import allowance for 1 person only.

Restricted articles: An import permit is necessary for all firearms and ammunition. Applications should be made well in advance to the Firearms Licensing Board.

PRACTICAL INFORMATION FOR THE VISITOR

1. Currency

Monetary Unit – lilageni, divided into 100 cents; and rand, divided into 100 cents (South African currency).
Notes – 1 lilageni, 2, 5, 10 and 20 emalageni. 1, 2, 5, 10, 20 rand.
Coins – 1, 2, 5, 10, 20, 50 cents; 1 lilageni. ½, 1, 2, 5, 10, 20, 50 cents (South African).

As a member of the Rand Monetary Area, the local currency is freely convertible at a par with the South African rand. Travellers' cheques and foreign exchange can be cashed at all banks and at Matsapa Airport. The Monetary Authority controls currency issue and banking policy. The Government has a 40% share of Barclays Bank of Swaziland and the Standard Bank of Swaziland.

Banking Hours
0830–1300 Monday to Friday
0800–1100 Saturday

Principal Commercial Banks in Swaziland
Bank of Credit and Commerce International S.A., Nkoseluhlaza Street, Manzini.
Barclays Bank of Swaziland Ltd., P.O. Box 669, Allister Millar Street, Mbabane.
Standard Bank of Swaziland Ltd., P.O. Box 68, 21 Allister Millar Street, Mbabane.
Swaziland Development and Savings Bank, P.O. Box 336, Mbabane.

2. Electricity Supply
230–250v AC 50Hz.

3. Weights and Measures
The metric system is in use.

4. Media
The Swaziland Broadcasting Service broadcasts a commercial service for 7 hours daily mainly in Siswati, but with some English programmes. Swazi Radio is a commercial service operating from South Africa and broadcasting in English, Afrikaans, Portuguese and several Indian languages. Subscribers in Mbabane and Manzini receive cable television.

Newspapers and Journals
The Times of Swaziland is the major newspaper, published daily in English. Many South African papers are available in the main towns. The Government Information Services issue a weekly, *News from Swaziland*, and a fortnightly, *Ummbiki*, in English and Siswati respectively.

SWAZILAND

5. Medical Care
There is a risk of malaria, particularly in the lowveld during the rainy season. Anti-malarial prophylactics should be taken. Bilharzia is endemic, and care should be taken not to swim or paddle in still or slow-moving waters.

Medical care is good. Mbabane has a Government hospital, a private clinic, several doctors and dentists.

6. Telephone, Telex and Postal Services
Telephone, telex and telegram services are available in the main centres. All mail, to and from Swaziland, should be despatched by air mail.

7. Public Holidays
1 January	New Year
25 April	National Flag Day
22 June	King's Birthday
6 September	Independence Day
24 October	United Nations Day
25 December	Christmas Day
26 December	Boxing Day

Incwala, the First Fruits Festival, occurs in December or January. The second Monday in June is *Commonwealth Day*. The last Monday in August is *Reed Dance/Mhlanga Day*. The following Christian holidays are also observed: *Ascension Day*, *Good Friday* and *Easter Monday*.

8. Time
GMT + 2.

9. Internal Transport

Air
Swaziland is too small for anyone likely to want to charter aircraft for internal use, but if this is necessary try Swaziland Air Services of Mbabane, ☎ 6302. Air Swazi also offer domestic services.

Airline Offices
Royal Swazi Airlines, P.O. Box 939, Manzini, ☎ 53151.
Royal Swazi National Airways Corporation, P.O. Box 1082, Mbabane.

Road
Swaziland is well served by 2,750km/1,000 miles of roads of which 640km/400 miles are asphalted, the rest being gravel or dirt. Minor roads may be impassable after heavy rains. Major routes enter Swaziland from South Africa, and Manzini and Mbabane are joined by a highway. Bus services are numerous but uncomfortable, and taxis are scarce even in the largest towns.

Traffic drives on the left, and an International Driving Licence is required. Self-drive cars are available.

Car Hire Firms
Hertz – Manzini ☎ 30.
        Mbabane ☎ 4256.
        Airport ☎ 52509.
Also Swazi Safaris, P.O. Box 680, Manzini.

10. Tipping
Taxis – 10% of the fare.

Hotels/restaurants – 10% of the bill.

USEFUL ADDRESSES (GENERAL)

British High Commission, Allister Millar Street, ☎ 2581.

Israeli Embassy, P.O. Box 146. ☎ 2626.

Taiwan Embassy, Embassy House, P.O. Box 56.

US Embassy, Allister Millar Street, P.O. Box 199, ☎ 2272.

Swaziland Government Tourist Office, P.O. Box 451, Mbabane, ☎ 2531.

Chief Immigration Officer, P.O. Box 372, Mbabane.

Chief Customs Officer, Dept. Customs and Excise, P.O. Box 489, Manzini.

University of Botswana and Swaziland, Swaziland Campus, Post Bag, Kavaluseni.

BUSINESS INFORMATION

Foreign investment is welcome, especially in major capital projects. Encouragement is given to potential investors, and services are continually improving as Swaziland seeks to expand its industrial base. An industrial estate off the major highway between Mbabane and Manzini offers fast connections to Maputo, and all sites are fully serviced. The major areas in which investment potential lies remain the processing of agricultural produce and mining. Tourism is also rapidly expanding, and the number of visitors and amount of revenue are increasing every year. Major development projects are especially encouraged if they are labour intensive and include provision for training. The general aim is to decentralise industry and develop export markets outside southern Africa. Swaziland has a relatively large manufacturing sector and machinery and transport equipment are in demand. Most of the domestic market is supplied by South Africa.

Import and Exchange Control Regulations

All goods imported from SACU member countries are free of import duties, otherwise import regulations follow those of South Africa. All goods not included in the free list require import permits. There is no exchange control between South Africa, Lesotho and Swaziland as they are constituent members of the RMA. Exchange control regulations are otherwise similar to those of South Africa.

Business Hours
Government Offices
0800–1645 Monday to Thursday
0800–1630 Friday

Business Houses
0800–1700 Monday to Friday
0800–1300 Saturday

BUSINESS SERVICES

Shipping
Royal Swazi Maritime Co Ltd (Swazimar), Mbabane.

Insurance
Since 1974 the only insurance company, in which the Government owns a 51% share, has been the *Swaziland Royal Insurance Corporation*, P.O. Box 917, Mbabane.

USEFUL ADDRESSES (BUSINESS)

Exchange Controller, Monetary Authority of Swaziland, P.O. Box 546, Mbabane.

Ministry of Works, Power and Communication, P.O. Box 58, Mbabane.

National Industrial Development Corporation of Swaziland (NIDCS), P.O. Box 866, Mbabane.

Small Enterprise Development Co. Ltd, P.O. Box A186, Mbabane.

Swaziland Chamber of Commerce, P.O. Box 72, Mbabane.

Swaziland Central Cooperatives Union, Manzini.

Swaziland Citrus Board, P.O. Box 343, Mbabane.

Swaziland Commercial Board, P.O. Box 509, Mbabane.

Swaziland Cotton Board, P.O. Box 160, Mbabane.

Swaziland Investment Corporation Ltd, P.O. Box 158, Manzini.

Swazi Meat Corporation Ltd, P.O. Box 446, Manzini.

Swaziland Railway Board, Swaziland Railway Building, Johnstone Street, P.O. Box 475, Mbabane.

Swaziland Sugar Association, P.O. Box 455, Mbabane.

MAJOR CITY

Mbabane

Mbabane, the administrative capital, is situated in the Dalengi Hills of the highveld overlooking the beautiful Ezulwini Valley. It is a growing commercial centre with a mixture of old and modern buildings in the town centre and spreading suburban development.

Hotels

There is no hotel rating system. In view of the limited number of rooms, it is advisable to book well in advance.

BEST WESTERN SWAZI INN, P.O. Box 121, ☎ 2235.
Cottage-style inn near Mbabane, at head of Ezulwini Valley.
Rooms: 40 ♪, 🍴, ☎, ♨, ♡.
Facilities: Restaurants, bars. Films. Swimming. Conference room.
Service: TC, FC. 🖃 Amex, Barclaycard, Diners Club, Master Charge. Dr. on call.

EZULWINI HOLIDAY INN, P.O. Box 412, ☎ 1201.
Modern hotel on Mbabane–Manzini highway, 11km/7 miles from Mbabane town centre, 23km/14 miles from Matsapo Airport.
Rooms: 120 ♪, 🍴, ☐, ☎, ♨, ♡ (0630–2230). Suites available.
Facilities: Restaurants, bars. Nightclub, casino. Car hire. Golf, tennis, sauna, squash, swimming, bowling, riding.
Services: TC, FC. 🖃Amex, Barclay Visa, Diners Club. Dr. on call. Audio-visual equipment.
Conference and banqueting rooms – max. capacity 60.

HIGHLAND VIEW HOTEL, P.O. Box 223, ☎ 2464.
Recently enlarged and modernised hotel.

SWAZILAND

Rooms: 60 ♒, ⌂, ⛉, ⛄, ☯.
Facilities: Restaurant, bar. Nightclub. Swimming pool.
Services: TC, FC. ▤ Amex, Barclaycard, Diners Club. Dr. on call.
Conference room – max. capacity 100.

JABULA INN, P.O. Box 15, ☏ 2406.
Traditional hotel in city centre.
Rooms: 25 ♒, ⌂, ⛁, ⛄, ☯ (0700–1900). Suites available.
Facilities: Restaurant, bars. Nightclub. Car hire.
Services: TC, FC. ▤ Amex, Barclaycard, Diners Club, Eurocard. Dr. on call. S, ♂. Audio-visual equipment.
Conference and banquet rooms – max. capacity 120.

LUGOGO HOLIDAY INN, P.O. Box 412, ☏ 2022.
Situated on main road 11km/7 miles from Mbabane, 27km/17 miles from Manzini, in Ezulwini Valley near Royal Swazi Hotel complex.
Rooms: 204 ♒, ⌂, ⛁, ⛉, ⛄, ⛟. Suites available.
Facilities: Restaurants, bars. Nightclub, casino. Swimming, health hydro. Tennis, bowling, riding. Car hire.
Services: TC, FC. ▤ Access, Amex, Barclaycard, Diners Club, Eurocard, Master Charge. Dr. on call. S, ♂.
Conference room – max. capacity 60.

ROYAL SWAZI HOTEL AND SPA, P.O. Box 412, ☏ 61001.
Modern and recently extended hotel complex, 18km/11 miles from Mbabane town centre in Ezulwini Valley. An expensive hotel.
Rooms: 149 ♒, ⌂, ⛁, ⛉, ⛄, ⛟. Suites available.
Facilities: Restaurants, bars. Nightclub, casino. Sauna, health hydro. Cinema.

Golf, swimming, tennis, squash, riding, bowling. Car hire.
Services: TC, FC. ▤ Access, Amex, Barclaycard, Diners Club, Eurocard, Master Charge. Dr. on call. S, ♂.

Restaurants
All hotel restaurants are open to non-residents. In addition to a Portuguese restaurant opposite the Tavern Hotel, there is a selection of Greek, Indian, German and Chinese restaurants in Mbabane and the Ezulwini Valley.

Nightclubs
There are 2 nightclubs in Mbabane: *The Penguin*, open every night, situated next to the Jabula Inn; and *The Highland View* nightclub, next to the Highland View Hotel. Several of the hotels stage cabaret acts in the evenings. The casino at the Royal Swazi Hotel is a big attraction for South African weekend visitors.

Entertainment
Outdoor sports and other pursuits are well catered for. Game parks are easily accessible and tours may be arranged in Mbabane or from the major hotels.

Shopping
Best buys: traditional Swazi handicrafts, especially woven grass and mats, wooden bowls, cloth garments.

Many of these goods are produced specifically for sale to tourists. The *Small Enterprises Development Company* (SEDCO) estate on the Mbabane–Manzini highway is worth a visit to see the craftsmen at work and to buy tie-dyed shirts, dresses and cloth. Mohair blankets are also on sale in many places. Other items include beadwork, basketware, gemstone jewellery and carved soapstone. Bargaining is acceptable in markets, but not in shops.

TANZANIA
United Republic of Tanzania

Geography	*420*
The Economy	*422*
How to Get There	*423*
Entry Regulations	*423*
Practical Information for the Visitor	*424*
Useful Addresses (General)	*426*
Business Information	*427*
Business Services	*428*
Useful Addresses (Business)	*428*
Dar es Salaam	*429*
National Parks	*430*

Size: 945,091 sq.km/364,900 sq.miles.

Population: 16.9 million (1978 est.).

Distribution: 7% in urban areas.

Density: 17 persons per sq.km/45 per sq.mile.

Population Rate: 3.0% p.a.

Ethnic Composition: Approximately 98% are Africans belonging to over 130 different tribes, mostly Bantu. There are also Indian and Pakistani minorities, living mainly in the towns; a small Arab population; and about 10,000 resident Europeans.

Capital: Dar es Salaam Pop. 600,000 (proposed change of capital to Dodoma circa 1983).

Major Cities/Towns: Tanga Pop. 98,000; Zanzibar Pop. 96,000; Mwanza Pop. 65,000; Arusha Pop. 61,000.

Language: Swahili is the national language. English is very widely spoken, as are a large number of African dialects, mainly Bantu.

Religion: Large numbers of Christians and Animists, with a small Hindu minority amongst the Asian community. The vast majority of Zanzibaris are Muslims.

Government: The President is elected by universal suffrage and appoints the Cabinet Ministers. The National Assembly is comprised of both appointed and elected members, the latter being in the minority. The Chama Cha Mapinduzi (Revolutionary Party) is the only authorised political party.

GEOGRAPHY

The total land area of Tanzania (945,091 sq.km/364,900 sq.miles) includes the islands of Zanzibar and Pemba in the Indian Ocean, which lie some 35 km/22 miles off the mainland. The country has about 53,483 sq.km/20,650 sq.miles of inland water, including large parts of Lakes Victoria and Tanganyika.

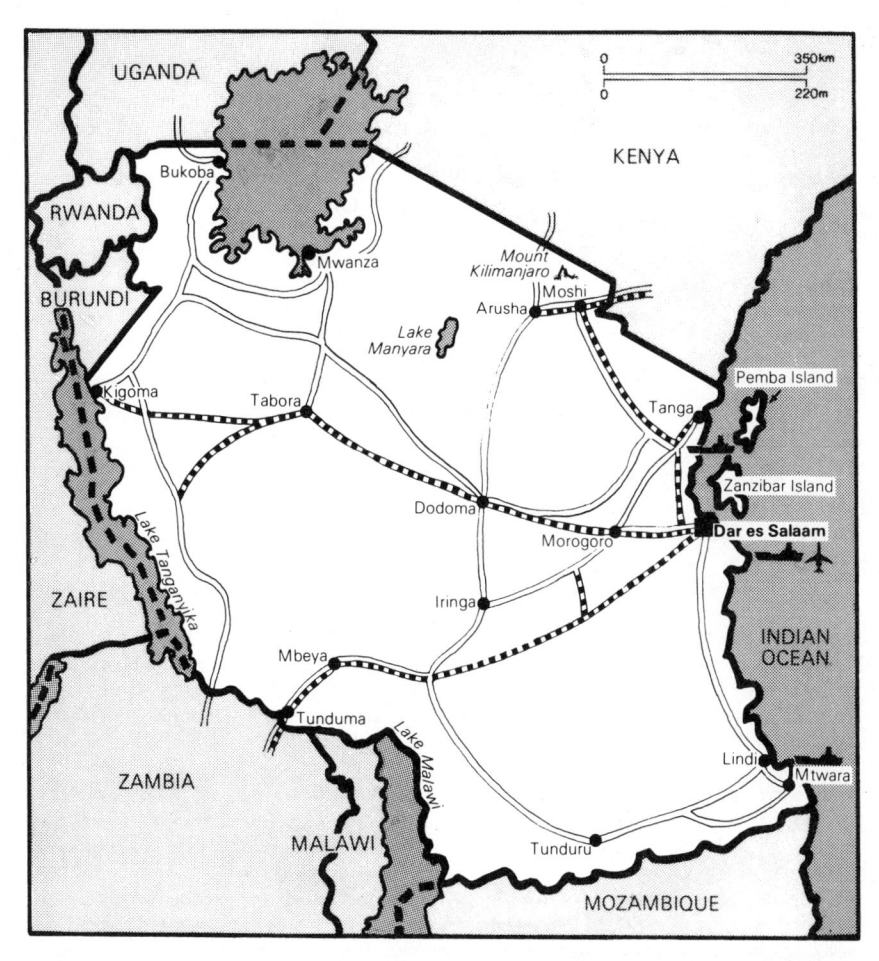

Mainland Tanzania consists of a narrow coastal plain; a high, arid central plateau; and scattered mountainous zones. The most fertile areas are the highlands to the north and south-west, the coastal region and the shores of Lake Victoria. Within Tanzania are the highest and lowest points of the whole African Continent: Mt Kilimanjaro (5,895m/19,347ft) and the floor of Lake Tanganyika.

Climate

Along the coastal strip the climate is usually hot and humid, with temperatures often exceeding 32°c/90°F from December to March and the humidity exceeding 90%; the cool season on the coast is from June to September, with temperatures between 15°c/60°F and 21°c/70°F – this is the best time to visit the coastal area. The main rains fall in April and May. The climate on the Central Plateau is warm and dry, with an average temperature of 27°c/80°F. In the highlands temperatures are lower, and it is usually very cool at night.

Agriculture

Only a small proportion of the total land area is under cultivation, although much of the country is very fertile. The Government launched a 20-year National Agricultural Development programme in 1978/79. Major projects include the development of intensive rice and sorghum production in designated areas and the expansion of coffee, tobacco and cotton production – all of which are important export items. Large amounts of foreign aid and investment are involved in these projects, with the World Bank playing a leading role.

Main Crops: cotton, coffee, sisal, cashew nuts, tea, tobacco, pyrethrum.

Mineral Resources: diamonds, gold, salt, gemstones, tin concentrates.

THE ECONOMY

Gross National Product (1978): US$4,504 million.

Per Capita Income (1978): US$230.

Gross Domestic Product in Purchasers' Values (1978): 33,466 million shillings.

Foreign Trade (1978): Total Imports – US$1,006.1 million. Total Exports – US$473.6 million.

Main Trading Partners: Imports – UK, Iran, West Germany, Japan, China, USA. Exports – West Germany, UK, USA, Singapore, Hong Kong, Italy, India.

The current Five-Year Plan (1978–83) places a strong emphasis on agricultural production and the achievement of self-suffiency in food; the development of basic industries is also being stressed to further import substitution and utilise domestic raw materials to a greater extent. The plan projects an annual growth rate of 6%.

Many key areas of the economy are state-owned, but certain industries (e.g., meat and petrol) have recently been returned to the private sector. The general policy now seems to be to encourage both public and private industries, with a greater interest in foreign participation in specified areas of development. Government control over new industrial activities is exercised by the National Development Corporation.

The main industrial sectors earmarked for expansion are iron and steel, cement, fibres and textiles, pulp and paper, tanneries, meat processing, fertilisers, chemicals and energy.

The disintegration of the East African Community, to which Tanzania belonged, has caused the country to develop its own infrastructure of telecommunications and transport facilities. Basic services such as electricity and water are still underdeveloped and insufficient for an economy set on industrialising. Some progress has been made, however, particularly in health and social services.

The tourist potential is enormous although the industry remains small (having virtually ceased to exist following the closure of the border with Kenya in 1977). Improvement in roads and transport will be an important factor in future developments.

Major Industries: food processing, mining, cement, cotton, cigarettes.

Main Commodities Traded: Imports – machinery and transport equipment, manufactured goods, textiles. Exports – cotton, coffee, diamonds, sisal, petroleum products, cloves, cashew nuts.

International Affiliations: UN, IBRD, OAU, ACP, ADB, Commonwealth, KRBO.

HOW TO GET THERE

Air
The following major airlines fly to Dar es Salaam: Aeroflot, Air France, Air India, Alitalia, British Airways, Egypt Air, KLM, Lufthansa, Pan Am, PIA, SAS, Sabena, Swissair, TWA and Zambia Airways.

An airport service charge of 20 shillings is payable by all passengers on both domestic and international flights.

Flying times to Dar es Salaam: from London, 11½ hours; from New York, 20 hours.

Dar es Salaam International Airport is 10km/6 miles from the city centre. There is also an international airport at Kilimanjaro.

ENTRY REGULATIONS

Visas
Visas are required by nationals of all countries except: (i) British Commonwealth other than persons of Asian descent with passports prefixed 'C' or 'D' – but a visitor's pass must be obtained before travelling; (ii) Denmark, Finland, Iceland, Republic of Ireland, Norway and Sweden – visitor's passes are not required.

Visas and visitor's passes are obtainable from Tanzanian high commissions and diplomatic missions abroad. Applications should be supported by a letter (usually from a travel agent or airline) giving details of the booking and confirming that return or onward tickets are held and that the applicant has sufficient funds for the stay. For business travel purposes, a letter from the applicant's firm is required detailing the business to be undertaken and confirming financial responsibility for the applicant.

Visitor's passes may be issued to *bona fide* business travellers at their point of entry into Tanzania on production of onward or return tickets.

Visas are valid for 3 months for a stay of varying lengths. The validity and length of stay of a visitor's pass varies according to circumstances. Allow 3 to 4 days for the issue of a visitor's pass.

If a passport contains stamps or visas of South Africa, the holder is advised to apply for a new one.

Bona fide business visitors require no entry certificate or visa, although it is necessary to have a passport. An entry permit can be obtained on arrival.

Health Regulations
All visitors must be in possession of a valid International Certificate of Vaccination against smallpox. Tanzania lies within the recognised yellow fever area, and although certificates of vaccination against yellow fever are not required on entry, it is advisable to have International Certificates of Vaccination against both yellow fever and cholera. These may be required when departing from certain areas of Tanzania.

Customs

Currency: There is no limit on the amount of foreign currency which may be brought in, but this must be declared on entry and all receipts for money spent in the country must be produced on departure. Tanzanian currency may not be imported, and there is a limit of 100 shillings on the amount of local currency which may be exported.

Duty-free articles: Personal effects. 250g of tobacco or the equivalent in cigars or cigarettes. 1 litre of spirits. One-half litre of perfume or toilet water, of which not more than a quarter may be perfume. Samples of no commercial value.

Articles liable to duty: Commercial samples of value may be imported on a temporary basis, subject to the appropriate duties and taxes being deposited or security given for the amount payable. The deposit is returned or the bond cancelled, provided the samples are re-exported within 6 months.

Prohibited articles: Certain types of firearms. Pornographic literature and printed matter. South African goods.

PRACTICAL INFORMATION FOR THE VISITOR

1. Currency
Monetary Unit – Tanzania shilling (Sh), divided into 100 cents.
Notes – 5, 10, 20, 100 shillings.
Coins – 5, 20, 50 cents; 1, 5 shillings.

Travellers' cheques may only be cashed at authorised dealers, i.e., banks, tourist hotels, etc. All exchange transactions should be recorded on the currency declaration form completed by the visitor on arrival.

Banking Hours
0830 – 1200 Monday to Friday
0830 – 1100 Saturday

All banks in Tanzania were nationalised in 1967. The *Bank of Tanzania*, 10 Mirambo Street, P.O. Box 2939, Dar es Salaam, is the central and sole issuing bank.

The principal state bank is the *National Bank of Commerce*, P.O. Box 1255, Dar es Salaam, ☎ 28671 – more than 100 branches throughout the country. In addition, there are a number of specialist Government-owned banks, including the *Tanzania Housing Bank*, *Tanzania Investment Bank* and *Tanzania Rural Development Bank*.

2. Electricity Supply
230v AC 50Hz.
Plugs: 3 round or square pins.

3. Weights and Measures
The metric system is in use.

4. Media
The media is Government-controlled. Television is available in Zanzibar and Pemba only. Radio Tanzania broadcasts programmes in Swahili; external broadcasts are in English, Afrikaans and several African languages. Spot announcements can be arranged.

Newspapers and Journals
The main daily papers are *The Daily News* (English), *Kipanga* and *Uhuru* (Swahili). *The Sunday News* and *Mzalendo* are Sunday weeklies. *Kiongozi* is published every fortnight in Swahili.

Ukulina wa Kisasa is an agricultural Swahili magazine published by the Ministry of Agriculture and has a relatively wide circulation.

5. Medical Care
Malaria is prevalent in many parts, although the risk is much smaller in

TANZANIA

higher areas. Visitors should seek advice from their doctor about anti-malarial precautions.

Visitors should avoid eating uncooked vegetables and unwashed salads and fruit; it is advisable to bring a suitable medication for dysentery. Water is safe to drink in the better hotels, but visitors should ensure that it has been boiled and filtered. Avoid swimming in lakes and rivers, most of which are infected with bilharzia.

Vaccination against cholera and TAB (typhoid and paratyphoid) injections are recommended, although not obligatory.

The principal Government-run hospitals in Dar es Salaam are the Aga Khan and Muhimbili Hospitals. Outside the capital, medical facilities are of a low standard. Several embassies in Dar es Salaam carry lists of doctors and dentists in private practice.

6. Telephone, Telex and Postal Services

A radio-telephone service is available between principal towns and most countries during certain specified hours, with a continuous service to a number of countries, e.g. the United Kingdom.

There are public telex facilities at the Kilimanjaro Hotel in Dar es Salaam – charges payable at the normal rates plus 50%.

All mail to and from Tanzania should be despatched by air. The P.O. box system is used; mail is distributed via locked, numbered boxes situated in post offices for collection by the addressee.

7. Public Holidays

12 January	*Zanzibar Revolution Day*
5 February	*Chama Cha Mapinduzi (CCM) Day*
26 April	*Union Day*
1 May	*Workers' Day*
7 July	*Peasants' Day*
9 December	*Independence Day*
25 December	*Christmas*

The following Muslim and Christian holidays are also observed: *Mouled*, *Eid el Fitr*, *Eid el Haj*, *Good Friday* and *Easter Monday*.

8. Time
GMT + 3.

9. Internal Transport

Air
Air Tanzania operates services between main towns. 2 main air charter companies fly to the smaller towns and bush air strips throughout Tanzania. All the national parks have their own air strips.

Airline Offices in Dar es Salaam

Aeroflot	☎ 23577.
Air France	☎ 20356/7.
Air India	☎ 23525.
British Airways	☎ 20322/3.
KLM	☎ 21497.
Lufthansa	☎ 22270.
Pan Am	☎ 21747, 23526.
PIA	☎ 26944.
Swissair	☎ 22539.
TWA	☎ 24185.

Aircraft Charter in Dar es Salaam

Tanzania Air Services	☎ 22032, 29974.
Tim – Air Charters	☎ 27128.

Rail
Tanzania Railways operate services between Dar es Salaam and Dodoma, Tanga and Arusha. There are refreshment facilities (restaurant or buffet cars) and sleeping accommodation on all long-distance trains.

Road
There are good tarred roads from Dar es Salaam to Moshi and Arusha, and from Dar es Salaam to Tunduma on the Zambian border. Road conditions vary; many are simple dirt tracks which are virtually impassable during the rainy season.

There are taxi stations in Dar es Salaam at the New Africa and Kilimanjaro Hotels; taxis associated with these stations operate at fixed and reasonable charges. There is also a large number of private taxis in the capital, and their fares are negotiable.

Traffic travels on the left-hand side of the road.

Self-drive and chauffeur-driven cars are available for hire in Dar es Salaam. A deposit of about 2,000 shillings is usually required. Some companies calculate the hire charge on a kilometre basis and ask for a deposit equal to three-quarters of the total estimated cost of hire.

An International Driving Licence or driving licence from the visitor's country is required.

Car-Hire Firms in Dar es Salaam
Riddoch Motors ☎ 20681.
Subzali Tours &
  Safaris ☎ 25907.
Tanzania Tours
  Ltd ☎ 25586, 28181, 25588.
Tanzania Taxi &
  Tour Services ☎ 21028.
Valji and Allibhai
  Ltd ☎ 20522, 26537.

10. Tipping
Tipping is generally frowned upon in Tanzania, however a number of hotels make a service charge and tips are generally expected by taxi drivers, hotel staff, etc. Tips should not be offered in Zanzibar.

Taxis – 10% of fare.

Porters – 50 cents per bag.

Hotels – Where no service charge is included, 5–10% of the bill divided between room and restaurant staff.

11. Social Customs
European customs prevail in business circles, but visitors should remember that their business contacts may be Hindus or Muslims, in which case they should not be offered alcoholic drinks or foods such as pork, bacon or ham; Sikhs should not be offered anything to smoke. The month of *Ramadan* should be avoided by business visitors as it is difficult to achieve much during this period.

The majority of Zanzibaris are Muslims and strictly adhere to the laws of their religion. In addition, they tend to be sensitive about clothing and male hair length. It is advisable for women to avoid wearing short skirts or any other articles of clothing which might be thought of as indecent.

12. Photography
Visitors should not attempt to photograph bridges, railway stations and government buildings, as these are regarded as security installations.

USEFUL ADDRESSES (GENERAL)

Dar es Salaam
Australian High Commission: 7th and 8th floors, Wing 'A' NIC Investment Building, Independence Avenue, P.O. Box 2996, ☎ 20244.

British High Commission: 5–8th floor, Permanent House, corner Makkaba Street and Independence Avenue, P.O. Box 9200, ☎ 29601.

Canadian High Commission: Pan Africa Insurance Building, Independence Avenue, P.O. Box 1002, ☎ 20651.

Dutch Embassy: IPS Building, 10th floor, Azikiwe Street, corner Independence Avenue, P.O. Box 9534, ☎ 26767/8.

French Embassy: Bagamoyo Road and Kulimani Road, P.O. Box 2349.

Japanese Embassy: Bagamoyo Road, P.O. Box 2577.

Swiss Embassy: 17 Kenyatta Drive, P.O. Box 2454, ☎ 67801.

US Embassy National Bank of Commerce Building, City Drive, P.O. Box 9123, ☎ 22775.

West German Embassy: NIC Investment House, Independence Avenue, P.O. Box 9541, ☎ 23286/87.

Tanzania Tourist Corporation: IPS Building, Independence Avenue, P.O. Box 2485, ☎ 27572.

British Council: Independence Avenue, Ohio Street, P.O. Box 9100, ☎ 22726/8.

Thomas Cook Authorised Representative: Bureau A.M.I., P.O. Box 9041, ☎ 27781/3.

Zanzibar
US Consulate: 83a Tuzungumzeni Square, P.O. Box 4, ☎ 2118.

BUSINESS INFORMATION

Importation into Tanzania is basically controlled by a number of parastatal companies operating in specific sectors of the economy. The most important of these are under the direction of the Board of Internal Trade. Others have a monopoly over the import of certain types of goods. Imports may also sometimes be handled by stockist-distributors and agents with limited stock-holding or servicing facilities; larger firms offering stockist-distributor and after-sales service often buy on their account and represent overseas principals handling a wide variety of goods. Such concerns usually have branches in most of the chief mainland towns.

Zanzibar manages its commercial affairs independently. The import trade is handled by State Purchasing Authorities.

Parastatal importing companies in Tanzania do not enter into agency agreements with overseas manufacturers on an exclusive basis, thus foreign suppliers should either pay regular visits to Tanzania to promote their goods through the parastatal concerns or appoint a representative to maintain contact with the parastatal organisations and relevant Government departments. Due to the uncertain nature of relations between Tanzania and Kenya, it is inadvisable for companies to cover the Tanzanian market from a base in Kenya.

Import and Exchange Control Regulations
The administration of import licensing is under the control of the Bank of Tanzania. The import licensing system is strict and ensures that non-essential and luxury goods are not imported into Tanzania. A limited number of items may be imported on Open General Licence and items requiring specific import licences may only be imported by the Board of Internal Trade's subsidiaries or with their endorsement.

The *Tanzania Import Export Directory*, published by the National Bank of Commerce, is a useful publication for those firms wishing to trade with Tanzania.

Exchange control is in operation in respect of all countries; applications for payments for all imports are considered by the National Bank of Commerce on presentation of the appropriate documents.

Business Hours

Government Offices
0730 – 1430   Monday to Friday
              (no lunch break)
0730 – 1200   Saturday

Business Houses
0730 – 1430   Monday to Friday
              (no lunch break)

Alternatively, some businesses take a lunch break from 1200 – 1400 and work until 1600 or 1630.

Business Events
An International Trade Fair, sponsored by the Tanzanian Government, is held every July in Dar es Salaam.

BUSINESS SERVICES

Advertising
The Tanzanian Advertising Corporation Ltd, P.O. Box 2704, Dar es Salaam.

Shipping
Tanzania Coastal Shipping Line Ltd, P.O. Box 9461, Dar es Salaam, ☎ 26192/3.

National Shipping Agencies Co. Ltd, P.O. Box 9082, Dar es Salaam, ☎ 27241/8 – branches in Tanga and Mtwara – forwarding/clearing agents.

Consultants
Industrial Management Services Ltd, NIC Investment House, Independence Avenue, 6th Floor wing B, P.O. Box 21011, Dar es Salaam, ☎ 31455.

USEFUL ADDRESSES (BUSINESS)

Tanzanian Association of Chambers of Commerce, P.O. Box 41, Dar es Salaam.

Dar es Salaam Chamber of Commerce, P.O. Box 41, Dar es Salaam.

Dar es Salaam Merchants' Chamber, P.O. Box 12, Dar es Salaam.

Arusha Chamber of Commerce and Agriculture, P.O. Box 141, Arusha.

Tanga Chamber of Commerce, P.O. Box 331, Tanga.

Southern Province Chamber of Commerce and Agriculture, P.O. Box 1063, Lindi.

Tanzanian Law Society, P.O. Box 2148, Dar es Salaam.

MAJOR CITY

Dar es Salaam

Dar es Salaam is an attractive city built around a picturesque port and harbour, with few modern skyscrapers and large office blocks.

The city is filled with flowering, scented trees and has an abundance of tropical flora. There is always some interesting activity to watch down at the harbour – the occasional Arab *dhow* may call in from the Persian Gulf and another unusual sight are the fishing boats or *ngalawas*, which are sail boats made from dugout canoes.

Hotels

There is no official hotel rating system.

MOTEL AGIP, P.O. Box 529, ☎ 23511.
1st-class motel in central location overlooking harbour.
Rooms: 57 ♫, ☎, ♠, ○.
Facilities: Restaurant, snack bar, roof terrace, lounge, cocktail bar.
Services: TC, FC. ⊟ Amex, Diners Club. Dr. on call. S, ♂.

BAHARI BEACH, P.O. Box 9312, ☎ 47101.
Modern, distinctive hotel and Bahari Beach (26km/16 miles from Dar es Salaam) in the style of a typical African village with accommodation in two-storey thatched circular cottages.
Rooms: 100 ♫, ☎, ♠, ○.
Facilities: Restaurant, coffee shop, lounge, bars. Car hire. Tennis, swimming, sailing and other water sports.
Services: TC, FC. ⊟ No credit cards accepted. Dr. on call.
Conference room – max. capacity 50.
Banquet rooms – max. capacity 500.

KILIMANJARO, P.O. Box 9574, ☎ 21281.
Modern superior 1st-class hotel in city centre, overlooking harbour and near to main business district.
Rooms: 200 ♫, ♠, ☎, ♠, ▥. Suites available.
Facilities: Restaurant, grill room, coffee shop, bars. Nightclub. Shopping arcade, service shops. Car hire. Airport transportation. Swimming.
Services: TC, FC. ⊟ Diners Club. Dr. on call. S on request.

Conference room – max. capacity 500.
Banquet rooms – max, capacity 250.

NEW AFRICA, Azikiwe Street, P.O. Box 9314, ☎ 29611.
Moderate 1st-class hotel in city centre, near seafront.
Rooms: 105 ♫, ♠, ☎. Suites available.
Facilities: Restaurant, grill, coffee shop, patio bar, cocktail lounge. Gift shop. Fishing and hunting excursions arranged. Conference and banquet facilities.

TWIGA, Independence Avenue, P.O. Box 1194, ☎ 22561.
Modern hotel on main street in city centre.
Rooms: 28 ♫, ☎, ♠, ○. Suites available.
Facilities: Restaurant, cocktail bar, roof garden, bars.
Services: TC. ⊟ Diners Club.

Restaurants

There are few restaurants in Dar es Salaam apart from the hotel restaurants, which tend to offer the highest standard of cuisine. Recommended restaurants include: *Hindu Lodge* and *Royal Restaurant* – Indian; *Bruno's*, Oyster Bay – Italian; *Twiga Room*, Twiga Hotel, Independence Avenue – seafood; *Joseph's* – seafood.

Nightclubs

Splendid Hotel – jazz, Fridays and Saturdays; *Simba Club*, Kilimanjaro Hotel – cabaret; *Margot's*; *Forodhani Hotel*.

Entertainment
There are several cinemas, including a drive-in, showing mainly Italian and Indian films. Theatre and dance productions are staged at the Theatre Arts Department of the University, and dance exhibitions are held on Sunday afternoons at the Village Museum on the Bagamoyo Road, 22½ km/14 miles from the city centre.

There are many good beaches around the capital area, and some of the beach hotels open their facilities to day visitors. The *Yacht Club*, 9½ km/6 miles north of the city, offers sailing, swimming and fishing; facilities for golf, tennis and cricket are available at the *Gymkhana Club*. A number of private clubs offer temporary membership to visitors.

National Parks
Almost one-quarter of Tanzania is set aside for national parks, game reserves and forest reserves. Among the most popular are: *Serengeti National Park* – Tanzania's largest and most famous game park; *Arusha National Park* – 32km/20 miles east of Arusha; *Lake Manyara National Park* – 128km/79 miles from Arusha; and the *Ngorongo Crater*.

Accommodation is available in many of the reserves and parks. All enquiries regarding safari tours and other excursions should be addressed to the Tanzania Tourist Corporation, IPS Building, Independence Avenue, P.O. Box 2485, Dar es Salaam, ☎ 27572.

Shopping
Best buys: jewellery, gemstones, wood and ivory carvings, brass, copper, animal skins.

There are a number of curio shops along Independence Avenue. Curios and handicrafts are also available at the Kariakoo and Ilala markets. The *National Arts Gallery* in the IPS Building on Independence Avenue has a wide range of goods on sale at fixed prices. Jewellery and leather goods can be purchased at the *Silver Curio Shop*, Azikiwe Street, and at *Peeras* on Independence Avenue.

TOGO
Republic of Togo

Geography	433
The Economy	433
How to Get There	435
Entry Regulations	435
Practical Information for the Visitor	436
Useful Addresses (General)	437
Business Information	438
Business Services	439
Useful Addresses (Business)	439
Lomé	440

Size: 56,000 sq.km/21,622 sq.miles.

Population: 2,410,000 (1978 est.).

Distribution: 15% in urban areas.

Density: 43 persons per sq.km/111 per sq.mile.

Population Growth Rate: 2.6% p.a.

Ethnic Composition: Of the 18 major ethnic groups, the largest are the Ewe and Mina in the south and the Kabyé in the north.

Capital: Lomé Pop. 230,000 (1977).

Major Towns: Sokodé Pop. 35,000; Palimé Pop. 25,000; Atakpamé Pop. 17,500; Anécho Pop. 11,000; Mango Pop. 9,000.

Languages: The official language is French. More than 40 indigenous languages are spoken of which the most important are Ewe, Kabyé, Twi and Hausa.

Religion: Some 20% are Christians, mostly Roman Catholic; about 20% are Muslim; and the remainder adhere to traditional beliefs.

Government: Togo became independent in April 1960 following a plebiscite in 1958 at which voting was in favour of independence from France, the administrative power of what was then a UN Trust Territory. President Olympio, leader of the Comité de l'Unité Togolaise (CUT), remained in power until a coup d'état in January 1963 led by Sergeant (later General) Eyadema reinstated former President Grunitzky. Eyadema led a second coup in 1967 to oust Grunitzky, and Eyadema has remained the effective ruler of Togo since then. In August 1969 the Rassemblement du Peuple Togolaise (RPT) was declared the sole political party. Despite offers to install a civilian government and draft a civil constitution, the Government continues to pursue policies of national unity with apparent popular approval.

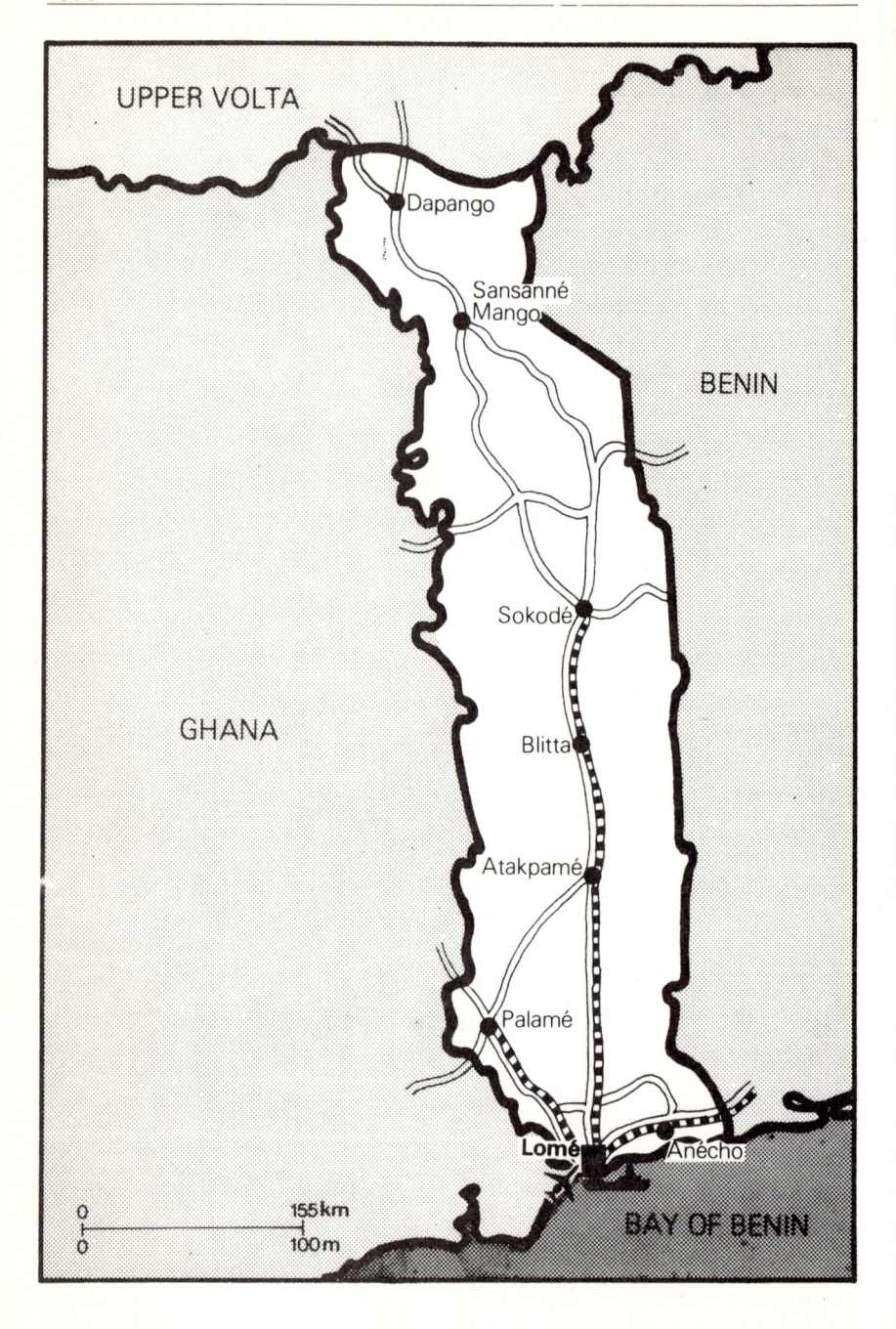

TOGO

GEOGRAPHY

Togo forms a narrow corridor of land which reaches some 550 km/340 miles inland from the Bay of Benin and averages 100 km/60 miles in width. Away from the coastal lagoons and swamps, the land rises slowly through a plateau to an area of forested hills covering much of the centre. Further inland the hills drop down to the savannah plains of the Oti plateau with a smalla rea of granite uplands in the far north.

Climate
There are 2 rainy seasons over most of Togo, the major one being from April to July and the other during October and November. The dry season is from December to March. July and August are the coolest months. In December and January the cool *harmattan* wind blows from the north. The coast is warm and humid with mean annual temperature in Lomé 27°c/80°F and rainfall at 782mm/31ins. Inland temperatures rise to annual averages of 30°c/86°F and above, with higher rainfall in the hills.

Agriculture
About 80% of the population engage in agriculture, the 2nd most important economic sector, contributing some 30% of the GDP and around 30% of export earnings. The major subsistence crops are cassava, yams, millet, sorghum, maize and rice, with meat supplements from fishing and small-scale livestock rearing. The major commercial crops are cocoa, coffee, palm kernels, groundnuts, cotton and copra. Production of cash crops has stagnated during the 1970s, and in the case of cotton has declined significantly. Cocoa, the principal export crop, is frequently smuggled into Togo from Ghana.

The 1976–80 5-Year Development Plan aimed for self-sufficiency in agricultural produce by 1980, but despite large projects undertaken with aid from the EDF, France, the World Bank and the IDA involving irrigated cultivation of new crops including sugar cane and fruits, the improvement of existing plantations, increasing mechanisation and the use of fertilisers, Togo cannot yet grow enough food in its good soils and favourable climate to feed its population adequately. Increasing food production is a major objective, though the diversification of export crops is also being encouraged. A Marketing Board has been established to help sell Togolese produce abroad, and a sugar estate with a mill capable of producing 25,000 tons per annum is under construction in the Sokodé region.

Main Crops: cocoa, coffee, cotton, palm kernels, groundnuts, cassava, millet, sorghum, maize, copra, rice, other roots and tubers.

Mineral Resources: phosphates, limestone, marble. Oil and uranium prospecting continues.

THE ECONOMY

Gross National Product (1978): US$790 million.

Per Capita Income (1978): US$329.

TOGO

Gross Domestic Product (1978 est.): US$900 million.

Foreign Trade (1977): Total Imports – US$284 million. Total Exports – US$159 million.

Main Trading Partners: Imports – France, West Germany, Netherlands, Japan, USA, Spain, Italy, Ivory Coast, Belgium/Luxembourg. Exports – Netherlands, France, West Germany, Poland, Yugoslavia, Belgium/Luxembourg, Mali, Japan, Nigeria.

Until the 1960s the economy was largely reliant upon agriculture, export earnings coming from the sale of the principal crops grown on the plantations since German colonisation. However, the mining of high-grade phosphate deposits at Akoupame since 1961 by CTMB has contributed an increasing share of export sales. In 1974, when CTMB was nationalised, phosphate exports amounted to some 75% of total export value. Although demand and prices on the world market fell after 1974, Togolese output is now exceeding 1974 levels. Limestone reserves estimated at 200 million tons are being exploited by CIMAO, who anticipate annual production of clinker to exceed 1 million tons in the early 1980s. Output is to be used in the manufacture of cement, and the project is financed and operated by interests from Ghana, Ivory Coast, France, UK, and Canada, the World Bank and the European Investment Bank in conjunction with the Togolese authorities. SOTOMA have mined marble at Gnaouion since 1970. Estimated reserves are being extracted at the rate of some 50,000 tons a year.

There is little manufacturing, though growth has been marked in recent years, especially in the Lomé area. Many factories are concerned with the processing of agricultural production, e.g., cotton ginning, palm oil extraction, flour milling, canning. Government policies to encourage import substitution have led to the development of some factories supplying the local market with cloth and footwear, beverages, tyres and some construction materials. An oil refinery has been operating since 1977 and a steelworks since 1979. A large fertiliser factory is planned.

The Government is eager to increase the number of tourists coming to the country, and several new hotels were built during the 1970s. Most of the tourists are from France, Germany and Switzerland.

Electricity production is steadily increasing from the thermal station in Lomé and the hydro-electric plant at Palimé. A new power station in Lomé using oil from the refinery is planned. Togo also imports electricity from Ghana. Togo's economic infrastructure is relatively well developed and continues to improve as the revenue position is good; nevertheless, aid is still necessary to make up a deficit on current payments. France is the main donor. The prospects for the Togolese economy are generally good and growth is steady.

Major Industries: brewing, soft drinks, bicycle and motor bike assembly, construction materials, textile printing, matches, agricultural and mineral processing.

Main Commodities Traded: Imports – machinery, transport equipment, cloth, petroleum products, metal goods, pharmaceutical supplies, tobacco, household and consumer items. Exports – phosphates, cocoa, coffee, cotton, palm kernels, printed cloth, seed cotton, tapioca, manioc starch and flour.

International Affiliations: UN, IBRD, OAU, ACP, ADB, ECOWAS, Franc Zone, OCAM.

TOGO

HOW TO GET THERE

Air
Air Afrique and UTA operate direct services from France (Paris via Nice) once a week, and other flights calling at Niamey (Niger), Ougadougou (Upper Volta) and Lagos (Nigeria). There are also services to Accra (Ghana), Abidjan, Cotonou and Douala.

Lomé Airport is 4 km/2½ miles from the town centre. Buses and taxis are available.

A Passenger Service Charge is levied on all passengers embarking in Togo and is payable at the airport or airline offices.

Road
The asphalted coastal road connects Lomé with Accra in the west and with Cotonou and Lagos to the east. The route south from Ougadougo to Lomé is being improved in the northern section.

Rail
There are railway services from Cotonou and Porto Novo (Benin).

ENTRY REGULATIONS

Visas
Visas are required of all visitors, except those from Francophone West African countries, Andorra, Belgium, Denmark, France, West Germany, Ghana, Italy, Luxembourg, Madagascar, Monaco, Netherlands, Nigeria, Norway, Sweden and Israel (if diplomatic or service passport holders). Visa exemptions are usually for a visit of up to 3 months.

Visas may be obtained from diplomatic representatives of Togo abroad. Re-entry permits must be obtained before departure from Togo if a visitor or alien resident wishes to return to Togo. All visitors leaving Togo after a stay exceeding 48 hours must obtain an exit permit from the Sûreté Nationale on confirmation of an outward journey. All visitors must hold an outward ticket or deposit an amount equivalent to the cost of such a ticket or carry a letter of assurance from employers in Togo confirming financial responsibility for the visitor. White nationals of South Africa are not admitted.

Health Regulations
International Certificates of Vaccination are required for smallpox and yellow fever if the visitor has been in an infected area within 6 days of arriving in Togo. Visitors arriving from an infected area must have a certificate of vaccination against cholera.

Customs
Currency: The import of foreign and local currency up to 1 million CFA francs or equivalent is allowed if declared on arrival. Local currency up to 25,000 CFA francs and foreign currency not exceeding the amount declared upon arrival may be exported.

Duty-free articles: Personal effects. 100 cigarettes or 50 cigars or 100g of tobacco. 1 litre of wine. 1 litre of spirits. ½ litre of toilet water. ¼ litre of perfume.

PRACTICAL INFORMATION FOR THE VISITOR

1. Currency
Monetary Unit – CFA franc (Communauté Financière Africaine).
Notes – 50, 100, 500, 1,000, 5,000 CFA francs.
Coins – 1, 2, 5, 10, 25, 50, 100, 500 CFA francs.

Banking Hours
0730–1130
1430–1530 Monday to Friday

The central bank and bank of issue for Togo and the 5 other West African States that are CFA members is the *Banque Centrale des Etats de l'Afrique de l'Ouest*, based in Cameroon, and at Avenue de la Victoire, B.P. 120, Lomé.

Principal Commercial Banks
Banque Arabe Libyenne-Togolaise du Commerce Extérieur (BALTEX), B.P. 4874, Lomé.
Banque Commerciale du Ghana SA, 14 Rue du Commerce, B.P. 1321 Lomé.
Banque Internationale de l'Afrique Occidentale, 13 Rue du Commerce, B.P. 346, Lomé.
Banque Togolaise pour le Commerce et l'Industrie (BTCI), 9 Rue du Commerce, B.P. 363, Lomé.

Other national banks include the *Caisse Centrale de Cooperation Economique*, Avenue de Sarakawa, B.P. 33, Lomé, and the *Caisse Nationale de Crédit Agricole*, B.P. 1386, Lomé. These banks provide credit for agricultural, industrial and other development projects.

2. Electricity Supply
220–240v AC 50Hz.

3. Weights and Measures
The metric system is in use.

4. Media
Télévision Togolaise operate 3 stations broadcasting in French and local African languages. Radiodiffusion du Togo transmits on 4 wavelengths in French, English and local African languages. No commercial advertising is accepted on the radio, and all services are Government-controlled.

Newspapers and Journals
The major dailies are *Journal Officiel de la République du Togo* and *Togo Presse*, published in French and Ewe, and carrying a small amount of advertising.

Several other periodicals are published in Togo, mainly by various Government ministries or religious organisations. These include: *Togo Dialogue*, a monthly from the Ministry of Information; *Bulletin de Statistique*, the monthly publication of the Ministry of Finance and Economic Affairs; *Image du Togo*; and the *Bulletin d'Information de l'Agence Togolaise de Presse*. The Togo Chamber of Commerce also publishes a monthly bulletin of news and announcements of interest to the business community.

5. Medical Care
Foreign visitors are advised to boil or filter tap water before drinking and to avoid eating uncooked foods as intestinal upsets are likely; suitable medicines should be carried as a precaution.

A malarial risk exists all year and anti-malarial prophylactics should be taken. TAB (typhoid and paratyphoid) injections are also recommended.

Hospital in Lomé
Hôpital de Tokoin ☎ 2501.

6. Telephone, Telex and Postal Services
Lomé is connected to Paris and Accra by radio telephone and to Cotonou and Lagos by direct line. All international calls are via Paris and should be booked well in advance.

Public telex facilities are available at the main post office in Lomé.

There is a reliable telegram service to all destinations, but, as a part of the French telegraph system, the service is quicker and cheaper to France and other Francophone African countries.

All mail, to and from Togo, should be despatched by air.

7. Public Holidays

1 January	*New Year's Day*
13 January	*Liberation Day*
27 April	*Independence Day*
1 May	*Labour Day*
15 August	*Assumption Day*
1 November	*All Saints Day*
25 December	*Christmas Day*

The Christian holidays of *Easter Monday*, *Ascension Day* and *Whit Monday* are also observed. The Muslim community observe *Ramadan* and the holidays of *Eid el Fitr* and *Tabaski*.

If a public holiday falls on a Sunday the next day is observed as a holiday.

8. Time
GMT.

9. Internal Transport

Air
Air Togo operate scheduled flights to Sokodé, Atakpamé, Dapango, Sansanné-Mango and Anécho from Lomé. Charter flights are also available.

Airline Offices in Lomé
Air Togo, 1 Avenue de la Libération, B.P. 1090 ☎ 3310.
Air Afrique, B.P. 111.

Rail
The major railway line runs north from Lomé to Blitta via Atakpamé. The coastal line runs from Lomé to Anécho and on into Benin; there is another section of line linking Lomé with Palimé to the north-west.

Road
There are good roads in the coastal region and the main coastal highway is asphalted; however, only some 10% of the total length of road is bitumenised and most roads are made of laterite or earth. Roads are passable at all times of the year in most places; only in the wettest weather or in the remoter areas does driving become impossible.

Taxis are available in the main towns and are often shared, especially on longer journeys. Lomé is well served by numerous cheap taxis. Regular bus services connect the main centres and operate in Lomé.

Self-drive cars and chauffeur-driven models can be hired in Lomé.

An International Driving Licence or foreign driving licence is required. Traffic travels on the right.

Car-Hire Firms in Lomé
Autogo,
  B.P. 1247   ☎ 4250
Télétaxi, Blvd.
  Circulaire,
  B.P. 1542   ☎ 3931
Garage du Centre ☎ 3010
Hertz, rue du
  Commerce,
  B.P. 2980   ☎ 6190

10. Tipping
Taxis – no tip.

Porters – 50–100 CFA francs per piece of luggage.

Hotel/restaurant – 10–15% of the bill.

USEFUL ADDRESSES (GENERAL)

Lomé
People's Republic of China Embassy, Tokoin Ouest, B.P. 2690.

Danish Embassy, Villa Klouto, Rte de l'Aviation, B.P. 2708.

TOGO

Egyptian Embassy, Angle Blvd Circulaire et Rte d'Anécho, B.P. 8.

French Embassy, 51 Rue du Colonel Derroux, B.P. 337, ☎ 2571/3.

Gabonese Embassy, B.P. 9118.

Ghanaian Embassy, Toikoin, Rte de Palimé, B.P. 92.

Libyan Embassy, B.P. 4872.

Nigerian Embassy, 311 Blvd Circulaire, B.P. 1189.

USSR Embassy, Rte d'Atakpamé, B.P. 389.

US Embassy, 68 Ave de la Victoire, B.P. 852. ☎ 2991.

West German Embassy, Marina Rte d'Aflao, B.P. 1175.

Zaïre Embassy, 325 Blvd Circulaire, B.P. 1102.

Dutch Consulate, Rte de la Frontière, Nyekonakpoe, B.P. 9092, ☎ 6168.

Haut Commissariat du Tourisme, Rte d'Anécho, B.P. 1289, ☎ 6410.

Office National Togolaise du Tourisme, B.P. 1177, Lomé, ☎ 2026.

BUSINESS INFORMATION

Togo's 'open door' policy for the supply of import requirements is non-discriminatory with regard to suppliers, although countries within the Franc Zone do not pay the same import duties as suppliers outside the Zone. The Government is pursuing a policy whereby state control is exercised in those sectors held to be of foremost national importance, and any investors in the fields of mining, agriculture, commerce and industrial development generally must accept large state holdings and Government control over policy. However, the *Code des Investissements* (1965) guarantees the right to transfer capital and revenue abroad for those foreign investors who are accepted. Fiscal advantages and other concessions are usually awarded only to local companies involved in key sectors of the economy. The Government aims to cut its imports bill, and continued attempts to build up local industry and encourage import substitution will make life harder for the exporter to Togo. There is a growing domestic market for consumer items, and their re-export is an important part of Togo's trade. SONACOM is the state-owned company with a monopoly on the import of food and industrial products.

All business correspondence should be in French.

Import and Exchange Control Regulations

As a member of the Franc Zone, Togo requires an import licence for all goods imported from outside the Zone. Licences are issued by the Ministry of Finance and Economic Affairs and the Office des Changes who will ensure that the necessary foreign exchange is available once authorisation is given. Imported goods exceeding 10,000 CFA francs in value must have prior authorisation, and notification should be given well in advance. Import licences are usually valid for imports cleared by customs within 6 months of approval. Goods sent over long distances or where delay in delivery is experienced may be eligible for licence extensions. A Taxe Forfaitaire, and in some cases a surtax, may be charged on certain imported goods.

TOGO

Business Hours
Government Offices
0700–1200
1430–1730 Monday to Friday

Business Houses
0800–1200
1430–1800 Monday to Friday
0730–1230 Saturday

BUSINESS SERVICES

Insurance
Groupement Togolaise d'Assurances, B.P. 3298, Lomé.

All insurance companies are to be nationalised under the national STAR company.

Transport
Chemin de Fer Togolais, B.P. 340, Lomé.
Compagnie Maritime des Chargeurs Reunis, 2 Rue de Maréchal Galliéni, B.P. 34, Lomé, ☎ 2612.
Société Nationale de Transports Routiers (TOGO-ROUTE), Rte d'Atakpamé, B.P. 4730, Lomé.

Shipping
Port Autonome de Lomé, B.P. 1225, Lomé.
Société Maritime Atlantique du Togo, B.P. 4086, Lomé.
Société Ouest Africaine d'Entreprises Maritimes, Togo, B.P. 3285, Lomé.
SOCOPAO-Togo, B.P. 821, 18 Rue du Commerce, Lomé.

Togo is also served by the *Société Agence Maritime de l'Ouest, Africaine Côte d'Ivoire, Société Ivoirienne de Transport Maritime* and the *Société Navale Chargeurs Delmas Vieljeux* (France).

USEFUL ADDRESSES (BUSINESS)

Compagnie Togolaise des Mines de Bénin (CTMB), B.P. 379, Lomé.

Chambre de Commerce, d'Agriculture et d'Industrie de la République Togolaise, Hôtel de la Chambre de Commerce, Ave Albert Sarraut, B.P. 360, Lomé, ☎ 2065.

Office National de Développement et d'Exploitation des Ressources Forestières, B.P. 334, Lomé.

Office National des Pêches, B.P. 1095, Lomé.

Office National des Produits Vivriers (TOGO GRAIN), B.P. 3039, Lomé.

Office des Produits Agricoles du Togo (OPAT), Angle Rue Branly et Ave 3, Lomé, B.P. 1334 – controls prices, sales of coffee and other export crops; sole exporter; promotes agricultural development; also sponsors research and grants loans.

Office Togolais des Phosphates, B.P. 3200, Route d'Atakpamé, Lomé.

Société des Ciments de l'Afrique de l'Ouest (CIMAO), B.P. 1687, Lomé.

Société Nationale de Commerce (SONACOM), B.P. 3009, 29 Blvd Circulaire, Lomé – state import company with monopoly; administers distribution of food and industrial products.

TOGO

MAJOR CITY

Lomé

Lomé, the national and regional capital, has been a busy trading port for several centuries and is now a growing commercial and industrial centre. Originally, Lomé and Aflao in Ghana constituted a single town divided in the partition of the former German colony by the French and British administrations after the First World War. The legacy of the French years of control is readily apparent, contributing to the distinctive character of the city. The atmosphere is relaxed on the west side in the wealthy residential districts with a number of flower gardens and national monuments in the area. To the east of the railway line, which splits the city in half, is the main business district. Lomé has become a resort town and is responding to increased numbers of visitors by expanding accommodation and improving facilities.

Hotels

There is no official hotel rating system in Togo.

HÔTEL DE LA PAIX, Route d'Anécho, B.P. 3452, ☎ 6265/9.
Modern resort hotel (1974) in an unusual style overlooking the beach and ocean, 3 km/2 miles from city centre.
Rooms: 216 🔔, 🌊, ☐, 🍸, △, 🚗. Suites.
Facilities: Restaurants, bars. Nightclub, casino. Car hire. Golf, tennis, swimming, private beach. Transport available to airport.
Services: TC, FC. 📧 Access, Amex, Diners Club, Eurocard, Master Charge. Dr. on call. 💲, ♂.
Conference room – max. capacity 250.
Banquet room – max. capacity 250.

HOTEL DU 2 FEVRIER
Situated near harbour.
Rooms: 400 🔔, 🌊, ☐, 🍸, △, 🚗. Suites available.
Facilities: Restaurants, bars.
Services: Conference room – max. capacity 450.

HÔTEL LE BENIN, Avenue Général de Gaulle, B.P. 128, ☎ 2485.
Good hotel facing the sea, 2 km/1 mile from city centre.
Rooms: 82 🔔, 🌊, ☐, 🍸, △, 🚗. Suites available.
Facilities: Restaurant, bars, open-air grill room. Garden. Private beach, swimming pool. Car hire. Shops. Transport available to the airport.
Services: TC, FC. 📧 Amex, Diners Club. Dr. on call. 💲, ♂.
Conference room – max. capacity 100.

HÔTEL DU GOLFE, 5 Rue du Commerce, B.P. 36, ☎ 5141.
Colonial period hotel near city centre and business district by the sea.
Rooms: 43.
Facilities: Restaurant.
Services: TC.

HÔTEL SARAKAWA
Large modern hotel complex near harbour.
Rooms: 367 🔔, 🌊, ☐, 🍸, △, 🚗. Suites available.
Facilities: Restaurants, bars. Nightclub.
Services: TC, FC.

HOTEL TROPICANA, B.P. 2724, ☎ 3404.
Modern villa style hotel (1972) situated 17km/11 miles east of Lomé, popular with German tourists.
Rooms: 200 🔔, 🌊, ☐, 🍸.
Facilities: Restaurant, bar. Nightclub, casino. Shops. Tennis, golf, riding, swimming.

Restaurants

Apart from those in the main hotels, other restaurants include: the *Café de la Poste*; *Mandarin* – Chinese; *Mini-Brasserie*; *Paris Snack*; *Las Palmas*;

4ᵉ Zone – Vietnamese; *Ramatou*; and *Las Vegas*.

Nightclubs
Lomé comes to life at night and amongst the many nightclubs are: *L'Abreuvoir*, Rue de la Gare; *Capri*, Avenue de la Libération; *Copa Cabana*, Blvd Circulaire at Rue de la Paix; *Forever Week-End*, Rte d'Atakpamé; *Kakadou*, Rte d'Atakpamé; *La Maquina-Loca*, 8 Avenue de Calais; *Number One*, 29 Rue de l'Eglise; *Le Rêve*, 27 Avenue des Alliés; *SOS Bafelo*, Rue de l'Eglise; *Watusi*.

Entertainment
There are several cinemas showing recent films, of which the Club Cinema is the best. Cultural events and films are put on at the Goethe Institute on the Rue de l'Eglise, at the Centre Culturel Francais, 19 Ave des Alliés, and at the Centre Culturel Américain, Rue Victor Hugo.

Football is the national game with matches in the National Stadium in Lomé. Various water sports facilities are provided at Porto Seguro, a short distance from Lomé, mainly for the tourists. The Herbert Kronton Museum in Lomé has a number of historical documents, photographs and artifacts relating mainly to the German period of government.

Shopping
Best buys: cloth, clothes, gold and silver jewellery, marbleware, wood carvings.

The outstanding place to shop in Lomé is the Asseganme 3-storey market (open every day until 1400) on Rue du Commerce. Other shops worth visiting for clothes and art works are *Galerie Africaine* on Rue de Maréchal Galliéni, *Les Arts Nègres* on Rue Maréchal Foch, *Pariscoa* and *SGGG*. *Togo a GoGo* and *La Gazelle Noire* are well-renowned boutiques selling Togolese crafts and some original fabric designs. Senegalese jewellery is on sale in many small shops.

TUNISIA
Republic of Tunis

Geography	442
The Economy	444
How to Get There	445
Entry Regulations	445
Practical Information for the Visitor	446
Useful Addresses (General)	448
Business Information	448
Business Services	449
Useful Addresses (Business)	449
Tunis	450

Size: 163,610 sq. km/63,170 sq.miles.

Population: 6.08 million (1978).

Distribution: 47% in urban areas.

Density: 36 persons per sq.km/93 persons per sq.mile.

Population Growth Rate: 2.3% p.a.

Ethnic Composition: The majority are Arabs and Berbers. The resident European population has continued to decrease since independence in 1956; today it numbers around 40,000 (mainly French and Italian) and is concentrated in and around Tunis.

Capital: Tunis Pop. 944,000.

Major Towns: Sfax Pop. 475,000; Sousse Pop. 255,000; Bizerte Pop. 62,000; Kairouan Pop. 54,000.

Language: Arabic is the official language. French is widely used in education, commerce and administration. English is rarely understood.

Religion: Most are Sunni Muslims. The European community is largely Roman Catholic, with Protestant, Greek Orthodox and Jewish minorities.

Government: Tunisia has a presidential regime. Executive power lies with the President, who chooses his own Prime Minister and Government ministers. The National Assembly is elected by direct universal suffrage every 5 years.

The Parti Socialiste Destourien (PSD) is the sole political party.

GEOGRAPHY

The country consists of 3 distinct physical regions. To the north are the mountains of the Tell Atlas (400–800m/1,320–2,640ft) and the Dorsale mountains near the Algerian border. The valley of the Medjerda lies between these 2 ranges. To the east are the fertile alluvial plains, extending from Bizerte to Sfax; this is the principal cultivated area as well as the most densely populated. South of the Dorsale range are the steppelands and the expanse of salt lakes known as *chotts*. The chief one is the Chott el-Djerid, which is surrounded by a number of oases and has now been partially developed for tourists. Further south lies the vast Sahara desert sector of Tunisia.

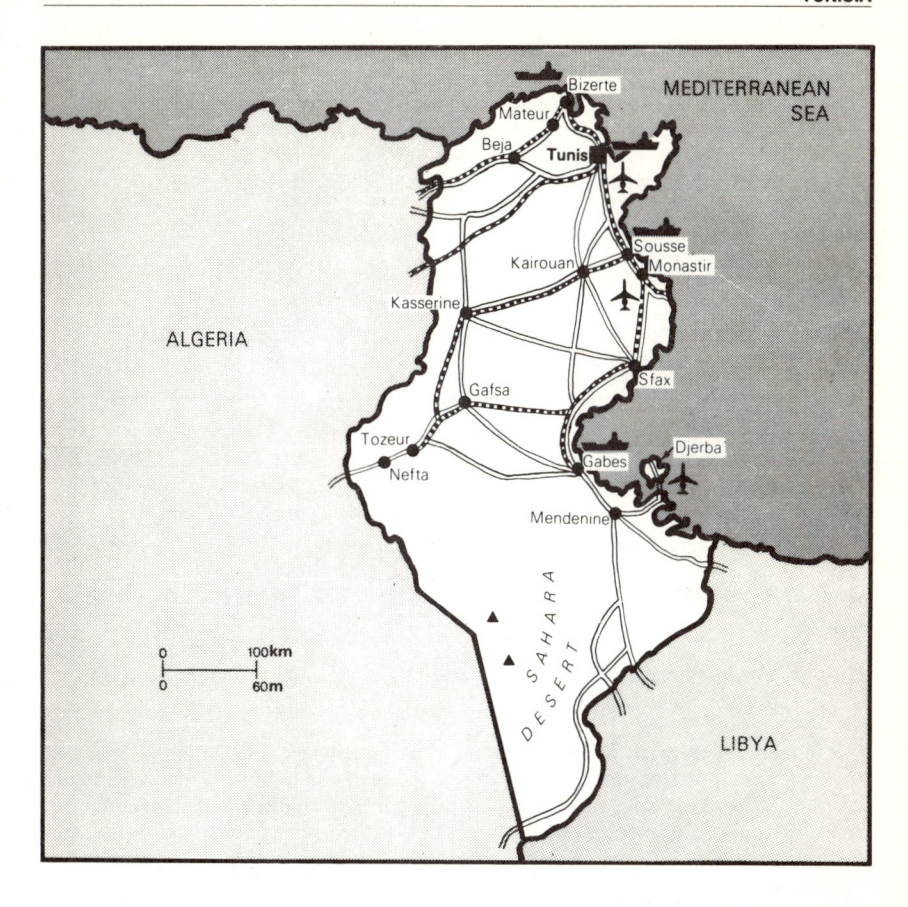

Climate
Northern and coastal Tunisia have a Mediterranean climate, with temperatures ranging from 30°C/85°F to 37°C/100°F in summer; the average temperature in winter is 13°C/55°F. Rainfall is concentrated in the winter months. Winter temperatures are generally cooler inland. Southern Tunisia has a desert climate and virtually no rainfall.

Agriculture
Approximately half of the population is dependent on agriculture for a livelihood, although the contribution of agriculture to the national income is declining.

Following independence, the Government nationalised European farms and introduced various co-operative schemes. Much of the state-owned land has now reverted to private ownership, and Government involvement is largely in the form of credit schemes.

Olives are the main agricultural export, and Tunisia is the world's 4th largest producer of olive oil.

A number of irrigation development schemes are being carried out in the north, partly financed by aid from West Germany and Canada in particular.

Main Crops: olives, wheat, barley, citrus fruits, dates, grapes, vegetables.

Mineral Resources: phosphates, iron ore, lead, zinc, oil.

THE ECONOMY

Gross National Product (1978): US$5.89 billion.

Per Capita Income (1978): US$967.

Gross Domestic Product (1978): TD 2,452 million.

Foreign Trade (1978): Total Imports – US$1.8 billion. Total Exports – US$894 million.

Main Trading Partners: Imports – France, West Germany, Italy, USA, Greece, USA. Exports – France, Italy, West Germany, Greece, USA.

The economy is primarily based on agriculture, although agriculture's importance as a foreign-exchange earner has declined. Mining is the main industrial activity, and the increase in the world price of phosphates, together with an increased demand for oil, has strengthened the economy considerably. Oil is the principal export by value, and the country has substantial oil and natural gas reserves.

Tunisia has been successful in attracting private investment and foreign aid – one of the main reasons for the former being the modest labour costs. This has enabled the implementation of ambitious economic development plans, particularly in the field of job creation which has been a major priority. A new focus on those manufacturing industries producing goods for export has also helped to alleviate the unemployment problem. Tourism plays an important role in the economy and has grown rapidly over the last decade.

Industry consists mainly of the processing of local raw materials with the state playing a dominant part in major industries such as mining and the associated chemical industry. Phosphates production continues to increase, and there has been recent growth in textiles and food-processing.

Major Industries: phosphates, chemicals and fertilisers, food processing, textiles, oil refining, cement and building materials, pulp and paper.

Main Commodities Traded: Imports – machinery and transport equipment, metal goods, sugar, wheat, industrial raw materials. Exports – petroleum, phosphates, olive oil, chemicals, wine.

International Affiliations: UN, IBRD, OAU, ADB, AL, BADEA.

HOW TO GET THERE

Air
Tunisia has 3 international airports, the principal one being Tunis-Carthage airport, 14km/9 miles from Tunis. The others are at Monastir and Djerba.

Major airlines serving Tunis-Carthage airport are Aeroflot, Air France, Alitalia, British Airways, British Caledonian, KLM, Lufthansa, SAS, Sabena and Swissair, with direct flights from Brussels, Frankfurt, London, Milan, Munich, Paris and Rome.

Tunis Air fly from French and other European cities, as well as from many Middle East capitals.

Flying times to Tunis: from London, 2¾ hours; from New York, 12 hours.

An airport tax of 1 dinar is payable on departure from Tunisia.

Sea
Regular passenger and car ferry services operate between Marseilles, Genoa, Naples, Palermo and Tunis. The main shipping lines involved are DFDS Seaways, the Tirrenia Line and the Société Nationale Maritime Corse Méditerranée (SNMCM).

Rail
Tunis has rail links with Annaba and Constantine in Algeria via Souk Ahras.

Road
There is access to Tunisia by road from both Algeria and Libya. Motorists need an International Driving Licence, log book and insurance (international green card).

ENTRY REGULATIONS

Visas
Visas are required by nationals of all countries, except UK and holders of passports which bear on the cover United Kingdom of Great Britain and Northern Ireland, Jersey, Guernsey and its dependencies, Hong Kong (1 month); also Barbados, Canada, Fiji, Ghana, Malaysia, Malta, Mauritius – for a stay of up to 3 months, except where otherwise stated. Also Algeria (unlimited stay), Austria, Belgium, Bulgaria (2 months), Chile, Denmark, Finland, France, West Germany (4 months), Greece (1 month), Guinea, Iceland, Iran, Republic of Ireland, Italy, Ivory Coast, Japan, South Korea (1 month), Kuwait, Liberia, Liechtenstein, Luxembourg, Mali, Mauritania, Monaco, Morocco (unlimited stay), Netherlands, Niger, Norway, Pakistan, Romania, San Marino, Senegal, Spain, Sweden, Switzerland, Turkey, USA (4 months) and Yugoslavia – for a stay of up to 3 months except where otherwise stated.

All other nationals require visas obtainable from Tunisian embassies and consulates abroad.

Transit visas are issued for a stay of up to 7 days.

Evidence in a passport of a previous or planned visit to Israel may adversely affect the granting of a visa.

Health Regulations
Visitors are advised to be in possession of a valid certificate of vaccination against smallpox. Certificates of vaccination against smallpox, cholera and yellow fever are

TUNISIA

required if arriving from an infected area. TAB (typhoid and paratyphoid) inoculations are recommended.

Customs
Currency: The import and export of Tunisian currency is prohibited. There is no limit to the amount of foreign currency which may be imported.

It is advisable to exchange foreign currency and travellers' cheques in small amounts, as it is often difficult to exchange back dinars and this will only be done on production of exchange slips from Tunisian banks. The amount of excess currency changed back into foreign currency must not exceed 30% of the foreign currency originally exchanged or 100 dinars, whichever is the greater.

Duty-free articles: Personal effects. 200 cigarettes or 50 cigars or 400g of tobacco. 1 litre of alcohol. Samples of no commercial value and those deemed unusable.

Samples of commercial value are admitted duty-free on payment of a deposit or the provision of a bond equivalent to the normal duties and taxes. The deposit is refunded or the bond cancelled if the samples are re-exported within 6 months.

PRACTICAL INFORMATION FOR THE VISITOR

1. Currency
Monetary Unit – Tunisian dinar (TD), divided into 1,000 millimes (m).
Notes – ½, 1, 5, 10 dinars.
Coins – 1, 2, 5, 10, 20, 50, 100, 500 millimes.

Banking Hours
Winter – 0800–1100
         1400–1600 Monday to Friday
Summer – 0730–1100 Monday to Friday
The *Banque Centrale de Tunisie*, 7 Place de la Monnaie, Tunis, is the central bank of issue.

Principal Domestic Banks in Tunis
Banque de Tunisie, 2 Avenue de la France.
Société Tunisienne de Banque, 1 Avenue Habib Thameur – correspondent of numerous foreign banks.
Union Internationale de Banque, 65 Avenue Habib Bourguiba.

Foreign Banks in Tunis
Arab Bank Ltd, 21 Rue al Djazira.
Chase Manhattan Bank, 3 Rue de Guinée, Place Jeanne d'Arc.

2. Electricity Supply
110v and 220v AC 50Hz.
Plugs: 2-pin.

3. Weights and Measures
The metric system is in use.

4. Media
Radiodiffusion Télévision Tunisienne broadcasts in Arabic, French and Italian. There is no commercial advertising on either radio or TV.

Newspapers and Journals
There are 5 national daily newspapers: *L'Action* (PSD), *La Presse de Tunisie, Le Temps, Al Amal* (PSD) and *Al Sabah.*

There are also a number of provincial daily newspapers as well as weekly and monthly journals. *Dialogue* and *Jeune Afrique* are the 2 main French-language weekly magazines.

5. Medical Care
The water supply in the main towns is drinkable, but mineral water is safer and readily available. Foreign visitors may suffer from stomach disorders, particularly during the hot summer months, and

are advised to take suitable precautionary medicines.

6. Telephone, Telex and Postal Services
Telexes can be sent from the Central Post Office.

Calls can be made from the Central Post Office, Rue Charles de Gaulle, Tunis, ☎ 245961, the Hilton Hotel in Tunis and from other large hotels.

The Central Post Office also has a 24-hour telegram service and *poste restante* facilities. There is a post office at Tunis-Carthage airport.

7. Public Holidays

1 January	New Year's Day
18 January	Anniversary of the National Revolution
20 March	Independence Day
9 April	Martyrs' Day
1 May	Labour Day
1 June	Fête de la Victoire
2 June	Fête de la Jeunesse
25 July	Republic Day
3 August	President's Birthday
13 August	Women's Day
3 September	Memorial Day
15 October	Evacuation Day

The following Muslim holidays are also observed: *Mouled, Eid el Fitr, Eid el Adha, El Hijra*. Business travellers are advised to avoid visiting Tunisia during the month of *Ramadan*.

8. Time
GMT + 1 (+ 2 May to September).

9. Internal Transport

Air
Tunis Air operates internal air services between Tunis and Monastir and Djerba. Unscheduled charter flights are operated by Tunisavia between Tunis and Sfax and other main towns.

Airline Offices in Tunis
Aeroflot	☎ 249779, 249773.
Air France	☎ 247922, 255422.
British Caledonian	☎ 244261, 246967.
KLM	☎ 242500.
Lufthansa	☎ 240714, 241905.
PIA	☎ 245785, 259189.
SAS	☎ 259800.
Swissair	☎ 242122.
Tunis Air	☎ 288100.

Rail
Most of the main towns are linked by railway services operated by the Société Nationale des Chemins de Fer Tunisiens.

Road
Self-drive cars are available for hire. An International Driving Licence is required. Traffic drives on the right-hand side of the road.

Long-distance taxis (*louages*) can be hired at reasonable rates for inter-town travel. These depart from fixed points in each town and the rates are fixed officially.

Within the towns an efficient form of travel is the *bébé* taxi – a small car operated as a taxi.

A radio taxi service operates in Tunis: Société Radio Taxi, 39 Boulevard Bechir Sfar, ☎ 282866.

Car-hire Firms in Tunis
Avis, 90 Avenue de la Liberté, ☎ 282508, 285734.
Europcar, 39 Avenue Kherredine Pacha, ☎ 287304.
Garage Excelsior, 53 Avenue de Paris, ☎ 245023.
Garage Majestic, 38 Avenue de Paris, ☎ 258228.
Hertz, 29 Avenue Habib Bourguiba, ☎ 248529.
Palace Garage, 15 Avenue de Madrid.

10. Tipping
Taxis – 100 millimes.

Porters – 100 millimes per bag.

Hotels/restaurants – 10% of the bill.

TUNISIA

11. Social Customs
Although Tunisia is a Muslim country, social customs and practices are less restrictive than in the stricter Muslim states, and life in the capital, Tunis, is relatively informal. Most mosques in Tunisia are open to non-Muslims.

USEFUL ADDRESSES (GENERAL)

Tunis

British Embassy: 5 Place de la Victoire, ☎ 245100, 245324.

Canadian Embassy: 2 Place Virgile, Notre-Dame de Tunis, B.P. 31 Belvédère, ☎ 286577.

Dutch Embassy: 24–6 Place de l'Afrique, ☎ 241481, 241561.

French Embassy: Place de l'Indépendance, B.P. 689.

Japanese Embassy: 16 Rue Djebel Aures, Notre-Dame, B.P. 1009, ☎ 285937, 285960.

Swiss Embassy: 17 Avenue de France, B.P. 501, ☎ 245003.

US Embassy: 144 Avenue de la Liberté, ☎ 282566.

West German Embassy: 18 Rue Felicien Challaye, B.P. 35, ☎ 281246.

Ministry of Cultural Affairs and Information: Place du Gouvernement, Tunis.

Office National du Tourisme Tunisien: 1 Avenue Mohammed V, Tunis, ☎ 259217/8.

American Express Authorised Representative: Tourafric, 52 Ave. Habib Bourguiba, Tunis, ☎ 245066.

Wagons-Lits: 65 Avenue Habib Bourguiba, Tunis, ☎ 242673/247320.

BUSINESS INFORMATION

The import of consumer goods is restricted by import licensing and import substitution. However, the import of raw materials and semi-finished goods, together with agricultural and industrial equipment, has increased significantly in recent years, partly financed by foreign aid.

The Tunisian market is a small one, but with the reduction in the advantages given to French goods it is now becoming more competitive. Most sales are made by personal contact between buyer and seller. Both stockist and commission agents are also used.

Several government organisations have been established to undertake agency work and have a monopoly or near-monopoly in their particular sectors. Many large-scale purchases are made by these organisations which also deal with government contracts.

Import and Exchange Control Regulations
Import licences are required for all permitted imports, and a few categories of goods may be imported only by state monopolies. Preferential quotas are available for certain imports from the EEC. Bilateral agreements provide for a number of products from France, Algeria, Morocco, Niger, Senegal and the Ivory Coast to enter at

preferential rates of duty. The EEC/Tunisian Trade Agreement provides for preferential duty rates for some goods of EEC origin.

The possession of an import licence guarantees that the appropriate foreign currency will be available for payment. An *authorisation préalable* constitutes a right for foreign exchange and authorises the importer to make all payments specified in the contract.

Business Hours
Government Offices
Winter – 0830–1300 / 1500–1745 Monday to Thursday
0830–1330 Friday and Saturday
Summer – 0730–1100 Monday to Saturday

Business Houses
Winter – 0800–1200 / 1430–1800 Monday to Friday
0800–1200 Saturday
Summer – 0700–1300 Monday to Saturday

Business Events
The Tunis International Trade Fair has been held at irregular intervals since 1953. Further details can be obtained from: Foire Internationale de Tunis, Palais de la Foire, Avenue Mohammed V, Tunis.

BUSINESS SERVICES

Forwarding/Clearing Agents
(including Collection and/or Despatch of Samples)

Agence Africaine de Consignation et Commerce, 5 Rue Champlain, Tunis.

Agence Bahri Said Ben Said, 16bis Avenue des Nations-Unies, Tunis.

Compagnie Tunisienne d'Armement, 10 Avenue Farhat Hached, Tunis.

Lasry Brothers, 6 Avenue de Carthage, Tunis.

Société Générale de Surveillance, 8 Rue Jean le Vacher, Tunis.

Socotu, 1 Rue des Glacières, Tunis.

Tunisie-Maritime, 1 Avenue des Nations-Unies, Tunis.

USEFUL ADDRESSES (BUSINESS)

Agence de Promotion des Investissements (API): 18 Avenue Mohammed V, Tunis, ☎ 256022.

Chambre de Commerce de Tunis: 1 Rue des Entrepreneurs, Tunis, ☎ 242872.

Chambre de Commerce du Centre: Rue Chadly Khaznadar, Sousse.

Chambre de Commerce du Nord: 12 Rue Ibn Khaldoun, Bizerte.

Chambre de Commerce du Sud: 21–3 Rue Habib Thameur, Sfax.

Chambre Tuniso-Française de Commerce et d'Industrie: 14 Rue de Vesoul, Tunis.

TUNISIA

MAJOR CITY

Tunis

The most interesting part of Tunis for the foreign visitor is the traditional Medina with its narrow, winding alleys, *souks* and mosques. Entrance to the Medina is through the gate known as Bab el-Bahar.

The Medina contains a wealth of architectural delights: vaulted and ceramic tiled courtyards or *zawias*, the 18th-century Palace of Dar Hussein, the 9th-century Great Mosque of Zitouna and the 11th-century el-Ksar Mosque. The Museum of Islamic Art (open daily) contains some fine pieces of art.

The Punic capital of Carthage was founded in 815 BC, but today is no more than a suburb of Tunis; all that remains of the former Roman town are the Baths of Antonius and the port. An extensive collection of Roman, Punic and Islamic art is housed in the Bardo Museum, about 5km/3 miles north of Tunis.

Hotels

The National Tourist Board grades hotels from 4-star de luxe, 4-star, etc., down to 1-star.

AFRICA MERIDIEN, 50 Avenue Habib Bourguiba, ☎ 247477.
Modern 4-star de luxe hotel in city centre, 15 minutes' drive from airport.
Rooms: 168 ♪, ⑩, ⚅, ☐, ☎, ⚄, ⊚.
Suites available.
Facilities: International restaurant, bar, rooftop restaurant and bar, brasserie, coffee shop. Shopping arcade. Cinema. Car hire. Golf, tennis, swimming, solarium.
Services: ⊟ Access, Amex, Carte Blanche, Diners Club, Eurocard, Master Charge. Dr. on call. **5**, ♂. Audio-visual equipment.
Conference room – max. capacity 500.

HILTON TUNIS, Avenue Salambo, P.O. Box 1160, ☎ 282000.
Modern 4-star de luxe hotel in Belvedere Park district, 5 minutes from city centre.
Rooms: 245 ♪, ⑩, ☐, ☎, ⊚. Suites available.
Facilities: Grill room, coffee shop, bars. Dinner dancing. Swimming. Golf, tennis and riding privileges at nearby clubs. Car hire.
Services: TC, FC. ⊟ Amex, Barclay Visa, Carte Blanche, Diners Club, Eurocard, Master Charge. **5**, ♂. Free transport to private beach and city centre. Audio-visual equipment.
Conference room – max. capacity 450.
Banquet rooms – max. capacity 300.

INTERNATIONAL TUNISIA, 49 Avenue Habib Bourguiba, ☎ 254855, 247854.
Modern 4-star de luxe hotel in business centre.
Rooms: 203 ♪, ⚅, ☐.
Facilities: 2 restaurants, café, bars. Nightclub.
Services: ⊟ Amex, Carte Blanche, Diners Club, Eurocard.
Conference and banquet facilities.

DU LAC, Avenue Habib Bourguiba, ☎ 258322.
Ultra-modern 3-star hotel in city centre, 15 minutes from airport.
Rooms: 200 ♪, ⑩, ☎, ⊙.
Facilities: Restaurant, bar, lounge. Golf, tennis, swimming. Ladies' and men's hairdressers.
Services: TC, FC. ⊟ Amex, Diners Club, Eurocard. Dr. on call. **5**, ♂.

Restaurants

In addition to the restuarants in the larger hotels, others are: *Chez Nous*, 5 Rue de Marseille; *Chez Slah*, Rue Pierre de Courbertin; *Hungaria*, 11 Rue Bach Hamba; *Le Malouf*, Rue de Yougoslavie – Tunisian; *M'Rabet*, Souk Ettrouk –

Tunisian; *Le Palais,* Avenue de Carthage – Tunisian; *Strasbourg,* 100 Rue de Yougoslavie – French.

Restaurants in the suburbs of Tunis include: *Les Dunes,* Gammarth; *Le Pêcheur,* Gammarth – seafood; *Le Pirate,* Sidi Bou Said; *Neptune,* Carthage.

Nightclubs
The Hilton and Africa Hotels have their own nightclubs. The *Café des Nattes* is a popular open-air nightclub at Sidi Bou Said. Several restaurants (including the *Palais, Malouf* and *M'Rabat*) have floor shows featuring belly-dancing.

Entertainment
The National Theatre in Tunis gives performances by local and visiting companies from November to May.

Opportunities for all watersports, including skin diving and deep-sea fishing, are very good. Horse racing takes place from October to May, and there is camel riding at the beach resorts. There is a golf course at La Soukra, 11km/7 miles from Tunis.

UGANDA
Republic of Uganda

Geography	452
The Economy	454
How to Get There	454
Entry Regulations	455
Practical Information for the Visitor	455
Useful Addresses (General)	456
Business Information	457
Useful Addresses (Business)	457
Kampala	457

Size: 241,139 sq.km/93,104 sq.miles.

Population: 12.4 million (1978 est.).

Distribution: 8% in urban areas.

Density: 51 persons per sq.km/133 per sq.mile.

Population Growth Rate: 3.4% p.a.

Ethnic Composition: There are many African tribes, the largest being the Baganda, the Iteso, the Banyankore and the Basoga.

Capital: Kampala Pop. 332,000.

Major Towns: Jinja Pop. 52,000; Mbale Pop. 23,000; Entebbe Pop. 21,000.

Language: English is the official language, and Swahili the national language.

Religion: Mainly Christian (Catholic and Anglican) with some Muslims and Animists.

Government: In April 1979 President Idi Amin was overthrown by Tanzanian troops. The provisional government which took office in July 1979 was deposed by the military; it is uncertain when the promised elections will be held.

GEOGRAPHY

Uganda is chiefly a land-locked plateau at an altitude of 900–1,500m/3,000–5,000 feet, with nearly one-fifth of its area covered by fresh water lakes or swamps. The western border is part of the east African rift system and includes the lowlands around Lakes Albert and Edward (renamed in 1972 Lakes Mobutu Sese Seko and Idi Amin Dada, although the latter is likely to be renamed). The White Nile rises in Lake Victoria and traverses the country. There are mountain groups on both eastern and western borders. In the south there is dense forest, while the north is mainly savannah with semi-desert areas in the north-east.

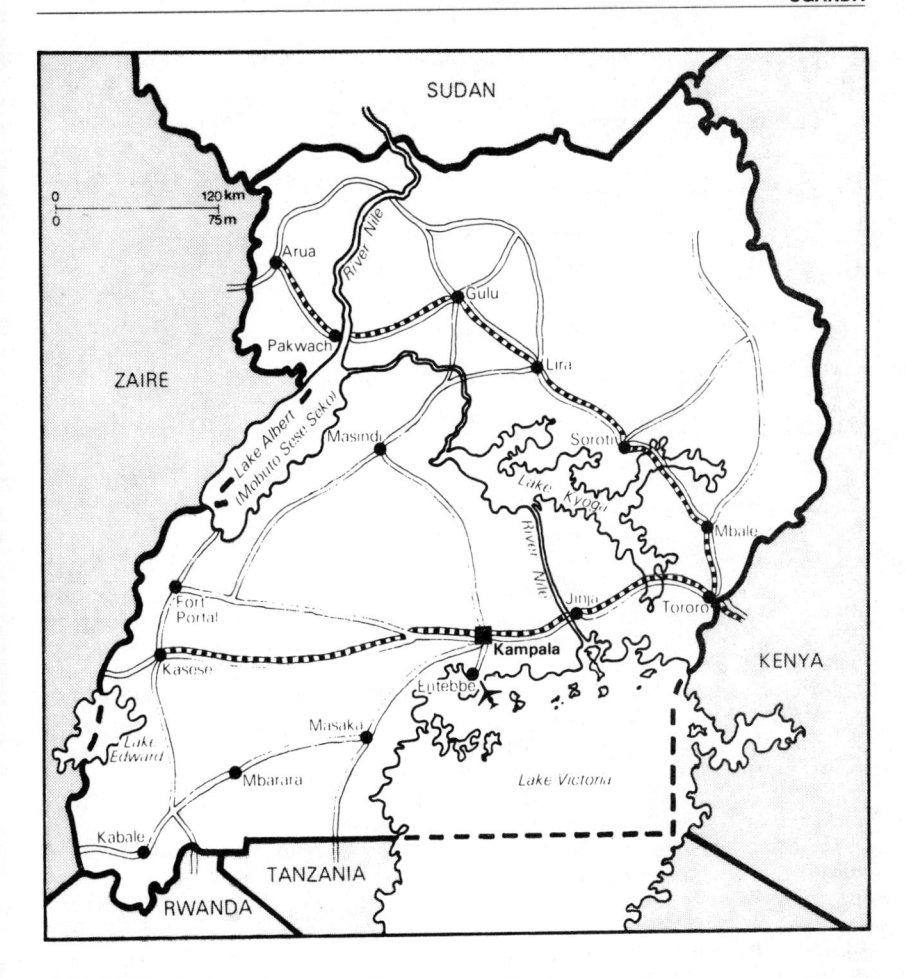

Climate
The climate is equatorial, modified to a pleasant level by altitude. Temperatures vary little throughout the year and range between 15°C/59°F at night to 26°C/78°F during the day. Principal rainy periods are March to May and October to November.

Agriculture
Agriculture dominates the Ugandan economy, employing about 90% of the population, mostly in subsistence farming. The main cash crops are coffee and cotton, with tea, tobacco and sugar of growing importance. Production declined drastically in the years 1972-7 when a number of farmers turned to subsistence-level cultivation for food, transport and maintenance problems multiplied and bad weather damaged the tobacco crops. In addition, growers smuggled large quantities of coffee, the principal export earner, into Kenya and Zaïre to take advantage of higher prices and foreign currency payments. These difficulties were partially and temporarily offset by the boom in world tea and, especially, coffee prices, but by the end of Amin's regime the agricultural sector and the economy as a whole was said to be in total disarray.

Main Crops: millet, plantains, sweet potatoes, cassava, maize, coffee, cotton, tea, sorghum, groundnuts, beans, sugar, tobacco.

Mineral Resources: copper, apatite, tungsten, tin, beryllium.

THE ECONOMY

Gross National Product (1978 est.): US$2.1 billion.

Per Capita Income (1978 est.): US$169.

Gross Domestic Product (1978 est.): US$3.7 billion.

Foreign Trade (1977): Total Imports – US$371 million. Total Exports – US$555 million.

Main Trading Partners (1977): Imports – Kenya, Tanzania, UK, West Germany, Italy, Hong Kong, Japan. Exports – US, UK, Netherlands, Japan, Spain, Australia.

Agriculture is the mainstay of the economy, with copper the only non-agricultural commodity of significance in export terms. Industry is concentrated on the processing of primary products, and import substitution (textiles, beer, cigarettes, bicycle parts, cement, metal implements).

Former President Amin's policies (particularly the expulsion of Asians in 1972 and nationalisation of foreign firms) contributed to a severe decline in all sectors of the economy throughout the 1970s. There was an extreme shortage of spare parts and skilled personnel, and plant and machinery fell into disrepair. Tourism dropped to nothing, and the acute fall in agricultural output resulted in a shortage of foreign exchange, so that by 1978 the economy was completely run down.

The country is naturally very fertile and the new Government, which is attracting much-needed foreign assistance, estimated that it would have the economy functioning again within 2 years of taking office.

Major Industries: food processing (sugar refining, tea, tobacco, cotton, dairy products), textiles, oil seed processing, tanning, copper refining, cement, fertilisers.

Main Commodities Traded: Imports – machinery, petroleum products, transport equipment, paper products. Exports – coffee, cotton, tea, tobacco, copper, hides and skins.

International Affiliations: UN, IBRD, OAU, ACP, ADB, Commonwealth.

HOW TO GET THERE

Air
Air France fly direct once weekly from Paris to Entebbe International Airport, and Sabena once weekly from Brussels to Entebbe. Inter-African services are provided by Air Zaïre, Ethiopian Airlines, Sudan Airways and the national airline, Uganda Airlines Corporation.

Flying time from Paris to Entebbe, 11 hours.
Entebbe Airport is 35km/22 miles from Kampala.
An airport tax of UGS 40 is payable on departure.

ENTRY REGULATIONS

Visas
Visa requirements for Uganda are continually changing, and visitors are therefore advised to check with their nearest Uganda consulate. Where visas are not required, passports must nevertheless be endorsed for Uganda. In addition, all business visitors must obtain a Visitor's Pass prior to arrival. It is also recommended that the Ministry of Foreign Affairs be kept informed of the details of the business visitor's travelling schedule, in order to help alleviate any problems that might arise.

Health Regulations
International Certificates of Vaccination are required against cholera, smallpox and yellow fever.

Customs
Currency: Unlimited foreign currency may be imported, provided it is declared. Foreign currency up to the amount imported and declared may be exported. Import and export of local currency is forbidden.

Duty-free articles: 250g of tobacco or 200 cigarettes; 1 bottle of spirits or wine; ½ litre of perfume and toilet water.

Dress: There have been varying restrictions on dress for visitors entering Uganda, ignorance of which resulted in a fine or imprisonment. It is not known whether all these restrictions still apply, but visitors are advised to check with their nearest Ugandan consulate.

PRACTICAL INFORMATION FOR THE VISITOR

1. Currency
Monetary Unit – Uganda shilling (UGS) divided into 100 cents.
Notes – 5, 10, 20, 50, 100 shillings.
Coins – 5, 10, 50 cents; 1 shilling.

Banking Hours
0800 – 1230 Monday to Friday
0800 – 1100 Saturday

Major Domestic Banks in Kampala
Bank of Uganda, P.O. Box 7120, 37–43 Kampala Road – *central bank and bank of issue.*
Uganda Commercial Bank, P.O. Box 973, 12 Kampala Road.

Foreign Commercial Banks in Kampala
Barclays Bank of Uganda, P.O. Box 2971, Kampala Road.
Grindlays Bank (Uganda), P.O. Box 7131, 45 Kampala Road.
Standard Bank Uganda, P.O. Box 311, Speke Road.

2. Electricity Supply
240v AC 50 Hz.
Plugs: 3 square or 2 round pins.

3. Weights and Measures
The metric system is in use.

4. Media

The Uganda Broadcasting Corporation broadcasts daily programmes in English, French, Swahili, Arabic and several African languages.

The Uganda Television Service transmits a commercial service from Kampala for the Ministry of Information and Broadcasting. Colour transmission was introduced in 1975.

Newspapers and Journals

The *Uganda Times* is published daily in English. There is a weekly government paper, the *Uganda Weekly News*, as well as several monthlies, including church publications and specialist papers such as the *Uganda Dairy Farmer*.

5. Medical Care

Tap water is safe to drink only in the cities. Anti-malarial precautions are strongly recommended, and visitors should be wary of swimming as bilharzia is present in most Ugandan lakes.

Medical facilities are not readily available outside Kampala.

6. Telephone, Telex and Postal Services

The postal service is adequate, but telephone, telex and telegraph services are reported to be less so. There is a direct dial service from Kampala to Nairobi (Kenya) and Dar-es-Salaam (Tanzania).

7. Public Holidays

1 January	*New Year's Day*
25 January	*Republic Day*
1 May	*Labour Day*
10 July	*National Day*
9 October	*Independence Day*

In addition, the main Christian and Muslim feasts are observed.

8. Time

GMT + 3.

9. Internal Transport

Air

Uganda Airlines connects Kampala (Entebbe) with Jinja, Kasese and Kabalega Falls. Charter services are available at Entebbe Airport.

Airline Offices in Kampala

Aeroflot	☎ 31703.
Air France	☎ 56056, 33495.
British Airways	☎ 57414, 56695.
Sabena	☎ 34200.

Road

All the main towns are connected by bitumen roads. Bus services cover much of the country, but are often overcrowded and unreliable. Collective taxis are available in and between most towns. Cars can be hired in Kampala. An international or national driver's licence is required and traffic travels on the left.

Car-Hire Firms in Kampala

Impala Tours	☎ 56931.
Hunts Travel Services	☎ 3616.
United Touring Company	☎ 3079.

USEFUL ADDRESSES (GENERAL)

Kampala

Dutch Consulate: 9–11 Seventh Street, c/o Shell and BP Uganda Ltd, P.O. Box 3087, ☎ 54061.

French Embassy: 25 Kampala Road, P.O. Box 7212, ☎ 42120.

Swiss Consulate: Baskerville Ave. 1 Kololo, P.O. Box 4187, ☎ 41574.

UK High Commission: 10–12 Parliament Ave.

US Embassy: 9–11 Parliament Ave, P.O. Box 7007, ☎ 54451.

West German Embassy: 9–11 Parliament Ave., P.O. Box 7016, ☎ 56767/8.

Uganda Tourist Development Corporation: P.O. Box 7211.

Uganda Wildlife Development Ltd: P.O. Box 1764.

BUSINESS INFORMATION

Import and Exchange Control Regulations
The Uganda Advisory Board of Trade and several state-owned specified companies control the importation of all goods on behalf of registered importers and manufacturers. Companies wishing to import goods must register with the Ministry of Commerce and Industry. Uganda is at present in the process of rebuilding its run-down economy with the help of foreign aid and companies or individuals wishing to conduct business in the country are advised to contact their nearest Ugandan embassy for up-to-date information.

Business Hours
Government Offices
0815 – 1245
1400 – 1600 Monday to Friday

Business Houses
0800 – 1230 Monday to Saturday
1400 – 1700 Monday to Friday

USEFUL ADDRESSES (BUSINESS)

National Chamber of Commerce and Industry, P.O. Box 2369, Kampala.

Uganda Advisory Board of Trade, P.O. Box 6877, Kampala.

Uganda Development Corporation Ltd, 9–11 Parliament Street, P.O. Box 442, Kampala.

MAJOR CITY

Kampala
Kampala is set on a cluster of hills, its skyline dominated by the Christian cathedrals, the Kibuli mosque, the palace complex of the old kings of Buganda and the modern International Hotel. The city has been the centre of a great deal of history and has an excellent National Museum. The Kabaka tombs on Kasubi Hill offer excellent examples of Buganda thatched buildings. Modern architecture of note includes the National Theatre and the Parliament buildings. The city also houses Makarere Univeristy, one of the oldest in Africa.

UGANDA

Hotels

Many of the city's hotels were looted in the final stages of the overthrow of Idi Amin and it is reported that few are yet up to their former standards. Few tourists have visited Uganda since 1971 but the Tourist Development Association is in the process of rehabilitating the country's tourist resources.

INTERNATIONAL, 11–15 Nile Avenue, P.O. Box 7041, ☎ 58022.
High-rise hotel in city centre.
Rooms: 300 ◉, ◻ (on request), ☎, ▲, ◪. Suites availabe.
Facilities: Restaurants, buffet with local cuisine, terrace lounge, bars, roof garden. Nightclub. Parking, car hire. Swimming, sauna.
Services: TC, FC. ▤ None accepted. Dr. on call. S. Audio-visual equipment.
Conference room – max. capacity 500.

LAKE VICTORIA, P.O. Box 15, Entebbe, ☎ 2644.
Situated in pleasant grounds overlooking Lake Victoria, 1½km/1 mile from airport, 33½ km/21 miles from Kampala.
Rooms: 106 ♪ (some).
Facilities: Dining room, bars. Dancing, swimming. Golf, tennis, sailing available.

UPPER VOLTA
Republic of Upper Volta

Geography	*459*
The Economy	*461*
How to Get There	*462*
Entry Regulations	*462*
Practical Information for the Visitor	*462*
Useful Addresses (General)	*464*
Business Information	*464*
Business Services	*465*
Useful Addresses (Business)	*465*
Ouagadougou	*465*

Size: 274,200 sq.km/105,870 sq.miles.

Population: 6.6 million (1978 est.).

Distribution: 11% in urban areas.

Density: 23 persons per sq.km/60 per sq.mile.

Population Growth Rate: 1.6% p.a.

Ethnic Composition: The two main groups are the Voltaic and the Mande. The principal Voltaic tribes are the Mossi (50% of the population) and the Gourma in the north, and the Bobo in the south-west. The Mande are mainly in the south-east. To the north are several nomadic tribes, the largest being the Fulani.

Capital: Ouagadougou Pop. 150,000.

Major Towns: Bobo-Dioulasso Pop. 90,000; Koudougou Pop. 40,000.

Language: French is the official language. The principal African tongues are Moré (spoken by the Mossi), Dioula and Gourmantche.

Religion: Most are Animists, with about 15% Muslim and 5% Christian, mainly Roman Catholic.

Government: In May 1978 General Sangoulé Lamizana was elected President, the office he had assumed in the military takeover in 1966. In accordance with the new Constitution (1977), general elections for the 57-member National Assembly were held in April 1978 and the Mossi-based Union Démocratique Voltaique-Rassemblement Démocratique Africain coalition won a majority of seats.

GEOGRAPHY

Upper Volta is a land-locked country in West Africa. In the south there are wooded savannahs; in the north the plains dry out into semi-desert. The most important rivers

UPPER VOLTA

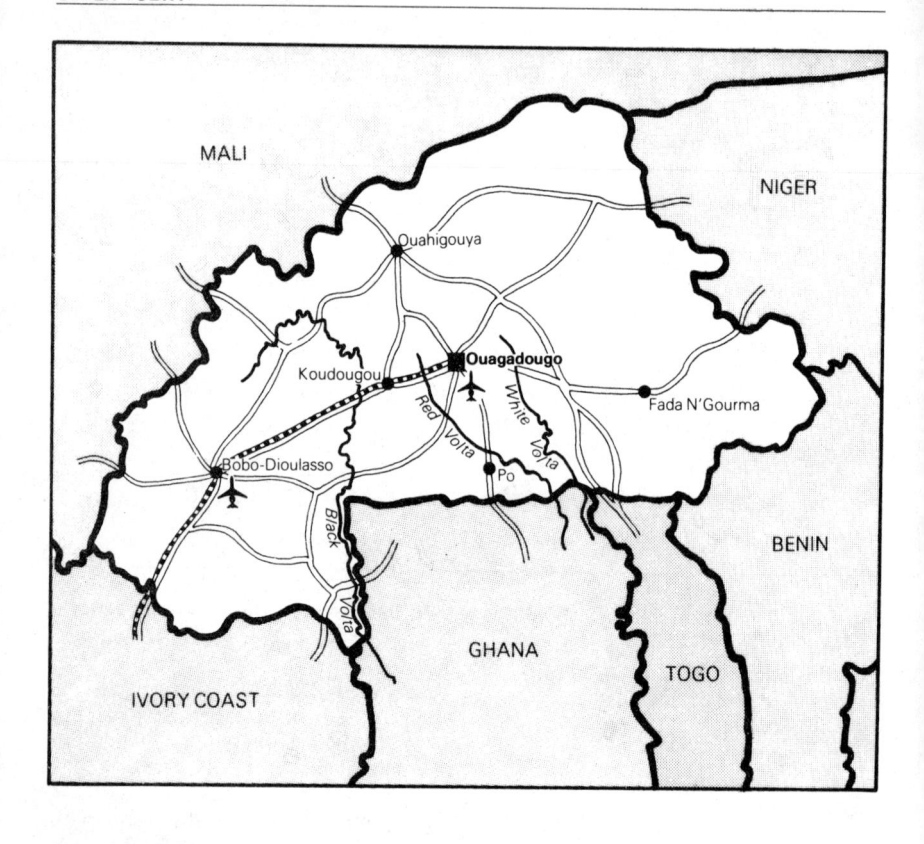

are the Red, Black and White Voltas, which dry to a trickle in summer making them impossible to navigate.

Climate
The country is uniformly hot and dry with a desert climate in the north. In the south the dry season runs from December to May and the rainy season from June to October, with violent storms in August. From November to January, the cooling, dusty *harmattan* blows from the east. Mean temperature between December and March is 27°c/81°F.

Agriculture
Agriculture accounts for over one-third of the GDP and is almost entirely at subsistence level, employing over 90% of the population. Crop production and livestock numbers have recovered from the 1973–4 drought, but inadequate irrigation development and the generally poor soils and climatic conditions continue to hinder agricultural development. The main subsistence crops are sorghum, millet, maize and, more recently, rice. Production of cash crops is increasing, with the help of Government investment in cotton, groundnuts, sugar and market gardening.

The country's 2.5 million cattle were its principal export until 1976 and continue to be of major importance, though over-grazing is now a serious problem in the north. There are, in addition, large numbers of sheep, goats, pigs and poultry.

Main Crops: sorghum, millet, cotton, groundnuts, sesame, maize, rice, karité nuts, sugar cane.

Mineral Resources: manganese, phosphate, limestone, gold, bauxite, zinc, lead, nickel.

THE ECONOMY

Gross National Product (1978): US$870 million.

Per Capita Income (1978): US$160.

Gross Domestic Product (1978 est.): US$1.1 billion.

Foreign Trade (1978): Total Imports – US$209 million. Total Exports – US$110.6 million.

Main Trading Partners: Imports – France, Ivory Coast, USA, West Germany, Netherlands. Exports – Ivory Coast, France, UK, West Germany, Japan.

Upper Volta is a poor country with large areas of infertile land and a high population density. Agriculture supports over 90% of the population and much of the industrial activity is agricultural processing – cotton ginneries, textiles and soap mills, slaughter houses, rice and flour mills, an oil-extraction plant, a sugar mill and a tannery. The remaining industrial output is chiefly concerned with import substitution (bicycle and motor assembly, cigarettes, paints, plastics, beer and soft drinks, ceramics and light metal goods).

Mining activity is still very limited with hopes for major development centred on the deposits of manganese ore near Tambao on the northern border. A Government-controlled company has been set up with Japanese, West German, US and French participation to exploit the ore, and prospecting continues for several other minerals.

Much of the current development plan is orientated towards the 'modern' sector of the economy, specifically mining development at Tambao, the railway extension to this area, further prospecting and the construction of a cement factory at Tin Hrassan. 31% of expenditure is earmarked for infrastructure development and only 13% for the rural sector.

Foreign aid and investment is crucial to the economy, which is still recovering from the devastation of the Sahel drought in the early 1970s. The country suffers a permanent trade deficit, which is substantially eased by the remittances of Voltaics working in other countries, principally the Ivory Coast.

Major Industries: food processing, textiles, tanning, footwear, bricks, bicycle assembly.

Main Commodities Traded: Imports – transport equipment, mechanical and electrical machinery, iron and steel, petroleum products, dairy produce, cereals. Exports – raw cotton, karité nuts, livestock products, groundnuts.

International Affiliations: UN, IBRD, OAU, ACP, ADB, CEAO, ECOWAS, Franc Zone, OCAM, NRC.

UPPER VOLTA

HOW TO GET THERE

Air
UTA operate regular flights to Ouagadougou from Paris, via Niamey in Niger. Flights to Ouagadougou and Bobo-Dioulasso from the African Continent are operated by Air Afrique, Air Mali and Ghana Airways.

Flying time to Ouagadougou from Paris is 6 hours.

Ouagadougou airport is 2km/1¼ miles from the city centre; ground transport to the city is available. Bobo-Dioulasso airport is 16km/10 miles from the city centre.

Rail
Ouagadougou is linked with Abidjan on the Ivory Coast via Bobo-Dioulasso. The express train with sleepers takes 27 hours.

ENTRY REGULATIONS

Visas are required by nationals of all countries, except: (i) Belgium, West Germany, Italy, Luxembourg, Netherlands – for a stay of up to 3 months; (ii) France and former French territories – for an unlimited stay.

All other nationals require visas, obtainable from Upper Volta embassies or French consulates. Visitors must hold a return ticket or repatriation guarantee. Business visitors should ensure that their passport is valid for at least 3 months beyond the date of issue of their visa.

Health Regulations
Valid International Certificates of Vaccination against smallpox and yellow fever are required by all persons entering Upper Volta. A cholera vaccination certificate is no longer obligatory, but is advisable.

Customs
Currency: There is no limit to the amount of local or foreign currency which may be imported or exported.

Duty-free articles: Personal effects. 200 cigarettes or 250g of tobacco. 1 bottle of wine. 1 bottle of spirits. A small amount of perfume. Samples of no commercial value. Samples of commercial value should be declared on arrival and these will be checked on departure.

PRACTICAL INFORMATION FOR THE VISITOR

1. Currency
Monetary Unit – CFA franc.
Notes – 50, 100, 500, 1,000 and 5,000 CFA francs.
Coins – 1, 2, 5, 10, 25, 50 and 100 CFA francs.

Upper Volta, together with Benin, Ivory Coast, Niger, Senegal and Togo, is a member of the *Banque Centrale des Etats de l'Afrique de l'Ouest*, B.P. 356 Ouagadougou.

UPPER VOLTA

Banking Hours
0800–1200 Monday to Friday.

Domestic Commercial Banks
Banque Internationale pour le Commerce, l'Industrie et l'Agriculture de la Haute Volta, B.P. 8, Rue de Marché, Ouagadougou – Bank of America affiliate.
Banque Internationale des Voltas, B.P. 362, Rue André Brunnel, Ouagadougou.

2. Electricity Supply
220/380v AC 50Hz.
Plugs: 2 round pins

3. Weights and Measures
The metric system is used.

4. Media
Voltavision is a Government-owned television service which transmits 3 days a week in the immediate Ouagadougou area. La Voix du Renouveau has 2 radio stations, in Ouagadougou and Bobo-Dioulasso, and broadcasts in French and 13 vernacular languages.

Newspapers and Journals
There are 3 daily publications in Ouagadougou: *L'Observateur*, *Notre Combat* and the *Bulletin Quotidien d'Information*, the latter issued by the Government Information Bureau simultaneously in the capital and in Bobo-Dioulasso.

Periodicals include the weekly *Journal Officiel de la République de Haute Volta*; the Government-sponsored twice monthly *Carrefour Africain*; and the Chamber of Commerce publications *Bulletin Douanier et Fiscal* and *Courrier Consulaire de la Haute Volta*.

5. Medical Care
Anti-malarial prophylactics should be taken, on the advice of a doctor. Typhoid vaccination is also recommended.
Tap water is generally not safe to drink and should be boiled; alternatively, drink bottled water. Visitors are advised to carry a preventative against stomach upset and to take care with uncooked fruit and vegetables. Ouagadougou has a partly modern hospital, and there is a hospital in Bobo-Dioulasso.

6. Telephone, Telex and Postal Services
There is a good quality telephone connection with Paris from Ouagadougou and Bobo-Dioulasso, and a direct automatic exchange between Bobo-Dioulasso and Abidjan on the Ivory Coast. An automatic intersuburban network connects Ouagadougou, Bobo-Dioulasso and Banfora.

The Hôtel Indépendance has telex facilities for its guests.

Post offices in Ouagadougou and Bobo-Dioulasso are open between 0830–1200 and 1500–1830, Monday to Saturday. There is no local delivery of mail in Upper Volta; all mail must be addressed with a post office box (*boîte postale*) number. All mail, to and from Upper Volta, should be sent by air.

7. Public Holidays
1 January	New Year's Day
3 January	Anniversary of the Revolution
1 May	May Day
15 August	Assumption
1 November	All Saints Day
11 December	Republic Day
25 December	Christmas Day

The following Muslim and Christians holidays are also observed: *Mouled*, *Eid el Fitr*, *Eid el Kabir*, *Easter Monday*, *Ascension Day* and *Whit Monday*.

8. Time
GMT.

9. Internal Transport

Air
Air Volta operates regular services from Ouagadougou to Bobo-Dioulasso and Tambao. UTA and Air Afrique also connect Ouagadougou and Bobo-

UPPER VOLTA

Dioulasso. Air taxi services are also available.

Airline Offices in Ouagadougou
Air Afrique ☎ 32438.
Air France ☎ 33387.
UTA ☎ 32216.
Air Volta ☎ 36155.

Road
Cheap taxis are available in Ouagadougou and Bobo-Dioulasso.

Self-drive cars are available for hire in Ouagadougou. A foreign licence or International Driving Licence is required.

Car-Hire Firms in Ouagadougou
Volta Auto
  Location ☎ 32720.
  Location Desplat ☎ 32219.

10. Tipping
Taxis – 10% of the fare.

Porters – 50 CFA francs per bag.

Hotels/restaurants – a service charge of 10–15% is usually added to the bill. It is customary to give a tip of 100 CFA francs to hotel room staff on departure.

11. Social Customs
It is essential to have a good working knowledge of the French language when visiting Upper Volta, as French is used exclusively in Government and business circles and English is rarely understood. French customs and manners predominate in the business and social life of the major towns; in the Muslim areas of the west and north, the usual Muslim protocol applies.

USEFUL ADDRESSES (GENERAL)

Office of the Canadian Embassy, B.P. 548, Ouagadougou, ☎ 32093.

Dutch Consulate, B.P. 379, Ouagadougou, ☎ 35206/7/8.

French Embassy, B.P. 504, Avenue de l'Indépendance, Ouagadougou, ☎ 32270/1/2.

US Embassy, B.P. 35, Ouagadougou, ☎ 35442/4/6.

West German Embassy, B.P. 600, Ouagadougou, ☎ 36094.

Office du Tourisme de la Haute Volta, B.P. 624, Ouagadougou, ☎ 32801.

BUSINESS INFORMATION

Large-scale foreign aid is necessary for virtually all development and there is still a relatively low level of commercial activity. France has retained considerable control of the economy since independence, and most companies are at least partly owned by French interests. Foreign investment is encouraged with generous incentives to promote the development of manufacturing industries, but nationals must own a majority of the shares in large or 'essential' enterprises.

As with its francophone neighbours, there is a natural orientation in Upper Volta towards French sources of supply. Most of the established French export and import companies have their headquarters and purchasing organisations in Paris. In general, most importers deal with a wide variety of goods and often act in a number of trading capacities. Commercial practice is based on the French commercial code. In addition to a visit to Upper Volta, foreign suppliers may find it advantageous to visit the headquarters or buying agencies of local firms either in Paris or elsewhere outside Upper Volta.

Import and Exchange Control Regulations
In general, all imports from countries outside the Franc Zone are subject to import authorisation. Following the signing of the Lomé Convention, there are special regulations for imports into Upper Volta from EEC countries.

Exchange control applies to all currencies other than the CFA franc and the French franc. Foreign exchange is made available under 3 main headings: the EEC, Bilateral Trade Agreements and Global Quotas.

Business Hours
Government Offices
0800–1230 Monday to Friday
1500–1730
Closed all day Saturday.

Business Houses
0800–1200 Monday to Saturday
1500–1830

The best time to visit Upper Volta is between November and May so as to avoid the rainy season. Peak buying period is around the end of the year and the beginning of the new year.

BUSINESS SERVICES

Insurance
Société Nationale d'Assurance et de Reassurance (SONARE), B.P. 406, Ouagadougou.

Shipping
Société Voltaique des Transports Routiers, B.P. 34, Ouagadougou – road haulage.
La Régie du Chemin de Fer Abidjan-Niger, B.P. 192, Ouagadougou – railway transport.

USEFUL ADDRESSES (BUSINESS)

Chambre de Commerce, d'Industrie et d'Agriculture de la Haute Volta, B.P. 502, Ouagadougou.

Office National du Commerce Exterieur (ONAC), B.P. 389, Ouagadougou.

Syndicat des Commerçants, Importateurs et Exportateurs, B.P. 552, Ouagadougou.

Syndicat des Entrepreneurs et Industriels de Haute Volta, B.P. 446, Ouagadougou.

MAJOR CITY

Ouagadougou
The capital of the Mossi empire from the 15th century onwards, Ouagadougou is today a modern city of 150,000 people. Both the former Governor's Palace and the Palace of the Emperor of the Mossi are in the city centre, and there is an interesting Ethnographical Museum near by.

Several day excursions to the surrounding area are worthwhile, with wildlife on view in Sabou, 50km/31 miles from Ouagadougou, and Po National Park, 145km/90 miles to the south.

Hotels
The Government classifies hotels using the international stars system.

HÔTEL INDEPENDANCE, B.P. 127, ☎ 2721.
Modern 5-star hotel in city centre with spacious, landscaped grounds.
Rooms: 135 ♪, ⚜, ☎, △, ♂. Suites available.
Facilities: Restaurant, cocktail lounge, bar. Parking, car hire. Tennis, swimming, solarium, bowling. Travel agency, dresser.
Services: TC, FC. ☐ Amex, Diners Club. Dr. on call. S, ♂.
Conference room – max. capacity 50.
Banquet room – max. capacity 150.

RAN HOTEL, B.P. 62, ☎ 3240.
Traditional 4-star hotel in city centre.
Rooms: 34 ♪, △, ♂. Suites available.
Facilities: Restaurant, bar. Parking, car hire. Swimming.
Services: TC, FC. ☐ None accepted.
No conference facilities.

Restaurants
In addition to the hotel restaurants, there are the *Volta Bar*, *L'Eau Vive* (run by a Catholic lay order) and *Escale*.

Nightclubs
Chez Maurice, the *Volta Club* and *Le Cave*.

Entertainment
Swimming and tennis are available at the hotels or by invitation at the *Volta Club*. Riding is available at the *Club Hippique*. There are 2 open-air cinemas.

Shopping
Best buys: African souvenirs, wooden carvings, jewellery, fabrics, leather goods, which can be bargained for in the traditional market. Visitors can also choose among the wide range of well-finished goods produced by the local tannery.

ZAIRE
Republic of Zaïre

Geography	*467*
The Economy	*469*
How to Get There	*470*
Entry Regulations	*470*
Practical Information for the Visitor	*471*
Useful Addresses (General)	*473*
Business Information	*474*
Business Services	*475*
Useful Addresses (Business)	*475*
Kinshasa	*475*

Size: 2,345,409 sq.km/905,562 sq.miles.

Population: 27.75 million (1978 est.).

Density: 11 persons per sq.km/29 per sq.mile.

Distribution: 30% in urban areas.

Population Growth Rate: 2.8% p.a.

Ethnic Composition: Some 200 tribal groups make up the population of Zaïre. The principal ones are the Bantu, Sudanese, Nilotics, Pygmies and Hamites. The non-African population numbers around 82,000, the largest foreign community being Belgian.

Capital: Kinshasa Pop. 2,443,876 (1976).

Major Cities/Towns: Kanaga Pop. 704,211; Lubumbashi Pop. 451,332; Mbuji-Mayi Pop. 382,000; Kisangani Pop. 339,210.

Language: French is the official language. A large number of other languages and dialects are spoken throughout Zaïre, of which Lingala, Tshiluba, Kikongo, Swahili and Kingwana are the most common.

Religion: About 50% adhere to traditional beliefs and practices, especially Animism. The remainder are mostly Christian (75% Roman Catholic), and there are a small number of Muslims.

Government: The Republic of Zaïre gained independence in 1960. The President is elected for a 7-year term of office and the single-chamber parliament, the National Legislative Council, is elected for 5 years. Real power lies with President Mobutu as head of the Political Bureau of Zaïre's only political party, the Mouvement Populaire de la Révolution (MPR).

GEOGRAPHY

Zaïre is a country of widely contrasting geographical features. A vast tropical rain forest basin covers much of the west and centre, and is drained by the River Zaïre which flows out into the Atlantic – the narrow strip of land north of the estuary being the only outlet to the sea. The east is an area of high mountains and lakes, with intervening rift valleys containing much of the country's fertile farmland. The southern province of Shaba consists of plateaux merging with savannah, while the north-west is an area of dense grasslands.

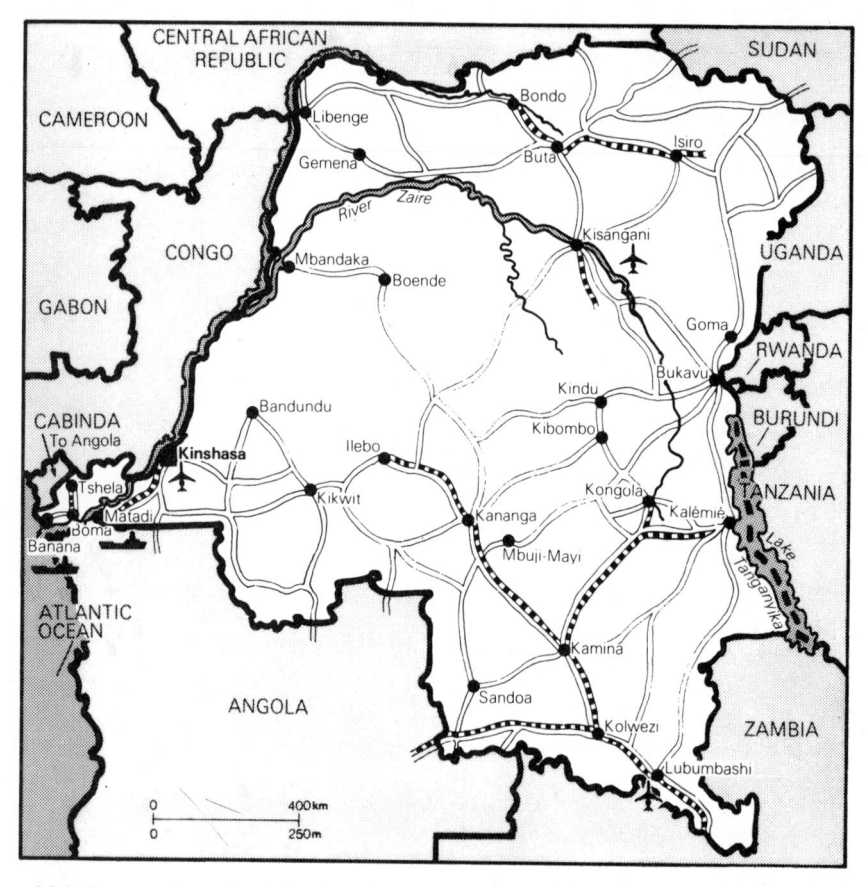

Climate
The western and central parts have an equatorial climate (hot and humid), with temperatures ranging between 20°C/68°F and 30°C/86°F. The higher areas of the east and south-east have a cooler climate, with temperatures ranging from 15°C/59°F to 25°C/77°F.

The principal rainy seasons are from October to April in the south and south-east; from October to May in the south-west (including Kinshasa); and from April to June and September to October in the north.

The best time to visit areas south of the equator is from June to September, and areas north of the equator November to March.

Agriculture
About 80% of the population is engaged in agriculure, much of it subsistence farming.

The country has enormous agricultural potential, but this sector of the economy has suffered from a severe lack of incentive, inadequate transport and marketing facilities, and the enormous political and economic upheavals which have occurred in Zaïre since independence in 1960. Less than 10% of the available land is under cultivation, necessitating the importation of large amounts of food. Of the important export crops, only cotton has shown a noticeable improvement in the 1970s. Production of both palm products and rubber has steadily declined; that of coffee, tea and cocoa has remained static.

With the announcement of financial reform at the end of 1977, President Mobutu declared agriculture a priority, and foreign aid and assistance are being employed with the aim of improving production methods and developing the necessary aids to effective marketing (e.g. transport).

Main Crops: cassava, plantain, palm products, sugar-cane, rice, citrus fruits, pineapples, coffee, bananas, rubber, cotton seed, vegetables, tea, cocoa.

Mineral Resources: copper, cobalt, industrial diamonds, coal, gold, manganese, crude petroleum, silver, zinc, cadmium, tungsten, cassiterite, uranium.

THE ECONOMY

Gross National Product (1978 est.): US$7.3 billion.

Per Capita Income (1978 est.): US$223.

Gross Domestic Product (1978 est.): US$9.1 billion.

Foreign Trade (1978): Total Imports – US$1.31 billion. Total Exports – US$1.61 billion.

Main Trading Partners: Imports – Belgium/Luxembourg, France, US, Canada, West Germany, Netherlands, Italy. Exports – Belgium/Luxembourg, US, Canada, Italy, France, Japan, West Germany, United Kingdom.

Zaïre is a country of enormous mineral wealth. It is one of the world's principal copper producers, exports some 80% of the world's cobalt production and has substantial reserves of industrial diamonds, platinum, uranium, tin, zinc and silver. Despite this wealth and because of it, Zaïre is one of the most heavily indebted countries in the world.

Political problems combined with the lack of administrative skills and organisation created enormous problems for the country's economy since independence in 1960. The secession of the mineral-rich province of Katanga (Shaba) contributed to a dramatic decline in production, and it was not until 1966 that domestic production returned to its 1959 level. Since then, the economy has suffered from a succession of contradictory Government policies. In 1973 President Mobutu introduced a policy of 'Zaïreanisation', the nationalisation of plantation companies, local shipping and the Belgian mining company MIBA – this policy was later extended to all significant importing, exporting, foreign-owned trading and wholesaling businesses. The policy foundered because of a lack of funds and expertise in the private sector and was reversed at the end of 1975, though businesses that were returned to foreign owners were required to sell off 40% of their holdings to Zaïrians.

ZAÏRE

In March 1976 President Mobutu announced a 42% devaluation. Inflation was running very high and has worsened since then. Several political factors have contributed to the problems since 1975. The troubles in Angola have closed the Benguela railway, which linked Shaba province with the Angolan port of Lobito, and satisfactory rerouting of exports has not yet been achieved. The invasions of Shaba province by Katangan dissidents in 1977 and 1978 have badly hit copper production, and the increase in oil prices and the collapse of copper prices have left Zaïre, which has had little trouble raising loans in view of its mineral wealth, with an appalling financial deficit.

At the end of 1978 the International Monetary Fund, together with a consortium of Western financiers representing Zaïre's creditors, presented the third IMF plan for Zaïrian stabilisation since 1975. This plan, which has been agreed to in principle by President Mobutu, requires strong IMF involvement in Zaïre's financial affairs, and its satisfactory progress is a prerequisite for further aid from Western countries. At present, however, manufacturing output and agricultural production continue to decline, and although cobalt, which is being exported by air, is fetching high prices, the level of export receipts remains disappointing and is contributing to a low level of imports and continuing inflation problems.

Major Industries: food processing, vegetable oil extraction, textiles, cotton processing, steel rolling, tobacco and wood processing, sulphuric acid and cement production.

Main Commodities Traded: Imports – consumer goods, food, chemicals, construction materials, transport equipment, machinery, petroleum products. Exports – copper, cobalt, diamonds, zinc, coffee, palm products, tin, gold, rubber, timber, cotton, cocoa, tea.

International Affiliations: UN, IBRD, OAU, ACP, ADB, CEPGL, KRBO.

HOW TO GET THERE

Air

Air Zaïre operates direct flights to Kinshasa from Athens, Brussels, Frankfurt, Geneva, London, Madrid, Paris and Rome. Other airlines operating flights from Europe include Alitalia, Iberia, Lufthansa, Sabena, Swissair, TAP and UTA.

Within Africa there are direct links between Kinshasa and Abidjan, Dakar, Dar es Salaam, Entebbe, Lagos, Libreville, Lomé, Luanda and Nairobi.

Flying times to Kinshasa: from London, 12 hours; from New York, 17 hours; from Sydney, 27 hours.

The main airport is N'djili International Airport, 29km/16 miles from Kinshasa. Transport to and from the airport is provided by Air Zaïre. Taxis are also available, although these tend to be very expensive.

ENTRY REGULATIONS

Visas

Visas are required by nationals of all countries and should be obtained before departure from the nearest embassy or consulate of the Republic of Zaïre. All visitors should be in possession of a valid passport and should ensure that the validity of their passport extends for at least 3 months beyond the date of issue of the visa.

Business visitors should support their visa application with a letter from their firm giving details of the business to be undertaken and confirming financial responsibility for the applicant. A letter from a travel agent or airline is also required, giving details of the booking together with a letter from the organisation to be visited in Zaïre confirming the arrangements. 3 photographs are also required.

The validity of a visa ranges from 3 to 6 months for a stay which varies according to requirements. Applications for a visa should be made at least 4 weeks before the proposed date of departure for Zaïre.

Transit visas are issued at the point of entry on presentation of the relevant entry documents for the country of destination. A transit visa is valid for up to 8 days.

Health Regulations

Valid International Certificates of Vaccination against smallpox, yellow fever and cholera are required by all persons entering Zaïre.

Customs

Currency: The import and export of local currency are strictly prohibited. There is no limit to the amount of foreign currency which may be imported or exported, but all foreign currency must be declared on arrival and Form DM1 of the National Bank must be completed. All exchange transactions should be entered on this form, which must be presented to the bank authorities on departure.

Duty-free articles: Personal effects. 200 cigarettes. 1 bottle of spirits. Samples of no commercial value.

Articles liable to duty: A cash deposit for the duty increased by 25% is required for samples of commercial value. Visitors may experience some difficulty in reclaiming the deposit on re-export of the samples.

PRACTICAL INFORMATION FOR THE VISITOR

1. Currency

Monetary Unit – zaïre (Z), divided into 100 makuta. (The singular of makuta is likuta; 1 likuta = 100 sengi.)
Notes – 10, 20, 50 makuta; 1, 5, 10 zaïres.
Coins – 10 sengi, 1 likuta, 5 makuta.

The *Banque de Zaïre,* B.P. 2697, Kinshasa, ☎ 30681, 30690, 30761, is the central bank and bank of issue.

Major Domestic Banks in Kinshasa

Banque Commerciale Zaïroise, Boulevard du 30 Juin, B.P. 2798, ☎ 26401/4.
Union Zaïroise de Banques, 19 Avenue de la Nation et des Aviateurs, B.P. 197, ☎ 25801/5.
Banque du Peuple, Boulevard du 30 Juin, B.P. 8822, ☎ 24204/5.
Banque de Kinshasa, Avenue Tombalbaye, Place du Marché, B.P. 8033, ☎ 25948/9.

Foreign Commercial Banks in Kinshasa

Banque de Paris et des Pays Bas, Immeuble Unibra, Avenue Colonel Ebeia, B.P. 1600, Kinshasa, ☎ 24745/7.
Barclays Bank Zaïre, 191 Avenue de l'Equateur, B.P. 1299, Kinshasa, ☎ 22536/22578/25777/21113.

ZAÏRE

Citibank, Centre de Commerce Internationale, Avenue Colonel Tshatshi, B.P. 9999, ☎ 32151, 23056, 32021.

2. Electricity Supply
220v AC 50Hz.

3. Weights and Measures
The metric system is in use.

4. Media
Zaïre Television is the Government-owned commercial television station. The Government-owned radio network, La Voix du Zaïre, broadcasts in French, Swahili, Lingala, Tshiluba and Kikongo.

Newspapers and Journals
Dailies: *Elima* (evening); *Le Courrier d'Afrique*; *MJUMBE*; Salongo. Epanza, Horizons 80, Taifa and *Zaïre* are published weekly. The official *Zaïre Magazine* is a fortnightly publication. *Cahiers Economiques et Sociaux* is a quarterly political and economic review.
Zaïre has no established trade press.

5. Medical Care
Tap water is not safe to drink unless it has been boiled and filtered; bottled mineral water is readily available. Avoid having ice cubes in drinks, especially outside Kinshasa. Care should also be taken with uncooked vegetables and unwashed salads and fruit.
Malaria is prevalent in many areas, and visitors are advised to take antimalarial prophylactics. Typhoid is another health hazard and it is advisable to have a TAB (typhoid and paratyphoid) inoculation. Avoid swimming in rivers and lakes because of the risk of bilharzia.
Medical services are adequate with relatively modern hospital facilities in the large cities and towns.

Medical Facilities in Kinshasa
Centre Medical de Kinshasa, Avenue des Wagenias, ☎ 23156/7.
Clinique de Ngaliema, Avenue des Cliniques, ☎ 30315/7.

Service Médical de la Présidence de la République, Mont Ngaliema, ☎ 59700/59644.

6. Telephone, Telex and Postal Services
Internal telephone services to tend to be unreliable, and international calls are often subject to lengthy delays.
Telex facilities are available in Kinshasa at the main post office and the Inter-Continental Hotel, and in Lubumbashi.
External postal services are fairly reliable, although the internal services are subject to delays. All mail to and from Zaïre should be despatched by air.

7. Public Holidays

1 January	New Year's Day
4 January	Martyrs of Independence
1 May	Labour Day
20 May	Anniversary of the MPR (Mouvement Populaire de la Révolution)
24 June	Promulgation of the Constitution
30 June	Independence Day
1 August	Parents' Day
27 October	Anniversary of Zaïre
17 November	National Army Day
24 November	Anniversary of the Regime

8. Time
GMT + 2, with the exception of the western provinces of Equateur and Bas-Zaïre, where local time is GMT + 1.

9. Internal Transport

Air
Air Zaïre operates regular services from N'djili International Airport (Kinshasa) to Lubumbashi, Bukavu, Boma, Mbuji-Mayi, Kisangani, Bandundu and other main towns. Air charter facilities are available at N'Dolo Airport just outside the centre of Kinshasa.

Passengers on internal flights in Zaïre are required to go through customs, immigration and health controls.

Airline Offices in Kinshasa

Air France/ UTA	☎ 25077.
Air Zaïre	☎ 24985/9.
British Caledonian	☎ 25651/6.
Iberia	☎ 22574.
Lufthansa	☎ 25233, 25290.
Pan Am	☎ 23371/2.
Sabena	☎ 25651.
Swissair	☎ 24682/3.

Rail

The main railway line runs from Lubumbashi northwards to Ilebo, with a branch line from Kamina to Kalémié on the shores of Lake Tanganyika. Kinshasa is connected by rail to the port of Matadi on the Atlantic Coast.

A number of river and lake car-ferry services link up with the main railway services, although the time taken to complete the journey is prohibitive for most business travellers. From Kinshasa to Kisangani takes 7 days; and to Ilebo 5 days. A much quicker boat service connects Bukavu and Boma across Lake Kivu, taking approximately 5 hours.

Road

Road conditions are poor with the exception of a handful of roads linking the main centres: Kinshasa/Matadi Road; Lubumbashi/Ndola (Zambia) Road; Lubumbashi/Kolwezi Road, serving the Copperbelt; Kisangani/Mambasa Road in eastern Zaïre.

Taxis are plentiful in the main towns; it is important to agree upon the fare before starting the journey.

Self-drive and chauffeur-driven cars are available for hire in the principal towns. An International Driving Licence is required. Traffic travels on the right-hand side of the road.

Car-Hire Firms in Kinshasa

Autoloc	☎ 23322.
Avis	☎ 31800 (Inter-Continental Hotel).
Hertz	☎ 32079, 32121.

10. Tipping

The standard tip given in Zaïre is 10% of the bill or fare. For small services a tip of 50 makuta is normally sufficient.

11. Social Customs

When addressing Zaïrians, it is important to use the title *Citoyen* for men and *Citoyenne* for women.

Most business is conducted in French and visitors to the country should have a good working knowledge of the language.

N.B. Kinshasa has a reputation for being a violent city and it is generally considered unsafe to wander about alone at night. Pickpockets are plentiful, particularly in the area of the main shops and hotels; visitors should keep a close watch on their personal belonging at all times.

Anyone encountering difficulties with the Zaïrian authorities should contact their nearest embassy or consulate. Passports should not be surrendered without first obtaining an official receipt.

USEFUL ADDRESSES (GENERAL)

Kinshasa

British Embassy: Barclays Bank International Building, 5th Floor, 9 Avenue de l'Equateur, B.P. 8049, ☎ 23483/6 and 23280.

Canadian Embassy: Edifice Shell, corner of Avenue Wangata and Boulevard du 30 Juin, B.P. 8341, ☎ 22706, 24346.

Dutch Embassy: Avenue Zongo Ntolo 11, B.P. 10299, Gombe, ☎ 30638, 30733.

French Embassy: 97 Avenue de la République du Tchad, B.P. 3093.

Japanese Embassy: Avenue Mbuji-May 3668, Gombe, B.P. 1810, ☎ 26913, 22118.

US Embassy: 310 Avenue des Aviateurs, B.P. 697, ☎ 25881/6.

West German Embassy: Résidence Le Flambeau, 10ème étage, 201 Avenue Lumpungu, B.P. 8400, ☎ 26933/4.

British Council: c/o British Embassy, 9 Avenue de l'Equateur, B.P. 8049, ☎ 23483/6.

Centre Culturel Du Zaïre: Balari No. 20, Bandalungwa, Kinshasa.

National Office for Tourism: Boulevard du 30 Juin, B.P. 9502, Kinshasa, ☎ 22417.

Other Addresses

British Consular Correspondent: c/o Barclays Bank Zaïre, 743 Avenue Marna Yeno, B.P. 2098 Lubumbashi, ☎ 5315.

British Consular Correspondent: c/o Sagrin, 26 Avenue de la Corniche, B.P. 190, Goma.

Wagons-Lits Tourisme Authorised Representative: Agence Maritime Internationale SA, Avenue des Aviateurs, B.P. 7597, Kinshasa, ☎ 24602, 23083; Avenue President Mobuto, B.P. 372, Goma, ☎ 514; Avenue Kasai, 781, B.P. 1047, Lubumbashi, ☎ 3101, 3107; Rue de la Poste 6, B.P. 264, Matadi, ☎ 2602/7.

BUSINESS INFORMATION

Any company operating in Zaïre for more than 5 years must have a Zaïrian chairman and managing director, and must observe the restrictions on the number of foreign personnel it can employ. Foreign companies may be expected to provide management training programmes for Zaïrian employees.

It is advisable, depending on the nature and scope of the business involved, to appoint an agent in Kinshasa or Lubumbashi; however, careful supervision through personal visits is very important, due to administrative and transportation problems. Certain sectors of commercial trade (importing, wholesaling, retailing, etc.) are reserved for Zaïrians, though exemptions are sometimes granted. There is a state monopoly on mining, energy, transport and forestry, but joint ventures with foreign companies in these areas are possible.

All business documentation and trade literature must be produced in French.

Import and Exchange Control Regulations

Essential goods (basic foodstuffs, pharmaceuticals, etc.) do not require import licences, but their import must have a banker's approval. All other goods require import licences, and Bank of Zaïre authorisation is required for goods which may compete with local industry. Special regulations cover the importation of arms, aircraft, transmitters, etc., as well as goods financed by foreign aid.

Suppliers are required to grant minimum credit terms of 90 or 180 days, depending on the nature of the goods. Freedom to repatriate capital and profits is guaranteed;

given the present economic climate, however, considerable delays are likely in any foreign exchange transactions.

Business Hours
Government Offices
0730–1330 Monday to Friday
0730–1200 Saturday

Business Houses
0730–1200 Monday to Friday
1430–1700
0730–1200 Saturday

Business Events
The Kinshasa International Trade Fair is held each year in July. For further information, contact: Foire Internationale de Kinshasa, B.P. 1397, Kinshasa.

BUSINESS SERVICES

Insurance
All foreign insurance companies were closed down in 1966.

Société Nationale d'Assurances (SONAS), Kinshasa.

Shipping
Compagnie Maritime Zaïroise SARL, B.P. 9496, Kinshasa – services to Antwerp and USA, and from Mediterranean ports to West Africa.

The *Compagnie Maritime Belge* operates a fortnightly cargo service from Antwerp to Matadi; *Elder Dempster Lines* and the *Palm Line* run cargo services to Zaïre.

USEFUL ADDRESSES (BUSINESS)

Association Nationale des Entreprises Zaïroises (ANEZA): 10 Avenue des Aviateurs, B.P. 7247, Kinshasa, ☎ 22565.

ANEZA HAUT-ZAIRE: B.P. 1407, Kisangani.

ANEZA KASAI-OCCIDENTAL: B.P. 194, Kananga.

ANEZA-SHABA: B.P. 1500, Lubumbashi.

MAJOR CITY

Kinshasa
Kinshasa, formerly Leopoldville, is the administrative and commercial centre of Zaïre. As with many African capitals, there is a clear division between the commercial area and the African workers' township, La Cité. The Government and business elite live in the spacious, hilly, residential area; near by, Mount Ngaliema has an elaborate presidential park with gardens open to the public, as well as the village and recreation grounds built for the OAU summit meeting in 1967.

ZAÏRE

Kinshasa National University has a Museum of African Culture and a geological museum. N'Sele, the President's experimental farm, is a short drive or boat ride away, Brazzaville (Congo) is an hour-long ferry trip across the Malebo Pool (a visa is required to enter the town). There are also public boats available for a full day's fishing and swimming excursion on the Pool.

Hotels

There is no official hotel rating system.

INTER-CONTINENTAL KINSHASA, Avenue des Batetela, B.P. 9529, ☎ 31800.
Modern de luxe hotel a few minutes' walk from the commercial centre of Kinshasa.
Rooms: 260 ✻, △, ◘.
Facilities: Restaurant, rooftop supper club, bar, cocktail lounge, poolside snack bar. Swimming, tennis, squash, health club. Shops, bank. Car hire.
Services: TC, FC. ☱ Amex, Carte Blanche, Diners Club, Master Charge. Dr. on call. Audio-visual equipment. Conference room – max. capacity 600. Banquet rooms – max. capacity 400.

MEMLING, 5D Avenue de la République de Tchad, B.P. 68, ☎ 23260/5.
Modern 1st-class hotel in city centre, overlooking River Zaïre.
Rooms: 212 ☎.
Facilities: Restaurant, bar.
Conference room – max. capacity 50.
Banquet room – max. capacity 40.

OKAPI, Zone de Gahema/Binza, B.P. 8697, ☎ 81444, 80222.
Modern 1st-class hotel in parkland, overlooking Kinshasa.
Rooms: 100 ✻, ☎.
Facilites: Restaurant, bar, cocktail lounge. Nightclub. Swimming.
Services: ☱ Amex, Carte Blanche, Diners Club.

Restaurants

Kinshasa offers a good selection of restaurants, but, as with most other things in the country, dining out is expensive.

La Devinière, Route de Binza, ☎ 81571; *La Raquette,* World Trade Centre, ☎ 32930; *Le Mandarin,* Immeuble INSS, 7ème étage, Boulevard du 30 Juin, ☎ 22068 – Chinese; *Restaurant du Zoo,* Avenue Kasavuby, ☎ 23395; *Chez Nicola,* Avenue de l'Ouganda, ☎ 30253 – Iranian; *La Pergola,* 16 Avenue du Bas – Zaïre, ☎ 23313; *La Terrasse,* Immeuble Sozacom, Boulevard du 30 Juin, ☎ 23763; *L'Esquinade,* 58 Avenue du Flambeau, ☎ 24733.

Nightclubs

Kinshasa's nightlife is varied and lively. The city has several good casinos – the *Kin Casino, Olympic* and *Casino National* – and nightclubs, among the more popular of which are: *Les Anges Noirs; Baninga; L'Etoile,* Hotel Inter-Continental, ☎ 31800; *Safari,* Binza; *VIP,* Avenue de la Mongala, ☎ 23283; *Chez Cara; Vatican.*

Entertainment

Kinshasa has a number of both air-conditioned and open-air cinemas showing recent films, mostly in French. There are good sporting facilities within the city and at the Organisation of African Unity village at Mount Ngaliema. Tennis can be played at the *Cercle de Kin, Familia Club, Athenée* and the *Funa* and *OAU* sports centres. The *Centre Hippique de Kin* and *L'Etrier* offer riding facilities, and sailing can be arranged through Kinshasa's 2 sailing clubs – the *Nautic Club of Kin* and the *Yacht Club.*

Shopping

Best buys: ivory and ebony carvings; crocodile and snakeskin bags, shoes, belts, etc., semi-precious stones.

A small souvenir market is situated near the Memling Hotel in the Avenue de la République du Tchad, and there are numerous curio shops on the main streets of the city.

ZAMBIA
Republic of Zambia

Geography	477
The Economy	479
How to Get There	480
Entry Regulations	480
Practical Information for the Visitor	481
Useful Addresses (General)	484
Business Information	484
Business Serivces	485
Useful Addresses (Business)	485
Lusaka	486
The Copperbelt	487

Size: 752,614 sq.km/290,586 sq.miles.

Population: 5.47 million (1978 est.).

Distribution: 40% in urban areas.

Density: 7 persons per sq.km/18 per sq. mile.

Population Growth Rate: 3.2% p.a.

Ethnic Composition: There are more than 50 different ethnic groups, the majority of which are Bantu-speaking tribes. The largest single group is the Tonga in the south. The non-African population numbers around 50,000.

Capital: Lusaka Pop. 520,000.

Major Cities/Towns: Ndola Pop. 350,000; Kitwe Pop. 295,100; Chingola Pop. 181,500.

Language: English is the official language. More than 70 different African languages and dialects are spoken, but 5 principal languages are used for educational and administrative purposes: Nyanja, Bemba, Lozi, Luvale and Tonga.

Religion: The majority of the African population adhere to traditional beliefs. The Christian community numbers around 700,000, and there are small groups of Hindus and Muslims.

Government: Zambia became an independent republic within the British Commonwealth in 1964. The President and National Assembly are elected by universal suffrage. However, the National Assembly has no powers to initiate or veto legislation.

The United National Independence Party (UNIP) is the only legal political party, and the party's Central Committee is the main policy-making body.

GEOGRAPHY

Zambia is a landlocked country situated in south-central Africa. The majority of the land area consists of a high plateau of savannah lying between 1,066m/3,500ft and

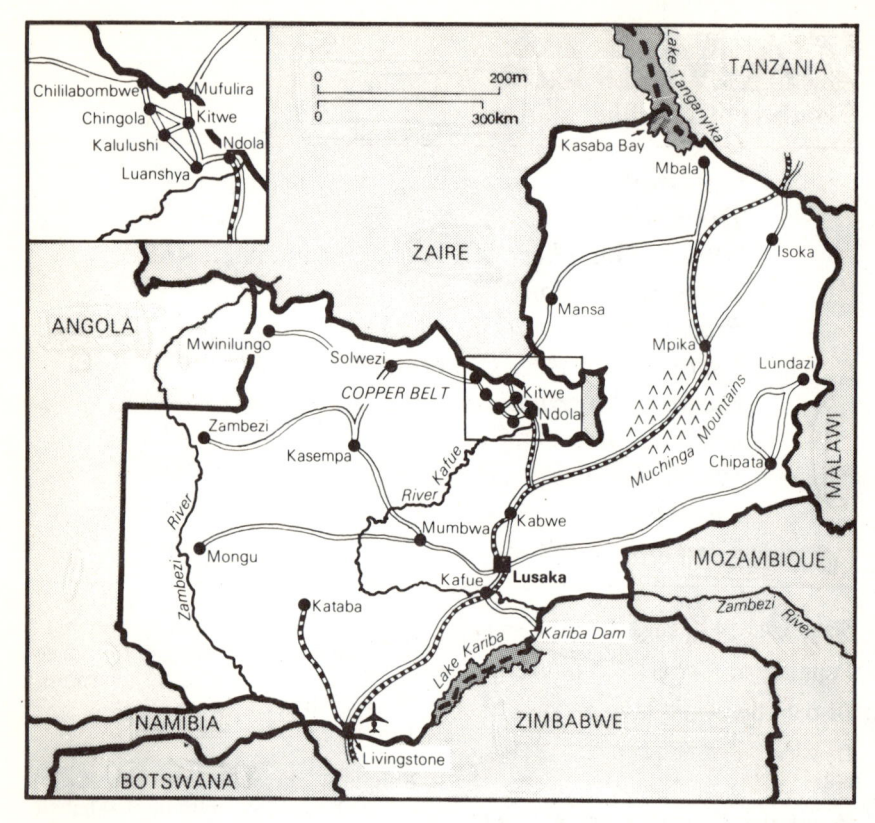

1,370m/4,500ft above sea level. In the northeast are the Muchinga Mountains, rising to a height of more than 2,130m/7,000ft. The Zambezi River marks the western frontier of Zambia, where there is a broad, fertile flood-plain.

Climate
Zambia lies within the tropics, but the elevated position of much of the country ensures that temperatures are seldom unpleasantly hot. The 3 main seasons are the cool, dry winter season (May to August), the hot, dry months of September, October and November, and the rainy season which lasts from November to April.

Average temperatures in Lusaka range from 31°c/88°F in October to 10°c/50°F in June with slightly lower temperatures on the Copperbelt. Rainfall is highest in the north, decreasing southwards.

The period from May to August is the best time to visit.

Agriculture
Zambia's agricultural potential is large, but recent attempts to increase production have been relatively unsuccessful. Large amounts of food are imported, while agricultural exports account for little more than 1% of total exports.

Maize and tobacco are the principal export crops, although tobacco production has gradually declined since independence in 1964, together with dairy and beef production.

Investment in agriculture has been largely inadequate despite significant amounts of foreign aid, although the 3rd National Development Plan (1979–84) allows for more resources to be allocated to the agricultural sector with the aim of increasing the productivity of the small and medium-scale farmers. A number of obstacles still remain in the path of agricultural development; there is a serious shortage of agricultural advisers and basic equipment, and the road system in many rural areas is still inadequate.

Expatriate farmers in Zambia produce more than half of the country's marketable produce, although price controls and shortages of equipment have led to a sharp decline in some agricultural production, particularly in the private farming sector.

Main Crops: tobacco, maize, groundnuts, cotton, sugar-cane.

Mineral Resources: copper, cobalt, lead, zinc, iron ore, coal.

THE ECONOMY

Gross National Product (1978): US$2.71 billion.

Per Capita Income (1978): US$480.

Gross Domestic Product (1978): 2.29 billion kwacha.

Foreign Trade (1978): Total Imports – US$621 million. Total Exports – US$828 million.

Main Trading Partners: Imports – UK, West Germany, USA, South Africa, Japan. Exports – Japan, UK, West Germany, USA.

The Zambian economy is dominated by the copper mining industry, which is 51% Government-owned and accounts for more than 90% of the country's foreign exchange earnings. Government interest in the mines is controlled by the Zambia Industrial and Mining Corporation Ltd (ZIMCO); the 2 operating companies involved are Nchanga Consolidated Copper Mines and Roan Consolidated Mines.

Following a series of reforms introduced between 1968 and 1972, the Government acquired a majority shareholding (51%) not only in the country's mines but in many commercial and industrial concerns, and today state-owned companies dominate the economy. The Industrial Development Corporation of Zambia Ltd (INDECO) is the Government holding company for state participation in industry and also acts as a development corporation while the State Finance and Development Corporation Ltd (FINDECO) controls state participation in banking, insurance and building societies.

The prolonged downward trend of copper prices since 1975 has seriously damaged Zambia's economy and resulted in a drastic fall in Government mineral revenues. The industry faces additional problems with the ever-increasing operating costs in the mines, declining ore grades and a shortage of technically skilled mineworkers. The shortage of expatriate staff in the mines has further damaged the industry.

The serious nature of the mining industry's problems, together with the continued slump in copper prices, have pinpointed the need for a greater diversification of Zambia's economy, with a new emphasis on the manufacturing industries and agriculture. In 1977 the country's economic crisis came to a head, and President Kaunda outlined a new economic policy designed to free Zambia from her dependence on copper. Increased agricultural production, reduction of staff in the public sector, a rural resettlement programme, reorganisation of state-owned companies and encouragement of local and international investment were major factors in the new economic policy. This was followed by a harsh budget in 1978 with large cuts in Government subsidies and capital and recurrent spending. Almost US$400 million was obtained in credit from the IMF in return for certain conditions, and further loans have been obtained from the United States and Britain.

The situation in Zimbabwe (formerly Rhodesia) has further contributed to Zambia's economic crisis and the settlement there should go some way towards easing some of the country's problems. The cost to Zambia of applying UN economic sanctions was enormous, but more serious damage was inflicted by the closure of the Rhodesian (Zimbabwe) border from 1973 to the beginning of 1980. Nearly all Zambia's copper and two-thirds of the country's imports were carried by Rhodesia Railways linking landlocked Zambia with the port of Beira in Mozambique. The Tanzania–Zambia Railway linked to the port of Dar es Salaam should eventually be capable of handling most of Zambia's copper exports and imports, although initial problems have resulted in a backlog of both exports and imports.

Major Industries: mining, food processing, textiles, furniture, construction materials.

Main Commodities Traded: Imports – machinery and transport equipment, petroleum products, manufactures, chemicals, foodstuffs. Exports – copper, lead, zinc, cobalt, tobacco. maize.

International Affiliations: UN, IBRD, OAU, ACP, ADB, Commonwealth.

HOW TO GET THERE

Air

Zambia Airways operate direct services to Lusaka from London and regular flights from Rome and Belgrade. Other international airlines flying to Lusaka include British Caledonian (London), Alitalia (Rome and Athens), UTA (Paris) and Lufthansa (Frankfurt). Daily flights are available to Nairobi from many European centres with regular connections to Lusaka.

Pan Am fly to Nairobi from New York with stopover connections to Lusaka.

Zambia Airways fly to Lusaka from Blantyre, Gaberone, Maputo (Mozambique), Port Louis (Mauritius), Dar es Salaam and Nairobi. There are no direct flights to Zambia from South Africa, Zimbabwe and Zaïre. Flights from South Africa are operative only via Malawi and Botswana.

Flying times to Lusaka: from London, 10 hours; from New York, 20 hours.

Lusaka International Airport is 26km/16 miles from the city centre. Taxis are readily available at the airport. A departure tax of K3 is payable by all passengers.

ENTRY REGULATIONS

Visas

Visas are required by nationals of all countries except the British Commonwealth and the Republic of Ireland, provided they are *not*: (i) persons ordinarily resident in South

Africa; (ii) entering Zambia from South Africa by road holding British passports; (iii) residents of Kenya, Uganda or Tanzania of Asian origin holding British passports.

Visas should be obtained from Zambia diplomatic missions abroad. A letter from a travel agent or airline is required giving details of bookings for the visit, and business travellers require a letter from their firm giving details of the business to be undertaken and confirming financial responsibility for the applicant.

Visas are valid for 3 months, usually for a stay of 30 days. Business visitors wishing to stay longer must obtain a work permit.

Nationals or residents of South Africa and those listed in (iii) above who wish to visit Zambia should apply directly to the Chief Immigration Officer, P.O. Box RW 300, Lusaka, allowing 4–6 weeks for their visa application to be processed.

Health Regulations

A valid International Certificate of Vaccination against smallpox is required by all persons entering Zambia. International Certificates of Vaccination against yellow fever and/or cholera are required by all persons arriving from infected areas. Air passengers are advised to be in possession of a yellow fever vaccination certificate in the event that their aircraft is unavoidably delayed in central Africa, where the disease is endemic.

Customs

Currency: The import and export of Zambian currency are prohibited. There is no limit to the amount of foreign currency which may be brought in, but this must be declared on arrival and the currency declaration form should be retained for inspection on departure. Up to the equivalent of K20 in foreign currency may be taken out of Zambia unless a receipt is produced to prove that the excess amount was originally imported.

Duty-free articles: Personal effects. 200 cigarettes or 450g of tobacco. 1 bottle of spirits.

Articles liable to duty: Duty on *bona fide* samples imported for the purpose of gaining orders is refunded if the samples are re-exported within 12 months. Business travellers should produce a list in duplicate to the Customs Authorities describing each sample in detail and showing its value and country of origin.

PRACTICAL INFORMATION FOR THE VISITOR

1. Currency

Monetary Unit – kwacha (K), divided into 100 ngwee.
Notes – 50 ngwee; 1, 2, 5, 10, 20 kwacha.
Coins – 1, 2, 5, 10, 20, 50 ngwee.

Visitors are advised to carry travellers' cheques in small denominations and to cash only a sufficient amount for current needs. All foreign exchange transactions must be endorsed by the commercial bank on the currency declaration form obtained on arrival.

A number of major credit cards are accepted by hotels in Zambia, although credit cards are not yet accepted in restaurants and shops.

Banking Hours

0815 – 1245 Monday, Tuesday, Wednesday, Friday
0815 – 1200 Thursday
0815 – 1100 Saturday

The *Bank of Zambia* is the central bank. The *State Finance and Development Corporation* (FINDECO) is responsible for state participation in banking, investments, insurance, building societies and industrial financing interests.

All foreign-owned commercial banks were incorporated in Zambia in 1972.

Main Commercial Banks
National Savings and Credit Bank of Zambia, Cairo Road, P.O. Box 67, Lusaka.
Zambia National Commercial Bank Ltd, Cairo Road, P.O. Box 2811, Lusaka.
Barclays Bank of Zambia Ltd, Cairo Road, P.O. Box 1936, Lusaka, ☎ 75171.
Grindlays Bank International (Zambia) Ltd, Woodgate House, Cairo Road, P.O. Box 1955, Lusaka, ☎ 75135/9 – branches in Chingola, Kitwe, Ndola and Kabwe.
Standard Bank Zambia Ltd, Cairo Road, P.O. Box 1934, Lusaka, ☎ 75151/7; corner Zambia Way and Oxford Avenue, P.O. Box 61, Kitwe, ☎ 4472; Buteko Avenue, P.O. Box 1665, Ndola, ☎ 3994.

2. Electricity Supply
230v AC 50Hz.
Plugs: 3 square pins, 13 amp fused; older buildings may have 2- or 3-pin round plugs.

3. Weights and Measures
The metric system is in use.

4. Media
Radio and television are controlled by the Government-owned Zambia Broadcasting Services. There are 4 television channels available in Lusaka, Kabwe, Livingstone and the Copperbelt.

Radio Zambia has 2 channels broadcasting in English and 7 African languages.

There is a limited amount of commercial advertising on both television and radio.

Newspapers and Journals
The Times of Zambia and *Zambia Daily Mail* are the 2 daily papers. A number of African newspapers are published by the Government for distribution in various parts of the country.

The Mining Mirror is a joint fortnightly publication of Road Consolidated Mines and Nchanga Consolidated Copper Mines. *Imbila* is a monthly publication of the Zambia Information Services. Principal trade publications include *Productive Farming* (monthly), *Enterprise*, and the *Journal of the Engineering Institution of Zambia* (both quarterly).

5. Medical Care
Zambia has a relatively healthy climate, although there are some risks outside the main cities and towns. Outside Lusaka and the Copperbelt towns, malaria is endemic and visitors are advised to take anti-malarial prophylactics. Bilharzia is also endemic; paddling and swimming should be avoided in all water-courses and dams. Tap water is safe to drink in the towns.

Visitors intending to spend time in any of the game parks are advised to take suitable protective clothing and an effective insect repellent.

The main urban areas are served by well-run hospitals and clinics open to outpatients 7 days a week.

6. Telephone, Telex and Postal Services
An adequate international telephone service is available and calls can be made to Europe. There is a direct radio-telephone link with most East African countries.

Direct-dialling is available between the main towns and the Copperbelt and a trunk service links the majority of telephone exchanges across the country, although services are not always reliable.

There is a public telex machine at the General Post Office in Lusaka. The main hotels also have telex facilities.

Telegrams can be sent from telegraph

offices from 0730 – 1630 Mondays to Saturdays and 0900 – 1000 on Sundays and public holidays. The Central Lusaka Telegraph Office will accept urgent telegrams up to 2100 hours, Monday to Saturday.

Internal mail services are slow. There is no street delivery service, so all mail should be addressed with the Post Office Box number.

All mail to and from Zambia should be despatched by air. Valuable documents sent to Zambia should be registered or sent via an insured letter service.

7. Public Holidays

1 January	New Year's Day
1 May	Labour Day
25 May	African Freedom Day
1st Monday in July	Heroes' Day
1st Tuesday in July	Unity Day
24 October	Independence Day
25 December	Christmas

Good Friday and *Easter Saturday* are also public holidays. *Youth Day* is observed some time in March.

When a public holiday falls on a Sunday, it is observed on the following Monday.

8. Time
GMT + 2.

9. Internal Transport

Air
Zambia Airways operate daily flights between Lusaka and Livingstone and twice weekly from Lusaka to Kasaba Bay and Ndola. From May to October weekly flights are available to Mafue Lodge in the Luangwa Valley. Flights are also available to some of the game reserves from Lusaka and Livingstone.

Light aircraft can be chartered; bookings should be made well in advance.

Airline Offices in Lusaka

Air France/UTA	☎ 72124/5.
Air India	☎ 81086.
British Airways	☎ 73187/8.
British Caledonian	☎ 72800.
Lufthansa	☎ 81280, 81555.
SAS	☎ 74273.
Swissair	☎ 74301, 74901.
Zambia Airways	☎ 74301, 74901.

Rail
The Tanzania–Zambia Railway was opened in 1975. An overnight sleeper service is operated by Zambia Railways from Livingstone to the border with Zaïre, via Lusaka.

Road
Tarmac roads link Livingstone and Lusaka with the Copperbelt, and there are good-quality roads connecting the towns within the Copperbelt. The Great North Road to the Tanzanian border and the Great East Road to the Malawian border are also tarmac. During the rainy season (November to April) visitors should check on driving conditions and avoid earth or gravel roads.

Taxis are scarce in the main centres and visitors are usually overcharged unless they have some prior knowledge of the city or town.

A number of car-hire firms are in operation in the main centres. It is advisable to hire a car in Lusaka where many of the better hotels are some distance from the city centre. Chauffeur-driven cars are also available for hire. A driving licence from the visitor's country of residence is valid for 90 days.

Car-Hire Firms
Lusaka

Central African Motors (CAMS)	☎ 73181.
Ridgeway Car Hire Service	☎ 73968.
Streamline Car Hire Ltd	☎ 75728.

Ndola
Central African
  Motors
  (CAMS)   ☎ 3621.
Corner Taxi &
  Car Hire   ☎ 2469.

Kitwe
Central African
  Motors
  (CAMS)   ☎ 2390.

10. Tipping
Tipping in hotels and restaurants has been abolished by law, and replaced by a 10% service charge. A sales tax of 10% is also levied on all bills.

11. Social Customs
Since independence in 1964, social and business customs in Zambia have moved away from the South African modes and are similar to those in other black African countries.

Europeans and South Africans are usually referred to as 'expatriates' and members of the Indian and Muslim communities as 'Asians'. Zambians should be referred to as such, and not called Africans.

Most business entertaining by residents takes place at home or at clubs. Foreign visitors can usually obtain club membership through a personal introduction. Visitors will find it most convenient to entertain in their hotel or in a restaurant.

The practice of exchanging cards is customary in Zambia, so business travellers should have a good supply of visiting cards.

USEFUL ADDRESSES (GENERAL)

Lusaka
Dutch Embassy: United Nations Avenue 5028, P.O. Box 1095, ☎ 50468, 50945.

French Embassy: Unity House, Corner of Katunjila Road and Freedom Way, P.O. Box 62.

Japanese Embassy: Haile Selassie Avenue 5218, P.O. Box 3390, ☎ 52244, 52454.

US Embassy: Corner of Independence and United Nations Avenue, P.O. Box 1617, ☎ 50222.

West German Embassy: United Nations Avenue, Stand No. 5209, P.O. Box RW 120, ☎ 51899, 51913.

British High Commission: Independence Avenue, Stand No. 5210, P.O. Box RW 50, ☎ 51122.

Canadian High Commission: c/o Barclays Bank – North End Branch, Cairo Road, P.O. Box 1313, ☎ 75187/8.

Swiss Consulate: c/o Diesel Electric (Zambia) Ltd, 4791/2 Chifinga Road, P.O. Box 73, ☎ 75233/4.

Zambia National Tourist Board: Century House, Cairo Road, P.O. Box 17, ☎ 72891/5.

British Council: Heroes Place, Cairo Road, P.O. Box 3571, ☎ 75341/2.

BUSINESS INFORMATION

There are many different methods of selling to Zambia, which vary according to the commodity being sold and the nature of the purchasing organisation.

As in many other African countries, a local company may act simultaneously in the capacity of agent, wholesaler, retailer and distributor. Although some types of goods can be sold direct to the purchaser, it is preferable to appoint an agent. The majority of agents deal with a wide variety of goods, and specialisation is rare. It is worth noting that commissions are usually high due to the cost of living in Zambia and the large distances between major population centres.

It is inadvisable to appoint an agent in South Africa to cover the Zambian market. Similarly companies with subsidiary organisations in Zambia should ensure that the subsidiary is directly responsible to the parent company and not to a subsidiary operating in South Africa.

It is expected that the National Import and Export Corporation Ltd will eventually take responsibility for all importing and distribution activities in Zambia, though this is unlikely to take effect for a number of years. In the meantime, several of the state trading corporations dealing with a particular type of commodity, such as consumer goods, prefer to buy direct from the manufacturer without using the services of an agent. Most Government purchases are put out to tender by the Central Supply and Tender Board in Lusaka, although organisations such as Zambia Railways and the Agricultural Marketing Board publish their own calls for tender.

Import and Exchange Control Regulations

Import licensing regulations remain relatively strict in an effort to conserve foreign exchange reserves. A specific licence, obtainable from the Technical Committee of the Ministry of Commerce and Foreign Trade, is required for each shipment of goods.

Due to a shortage of foreign exchange, no payments for imported goods will be made without a valid import licence. Remittances are subject to lengthy delays.

Business Hours

Government Offices
0800 – 1300
1400 – 1700 Monday to Friday

Business Houses
0800 – 1230
1400 – 1630 Monday to Friday

BUSINESS SERVICES

Insurance
Zambia State Insurance Corporation Ltd, 1st Floor, Kafue House, Cairo Road, P.O. Box 894, Lusaka.

Road Transport
National Transport Corporation of Zambia Ltd, P.O. Box 2607, Lusaka.
Zambia-Tanzania Road Services, P.O. Box 2581, Lusaka.

USEFUL ADDRESSES (BUSINESS)

Chingola Chamber of Commerce and Industry, P.O. Box 722, Chingola, ☎ 2466, 2353.

Copper Industry Service Bureau Ltd, P.O. Box 2100, Kitwe – formerly Chamber of Mines.

Industrial Development Corporation of Zambia Ltd (INDECO), P.O. Box 1935, Lusaka.

Kabwe Chamber of Commerce and Industry, P.O. Box 132, Kabwe, ☎ 3773, 5301.

Kitwe and District Chamber of Commerce and Industry, Zambia State Insurance Building, Room 510, P.O. Box 672, Kitwe, ☎ 2723.

Livingstone Chamber of Commerce and Industry, P.O. Box 497, Livingstone.

Luanshya Chamber of Commerce and Industry, P.O. Box 164, Luanshya.

Lusaka Chamber of Commerce and Industry, P.O. Box 844, Lusaka, ☎ 81796.

Ministry of Commerce and Foreign Trade, Philips House, Cairo Road, P.O. Box 1968, Lusaka, ☎ 75195, 73676.

Ministry of Mines, Chilufya Mulenga Road, P.O. Box 1969, Lusaka, ☎ 53122.

National Import and Export Corporation, National Housing Authority Building, P.O. Box 283, Lusaka.

Ndola and District Chamber of Commerce and Industry, P.O. Box 6041, Ndola, ☎ 3026.

Zambia Industrial and Commercial Association, Ranchhod Building, Cha Cha Cha Road, P.O. Box 844, Lusaka, ☎ 81796, 81543.

Zambia Industrial and Mining Corporation (ZIMCO), P.O. Box 90, Lusaka.

MAJOR CITY AND TOWNS

Lusaka

Lusaka, the capital of Zambia, stretches out over a large area with no central focal point. The main shopping area is the Cairo Road where most of the banks, airline offices and commercial buildings are situated, while the principal administrative centre lies some 4km/2½ miles away.

There are several buildings and places of interest to the visitor, including the domed National Assembly building on the airport road, the Cathedral, the residence of the President and the Geological Survey Museum, which houses exhibits from Zambia's copper industry as well as a collection of the many gemstones to be found in Zambia such as garnets, emeralds and amethysts.

Other places of interest are the Munda Wanga Botanical Gardens and the Zambian Wildlife, Fisheries and National Parks Department at Chilanga. At the Cultural Village in Lusaka, visitors can see regular performances of traditional dancing and ceremonial rites.

Lusaka has an international conference hall, which is situated on the airport road near the National Assembly.

Hotels
The Tourist Board hotel classification ranges from 5 star to 1 star.

ANDREWS MOTEL, P.O. BOX 475, ☎ 74966.

Modern 3-star motel situated on main access road south of Lusaka, 8km/5 miles from city centre.
Rooms: 82 ♌, ♉, ♍. Suites available.
Facilities: Restaurants, bars. Entertainment. Swimming, tennis, mini-golf.

Drive-in cinema adjacent. Transport to airport and city centre.
Services: TC, FC, ▣ Amex, S, ♂.
Conference room – max. capacity 100.
Banquet rooms – max. capacity 100.

INTER-CONTINENTAL LUSAKA, Haile Selassie Avenue, P.O. Box 2201, ☎ 51000.
Modern de luxe (5-star) hotel in residential area of Lusaka, 5 minutes' drive from commercial and business district.
Rooms: 210 ♪, ●, ▭, ☎, ☗, ▽. Suites available.
Facilities: Rooftop restaurant, other restaurants, supper club, bars, cocktail lounge, coffee shop. Casino. Swimming, sauna. Shopping gallery.
Services: TC, FC. ▣ Amex, Bankamericard, Carte Blanche, Diners Club, Eurocard, Master Charge. Dr. on call.
Conference room – max. capacity 400.

RIDGEWAY, P.O. Box 666, ☎ 51699.
Modernised 1st-class (4-star) hotel near administrative centre, 24km/15 miles from airport.
Rooms: 130 ♪. Suites available.
Facilities: 2 restaurants, bars. Resident orchestra. Swimming, tennis. Airport bus.

Services: ▣ Amex, Diners Club.
Conference rooms and private dining room.

Restaurants
Apart from those in the main hotels, other restaurants include the *Fresco Restaurant, Woodpecker Inn, Kudu Inn*, and the *Shanghai* – Chinese.

Entertainment
The larger hotels have live floor shows and dancing, and there is a casino at the Inter-Continental Hotel. Lusaka has a theatre and several cinemas, including a drive-in. There are a number of sporting clubs in and around the city, and temporary membership is usually available to foreign visitors.

Shopping
Best buys: wood carvings, beadwork, copperware, pottery.
Lusaka has a colourful open-air market where a wide range of handicrafts are on sale. There are several boutiques in the city selling copper goods. Local gemstones can be purchased at the *Gemstones Polishing Works*.

The Copperbelt
The Copperbelt, the centre of Zambia's mining industry, is made up of the mining towns of Chililabombwe, Chingola, Kalulushi, Kitwe, Luanshya, Mufulira and Ndola. Kitwe and Ndola, in particular, have grown with the development of the copper industry into modern, industrial centres with good communications with the rest of the country.
Visits to the copper mines in the area can be arranged through the Zambian National Tourist Bureau, Century House, Cairo Road, Lusaka, ☎ 72891/5 (bookings should be made in advance in Lusaka). Other places of interest in the Copperbelt are the Dag Hammarskjold Memorial and the Sunken Lake and Slave Tree outside Ndola.
Ndola Airport is 6½km/4 miles from the centre of Ndola.

Hotels

Kitwe
HOTEL EDINBURGH, P.O. Box 1800, ☎ 3416.
Modern 1st class (4-star) hotel in town centre.

Rooms: 72 ♪, ⊞, ●, ☎. Suites available.
Facilities: Restaurant, bars. Terrace. Service shops.
Conference rooms.

NKANA, P.O. Box 664, ☎ 2410/2358.

ZAMBIA

Ndola
SAVOY, Buteko Avenue, P.O. Box 1800, ☎ 3771.
Modern hotel in town centre.
Rooms: 78 ☎.
Facilities: Restaurant, cocktail lounge. Dancing. Golf course near by. Travel agency.
Banquet room.

COPPERSMITH ARMS, P.O. Box 1063, ☎ 2395.

ZIMBABWE
Republic of Zimbabwe

Geography	*490*
The Economy	*491*
How to Get There	*492*
Entry Regulations	*493*
Practical Information for the Visitor	*493*
Useful Addresses (General)	*495*
Business Information	*495*
Business Services	*496*
Useful Addresses (Business)	*496*
Salisbury	*496*
Bulawayo	*498*

Size: 390,272 sq.km/150,685 sq.miles.

Population: 7.14 million (mid-1979).

Distribution: 20% in urban areas.

Density: 18.3 persons per sq.km/47.4 per sq.mile.

Population Growth Rate: 3.5 % p.a.

Ethnic Composition: Some 95% of the population are of African descent, the main tribal groups being Shona, Ndebele, Tonga, Sena, Hlengwe, Venda and Sotho. About 4% are European settlers and their descendants. There is also a small Asian community.

Capital: Salisbury Pop. 610,000 (1978 est.).

Major Towns: Bulawayo Pop. 358,000; Gwelo Pop. 69,000; Umtali Pop. 62,000; Que Que Pop. 54,000; Gatooma Pop. 33,000; Wankie Pop. 32,000 (1978 ests.).

Language: English is the official language. Shona and Ndebele are the major African languages.

Religion: Most people adhere to traditional beliefs. Some 20% are Christians, mostly Protestant.

Government: From 11 November 1965, when the Unilateral Declaration of Independence from Britain was proclaimed, until 1st June 1979 Ian Smith was Prime Minister of Rhodesia and leader of the Rhodesian Front political party. African resistance to the entrenched rebel regime of Mr Smith heightened over the years turning into a full-scale guerrilla war conducted with increasing success by the ZAPU and ZIPRA forces. On 3 March 1978 Smith negotiated the so-called 'internal settlement' which resulted in Bishop Abel Muzorewa becoming Prime Minister. However, there was no let-up in the guerrilla war despite some small concessions to the African majority, and after a fresh initiative from the newly elected Conservative government in Britain the Lancaster House talks were held in London and a cease-fire, constitution and

ZIMBABWE

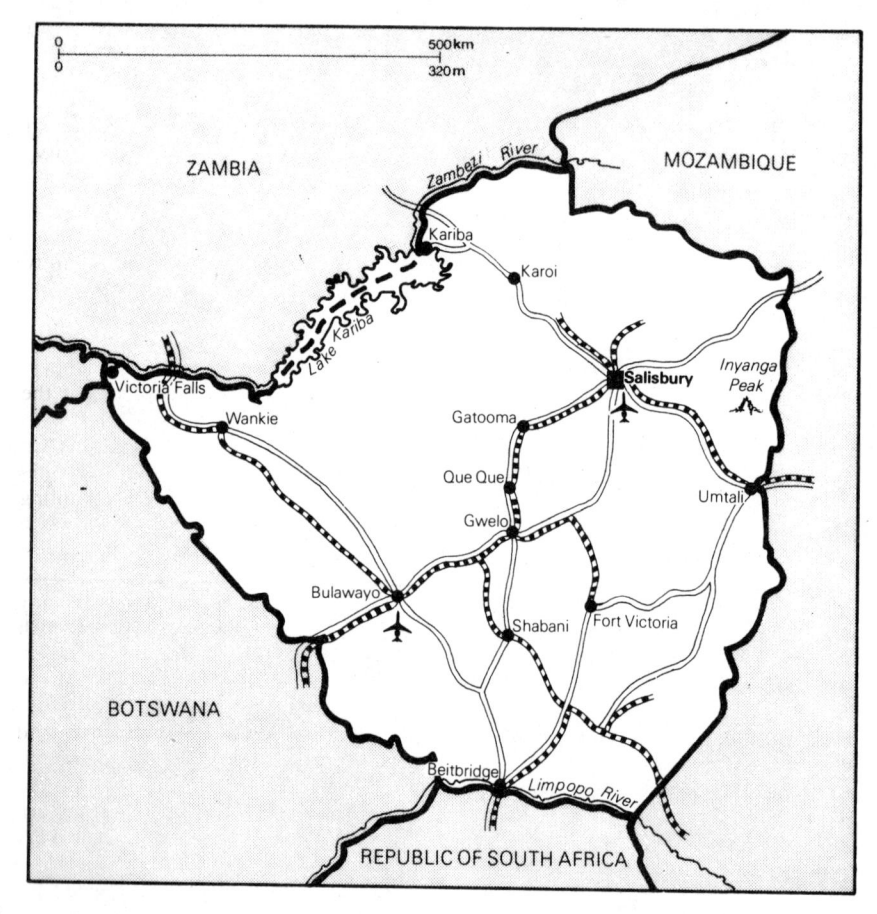

the basis for elections were agreed and enacted. Elections were supervised by a United Kingdom and Commonwealth monitoring force, while rule passed temporarily into the hands of a British Governor, Lord Soames. The vote resulted in a comfortable majority for Robert Mugabe, who then formed a government of national unity, announcing a cabinet composed of members of his own ZANU (PF) and other parties on 11 March 1980, with ministers representing all regional, tribal and racial elements of the Zimbabwean population. Independence was formally declared on 18 April.

GEOGRAPHY

Much of Zimbabwe consists of high plateaux above 1,000m/3,280 feet gently sloping down to the lowveld around the Zambezi Valley to the north and to the valleys of the Limpopo, Save and their tributaries in the south. There are numerous granite outcrops (*kopjes*) which stand out above the highveld landscape, and hills mark the watershed between the 2 river systems to the north and the south. The highest peak is Inyangi at

2,594m/8,500 feet in the mountainous region along the extreme eastern border with Mozambique.

Climate
Altitude moderates temperature and rainfall. From August to November it is hot and dry, with October average temperatures ranging from 30°c/86°F in the Zambesi Valley to 20°c/68°F on the upland plateaux. The wet season is from November to April, with the heaviest rainfall in December and January. The eastern highlands are the wettest, and the southern valleys the driest regions. Between May and July conditions are dry and cool, with average temperatures between 13°c/55°F and 18°c/65°F. It is rarely humid in Zimbabwe.

Agriculture
Although agriculture contributes only 17% to the GDP and is relatively underdeveloped (due in part to a lack of reliable rain and poor soil over much of the country), it provides employment for 70% of the population. Over 60% of Africans live in the rural areas and are dependent upon subsistence agriculture, the main crop being maize. The Land Apportionment Act of 1930 and the Land Tenure Act of 1969 were the legal basis of land ownership and management for almost 50 years, enabling disproportionate areas of land with the best agricultural potential to be held by white settlers while prohibiting African commercial farming. In the post-independence period the question of land ownership is bound to cause problems for the Mugabe Government which is faced with the dilemma of having to satisfy the demands of many Africans by acquiring the formerly white-held lands either by confiscation (which would result in a rapid exodus of many whites) or by payment of compensation (which would impose a strain on insufficient funds needed for other projects) while at the same time maintaining productivity.

The commercial agricultural sector produces food and cash crops for domestic and export markets; the main crops are tobacco, coffee, cotton, tea, groundnuts, wheat, sugar-cane. A campaign of diversification has encouraged wheat, cotton and sugar production at the expense of tobacco, which nevertheless remains the major export. Livestock raising is also important and, in addition to providing meat and dairy products for the home market, some meat products are exported. There are some 6 million head of cattle in Zimbabwe, but the war damage to pest control, fencing, etc., has yet to be repaired.

Main Crops: sugar-cane, maize, wheat, tobacco, millet, groundnuts, soya-beans, cotton, tea, sorghum, pyrethrum, potatoes, beans, oranges, other fruits.

Mineral Resources: chrome, nickel, iron ore, coal, copper, asbestos, gold.

THE ECONOMY

Gross National Product (1978): US$3 billion.

Per Capita Income (1978): US$452.

Gross Domestic Product (1978 est.): US$3.32 billion.

Foreign Trade (1973): Total Imports – US$541 million. Total Exports – US$652 million.

Main Trading Partners: South Africa, UK, USA, West Germany.

During the late 1960s and early 1970s, the economy continued to function fairly effectively as the multinational subsidiaries and local entrepreneurs found ways around the trade sanctions. Indeed, certain sectors, notably manufacturing, grew as new industries were established to supply the domestic market. Economic growth declined sharply after 1975 as the war intensified, diverting labour and supplies to the war effort, and the strain of isolation began to be felt. Deteriorating plant led to reduced productivity, and budgetary deficits grew as defence spending rose. One side effect of this isolation was a relatively low rate of inflation, now estimated to be at around 13%.

Mineral production, which provided some 10% of total export value in 1965, reached a peak in 1976 and is expected to continue to rise as a percentage of exports and GDP over the next few years as transport routes are re-opened. Mining potential is great, with ferro-chrome and asbestos the most important. Zimbabwe is one of the world's top 10 gold producers; and its reserves of copper and nickel are substantial, with output expected to increase significantly. High-quality reserves of coal at Wankie are to be used for domestic power production and for exportation.

Manufacturing is relatively well developed in Zimbabwe, having remained (apart from export goods) comparatively unaffected by the war. This is now the most important sector of the economy, accounting for 20% of the GDP. Local raw materials are used in food and metal processing, and there is every hope of increased investment and output in this sector.

Agriculture was the most severely damaged area of the economy during the war, and the Government are planning to make special efforts to improve productivity so that exports can pick up and domestic food demands be met, in this way reducing foreign exchange expenditure. The establishment of a nitrogenous fertiliser factory at Que Que has been a notable exception to the general atmosphere of gloom prevailing in this sector over the last few years.

A substantial part of the cost of economic reconstruction is expected to be provided as aid by several donor nations and international organisations.

Major Industries: mineral and food processing, textiles, paper, printing, construction materials.

Main Commodities Traded: Imports – transport equipment and machinery, fuels. Exports – asbestos, nickel, copper, gold, chrome, pig iron, cereals, tobacco, tea, cotton, sugar, meat products, clothing, shoes, furniture.

International Affiliations: Commonwealth. At the time of writing, Zimbabwe has applied to join the UN and OAU.

HOW TO GET THERE

Air

Air Zimbabwe operate services twice a week from London to Salisbury, from Johannesburg 7 days a week and from Durban twice weekly. There are also 2 flights a week from Johannesburg to Bulawayo.

British Airways connect London with Salisbury twice a week and also fly from Geneva and Hamburg.

South African Airways fly to Salisbury from Berlin (once weekly), Durban (once weekly), Frankfurt (twice a week), Hamburg (twice weekly), Johannesburg (every day), New York (thrice weekly), Rome (once weekly) and Zürich. SAA also fly from Johannesburg and Paris to Bulawayo Airport.

Zambia Airways have direct flights to Salisbury from Lusaka 2 times a week and DETA (Mozambique) operate services to Salisbury from Beira (once weekly) and Maputo (once weekly).

Lufthansa fly to Salisbury direct from Hamburg, Hanover and Munich, while Swissair fly from Zürich and Geneva. Alitalia operate a stopping service to Salisbury from Rome; Pan American fly direct from West Berlin; and Air Malawi from Blantyre – all once weekly.

Salisbury International Airport is 13km/8 miles from the city centre.
Bulawayo International Airport is 24km/15 miles from the town.

Road
Good roads exist into Zimbabwe from Botswana, Zambia, Mozambique and South Africa. Fast bus services are provided from Johannesburg to Salisbury.

Rail
Rail routes carry passenger and goods services from South Africa via Mafeking or Beit Bridge. It is hoped that rail services to Beira (Mozambique) will be re-opened.

ENTRY REGULATIONS

Visas
Visas are required of all visitors to Zimbabwe, except for nationals of Commonwealth countries, western European countries (not France, West Germany, Finland and Spain), Bahrain, South Africa, USA.

Apart from nationals of certain specified countries, visas may be obtained upon arrival in Zimbabwe if proof of purchase of an onward ticket or sufficient funds to purchase such a ticket can be provided. Visas may also be obtained from Zimbabwean representatives abroad.

Health Regulations
International Certificates of Vaccination against smallpox, yellow fever and cholera are required if arriving within 6 days of leaving an infected area.

Customs
Currency: Foreign currency import is unrestricted if declared upon arrival; export is allowed up to the amount declared. The import and export of local currency up to ZD 20 are permitted.

Duty-free articles: 100 cigarettes or 115g tobacco. 5 litres of alcoholic beverages, of which 2 litres can be spirits. Goods to the value of ZD 50 per person.

PRACTICAL INFORMATION FOR THE VISITOR

1. Currency
Monetary Unit – Zimbabwe dollar (ZD) divided into 100 cents.

Notes – 1, 2, 5, 10 ZD.
Coins – ½, 1, 2½, 5, 10, 20, 25 cents.

All main commercial banks have branches throughout Zimbabwe.

Banking Hours
0830–1400 Monday to Friday
0830–1200 Wednesday
0830–1100 Saturday

The *Reserve Bank of Zimbabwe* is the central bank and bank of issue.

Principal Commercial Banks
Barclays Bank International Ltd, Manica Road, P.O. Box 1279, Salisbury.
Grindlays Bank Ltd, 59 Jameson Avenue, Salisbury.
Standard Bank Ltd, John Boyne House, corner Speke Avenue and Inez Terrace, P.O. Box 3693, Salisbury.
Zimbabwe Banking Corporation Ltd, 46 Speke Avenue, P.O. Box 3198, Salisbury.

Domestic Bank
Reserve Bank of Zimbabwe, P.O. Box 1283, Salisbury.

2. Electricity Supply
230v AC 50Hz.

3. Weights and Measures
The metric system is soon to replace Imperial standards.

4. Media
The Zimbabwe Broadcasting Corporation controls radio and television broadcasting. The commercial radio and television services are operated from studios in Salisbury and Bulawayo in English and in African languages.

Newspapers and Journals
The Herald is the Salisbury English-language daily paper. *The Chronicle* is the Bulawayo daily. Other newspapers include: *African Times* – fortnightly, *Country Times, Midlands Observer* (Que Que), *The National Observer, Sunday Mail, Sunday News* (Bulawayo), *The Times* (Gwelo), There are several local newspapers, and a number of trade and business journals including *Cattle World, Development Magazine, Industrial Review* and *Modern Farming*.

5. Medical Care
Malaria is endemic over much of the country and is especially prevalent in the lowland areas. Swimming and bathing in rivers and lakes should be avoided because of the risk of bilharzia. Water is safe to drink in towns but should be boiled or filtered in rural areas. Hospitals are good in the main centres but the war has severely damaged rural medical facilities.

6. Telephone, Telex and Postal Services
The telephone system is extensive, and there should be little or no delay on international calls.

Telex facilities are likewise plentiful and available for public use at the larger hotels.

The domestic postal service is satisfactory. All overseas mail should be despatched by air.

7. Public Holidays
1 January   *New Year's Day*
18 April   *Independence Day*
25–6 December   *Christmas*
Good Friday, Easter Monday and *Whit Monday* are also observed as public holidays.

Other national holidays may be declared soon.

8. Time
GMT + 2.

9. Internal Transport
Air
Air Zimbabwe operate frequent scheduled domestic flights between Salisbury, Bulawayo, Gwelo, Kariba, Buffalo Range, Umtali, Victoria Falls and Fort Victoria.

There are many smaller airstrips throughout the country and air charter facilities are available.

Air Charter Firm
Air Trans Africa (Pvt.) Ltd, P.O. Box 655, Salisbury.

Airline Offices in Salisbury
Air Zimbabwe, P.O. Box AP1, ☎ 52601.
British Airways, Roslin Ho., Baker Ave., ☎ 794616.
Sabena, Ambassador Ho., Union Ave., P.O. Box 3192, ☎ 26504.

Road
Zimbabwe has an extensive road network of 80,000km/50,000 miles, of which 8,500km/5,600 miles are asphalted. There are good roads linking all the main centres, and war damage is to be repaired as soon as possible.

Bus services are frequent in and between the larger towns.

Metered taxis are available in the main towns and self-drive cars can be hired from a number of agents. All drivers require a foreign or International Driving Licence. Traffic travels on the left-hand side of the road.

Car-Hire Firms
Hertz
- Salisbury ☎ 704915, 793701.
- Bulawayo ☎ 61402, 26311.
- Umtali ☎ 64711.
- Gwelo ☎ 3366.
- Fort Victoria ☎ 2054/5.

Avis
- Salisbury ☎ 20361.
- Bulawayo ☎ 68571.

Europcar
- Salisbury ☎ 70222.
- Bulawayo ☎ 87925.

Rail
Scheduled passenger and goods services operate between the major towns of Salisbury, Bulawayo, Umtali, Wankie, Gwelo, Gatooma and Fort Victoria.

10. Tipping
Taxis – 10%.

Hotels/restaurants – 10–15% of the bill.

USEFUL ADDRESSES (GENERAL)

British Government Representative Office, Mrimba House, Mrimba Close, P.O. Chisipite, Salisbury.

Department of Tourism, Cecil House, 95 Stanley Avenue, Causeway, P.O. Box 8052, Salisbury, ☎ 706511.

University of Zimbabwe, P.O. Box MP167, Mount Pleasant, Salisbury.

BUSINESS INFORMATION

It is anticipated that foreign investment and assistance in the reconstruction of the economy will be welcomed by the Government, particularly joint participation in projects accorded priority; however, many of the details of policy towards foreign companies and subsidiaries in Zimbabwe have yet to be decided. The Government has expressed its intention to take a greater share in the management of the large enterprises operated by the multinationals in Zimbabwe. The trend will be towards a greater 'Africanisation' of management positions and towards higher wages.

Import and Exchange Control Regulations
Strict import controls are likely to remain in force for some time yet, and licences are needed before payments can be made. The exact conditions to be imposed upon

importers and specific moves to encourage economic growth have yet to be worked out.

Business Hours
Government Offices
0830–1700 Monday to Friday.

Business Houses
0800–1700 Monday to Saturday.

BUSINESS SERVICES

Insurance
Insurance Corporation of Zimbabwe Ltd, corner Manica Road and Angwa Street, P.O. Box 2417, Salisbury.

Old Mutual Fire and General Insurance Co, Speke Avenue, P.O. Box 2101, Salisbury.

Railway
Zimbabwe/Rhodesia Railways, Metcalfe Square, P.O. Box 596, Bulawayo.

USEFUL ADDRESSES (BUSINESS)

Agricultural Marketing Authority, P.O. Box 8094, Salisbury.

Associated Chambers of Commerce of Zimbabwe, 5th Floor, Equity House, Rezende Street, P.O. Box 1934, Salisbury.

Bulawayo Chamber of Industries, P.O. Box 2317, Bulawayo.

Bulawayo Farmers Association, P. O. Box 9003, Hillside, Bulawayo.

Bulawayo Trade Fair and Agricultural Society, P.O. Famona, Bulawayo.

Industrial Association of Zimbabwe, 109 Rotten Row, Salisbury.

Industrial Council of the Meat Trade, P.O. Box 1084, Bulawayo.

Midlands Chamber of Industries, P.O. Box 293, Gwelo.

National Industrial Council for the Engineering and Iron and Steel Industry, Chancellor House, Jameson Avenue, P.O. Box 1922, Salisbury.

Que Que Farmers Association, P.O. Box 240, Que Que.

Tobacco Association, Baker Avenue, P.O. Box 1781, Salisbury.

Umtali District Farmers Association, P.O. Box 29, Umtali.

MAJOR CITY AND TOWNS

Salisbury
The capital city is the regional and national commercial centre. The compact central business district gives way to spacious sprawling suburbs and the large African town-

ZIMBABWE

ships which have spread as a result of the influx of people from the rural areas during the war years. Salisbury is a city of modern western-style building and wide avenues with a pleasant sunny climate.

Hotels
Hotels are rated from 1 to 4 stars in the Tourist Board Classifications.

AMBASSADOR HOTEL, Union Avenue, P.O. Box 872, ☎ 793666.
3-star hotel (1955) in city centre within the main shopping district, situated 10km/6 miles from airport.
Rooms: 80 ☎, ⌑, ♨, ♿, 🅿. Suites available.
Facilities: Restaurants, bars. Shops. Car hire. Fishing trips, safaris arranged.
Services: TC, FC. ☐ Amex, Diners Club. Dr. on call. S, ♂. Audio-visual equipment.
Conference and banqueting rooms – max. 150 persons.

JAMESON HOTEL, Jameson Avenue, P.O. Box 2833, ☎ 794641.
4-star hotel (1958) in city centre, near commercial area.
Rooms: 128 ☎, ☎, ⌑, ♨, ♿, 🅿. Suites available.
Facilities: Restaurants, bars.
Services: TC, FC. ☐ Amex, Barclay Visa, Diners Club. Dr. on call. ♂, S.
Conference rooms – max. capacity 200.
Banqueting rooms – max. capacity 150.

MEIKLES HOTEL, Stanley Avenue, P.O. Box 594, ☎ 707721.
Modernised 4-star hotel (1959) in commercial district.
Rooms: 112 ☎ (some), ☎, ⌑, ♨, ♿, 🅿.
Facilities: Restaurants, bars.
Services: TC, FC. ☐ Amex, Diners Club. Dr. on call. ♂, S. Audio-visual equipment.
Conference rooms – max. capacity 500.
Banqueting rooms – max. capacity 350.

MONOMATAPA HOTEL, 54 Park Lane, P.O. Box 2445, ☎ 704501.
Modern 4-star hotel in city centre with adjacent 35-acre garden park.
Rooms: 300 ☎, ☎, ⌑, ♨, ♿, 🅿. Suites available.
Facilities: Restaurants, bars, private dining salons. Nightclub. Parking, car hire. Swimming pool. Shops.
Services: TC, FC. ☐ Amex, Diners Club. Dr. on call. S.
Conference room – max. capacity 396.

PARK LANE HOTEL, Jameson Avenue East, P.O. Box HG192, ☎ 707631.
Modern motel 2km/1 mile from city centre.
Rooms: 36 ☎, ⌑, ♨, ♿, ♡.
Facilities: Restaurants, bar. Extensive grounds. Swimming pool, golf.
Services: TC, FC. ☐ Amex.

Restaurants
Many of the hotels in Salisbury have good restaurants. There are also several good African, Asian and European restaurants; however, shortages as a result of the war have reduced the variety and quality of meals available. The *Bamboo Inn*, Manica Road, serves Chinese cuisine.

Nightclubs
Nightlife is limited, confined mostly to the hotel bars and the few nightclubs remaining open in Salisbury.

Entertainment
Salisbury has several museums, including: the Queen Victoria Museum, which houses an excellent natural history collection; the National Gallery, with exhibitions of the work of local artists and craftsmen; and the National Archives Building, containing a wealth of material on public view about the history of the country. Salisbury Botanical Gardens are also worth a visit, as is the

ZIMBABWE

Ewanrigg National Park, 40km/25 miles north of Salisbury, where the aloes and cacti flower over 60 acres from June to August.

Lake McIlwaine, 30km/20 miles south-west of the city, is a favourite place for watersports.

Shopping

Best buys: copperware, jewellery, stone and wood carvings.

African artists working in soapstone and granite sell their ceramics and sculpture at the *National Gallery Workshop* sale rooms.

Bulawayo

The 2nd largest city in Zimbabwe is a regional centre of considerable industrial and commercial importance. Founded in 1893, the town has increased in population as the nearby townships have grown. A certain amount of dereliction has set in as a result of the general economic decline in recent years, but the wide streets and large colonial offices and houses remain.

The National Museum in Bulawayo contains large collections of zoological and geological exhibits and 'pioneer' memorabilia. Matopos National Park, south of the city, contains numerous examples of Bushman cave paintings, of which Nswatugi Cave is the best known. The Khami Ruins, 20km/12 miles from Bulawayo, are another local attraction, attesting to the presence of a flourishing culture in this region several centuries before the European encroachment. The Art and Craft Centre in Mzilikazi Village, near Bulawayo, has exhibitions and sales of local pottery and stone and wood carvings.

Hotels

SOUTHERN SUN HOTEL, 10th Avenue, P.O. Box 654, ☎ 60101.
3-star hotel in colonial style near city centre.
Rooms: 192 ♫, ♠, ☐, ♋, ♥. Suites available.

Facilities: Restaurant, bars, grill. Nightclub. Shops. Sauna. Parking.
Services: TC, FC. ⊟ Amex, Diners Club. S.
Conference rooms – max. capacity 500.

APPENDICES

Metric Measures and Equivalents 500
Imperial Measures and Equivalents 501
Conversion Tables 502
Temperatures 505
World Time Zones 506
Index to Places 508

APPENDICES

METRIC MEASURES AND EQUIVALENTS

Length

1 millimetre (mm)		= 0·0394in
1 centimetre (cm)	= 10mm	= 0·3937in
1 metre (m)	= 1000mm	= 1·0936 yards
1 kilometre (km)	= 1000m	= 0·6214 mile

Surface or area

1 sq cm (cm²)	= 100mm²	= 0·1550sq in
1 sq metre (m²)	= 10000cm²	= 1·1960sq yds
1 hectare (ha)	= 10000m²	= 2·4711 acres
1 sq km (km²)	= 100 hectares	= 0·3861sq mile

Capacity

1 cu cm (cm³)		= 0·0610cu in
1 cu decimetre (dm³)	= 1000cm³	= 0·0353cu ft
1 cu metre (m³)	= 1000dm³	= 1·3079cu yds
1 litre (l)	= 1dm³	= 0·2642 US gal
1 litre (l)		= 0·2200 Imp gal
1 hectolitre (hl)	= 100 litres	= 2·8378 US bus
1 hectolitre (hl)		= 2·7497 Imp bus

Weight

1 milligramme (mg)		= 0·0154 grain
1 gramme (g)	= 1000mg	= 0·0353oz
1 kilogramme (kg)	= 1000g	= 2·2046lb
1 tonne (t)	= 1000kg	= 1·1023 short tons
1 tonne (t)		= 0·9842 long tons

IMPERIAL MEASURES AND EQUIVALENTS

Length
1 inch (in)   = 2·5400 cm
1 foot (ft)   = 12 in   = 0·3048 m
1 yard (yd)   = 3 ft   = 0·9144 m
1 mile   = 1760 yd   = 1·6093 km

Surface or area
1 sq inch   = 6·4516 cm^2
1 sq yard   = 9 sq ft   = 0·8361 m^2
1 acre   = 4840 sq yd   = 4046·86 m^2
1 sq mile   = 640 acres   = 259·0 hectares

Capacity
1 cu inch   = 16·387 cm^3
1 cu yard   = 27 cu ft   = 0·7646 m^3

US dry measures
1 pint   = 0·9689 Imp pt   = 0·5506 litres

US liquid measures
1 pint   = 0·8327 Imp pt   = 0·4732 litres
1 gallon   = 8 pints   = 3·7853 litres

Imperial liquid measures
1 pint   = 1·0321 US pt   = 0·5683 litres
1 gallon   = 8 pints   = 4·5461 litres

Weight (Avoirdupois)
1 ounce (oz)   = 437·5 grains   = 28·350 g
1 pound (lb)   = 16 oz   = 0·4536 kg
1 short cwt   = 100 lb   = 45·359 kg
1 long cwt   = 112 lb   = 50·802 kg
1 short ton   = 2000 lb   = 0·9072 tonnes
1 long ton   = 2240 lb   = 1·0161 tonnes

APPENDICES

CONVERSION TABLES

Length

centimetres	No.	inches	metres	No.	yards
2.540	1	0.394	0.914	1	1.094
5.080	2	0.787	1.829	2	2.187
7.620	3	1.181	2.743	3	3.281
10.160	4	1.575	3.658	4	4.374
12.700	5	1.969	4.572	5	5.468
15.240	6	2.362	5.486	6	6.562
17.780	7	2.756	6.401	7	7.655
20.320	8	3.150	7.315	8	8.749
22.860	9	3.543	8.230	9	9.843
25.400	10	3.937	9.144	10	10.936
50.800	20	7.874	18.288	20	21.872
76.200	30	11.811	27.432	30	32.808
101.600	40	15.748	36.576	40	43.745
127.000	50	19.685	45.720	50	54.681
152.400	60	23.622	54.864	60	65.617
177.800	70	27.559	64.008	70	76.553
203.200	80	31.496	73.152	80	87.489
228.600	90	35.433	82.296	90	98.425
254.000	100	39.370	91.440	100	109.361

kilometres	No.	miles			
1.609	1	0.621	32.187	20	12.427
3.219	2	1.243	48.281	30	18.641
4.828	3	1.864	64.374	40	24.854
6.437	4	2.485	80.468	50	31.068
8.047	5	3.107	96.562	60	37.282
9.656	6	3.728	112.655	70	43.495
11.266	7	4.350	128.749	80	49.709
12.875	8	4.971	144.842	90	55.922
14.484	9	5.592	160.936	100	62.136
16.094	10	6.214			

Area

sq. kilometres	No.	sq. miles			
2.590	1	0.386	51.800	20	7.722
5.180	2	0.772	77.699	30	11.583
7.770	3	1.158	103.598	40	15.444
10.360	4	1.544	129.498	50	19.306
12.950	5	1.931	155.397	60	23.167
15.540	6	2.317	181.297	70	27.028
18.130	7	2.703	207.196	80	30.889
20.720	8	3.089	233.096	90	34.750
23.310	9	3.475	258.995	100	38.611
25.900	10	3.861			

APPENDICES

hectares	No.	acres			
0.41	1	2.47	8.09	20	49.42
0.81	2	4.94	12.14	30	74.13
1.21	3	7.41	16.19	40	98.84
1.62	4	9.88	20.23	50	123.60
2.02	5	12.36	24.28	60	148.30
2.43	6	14.83	28.33	70	173.00
2.83	7	17.30	32.38	80	197.70
3.24	8	19.77	36.42	90	222.40
3.64	9	22.24	40.47	100	247.10
4.05	10	24.71			

Capacity

litres	No.	Imperial pints	litres	No.	Imperial gallons
0.568	1	1.760	4.546	1	0.220
1.136	2	3.520	9.092	2	0.440
1.705	3	5.279	13.638	3	0.660
2.273	4	7.039	18.184	4	0.880
2.841	5	8.799	22.730	5	1.100
3.409	6	10.559	27.276	6	1.320
3.978	7	12.319	31.822	7	1.540
4.546	8	14.078	36.368	8	1.760
5.114	9	15.838	40.914	9	1.980
5.682	10	17.598	45.460	10	2.200
11.365	20	35.196	90.919	20	4.399
17.047	30	52.794	136.379	30	6.599
22.730	40	70.392	181.838	40	8.799
28.412	50	87.990	227.298	50	10.999
34.094	60	105.588	272.758	60	13.198
39.777	70	123.186	318.217	70	15.398
45.459	80	140.784	363.677	80	17.598
51.142	90	158.382	409.136	90	19.797
56.824	100	175.980	454.596	100	21.997

US gallons	No.	litres			
0.264	1	3.785	5.284	20	75.706
0.528	2	7.571	7.925	30	113.559
0.793	3	11.356	10.567	40	151.412
1.057	4	15.141	13.209	50	189.265
1.321	5	18.927	15.851	60	227.118
1.585	6	22.712	18.493	70	264.971
1.849	7	26.497	21.134	80	302.824
2.113	8	30.282	23.776	90	340.678
2.378	9	34.068	26.418	100	378.531
2.642	10	37.853			

APPENDICES

US gallons	No.	Imperial gallons				
1.201	1	0.833				
2.402	2	1.665	24.019	20	16.654
3.603	3	2.498	36.028	30	24.980
4.804	4	3.331	48.038	40	33.307
6.005	5	4.163	60.047	50	41.634
7.206	6	4.996	72.057	60	49.961
8.407	7	5.829	84.066	70	58.287
9.608	8	6.661	96.076	80	66.614
10.809	9	7.494	108.085	90	74.941
12.010	10	8.327	120.095	100	83.267

Weight

kilogrammes	No.	pounds	tonnes	No.	long tons
0.454	1	2.205	1.016	1	0.984
0.907	2	4.409	2.032	2	1.968
1.361	3	6.614	3.048	3	2.953
1.814	4	8.818	4.064	4	3.937
2.268	5	11.023	5.080	5	4.921
2.722	6	13.228	6.096	6	5.905
3.175	7	15.432	7.112	7	6.889
3.629	8	17.637	8.128	8	7.874
4.082	9	19.842	9.144	9	8.858
4.536	10	22.046	10.161	10	9.842
9.072	20	44.092	20.321	20	19.684
13.608	30	66.139	30.482	30	29.526
18.144	40	88.185	40.642	40	39.368
22.680	50	110.231	50.803	50	49.211
27.216	60	132.277	60.963	60	59.053
31.751	70	154.324	71.124	70	68.895
36.287	80	176.370	81.284	80	78.737
40.823	90	198.416	91.445	90	88.579
45.359	100	220.462	101.605	100	98.421

Volume

cu. metres	No.	cu. yards			
0.765	1	1.308	7.646	10	13.080
1.529	2	2.616	15.291	20	26.159
2.294	3	3.924	22.937	30	39.239
3.058	4	5.232	30.582	40	52.318
3.823	5	6.540	38.228	50	65.398
4.587	6	7.848	45.873	60	78.477
5.352	7	9.156	53.519	70	91.557
6.116	8	10.464	61.164	80	104.636
6.881	9	11.772	68.810	90	117.716
			76.455	100	130.795

APPENDICES

TEMPERATURES

°C	No.	°F	°C	No.	°F	°C	No.	°F
−17·8	0	+32·0	4·4	40	104·0	26·7	80	176·0
17·2	1	33·8	5·0	41	105·8	27·2	81	177·8
16·7	2	35·6	5·6	42	107·6	27·8	82	179·6
16·1	3	37·4	6·1	43	109·4	28·3	83	181·4
15·6	4	39·2	6·7	44	111·2	28·9	84	183·2
15·0	5	41·0	7·2	45	113·0	29·4	85	185·0
14·4	6	42·8	7·8	46	114·8	30·0	86	186·8
13·9	7	44·6	8·3	47	116·6	30·6	87	188·6
13·3	8	46·4	8·9	48	118·4	31·1	88	190·4
12·8	9	48·2	9·4	49	120·2	31·7	89	192·2
12·2	10	50·0	10·0	50	122·0	32·2	90	194·0
11·7	11	51·8	10·6	51	123·8	32·8	91	195·8
11·1	12	53·6	11·1	52	125·6	33·3	92	197·6
10·6	13	55·4	11·7	53	127·4	33·9	93	199·4
10·0	14	57·2	12·2	54	129·2	34·4	94	201·2
9·4	15	59·0	12·8	55	131·0	35·0	95	203·0
8·9	16	60·8	13·3	56	132·8	35·6	96	204·8
8·3	17	62·6	13·9	57	134·6	36·1	97	206·6
7·8	18	64·4	14·4	58	136·4	36·7	98	208·4
7·2	19	66·2	15·0	59	138·2	36·9	98·4	209·1
6·7	20	68·0	15·6	60	140·0	37·2	99	210·2
6·1	21	69·8	16·1	61	141·8	37·8	100	212·0
5·6	22	71·6	16·7	62	143·6	38·3	101	213·8
5·0	23	73·4	17·2	63	145·4	38·9	102	215·6
4·4	24	75·2	17·8	64	147·2	39·4	103	217·4
3·9	25	77·0	18·3	65	149·0	40·0	104	219·2
3·3	26	78·8	18·9	66	150·8	40·6	105	221·0
2·8	27	80·6	19·4	67	152·6	41·1	106	222·8
2·2	28	82·4	20·0	68	154·4	41·7	107	224·6
1·7	29	84·2	20·6	69	156·2	42·2	108	226·4
1·1	30	86·0	21·1	70	158·0	42·8	109	228·2
0·6	31	87·8	21·7	71	159·8	43·3	110	230·0
0·0	32	89·6	22·2	72	161·6	43·9	111	231·8
+0·6	33	91·4	22·8	73	163·4	44·4	112	233·6
1·1	34	93·2	23·3	74	165·2	65·6	150	302·0
1·7	35	95·0	23·9	75	167·0	93·3	200	392·0
2·2	36	96·8	24·4	76	168·8	100·0	212	413·6
2·8	37	98·6	25·0	77	170·6	121·1	250	482·0
3·3	38	100·4	25·6	78	172·4	537·8	1000	1832·0
3·9	39	102·2	26·1	79	174·2	1648·9	3000	5432·0

APPENDICES

WORLD TIME ZONES

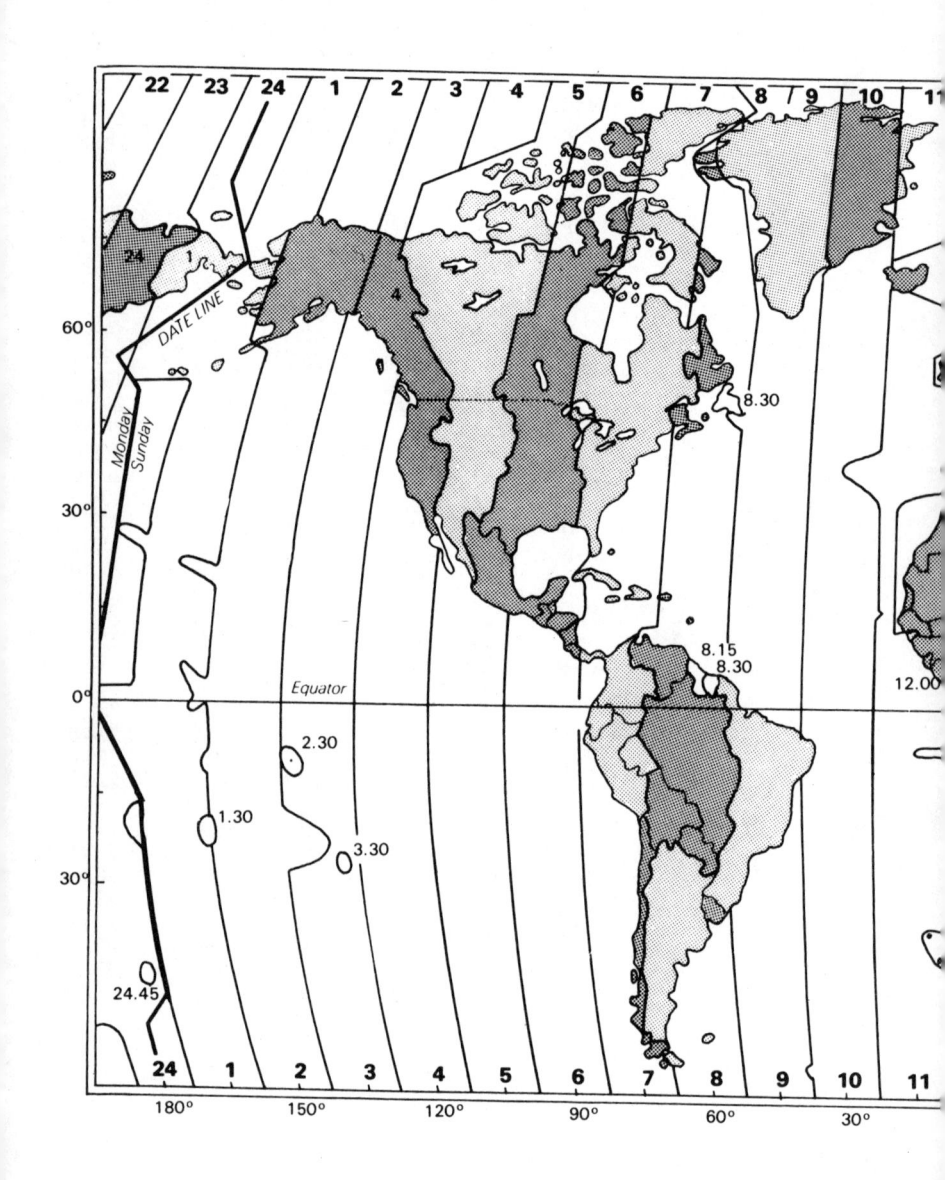

APPENDICES

This map shows the Standard Times observed in the 24 time zones of the world as compared with 1200 hours (midday) Greenwich Mean Time. Daylight Saving Time, usually one hour ahead of local Standard Time, is not shown on this map.

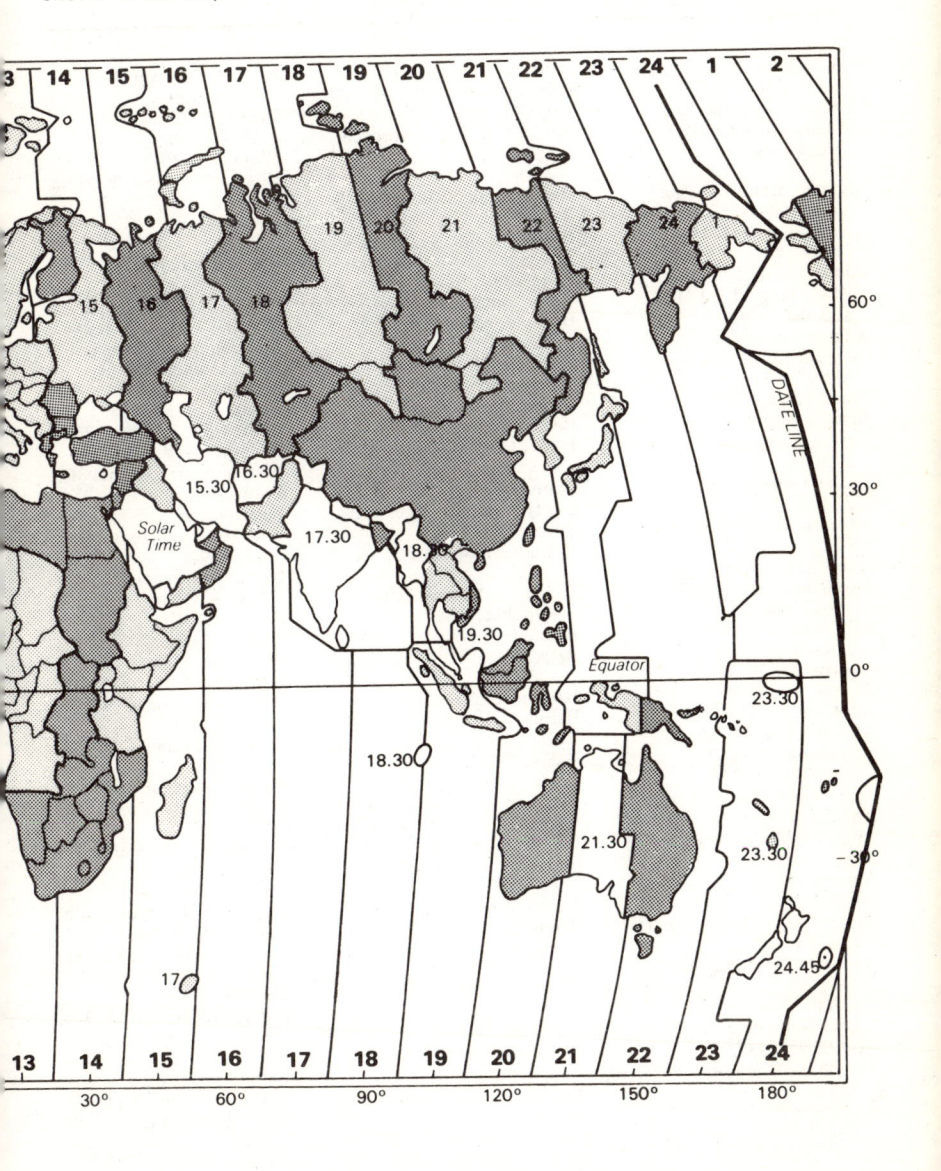

507

INDEX TO PLACES

Aba, Nigeria, 332
Abéché, Chad, 89, 94
Abeokuta, Nigeria, 322
Abidjan, Ivory Coast, 94, 162, 186–7, 189–95, 317, 320, 462
Abomey, Benin, 45, 50
Abomey-Calavi, Benin, 53
Accra, Ghana, 51, 159–160, 162–8, 435
Addis Ababa, Ethiopia, 21–2, 109, 112, 131, 133–40
Adjamé, Ivory Coast, 194
Adrar des Iforas Massif, Mali, 258
Aflao, Ghana, 440
Agadez, Niger, 319
Agadir, Morocco, 288, 290, 292
Agalega island, Mauritius, 274
Akjoujt, Mauritania, 269, 272
Akosombo, Ghana, 164
Akoupame, Togo, 434
Akouta, Niger, 317
Alexandria, Egypt, 115, 117, 119–25
Algeria, 24, 29–38
Algiers, 29, 32–7, 231
Al Hoceima, Morocco, 290
Ali-Sabreh, Djibouti, 107
Ambatondrazaka, Madagascar, 244
Am Timan, Chad, 94
Anécho, Togo, 431, 437
Angoche, Mozambique, 303
Angola, 11, 39–44
Annaba, Algeria, 29, 32, 34, 445
Antananarivo, Madagascar, 238, 241–7
Anteranana, Madagascar, 238, 244
Antsirabé, Madagascar, 243
Apapa, Nigeria, 332
Arlit, Niger, 317, 319
Arusha, Tanzania, 420, 425, 428
Asmara, Ethiopia, 131, 134–9, 141
Aswan, Egypt, 115, 120–1, 125
  High Dam, 117
Atakora Mountains, Benin, 47

Atakpamé, Togo, 431, 437
Atbara, Sudan, 401, 407–8
Ati, Chad, 94
Atlas Mountains, Morocco, 286

Bafata, Guinea-Bissau, 178
Bafoussam, Cameroon, 77
Bakayu, Zaïre, 472
Bakouma, Central African Republic, 84
Balia, Cameroon, 77
Bamako, Mali, 258–9, 261–6, 347
Bambari, Central African Republic, 86
Bandundu, Zaïre, 472
Banforo, Upper Volta, 463
Bagui, Central African Republic, 26, 27, 82–8, 94
Banjul, Gambia, 151–8
Bardj Mokhtar, Algeria, 32
Baro, Nigeria, 329
Barra, Gambia, 153, 155, 157
Basongoa, Central African Republic, 82
Basse, Gambia, 151, 155
Bata, Equatorial Guinea, 126–30
Batouri, Cameroon, 77
Bausang, Gambia, 151
Beau-Bassin, Mauritius, 274, 284
Beida, Libya, 233
Beira, Mozambique, 254, 298, 301–3, 306, 480, 493
Beit Bridge, Zimbabwe, 493
Benghazi, Libya, 228, 230–5, 237
Benguela, Angola, 39
Benin, 24, 45–54
Benin, Bay of, Togo, 433
Benin City, Nigeria, 327–9, 332
Berbera, Somalia, 372–5, 377–8
Berbérati, Central African Republic, 82, 86
Big Bend, Swaziland, 411
Bijagos Archipelago, Guinea-Bissau, 178
Bird Island, Seychelles, 359
Bissau City, Guinea-Bissau, 178–9, 181–5
Bitam, Gabon, 147
Bizerte, Tunisia, 442, 449

Black Volta river, Upper Volta, 460
Blantyre, Malawi, 248, 251–7, 302
Blitta, Togo, 437
Bloemfontein, South Africa, 380, 387
Blue Nile river, 132, 402–3, 409
Bo, Sierra Leone, 363, 367–9
Bobo-Dioulasso, Upper Volta, 190, 459, 462–4
Boe, Guinea-Bissau, 181
Boké, Guinea, 171
Bol Chad, 94, 97
Boma, Zaïre, 472–3
Bomi Hills, Liberia, 224
Bongor, Chad, 94
Bonthe, Sierre Leone, 368
Booué, Gabon, 147
Botswana, 27, 55–63
Bouaké, Ivory Coast, 186, 188, 191
Bouar, Central African Republic, 86
Bouenza, Congo, 101
Bougie, Algeria, 35
Bougouni, Mali, 263
Boukhof, Morocco, 288
Brazzaville, Congo, 94, 98, 101–6, 311
Buchanan, Liberia, 219, 224–5
Buéa, Cameroon, 76–7
Buffalo Range, Zimbabwe, 494
Bujumbura, Burundi, 64, 67–71, 339
Bukavu, Zaïre, 473
Bulawayo, Zimbabwe, 489, 492, 494–6, 498
Bunce Island, Sierra Leone, 370
Burundi, 26, 64–71
Butare, Rwanda, 336, 341, 343

Cabora Bassa dam, Mozambique, 301
Cairo, Egypt, 115, 117–24, 231
Calabar, Nigeria, 327–9
Cameroon, 26, 27, 72–81
Cameroon, Mount, Cameroon, 73, 80
Cape Coast, Ghana, 163

508

INDEX

Cape Town, South Africa, 380, 384–9, 392–5
Cape Verde, Senegal, 352–3
Casablanca, Morocco, 32, 231, 285, 288–96
Central African Republic, 27, 82–8
Cerf Island, Seychelles, 361
Ceutimbo, Mozambique, 303
Chad, 11, 26, 27, 89–97
Chad, Lake, 90–1, 97
Chellah, Morocco, 294
Chichiri, Malawi, 256
Chililabombwe, Zambia, 487
Chilumba, Malawi, 253
Chingola, Zambia, 477, 482, 485, 487
Chipoka, Malawi, 254
Chott el-Dierid, Tunisia, 443
Cocody, Ivory Coast, 194–5
Conakry, Guinea, 169, 172–7
Congo, The, 27, 98–106
Congo river, 99, 102, 105–6
Constantine, Algeria, 29, 32, 34, 445
Copperbelt, The, Zambia, 482–3, 487–8
Cotonou, Benin, 45, 47–8, 50–4, 435
Cumere, Guinea-Bissau, 180
Curepipe, Mauritius, 274, 278, 280–1, 284

Dakar, Senegal, 27, 155, 182, 261, 272, 344, 346–53
Dalengi Hill, Swaziland, 418
Daloa, Ivory Coast, 186, 191
Dapango, Togo, 437
Dar es Salaam, Tanzania, 302, 420, 423–30, 480
Debre Zeyt (Bishoftu), Ethiopia, 141
Denis Island, Seychelles, 359
Dessie, Ethiopia, 131, 135
Dikhul, Djibouti, 107
Dire Dawa, Ethiopia, 109, 131, 138
Djerba, Tunisia, 445, 447
Djibouti, 23, 107–14
Djibouti, Djibouti, 107 109–14
Djoue, Congo, 101
Dodoma, Tanzania, 420, 425
Dorsale mountains, Tunisia, 442–3
Douala, Cameroon, 72–3, 75–81, 84, 94, 129, 344, 346–53

Drakensberg mountains, 211, 382
Dschang, Cameroon, 77
Durban, South Africa, 380, 382, 386–7, 389–90, 392, 395–6

East London, South Africa, 386–7, 389, 392
Ebutte Metta, Nigeria, 332
Edea, Cameroon, 74, 77
Egypt, 115–25
El Golea, Algeria, 34
El Kala, Algeria, 32
El Obeid, Sudan, 401, 407
Entebbe, Uganda, 452, 455
Enugu, Nigeria, 328–9, 332
Equatorial Guinea, 126–30
Eritrea, Ethiopia, 134, 137, 141
Ethiopia, 110, 131–41
Etosha Pan, Namibia, 308
Ezulwini Valley, Swaziland, 418–19

Faranah, Guinea, 174
Faya-Largeau, Chad, 94
Fébé, Mount, Cameroon, 81
Ferkesedougou, Ivory Coast, 191
Fernando Po, Equatorial Guinea, 126–30
Fez, Morocco, 285, 288–90, 295
Fianarantsoa, Madagascar, 244
Fort Thiriet, Algeria, 32
Fort Victoria, Zimbabwe, 494–5
Foumban, Cameroon, 72, 77
Fouta Djallon, Guinea, 169
Franceville, Gabon, 147
Francistown, Botswana, 55, 58, 60, 63
Freetown, Sierra Leone, 26, 363–4, 366–71

Gabon, 24, 27, 142–150
Gaborone, Botswana, 55, 58–63
Gambia, The, 26, 151–8
Gambia river, 26, 151
Ganvie, Benin, 53
Gao, Mali, 263
Garoua, Cameroon, 76–7
Gatooma, Zimbabwe, 489, 495
Gbangbatoke, Sierra Leone, 368
Georgetown, Gambia, 151, 155
Ghadames, Libya, 233
Ghana, 159–68
Gisenye, Rwanda, 341, 343
Gitenga, Burundi, 64

Giza, Egypt, 115, 123–4
Goma, Zaïre, 474
Gorée, Island of, Senegal, 351, 353
Goundam, Mali, 263
Grand Anse, Seychelles, 358
Grand Bassam, Ivory Coast, 186
Greenville, Liberia, 226
Grootfontein, Namibia, 312
Guinea, 169–77
Guinea Highlands, Guinea, 169
Guinea-Bissau, 11, 178–85
Gwelo, Zimbabwe, 489, 494–6

Harar, Ethiopia, 131
Harbel, Liberia, 219, 223–4
Hargeisa, Somalia, 372, 375–7
Harper, Liberia, 224, 226
High Atlas Mountains, Morocco, 286
Hottentots Holland Mountains, South Africa, 394
Huambo, Angola, 39

Ibadan, Nigeria, 322, 327–30, 332, 335
Idi Amin Dada, Lake, Uganda, 452
Ilebo, Zaïre, 473
Iles de Los, Guinea, 176
Ilorum, Nigeria, 322, 328
Ikeja, Nigeria, 325, 328–9, 331
Ikoyi Island, Nigeria, 333
Impfondo, Congo, 103
In Guezzam, Algeria, 32
Int'ot'o mountains, Ethiopia, 140–1
Inyangi mountain, Zimbabwe, 490
Ivory Coast, 186–95

Jebel, Libya, 228
Jinja, Uganda, 452, 456
Johannesburg, South Africa, 302, 380, 382, 384–93, 397–8, 493
Jos, Nigeria, 328–9, 332–3
Juba river, Somalia, 373–4
Juba, Sudan, 401, 407
Jwaneng, Botswana, 57

Kabala, Sierra Leone, 368
Kabalenga Falls, Uganda, 456
Kabwe, Zambia, 482, 486
Kaduna, Nigeria, 322, 328–31
Kaédi, Mauritania, 267
Kailahun, Sierra Leone, 367
Kairouan, Tunisia, 442

509

INDEX

Kalahari Desert, 55, 308–9
Kalémié, Zaïre, 473
Kaloum Peninsula, Guinea, 176
Kalulushi, Zambia, 487
Kamembe, Rwanda, 341
Kamina, Zaïre, 473
Kampala, Uganda, 452–8
Kanaga, Zaïre, 467, 475
Kandi, Benin, 50
Kankan, Guinea, 169, 174
Kano, Nigeria, 322, 327, 329, 332
Kanye, Botswana, 55, 60
Kaolack, Senegal, 344, 350–1
Kariba, Zimbabwe, 494
Karisimbi, Rwanda, 337
Karonga, Malawi, 253
Kasaba Bay, Zambia, 483
Kasese, Uganda, 452–8
Kassala, Sudan, 407
Kasungu, Malawi, 253
Kau'r, Gambia, 151
Kaura Namoda, Nigeria, 329
Kavaluseni, Swaziland, 417
Kayes, Congo, 98, 103
Kayes, Mali, 258, 261, 263, 265
Kazungula, Botswana, 58, 60
Keetmanshoop, Namibia, 307, 310, 312
Kenema, Sierra Leone, 363, 367–9
Kenya, 196–209
Kericho, Kenya, 204
Kerrewan, Gambia, 155
Khartoum, Sudan, 23, 94, 136, 401–3, 405–10
Khartoum North, Sudan, 401, 405, 409
Khomas-Hochland highlands, Namibia, 313
Kigali, Rwanda, 336, 338–43
Kigoma, Tanzania, 67
Kilimanjaro, Tanzania, 423
Kilimanjaro, Mount, Tanzania, 421
Kimberley, South Africa, 387
Kindia, Guinea, 171, 174
Kinshasa, Zaïre, 106, 467–8, 470–6
Kisangani, Zaïre, 467, 472–3, 475
Kisenyi, Rwanda, 26
Kismayu, Somalia, 374, 377
Kissidougou, Guinea, 174
Kisumu, Kenya, 196, 202, 204
Kitimba Dam, Rwanda, 339
Kitwe, Zambia, 477, 482, 484–7

Kivu Lake, Rwanda, 26, 64, 338, 473
Koidu, Sierra Leone, 367
Kolwezi Road, Zaïre, 473
Kono, Sierra Leone, 367
Korhogo, Ivory Coast, 186, 191
Kosti, Sudan, 407
Koudougou, Upper Volta, 459
Kouilou Dam, Congo, 101
Koutaba, Cameroon, 77
Kufrah, Libya, 233
Kumasi, Ghana, 159, 163–4
Kumba, Cameroon, 72, 77, 80
Kuntaur, Gambia, 151

Labé, Guinea, 174
La Digue Island, Seychelles, 359
Lagos, Nigeria, 25, 51, 94, 162, 320, 322, 325–30, 332–4, 435
Lagos Island, Nigeria, 333–4
Lambáréne, Gabon, 101, 142, 147
Legon, Ghana, 163
Lesotho, 27, 210–19
Letlhakane, Botswana, 57
Letseng-La-Terai, Lesotho, 212
Liberia, 26, 219–27
Libreville, Gabon, 129, 142, 145–50
Libya, 24, 228–37
Lichinge, Mozambique, 303
Lilongwe, Malawi, 248, 253, 255–6
Limbe, Malawi, 253, 256–7
Limpopo river, 300, 490
Lindi, Tanzania, 428
Livingstone, Zambia, 482–3, 486
Lobatse, Botswana, 55, 58, 60, 62
Lobita, Angola, 39, 470
Lomé, Togo, 51, 162, 431, 434–41
Loubomo, Congo, 98, 101, 103
Loukolela, Congo, 103
Luanda, Angola, 39, 41–4, 311
Luangwa Valley, Zambia, 483
Luanshya, Zambia, 486–7
Luba, Equatorial Guinea, 130
Lubango, Angola, 39
Lubumbashi, Zaïre, 467, 472–5
Luderitz, Namibia, 307
Lusaka, Zambia, 302, 311, 477–8, 480, 482–8

Luxor, Egypt, 120–1

Macias Nguema, *see* Fernando Po
Madagascar, 238–47
Mafeking, Zimbabwe, 493
Mafue Lodge, Zambia, 483
Mahajanga, Madagascar, 238
Mahalapye, Botswana, 58, 60
Mahe, Seychelles, 354–5, 357, 359–62
Maiduguri, Nigeria, 329, 332
Makabana, Congo, 103
Makeni, Sierra Leone, 363
Makgadikgadi Salt Pans, Botswana, 56, 63
Makokou, Gabon, 147
Malabo, Equatorial Guinea, 126–30
Malanje, Angola, 39
Malawi, 248–57
Malawi, Lake, 248, 253–4, 300
Mali, 25, 27, 258–66
Malindi, Kenya, 202
Maloti mountains, Lesotho, 211
Mambassa Road, Zaïre, 473
Mamfé, Cameroon, 77
Mamou, Guinea, 174
Man, Ivory Coast, 191
Manakara, Madagascar, 244
Manantali Dam, Mali, 260
Mango, Togo, 431
Mangochi, Malawi, 253
Mansôa, Guinea-Bissau, 180
Mansoura, Egypt, 115
Manzini, Swaziland, 411, 414–16
Mao, Chad, 94
Maputo, Mozambique, 298, 301–6, 417
Maradi, Niger, 315, 319
Marampa, Sierra Leone, 365
Maroua, Cameroon, 77
Marrakech, Morocco, 285, 288–90, 292, 295
Marsa Brega, Libya, 233
Marshalltown, South Africa, 393
Mascarene archipelago, Mauritius, 275
Maseru, Lesotho, 210, 213–18
Matadi, Zaïre, 473–4
Maun, Botswana, 60
Mauritania, 27, 267–73
Mauritius, 9, 274–84
Mbabane, Swaziland, 411, 414–19
Mbale, Uganda, 452
Mbalmayo, Cameroon, 81

INDEX

Mbinda, Congo, 103
Mbini, see Rio Benito
Mbuji-Mayi, Zaïre, 467, 472
McIlwaine, Lake, Zimbabwe, 498
Medjerda valley, Tunisia, 442
Mekambo, Gabon, 147
Meknes, Morocco, 285, 288, 290, 292
Menara, Morocco, 288
Mezergues, Morocco, 288
Moanola, Gabon, 147
Mobutu Sese Seko, Lake, Uganda, 452
Mochudi, Botswana, 55
Mogadishu, Somalia, 372, 374–9
Moka, Mauritius, 284
Molepolole, Botswana, 55, 57
Mombasso, Kenya, 196, 199, 201–5, 207–8
Monastir, Tunisia, 445, 447
Mongo, Chad, 94
Monrovia, Liberia, 219, 221–7
Mont-aux-Sources, South Africa, 382
Mopti, Mali, 258, 263
Morne Seychelloise, 355
Morocco, 285–97
Moshi, Tanzania, 420
Moundou, Chad, 89, 91, 94
Moyenne Island, Seychelles, 361
Mozambique, 11, 298–306
Mpaka, Swaziland, 414
Muchinga Mountains, Zambia, 478
Mufulira, Zambia, 487
Muizenberg, South Africa, 394
Mulanje, Mount, Malawi, 248, 256
Mwanza, Tanzania, 420
Mzuzu, Malawi, 253

Nairobi, Kenya, 196, 199–207, 302, 359
Nakuru, Kenya, 196, 202, 204
Namib Desert, Namibia, 308–9
Namibia, 11, 21, 307–14
Nampula, Mozambique, 298, 303
Nanyuki, Kenya, 202
Nara, Mali, 263
Natitingou, Benin, 50
Ndende, Gabon, 147
N'djaména, Chad, 26, 89–97
Ndjolé, Gabon, 147
Ndolo, Zambia, 473, 477, 482–4, 486–8

Newlands, South Africa, 393
Ngaoundéré, Cameroon, 77
Nguru, Nigeria, 329
Nhlangano, Swaziland, 411
Niamey, Niger, 26, 315, 317–21
Niari Valley, Congo, 99–100
Niger, 26, 315–21
Niger river, 26, 259–60, 265–6, 315, 321
Nigeria, 24, 25, 26, 322–35
Nile river, 401–2
Nile Valley and Delta, 115–17, 123
Nimba Mountains, Liberia, 226
Nioro du Sahel, Mali, 263
Njala, Sierra Leone, 367
Nkhotakota, Malawi, 353
Nkongsamba, Cameroon, 72, 77
Nouadhibou, Mauritania, 267, 269–72
Nouakchott, Mauritania, 267, 269–73
Nsanje, Malawi, 253
Nyala, Sudan, 407
Nyeri, Kenya, 202
Nyong river, Cameroon, 81

Obock, Djibouti, 107
Ogaden Desert, 11, 110, 134, 374
Okahanda, Namibia, 312
Okavango Basin, Botswana, 56
Omdurman, Sudan, 401, 405, 409
Onigbolo, Benin, 47
Oran, Algeria, 29, 32, 34, 38, 288
Orapa, Botswana, 57, 60
Oti plateau, Togo, 433
Otjiwarongo, Namibia, 312
Ouagadougou, Upper Volta, 25, 191, 459, 462–6
Ouargala, Algeria, 34
Ouessa, Congo, 103
Ougadougo, Togo, 435
Ouidah, Benin, 45
Oujda, Morocco, 290, 292
Outjo, Namibia, 312

Paerl, South Africa, 394
Pala, Chad, 94
Palimé, Togo, 431, 434, 437
Pamplemousses, Mauritius, 280
Parakou, Benin, 50
Pemba, Tanzania, 420, 424
Phoenix, Mauritius, 274, 284
Piggs Peak, Swaziland, 411
Piton de la Rivière Noire, Mauritius, 275
Pointe Indienne, Congo, 100

Pointe Noire, Congo, 98, 101, 103–5
Port Elizabeth, South Africa, 380, 386–7, 389, 393, 399
Port Gentil, Gabon, 142, 147–8
Port Harcourt, Nigeria, 91, 321, 322, 327–9, 331–3
Port Louis, Mauritius, 274, 278–83
Port Said, Egypt, 115, 117, 121
Port Sudan, Sudan, 401, 407, 409
Porto Novo, Benin, 45, 50–1, 53, 435
Poto-Poto, Congo, 106
Prasline, Seychelles, 358–9
Pretoria, South Africa, 380, 382, 384, 386, 388–91, 393, 399–400

Quatre-Bornes, Mauritius, 274, 284
Que Que, Zimbabwe, 489, 492, 496
Quilimane, Mozambique, 303

Rabat, Morocco, 285, 288–91, 294–5
Red Volta river, Upper Volta, 460
Richards Bay, South Africa, 383, 414
Rift Valley, 64–5, 132, 197, 248
Rio Benito, Equatorial Guinea, 129
Rio Muni, Equatorial Guinea, 126–7
Robertsport, Liberia, 224
Roderigues Island, Mauritius, 274
Roseires Dam, Sudan, 403
Rose Hill, Mauritius, 274, 281, 284
Rosso, Mauritania, 272
Roume, Guinea, 176
Ruhengeri, Rwanda, 341
Ruzizi river, Burundi, 26, 64
Rwanda, 26, 336–43

Sabou, Upper Volta, 466
Sahara Desert, 268, 286, 323–4, 443
St Brandon Island, Mauritius, 274
St James, South Africa, 394
Saint Louis, Senegal, 344, 349
Sainte Anne, Seychelles, 361
Sais, Morocco, 288
Saldanha Bay, South Africa, 383

511

INDEX

Sale, Morocco, 288
Salima, Malawi, 253–4
Salisbury, Zimbabwe, 489, 492–8
Saltinho, Guinea-Bissau, 181
Sangmelina, Cameroon, 77
San Pedro, Ivory Coast, 186, 191–2
Sansanné-Mango, Togo, 437
Santa Isabel, *see* Malabo
Sarh, Chad, 89, 91, 94
Sassandra, Ivory Coast, 191–2
Sategui-Deressia, Chad, 91
Savé, Benin, 47
Save river, 300, 490
Sebha, Libya, 228, 233
Ségou, Mali, 258, 263
Sekondi-Takoradi, Ghana, 157
Selebi-Pikwe, Botswana, 55, 57–8, 60
Selingué Dam, Mali, 260
Senegal, 26, 27, 344–53
Senegal river, 27, 260, 267, 269, 346
Sennar Dam, Sudan, 403
Serowe, Botswana, 55
Seychelles, 9, 354–62
Sfax, Tunisia, 442, 447, 449
Shangugu, Rwanda, 343
Shebelli river, Somalia, 373–4
Sierra Leone, 26, 363–71
Sikasso, Mali, 263
Simonstown, South Africa, 394
Siteki, Swaziland, 411
Skikela, Algeria, 34
Sokodé, Togo, 431, 437
Sokoto, Nigeria, 329
Soma, Senegal, 155
Somalia, 22, 110, 372–9
Souk Ahras, Algeria, 32, 445
Sousse, Tunisia, 442, 449
South Africa, 27, 212–13, 217, 307–8, 312, 380–400
Stanley (Malebo) Pool, Congo, 105–6
Stellenbosch, South Africa, 394
Suarez, Madagascar, 238
Sudan, 401–10
Suez, Egypt, 115, 117, 121
Suez Canal, 109–10, 116, 374
Sunyani, Ghana, 164
Swakopmund, Namibia, 307, 312

Swaziland, 27, 411–19

Table Mountain, South Africa, 393
Tabou, Ivory Coast, 191
Tadjoura, Djibouti, 107
Tahat, Mount, Algeria, 29
Tahoua, Niger, 315, 319
Takoradi, Ghana, 163–4
Tamale, Ghana, 159, 164
Tamanrasset, Algeria, 34
Tamara Island, Guinea, 176
Tambacounda, Senegal, 349
Tambao, Upper Volta, 461, 463
Tananarive, Madagascar, 302
Tanganyika, Lake, 26, 64–7, 70, 337, 421, 473
Tanga, Tanzania, 420, 425, 428
Tangier, Morocco, 285, 288–90, 292–3, 296–7
Tanzania, 26, 420–30
Tchibanga, Gabon, 147
Tebessa, Algeria, 32
Tell Atlas mountains, 442
Tema, Ghana, 159, 164, 167
Tete, Mozambique, 303
Tetouan, Morocco, 290
Teyateyaneng, Lesotho, 210
Thiès, Senegal, 344
Tigray, Ethiopia, 141
Tiko, Cameroon, 77
Tin Hrassan, Upper Volta, 461
Toamasina, Madagascar, 238, 241, 243–4
Tobruk, Libya, 233
Togo, 24, 431–41
Tombouctou, Mali, 263
Touggourt, Algeria, 34
Tripoli, Libya, 228, 230–6
Tsaratanana, Mount, Madagascar, 239
Tsumeb, Namibia, 312
Tumbo Island, Guinea, 176
Tunduma, Tanzania, 425
Tunis, Tunisia, 32, 231, 442, 446–51
Tunisia, 442–51

Uganda, 11, 452–8
Umhlanga Rocks, South Africa, 396
Umtali, Zimbabwe, 489, 494–6
Upper Volta, 459–66

Vacoas, Mauritius, 274, 284

Victoria, Cameroon, 76–7, 79–80
Victoria Falls, Zimbabwe, 494
Victoria Island, Nigeria, 333–4
Victoria, Lake, 197, 421, 452
Victoria, Seychelles, 354, 357–62
Virunga, Rwanda, 337
Voi, Kenya, 203
Volta river and delta, 160

Wad Medani, Suda, 401, 407–8
Wadi Halfa, Sudan, 407
Walvis Bay, Namibia, 307, 312
Wankie, Zimbabwe, 489, 492, 495
Warri, Nigeria, 331–2
Wau, Sudan, 407
Welkom, South Africa, 391
White Nile river, 402–3, 409, 452
White Volta river, Upper Volta, 460
Windhoek (Otjomuise), Namibia, 307, 312
Wouri, Cameroon, 72

Yaba, Nigeria, 332
Yaoundé, Cameroon, 72, 75–9, 81
Yengema, Sierre Leone, 368
Yoff, Senegal, 347
Yola, Nigeria, 329
Youpougou, Ivory Coast, 194
Yundum Airport, Gambia, 153

Zaïre, 26, 467–76
Zaïre river, 467
Zakouma, Chad, 94
Zambezi river, 300, 478, 490
Zambia, 477–88
Zanzibar, Tanzania, 420, 424, 427
Ziguinchor, Senegal, 155, 181, 344, 349–51
Zimbabwe, 11, 22, 489–98
Zinder, Niger, 315, 319
Zomba, Malawi, 248, 253
Zomba, Mount, Malawi, 248
Zouérate, Mauritania, 267, 269